How to Survive and Thrive During Hard Times

Robert Wayne Atkins, P.E.
(Grandpappy)

Practical Advice
for Surviving
an Economic Depression
or a
Natural or Manmade Disaster
that Disrupts Commerce

How to Survive and Thrive During Hard Times
Robert Wayne Atkins, P.E. (Grandpappy)

Copyright © 2011 by Robert Wayne Atkins, P.E. All rights reserved. No part of this book may be used or reproduced in any manner without the written permission of the author except for brief quotes that are included as part of a review article. For additional information contact the author at: P.O. Box 225, Talking Rock, Georgia, USA 30175.

Some of the picture images in this book are from the Corel Mega Gallery © 1996 by Corel Corporation. The images are used with permission granted by Corel Corporation to the author of this book as the original purchaser and user of the original software and the original CDs.

Bible scripture verses are from one of the following three translations of the Holy Bible:
Holy Bible, King James Version.
(Pages 437-440.)
Holy Bible, New King James Version, Copyright © 1995 by Thomas Nelson, Inc.
(Pages 115, 129, 182, 363, 418, 427-429.)
Holy Bible, New International Version, Copyright © 1978 by New York International Bible Society.
(Pages 431-435, 441-454.)

First Edition published by Grandpappy, Inc.

Practical Advice
for Surviving
an Economic Depression
or a Natural or Manmade Disaster
that Disrupts Commerce.

ISBN: 978-0-615-47657-5

Printed in the United States of America.
10 9 8 7 6 5 4 3 2

Preface to

How to Survive and Thrive During Hard Times

This book contains suggestions and alternatives for you to consider so you can make the best possible choices for the continued comfort and survival of your family during hard times.

The book will **not** tell you exactly what you should do. This book does not assume to know your family's specific circumstances, or what skills and abilities you and your family members possess, or what special needs you or your family members require. Only you know the answers to these questions and therefore only you can strategically customize a strategy that would have the maximum chance of being successful for you and your family.

If you are looking for a book that makes specific recommendations about exactly where you should live, and exactly what foods and other items you should buy, and the exact type of firearms and ammunition you should purchase, then this is **not** that book. If that is the type of advice you are seeking then there are a multitude of books that have been written on this topic by a variety of other authors who do know exactly what you should be doing. You should purchase one of those other books instead of this one.

This book assumes you are an intelligent individual who is capable of making your own decisions. It assumes you simply want to know what the current options and alternatives are, along with the specific advantages and disadvantages of each alternative. Once you have all this information in your possession then you know you can make the best choice about which options would be the most logical for your family's long-term survival during hard times. The author of this book cannot make that decision for you. That is a decision you will need to make for your own family based on your intimate knowledge of the strengths and weaknesses of your family unit.

This book will provide you with a variety of options to consider in the areas of water and food procurement, gardening options, personal hygiene alternatives, practical battery operated electronic equipment, practical information on the importance of fire, a reasonable summary of the relevant issues related to firearm selection, how to make your own ammunition at home, a common sense discussion of the pros and cons of a variety of different long-term survival strategies, some spiritual encouragement, and some recommendations for your family's continued education and entertainment.

If the above is the type of information you believe would be useful to you then this book might be a practical addition to your home library. However, this is **not** a stand-alone reference book. This book presents a concise clear overview about a wide variety of different topics but it does not go into extensive depth in every topic area. You will need to acquire a book written exclusively about a specific topic if you decide you wish to know more about that subject. For example, this book contains a very good explanation of how to use commercial quality steel traps to capture wild game animals for food. But if you decide you want to know more about the trapping profession then you will need to purchase a book written exclusively on the topic of trapping, or you will need to download the recommended "State of Michigan Trapper's Instruction Manual" from their web site as explained in the Trapping Chapter in this book.

If you are seriously considering the purchase of this book then I strongly recommend that you examine the Table of Contents of this book and read the list of topics that are discussed in this book. If the topics are ones you are specifically interested in then this book might be worthy of a place in your home library.

Please let me explain why I believe I am qualified to write a book such as this one. To begin with, I am not one of those people who simply writes about hard times and who has never really experienced hard times. I spent approximately six-months living deep in the backwoods of Maine with my wife and our three small preschool age children from June to November of 1975 while I was building a rustic log cabin using pine trees that grew on the 12 acres of land we had purchased. I wore a pistol every day while I was building our cabin in that primitive wilderness environment. I hunted with a bolt-action rifle and I used steel traps to capture wild game animals. We cooked our meals over a campfire every day. After returning to "civilization" in late

November of 1975 I continued to study about pioneer life and hard times survival. During the past thirty-five years I have personally tested a wide variety of "textbook procedures" and I have discovered which ones are truly reliable and which ones are almost completely worthless from a practical perspective. Therefore I have accumulated a tremendous amount of practical hands-on knowledge and experience on this topic. And it has all been tempered by my actual experience of living a primitive existence in the backwoods of Maine during the summer and fall of 1975.

My primary objective for the past 35 years has been to discover practical reliable methods that could be used in a long-term survival situation when a family did not have the option to conveniently replenish their supplies on a regular basis.

The chapters in this book were not simply copied from another source. Although some of the information in this book can be found elsewhere, most of information in each of the chapters is from my own personal files and it is based on my own personal life experiences.

One of the advantages of receiving hard times survival instruction from an old man is that he no longer has the desire to prove that he can survive on a day-to-day basis with nothing more than a good knife, a good rifle, and the will to survive. An old man more fully appreciates the comforts of civilization and the advantages of modern technology. Therefore he will employ as much of that technology as is reasonably possible to make the living conditions for his family as enjoyable as possible. If this is also your objective then this book might help you to achieve your goal.

Respectfully,
Grandpappy
July 1, 2011

Table of Contents

Chapter   **Page**

Section One: Introduction
1. A Simultaneous Worldwide Depression, and a Worldwide Famine, and World War III 1
2. A List of 20 Common Mistakes That Should Be Avoided 7

Section Two: Basic Survival
3. Why Prepare for Something That May Never Happen? 11
4. Realistic Self-Sufficiency 13
5. A Simple But Effective Survival Plan 17
6. How to Start Preparing for Hard Times on a Very Modest Budget 21

Section Three: Water
7. How to Build a Very Effective Water Filter System for Approximately $75 31
8. How to Find Water and How to Make Water Safe to Drink 33

Section Four: Food
9. Introduction to Emergency Food Storage 53
10. 30-Day Emergency Food Supply 63
11. One-Year Emergency Food Supply 69
12. Some Practical Places Where You Can Store and Hide Your Emergency Food 71
13. Some Simple Options for Heating Canned Foods 77
14. Cast Iron Cookware 79
15. Pure Salt, Table Salt, and Sea Salt 87
16. Black Pepper, Peppercorns, and Peppercorn Grinders 89
17. Coffee, Coffee Pots, and Coffee Grinders 91
18. Meat Grinder 95
19. Wheat Grinder: Hand Crank and Electric 97

Section Five: Gardening
20. During Hard Times Should You Know Some Basic Gardening Skills 99
21. Vegetable Recommendations for New Gardeners 101
22. How to Grow Each Type of Vegetable and Each Type of Vegetable Seed 107
23. How to Harvest, Process, and Store Vegetable Seeds 115
24. How to Grow Fruits, Nuts, Grapes, and Berries 119
25. How to Grow Fruit Trees From Seed 129
26. How to Preserve Food Using Three Simple Old Fashioned Methods 133
27. How to Convert Human Waste into a Safe Garden Compost Fertilizer 139
28. The Advantages of Mulch in a Garden 143
29. Ant Hills: A Simple Solution 145

Section Six: Shelter
30. Use Common Sense to Compare Your Current Location to Another Location 147
31. How to Select the Optimal Retreat Location 151
32. The Advantages and Disadvantages of Recreational Vehicles and Campers 155
33. How to Build a Safe Temporary Shelter 159
34. Grandpappy's Wilderness Cabin Cave 167

Section Seven: Clothing and Shoes
35 Clothing 177
36 Shoes and Boots 183

Section Eight: Personal Hygiene
37 Personal Hygiene Items 185
38 Toilet Tissue 187

Section Nine: Emergency First Aid and Home Remedies
39 Emergency First Aid 191
40 Aspirin 195
41 Herbal Home Remedies 199
42 Colloidal Silver 201
43 Home Remedies for Insect Stings, Ticks, Chiggers, Head Lice, and Skunk Deodorizer 203

Section Ten: Electronics
44 Rechargeable NiMH Batteries and a Solar Battery Charger 209
45 Flashlights 217
46 Emerson AM/FM Instant Weather Portable Radio 219
47 Grundig "Eton" S350DL Deluxe AM/FM/Shortwave Radio 221
48 Grundig "Eton" G6 Buzz Aldrin AM/FM/Aircraft/Shortwave Portable Radio 223
49 The Basics of Shortwave Radio 225
50 Cell Phones, Satellite Phones, and Two-Way Radios 227
51 The Basics of Solar Power and How to Build a Portable Solar Power Generator 231

Section Eleven: Basic Skills
52 How to Build a Safe Fire and Why Fire Is So Important 237
53 How to Start an Emergency Fire Using the Gunpowder from a Bullet 241
54 How to Build a Simple Sundial 243
55 Grandpappy's Homemade Soap Recipe 245
56 Other Basic Skills: How to Make Charcoal and How to Make Maple Syrup 257

Section Twelve: Firearms
57 Self-Defense 259
58 Should You Own a Firearm? 261
59 Should You Have a Concealed Carry Firearm License? 265
60 Firearm Safety Rules 266
61 Bolt-Action Rifle or Semi-Auto Rifle? 267
62 How to Hit the Target Bull's-Eye 275
63 Should You Install a Laser Sight on Your Firearm? 301
64 Cost Comparison: Factory-Loaded Ammunition and Hand-Reloaded Ammunition 307
65 How to Make Your Own Ammunition 309
66 Pellet Rifles: 22 Caliber and 177 Caliber 335

Section Thirteen: Hard Times Survival
67 An Emergency Backpack or Bug-Out-Bag (B.O.B.) 339
68 Bicycles for Emergency Transportation 343
69 Basic Hand Tools 353
70 Firewood, Fireplaces, and Cast Iron Stoves 355
71 Charity During Hard Times 363
72 Pets and Livestock 367

Section Fourteen: Wilderness Survival

73	The Three Most Important Wilderness Survival Items	371
74	Compass Instructions and Alternatives	375
75	Homemade Bow and Arrows	381
76	How to Catch Wild Game Using Professional Quality Snares and Steel Traps	385
77	Gill Nets: The Easy, Efficient Way to Catch Fish	391

Section Fifteen: Social Breakdown

78	Are You Prepared for a Worst Case Breakdown in Society?	399
79	The Basic Rules of Survival During Hard Times	407

Section Sixteen: Spiritual

80	During Hard Times Will You Accept God's Help?	417
81	The Reasons I Decided to Become a Christian	419
82	How to Become a Christian	427
83	Is Salvation by Faith Alone or is Something More Required?	431
84	The Rapture	437
85	What Does the Bible Say About Alcohol?	441
86	What Does the Bible Say About Giving?	447

Section Seventeen: Education and Entertainment

87	Recommended Schoolbooks for the Education of the Ones You Love	457
88	Recommended Books for Hard Times Survival	461
89	Paperback Novels for Entertainment	465
90	Music for Entertainment	467
91	A Deck of 52 Playing Cards and Some Card Game Books and Five Ordinary Dice	469

Section Eighteen: Conclusion

92	What to Do Right Now if the Hard Times Have Begun and You are Not Prepared	471

Index	487
About the Author	492

Page Numbers for Christian Poems

Poem Title	**Page**
Prepare or Perish	10
A Traveling Bag	16
The Truth	30
In the Beginning	62
I Need a Hug	76
A Humble Birth	86
His Last Day	94
One Wish and Not Three	106
Do You Understand?	118
One Precious Life	138
Are You a Nobody?	144
Missing Teeth	194
Two-Way Communication	230
The Words of God	236
Self-Defense	264
Victory	306
Ordinary People	362
The Book	366
The First Commandment	374
Star Travel	380
What Does God Look Like?	398
The Good Old Days	416
So Many Religions	426
The Tree of Life	430
The Rapture	436
The Mark of the Beast	456
Can You Imagine?	464
The Great Resurrection	468
Say Your Sorry Before It's Too Late	470
The Adventure: A True Story	486

Chapter One

A Simultaneous Worldwide Depression, and a Worldwide Famine, and World War III

Following is a very brief summary of a few of the major events of the Great Depression of the 1930s and World War II:

1. On "Black Tuesday" October 29, 1929 the stock market crashed for two fundamental reasons. First, stock prices were artificially inflated. Stock prices were not directly related to the true value of the stock, such as the stock's dividend yield or the stock's price-earnings ratio. Instead stock prices were based on "faith" that the stock could be sold at an even higher price to someone else in the very near future. Second, most stocks were bought on margin, which meant that the investor only owned a very small piece of the stock because borrowed money had paid for the bulk of the purchase price. As long as stock prices remained stable or increased, then the investor was okay. However, when stock prices began to adjust downwards towards their true market value, the investors could not meet their margin calls and their loans were automatically closed out and their stocks sold. This snowballed into an avalanche of selling as stock prices continued to crash and "paper fortunes" were lost. (Note: The real estate price bubble of the year 2008 can be directly compared to the stock market price bubble of 1929.)

2. Beginning in late 1929 many different businesses began to fail and unemployment began to skyrocket.

3. Between 1930 and 1931 approximately 2,300 United States Banks went bankrupt and their investors and depositors lost all the money they had entrusted to those banks. This was just the beginning and over the next few years thousands of additional banks also went bankrupt.

4. On April 5, 1933, under Presidential Executive Order 6102, the United States Government seized all the gold owned by its citizens. The government also seized everyone's bank safe deposit box and then declared that those boxes could not be opened except in the presence of a representative of the United States Government. Although this action made the government, its officials, and the surviving bankers richer it did nothing to help relieve the suffering of ordinary people. The Depression continued to get worse for approximately 12 more years.

5. People were gradually and systematically evicted from their homes and their farms. This action helped to enrich the bank owners but it made the Depression worse because the experienced food growers were evicted from their farms. Therefore food production declined and the famine became worse worldwide.

6. Food became a very precious commodity. Government officials and bankers could still afford to buy food but ordinary people could not. Fortunately in many small communities and in most large cities there were charitable soup kitchens that provided starving people with one small free meal per day. That meal usually consisted of a bowl of soup and a piece of bread. These soup kitchens were supported by the compassion and generosity of the people in each local community who still had some type of regular income.

7. On September 1, 1939 World War II began in Europe. The United States was drawn into the War with the bombing of Pearl Harbor on December 7, 1941. During the War many items disappeared from the stores and there was strict rationing of most of the remaining products. During World War II there was a massive loss of life and property.

8. On September 2, 1945 World War II ended. The people who survived the War were able to find work rebuilding the farms, homes, cities, and infrastructures that were destroyed during the War. The United States did not suffer the property damage inflicted on other nations so they were in a much better position

to "recover" from the War. The Great Depression of the 1930s was at an end and the "Baby Boom" generation was just beginning.

Following is a brief summary on the "legal impact" of the Great Depression of the 1930s on ordinary people, just like you and me:

1. The life savings of millions of individuals systematically disappeared as thousands of banks permanently closed their doors. These banks were declared legally insolvent and they were therefore legally exempt from paying their debts to their depositors. In many cases the depositors received nothing or they received a few pennies for each dollar they had originally entrusted to those banks. (Personal Note: My great-grandparents lost their life savings when their local bank went bankrupt. My great-grandparents were just ordinary people: a Baptist Preacher and his wife.)

2. The farm mortgages and home mortgages held by those "insolvent" banks survived because they were legally transferred to a few "solvent" banks. The government declared that those mortgages were still legally binding debts and that the solvent banks had a right to collect on them. In addition, the solvent banks could keep the proceeds from those mortgages and they did not have to reimburse the depositors of the original "insolvent" banks whose money had originally been used to finance those mortgages.

3. Many families lost their homes and their farms when the "solvent" banks foreclosed on them and kicked them out into the streets.

4. The end result was that most individuals not only lost their life savings but they also lost their homes and their family farms. And a few "solvent" banks grew very rich and powerful during this process because it was all done legally and with the blessing and support of the government.

Occasionally people want to compare the Next Great Depression to the Great Depression of the 1930s (as briefly described above). Although this is an interesting intellectual exercise, it is a waste of time in my opinion because the Next Great Depression will be significantly different from the Great Depression of the 1930s for the reasons that are summarized on the next few pages.

**Some Observations About
Moral Values, the Next Worldwide Depression,
the Next Worldwide Famine, and World War III**

Moral Values:

1. Since about 1965 there has been a gradual and steady decline in moral values at all levels in society (individuals, business leaders, and government officials). There is no universal concept of basic right and wrong in the minds of many people around the world. Right and wrong is now loosely defined based on the current situation.

2. The entertainment industry has made "heroes" out of "normal individuals" when they behaved in a selfish manner during a life threatening situation. These movie heroes sometimes drive cars at high speed through traffic (or onto the sidewalk) and they frequently cause accidents to other drivers who are simply on the same highway as the "hero." However, the audience doesn't know the names of those victims (or how many children are in the car that flips over or crashes into a wall) and our attention is only focused on the efforts of the hero to survive regardless of how much damage the hero does to everyone else on the highway (or on the sidewalk). *The movie's message is a simple one: "Only your life is important and everyone else is expendable if it means your escape and survival."* In the 1930s this type of movie would have been shocking and morally repulsive. People today, however, casually watch these movies without uttering one word of moral disapproval.

3. After several decades of this type of intellectual brainwashing, how do you think "normal people" are going to react if they discover they are in a life threatening situation? Will they consider your life and the lives of your children to be of any value? Movies originally made in the United States have been viewed in almost every part of the world for many years so no nation is exempt from this type of subtle but voluntary mind conditioning.

4. Although there are still a large number of very ethical people in every nation around the world, their numbers are at least equally matched by individuals who have no ethical values and who will do anything and everything they believe they can get away with, including theft, murder, rape, and the destruction of property. During a disaster event these unethical individuals blend in with everyone else until they see a situation where they can do as they wish without any fear of being caught or punished.

The Next Worldwide Depression:

1. Let's use a hypothetical Used Car Lot to illustrate the economic forces that bring on a Depression. In our example let's assume that the Used Car Lot owner has 50 used cars on his lot which he bought with a 10% down payment and 90% financing. He then sells each used car for approximately 20% more than his total investment in the car. Each month he replaces any used cars he sells, and he pays his monthly finance fees, and the rent and utilities on his car lot. Any money left over each month is his profit. However, if the economy does poorly and he only sells two used cars per month then his profit on those two sales will 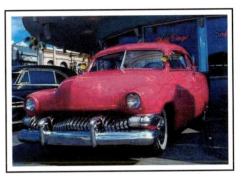 not be enough to pay his finance fees, rent, and utilities. He will have to borrow money to pay his other bills. But soon he will not be able to get a loan. The finance company will realize he has inadequate income. The finance company will foreclose on his loan and he will lose his meager source of income and his original 10% investment in the 50 used cars. The finance company will also lose because they will not be able to sell the 50 used cars for the amount of money they have invested in them. The reason is because during a Depression the price of all used cars will have fallen by at least 30%. In this type of situation everyone loses. The problem for the Used Car Lot owner was not his stable **Balance Sheet** which always showed 50 used cars. Instead his real problem was that his **monthly income** declined below the amount necessary to pay all his monthly bills.

2. The banking system of the entire world is currently not receiving enough **monthly income** to pay their monthly bills. And their **Balance Sheet** assets are at least 40 percent over-valued because they are based on unsecured credit card debts and loans on real estate at artificially inflated prices.

3. When the banks are eventually forced to declare bankruptcy it may take months or years to resolve the mess. During this period of time people will not be able to access their money in those banks and therefore they will not be able to pay their bills. However they will still be required to pay those bills or suffer the legal consequences. Do you think most people today will accept this situation in the same way that people did during the Great Depression of the 1930s?

4. One quick solution to this problem would be for the government to simply print more money and then give each depositor the full value of their insured deposits in cash. The government could once again print larger denomination bills, such as a $500 and a $1,000 bill. This would result in a tremendous increase in cash in circulation but there would be no corresponding increase in the amount of basic necessities, such as gasoline, food, and clothing. Prices would therefore rapidly increase and hyperinflation would result. Although people could no longer complain about the loss of their money within the banking system, they would now be complaining that prices were 5 or 10 or 100 times higher than before.

5. Another less obvious solution would be to create a "new" special electronic bank and completely eliminate all cash and all checks. The recent Zimbabwe experience could be used to justify the elimination of cash.

Chapter One: Depression, Famine, and World War III

With widespread media support many people might actually believe the government's claim that this new "cash elimination" policy would prevent future inflation. The individual deposit accounts and savings accounts from the old "insolvent" banks, up to $100,000 each (or more), could then be immediately transferred into this new bank. And all the mortgages from the failed banks could also be immediately transferred to this new electronic bank. Then the new bank could mail each of its new depositors an ATM debit card so they could continue to pay their bills. All transactions would therefore clear through this "new" electronic bank. This would allow the government to easily monitor the selling price of all goods and services and thereby theoretically "control" prices. And then business could resume as usual **except** no one could buy or sell unless he or she had one of these new ATM debit cards and either an individual or a business account with the "new" electronic bank. The new ATM debit cards for individuals would have monthly spending limits. The government could claim that this "temporary spending limit" was necessary to control inflation. However its real objective would be to force people to remain **forever dependent** on the government and its "new" bank for their continued long-term survival. This solution would effectively "freeze or steal" everyone's money because each person would only be permitted to spend just enough of his or her money each month to buy "necessities as defined by the government" and pay the minimum payment on their current mortgages and other legal debts. This would create the "illusion" of wealth because each person could see the "balance of money" in his or her "new electronic bank" account. However, for one official reason or another, nobody would **ever** be allowed to spend that money. Each person's monthly spending allowance would be directly related to that person's monthly income. If a person did not work, then their monthly spending allowance would be drastically reduced and they would be in danger of losing their home or apartment. The government could claim this was necessary to end the depression and force people to find some type of job. Therefore each person would have a very strong incentive to support this solution or suffer the following two consequences: (1) they would starve to death, and (2) they would lose their home and their life savings (which they have already lost but this solution would allow them to continue in a state of intellectual denial). This solution would save the government and the "real" bankers because they need peasants in order to exist. If all the peasants disappear then there is no need for a government or a bank. The quality of life can only be defined in relation to what other people have, or don't have, at any time in history.

The Next Worldwide Famine:

1. None of the governments of the world have enough food stockpiled to survive one poor harvest year. Unless there is a reasonable worldwide food harvest each and every year then a worldwide famine is inevitable.

2. Governments cannot hide the existence of a worldwide famine. Government propaganda will not be effective. People know when they are starving to death and the media will not be able to divert their attention to any other issue or topic. People quickly become painfully aware of their hunger, their weight loss, and their crying children. People will no longer be concerned about the private lives of famous celebrities. Their only concern will be about food prices and food availability. Everything else will become irrelevant by comparison.

3. During the next worldwide famine there will not be enough food for everyone. Therefore there will be no free food for anyone. Unlike the Great Depression of the 1930s, there will be no free soup kitchens and no food pantries or churches distributing free food to needy families. Regardless of how pure your motives and intentions may be, it will be impossible to be charitable if you have nothing to give except sympathy.

4. The lack of food will result in a dramatic increase in food prices worldwide. Food is not an optional or discretionary expense. Everyone has to eat and food prices will rise because of the diminishing supply of food while the demand for food remains constant. There will not be enough food for everyone and

Chapter One: Depression, Famine, and World War III

therefore the poorer people of the world will have to do without because they will not be able to afford to pay $50 for one loaf of bread. The resulting worldwide famine will force the starving people within each nation to take some type of action in order to stay alive. If they do nothing then they will slowly and painfully starve to death. However, if they do something, even if it dangerous and morally wrong, then there will be at least some small chance they might survive.

World War III:

1. There is only one long-term solution to a worldwide famine. *One way or another the world population must be brought into equilibrium with the available world food supply.*

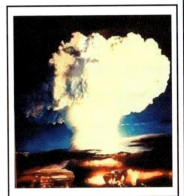

2. When the "Great Depression" began in 1930 the world was still recovering from World War I and it was not yet ready for another global war. Today, however, there are a multitude of significant trouble spots all over the world. For example, China and Taiwan, India and Pakistan, United States and Iraq, United States and Afghanistan, Iran and Israel, Syria and Israel, Russia and its former satellites, Europe and its Muslin population. Almost any event anywhere could easily be used as an excuse to start World War III. *During a World War food production always suffers significantly.* Therefore World War III would seriously disrupt the production and distribution of food. The combination of World War III and a worldwide famine would result in an astronomically high death toll. Unfortunately this may work to the advantage of every government in the world. Each government would have fewer people to manage and fewer mouths to feed.

3. Any nation that refused to participate in the war and which preferred to devote their attention to food production would not survive for very long. They would become an immediate target for any nation with sufficient military might and few food resources. Therefore a peaceful nation would be forced into becoming an unwilling participant in World War III in order to protect its food supplies.

4. The chance of the United States surviving World War III without any damage to its cities or infrastructure is approximately zero. For example, one terrorist could start several large fires inside a big city on a windy day and the city would burn to the ground. A city's fire fighting system cannot handle several major fires in several different locations simultaneously.

Summary

Since morals and ethics have seriously declined since the 1960s, the upcoming "hard times" will not unfold in the same orderly and peaceful manner as the Great Depression of the 1930s. The crime rate in every nation will increase in direct proportion to the lack of jobs and the lack of food in that nation.

Most people depend on the "system" for survival (electricity, computers, cheap transportation, and just-in-time food deliveries). They do not know how to survive without these "basic necessities of life." If these "necessities" become undependable or unavailable, many people will honestly believe they have been betrayed by their leaders and that they deserve whatever they can steal from anyone and from anywhere. The "law of the jungle" and "survival of the fittest" will become the battle cry of these individuals. Therefore, ordinary honest people will be in mortal danger from the less ethical members of their own communities.

During periods of famine, high unemployment, and high crime rates, many young men and women voluntarily join their nation's military because the military advertises that they will feed them, house them, give them a little spending money, and provide them with a firearm and the training to use that weapon. From a young person's point of view this increases their chance of survival during the hard times. However, in exchange these young people give up their right to make their own decisions and they must do whatever they are told to do or face a military firing squad. These young people are almost immediately transferred to a "hot" conflict area, or onto a front battle line, where most of them eventually die. As their life force gradually fades and flickers, these young people become painfully aware that their decision to join the military did not result in their survival during the hard times. Instead their lives, and the lives of the enemy soldiers they have killed, are being sacrificed to reduce future birth rates and to reduce the current demand on limited food resources.

Except in the United States, the citizens of most other nations have been stripped of their ability to protect themselves from anyone, including armed criminals and invading enemy soldiers. Therefore in most nations the first people to die will be the moral, ethical, law abiding residents of the nation. Once most of the peasants are dead, there will only be government officials, its military, and the criminal element of society. None of these groups actually produces anything. It was the peasants who did all the real work and when they are gone that society will be doomed. Each nation will start attacking its neighbors in a fight over the few remaining resources.

Therefore the coming "hard times" will be an extremely dangerous period and, when it is over, there is a chance that only a few honest, moral people will have survived. Hopefully you and your family will be among the survivors.

Conclusion

In conclusion, a prudent individual will carefully consider:

1. The chance of one of these events occurring, and
2. The impact that event could have on his or her life.

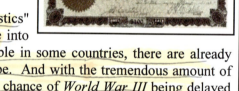

If an event has a high chance of occurrence but its impact would be minor then it does not require a contingency plan.

If an event has a low chance of occurrence but it could have a drastic impact on your life, then a contingency plan would be appropriate.

Even though the media and most world government "official statistics" say otherwise, our world is quickly sliding from the recession phase into the *depression phase*. And although there is still some food available in some countries, there are already *severe food shortages and food riots* in many nations around the globe. And with the tremendous amount of social unrest in so many different trouble spots all over the earth, the chance of *World War III* being delayed much longer is very slim.

In the 1930s the above events gradually unfolded over a period of about ten years. However there is a very good chance that all three of these events may occur simultaneously in the very near future.

Therefore my recommendation is that you make the appropriate contingency plans for the continued survival of your family in the event of a simultaneous worldwide depression, and a worldwide famine, and World War III. You might want to consider one of the following strategies:

1. Become a part of a small farming community that still has a functioning local government and a basic infrastructure, such as a doctor, dentist, sheriff, general store, shoe maker, carpenter, plumber, seamstress, etc. The farming community should also be one where its citizens still have the right to legally own weapons and where they have the right to work together to defend themselves against attack from organized gangs of criminals and from enemy forces from foreign countries.

2. Disappear into the wilderness for a few years until World War III has run its course and honest people once again have a chance to live together in peace.

Perhaps the most logical choice would be to implement option one above and then wait and see how future events gradually unfold. If at some future date you become a target for elimination due to your ethnic heritage, or religious or political beliefs, then you could switch to option two above. Option two is a much more challenging option because it is a very difficult, lonely, and unpredictable way to live. However, in my opinion, option two would be better than facing a firing squad, or the gas chamber, or the guillotine.

Chapter Two

A List of 20 Common Mistakes That Should Be Avoided

When people first become aware that our current worldwide economy is far more unstable than they previously realized, and that their life style could change rather drastically in a very short period of time, then they usually panic and they start doing things they would never have done if they had taken the time to carefully think things through to their logical conclusion.

The following suggestions may help you to avoid making some really serious mistakes that you may quickly regret.

1. Do not quit your job. Do not quit your job. Do not quit your job. **It is okay to have a job in a big city.** But you do not have to live inside a big city unless there is no other option. Think carefully about all your options and then pick the best option that is just right for you and your family. Pick an option that balances your risks and your benefits (your paycheck). Life without a paycheck will quickly bring on the hard times you are trying to avoid.

2. Do not be motivated by fear. If you do something then do it because it is the most reasonable course of action and not because you are afraid that if you don't do it then something bad will happen to you.

3. Do not spend your life savings. There is a big difference between spending and investing. Make sure you maintain a reasonable balance between the two.

4. Do not invest in anything that will consume a huge piece of your life's savings unless you can justify it based on several totally different but extremely valid reasons. Putting the majority of your life savings into one investment is almost never a smart thing to do.

5. Do not buy a ranch or a farm unless you have previous ranching or farming experience. It is okay to invest in vacant farm land or a deserted ranch if it meets your true needs and if you are very knowledgeable about what you are buying. However, the vast majority of people will get swindled investing in property they are not intimately knowledgeable about. Anyone who is trying to sell you property probably does not have your best interests at heart. You should seek out advice from people you know and trust and who have extensive real estate experience and who have nothing to gain or lose one way or the other.

6. Do not move to an area where there are very few people and where the winters are horrible based on the false illusion that you will be safer there. There are two reasons why this is not a good idea. First, it only takes one pervert who is mentally deranged, or who is a truly evil person, to kill you and your entire family. And there is no place on the face of the earth where perverts do not live among us. Second, each year severe winter weather kills a lot of people. If you intentionally move to an area that has a history of long horrible winters then your family could easily perish as a result of the bad weather.

7. Do not move into the wilderness. Moving into the wilderness should be your last option and it should not be done until after you have completely exhausted all your other options and there is absolutely no other place where you can live in safety. Almost any small community is infinitely better than the wilderness. (Note: Although moving into the wilderness should be your last option, it should still be one of your options. In times of great hardship the wilderness is sometimes the best choice for long-term survival. History is filled with examples of people who were terminated by their own governments because of their

ethnic background, or religious beliefs, or political beliefs. In this type of situation the only logical alternative is to disappear into the wilderness until the danger has passed and true justice is restored. If you wish to have any reasonable chance of success living in the wilderness then you should have made some definite plans on where you will go and what you will take with you.)

8. Do not buy more food or guns or ammunition than you need. On the other hand, you should have enough food and guns and ammunition to last several years. But resist the temptation to acquire enough food to feed 100 people for 20 years, or to build an arsenal of weapons that could equip a small army.

9. Do not buy gold and silver until after you have first acquired the basic fundamental necessities for long term survival.

10. Do not believe everything you hear or everything you read. Use common sense to evaluate all the advice you encounter including this advice you are now reading.

11. Beware of "group think." It is easy to find other people who will agree with your opinions. **But that doesn't mean anything.** Do not discredit information just because it doesn't conform to your beliefs. Carefully reflect on conflicting data and make sure you have a valid reason for rejecting that information, such as you know it is biased or you know it is simply wrong.

12. Beware of advice from the government and from any group or person that has a "hidden agenda." Whenever possible get several different opinions from a variety of different sources. Those sources should be independent and not related in any way.

13. Beware of advice that is accompanied by an offer to sell you something you really need.

14. Beware of advice from sincere individuals who speak convincingly and who are absolutely certain they know exactly what you should be doing.

15. Beware of advice from people who have never actually done what they are recommending but who are simply repeating what they heard or read somewhere else. The overwhelming vast majority of the survival advice I currently read on the internet is extremely well written, and it is presented in a very logical and convincing manner, but it is completely wrong. However, some of the survival advice I read is remarkably accurate and of a superior quality. This is where you need some practical real world experience in addition to common sense in order to separate the good advice from the bad advice.

16. Beware of advice from people who have just done something or have just made some type of purchase. These people usually need positive feedback to help them feel "good" about their decision. Therefore they will normally tell anyone who will listen what a good decision they made, and how happy they are that they did what they did, and what a good deal they got. My suggestion is that you wait several months and then ask that person for some honest feedback about their decision. For example, most people who invest in goats are absolutely delighted with their decision for a few days or weeks. But a few months later you will discover that almost every one of them has sold their goats at a loss and, if they are honest, they will advise you to not make the same mistake they made. On the other hand, if they have ego issues then they will explain their decision to sell their goats based on some really logical reason that does not negatively reflect on their original decision to buy the goats.

17. There is no perfect strategy that is just right for everyone. Each of us has our own unique skills and abilities, and family responsibilities, and health issues, and each one of us will need a plan that we customize to meet our specific circumstances. The plan that is just right for your best friend will probably be totally wrong for you and your family. And the plan you develop that is just right for you will probably not be appropriate for anyone else.

18. Do not believe in one and only one possible future. Anything could happen. Things could continue exactly the same as they are right now for several years, or things could start to get significantly better, or things could deteriorate into a "Hollywood movie disaster scenario." In my opinion you should be prepared for a good future, as well as a bad future, and for something in between.

Chapter Two: 20 Common Mistakes

19. Nobody knows how the future will unfold except God. Beware of anyone who tells you they are certain that some future event is going to happen, or they know exactly when something is going to happen. If they should get it right then it is luck and nothing more. In other words, it is similar to winning the state lottery. They have one chance in about 9 million of being correct. Almost anyone can make a vague general prediction about the future and then wait for the future to unfold and then select something very specific that has just happened and then claim that specific event as being the fulfillment of their prophecy. **Only God knows the future.** Everyone else is just guessing.

20. Do not trust your emotions. Trust God instead. Pray every day for guidance.

The Handwriting on the Wall
Holy Bible: Daniel Chapter 5

Prepare of Perish

If Noah had not obeyed God and built a huge ark using pitch and wood,
Then he, his family, and all the animals would have perished in the flood.

If Joseph had not stored extra food during the seven years of prosperity,
Then Egypt would have perished during the seven years of adversity.

A prudent person will prepare for a "rainy day" or some other calamity,
But a foolish man will do nothing and he will perish during a catastrophe.

Jesus told a parable about five girls who had oil and five who did not,
Jesus said the five wise girls had plenty but the five foolish girls ran out.

God also loves the birds of the air and all the birds are precious to Him.
But the birds must hunt for their food -- God does not take food to them.

It is easy to say "I trust God" and then use that as an excuse to do naught,
But it is better to "obey God" and be like Noah and prepare as you ought.

Scripture References: Genesis 6:11-14, Genesis 41:29-30, Proverbs 27:12, Matthew 25:1-13, Matthew 10:29, Luke 12:2, Second Thessalonians 3:10, James 1:22.

Chapter Three

Why Prepare for Something That May Never Happen?

Assume you just heard the following announcement on your radio or television:

Special Winter Weather Advisory: *A winter blizzard will hit our area tomorrow afternoon. Based on our current projections it will be the worst winter blizzard we have had for over 100 years. You should be prepared to be snowed in and unable to travel for at least one week.*

What would you do after you heard the above warning?

1. Would you completely ignore the "Winter Advisory Warning?"
2. Would you make a special trip to the store to purchase enough food and supplies to last a week?
3. Would you make sure you had enough extra water in case the water lines should freeze?
4. If you have a fireplace, would you also purchase some fire logs in the event the electricity goes off?

If you **do nothing** and the blizzard hits as predicted then you will either be extremely miserable for about one week, or you may die as a result of exposure. After each winter blizzard has passed we are usually told how many people froze to death as a result of the extremely low temperatures.

If you **do something before the blizzard hits** then you will at least have a chance to survive the blizzard. Depending on what you do you may even be able to survive without suffering any really serious hardships.

In the above scenario the overwhelming vast majority of people will decide to do something in order to prepare for the blizzard before it actually hits. Unfortunately these same logical individuals will not make any preparations for a hard times event unless they are specifically told on the news that something is about to happen.

The fundamental problem is that **occasionally** there is no advance warning of a hard times event. For example, an earthquake or a tornado may devastate an area without any advance notice.

Therefore a wise person will make some simple preparations for an unexpected hard times event during normal times when there is no threat of impending doom. This wise person would then be prepared to continue a relatively normal life style if an unexpected hard times event occurs. But almost everyone else will be desperately trying to find something to eat and some clean water to drink (the basic necessities of life).

If the hard times event is a serious one, such as a suitcase nuclear bomb being detonated in a big city, then living conditions after the event may become chaotic and unstable for a very long period of time. Many normal average people will resort to the "law of the jungle" and "survival of the fittest" and the vast majority of the weaker, kinder people will not survive the event. Therefore a wise person will think about this topic before a hard times tragedy actually unfolds.

There is no single strategy that would be appropriate for every possible hard times event. However, there are some things that would useful regardless of the type of hard times event. This would include all the following:

1. A reasonable inventory of canned food for your family to eat.
2. A way to replenish your water on a continuous basis for several years.
3. Some basic first aid supplies and medicines.
4. Some way to protect your family from ruthless looters and/or killers.
5. Some type of shelter or home where you can survive until things return to normal.

Let's examine the shelter option in a little more detail. (Note: The other four topics will be discussed in more detail in future chapters.)

1. You could try to survive at your current home or apartment.

2. You could try to survive after abandoning your home or apartment.

A wise person will realize that staying at home **and** abandoning your home both have advantages and disadvantages depending on the circumstances. If either alternative is completely ignored then the only other alternative may be death. To maximize your chances for long-term survival you will need to carefully evaluate your current residence in relationship to the actual event you are trying to survive.

For example, if a fire was headed your way and you knew there was a 99.99% chance your home was going to burn to the ground, then staying in your home would not be the best choice for someone who wanted to survive.

On the other hand, if a winter blizzard was coming your way and the weather forecast was for three-feet of snow that would be on the ground for at least six weeks, then a decision to abandon your home would not be the best choice.

Therefore neither staying at home nor abandoning your home would always be the best choice in every possible scenario. A person who wishes to maximize his or her chances for long-term survival should be able to quickly and effectively execute either option depending on the actual circumstances at the time the decision needed to be made.

This remainder of this book will help you to systematically develop a contingency plan that will work well in almost any type of hard times event. And the plan you gradually develop will work if you stay at home or if you are forced to abandon your home.

Chapter Four

Realistic Self-Sufficiency

One of the first things that needs to be carefully considered in order to create a practical survival plan is the issue of self-sufficiency.

The concept of becoming 100% self-sufficient is a very basic emotion that appeals to most people's survival instinct. It is the primary ingredient of a variety of pleasant daydreams where we picture ourselves independent of society and surviving in a comfortable although somewhat modest fashion. However, the reality of self-sufficiency is completely different from the vision we conjure up for ourselves whenever this topic intrudes into our minds.

For example, think about your last visit to the dentist. You sat in a relatively comfortable chair in a temperature controlled office and the dentist repaired your tooth in an almost painless procedure while your jaw was temporarily numbed from an injection a few minutes earlier. Now think about having a tooth removed under primitive conditions without any pain killer by an auto-mechanic using a pair of vise-grip pliers. Sometimes the realities of self-sufficiency are quite different from our romantic notions of living a more primitive existence.

The chapters in this book about self-sufficiency are based on my own personal viewpoints on each of the topics. In almost every case I am writing based on my own personal first-hand experience in each of the topic areas discussed.

The primary problem faced by our ancestors will be the same problem we would face today if we try to become 100% self-sufficient. There is simply not enough time in a normal workday to accomplish everything that would need to be done during that day. Therefore each of us would have to prioritize our daily work schedule and do those tasks that absolutely must be done that day. Even under these conditions most of us would still not be able to do everything if our goal was to be 100% self-sufficient.

However, if we were to reconsider our original objective and **not** try to become 100% self-sufficient in everything, then it is possible for the average person to achieve some reasonable level of self-sufficiency -- just not 100%.

For example, it would be far more cost efficient and practical for the average person to simply purchase a good quality stainless steel hunting knife instead of trying to locate the proper type of raw ore, and then dig that ore out of the ground, and then smelt the raw ore into metal, and then forge that metal into a knife. The average person would be better advised to simply purchase a good hunting knife at a local sporting goods store. The only two reasons why a person would want to make his or her own knife completely 100% from scratch would be if that person: (1) enjoyed knife making as a hobby, or (2) did not have the foresight to buy a good knife before knives became unavailable for some hypothetical reason.

The suggestions in this book are based on the assumption of partial self-sufficiency as opposed to 100% self-sufficiency. This book will explain which items to purchase now (such as a good hunting knife) and which items you could learn to provide for yourself if you have the knowledge and a few basic tools and pieces of equipment.

An Early Life Lesson In Self-Sufficiency

When I was seven-years old my grandfather bought each of his three grandsons our own brand-new fishing poles and reels. Then we dug up some worms from our garden area, and my father, grandfather, and the three of us boys traveled in an old car to a nearby lake where there was a rowboat for rent. We rented the rowboat and my father rowed us towards one of the shaded banks of the lake. The three of us boys were then instructed on how to put a worm on a fishhook, and how to cast the weighted bait out into the lake without interfering with anyone else in the boat. We fished for about three-hours but we only succeeded in catching a few really, really small fish which the adults immediately removed from our hooks and tossed back into the lake. Then my father rowed us back to the boat dock.

When we arrived there was a blonde-haired boy about five-years old fishing off the end of the dock with an old cane fishing pole and a small box of hand-tied fishing flies. He had no fishing reel -- just a piece of fishing line tied to the end of his cane fishing pole. He was wearing a pair of cut-off faded ragged blue jean shorts and nothing else. No shirt. No shoes. His shoulders had been blistered by the sun and were in the process of healing. As we passed him he pulled up his catch of fish for us to see -- about four or five really nice looking large fish. He never said a word. Then he lowered his catch of fish back down into the water. As we were walking towards the car my grandfather remarked that those fish were probably all that boy's family were going to have to eat that evening for supper. I was permanently impressed by two things. First, that a small five-year old boy was providing food for his family. And second, that the boy had caught several large fish with an old cane pole and a few hand-tied fishing flies. As I grew older I reflected on that scene many times inside my mind and I gradually realized that **knowledge and experience** are more important factors for success than expensive fishing gear and high performance fishing boats.

Quality and Cost

When you think about long-term self-sufficiency, think about how long your planned future investment will last before it gradually wears out.

1. It would be much better to have one or two high quality items instead of several cheaper items.
2. It would also probably be better to have high quality stainless steel items instead of items made from other materials which may rust, or break, or more quickly wear out.

Trade Items (or Barter Items) are Not Self-Sufficiency Items

One of the suggestions you will hear sooner or later is to purchase "trade or barter items" before the hard times begin. Some of the typical "trade and barter items" that are recommended are salt, first aid supplies, toilet tissue, and 22LR ammunition. The general reasoning behind this "trade and barter strategy" is as follows:

1. At the current time these "items" are widely available and reasonably priced.
2. During really hard times these items will become scarce or very expensive.
3. When that happens almost everyone will be desperate to obtain these items.
4. You will therefore be able to trade these "items" for the things you really need.

At first glance the above logic appears to be reasonable. However, there are several flaws with the above strategy such as:

1. The items you will eventually need during a hard times event will also probably be very scarce or very expensive.
2. You will have a very slim chance of finding someone who has what you need and who is also willing to trade for what you have to offer.
3. The overwhelming vast majority of the people who desperately need your "items" will probably have nothing to trade that you really want.

Chapter Four: Realistic Self-Sufficiency

4. Once it becomes known that you have an inventory of "extra items" you will become a high-priority target for thieves and criminals.

Therefore I suggest that you think very carefully about investing your money in "trade or barter items" for future trading purposes during a hard times tragedy event.

In my opinion a better strategy would be to simply invest your money in the things you know you will need. If you have all the things you will need during a hard times tragedy event then you will not be forced to leave your home and expose yourself to unnecessary risk by traveling to some remote "barter location" in the hope of being able to find someone who has what you need and who is willing to trade for what you have. In other words, you will already be self-sufficient at your current location and you will not be forced to invest precious time and energy in trying to find the things you should have purchased before the hard times begin.

Conclusion

The key to successful self-sufficiency is knowledge and experience. However, the amount of work required to become 100% self-sufficient far exceeds the amount of time that any one family would have to devote to these activities. Therefore it is important to know which skills are critical to learn immediately, and which skills can be safely learned at some future date if and when the need should eventually arise.

The purpose of this book is to help you acquire the **knowledge** in a variety of practical skill areas. But, due to time constraints, you will probably **not** be able to immediately gain practical **hands-on experience** in every skill area. You will need to prioritize. The suggestions in this book will help you prioritize in the most important survival skill areas. Later, as time permits and the situation requires it, you could gradually gain hands-on experience in a variety of other skill areas.

A Traveling Bag

When Jesus first sent His Disciples out to preach the good news,
He said, "Do **not** take a bag, food, money, staff, or extra clothes."

A bag could be used to carry supplies and other items for self-sufficiency.
A walking staff could be used for self-defense if it became necessary.

Just before He was crucified Jesus revised His instructions and He said,
"Take a bag, some money, and a sword with you wherever you feel led."

Jesus wanted His Disciples to be self-sufficient and to not live in fear,
or be a burden to those who for the first time the Gospel they would hear.

- - - - - - -

When Paul left Troas, his winter cloak and his scrolls he did not take.
This he later regretted and he asked Timothy to help him correct his mistake.

- - - - - - -

We should ask God for the things we need that He has not yet provided,
but we should take good care of those things He has already supplied.

If we are careless with the things that God has already to us given,
then He may not replace them when we once again truly need them.

Therefore pack a traveling bag with all the things you might really need,
and take it with you when traveling if Jesus' Words you wish to heed.

  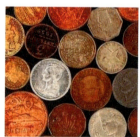

Scripture References: Matthew 10:5-10, Mark 6:6-11, Luke 9:1-6, Luke 22:35-36, Second Timothy 4:9-13, Second Timothy 4:21.

Poem: A Traveling Bag

Chapter Five

A Simple But Effective Survival Plan

Introduction

Your family's survival plan should meet both of the following minimum standards:

1. There is a very **small** probability that any member of your family will be hurt or injured in any way.
2. There is a very **high** probability that your plan will succeed.

One of the most difficult things to do when evaluating a survival plan is to be completely honest about the strengths and weaknesses of our plan. It is a natural human tendency to downplay any negatives and to focus exclusively on the positives. Although this may help to relieve some of our current anxiety about our family's future, this type of "tunnel vision" in not in the best interests of our family. If we truly desire to create a reasonable survival plan then we need to be honest and we need to own up to any shortcomings in our plan and we need to try and think of ways to minimize those negative aspects.

In my opinion a reasonable survival plan for your family should include:

1. Enough supplies to last at least fourteen-days at your current location.
2. Enough supplies to last at least six-months at either your current location or at a more desirable location.
3. The ability to provide additional water and food and clothing for at least twenty-years.
4. The desire to survive extremely difficult circumstances without compromising your humanity or your religious beliefs.

Let's examine each of the above four points one-at-a-time.

At Least Fourteen-Days of Supplies

Your family should have the option to stay exactly where you are or to evacuate your home immediately. Your family should have the option to carefully evaluate the current situation and then make an intelligent decision about the best way to maximize your family's chances for long-term survival.

Let's consider two hypothetical situations: (1) a nuclear explosion, and (2) a fire.

1. If a nuclear device was detonated a "safe distance" away from your location and the blast did not destroy or damage your neighborhood, then it probably will not be too long before radioactive fallout makes any type of travel extremely dangerous. After a nuclear explosion the prevailing wind patterns may shift suddenly and unexpectedly and you could easily find yourself surrounded by nuclear fallout. To venture outdoors in this situation would be stupid. A family's best chance for long-term survival would be to immediately build a small safe improvised shelter inside your current residence with as much weight (furniture, books, food, water, whatever) between you and the outside. Your family should then remain inside your improvised shelter for at least two-weeks to give most of the radioactive particles a chance to gradually burn themselves out. If possible, you should remain inside your improvised shelter for even longer but that is a decision you would need to make based on the specific circumstances at that time.

2. If a fire was headed your way and you knew the fire was going to reach and completely destroy your home in about one-hour, then you either abandon your home or you die. It this situation it should only take you a few minutes to put your "bug-out-bags" into your escape vehicle, along with several cases of food, and then you could head away from the danger zone.

If you had at least fourteen-days of supplies in your home then you could quickly and easily implement either one of the above two strategies, depending on which strategy was your best option at the time the decision actually needed to be made.

At Least Six-Months of Supplies

If you are suddenly and unexpectedly thrust into a situation that is completely different from today then it would be highly desirable if you did not have to worry about your family starving to death for at least six-months. This would give you time to more completely analyze the situation and determine what all your options are and which options have the best chance for long-term survival.

On the other hand, if your family has no food then you will be forced to search for food and this could expose you and your family to an overwhelming multitude of dangerous situations.

Therefore, which would you prefer:

1. Having six-months to carefully consider and develop a feasible long-term survival plan, or
2. Having to immediately search everywhere for food along with 99% of the rest of the people in the world and frequently getting caught in life-or-death fights over whatever food you might find.

The Ability to Be Self-Sustaining for at least Twenty-Years

Your objective should be long-term survival and not just for fourteen-days or for six-months. Therefore before a hard times event occurs you should have thought about how you will replenish your supplies on an on-going basis.

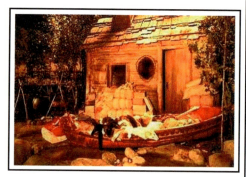

This will require that you have the following **minimum** items in your possession **before** the hard times event begins:

1. At least one good quality water filter element (about $50) that will process at least 10,000 gallons of water and remove harmful microorganisms and tiny radioactive nuclear particles. If you can afford it you should have three or four of these replacement water filter elements.
2. A comprehensive first aid kit, a good first aid/medical reference book, and a reasonable supply of the over-the-counter medicines your family has used in the past.
3. At least 5,000 paper matches (vacuum sealed in groups of eight match books or 160 matches per vacuum bag) and at least five new butane lighters.
4. A reasonable assortment of heirloom vegetable seeds and the knowledge of how to plant and harvest those crops, and how to save the new seeds for the following year.
5. At least one good quality gill net and at least 200 yards of extra fishing line so you can repair your net. This would allow you to easily harvest fresh fish for your family to eat.
6. A reasonable assortment of snares and traps along with at least one good trapping manual. This would permit you to silently harvest wild game animals for their meat and their hides.
7. At least one good semi-automatic hunting rifle (and scope) that will successfully terminate the largest wild game animal in your area and at least 1,000 rounds of ammunition for that rifle.
8. At least one good semi-automatic handgun and a good holster and at least 1,000 rounds of ammunition for that handgun.
9. At least one good 22LR semi-automatic rifle and at least 5,000 rounds of ammunition for that rifle.
10. At least one good hunting knife for each member of your family.
11. One good book on how to convert animals hides into buckskins so you can make your own clothes and moccasins with the passing years.
12. One good book on how to preserve food for winter consumption (smoking, drying, root cellars, etc.).

Chapter Five: A Simple But Effective Survival Plan

13. One good quality portable comprehensive tool kit that contains the most commonly used hand tools such as screwdrivers, wrenches, hammer, pliers, etc.
14. One good quality wood saw with at least a ten-inch blade. A fifteen-inch blade would be even better.
15. One good quality digging shovel (spade) with a pointed tip. The distance from the tip of the shovel to the end of its handle should be at least 54 inches long.
16. At least four heavy-duty tarps (10 mil thick). The sizes of these tarps should be between 10 feet by 12 feet up to approximately 16 feet by 30 feet. You should also have several hundred feet of strong nylon or polypropylene twine and several hundred feet of 20 gauge wire.
17. One good battery operated portable radio and one solar battery charger and several sets of replacement rechargeable batteries for that radio. This will allow you to listen to the news on a regular basis.
18. A good copy of the Holy Bible such as the New King James Version Study Bible.

The above items are not very big and they could easily be packed into your escape vehicle and taken with you. If you had all the above items with you then you would have the knowledge and the necessary equipment to provide for your family for at least twenty-years. This would take a lot of stress off you so you could focus your thoughts on other issues that might endanger your family's survival.

Your Personally Integrity and Morality

If a hard times event occurs unexpectedly then at least 99% of the people in the world will not be prepared for it. These individuals will engage one another in a life-or-death struggle over the supplies that existed at the beginning of the hard times event. You do not need to be in competition with these individuals. The odds will be too great against you (99 to 1).

Most of these individuals would never have believed that they could kill someone over a few cans of food. However, after starvation gradually weakens their bodies and their morals, then killing will no longer be considered murder -- it will be considered absolutely necessary for ordinary day-to-day survival.

If you have reflected on this prior to the onset of a serious society changing hard times event, then hopefully you will have made the decision that you and your family are not going to participate in the above fight over scarce resources. Hopefully you will have made some plans on where you could survive while the overwhelming majority of the world's population destroy one another.

If you make these plans now then you could retain your moral principles and your religious beliefs. If you don't make any plans now, then be prepared for a radical change in what you consider acceptable behavior after a serious hard times event begins.

Conclusion

At the current time the amount of really bad survival advice on the internet far exceeds the amount of good survival advice. I have seen this bad advice repeated again and again by a variety of different individuals on multiple internet forums and blogs. I am simply amazed at what the vast majority of people will accept on faith without first subjecting it to any type of in-depth critical analysis. Since they read the same bad advice again and again on different internet forums and since it is posted by individuals with the very best intentions, most people eventually accept the bad advice as being really good advice.

The problem is that the basic flaws in the bad advice won't become apparent until you actually put it into practice and then you will discover the obvious shortcomings that you should have had the wisdom to foresee if you had just taken the time to think about it ahead of time.

Therefore I strongly recommend that you carefully reflect on everything you read and that includes **all** the information in this book, including this chapter you are now reading. If you will just take the time to think things through to their logical conclusion you should be able to separate the really bad advice from the good advice and thereby help your family avoid a lot of potentially devastating heartbreaking events at some point in the future.

Hard times survival will be hard work. It will be hard work every day. There are several things you can do now to minimize the amount of future hard work but there is no "secret" that will eliminate the hard work. May I humbly suggest that you stop looking for some "secret" and instead accept the fact that if a hard times event occurs then you will need to work hard every day just to survive. If you can accept this basic truth then you will be far ahead of the vast majority of "survivalists" who think they have some "gadget" or "strategy" or "plan" that is going to make their life easier during the coming hard times.

May I also suggest that you stop adding more future work to your survival plan. Each new idea that you include in your future daily "adventure" will require more work each day and not less work. Too many new "survivalists" already have a survival plan that is far too complicated to be successful. And each day they add something new to their plan. The shear complexity of their survival plan currently exceeds the amount of work they can do each day. When they eventually try to put their plan into action they will discover this truth and they will wonder why they couldn't see this ahead of time. Please don't become one of those people whose survival plan is too complex to be successful on a practical level.

Footnote: An Example of Unnecessary Complexity

If you visit several different survival web sites on a regular basis then the chances are extremely high that you have seen a "homemade laundry detergent" formula on one or more of those web sites. Most of these formulas include Borax, which is a laundry detergent, plus two other items. The formula then explains how to mix these three ingredients together to make your own homemade laundry detergent.

Now stop and think about this formula from an honest perspective. Why would you want to buy three chemicals, one of which is a laundry detergent, to make your own homemade laundry detergent? Why not just buy regular laundry detergent that is ready to use right out of the box? Better still, why not follow the suggestion at several places on my web site and just buy some bars of pure Ivory soap, and then use that Ivory soap for everything (bath soap, hand soap, dish soap, laundry soap, and shampoo)? You can make liquid soap by shaving some of the soap off the bar of Ivory soap and then putting those shavings into some boiling water. After it cools you would then have pure liquid soap that may be used to wash your dishes, or your laundry, or your hair, or even a baby if your family is not allergic to Ivory soap.

Please don't make the hard times more difficult than they need to be. Think about what you read and then use common sense to make your own decision. Don't immediately accept something just because it appears on a really popular survival forum. This also applies to my web site. Don't simply accept everything I write as being the best solution for your family. I know the information I share is the best option for my family because I have actually tried it and it works well for us. I have also tried a lot of other things that didn't work well but I don't mention them on my web site.

Therefore please use common sense and select the best overall strategies for your family's survival, which will probably also include some really good information you find elsewhere. However, before you reject one my suggestions, please compare all your options in an honest manner as they specifically apply to your family's needs in your family's specific circumstances.

Chapter Six

How to Start Preparing for Hard Times on a Very Modest Budget

On February 11, 2010 I begin discussing the above topic on the "Survival Corner," a two-hour talk radio show on the Texas Broadcasting Network.

On February 25, 2010 I finished discussing the above topic on the Texas Broadcasting Network. A summary of some of my comments from both of those two-hour radio shows is included in this chapter.

Introduction

Nobody knows how the future will unfold. And that includes myself. Next month may be the same as this month, or it may be a lot better, or it may be a lot worse. There is no way to know what next month will bring until it actually gets here. Therefore it would probably be a good idea to have a variety of contingency plans instead of simply believing in one and only one possible future.

For example, it would be sad if you invested your life savings in preparing for an "end-of-the-world event" only to discover that the world doesn't come to an end and that the economy slowly but gradually starts to improve.

On the other hand, it would also be sad if you didn't make a few simple inexpensive investments so your family could survive an "unexpected hard times event" with the least amount of discomfort. That is the purpose of this chapter. This chapter will review a few basic things a person could do prior to an actual hard times event so his or her family could survive an unexpected hard times event and be in a better position to have their lives return to "normal" after the event has passed.

With this in mind the following topics will be discussed one at a time:

1. Where to Start When You Don't Have Much Money
2. Safety Is More Important Than You Think.
3. Where Will You Live?
4. Always Have a Backup Plan.
5. Secrecy and Other People.
6. Things to Avoid.

I Don't Have Much Money and I Really Don't Know Where I Should Start

Do you remember the moral of Aesop's Fable of "The Race between the Turtle and the Rabbit?" The moral of the story was: "Slow and steady wins the race." But how does that moral apply to preparing for hard times? The answer is simple:

1. Relax. Don't panic.
2. Avoid impulse purchases motivated by fear.
3. Relax. But don't procrastinate. Start today.
4. Start by making a plan and then gradually and systematically work your plan.
5. In other words, proceed at a slow but steady pace.

For example, you could design a hard times survival plan that was customized for your family's specific needs by doing the following:

1. Start with a very brief list of the most important broad categories of things your family would need to survive a hard times tragedy event, such as water, food, and clothing.

2. Under each broad category add a more detailed list of the things you would like to have within that category. This is a wish list. Don't be ashamed to add things to your wish list. You can prune your list later.
3. Do a little internet window shopping and find out where you could buy each item on your list along with its price at each internet store. Make sure you copy and save the internet address of each store you visit in a special file so you can find that store again later if you decide to buy something from them.
4. Carefully analyze your list and prioritize your spending.
5. Don't go overboard in a single category. In other words, if you really like clothes then don't invest every spare dollar you have in clothes. If you really like firearms then don't invest every spare dollar you have in firearms. Instead systematically make investments in all of the major categories as money becomes available.
6. Take the time to carefully think about each of your purchases before you invest your money.

Safety is More Important Than You Think

Remember your primary objective is to survive a hard times tragedy event and live to a ripe old age. This objective can be achieved if you will be extra careful whenever you are trying to learn a new skill, and whenever you are trying to learn how to use any type of equipment you have never used before.

For example, most of the following accidents could be avoided if you first take the time to learn and follow the appropriate safety rules:

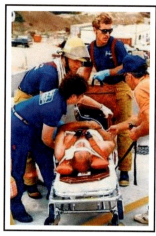

1. Buying some basic hand tools you have never owned or used before, including a hammer, and then severely smashing your thumb the first time you use the hammer.
2. Buying your very first firearm and then accidentally shooting yourself or someone in your family.
3. Trying to learn how to sharpen a knife using a sharpening stone and then accidentally slicing a huge piece off one of your fingers.
4. Buying your first chain saw so you can cut your own firewood and then you become permanently crippled by an accident that could have been avoided if you had just taken the time to receive some proper training in the safe way to use a chain saw.

Safety is always important but it is of critical importance during a hard times event because professional emergency medical care may not be immediately available. Therefore always begin by learning and practicing all the relevant safety rules for whatever you are attempting to do.

The following two universal safety rules are always important but they are even more important during hard times:

1. **Always wear safety glasses.** Your eyes are too important to your survival to lose one or both of them. Therefore during a hard times tragedy event always wear safety glasses, even when you are just sitting down and doing nothing. You can purchase a good pair of safety glasses for less than $5 at almost any store that sells hand tools. Aren't your eyes worth a simple $5 investment? (**Note:** On two different occasions during my life I have had an extremely tiny object embed itself in one of my eyes. The object was so small that I couldn't see it in a mirror but it was very uncomfortable and my eye watered continuously. On both occasions I tried flushing the object out but it was embedded and it would not come out. I had to visit an eye doctor and have my eye numbed while he located the object and then extracted it. The first time I was outdoors and a sudden strong wind blew the tiny object into my eye. The second time something heavy fell on the ground beside me and the impact sent a tiny object flying upwards into my eye. Both of these painful experiences could have been avoided if I had been wearing safety glasses.)

Chapter Six: How to Start Preparing For Hard Times

2. **Be careful when lifting or moving anything bulky or heavy.** Don't injure your back and then live in pain for the rest of your life. My father was in the Accident Insurance Business for thirty-years and he told me that one of the most common accidents was when a woman who was at least 40 years old attempted to move or rearrange a mattress on a bed. The mattress was too big to get a good grasp on it and the lady would bend over into a really bad lifting position and then throw her back out of alignment. You can avoid a similar injury by learning the basic rules about how to lift things using your legs instead of your back, and then not lifting anything that is too heavy or too awkward to be easily moved by one person.

Where Will You Live?

In my opinion the safest place for most families to live would probably be the home or apartment where they now live. However, depending on the type of hard times event, it might be better if you abandoned your home. This is the type of decision that would need to be made based on a variety of different variables that you would not know until the decision actually needed to be made.

For example, if a forest fire was headed in your direction then a decision to stay where you are could prove to be fatal. Therefore it would be good idea to have at least one or two backup locations that you could retreat to in the event that it becomes necessary.

For most families the most obvious choice would be the home or apartment of another close family member, such as your parents, or a brother, or a sister, or maybe even the home of one of your children.

However, in addition to this obvious first choice, you should also have considered the possibility that your first choice might not exist at the time you really needed it. For example, three days earlier an earthquake could have destroyed the place you had originally planned to retreat to. Therefore you should have a second option to fall back on. For most families this may mean living inside their vehicle or inside a tent. Let's examine both options:

1. **Vehicle:** Most vehicles are too small to be comfortable for more than two people. Even two people will usually find that the space inside a vehicle is not adequate for a long period of time. However, if you have a mini-van or a regular size van then you may actually be able to live inside it for period of time until you can locate more suitable arrangements. After removing the rear seats, a van will allow you to store a lot of your belongings in plastic tote containers or plastic buckets on the floor of the van. You could then put a full size or queen size mattress on top of those containers. The size of the mattress would depend on

the size of the van. This would give you a place to sleep at night if the weather outside was not too cold. (Note: If your containers and buckets are a variety of different sizes then you may need to put a flat sheet of thin plywood on top of the taller containers and then put your mattress on the plywood.)

2. **Tent:** If you have children then a tent is a better option than living inside your vehicle. However, it will only be acceptable for a short period of time, and then only if the weather outside is not too cold. However, it would allow you to lie down at night on an air mattress or a folding cot and get some sleep. The major disadvantage of a tent is that it is not as secure or safe as sleeping inside a vehicle.

Sleep Deprivation: Regardless of which of the above two options you select, one of the most important considerations will be your ability to get some sleep at night. Sleep deprivation during a hard times event will

Chapter Six: How to Start Preparing For Hard Times

gradually reduce your ability to make good decisions. Therefore, whichever option you select you will need to think about the sleeping arrangements very carefully and make sure you have a regular mattress, or a folding cot, or an air mattress for each family member, along with the corresponding number of pillows, sheets, blankets, or sleeping bags. (**Note:** Sleep deprivation is one of the reasons that most government shelters would be unacceptable as a backup alternative during a hard times event.)

Government Shelters: If you are absolutely certain that the hard times event will be over in a week or two, then a temporary government shelter might be okay. The major problems will be that those shelters will be very crowded, and the shelters will house people that you absolutely would never allow your family to associate with during normal times, such as alcoholics, prostitutes, sex offenders, drug addicts, and hardened criminals who just happen to be between visits at the state penitentiary. Therefore you need to think very carefully before you enter any type of government shelter. If the shelter is a "temporary" shelter inside a local church or public school then it might be a little better than the typical government run shelter. If you know from the beginning that the hard times event is going to last a very long time then I suggest that you not enter any type of shelter. Once you are inside the shelter you may not be allowed to leave regardless of what you may have been told when you voluntarily walked through the front door. The people you will meet inside the shelter will have nothing to say except to repeat their heart-breaking stories. You will also find yourself among a group of people who have rarely ever worked but who are exceptionally well skilled at knowing how to survive by stealing from others.

Cabin Cave: If the hard times event is one that will be relatively long in duration, such as several years, then your vehicle or tent or a government shelter will not be acceptable. If you try to live inside a tent or your vehicle then your family will freeze to death during the winter months. During a long-term tragedy event a "cabin cave" would probably be your best long-term solution. To build a "cabin cave" you will need a shovel, a good saw, a hatchet, some wire, and a few tarps. Complete instructions for building a "cabin cave" are discussed in another chapter in this book.

Always Have a Backup Plan

By this time you have probably noticed that for almost every topic that has been discussed there have been several different options for you to consider. Having options, or a backup plan, significantly increases the chances of your family's long-term survival. You and your spouse should take the time to seriously discuss your backup plan and the two of you should agree on what would work best for your family.

Close Relatives: If your backup plan involves going to live with some of your very close relatives in the country then you should discuss this possibility with those relatives now. Get their permission that it would be okay with them. Then ask them if it would also be okay if you could please store some basic food items, some clothes, and a firearm and some ammunition at their location. This would demonstrate that you do not intend to become a burden to them but you will do everything within your power to provide for the needs of your own family members if an unexpected hard times event forces you to come live with them.

Note 1: Every member of your family will need to adjust their life style and their habits and everyone will need to 100% comply with any and all of the rules of the head of the household at your backup location regardless of whether or not you agree with those rules. Please explain to each member of your family that you will not be waited on hand and foot and you will not have your every whim instantly gratified. Instead your family will be temporary residents that can be instantly evicted if everyone does not behave in a manner that is acceptable to your relatives. It will just take one rebellious family member to get everyone evicted. Explain to your family that if you are evicted then your next location living under a bridge will be significantly worse than where you currently are.

Chapter Six: How to Start Preparing For Hard Times

Note 2: If you are the family member who still has a safe place to live and some of your close relatives ask your permission to come live with you then you need to decide whether or not this will be acceptable to your entire family. If you say "yes" then please make sure that everyone in that other family 100% understands the information in the above paragraph, and that they will be asked to immediately leave if they do not follow all the rules you have established for your household. Your rules are not open for negotiation. In addition, everyone who comes to live with you will have assigned chores that they must do every day, such as: sweep the floor, wash the dishes, do the laundry, or work in the garden. And every adult will need to find some type of job even if it only pays minimum wage. Every adult should be given a reasonable period of time to find a full-time or part-time job, such as two or three-weeks. One-third of every person's paycheck, whether it is a big paycheck or a little tiny paycheck, will be given to you as "rent" to help you pay a portion of your normal household expenses, such as your mortgage payment and your utility bills. These "rent payments" will not give the other family part ownership in your home or the right to misuse the utilities or the right to start making their own rules. The "rent payment" will also not include free food. The other two-thirds of each person's paycheck should be used by the other family to purchase food, and gasoline, and other necessities for themselves. If your close relatives do not like these arrangements then they will need to find some place else to live. I suggest you think very carefully about who you allow to come live with you because every family, including my own, has some people who are lazy and they always have some reason why they can't find a job, or why they had to quit the job they just had, or why they can't do the chores assigned to them. If you have one or more of these people living with you, or someone who always gripes and complains, then you will need to evict them from your household the minute you get fed up with their behavior. In my opinion the hard times are probably going to get a lot, lot worse before they gradually start to improve and these types of individuals will significantly reduce the chances for the long-term survival of your spouse and children. In my opinion, if you suspect there is a very small chance that things would work out in the long run with the another family living with you, then you should not allow them to move in with you to begin with. Instead you should say "no" when they first ask and then explain why using one or more of the following reasons:

1. There is not enough space in your house for the other family, not even for one night.
2. You can't afford to feed the other family.
3. You can't allow all of your close relatives and friends to live in your home and instead of making an exception for one family and showing favoritism you must treat everyone the same and you must say no to everyone who asks. If you take in one family and then refuse to take in another family then that other family will hate you for the rest of their lives and they will blame every bad thing that happens to them from that day forward on your refusal to take them in.

There will be fewer long-term bad feelings if you do not start a dependency relationship than if you start one and then have to stop it. You and your spouse should seriously discuss this now and together you will need to decide if you will say no to another family or to all the other families that ask. If you say no then do not let the other family load you down with guilt and pity for not taking them in. After you say no you will need to bring the conversation to a close as soon as possible to prevent the conversation from going downhill and having things said that should never have been said. It may become necessary to politely say, "I have to go now. Good-bye." and then immediately hang up the phone very gently while the other person is still complaining, or immediately but gently close the door to your home while the other person is still trying to get you to change your mind. If they are at the front door to your home and they keep banging on your door and they refuse to leave then politely and calmly say through the closed door, "You are creating a disturbance. I am calling 911 now. The police will be here in a few minutes to escort you off this property." Then call 911 and explain the situation to them and let the proper authorities handle the situation in the same manner that they have probably handled dozens of similar situations in the past few days. This will be much easier if you have kept the other family standing outside the door to your home instead of inviting them inside to explain their situation to you. Let the other family make their request outside at the door to your home and not inside your living room.

Rental Storage Building: Another type of backup plan would be to rent a small storage area in a temperature controlled building in a small rural town that you consider a reasonable place to live and raise your family.

The cost of the storage area will usually be somewhere between $35 to $70 per month depending on the size of the storage area. You will probably need an area that is at least 6-feet wide by 8-feet deep by 8-feet tall. You will be allowed to put your own padlock on the storage area door so you would be the only one who would have access to that storage area as long as you keep your rent payments up to date. I suggest that you always keep your rent paid at least three months in advance. You could then store a variety of long shelf life food items, clothing, kitchen utensils, sheets, pillows, air mattresses or cots, and camping gear inside your storage area. This could be your "Plan B" in the event you had to quickly abandon your current location. Later in this book I will provide some more detailed information about to "How to Select the Optimal Retreat Location."

Emergency Gasoline for your Primary Vehicle: If a hard times event strikes suddenly and unexpectedly then you may need some gasoline to get to your "Plan B" location. However, storing gasoline is dangerous and therefore you should consider the following:

1. Always comply with your local fire safety laws.
2. Purchase and store either one or two 5-gallon containers of gas. These should be containers that are specifically designed for the safe storage of gasoline.
3. Store your gasoline in a safe location and avoid breathing the gas fumes. A reasonable location might be the same place you store your lawn mower. The storage area should have a lock on it to prevent the loss of your lawn mower and your gasoline.
4. It is best to purchase your gasoline during the cold winter months because the winter gas formula is better than the warm weather gas formula for long-term gas storage.
5. Buy the highest octane available, such as 93 octane. The higher the octane rating the longer the gas will remain effective in storage.
6. Treat your gasoline before you put it into storage. In my opinion PRI-G is the best gas treatment available. A 16-ounce container costs about $22 and it will treat 216 gallons of gas. PRI-G may also sometimes be used to rejuvenate old gas that has gone stale, One internet store that sells PRI-G is: http://www.wisementrading.com/farm/pri.htm
7. Each winter put the one-year old gasoline that you have in storage inside your vehicle and use it. Then refill your gas containers with fresh gasoline and immediately treat that fresh gasoline with PRI-G gas treatment following the instructions on the PRI-G container.

Secrecy

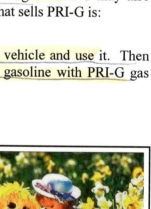

1. Don't discuss your disaster plans with anyone except your spouse. Don't even discuss your plans with your children because children like to brag about their parents and it won't be long before everyone knows everything about your plans.
2. Most people will not prepare but they will remember that you talked about it and that you are prepared.
3. When their children get hungry they will come knocking on your door.
4. They will politely ask you to share everything you have with them. If you don't share what do you think they will do next?
5. If you do share then they will keep coming back every day for another handout.
6. They will also tell anyone who asks them exactly where they got their free supplies. If they don't tell where they got their supplies what do you think would happen to them? Will they put your family's safety above the safety of their own family?

Chapter Six: How to Start Preparing For Hard Times

7. How many different families can you feed and how long can you feed them?
8. After you run out of supplies trying to feed dozens of families, what will happen to your family?

Other People

People generally fall into one of three very broad groups as follows:

1. A very small but very powerful group of "elite" families who have control over a significant portion of the world's resources.
2. People who are "too smart" to work because they know:
   a. They can get the "entitlement welfare system" to provide for some of their needs, plus
   b. They can get honest hard working people to provide for some of their needs due to "pity," plus
   c. They will steal what they want when they see they can get away with it and there is no chance of their being caught or punished.
3. Honest people who do all the honest necessary jobs within the society, such as an emergency room physician, an automobile repair mechanic, and a restaurant worker who earns minimum wage. These individuals normally would rather work than beg. Therefore they end up supporting both of the above two groups of people.

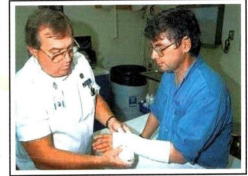

Hard times occur when a large percentage of the honest hard-working people lose their jobs and they are unable to find any type of work of any nature. This creates significant problems for a society for three basic reasons:

1. There is not enough tax revenue to support the government in its current size. Therefore governments must either increase the tax burden on its citizens who are still working, or downsize its operations.
2. The amount of "entitlement" benefits cannot be maintained at their former level and therefore the system cannot add all the honest hard-working people who have lost their jobs into the "entitlement welfare programs." Therefore the government must come up with some "creative reasons" why the honest people who are now out of work are not qualified for the same benefits as the people who have never worked.
3. The amount of "freewill charity" is drastically reduced because people can just barely support themselves and their extended family members who are now living with them. Freewill charity consists of voluntary donations to organizations such as the United Way and Food Pantries that distribute free food to needy families.

During a serious hard times tragedy event other people will quickly become one of the most dangerous problems you will have to deal with. Please don't lie to yourself about what other people are capable of doing when they are faced with a life threatening situation. You should be emotionally prepared to see the **dark side** of people you may have known for many years. People will do whatever they believe is necessary to save themselves and their children from starvation or death.

To survive a serious long-term tragedy event you will need to become part of a small close-knit community, or your family will need to live by yourselves in the middle of a wilderness area for both of the following reasons:

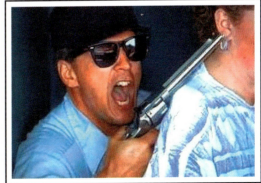

1. Some members of our society are evil and they are just waiting for some type of disaster to happen so they can do all the unspeakable things they have been wanting to do for many years but they were afraid to do because they might get caught and punished. When there is a very, very small chance of being caught and punished then these individuals

Chapter Six: How to Start Preparing For Hard Times

will start doing horrible things because they know they have nothing to fear from honest law-abiding citizens because honest people would never consider harming them in any way. Therefore it will be extremely easy for these evil individuals to gain the trust of honest people through some type of "hard luck story" and then when their guard is down to quickly and easily kill all of them and then take everything they have.

2. The overwhelming vast majority of the people in the United States are "spoiled" and they have never had to live for any extended period of time in conditions that people in third world countries would be very happy with but which people here in the United States would find totally unacceptable. This will be a significant problem during the first few months of a serious hard times tragedy event. Most people will not be able to adjust and accept a lower standard of living that only includes clothes to wear, a safe place to sleep at night, one or two decent meals every day, and a lot of spare time to read or relax. Their past life experiences will not allow them to accept this basic level of survival and they will look for some way to improve their daily lives, even if it is only for a very brief period of time. Their refusal to be content with the basic essentials of life will be the primary reason they will not live very long, and it will also be the reason that anyone who is associated with them will also have a very short life expectancy. I suggest that you think about this very carefully and then make your own decision on whether or not you are emotionally prepared to live in a more primitive 1800s lifestyle until you reach a ripe old age.

Things to Avoid

1. **Avoid becoming a prisoner:**
   a. During a hard times tragedy event don't become a prisoner.
   b. Don't become a prisoner of the government, or a group of criminals, or another person.
   c. During a hard times tragedy event the vast majority of prisoners don't survive.
   d. The living conditions within a prisoner-of-war camp are horrible. There is no running water or sewer systems. But every prisoner still needs to relieve himself at least once a day and therefore the ground gradually fills up with human waste. This human waste attracts flies and other disgusting creatures. A variety of diseases rapidly spread throughout the entire prison camp. And there is nothing the prisoners can do about it.

   e. There are no "real" statistics on prisoner survival because no nation would admit to what really happened to the prisoners under their control.
   f. But the reality is that there is no spare food or extra medicine to give to prisoners.
   g. And if the prisoners are kept hungry and weak then it makes it easier to control them and it helps to avoid any type of uprising or revolt or escape attempt.
   h. Starving prisoners are not able to think as clearly as healthy people. Starving prisoners make more serious mistakes.
   i. Starving prisoners will gradually die from natural causes, such as dysentery. This makes space for the next group of prisoners.
   j. Therefore don't become a prisoner during a hard times tragedy event.

2. **Avoid becoming a refugee:**
   a. A refugee is an individual who has had to abandon his or her home in order to stay alive.
   b. A refugee only has what he could carry with him. This may be nothing more than the clothes he is wearing but most of the time it also includes a few things he was able to salvage from his home before abandoning it.
   c. A refugee's only hope for survival is to accept whatever donations and charity he may receive from the

government, and from relief organizations, and from the citizens of the surrounding area.

d. Refugees are not able to find any type of work and therefore they can't support themselves or provide their own food.
e. The living conditions in a refugee camp are horrible. Human waste quickly accumulates on the ground and disease rapidly spreads throughout the refugee area.
f. The average life expectancy of the vast majority of the refugees can be measured in weeks. Some die during the first few days but some survive for several months.
g. When we watch the aftermath of a disaster event on television we normally only see the impact of relief efforts for the first few weeks in the disaster area. What we don't see on television is what happens when the media gradually shifts its attention away from the disaster area and the voluntary donations to the disaster area are gradually used up and the people are once again forced to provide for themselves. When that happens the average life expectancy of the surviving refugees can be measured in days or weeks.
h. Don't become a refugee. Always have a backup plan that includes a reasonable destination to flee to where you have previously stored some basic food, supplies, and equipment before the disaster event occurred.
i. If 100% of your emergency supplies are stored at your current residence then you will have created the perfect conditions for you and your family members to become homeless, helpless refugees if an unexpected disaster event destroys your home, or forces you to quickly abandon your home.

3. **Avoid farm livestock and household pets:** The reasons are discussed in detail in the "pet and livestock" chapter of this book.

4. **Avoid a huge garden and a green house:** This is an open invitation to everyone to come and steal from you because you obviously have far more than you need.

5. **Avoid a specialty skill that is difficult or time consuming to learn:** This would be any skill that requires a investment in equipment and many years of training that will far exceed the price of the item you are trying to make yourself. For example, which of the following activities would be the best use of your time and your money?

   a. Buy some cotton seeds. Plant those seeds. Take care of your cotton plants while they grow. Water them if they need it. Learn how to pick cotton without destroying your hands. Buy a spinning wheel. Learn how to spin cotton into thread on the spinning wheel. When you are finished you will have some homemade yarn or some homemade thread. It may not be the best quality you have ever seen but you will be proud of it because you will have invested more than one year in learning how to make it yourself.

   or:

   b. Visit the sewing goods department at your local Walmart store and buy one 1,200 yard spool of high quality thread for $4.97 per spool. The 1,200 yard spool of thread will probably be sufficient for all your family's sewing needs for at least ten years during a hard times tragedy event.

When you take the time to carefully think about the above and you use simple common sense to compare the two options, isn't the best answer obvious?

Chapter Six: How to Start Preparing For Hard Times

The Truth

Sometimes the truth is visible to everyone and
    sometimes the truth is hidden from our eyes.
Sometimes the truth is mixed in with rumors,
    misinformation, half-truths, and intentional lies.

If a person impulsively decides what he or she wants to believe,
    then it is very easy to justify that point of view.
You simply accept anything that supports your belief,
    and then you discard everything else as being untrue.

But a person who honestly seeks to know the truth
    will not form an opinion until all has been revealed.
And then that person will carefully separate the truth
    from all the lies in which it has been carefully concealed.

The origin of lies is Satan and he still tempts people to lie
    in his ongoing effort to bury the truth in obscurity.
Even our historical past which should be known for certain
    is sometimes rewritten to support the latest philosophy.

In a world where lies frequently outnumber the truth
    where can we go to be certain we are not being deceived?
There is only **one** place and that is the Holy Bible.
    Read it carefully and the truth will set you free.

Scripture References: John 8:44, Second Timothy 2:1, Ephesians 1:13-14, Ephesians 6:13-17, Second Timothy 3:16-17, Second Peter 1:21, Isaiah 34:16, Matthew 24:55, John 17:17, John 8:31-32.

Poem: The Truth

Chapter Seven

How to Build a Very Effective
Water Filter System for Approximately $75

An effective water filter system that will process about 10,000 gallons of drinking water can be made using:

1. A replacement water filter cartridge such as the ones made by Berkefeld or Aquarain (about $50).
2. A plastic food grade five or six-gallon pail or bucket (about $3).
3. One or two heavy duty tarps (about $10 each).
4. One or two heavy duty plastic tote containers (about $8 each).
5. Some strong nylon or polypropylene cord or twine (about $4).

The first step is to capture rainwater using heavy-duty tarps. You will also need some strong nylon or polypropylene cord or twine to secure the grommets in the outside edges of a tarp to some nearby objects (such as trees or buildings) so the tarp will hang down in a "U" or "V" shaped pattern from side to side and with the rear of the tarp about one-foot higher than the front of the tarp. Place a large clean empty plastic tote container at the front end of the tarp at the center of the "V" to catch the rainwater as it pours out the front end of the tarp.

As a practical example, if it rains one-inch and you have the tarp arranged in a "U" or "V" shape then:

1. A single 9-foot by 10-foot tarp will collect approximately 50 gallons of rainwater.
2. A single 10-foot by 12-foot tarp will collect approximately 70 gallons of rainwater.

For planning purposes you will need approximately one-gallon of water per day per person. This is enough water for drinking and for brushing your teeth. It is not enough for cooking, or bathing, or washing the dishes, or doing the laundry. These activities will require significantly more water. You should have enough drinking water for each member of your household to last at least 30-days.

Rainwater is safe to drink if you can catch it before it comes in contact with anything else. In other words, if you stand outside with your mouth open and the rain falls straight down from a cloud in the sky into your mouth then you could swallow that water and not worry about getting sick (assuming the air was not full of smog or something else).

However, if the water makes contact with anything else, such as the leaves on a tree, then you will need to process that water before you drink it. There are also several other factors that may force you to process your rainwater before you can drink it. Some examples would be:

1. A limited nuclear war, or a nuclear power plant meltdown, anywhere on the face of the earth. The tiny nuclear particles can travel extraordinary distances after they have entered the upper atmosphere.
2. A volcanic explosion that pumps huge amounts of volcanic debris into the upper atmosphere.
3. A small meteor that hits the earth and sends huge amounts of debris into the upper atmosphere.

If any of the above events occur then it would not be safe to drink rainwater until after you have filtered it.

The simple inexpensive solution to the water filter problem would be to purchase one good quality gravity water filter. A good quality water filter will process about 10,000 to 12,000 gallons of water before it wears out if you pre-filter the water through a clean cloth before putting it through your water filter. One good water filter will provide about six gallons of drinking water each day.

The type of water filter I recommend is the "replacement" filter that you would install in a $250 to $350 gravity fed water filter system such as the **British Berkefeld** or the **AquaRain**. If money is not an issue then you could buy one of these complete systems. But if you need to be very careful about how you spend your money then all you really need is one replacement water filter for about $50. One water filter will process about 10,000 gallons of water at a rate of approximately six gallons per day.

When you order your water filter please be sure to specifically request that they ship the filter with a new "O" ring and a new "wing nut" for the bottom of the filter. With a new water filter, and an "O" ring seal, and a "wing nut" you can install your filter on anything that will hold at least one-gallon of water, and is also at least as tall as the filter itself. For example, you could install a water filter in a food grade 5 or 6 gallon plastic bucket, or a plastic tote container, or an empty one-gallon plastic water bottle (after you cut the top off the bottle). The container must have a flat bottom surface at the position where you will install the water filter. Simply drill a one-half inch diameter hole in the bottom center of the container and then put the "O" ring tight against the filter on the inside of the container and then screw the "wing nut" to the filter on the outside of the container. Then put the modified water filter container over another clean container that will catch the filtered water and fill the water filter container with water. Then relax and wait for gravity to move the water through your water filter into the lower container.

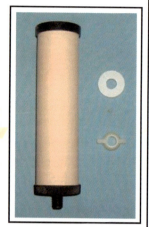

The lower container below your water filter container could be an ordinary water cooler with a normal water spout. These plastic water coolers are frequently sold in the camping section of stores. The advantage of one of these water coolers is that they have an airtight plastic lid that you can put on top of the water cooler after you remove your water filter container. This lid will help to keep the filtered water inside your water cooler clean. When you need some drinking water you could activate the bottom spout on the water cooler and clean water would flow out of the water cooler, through the spout, and into your drinking glass.

If you are filtering out radioactive particles then position your water filter system far enough away from your living quarters so the tiny radioactive particles that will get trapped inside the water filter cannot slowly poison your family members. Radiation only kills living organisms. It does not kill non-living things such as water or canned food. However, if you ingest water or food that contains radioactive particles then you will get sick and eventually die. However, if you remove the radioactive particles from the water then the water will be safe to drink. In other words, after you have removed the radioactive particles from the water then the water could be brought into your home but the water filter that trapped the radioactive particles should not be brought into your home.

One cheap way to store a lot of water is to use 5-gallon food grade plastic buckets or clean empty large heavy-duty plastic tote containers. Please remember that water is very heavy so please don't try to move a heavy plastic tote full of water. You could easily injure your spinal column. If you must move the water then move it a few gallons at a time by transferring it with cook pots to the new location.

Or you could store your extra water in clean empty two-liter soft drink plastic bottles with screw on caps. Or you could refill empty plastic water bottles that you saved for this purpose. These would be the 16-ounce to 20-ounce clear plastic water bottles that are sold by the case.

One quick final comment about water: your body needs water in order to digest food. Therefore if you don't have any water then don't eat.

Chapter Seven: A Homemade Water Filter

Chapter Eight

How to Find Water and How to Make Water Safe to Drink

The three basic necessities that sustain life are:

1. air,
2. water, and
3. food.

The **Rule of Threes** states that a person can live for:

three-minutes without air,
three-days without water, and
three-weeks without food.

Without water or any other fluids, a person will die in about three days. Therefore, since water is one of life's most basic necessities, it is a subject we should not take for granted.

Some Interesting Facts About Water and The Human Body

1. The human body:

    60% of our body is water.
    75% of our brain is water.
    83% of our blood is water and it transports nutrients and oxygen to the cells of our body.

2. Water is necessary to properly digest food. (Note: If you don't have water, then do **not** eat regardless of how hungry you become.)
3. Our urine is almost all water and it is how our body flushes and rids itself of toxic wastes.
4. Water facilitates normal bowel movements which helps prevent constipation.
5. In one day the average person loses between two to three quarts of water through their urine, sweat, and normal breathing. If a person doesn't replace that lost water then dehydration begins to occur.

    At 2% dehydration thirst is perceived.
    At 5% dehydration a person becomes hot and tired, and strength and endurance decrease.
    At 10% dehydration delirium and blurred vision become a problem.
    At 20% dehydration a person dies.

Pause and reflect on that for a moment. A person loses two to three quarts of water every day as a result of normal body functions. This means if a person doesn't get any fluids for about three days then that person will die. Most people have never thought about this because they have **never** been personally confronted with a extended shortage of fresh safe drinking water at any time in their lives.

Some More Facts About Water

1. Water is **very** heavy.
2. One gallon of water weighs about 8.5 pounds inside a thin-walled clear plastic water jug.
3. You can't carry enough water with you between locations to last for very long.
4. If one person consumes 2.75 quarts of water each day, then one person will need 250 gallons of water per year. A family of four will need 1,000 gallons of water per year. One-thousand gallons of water weighs about 4.25 tons. (And that does **not** include water for washing your hands or for washing dishes.)
5. With the passage of time bottled water will gradually become unfit to drink for a variety of reasons.

However, it can be reprocessed to make it fit for human consumption. Several different options are discussed later in this chapter.

If commerce were disrupted by either a natural or manmade disaster, one of the first things a person should do is evaluate their water situation. This involves three different but related issues:

1. How much water is on hand right now?
2. Where can more water be obtained?
3. How can that water be made safe to drink?

Drinking Water Available Immediately

If you are at home when the emergency occurs, then immediately check to see if the faucet water pressure is still on. If it is then fill every possible container in the house that will hold water and not leak. For example: pots, pans, plastic containers, drinking glasses and drinking cups, bowls, and every sink and bathtub.

If the water is off you will still have three sources of clean drinking water:

1. Ice cubes in the freezer, and
2. Water inside your water pipes, and
3. Water inside the hot water heater.

Even if the water pressure is off there is still some water inside the water pipes in your home or apartment. That water can be drained from the water pipes (using gravity) by opening the **lowest** cold water faucet in your home, which will usually be on the first floor, or the basement, or an outside water faucet. However, you will also need to open the highest cold water faucet in your home to allow air to enter the cold water pipes so the water can flow out the lowest water faucet into your collection container. This will drain all the water out of your cold water pipes but **not** your hot water pipes.

Most hot water heaters contain 40 gallons of clean water. However, **before** you remove that water you **must** turn off the power or turn off the gas to your hot water heater or you could start a fire. Then open the faucet at the bottom of the water heater to gain immediate access to 40 gallons of reserve clean drinking water. This is enough emergency water to last a family of four for 20 days if they **only** drink the water and don't wash with it. This is the **best** source of reserve drinking water for the average family because it is constantly being used and replaced inside the hot water heater prior to the emergency. Therefore it will be fresh and clean at the beginning of an emergency. (Note: Some hot water heaters do **not** have an easy access water value at their base. Prior to an emergency you should take a look at your hot water heater and determine if you can get to the water inside your heater. If you can't, then you might consider having a plumber install a standard water faucet value in the water line at the bottom of the hot water heater.)

Another source of water is canned foods because many canned foods are packed in water. When you open a can, serve the water in the can with the food. Never throw the canned water away if you are low on water.

Water that isn't safe to drink is toilet tank water and water inside the mattress of a water bed.

If you had the foresight to plan for an unexpected emergency then you should have a stash of clean empty 2-liter plastic soda bottles stored somewhere out-of-sight. They are really nice for storing water because they are free (after you drink the soda), they are made of food grade plastic, they don't leak, they have a screw on cap to keep the water clean, they have an extremely long shelf life, and they are a convenient size to handle and use. The major disadvantage of the 2-liter bottles is that don't stack well on top of one another.

If you purchase bottled water by the case then after you drink the water, screw the clean caps back onto the clean empty plastic bottles, and put the empty plastic bottles back onto the cardboard flat. These cardboard flats of empty plastic water bottles will stack nicely on top of one another.

If you have empty one-gallon plastic water jugs then you should also consider saving them for a future emergency. However, clean empty plastic milk jugs are **not** a good option because they will deteriorate with the passage of time and begin to leak.

After inventorying your water the next step is to ration your water. During normal times one person consumes about 3 quarts of water per day. No one I know drinks that much water each day. However, all of us drink some water, plus a variety of other fluids (coffee, tea, soda, juice, or whatever appeals to you). During hardship conditions, a person can survive on two quarts of water per day (two quarts is one-half gallon). If water is really in short supply then one quart per day will keep a person alive but that person will begin to slowly dehydrate.

Everyone knows better but after an extended period of time with little or no water a person will drink all the water he or she can when it suddenly becomes available. If you do this you will get sick. Force yourself to . . . S l o w - - d o w n. Drink one cup of water every 10 minutes. Give your system a chance to absorb the water and send it where it is needed most. Don't overload your system and kill yourself.

Where to Find More Water

You have inventoried and carefully rationed your water but the emergency continues longer than you anticipated and you are running low on water. Before your water completely runs out you should start replenishing it. Let's examine a number of different alternatives.

Well Water: If you live in the country, or if you have a water well on your property, then you already know there is water in the bottom of that well. Drilled wells can be anywhere from about 25 feet deep up to a thousand feet deep or more. For approximately $1,000 it is possible to purchase a heavy-duty manually-operated complete hand water pump for wells that are 200 feet deep or less. It is not possible to hand-pump water from wells much deeper than about 200 feet. However, there is a **very** cheap way to get water out of almost any well, regardless of its depth.

If you know your electricity is going to be off for an extended period of time, and you are out of drinking water, and you have no other way to get drinking water, then you can manually remove the water from your well.

There are many different well configurations but a typical one is illustrated in the picture on the right. First you **must** turn off the electrical power at the main circuit breaker box, even if the electricity is off. Then disconnect the electrical wires at the top of the well and protect them so they do not touch one another or any other object. You may also need to disconnect the plastic pipe or hose connected to the top of the well piece. Next you will need the correct size wrench to remove the large bolts that secure the top piece to the well. After removing the bolts also remove the top piece and you will probably find three things: a very long flexible heavy-duty hose, a water-resistant rope, and some electrical wiring, all of which go down into your well and are attached to the well pump in the bottom of the well. You can gradually pull up on the rope (or the flexible hose if absolutely necessary) and it will bring the well pump up out of the well. Don't pull on the electrical wiring because it is not intended for that purpose. After removing the well pump you will have exposed the entire shaft down to where your water is.

Depending on the depth of the well, the diameter at the **bottom** of the well shaft will probably be a little **smaller** than the visible diameter at the top of the well shaft. Therefore, select a container that is at least one or two inches smaller in diameter than the well opening at its top. The container can be almost any length up to about 18 inches. The container should have a large mouth on top to allow water to enter and air to escape. One option would be an empty two-liter plastic soda bottle with its top cut off.

The next step is of critical importance. Untie the wet end of the well rope from the well pump. Tie the opposite dry end of the rope to a secure object. This will keep the rope from falling into the well if you lose your grip. Then **securely** attach the wet end of the well rope to the container. If the container somehow works itself loose from the rope then you will **not** be able to get the container out of your well shaft. Also remember the container is going to be **heavy** with water when you pull it up. One option would be to make a strong net and put your container inside the net. Then tie the rope securely to the net.

Then put a relatively heavy clean, sterile object in the bottom of the container so the container will sink when it reaches the water level. Then slowly lower the container on the end of the rope by hand until it reaches the bottom of the well. You will know you have hit bottom when the rope has some slack in it. Wait for the container to fill with water and then pull it up. Repeat as often as required. When you are finished cover the exposed well head to prevent foreign materials from entering and contaminating your well water.

Rain Water: For the average person the best source of replacement drinking water will probably be rain water. Although this is an excellent source of safe drinking water, it is unpredictable in regards to timing and quantity. However, for most people this is probably the cleanest source of replenishment drinking water they will have access to on a regular but intermittent basis.

Regardless of where you live in the world, if you can catch the rain water **before** it comes in contact with anything then it is safe to drink without any special treatments. Even when you take acid rain into consideration, this is still a true statement. However, if there is a nuclear, chemical, or biological war at some point in the future, then rain water may not be safe to drink for some period of time. You will have to use your own judgment in that situation. Distillation or one of the portable commercial water filters described later in this chapter might be appropriate in those types of unusual and hazardous situations.

If the air contains smog, pollen, or any other unpleasant stuff, then the rain will usually clean that stuff out of the air during the first 20 to 30 minutes of a good rain shower. Therefore when it begins to rain you should wait about 30 minutes and then start collecting the clean rain water in a container. (Note: If you are seriously low on water and you are forced to collect the rain water during the first few minutes when it starts to rain, then you should process that water through one of the water filters described later in this chapter.)

Be creative. Think about what you have available that you can put outside to catch and hold rain water, or channel rain water through a partially open window into a big pot. Remember that it usually rains one-inch or less each time it rains. You need a large surface area to collect enough rain water to drink. A drinking cup or glass will not be enough. Even a 5-gallon cook pot is too small to just put outside by itself because it will only collect one-inch of water in the bottom of the pot.

Something like a child's inflatable swimming pool would be ideal, if your family already owns one. A 6-foot diameter pool would collect about 17 gallons of water if it rained one-inch. An 8-foot diameter pool would collect about 31 gallons of water if it rained one-inch. (Note: One gallon of water = 231 cubic inches of water.)

Or you could secure a clean 10-foot by 12-foot tarpaulin (or a clean thick sheet of plastic) in a manner where it slopes downward into a "V" shape towards a large 5-gallon pot (or other large container). Tarpaulins are commonly called tarps. With this size tarp you could collect about 70 gallons of water if it rains one-inch in your area (if you keep emptying and replacing your 5-gallon pot). However, you will need to secure your tarp very carefully because it is frequently very windy during a rain storm. Determine the primary direction in which the wind is blowing and then secure your tarp facing the wind at an upwards angle so the wind will blow a lot of the rain onto the surface of your tarp where it can collect and be channeled down into your water storage container.

In many areas it usually rains **less** than one-inch each time it rains, so it would probably be a good idea to use several tarps to collect rain water when it does rain. Many different tarp sizes are available but for collecting rain water a tarp between 6-foot by 8-foot up to about 10-foot by 12-foot would be ideal. Smaller tarps don't cover enough area nor do they have very many other practical uses. Larger tarps are too heavy and they also have a limited number of other useful applications.

If you are trying to decide between an inflatable swimming pool or a good tarp then the tarp would be the better choice. It is usually less expensive, more durable, easier to transport between locations, easier to set up and take down, requires less storage space when not in use, and it will provide an overhead shelter if you need to do some unexpected camping. When camping the two most useful items are a good hunting knife and a high quality tarp.

Another option for collecting rain water would be to put clean bed sheets outside your windows. Let them get drenched in the rain and then bring them inside and ring the water out of them by hand into a pot. Then stick them back out into the rain again. This is **not** the best method but it will provide some drinking water.

If you live in a tall apartment building with a flat roof then you might consider collecting rain water on the roof of your building using the large tarp or heavy-duty plastic sheet described above.

If you live in a house, you could collect the rain water from your roof gutters at the end of the down spouts. However, since the rain water has already been in contact with your roof, you will need to process it using one of the methods described later in this chapter. The easiest way to collect roof rain water is to remove a few feet from the bottom of the gutter downspout and then put a large plastic container (or water barrel) directly beneath the shortened gutter downspout. The first few minutes of rain will wash a lot of stuff off your roof and down your gutter. Therefore don't position the water collection container below the downspout until after it has rained about twenty-minutes.

If you are camping then you will probably be sleeping under a weatherproof tarp, or you will have a rain fly above your tent. By using a little creative thinking you can frequently set things up so the rain water runs off your shelter into a big pot or other container. This requires a little ingenuity on your part depending on what you have available but I mention it because some of you will figure out a way to make this idea work for you.

Regardless of which method you use to collect the rain water you will need to save the majority of your rain water until the next time it rains. Once again, if you have anticipated the possibility and seriousness of this type of unexpected emergency, then you should already have a reserve supply of clean empty two-liter soda bottles, or clean empty plastic water bottles on a cardboard flat, or empty one-gallon plastic water jugs, so you can easily store your rain water.

The Morning Dew: If it doesn't rain then you could go outside at dawn and collect the morning dew. How? Take a clean thin dish cloth or thin wash cloth and wipe it gently over the damp grass and other non-poisonous flowers and shrubs. Periodically ring the water out of the cloth into a bowl. Repeat. This is very hard work that yields very small quantities of water. However, if you are low on water this may be your only way to stay alive. You will also need to purify the water using one of the techniques described later.

Snow or Ice: Bring the snow or ice inside your house and melt it down into water. You will be surprised at the small quantity of water you get from a big bucket of snow. If you are in the woods put the pot of snow near the campfire and wait for it to melt. If you have a black plastic trash bag then put some snow inside the bag and place it in the direct sunlight to melt the snow. If necessary you can put the snow inside a small or medium size container. Then put the capped container inside your clothing (but not next to your skin) and your body heat will gradually melt the snow into water. If you are concerned about the cleanliness of the snow then you can boil the resulting water for 1 or 2 minutes before you drink it. Never melt snow or ice inside your mouth. It will **not** relieve your thirst and you will dehydrate more quickly. Always melt the snow or ice first and then drink the resulting water.

Ground Water (or Surface Water): Ground water is almost always contaminated. If you live in the country then ground water is lake, pond, creek, stream, or river water. In the city it is water flowing beside the sidewalks during a heavy rain. If no other source of water is available then you may be forced to collect the only water you can find. But don't drink it until you purify it. Even if the water looks crystal clear in a glass it may still contain tiny organisms that will make you sick. You don't need a severe case of diarrhea or a high fever during difficult times. Like the old saying goes, it is better to be safe than sorry.

Wilderness Areas: All sorts of animals, bugs, and birds live in the woods. When they get the urge to use the bathroom they let it go wherever they happen to be at the time (as long as it isn't inside their nests). Later, when it rains, that waste material washes down into the nearest pond, lake, stream, creek, or river. Think about that if you are tempted to drink ground water without purifying it first. The chances are pretty high you will get sick even though there is no industrial pollution anywhere in the vicinity. You **must** purify ground water using one of the methods that will be described later.

Moving Water or Stationary Water: Water that is flowing swiftly over rocks is normally much cleaner than water in stagnant pools. If you have a choice, collect your water from a fast moving stream and then purify the water using one of the techniques described later.

When to Collect Ground Water: Immediately after a rain the water in most streams and creeks will be muddy for a short period of time. At the very beginning of a rain shower you should check your water containers and fill them up if necessary before your normal water source (creek) gets really muddy.

Spring Water (doesn't refer to the time of year): When it rains the water does two things. Some of it travels along the top surface of the ground and ends up in creeks and streams. But a lot of it soaks into the earth and some of it makes its way down to the natural water table in the area. The earth is an excellent water filter. If the water table is 100 feet or more beneath the surface then the water there is usually safe for human consumption without any treatment. That's why people in the country drill deep wells -- they want clean water that doesn't need treatment.

The next question is, how does a person get to that deep water out in the middle of the woods? Do **not** waste your time trying to dig for it. It isn't worth the effort.

The best way is to find a spring head. Let me explain. Because of gravity water seeks the lowest possible level. You can usually find a stream or creek at the bottom of most hills or mountains. When you find one, begin walking upstream. Every now and then you will find a tiny feeder stream flowing into the main stream. The main stream will continue along the foot of the hill. Follow the tiny feeder stream up the side of the hill. Sooner or later you will eventually come to its source. It will just emerge from the ground. This is called the "head of the spring." The underground water table in this area is very close to the surface of the earth at this one spot and this particular exit point just happened as a result of nature. The water at the head of the spring hasn't had a chance to become polluted with lots of animal waste so it is the purest water you will find in the woods.

Spring Head inside White Oval. Water Flows in Direction of Arrow.

The head of a spring is normally a reasonable distance up the side of a hill or mountain. If there is any level ground near the spring head then this is usually an excellent place to set up camp. You avoid both the peak and bottom of the hill (high winds and flooding waters), and you are near a really clean reliable source of good water.

Usually (not always) this spring water it so clean it doesn't need to be boiled. I only know of one way to determine if the spring water contains harmful micro-organisms (called pathogens). Take a small water

Chapter Eight: Water

sample to your local water authority (county water service) and have it tested. They will tell you if it is fit for human consumption without being treated.

There is one more important consideration. After a really good rain shower there are usually many, many feeder springs running into the main stream at the bottom of the hill. The water table rises and it leaks out all the holes near the surface of the earth. After a short period of time most of these holes run dry because the water table falls back to its normal level. Therefore the best time to look for the head of a spring isn't after a good rain. At that time they are easy to find but most will be undependable for the long haul. Wait until you have had a few good sunny days and then look for a spring head that is still running strong.

Water Caught in Rock Depressions: Most rain water will flow into a stream or soak into the earth. However, some of it will be caught in large natural depressions in boulders and other large rocks. Depending on the size of the depression (and other factors such as how long the water is in the shade each day, and how much of the rock is above ground to absorb the sun's rays, etc.) the rain water may not evaporate for many days after a rain. If you are trying to become familiar with a particular area of the woods then you should mentally note these large depressions in a rock when you see them (even if they aren't filled with rain water at the time).

Dry Spring Bed Water: After a long dry spell many springs and steams will run dry. If you are really desperate for water then try digging in the lowest part of a dry spring or stream bed. Sometimes you will hit the water table two or three feet below the surface.

Wildlife Watering Holes: All of God's creatures need water to live. If you follow a heavily worn animal path downhill in the woods it will probably lead to water. If you hear frogs in the distance they are probably real close to some water. If you hear geese or ducks in the distance they are probably real close to some water. Follow the animals and you will have a pretty good chance of finding where they get their drinking water. (Note: Bees also need water and they will build their hive in close proximity to a water source. If you see a bee then observe where it goes when it leaves the flower. It will either be heading to another flower or to its hive. When returning to its hive a bee always flies in a straight line, or the proverbial bee line. Remember, the bee's hive is near some water.)

Condensation From Green Leaf Vegetation: Put a large plastic bag around the leaves of a non-poisonous bush or shrub in the early morning and secure the open end of the bag to the wood branch with a string. During the heat of the day the green vegetation inside the plastic bag will release water vapor which will collect on the inside of your plastic bag and gradually drain down to the lowest edge of the plastic bag. When you check your bag at the end of the day you will discover about one-ounce of water (or less) in the lowest corner of the bag. Therefore for this method to be of any practical value you would need to have a lot of these bags attached to a lot of different plants every day.

Solar Still

I have read about solar stills but I have never personally experimented with one. However, I am passing this information on to you so you will know everything I know about water.

You will need a large plastic sheet or tarp to make a solar still. Dig a conical hole about four-feet wide at the top and coming to a point about two-feet deep. The bottom of the hole should be in the very center (equal distance from all sides). The slope of the sides isn't critical. Put a medium size pot at the very bottom of the hole. Then lay your plastic sheet over the top of the hole and put a medium size rock (about one-pound) in the center of the sheet just above the pot which will be directly underneath the sheet. Put heavy rocks on top of your plastic sheet all around the outside of the hole to keep the sheet from touching the inner sloping sides of the hole. The center of the sheet should be about 18 inches below the surface of the ground but about 6 inches above the pot. Wait 24 hours. Water vapor will form on the underside of your tarp and drain down to its lowest point (beneath your one-pound rock) and then drip into your pot in the bottom of the hole. On hot days and cold nights you can collect about one-pint of water per 24-hour period. I read somewhere that you can put moist green non-poisonous vegetation (leaves) near the bottom of the hole (but not in the pot) and this will increase the water yield from your still.

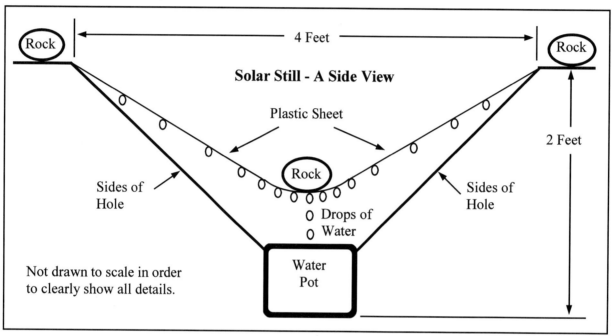

Solar still water is naturally distilled and it may be safe to drink without any treatments (such as boiling or chlorine). However, to avoid the possibility of getting sick it is a good idea to process the still water using one of the methods detailed later in this chapter.

You will have to move your solar still every two or three days because you will have pulled all the available water from that hole until the next time it rains.

If you want to buy a plastic sheet to take with you when you go camping then you can find them in the house paint section of most stores, including Walmart and most hardware stores. They are used by painters as drop-cloths to keep paint off the floor. They come in a variety of sizes and thicknesses. For durability the 2-mil thickness is probably best. I have never built a solar water still but I have used these plastic sheets before. The 3-mil stuff will last longer but it is heavier and therefore you will burn more calories carrying it around in your backpack. The 1-mil stuff is lighter but it is very easily damaged (torn).

What Makes Water Unsafe to Drink?
For educational purposes only.
This is not intended to be used as medical advice.

There are three different types of waterborne pathogens that make water unsafe to drink: protozoa, bacteria, and viruses.

1. **Protozoa:** They live in insects, or in cysts when on the outside of an animal. Examples of common waterborne protozoa are amoeba, giardia, and crypto(sporidium). Protozoa range in size from 1 to 100

microns, with the average being around 16 microns. They are easily removed from water by boiling. Because of their large size most of them are also easily removed by commercially available water filters (with the exception of the very small crypto). Some are relatively resistant to both chlorine and iodine chemical treatment methods. It has been estimated that 90% of the surface water in the United States is contaminated with protozoa.

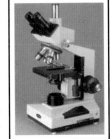

2. **Bacteria:** A one-celled organism that can exist in the air and in water. The average size of bacteria is between 0.2 to 1.5 microns with some as large as 10 microns. They are easily removed by boiling, by chemical treatments, or by most good water filters. Fortunately, not all bacteria are life threatening. However, the most common life-threatening waterborne bacteria are dysentery (diarrhea), typhoid, (vibrio)cholera, campylobacter, E. coli (escherichia), and salmonella.

3. **Viruses:** The most common waterborne viruses are hepatitis, yellow fever, polio(myelitis), rotavirus, and norwalk. Viruses are much smaller than bacteria. The average size of a virus is from 0.004 to 0.100 microns. They are easily removed by boiling or by chemical treatments. However, because of their extremely small size they can pass through most water filters. However, some viruses will cling to other larger particles in the water which can be filtered out.

The incubation period prior to becoming extremely sick as a result of ingesting one of the above pathogens varies from a few hours to a few weeks, depending on the pathogen itself and the concentration ingested. Common symptoms include fatigue, fever, cramps, diarrhea, dehydration, and nausea. If not properly treated by a medical professional these pathogens can eventually result in a person's death.

If you are in a remote area or if you can't get to a doctor quickly, then stay warm, drink plenty of safe fluids, and rest. You can help control the diarrhea with over-the-counter antidiarrheal medicines, and you can take over-the-counter pain relievers to help reduce the fever and minimize other associated discomforts. However, you should plan to get to a medical doctor as soon as possible.

How to Make Water Safe to Drink

Pure clean water should be used:

1. to drink,
2. to make a beverage,
3. to cook with,
4. to brush your teeth,
5. to wash your hands and face, and
6. to wash your eating dishes and cook pots.

After you have purified your water using one of the following techniques, do **not** contaminate your water by allowing it to touch a pot, or spoon, or anything else that has been in contact with the unpurified water.

If your source of water is relatively cloudy or muddy (high turbidity) then allow it to stand in a large pot for twelve-hours to give the foreign particles an opportunity to settle to the bottom of the pot. Then slowly and carefully scoop the water out of the top of the pot without disturbing the sediment on the bottom of the pot.

Regardless of which of the following methods you use to purify your water the first step is always the same. Begin by pouring your water through a standard paper coffee filter, or through a clean pillow case, or through a piece of denim cloth material. This will trap and remove any large impurities in the water. The same coffee filter can be used over and over again for several days (unless the water is muddy or dirty).

After you have pre-filtered your water then you may use one of the following options to purify your water. The following alternatives are presented in order from the cheapest to the most expensive method.

Boiling
Kills Protozoa, Bacteria, and Viruses
Does Not Neutralize Harmful Chemicals or Radioactive Particles

Boiling is the BEST method for killing **all** the pathogens in the water. Even the most expensive commercially available water filter can't make that claim. Therefore let's examine this method very carefully.

Water boils at approximately 212°F (100°C) at sea level at a barometric pressure of approximately 30.3 inches of mercury. The boiling point of water decreases as the barometric pressure decreases. Therefore the changing barometric pressure in your area has as much impact on the boiling point of water as the altitude at which you live. The following table illustrates this relationship:

The Boiling Point of Water at Different Altitudes at Different Barometric Pressures

Altitude	30" Mercury	29" Mercury	28" Mercury	27" Mercury
Sea Level	211.5 °F	209.8 °F	208.0 °F	206.2 °F
2,000 Feet	208.0 °F	206.2 °F	204.4 °F	202.5 °F
4,000 Feet	204.4 °F	202.5 °F	200.5 °F	198.4 °F
6,000 Feet	200.5 °F	198.4 °F	196.3 °F	194.1 °F
8,000 Feet	196.3 °F	194.1 °F	191.8 °F	189.4 °F
10,000 Feet	191.8 °F	189.4 °F	186.9 °F	184.3 °F

All pathogens die rapidly at 185°F (or 85°C). Some pathogens die at lower temperatures. By the time the water has reached its boiling point (even at low barometric pressures), all the pathogens in the water are already neutralized.

Therefore bring your water to a boil and let it hard boil for 1 minute. Or hard boil for 2 minutes on top of an extremely high mountain at very low barometric pressures. Boiling for more time doesn't help, and it results in more water being lost as steam, and it makes the water taste flatter. All the pathogens are already dead by the time the water reaches its boiling point. There is no benefit to a pathogen being "more" dead.

Wait patiently for the water to gradually cool to a comfortable drinking temperature.

How to Improve the Taste of Boiled Water:

1. Stir the water to add oxygen back into the water.
2. Or pour the water from one clean sterile container into another sterile container several times.
3. Or add a little salt to the water.
4. Or add 50 mg of Vitamin C to a quart of water.
5. Or add Kool-Aid (10% Vitamin C) or Tang (100% Vitamin C) to the water.

Now let's look at some other ways to improve the quality of your drinking water. But don't forget, **Boiling is Best,** if you intend to actually drink the water in the next 24 hours or so. However, if you plan to store the water for an extended period of time then one of the following methods should be considered.

Liquid Chlorine Bleach (Sodium Hypochlorite) - Either 5.25% or 6% Strength
Kills Bacteria and Viruses
Not effective against all Protozoa
Does Not Neutralize Harmful Chemicals or Radioactive Particles

1. **Relatively Clear Water:** Use 2 drops of bleach per quart of water or 8 drops per gallon (or 1 teaspoon per 10 gallons).
2. **Cloudy Water:** Use 4 drops of bleach per quart of water or 16 drops per gallon (or 2 teaspoons per 10 gallons).

The water should not be too cool. The water temperature should be 70°F (or 21°C) or higher. If necessary put the water in direct sunlight to raise the water temperature. The effectiveness of chlorine at killing pathogens diminishes rapidly at lower temperatures.

Add the required number of drops of chlorine liquid bleach (Clorox or store brand, unscented) to the water and wait one hour for the bleach to kill all the tiny organisms. If you can detect a faint chlorine smell in the water at the end of one hour, then it is safe to drink. If you can't smell the chlorine then add the same amount of bleach a second time and wait another hour. If you can detect a faint chlorine smell then the water is safe to drink. If you still can't detect the smell of chlorine then discard the water because it contains too many germs. (Note: Always start with the minimum recommended amount of bleach and add a little more if necessary. Too much chlorine is harmful to your body.)

Dry 68% Calcium Hypochlorite Granules
This is the shock treatment chemical used in swimming pools
Kills Bacteria and Viruses
Not effective against all Protozoa
Does Not Neutralize Harmful Chemicals or Radioactive Particles

The water should not be too cool. The water temperature should be 70°F (or 21°C) or higher. If necessary put the water in direct sunlight to raise the water temperature. The effectiveness of chlorine at killing pathogens diminishes rapidly at lower temperatures.

Put 1/96 of an ounce (a pinch between thumb and finger) of 68% Calcium Hypochlorite granules into one gallon of water. Wait one-hour. If you can detect a faint chlorine smell in the water then it is safe to drink. If you can't smell the chlorine then add another "pinch" and wait another hour. If you can detect a faint chlorine smell then the water is safe to drink. If you still can't detect the smell of chlorine then discard the water because it contains too many germs. (Note: Always start with a small amount of Calcium Hypochlorite and add a little more if necessary. Too much chlorine is harmful to your body.)

The shelf life of liquid bleach (sodium hypochlorite) is much shorter than the dry 68% Calcium Hypochlorite granules. Therefore if you wish to store hypochlorite for emergency purposes then the best choice is the dry granules.

Liquid Bleach: If you have dry 68% Calcium Hypochlorite granules and for some reason you need liquid bleach, then you may dissolve one-ounce of 68% granules in one-pint of water and you will have a 5.25% liquid bleach solution.

Liquid 2% Tincture of Iodine
Kills Bacteria and Viruses
Not effective against all Protozoa
Does Not Neutralize Harmful Chemicals or Radioactive Particles

1. **Relatively Clear Water:** Use 4 drops of iodine per quart of water or 16 drops per gallon.
2. **Cloudy Water:** Use 8 drops of iodine per quart of water or 32 drops per gallon.

The water should not be too cool. The water temperature should be 70°F (or 21°C) or higher. If necessary put the water in direct sunlight to raise the water temperature. The effectiveness of iodine at killing pathogens diminishes rapidly at lower temperatures.

Add the required number of drops of iodine to the water and wait one hour.

Iodine has a printed expiration date on the bottle. When that date has expired the iodine will have lost some or most of its original strength. Therefore iodine is generally not the chemical of choice for long-term survival situations.

Caution: Iodine water treatment methods can **not** be used by pregnant women, or nursing mothers, or individuals with thyroid conditions. In addition, long-term exposure to iodine can contribute to liver damage.

Although iodine is one way to purify water, it is **not** a preferred method. Any of the above methods is superior to the use of iodine.

Commercial Water Purification Tablets

Most commercially available water purification tablets are based on the use of either chlorine or iodine as their primary active ingredient. Both chlorine and iodine have a relatively short shelf life before they begin to lose their full strength and effectiveness. If you happen to have some of these tablets and they have passed their expiration date then you should replace them.

Commercial Portable Water Filters
**Removes Protozoa, Bacteria, Most Viruses, Many Harmful Chemicals and Some Radioactive Particles
To remove ALL Viruses, you must Boil the Water or Add Chlorine or Iodine**

The best overall method for improving the quality of water, but also the most expensive, is to use a commercial water filter, but not one that permanently connects to your home water system because it requires water pressure to function properly.

The one **potential** disadvantage of commercial water filters (not purifiers) is that they cannot remove 100% of **all** virus pathogens. Fortunately, waterborne virus pathogens are **not** a common problem in most areas. Therefore unless there has been an outbreak of viral diseases in your area, then waterborne viruses will probably not be a problem with your water supply. However, if there has been a recent outbreak of viral diseases then add the appropriate quantity of chlorine to the water, wait one-hour, and then put that treated water through one of the following filters.

Two Quick Definitions:
1. **Portable:** Easy to move from place to place.
2. **Potable:** Okay to drink.

Commercial water filters are normally purchased for one of three reasons:
1. To improve the taste and quality of the normal home water supply.
2. To provide drinking water during a short-term emergency.
3. To provide drinking water for long-term survival.

Many people add a variety of water softeners, water filters, and water purifiers to the plumbing in their homes to improve the quality of the water normally available at their place of residence. These filters depend on water pressure and/or electricity to function properly. Neither water pressure nor electricity can be depended on during either short-term or long-term survival scenarios so these types of water filters will not be discussed here.

1. **Short-term emergencies,** such as hurricanes or tornados, are extremely serious but life gradually returns to normal after the danger has passed. Unless your area was completely demolished most services are restored in days, or weeks, or sometimes a little longer.

2. **Long-term survival,** such as a World War being fought within your nation's borders, is a more challenging situation because you may not have any outside help or assistance for an extended period of time. Your survival will depend completely on the resources you had available before the situation developed.

Some water filters perform very well during short-term emergencies but they are not designed for long-term survival situations. Other water filters are specifically engineered for long-term survival scenarios. Fortunately, those same filters will also function exceedingly well during short-term emergencies. Consequently, the following recommendations are for long-term survival water filters, which will also serve in a short-term emergency if required.

In a long-term survival situation the primary source of life-threatening pathogens entering the water supply is through human waste (fecal matter). Since the normal sewage system is not functioning the way it was designed to, human waste is **not** disposed of properly. It is frequently thrown into the streets to get it out of people's homes. The next rain washes significant amounts of that human waste into the nearest water collection area. Disease, sickness, and death soon follow. Even if you are in or near a crowded camping area during a long-term survival scenario the same tragic drama unfolds. To survive in a situation such as this you need to filter all your drinking water and then boil it. (Note: The proper way to deal with human waste while camping is to bury it.)

Three different water filters will be discussed below. None of them require water pressure or electricity.

1. The first model is a **Swiss Katadyn Pocket Water Filter**. Its advantages are that is more affordable, lighter weight, and extremely portable. It comes with one 0.2 micron filter element that will yield one-quart of drinking water per minute and the filter has a maximum rated life of 13,000 gallons of water under good conditions. Its disadvantages are that it must be hand pumped, and if its one filter is damaged in any way then it makes the unit of questionable value. However, if you perceive a survival scenario where you will be frequently moving between locations by walking or by bicycle, then it is probably your best choice because it is both small and light weight. (Note: There are several other cheaper Katadyn water filters available, such as the Hiker and the Guide, but they are **not** designed for long-term survival scenarios.)

2. The second model is a British **Berkefeld Big Berkey.** Its advantages are that it uses gravity to filter the water and it comes with four 0.9 micron nine-inch filters. Each filter has a maximum rated life of 12,000 gallons of water under good conditions (or 48,000 gallons of water from all four filters). It weighs about 9 pounds and it has exterior dimensions of about 8.5" diameter and 20.5" tall. It may be used with one, two, three, or all four filters installed. In a survival situation one filter will provide about six gallons of drinking water per day. That would leave three unused filters in reserve as replacements when the first filter wears out, or if anything should happen to the first filter. It only costs about $80 more than the above Katadyn filter and therefore it is probably the best choice if you perceive a survival scenario where you will be at the same location most of the time, or if your plans to move between locations will be by automobile or truck.

3. The third model is an American **AquaRain Model 400 Water Filter**. It advantages are that is uses gravity to filter the water and it comes with four 0.3 micron filters. Each filter has a maximum rated life of 10,000 gallons of water under good conditions. It weighs about 10 pounds and it has exterior dimensions of 10.5" diameter and 22" tall. It can be used with one, two, three, or all four filters installed. The current AquaRain filters do have a silvered carbon core. The filters need to be periodically removed and boiled for 15 minutes and then allowed to cool. The AquaRain is a newer model than the two above units and therefore it does **not** have the proven track record of successful use with contaminated water in third-world countries. However, it was designed for use in those types of difficult conditions.

Swiss Katadyn Pocket Water Filter

1. No water pressure required.
2. No electricity required.
3. **Output:** 1 quart per minute via hand-pumping.
4. **Weight:** 24 oz. inside its carrying case with all its attachments.
5. **Size:** 3" x 10.5" inside its carrying case with all its attachments.
6. **Expected Life:** Up to 13,000 gallons of water from **one** filter depending on the quality of the incoming water source.
   The maximum filter life can be achieved if the incoming water is pre-filtered through a clean cloth before putting it through the Katadyn filter.
7. **Life-time warranty.**
8. **Filter Element:** One 0.2 micron porosity ceramic filter.
   Self-disinfecting due to fine silver embedded throughout the Katadyn filter which prevents the growth of

bacteria. Will remove **all** bacteria and **all** Protozoa, including:
   100% Giardia Protozoa.
   100% Cryptosporidium Protozoa.
9. Removes asbestos fibers, nuclear explosion debris, invisible dust particles, and pollen.
10. Does **not** remove 99.9% of all viruses.
11. Does **not** remove dissolved minerals or chemicals.
   Therefore it can not be used to desalinate sea water.
12. No carbon is included inside the filter.
   If you wish, you can purchase separately a Universal Carbon Cartridge Filter Unit for use with any water filter at a cost of about $11.95 on the internet.
13. The filter may be cleaned with one of the two cleaning pads which are included.

British Berkefeld "Big Berkey" Gravity Water Filter with Four 9-inch Super Sterasyl Candles

1. Used by missionaries around the world.
2. No water pressure required.
3. No electricity required.
4. Stainless Steel Construction.
5. **Output:** 6 gallons per day from **one** filter, or 24 gallons per day using all **four** filters at the same time.
   Water is filtered automatically by the use of gravity.
   Lower Tank Holding Capacity: 2.4 gallons.
6. **Weight:** About 9 pounds without water.
7. **Size Unassembled in Box:** 9" x 9" x 13½"
   Size Assembled: 8.5" Diameter by 20.5" Tall.
8. **Expected Life:** Between 2,000 to 12,000 gallons **per filter** of pure water depending on the quality of the incoming water.
   The maximum filter life can be achieved if the incoming water is pre-filtered through a clean cloth before putting it through the Berkefeld filter.
9. **Filter Elements:** Four 0.9 micron **Nine-Inch Super** Sterasyl Candle Filters
   Self-disinfecting due to fine particles of silver evenly distributed throughout the Sterasyl filter which prevents the growth of bacteria.
   Sterasyl Candles form a barrier to all particles 0.9 microns or larger in size.
   Super Sterasyl Candles have an **activated carbon** filling which removes chemical and organic compounds from the water, reduces herbicides and pesticides, eliminates unpleasant odors, and improves the taste.
   This unit may be priced and sold with either 7" or 9" Sterasyl Candles. Verify you are getting 9" filters before you buy.
   This unit may be priced and sold with either Regular Sterasyl Candles or Super Sterasyl Candles. Verify you are getting four 9" Super Sterasyl Candle filters before you buy.
   All Sterasyl filters will remove:
      More than 99.99% E. Coli (escherichia) Bacteria
      More than 99.99% Cholera Bacteria
      More than 99.99% Fecal Coliform Bacteria
      More than 99.99% Shigetta Bacteria
      More than 99.99% Salmonella Bacteria
      More than 99.99% Typhoid Bacteria
      100% Giardia Protozoa
      100% Cryptosporidium Protozoa
      Reduces turbidity more than 99.7%

Chapter Eight: Water

10. Does **not** remove 99.9% of all viruses.
11. Does **not** remove dissolved minerals or chemicals.
    Therefore it can not be used to desalinate sea water.
12. The durable filters element may be cleaned many times with a Scotch Brite pad, purchased separately.
13. Shipped with two rubber hole plugs to permit the use of two filters. To use more than two filters at the same time, remove the rubber hole plugs. To use only one filter, an additional cork or hole plug will need to be purchased separately.

AquaRain Model 400 Gravity Water Filter
with Four Ceramic Filters

1. No water pressure required.
2. No electricity required.
3. Seamless Heavy-Duty 18 Gauge Stainless Steel One-Piece Construction.
4. **Output:** 6 gallons per day from one filter, or 24 gallons per day using all four filters at the same time.
   Water is filtered automatically by the use of gravity.
   Lower Tank Holding Capacity: 3 gallons.
5. **Weight:** About 10 pounds without water.
6. **Size Unassembled in Box:** 10.75" x10.75" x 11.75"
   Size Assembled: 10" Diameter by 22" Tall.
7. **Expected Life:** Between 2,500 to 10,000 gallons **per filter** of pure water depending on the quality of the incoming water.
   The maximum filter life can be achieved if the incoming water is pre-filtered through a clean cloth before putting it through the AquaRain filter.
8. **Filter Elements:** Four 0.3 micron Ceramic Filters
   Each filters has an **activated carbon** filling which removes chemical and organic compounds from the water, reduces MTBE, herbicides and pesticides, eliminates unpleasant odors, and improves the taste.
   Will remove **all** bacteria and **all** Protozoa, including:
   - 100% Giardia Protozoa
   - 100% Cryptosporidium Protozoa
9. Does **not** remove 99.9% of all viruses.
10. Does **not** remove dissolved minerals or chemicals.
    Therefore it can not be used to desalinate sea water.
11. The durable filters element may be cleaned up to 200 times with the included cleaning pad.
12. Shipped with two silicone hole plugs to permit the use of two filters. To use more than two filters at the same time, remove the silicone hole plugs. To use only one filter, an additional cork or hole plug will need to be purchased separately.
13. **Special Care:** The filters should be periodically removed and boiled for 15 minutes and allowed to cool before replacing them in the unit.

Silver

At the current time all three of the above water filters are saturated with fine particles of silver to prevent and retard the growth of pathogens. Early American pioneers frequently put a silver dollar into their water barrels and they left it there because they had learned from experience that it helped to reduce the number of health related problems within their families.

Selecting a Water Filter

The Berkey filters, and the Katadyn filters, actually have the silver in the filter element itself. This means any pathogens trapped in the filter will generally not survive because of the silver.

The AquaRain filter has the silver deep inside its filter mixed with its carbon core. The silver is not on the outside of the filter where most of the pathogens will be trapped. Therefore the pathogens can continue their normal life cycle after they are trapped in the exterior filter element. This is probably the reason that AquaRain recommends that you remove and boil their filters once every one or two weeks in order to kill those trapped pathogens.

In a life-threatening emergency I would first hard boil my water for one-minute and then I would let it gradually cool down to room temperature. Boiling would kill the pathogens in the water. Then I would use one of the above water filters to further enhance the quality of the water. Then I would feel safer about drinking the water.

How to Distill Water

Equipment Needed:
1. Pressure Cooker (any size).
2. Copper Tubing (12 to 15 feet).
3. Cooling Bucket (a wide shallow bucket is better than a thin tall bucket) (2 to 5 gallons).
4. Clean Cook Pot or Clean Water Bucket.

The copper tubing should have an **inside** diameter that matches the **outside** diameter of the steam exhaust port on your pressure cooker. Leave about four-feet at both ends of the copper tubing relatively straight. Wrap the center of the copper tubing into a coil around any cylindrical object that is a few inches smaller in diameter than the inside of the cooling bucket (item 3 above). Remove and aside the cylindrical object after you have successfully coiled the middle of the copper tubing.

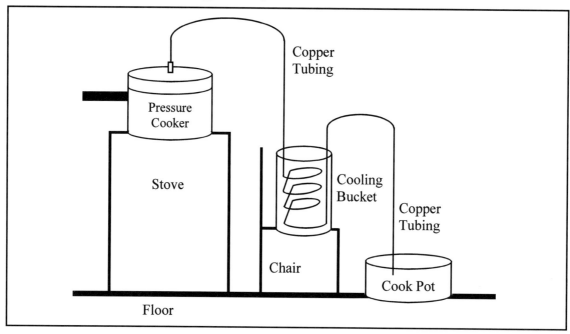

Instructions for Distilling Water:

1. Follow all the standard safety instructions for a pressure cooker.
2. Pour some water through a clean cloth to pre-filter the water and remove any large impurities.
3. Fill the pressure cooker between 1/2 to 3/4 full of pre-filtered water.
4. Put the pressure cooker on the stove top but do **not** turn on the heat yet.
5. Put a cooling bucket on a chair near the stove. Fill the cooling bucket with cool water.
6. Place an empty clean cook pot or clean water bucket on the floor.
7. Attach one end of the copper tubing to the steam exhaust port on top of the pressure cooker. Place the

center coil of the cooper tubing inside the cool water in the cooling bucket. Place the other end of the copper tubing in the clean cook pot on the floor.
8. Turn on the heat to the pressure cooker. The water inside the pressure cooker will gradually turn into steam and travel up through the steam exhaust port into the copper tubing. The steam will enter the cooling coil and cool down and become water again. It will then flow into the cook pot on the floor.
9. You may reduce the heat to the pressure cooker after water starts flowing into the cook pot on the floor. Do **not** touch the pressure cooker or the copper tubing while either one is **hot**.

The above procedure will make distilled water but it uses a lot of energy.

Other Methods of Making Water Safe to Drink

There are a variety of other methods for making water safe to drink, such as reverse osmosis and ultraviolet. However, those methods are better suited to normal situations that don't involve long-term survival and the possible absence of electricity.

A Practical and Inexpensive Method for Replenishing Water while Hiking

If you have enough Katadyn Pocket Water Filters for everyone in your group then you may skip this section. However, if some of the people in your party don't have their own Pocket Water Filter then the following information may be of use to you.

It is not practical to attach items to the belt that holds your pants up. If you do then those items will pull your pants down as you walk and rub blisters on your hips. Not only is it painful but it is also very annoying. Therefore let your normal belt (or suspenders) hold your pants up. Then use another belt for your knife, pistol, first aid kit, and canteen, but don't put that belt through the belt loops on your pants. A belt canteen is usually preferred to a shoulder strap canteen because the shoulder strap wears a blister on your shoulder in a very short time, even when you keep changing shoulders.

Most canteens are made of light-weight plastic. You can find them at most Army-Navy Surplus Stores. They also usually carry the canteen pouch and the equipment (canteen) belt. Sometimes you can also find a collapsible metal cup that will fit on the bottom of the plastic canteen and fit inside the cloth canteen pouch. The handle of the metal cup is on a hinge and it will fold down and under the cup out-of-the-way. (Note: If you decide to visit an Army-Navy Surplus Store then ask for an "Alice" type belt with shoulder harness suspender straps. It will cost a little more money but if you do **any** hiking you will probably never regret spending that money. If you purchase the Alice belt then you should also check out the different types of small equipment bags they sell that can be attached to that belt. Each small bag can be used to store something different, such as first aid supplies, dehydrated or freeze-dried food, personal care items, or small miscellaneous survival gear such as snare wires and fishing tackle.)

When full of water the canteen weighs about 2.5 pounds. However, as you walk you will periodically drink some of your water. And if the unexpected occurs, then you may not be able to return to your primary area of safety before nightfall. Therefore you should also carry the means to replace your drinking water if necessary.

If you add a clean cloth (folded inside a heavy-duty freezer bag) to the inside of your canteen pouch with your canteen, then you will have a method to pre-filter your water. The heavy-duty freezer bag can be used to collect the water, even from a very shallow area. The water can then be poured from the freezer bag through the cloth into your metal cup. This pre-filters the water and removes any large impurities.

You then have two options:

1. If you have water purification tablets then you could put the appropriate number inside the water in your cup and wait the specified time. Then you can pour the water into your canteen.

Chapter Eight: Water

2. Or you could start a fire **if** you have a small butane lighter. Of course you would also need to find some combustible material but in most areas that is not too difficult. Then you can heat the water in your metal cup over the coals from the fire until the water boils. Let it boil for 1 minute (or 2 minutes if you are at the top of an extremely high mountain). Then wait patiently for the water to cool to a safe temperature. Then pour the safe water into your canteen.

You would either boil your water **or** you would use your water purification tablets, but you would **not** do both at the same time because they both accomplish the same basic objective. Of the two methods, **boiling is best** because it positively kills every pathogen in your water source whereas the purification tablets will not be successful against all viruses.

The cloth canteen pouches sold at most Army-Navy Surplus Stores have a small pocket attached to the outside of the canteen pouch. This exterior pocket can be used to store your bottle of water purification tablets which should be placed inside a plastic sandwich bag. And it can also be used to store a miniature butane lighter in a separate plastic sandwich bag. The purpose of the sandwich bags is to protect those items from the condensation moisture from your canteen which will saturate your canteen pouch, or from the rain if it should start to rain unexpectedly while you are hiking.

Water Conservation Recommendations for Personal Hygiene Activities

Bathing: If you are low on water then don't waste it bathing. I know cleanliness is important but most of us overdo it in the United States. Just wash your hands, face, and feet periodically. Use the two-pot method for bathing. Fill one pot with water and use it as the first rinse after washing your hands with soap, or after bathing with a sponge or wash cloth. Fill another pot with water and use it as the second rinse. Don't discard the wash water in the first pot until it is too dirty to be safely used, and then pour it into the **back** of your toilet tank so you can use it to flush your toilet, if your sewer system is still working. Then use the second pot as your first rinse and start a new pot of clean water as your second rinse. (Note: The average person probably won't appreciate the true value of their feet until they are confronted with a difficult situation. Then they will suddenly realize that their long-term survival depends on the condition of their feet.)

If you have water pressure and you prefer to take showers, then take a military shower. Close the bath tub drain or put a flat round flexible plastic drain cover over the shower drain. Turn the water **on**, quickly get soaking wet all over, and then turn the water **off**. Use some soap to wash your body and use some shampoo on your hair while the water is **off**. When you have finished washing and shampooing, turn the water **on** and quickly rinse the shampoo out of your hair and the soap off your body. Then turn the water **off**. If you practice this method you will discover you can take a good shower with only three or four gallons of water, and you can then use the shower water that is in the bottom of the tub or shower to flush your toilet, if your sewer system is still working.

Teeth Brushing: Always brush your teeth at least once per day. It doesn't take much water, just a little in a small cup. If you still have water pressure, then do not let the water run while you are brushing your teeth. (Note: Also do not let the water run while you are shaving.) Instead turn the faucet on and put about 2 or 3 ounces of water into a small cup. Then turn the faucet off. Only use a little toothpaste each time and not the amount you normally use. Your toothpaste will last four to six times longer this way with no compromise in dental hygiene. If your sewer system is still working then spit the used mouthful of toothpaste into the toilet bowl. If your sewer system is not working then spit the toothpaste into the trash can. Rinse your mouth thoroughly after brushing with a small amount of water and spit it into the sink. (Note: If you have a limited amount of water then you do not want to run the risk of having your toothpaste slowly accumulate inside your sink drain and gradually dry out and form a soap block that prevents your drain from working properly. That is the reason you should consider spitting the toothpaste into the toilet stool or trash can.)

Washing Dishes: Use the three-pot method to wash your eating dishes. Wash your dishes in the first pot of water with dish soap. Rinse the dishes in a second pot. Rinse the dishes again in a third pot. When the dish water in the first pot gets really nasty, pour it down the **front** of your toilet stool to flush it, if your sewer system is still working. (Note: Dish water usually contains too much food residue and grease to put it in the back of the toilet tank but it can be poured into the front toilet bowl to help flush the stool.) Then put dish soap in the second pot and use it as the initial wash pot. Use the third pot as your first rinse. Add a new pot with clean water as the final rinse.

Hot water, or even warm water, makes it easier to wash your dishes by hand. However, the effort and energy required to heat the water may sometimes exceed the extra manual effort required to simply scrub the dishes a little harder by hand in cold water. That trade-off decision will need to be made by each person based on their own personal circumstances. (Note: Warm water doesn't kill germs. Boiling water kills germs. However, warm water does make grease removal from the dishes much easier. Or you could use enamel coated camping dishes which clean up nicely even in cold water. However, long-term exposure to citric acid will stain the enamel coating on enamel dishes.)

Washing Clothes: If you are using a standard electric washing machine then do **not** discard your washing machine water directly into the drain. Move the drain hose to a position above a large empty water container to catch the used wash water. After the first wash cycle, allow the wash water to drain into your water storage container. This **soapy wash water** can be used in the back of your toilet stool to flush your toilets, if your sewer system is still working. After the washing machine rinse cycle, allow the rinse water to drain into another water storage container. After the washing machine spin cycle is complete, remove your clean clothes, and then transfer the **rinse water** back into your washing machine. This water is relatively clean and it only contains a little soap residue which will be of use during the next wash cycle. If you will follow this method you will not be wasting any water to wash your clothes because all of the water will eventually be used to flush your toilets.

The Common Household Toilet Stool: If your sewer system is **not** working then you may use the two pot method for human waste collection and disposal. You will need two large five-gallon containers with lids. When you need to use the toilet then do so inside one of the two containers. Liquid waste should go into one container and solid waste in the other container. Then immediately replace the lid so most of the odor remains inside the containers. Your local public health authorities will tell you where and how to periodically dispose of this human waste to prevent the spread of a multitude of life threatening diseases.

If your sewer system is working then you may use your toilet. Most **new** toilet stools are very water efficient and they only require the absolute minimum amount of water per flush. If you have an **older** toilet stool then it probably uses between four to six gallons of water per flush, which is excessive. However, you can easily reduce the amount of water required per flush. Fill a clean empty 16 to 24 ounce plastic bottle (soft drink or water) with small rocks or pebbles as full as you can, and then finish filling the plastic bottle with water. Replace the bottle cap tightly. Carefully remove the top piece off the rear of your toilet tank and place the full weighted plastic bottle inside the tank. If necessary, secure it with some wire or string inside the toilet tank so that it does not interfere with the normal flushing operation of the toilet. Then flush the toilet to make sure it flushes properly. If you still have some space, then you may add a second and a third filled plastic bottle inside the toilet tank. Just be careful that you do not interfere with the normal flushing operation of the toilet. (Note: Or you could put a brick inside a plastic freezer bag and put it inside the toilet tank instead of using a plastic bottle. Or you could simply **replace your old toilet with a new water efficient toilet that uses about 1.6 gallons per flush.**)

Only flush human waste and used toilet tissue down your toilet stool. Do not put makeup removal tissues or any other type of used paper in your toilet stool. Instead dispose of these other types of used paper products in an ordinary trash can.

Flushing the toilet each time you use it is **not** a good idea under hardship conditions. In the country when people occasionally find themselves short on water they follow a very simple rule:

If it is yellow, let it mellow.
If it is brown, flush it down.

Chapter Eight: Water

Conclusion

Our bodies are mostly water. Most of the earth's surface is covered with water. Unfortunately, most of it isn't fit to drink. But without water we will all be dead in about three days. Therefore any information you can acquire about how and where to get drinking water takes you one step closer to being an independent, resourceful human being in God's natural order of things.

Chapter Nine

Introduction to Emergency Food Storage

Normal commerce could be easily and unexpectedly disrupted by hurricanes, tornadoes, floods, snow, ice, or a man-made disaster. In situations like these your family may need to survive for days (or weeks) on the food you had the wisdom to purchase and store **before** the unexpected event occurred.

A basic emergency food storage plan should be simple and economical. It should include:

1. foods you eat on a regular basis,
2. foods that have a long shelf life,
3. foods which can become part of a balanced and nutritious meal, and
4. foods that do not have to be refrigerated or frozen.

Appetite Fatigue: Your emergency food supply must have a reasonable variety of different food items. If you only have a limited number of different food items to eat then appetite fatigue will result in your starvation even though you have food. Your mind and your body will simply reject the thought of eating the same food again and again and again. If you doubt the truth of this statement then conduct a simple test. Pick your favorite four food items that you enjoy eating more than anything else and then only eat those four food items for one-month. Before one-week has passed you will be repulsed at the thought of eating those foods again. Try it and see if you can force yourself to only eat those four foods for an entire month.

Appetite fatigue does not occur when there is no food available. For example, long-term war prisoners in a P.O.W. camp will generally eat almost anything. Each day they do not have the option to eat or not eat. On many days they get nothing to eat. When they do get fed there is never enough food to satisfy their hunger and therefore they will eat almost anything at any time and be grateful for whatever it happens to be.

Appetite fatigue occurs when you have food to eat and you have the choice to eat or not eat. This is one of the reasons old people in a retirement home usually lose weight and their health. The cafeteria serves the same basic bland food over and over again.

To avoid appetite fatigue you should have some reasonable variety in your emergency food supplies.

Substitutions: If you are allergic to a food then do not buy it. If you do not enjoy the taste of one of the recommended foods then do not buy it. Feel free to substitute any food item and name brands you prefer. However, you should try to keep a reasonable balance of meat, carbohydrates, vegetables, fruits, grains, and dairy products.

For example, instead of buying 48 cans of Fruit Cocktail you may wish to buy a few cans of apples, peaches, pears, cherries, and pineapple based on your own individual taste preferences. The important issue is to have some canned fruits in your food storage plan.

The same concept applies to vegetables. The emergency food list recommended later in this book contains 180 cans of mixed vegetables, 96 cans of beans, 12 boxes of instant potatoes, 48 cans of beef stew (meat, potatoes, and carrots), 48 cans of roast beef hash (meat and potatoes), and 48 cans of chili with beans. If you like the canned "Mixed Vegetables" then purchase them. But you could purchase cans of corn, peas, spinach, or any other vegetable you wish. However, you should consider the nutritional value of each vegetable by reading the nutrition label. For example, green beans cost almost the same as all the other vegetables but they have very few calories. Therefore green beans would be a poor choice from a nutritional value standpoint. There would be nothing wrong with having a few cans of green beans in your pantry for variety but the number of those cans should be very small compared to the other vegetables. However, most other canned beans have relatively high levels of protein and calories.

You should also adjust the recommended quantities based on your family's actual needs. If you have several family members who drink a lot of milk then you should buy more dry milk powder than suggested.

Chapter Nine: Introduction to Emergency Food Storage

Calories: An active adult engaged in normal physical labor can burn 3,000 calories per day without gaining weight. However, an adult who has a desk job would gain weight. Therefore the concept of a "One-Year Food Supply" is based on the average physically active adult. If you were not very active during a disaster event then you could easily reduce your calorie intake to 2,000 calories per day and still maintain your weight. Therefore the recommended food reserves would last a non-active adult for 18 months with no weight loss. If you wanted to lose a little weight then your emergency food could last for 24 to 30 months.

Brand Names: All the foods in the recommended emergency food list are generic brand or store brand except where brand names are specifically indicated. For example, in my opinion Armour Brand Beef Stew is pleasant to eat but the cheaper brands are disgusting. Therefore purchase and eat one can of each of the recommended food items to see if the flavor of that brand is agreeable to you before you purchase a year's supply of that item and then discover it tastes horrible.

Taste is a very personal experience. Two people can have entirely different opinions about the same exact food. The limited number of brand name foods I recommend are based on my individual taste preferences and I do not have any financial interest in any of those food companies. You will need to make your own decision about which brands of food you prefer.

If you are already happy with a specific name brand then it would probably be a better investment than a generic brand you are not familiar with. However, if there is a big price difference between the brands, such as 52 cents for the generic and 94 cents for your brand, then it would be a good idea to buy one can of the generic brand and take it home and eat it to see how it compares to your preferred name brand food item.

Prices: All food prices are the average retail price in United States Dollars in the southeast United States. None of the prices are special temporary sale prices. If you can find any of the recommended food items offered at a really good discount then you should stock up on that item during the week it is on sale.

Package Sizes: Larger packages are usually a little cheaper per ounce but if half the package spoils after you open it and before it can all be used, then you lose. Therefore resist the temptation to buy the large one-gallon size cans of food. If you need more food per meal than one regular size can then you can always open two cans. However, instead of opening two cans of the same thing you might consider opening one can of two different food items to provide more variety during the meal.

Mix It Up: If you are storing canned foods for an emergency and most of your cans are approximately the same size such as 15 ounces, then you should consider mixing your canned foods together on a single cardboard flat. For example, some people have canned corn, pinto beans, mixed vegetables, fruit cocktail, spaghetti with meatballs, and chili with beans, and these cans are stored 24 cans per cardboard flat. However, instead of having 24 cans of exactly the same thing on a single cardboard flat it would be smarter to mix the canned foods together and put some of each type of canned food on each cardboard flat. For example, a cardboard flat that contains 24 cans could hold:

- 4 cans of corn,
- 4 cans of pinto beans,
- 4 cans of mixed vegetables,
- 4 cans of fruit cocktail,
- 4 cans of spaghetti with meatballs, and
- 4 cans of chili with beans.

This would be advantageous for all the following reasons:

1. **Plan A (Staying Home):** If a hard times tragedy event were to occur and you were forced to start consuming your emergency food then some of each type of food would be in the cardboard flat on top of a stack. You would not have to move everything to get to a food item that was on the bottom of the stack. This would also help you to use your emergency food in a more balanced nutritional manner because you would know that you should consume all the food on one cardboard flat before eating food items off the next cardboard flat.

2. **Plan B (Living with a Relative):** If you were going to transfer some of your canned food to the home of a close relative, or into a storage area at a distant small rural town, then you could move a few cardboard flats of food to that location and you would know you had a reasonable assortment of foods on each cardboard flat.
3. **Plan C (Disappearing into the Wilderness):** If you were forced to quickly evacuate your current home and you only had a few minutes to load your vehicle, then you could add as many cardboard flats of food as you could and you would know each cardboard flat contained a reasonable variety of canned foods.

Storage Area: You should carefully consider where you will keep your emergency food stored for the following reasons:

1. It takes a lot of space to store a one-year supply of food.
2. It will take a significant amount of time and effort to move all the food between locations.
3. The food should not be located where it may be accidentally discovered by anyone.
4. Absolutely no one, except your spouse, should know about your emergency food reserves.
5. The recommended foods need to be stored in a temperature controlled environment for a variety of reasons.
6. If a disaster unfolds rapidly and unexpectedly then you will need to be able to get to your food without drawing attention to your family.

If possible always purchase your food on cardboard flats for easy convenient stacking when you put it into a storage area. In other words, purchase canned goods in multiples of 6, 12, or 24 depending on the number that fit onto a standard cardboard flat. Take the cardboard flat with you through the check-out line when you pay for the food. If your store cuts one side off the front of the cardboard flats then take two cardboard flats and turn them end-to-end one inside the other to make one new cardboard flat that will hold your canned goods without collapsing.

When items are on sale at your local grocery store they sometimes leave them on cardboard flats at the end of an aisle. Just pick up an entire cardboard flat of food and put it into your shopping cart. If appropriate, put two, three, or more flats of food into your shopping cart and then pay for them at the cashier station. It would not hurt to have a little more food than you think you might need.

Usually it is much easier to buy large quantities of food at a place like Sam's Club or Costco. You can pick up entire cases of food already enclosed in plastic wrap and put them on your flatbed cart and take them to the checkout area. However, food items are very, very heavy so resist the temptation to purchase an entire year's food supply in one trip. Your vehicle may not be able to move 2,000 pounds of food in one trip. The only disadvantage of purchasing at a "Membership Warehouse" is that the store keeps a permanent record of all your purchases in its computer, even if you pay with cash. On the other hand, if you pay with cash at a grocery store and do not use a "Store Shopping Card" then there will be no permanent record of your food purchases. The lack of an electronic trail to your emergency food supplies may allow you to keep your food if the government decides to collect all the food purchased by "unethical hoarders" who made their food purchases just prior to a worldwide food shortage. If you need to use a credit card to finance your food purchases, then you should consider going to your local bank and asking your bank teller to give you a "cash advance" against your credit card. Most banks will do this regardless of which bank issued the credit card.

Each time you go to the store it is usually better to purchase food in more than one food category instead of investing all your money in only one food item. This way you could gradually build your emergency food reserves. If a disaster were to occur before you finished then you would still have some food in each major food group, instead of having lots of rice and no vegetables, as an example.

Either write or tape a simple label onto each cardboard flat of food indicating the date you purchased it.

It is very easy to forget what you have already purchased so you should keep a written list of all the food items you have added to your reserves. This list will help you to strategically build your food stores without overlooking something or buying too much of something else.

The shelf life of most of the recommended food items is five years or more, regardless of the expiration date printed on the package.

Store food at temperatures between 40°F to 70°F (4°C to 21°C) if possible. Higher storage temperatures shortens the shelf life, reduces the vitamins and calories, and changes the taste.

Rotation: Long-term food storage advice usually includes the recommendation that you use your emergency food on a regular basis and replace it as you use it by employing a first-in first-out inventory strategy. This is good advice but it is very difficult for most families to execute. The sheer volume of any reasonable emergency food supply makes it very difficult to rotate your food without a tremendous investment in time and energy. Therefore most families simply buy their emergency food, put it into a suitable storage area, and then forget about it. May I suggest a compromise between these two extremes. Most of the recommended long-term storage food items have a shelf life of five-years or longer. The major exceptions are yeast, spices, lemon juice, fresh butter, Velvetta Brand cheese, flour, and corn meal. If you will store these items where you can easily get to them then you could gradually use these items and replace them as they are consumed. If you discover that two or three years have passed and some of these items have not been used then you should consider replacing them with fresh food. However, the balance of your emergency storage food should still be safe and enjoyable to eat, even though you did not rotate it the same way you did your short shelf life foods.

Consumption: Carefully ration your food at the beginning of hard times. Don't wait until half your food is gone before you consider rationing.

Chef Boyardee Macaroni and Cheese: The Chef Boyardee brand Macaroni and Cheese is recommended instead of the boxed macaroni and cheese because it contains almost twice the calories and it is already cooked so it only needs to be heated before you eat it (you don't have to add milk or butter to cook it). In addition, the powdered cheese packages in the boxes of macaroni and cheese have a relatively short shelf life and they will go bad long before the dry macaroni noodles. Therefore the canned macaroni and cheese is a better value from a nutritional perspective, and an ease of preparation perspective, and a shelf life perspective.

Campbell's Chunky Brand Soup: Canned chicken was removed from the list because many families, including my own, do not find the taste of canned chicken to be very enjoyable. However, the Campbell's Chunky Brand Soups that contain chicken also contain a lot of other tasty foods, and they have more volume, and they have more nutrients, and they cost less than a can of chicken. Therefore in order to add chicken to the menu in addition to beef, tuna, and ham, the Campbell's Chunky Brand Chicken Based Soups are perfect. Some examples would be: Chicken Broccoli Cheese with Potato, Chicken Corn Chowder, Chicken and Dumplings, Grilled Chicken and Sausage Gumbo, and Fajita Chicken with Rice and Beans.

Cooking From Scratch: At the current time you may not use some of the food items in the recommended food list. However, in the event of an emergency you will probably discover you will need all the foods in the list, including the spices. During an actual emergency the recipes in my **Hard Times Cook Book** plus the recommended spices will help you to prepare an interesting and pleasant variety of meals using the basic staple foods and spices in the recommended list of foods.

Additional Food Items: If you have the money and the space then purchase extra white rice, beans, and wheat.

White Rice: Ordinary white rice should be one of the primary emergency foods every family has stored in their home. White rice goes well as a side dish with almost any meal (including wild game and fresh fish). White rice is normally enriched with several vitamins and it is a complex carbohydrate which is something the human body needs.

White rice is extremely cheap when compared to other foods. A ten-pound bag of white rice can be purchased at many grocery stores for about six-dollars (or a twenty-pound bag for about twelve-dollars). At approximately 60-cents per pound you are buying 1,500 calories per pound or 15,000 calories per ten-pound bag. That is a true bargain. And white rice has a shelf life between twenty to thirty-years if stored in a cool, dry area that is kept between 40°F to 70°F (4°C to 21°C) year round. (Note: Brown rice has a shelf life of six-months or less.)

In a hard times survival situation a ten-pound bag of white rice would feed one person for about 52 days if the person ate 1.5-cup of cooked rice per day (equal to 1/2 cup uncooked rice). This would be approximately 300 calories per day from rice. A recommended one-year food supply of white rice for one person would be approximately 70 pounds. Obviously other foods would also need to be eaten but the white rice could serve as an inexpensive part of the daily menu.

However it should be noted that white rice has two **disadvantages** in a hard times survival situation:

1. White rice needs to be prepared with fresh clean water. Therefore each family must determine how they are going to address the water issue. Additional information about water is explained in the Water Chapter in this book.
2. White rice has a tendency to become very unexciting after it has been eaten on a regular basis for an extended period of time.

There are a vast multitude of recipes that use white rice as a primary ingredient. Unfortunately most of those recipes require an assortment of herbs, spices, and many other ingredients that most of us don't have in our kitchen pantries. The recipes listed in my **Grandpappy's Recipes for Hard Times** cookbook are unique in that respect. Most of the white rice recipes in my cookbook only require a few ingredients and many of those ingredients are ones that most of us already have in our kitchen pantries. Therefore those white rice recipes can help to relieve the problem of dietary boredom or appetite fatigue.

Beans: A small quantity of dry beans may be substituted for some of the canned beans. Dry beans can be planted as seed in a garden and they will produce a new crop of beans at the end of the summer growing season. Dry beans are sold at most grocery stores inside 1, 2, and 4 pound plastic bags. However, it should be noted that dry beans will continue to get drier and drier with the passage of time and they will gradually become too hard to cook and eat after about 3 or 4 years in storage. Therefore if you anticipate storing your beans for an extended period of time then the canned beans are a better option. Canned beans are already fully cooked inside the can and they will be edible many, many years after the printed expiration date on the can. (Note: I have personally eaten canned beans that were ten years old and they tasted just like they had been recently canned.)

Salt: The suggested food list recommends the purchase of more salt than you would need in one-year because almost all the canned and processed foods already contain adequate salt. The reason salt is on the list is to provide the option to cook, season, and/or preserve any fresh vegetables or meat that you may be able to obtain during a long-term disaster event. Salt is one of the basic ingredients the human body requires to maintain good long-term health. At the present time salt is very cheap but during a disaster event it may become very difficult to acquire.

Pure Salt may be used to help preserve food. Iodized salt should not be used as a food preservative. However, iodized salt is the best salt to use when adding salt to your food just before you eat it. Your body needs a little iodine on a regular basis and a good way to get that iodine is by adding a little iodized salt onto your food at the table. I recommend the Morton Lite Iodized Salt because it can also be used to create an "electrolyte beverage." Therefore, in addition to Pure Salt, it would probably also be a good idea to purchase one or two 11-ounce Morton Lite Salt containers and add them to your one-year emergency food supply.

Pepper: If your family enjoys the taste of pepper then you will need to store some pepper as part of your emergency food supplies. You have two options: ground black pepper or whole peppercorns. Whole peppercorns have an indefinite shelf life if stored in their original packaging in the dark in a temperature controlled environment. Or you can vacuum seal the peppercorns to completely eliminate any aroma or taste loss as a result of exposure to the air or humidity. If you invest in peppercorns then you will also need to invest in a pepper grinder. I suggest you purchase a refillable normal pepper grinder and not one of those little pepper grinders in the spice rack of your grocery store that contains a small amount of peppercorns. The majority of those little pepper grinders cannot be opened and refilled.

Yeast: Freeze store bought yeast until it is needed. Stir a little crumbled yeast into some warm water (105°F to 115°F or 40°C to 46°C). Test the water on your wrist. It should feel warm but not hot. If the water is too hot it will kill the yeast. If the water is too cold it will slow down the process. Adding a little sugar to the water will speed up the process. Adding salt or fat will slow it down. Good yeast will become foamy and creamy after about 10 to 12 minutes.

Don't waste your package yeast. After you have added yeast to some bread dough, pinch off one handful of the bread dough **after the first rise** and save it in an airtight container in a cool dark place. The next day thoroughly mix (knead) the old dough into a new batch of dough. The yeast will multiply and spread throughout the new batch. After the first rise, pinch off a handful of dough and save it. Continue this process each time you make yeast bread and you will be able to make bread for a very long time from that one original package of yeast.

Baking Powder: Both yeast and baking powder will cause your bread dough to rise. But both yeast and baking powder have relatively short shelf lives. The good news is that you can make your own baking powder as follows:

1 part baking soda.
1 part corn starch.
2 parts cream of tartar.
Mix together to make fresh baking powder.

Baking soda, corn starch, and cream of tartar have an indefinite shelf life if properly stored. However, after you mix them together a slow chemical reaction begins and the shelf life of the resulting baking powder is much less. Therefore make your baking powder as you need it and do **not** make more than you will need in a specific recipe.

Baking Options: During a serious hard times event you may need to cook and bake using a wood burning fire. For baking you have two options as follows:

1. **Cast Iron Dutch Oven:** Instructions for using a Dutch oven for baking are in the Cast Iron Cookware Chapter of this book.
2. **Folding Camp Oven:** You could purchase a folding metal camp oven and bake over a propane stove or a campfire. These folding ovens come in a variety of different sizes and they may be purchased at some Army/Navy stores, some hardware stores, and some Walmarts.

Seasoned Meat Tenderizer: The reason seasoned meat tenderizer is recommended is because it is really cheap at the current time and it will make it a lot easier for your entire family to gradually adjust to the flavor of any "wild game meat" you may be able to acquire during a long-term hard times event.

Bouillon Cubes: Bouillon cubes are a seasoning. A large cube should be cut into quarter sections so each piece is the same size as a regular small cube. These cubes may be used to enhance or improve the flavor of a variety of different foods. For example, a cube may be used to enhance the flavor of white rice by adding it to some boiling water before you add the white rice, or it may be used to enhance the flavor of a casserole. A large cube only contains twenty calories and a small cube only contains five calories. Some of the different brands of cubes do not contain any calories. Bouillon cubes do **not** contain any carbohydrates, or protein, or vitamins. Therefore their food value is negligible, the same as any other seasoning or flavoring. If you simply add a bouillon cube to some water then you will change the taste of that water but you will **not** be creating a full-bodied soup that will sustain you and restore your energy. You will only be creating some flavored water.

Long-Term Storage Foods: Freeze-dried and dehydrated foods are also an outstanding choice for long-term food storage and you should include them in your food storage plan if you can find them available at a price you can afford. Occasionally these items are on backorder and it may take weeks or months before the food is delivered to you. That is one of the advantages of buying food at your local grocery store. You take possession of your food immediately and you don't have to worry about receiving a very polite notice at some future date that your order has been canceled and it will not be shipped to you for reasons beyond the control of the seller.

Chapter Nine: Introduction to Emergency Food Storage

Vitamins

The following is **not** medical advice nor is it a medical recommendation. If you have a medical question then please consult a licensed medical professional.

During a long-term hard times event the nutritional value of your daily meals will probably not be as high as during normal times. To help maintain your health and to help prevent a number of vitamin deficiency health problems, your family should have a reasonable supply of complete multivitamins. The health benefits of vitamins is usually not fully appreciated by people in the United States until they have a vitamin deficiency and a health problem develops as a result of that deficiency, such as bleeding gums and loose teeth. Therefore each member of your family should take a complete multivitamin on a regular basis, unless they have been advised not to by a medical professional.

During a hard times event if you are not sure how long it will be before you can replenish your supply of vitamins then you may need to ration your vitamins and only take one vitamin every two or three days. This is a decision you will need to make yourself.

Vacuum Food Sealer

1. Many foods can be protected from insects, oxygen, and humidity by sealing them inside vacuum seal bags. Some examples would be salt, peppercorns, baking soda, corn starch, corn meal, sugar, dry noodles, grits, instant potatoes, instant milk, oatmeal flakes, white rice, tootsie rolls, and hard candies.
2. Vacuum sealing will preserve the freshness and the original flavor of the sealed food approximately three to five times longer than if the food is not sealed.
3. Vacuum sealing will also significantly extend the shelf life of some foods because you eliminate the oxygen and the humidity that can gradually destroy the food.
4. If you use vacuum sealed storage bags you will not need to purchase any of the "oxygen absorber packets" because the vacuum sealing process will remove all the oxygen from inside the specially designed bags.

A cheap good quality food vacuum sealer will cost about $40 and a two-roll box of vacuum seal bags will cost about $22. If you buy the 11-inch wide rolls that are 16-feet long then you can cut individuals bags from the roll to the exact length you need. Therefore there will be very little waste because:

1. You won't need to seal a small item inside a large bag, and
2. You can seal the foods in the quantities you think you will need so you can open one bag at a time and the rest of your food will remain fresh inside its own vacuum sealed bag.

Immediately after you vacuum seal an item inside a vacuum storage bag use a medium tip permanent black magic marker to write a brief description of the contents on the top of the bag and the date you sealed the bag, such as: *16 ounces Pure Salt, Sealed March 2010.*

If you are sealing clothes to protect them from mold and mildew then you could write:
Men's Jeans, Size 36 x 30, Sealed March 2010.

A vacuum food sealer can also be used to protect any books you purchased for the future education of your children and grandchildren. If you vacuum seal these books then you will protect them from moisture and humidity damage and they will remain in very good condition the entire time they are vacuum sealed.

Note: Vacuum sealing is not a substitute for refrigeration or freezing. Any food item than needs to be refrigerated or frozen will still need to be kept in the refrigerator or freezer after you vacuum seal it. However, vacuum sealing will help that food item to remain edible about 3 to 5 times longer than if it wasn't sealed. It will eliminate the problem with freezer burn because you will have isolated the food from the cold dry air inside the freezer.

Chapter Nine: Introduction to Emergency Food Storage

Instant Non-Fat Dry Powdered Milk

Instant Nonfat Powdered Milk will last at least 20 years if properly stored. The easiest way to store and preserve instant milk for future consumption is to use a vacuum food sealer. However, if you simply pour some instant milk powder into a vacuum seal bag and then you attempt to draw a vacuum on the bag you will discover that some of the milk powder will be sucked into the seam area. This will result in the bag not being properly sealed and air will gradually enter the bag and your instant milk will deteriorate more rapidly.

The simple solution to this problem is to purchase instant powdered milk in the one-quart paper packs. There are usually several of these one-quart packs in a box of instant milk. Open the box and remove the one-quart packs of instant milk. Select a vacuum bag of a matching size or cut a bag that will work from a long roll of vacuum seal material. Either two or four of the one-quart instant milk packs will usually fit nicely in one vacuum bag, depending on the size of the bag. Use some scissors to snip a very short cut (about 1/4 inch long) into the edge of each paper milk pack to break the seal of the pack. Then place the milk packs inside the vacuum bag and draw a vacuum on the bag. The air inside the paper milk packs will be withdrawn but almost none of the dry milk powder will escape. This means you will have succeeded in vacuum sealing your instant milk. Then store your sealed instant milk inside a suitable container with a lid in a dark cool dry place.

Wheat Berries

I recommend the Golden 86 or White Wheat in a six-gallon pail. This type of wheat is closer in flavor to the average bread that most people in the United States now eat. A six-gallon pail of wheat berries will cost about $72 (which includes the shipping fee) and a six-gallon pail contains about 72,000 calories.

One internet store that sells wheat berries is: http://www.pleasanthillgrain.com/

The wheat is vacuum sealed inside a mylar bag and then sealed inside the six-gallon pail. Therefore the shelf life of the wheat inside one of these pails will be more than 30 years. You will also need a hand-operated wheat grinder.

If you can afford it then you should consider buying an equal amount of red wheat berries and white wheat berries. One type of wheat is better for loaves of bread and one type of wheat is better for cakes, cookies, and donuts. The above web site has some good information on the different types of wheat berries.

Unlike some of the other food items, if a hard times event does not force you to eat your wheat berries, then your wheat pails can be an investment that you can pass on to your children and grandchildren.

Frozen Foods and a Food Freezer

Do **not** invest in frozen foods for a long-term hard times event. Do **not** invest in a big freezer for a long-term hard times event. During a long-term hard times event you may not have any electricity. If you produce your own electricity using solar panels or a generator then you will need to use that electricity in the most efficient manner possible. A food freezer is not a good way to use that electricity. The reason is because you can currently purchase a huge variety of delicious foods that do not require refrigeration or freezing. The money you would have invested in a food freezer would be much better invested in a larger inventory of foods that do not need to be refrigerated or frozen.

Can Opener

Every family should invest in an old-fashioned manually operated can opener. This type of can opener is placed on the top of the can, then the handles are squeezed together to puncture a hole in the top of the can, and then the crank is rotated to open the can. If the electricity is off then you will be very glad that you have one of these manually operated can openers. It is okay to have a "Dollar Store" quality manual can opener as a backup but each family should also own a high quality stainless steel can opener. Being able to open your canned foods safely and quickly will help to prevent a wide variety of accidents during hard times. (Note: Rinse the piercing/cutting edge in clean water after each use to keep the can opener clean and sanitary and to significantly extend its useful life.)

Chapter Nine: Introduction to Emergency Food Storage

Reasonable Food Safety Precautions

1. Do not buy dented cans of food or canned foods that show any sign of aging such as rust on the outside of the can, or labels that show visible signs of aging.
2. If you do not protect the exterior of the cans from the natural moisture and humidity in the air then the cans will gradually rust and the food inside will be lost. One easy way to protect a case of canned foods from moisture and humidity is to place the entire case of food inside a standard kitchen sized garbage bag and then carefully force all the air out of the bag and either twist tie it closed or tape the bag down tight against itself so air cannot enter the bag easily.
3. Some canned foods are packed in water and the moisture in those cans may find a weak spot on the inside coating of the can and gradually eat its way through the can. If this happens then you will need to discard the entire can of food.
4. High acidic foods, such as tomatoes, will gradually eat right through the can. However, some canning companies use a special coating inside their high acidic food cans to help minimize this problem.
5. When selecting moisture packed canned foods, purchase and open one of the cans and then carefully examine the inside coating of the can to determine if the canning company is using a quality coating on the inside of their cans. If you are satisfied with the coating on the inside of the can then you could purchase additional quantities of that food item for long-term food storage.
6. Before using any item that has been in storage for a long time, open it and then carefully examine it. It should look okay and it should smell okay. If it doesn't look and smell okay then it is probably not safe to eat. Never, never eat any food that has an offensive or unusual odor, or that has something growing on it.
7. Boiling a food item before you eat it, or cooking it until its internal temperature exceeds at least 200°F (93°C), will kill almost every harmful microorganism that *might* be present in the food item. Therefore all canned meats and all canned vegetables and soups should be cooked at a high temperature before eating them.

A Brief Summary of Several Shelf Life Food Studies on a Variety of Food Items

(The following information is being presented for fair use and educational purposes only.)

The following list of foods have an indefinite shelf life if the food is sealed, kept dry, stored in a dark place, and it is not exposed to high heat. In other words, the following foods will still be edible many, many decades from now if the above conditions are met:

- Salt
- Peppercorns
- Granulated Sugar
- Brown Sugar
- Confectioners Sugar
- 100% Maple Syrup
- Baking Soda
- Corn Starch
- Cream of Tartar
- Extra Virgin Olive Oil
- Vanilla Extract
- Wheat Berries

Honey (Note: If the honey begins to crystallize into sugar then put the jar of honey into some very warm or hot water, but not boiling water, and the honey will gradually melt back into a honey consistency.)

The following foods will still be edible for at least 30 years if all the above conditions are met:

- White Rice
- Rolled Oats
- Dry Pasta (Spaghetti and Macaroni)
- Canned Jelly or Jam or Preserves
- Potato Flakes
- Dried Corn
- Canned Meats
- Canned Vegetables

Instant Nonfat Powdered Milk will last at least 20 years if properly stored.

In the Beginning

There are three simple questions that have often puzzled me:
Questions about water, and air, and animals -- just these three.

Outer space is a huge airless vacuum for as far as the eye can see,
With asteroids, comets, planets and stars sprinkled randomly.

So where did the water come from that fills our oceans and our seas?
And where did all the air come from that all animals need to breathe?

And there are animals and fish and insects and plant life everywhere,
All coexisting and supporting one another just by simply being here.

Why do people and animals breathe air and then carbon dioxide exhale?
Why do plants absorb carbon dioxide and give back the air we inhale?

Why do people and animals eat and digest plants and expel the residue?
Why do plants convert animal manure into food fit for me and for you?

Since space is a lifeless vacuum, how did all these things happen to be?
And how did our entire planet get to be in such perfect harmony?

There is an answer to these questions about our planet's origin or birth --
In the beginning God created the Heavens and the Earth.

This Poem is Dedicated to My Granddaughter **Gracie Leigh McClintock.**

Scripture References: Genesis 1:1-31, Genesis 2:1-4, Psalm 33:6, Nehemiah 9:6.

Poem: In the Beginning

Chapter Ten

A 30-Day Emergency Food Supply For One Adult
(3,000 Calories per Day)

Introduction

It would be nice to have two different types of emergency food supplies as follows:

1. A 30-day or one-month emergency food supply.
2. A one-year emergency food supply.

Some emergencies are short-term and they do not last very long. A 30-day food supply would be very useful in this type of situation. In most short-term emergencies electrical power is not available and water may or may not be available. Under these conditions cooking a meal from scratch would be extremely challenging. In this type of situation it would be nice if you had a decent variety of canned foods that you could simply heat and eat.

On the other hand, a long-term hard times event is different. Although eating from a can is a reasonable option for a short period of time, after awhile it becomes very boring. That is when your body will crave "real food" that you prepare from scratch. Therefore a one-year emergency food supply will need to contain a broad variety of food items that include some canned foods and some foods you can prepare from scratch, such as a loaf of fresh baked bread.

One reasonable option for storing your emergency food supplies would be as follows:

1. Store your 30-day food supply at your current residence. If something unexpected happens then you would have immediate access to your food and you could make the decision to either stay exactly where you are, or you could quickly load your 30-day food supply into your car and go somewhere safer.
2. Store your one-year food supply with your parents or children or close relatives who live in a country area. You could arrange this with them ahead of time and perhaps they could set aside a spare bedroom just for your family in the event of an emergency. Then you could stack your one-year emergency food supply in the closet of that bedroom, or put some of it under the bed or beds in that bedroom. This would provide you with food to eat when you arrived at your more desirable back-up location. (Or you could store some of your food at a temperature controlled warehouse in a distant small rural town.)

Important Criteria for Selecting Food Items
for an Emergency 30-Day Food Supply

If an emergency were to occur unexpectedly and you had to provide for your family until the emergency was over, then you should have enough fresh drinking water and enough food stored ahead of time to get you through the emergency.

If the electrical power is off then cooking a meal from scratch would be far more challenging than simply opening a can of food, heating it, and then serving it to your family. In this type of situation your canned foods should meet all of the following criteria:

1. The food item should be one that your family members have enjoyed eating in the past. During a short-term emergency it would be really nice if your family knew that their daily meals would be something they have enjoyed eating in the past. It is okay if different members of your family have different taste preferences. You should consider purchasing and storing the food items that each person in your family really likes because in most situations one can of food is just barely enough for one person.

2. The food item should have a reasonably long shelf life, preferably at least five-years or more.
3. The food item should not require refrigeration or freezing. You should be able to safely store the food item at normal room temperatures.
4. The food item should be relatively affordable.
5. The food item should be ready to heat and eat.
6. The food item should be a complete meal in a can that includes meat, vegetables, and a few vitamins.
7. The food item should contain a lot of calories, fat, carbohydrates, and protein. Your body will need and crave all of these basic ingredients and therefore your food items should contain all of them. In other words, don't just look at the calorie content of the food item. Also consider the fat, carbohydrates, and protein of the food in order to provide a truly balanced meal that will satisfy your family's hunger. After you have eaten a meal you should not feel hungry again for several hours. This is extremely important because some foods only relieve your hunger for a very short period of time and you become extremely hungry again rather quickly. Therefore the foods you select should be ones that can keep you from feeling hunger for at least 5 or 6 hours. If the food contains reasonable levels of calories, fat, carbohydrates, and protein then hunger should not be a problem for several hours.
8. For each food item read the nutritional data on the label. Multiply the number of servings in the container by the number of calories, fat, carbohydrates, and protein per serving. This will yield the total nutritional value of the entire food container. This is important because different canned foods show a different number of "servings per can" and therefore you must convert this into the total food value of the can instead of just comparing the food value per serving. For example, consider the following:

Food Item	Servings Per Can	Calories Per Serving	Total Calories Per Can
18.8 ounces Chunky Soup	2	170	340
12.5 ounces Canned Chicken	6	60	360
15 ounces Canned Pasta	2	250	500
16 ounces Canned Ham	8	80	640
15 ounces Chili with Beans	2	350	700
12 ounces Canned Spam	6	180	1,080

The last column in the above table is the important column because it shows the Total Calories in the entire Can. You would need to do the same calculation for the Total Fat per Can, the Total Carbohydrates per Can, and the Total Protein per Can.

Your food supply should contain a wide assortment of foods. If possible, you should not have to eat the same exact food item until at least seven days have passed. This means you should have enough variety so you could serve different meals to your family every day for one week.

A Recommended 30-Day Emergency Food Supply for One Adult

In my opinion the following food items are ones you should consider for your 30-day emergency food supply. I strongly recommend that you purchase one can of each of the following foods and serve it to your family during normal times to determine if they enjoy it. If they like it then you could purchase additional cans of that food item for your 30-day emergency food supply.

The following suggestions would be a reasonable starting position for the average family. However, since each family has unique taste and dietary requirements, each family will probably need to remove some items from the following list and add other items they enjoy more.

Note: All the data in the table on the next page was obtained on January 3, 2011.

Abbreviations used in the column headings of the following table:

Oz. = Ounces
CC = Calories per Can
FC = Fat per Can
AC = Carbohydrates per Can
PC = Protein per Can
TC = Total Calories
TF = Total Fat
TA = Total Carbohydrates
TP = Total Protein

Number	Oz.	Item Description	CC	FC	AC	PC	TC	TF	TA	TP
3 Cans	18.8	Campbell's Chunky Beef Soup	280	9	38	14	840	27	114	42
3 Cans	18.8	Campbell's Chunky Chicken Soup	360	16	38	16	1080	48	114	48
2 Cans	18.8	Campbell's Chunky Other Soup	380	5	60	24	760	10	120	48
8 Cans	15	Chef Boyardee Pasta Assortment	500	24	54	18	4000	192	432	144
4 Cans	42	LaChoy Asian Meat & Vegetables	360	10	54	15	1440	40	216	60
4 Cans	24	Armour Beef Stew	630	33	60	24	2520	132	240	96
4 Cans	15	Hormel Roast Beef Hash	780	48	44	42	3120	192	176	168
4 Cans	15	Van Camps Chili with Beans	700	36	62	34	2800	144	248	136
2 Cans	15	Black Beans (or Pinto or Kidney)	385	2	66	21	770	4	132	42
2 Cans	16	Taco Bell Refried Beans	420	3	70	24	840	6	140	48
4 Packs	1.25	Taco Bell Taco Seasoning Mix	120	0	18	0	480	0	73	0
4 Cans	12	Hereford Roast Beef	350	7	5	65	1400	28	20	260
2 Cans	15	Van Camps Pork and Beans	385	3	88	21	770	6	176	42
4 Cans	5	Armour Vienna Sausage	330	30	3	15	1320	120	12	60
4 Cans	15	Vegetables (Corn, Peas, Carrots)	140	0	28	3	560	0	112	12
6 Packs	4	Instant Potatoes (Add water only)	440	12	80	8	2640	72	480	48
2 Bags	16	Enriched White Rice	1600	0	350	30	3200	0	700	60
2 Boxes	?	Bouillon Cubes (beef & chicken)	100	0	0	0	200	0	0	0
4 Packs	2.65	County Gravy Dry Mix (or brown)	320	16	40	8	1280	64	160	32
8 Cans	15	Chef Boyardee Mac & Cheese	480	20	56	18	3840	160	448	144
4 Cans	14.75	Double "Q" Pink Alaskan Salmon	630	21	0	100	2520	84	0	400
4 Cans	5	Bumble Bee Solid White Albacore	160	6	0	28	640	24	0	112
4 Cans	12.5	Chunk Chicken Breast	360	6	6	66	1440	24	24	264
4 Cans	12	Spam Meat (or Dak Canned Ham)	1080	96	6	42	4320	384	24	168
1 Box	42	Quaker Quick Oats	4500	90	810	150	4500	90	810	150
4 Cans	20	Tang Orange Drink Mix	2160	0	520	0	8640	0	2080	0
15 Each	0.13	Kool-Aid Drink Mix	0	0	0	0	0	0	0	0
10 lbs.	80	Granulated Sugar	8500	0	2270	0	17000	0	4540	0
1 Box	64	Instant Powdered Milk	6400	0	960	640	6400	0	960	640
1 Can	8	Hershey's Cocoa Powder	900	22	135	45	900	22	135	45
8 Cans	4	Fruit Cocktail (or Peaches, Pears)	350	0	84	0	2800	0	672	0
3.5 lbs.	-	Candy Assortment (150 Pieces)	6000	150	1350	50	6000	150	1350	50
30 Each	-	Complete Multivitamin Tablets	0	0	0	0	0	0	0	0

Totals:
89,020 Total Calories
2,023   Total Fat
14,707 Total Carbohydrates
3,319   Total Protein
$191   Total Cost on January 3, 2011

If you do not want to cook then omit the rice and potatoes and buy more of the complete meals in a can (Chunky Soups, Pasta, Chili with Beans, Beef Stew, etc.).

Usually one can of food is just enough for one good meal for one person. However, some of the above canned foods contain enough food for two meals (lunch and supper), or for two people at the same time.

Discussion of Some of the Recommended Food Items

1. The powdered milk and the cocoa powder may be used to make either chocolate milk or hot chocolate. On the other hand, if your family doesn't like milk then don't buy it. If you prefer coffee or tea then buy it instead.
2. If you don't like Kool-Aid or Tang and you prefer soft drinks or beer or wine then buy them instead.
3. White rice can be enhanced with bouillon cubes (either beef or chicken) or with gravy (either white country gravy or brown gravy).
4. Instant potatoes can be enhanced with brown gravy or white country gravy.
5. Armour Roast Beef can be converted into a "Mexican" meal by combining it with approximately one-half package of Taco Mix and then serving it with either Refried Beans or Black Beans.
6. If you have some flour then you could make a burrito or tortilla shell.
7. Chef Boyardee Macaroni and Cheese may be eaten as a side dish by itself, or it can be converted into a casserole by adding canned tuna, or canned chicken, or sliced Vienna Sausages, or diced Spam.
8. Pork and Beans can be made into "Beanie Wienies" by adding sliced pieces of Vienna Sausage.
9. The Vienna Sausages may be eaten as a simple meat item, or converted into "mini corn dogs" if you have some cornmeal, or into "pigs in a blanket" if you have some flour.
10. The Spam may be sliced and fried for breakfast, lunch, or supper.
11. The Salmon can be made into "Salmon Patties" if you add a little cornmeal.
12. Canned fruit may be eaten as a dessert item, or you could eat from the bag of candy.
13. The candy could be hard candies (peppermints, spearmints, butterscotch disks, or cinnamon disks), or caramels, or tootsie rolls, or any combination your family prefers.

Note: If you use a standard Vacuum Food Sealer to vacuum seal some of the above items (candy, vitamins, white rice, instant milk, sugar, cocoa powder, and quick oats), then you could extend the normal shelf life of these items by a multiple of approximately five.

Suggestions for Preparing Meals During a Short-Term Hard Times Event

To prepare a meal from scratch normally takes more time, more fuel, and as the food slowly cooks it emits a stronger aroma than when you simply open a can of food, heat it, and then immediately eat it.

Therefore having canned foods that you simply heat and eat means you will need less cooking fuel and you will be keeping your cooking aromas to the absolute minimum. The absence of strong cooking aromas may help you to avoid attracting unnecessary attention to your family during a difficult short-term hard times event. As a practical example:

1. **Breakfast** could be oatmeal, or breakfast bars, or fried Spam or fried ham, or you could skip breakfast and eat lunch at 10:00 AM and supper at 5:00 PM.
2. **Lunch** could be a complete meal from a can.
3. **Supper** could be more like a normal meal such as boiled rice or instant potatoes or beans or vegetables, plus a meat item from a can, such as salmon patties.

Remember, canned foods have been fully cooked and they only need to be heated and served. However, whenever possible it is advisable to heat your food to at least 185 degrees Fahrenheit (85 degrees Celsius) to kill any potential harmful microorganisms that might be in the food.

It would also be a good idea to put a lid on the cook pot or skillet when you are heating the food. The lid will help to keep the heat and the aroma inside the cook pot. This means you will need less fuel to heat the food to an acceptable temperature, and it will prevent most of the delicious cooking aromas (odors) from escaping and attracting unnecessary attention to your location.

It should also be noted that some foods emit a powerful aroma while they are being prepared, such as coffee and bacon. Therefore if you truly love coffee then during a short-term emergency it might be advisable to have a small supply of "instant coffee" instead of "regular coffee." I know there is a difference between the flavor of instant coffee and regular coffee but you need to consider your priorities during a short-term emergency. For example:

1. Would a cup of instant coffee be okay if it did not attract any attention to your location?
2. Or would you prefer for everyone within a half-block radius to be knocking on your door and asking you to please, please share some of your fresh brewed coffee?

Conclusion

There may not be very much to do during a short-term emergency and everyone in your family will be truly looking forward to each meal in order to relieve their boredom and to satisfy their hunger.

It is okay to talk about unpleasant topics at other times during the day but each member of your family should understand that all discussions at the dining table will be about pleasant topics. This will facilitate their enjoyment of their meal and it will aid in the digestive process.

Finally, please remember to thank God for every meal before your family starts eating.

Footnote:
Additional Nutritional Information on Some Canned Food Items

Campbell's Chunky "Beef Base" Soup (18.8 ounce cans)

Food Item	Calories	Fat	Carbs	Protein
Baked Potato, Steak & Cheese	400	18	42	16
Italian Style Wedding Meatballs & Spinach	320	6	48	16
Salisbury Steak w/ Mushrooms & Onions	280	9	38	14
Beef with White & Wild Rice	280	3	48	16
Beef & Dumplings & Vegetables	260	3	40	16
Grilled Sirloin Steak with Vegetables	260	4	38	26
Sirloin Burger with Country Vegetables	260	4	38	9
Steak and Potato	240	4	30	16
Slow Roasted Beef with Mushrooms	240	3	36	16
Beef Rib Roast with Potatoes & Herbs	220	2	34	14

Campbell's Chunky "Chicken Base" Soups (18.8 ounce cans)

Food Item	Calories	Fat	Carbs	Protein
Chicken Broccoli Cheese with Potato	420	22	4	14
Chicken Corn Chowder	400	20	40	14
Chicken and Dumplings	360	16	38	16
Grilled Chicken and Sausage Gumbo	280	6	42	16
Fajita Chicken with Rice & Beans	260	3	46	14
Savory Chicken with White & Wild Rice	220	4	36	12

Campbell's Chunky "Other Base" Soup (18.8 ounce cans)

Food Item	Calories	Fat	Carbs	Protein
New England Clam Chowder	460	26	40	14
Potato Ham Chowder	380	22	34	12
Split Pea & Ham	380	5	60	24
Hearty Bean & Ham	360	4	60	22

Chapter Ten: 30-Day Emergency Food Supply

La Choy Asian Meals (42 ounce cans)

Food Item	Calories	Fat	Carbs	Protein
Chicken Sweet & Sour with Asian Style Vegetables	540	4	105	15
Chicken Teriyaki with Asian Style Vegetables	360	10	54	15
Chicken Chow Mein with Asian Style Vegetables	300	12	33	15
Beef Pepper Oriental with Asian Style Vegetables	240	3	33	21

Chef Boyardee Pasta (15 ounce cans)

Food Item	Calories	Fat	Carbs	Protein
Mini Beef Ravioli & Meatballs	560	24	64	20
Lasagna	540	20	72	18
Chili Mac	500	24	54	18
Pepperoni Pizzazaroli	500	14	76	18
Mini Spaghetti & Meatballs	480	20	58	18
Cheesy Nacho Twistaroni	440	14	64	16
Cheesy Burger Macaroni	400	12	56	18
Mac & Cheese	480	20	56	18

Chef Boyardee Canned Pasta Note: I have tried the Overstuffed Ravioli, and the Giant Meatballs, and the Regular Ravioli, and the Mini Ravioli, and the Mini Spaghetti with Meatballs. In my opinion the Mini Ravioli and the Mini Spaghetti with Meatballs are better than the regular pastas or the giant pastas. The "mini pastas" contain more sauce, and all the food heats more evenly in less time, and the overall taste is superior. Therefore I strongly recommend the "mini pastas" instead of the regular pastas or the giant pastas. However, since taste is a very individual experience, your family may completely disagree with me and there is nothing wrong with that.

If you have young children then they will probably prefer the Chef Boyardee "ABC" and "Dinosaur" pastas because they are significantly more fun to eat. The nutritional value of these pastas is almost the same as the other pastas so there is nothing wrong will adding these special pastas to your emergency food supply for your young children.

Chapter Eleven

One-Year Emergency Food Supply For One Adult
(3,000 Calories per Day)

At the beginning of the year 2008 the retail **Cost** of the "One-Year Emergency Food Supply" was equal to $1,385 on January 9, 2008.

2008 Inflation: The **total cost** of the one-year emergency food supply **increased** in price by **15.3%** or **$212** in **twelve-months** from January 9, 2008 ($1,385) to January 3, 2009 ($1,597).

2009 Inflation: The **total cost** of the one-year emergency food supply **increased** in price by **6.1%** or **$97** in **twelve-months** from January 3, 2009 ($1,597) to January 4, 2010 ($1,694).

2010 Deflation: The **total cost** of the one-year emergency food supply **decreased** in price by **–4.1%** or **$-23** in **twelve-months** from January 4, 2010 ($1,694) to January 3, 2011 ($1,671).

The retail cost of the "One-Year Emergency Food Supply" on the next page is based on prices as of **January 3, 2011.**

Comfort Foods: The list on the next page contains 60 different food items. However, you should also purchase some Kool-Aid, Tang, Coffee, Tea, Soft Drinks, Beer, Wine, Miniature Tootsie Rolls, Caramels, Assorted Hard Candies, or whatever else appeals to you. These are referred to as "comfort foods" and they can definitely help make the hard times more bearable.

Quantities: You should have enough food for each member of your family for at least six-months. If you are an experienced farmer or rancher living on your own land then you should also have enough **seeds** to replenish your food supplies on an annual basis. You will also need your own canning jars and lids or you will need to know how your ancestors preserved food without electricity or canning jars. If you have no previous experience with farming then you would probably be better off with a two or three-years supply of food for each family member.

Special Note: On January 3, 2011 a few minor changes were made to the list on the next page. During the year 2010 some package sizes were discontinued by the manufacturer and they were replaced by other package sizes. Therefore the data on the next page needed to be revised to match the package sizes currently available for sale. This changed the total price of the one-year emergency food supply from $1,671 to $1,768. This change was not the result of inflation. Instead it was the result of the change in the package sizes that were available for sale.

Quantity	Calories	Cost	Item (Number in Parenthesis = Total Calories per One Bag, Jar, or Can)
70 Pounds	105,000	$ 42	Long Grain White Rice (10 or 20 pound bags) (long shelf life) (15,000 Calories per 10 lbs.)
70 Pounds	105,000	$ 22	Whole Wheat Berries or Flour (not self-rising) (7,500 per 5 lb. Bag)
30 Pounds	48,240	$ 14	5 lb. Bag Corn Meal (8,040 per 5 lb. Bag)
4 Boxes	12,800	$ 9	32 oz. Box Aunt Jemima Buttermilk Complete Pancake/Waffle Mix (3,200)
4 Boxes	18,000	$ 13	42 oz. Box Quaker Quick 1 Minute Oats (4,500)
4 Boxes	31,720	$ 9	5 lb. Box Quaker Quick Grits (7,930)
36 Boxes	60,480	$ 36	16 oz. Box Spaghetti Noodles (Angel hair or thin cooks faster) (1,680)
24 Cans	11,520	$ 24	15 oz. Can Chef Boyardee Brand Macaroni and Cheese (480)
24 Cans	12,000	$ 24	15 oz. Can Chef Boyardee Pasta (lasagna, ravioli, spaghetti with meatballs, etc.) (500)
24 Cans	8,640	$ 36	18.8 oz. Can Campbell's Chunky Soup (buy the soups with chicken) (360)
48 Cans	9,000	$ 66	5 oz. Can Bumble Bee Brand Tuna in Oil (water pack has fewer calories) (187)
12 Cans	9,600	$ 42	16 oz. Can Dak Brand Canned Ham (no refrigeration required) (800)
24 Cans	24,480	$ 59	12 oz. Can Spam (1020)
24 Cans	9,000	$ 11	5 oz. Can Vienna Sausage (375)
24 Cans	9,000	$ 75	12 oz. Can Roast Beef (375)
24 Cans	18,720	$ 48	15 oz. Can Hormel Roast Beef Hash (or Corned Beef Hash) (beef and potatoes) (780)
48 Cans	30,240	$ 109	24 oz. Can Armour Brand Beef Stew (with potatoes and carrots) (630)
48 Cans	33,600	$ 56	15 oz. Can Van Camps Chili with Beans (700)
96 Cans	35,520	$ 65	15 oz. Can Beans (assorted different varieties) (370)
180 Cans	25,200	$ 121	15 oz. Can Mixed Vegetables (note: green beans have very few calories) (140)
12 Boxes	41,280	$ 30	32 oz. Box Instant Potatoes (add water only preferred) (3,440)
48 Cans	15,120	$ 47	15 oz. Can Fruit Cocktail (or peaches, pears, pineapple, etc.) (315)
24 Cans	3,000	$ 10	6 oz. Can Tomato Paste (125)
36 Cans	15,120	$ 35	26.5 oz. Can Delmonte Spaghetti Sauce (Do not buy the Hunt's Brand) (420)
12 Cans	480	$ 9	4 oz. Can Sliced Mushrooms (not pieces) (40)
12 Cans	3,600	$ 9	10.75 oz. Can Cream of Chicken Soup (or Chicken Noodle) (to eat if you get sick) (300)
12 Boxes	76,800	$ 188	64 oz. Box Powdered Instant Non-Fat Dry Milk (long shelf life) (6,400)
24 Cans	11,520	$ 19	12 oz. Can Evaporated Milk (480)
3 Boxes	7,680	$ 15	32 oz. Box Velvetta Brand Cheese (short shelf life) (2,560)
12 Boxes	38,400	$ 30	1 lb. Box Butter (short shelf life unless frozen) (no margarine) (3,200)
5 Jars	60,000	$ 61	50.7 oz. Jar Extra-Virgin Olive Oil (indefinite shelf life) (12,000)
2 Cans	24,860	$ 9	3 lb. Can Crisco Shortening (very short shelf life) (12,430)
12 Cans	10,800	$ 36	8 oz. Container Hershey's Cocoa Powder (900)
8 Cans	9,600	$ 13	16 oz. Can Hershey's Cocoa Syrup (1,200)
25 Pounds	42,500	$ 13	5 lb. Bag White Granulated Sugar (indefinite shelf life) (8,500)
12 Pounds	10,200	$ 13	1 lb. Box Light Brown or Dark Brown Sugar (indefinite shelf life) (1,700)
12 Pounds	10,800	$ 13	1 lb. Box Confectioners 10X Sugar (indefinite shelf life) (1,800)
12 Boxes	26,400	$ 17	20 oz. Box Brownie Mix (or Cake Mix) (2,200)
6 Jars	11,520	$ 9	16 oz. Jar Light Corn Syrup (indefinite shelf life) (1,920)
6 Jars	7,200	$ 37	12.5 oz. Jar 100% Pure Maple Syrup (indefinite shelf life) (1,200)
9 Jars	10,240	$ 50	16 oz. Jar Sue Bee Brand Honey (indefinite shelf life) (1,280)
12 Jars	36,480	$ 21	18 oz. Jar Peanut Butter (3,040)
12 Jars	15,600	$ 15	16 oz. Jar Jelly or Preserves (long shelf life) (1,300)
48 Each	960	$ 13	Beef Bouillon Large Cubes (20 per large cube) (1 large cube = 4 small cubes)
48 Each	960	$ 13	Chicken Bouillon Large Cubes (20 per large cube) (1 large cube = 4 small cubes)
12 Boxes	20,160	$ 12	16 oz. Box Corn Starch (indefinite shelf life) (1,680)
24 Boxes	0	$ 17	16 oz. Box Baking Soda (indefinite shelf life)
12 Jars	0	$ 56	2 oz. Jar Cream of Tartar (indefinite shelf life)
24 Pkgs.	0	$ 12	5/16 oz. Package Yeast (Hodgson Mill Brand) (Store in Ziploc bag in freezer)
6 Bottles	0	$ 22	2 oz. Bottle Vanilla Extract (indefinite shelf life)
24 Pounds	0	$ 7	4 lb. Box Pure Salt (Morton Canning and Pickling Salt) (indefinite shelf life)
12 Jars	0	$ 12	2.6 oz. Ground Black Pepper (or Whole Peppercorns have an indefinite shelf life) (Walmart)
12 Jars	0	$ 6	5.5 oz. Seasoned Meat Tenderizer (Walmart)
12 Jars	0	$ 6	3.12 oz. Onion Powder (Walmart)
2 Jars	0	$ 1	0.9 oz. Oregano (Walmart)
2 Jars	0	$ 1	2.5 oz. Garlic Powder (or Garlic Salt) (Walmart)
2 Jars	0	$ 1	2.37 oz. Cinnamon (Walmart)
1 Jar	0	$ 5	1.75 oz. Cayenne Red Pepper
2 Bottles	0	$ 4	15 oz. Lemon Juice (short shelf life)
1 Jug	0	$ 3	1 Gallon Jug White Distilled Vinegar (indefinite shelf life in glass jar at 40°-70°F in the dark)
Totals =	1,129,040	$ 1,768	

Chapter Eleven: One-Year Emergency Food Supply

Chapter Twelve

Some Practical Places Where You Can Store and Hide Your Emergency Food

You do not want anyone, except your spouse, to know about your emergency food. If anyone knows that you have some extra food stored then they will come to your home during a long-term hard times event and politely ask you to share all of your food with them. If you politely refuse then there is an extremely high chance they will return in the middle of the night with a large group of heavily armed individuals and they will quickly break into your home from as many different directions as possible, all at the same time, and they will kill everyone in your home before you can resist and defend yourself. Then they will take your emergency food and divide it among themselves.

Therefore in order to protect your food investment you should consider storing it in an area where it will **not** be seen by anyone who might enter your home during normal times or during hard times. This would include relatives, friends, neighbors, landlords, building inspectors, neighborhood children, and thieves.

One Simple Storage Area

Depending on your specific situation the simple solution may be to store your emergency food inside your bedroom closet. This would be the easiest way to hide your food but it might not be the best way depending on your location and a variety of other factors. But before we examine some more creative ways to hide your food, let's begin with your bedroom closet.

Your Bedroom Closet: Put a regular front door lock on your bedroom closet door. This would be a normal key operated lock that you might put on the front door to a home. It is relatively easy to install with just a Phillips four-slotted head screwdriver. Remove the existing closet door knob that is held in place with two screws and then remove the side latch two screws and the existing door knob will come out of the door. Then replace it with the same size front door lock in the reverse order. Install the side latch with two screws and then install the door lock with the key hole facing into the bedroom. This can be done for an investment of about $10 to $30 depending on the lock. The new door lock does **not** need to be burglar proof -- it just needs to be a simple key operated lock. (Note: Save the old closet door knob so you can replace it in the closet door when you move.)

Transfer most of what you currently have in your bedroom closet to another place. Then carefully stack your food on the floor of the closet all the way to the ceiling of the closet. If necessary, you can remove the closet shelf to make room for your food. Then put a **copy** of your "Last Will and Testament" and **copies** of whatever "Insurance Papers" you may have inside the closet with your food. Also put a few family pictures in the closet. Then lock the closet door.

Neighbor questions? If anyone asks you why you have a locked closet in your bedroom, then tell them the truth. Begin by saying that you don't have anything valuable in the closet. Tell them you do **not** have a bank safe deposit box and therefore you keep your "Will" and "Insurance Papers" and some other very personal papers (such as family photographs) in the closet and you don't want a thief or anyone else to be able to easily get to them without breaking down the door. Then immediately change the subject and start talking about something else. If the person asks again about the locked closet simply repeat your original comment and then add, "That's all I want to say about my personal papers. I don't have any cash or other valuable items in that closet. The only stuff in that closet are my personal possessions and I don't want to lose them or be forced to replace them. Now let's talk about something else." And if someone asks to look inside your closet then politely say that you put a lock on the closet door to prevent curious people from going through your personal possessions and you don't intend to make an exception for anyone.

The lock on your bedroom closet door will **not** keep a determined thief out of your closet. He or she will simply pry the door open or break the door down. The purpose of the locked closet door is to prevent curious people from accidentally seeing your emergency food supplies and other hard times survival items. If you can keep your emergency survival items a "secret" then you will have a much better chance of surviving a hard times tragedy event.

Some More Sophisticated Storage Areas

Now let's consider some more creative areas where you could hide your emergency food. The purpose of your emergency food is to keep you and your family members alive during a long term hard times event. Depending on your morals and ethics, you may decide to periodically donate some of your emergency food to your local church or food pantry. You should **never** give food directly to anyone during a long-term hard times event. Your food donations should always be anonymous to avoid serious complications. Please read the chapter on charitable donations for more information on this topic.

Your act of charity should be a voluntary decision on your part and you should not be forced by anyone, or by any organization, or by the government, to surrender your emergency food to them. You paid for your emergency food and it belongs to you, just like the shoes you are wearing and the bed you sleep in. You should not be forced to give up the things that belong to you.

During a long-term hard times famine event, one or more of following will **always** occur:

1. The government will try to collect all the food in an area for itself.
2. A powerful group or organization will try to collect all the food in an area for its members.
3. Your neighbors will try to collect all the food in an area for themselves.

History has repeated itself so many times during the last two-thousand years that it would be naive to believe that people will simply just starve to death without doing anything and everything they can to survive. Therefore in a worst case breakdown of society, if you intend to remain in a fixed location, then you will need to be very ingenious about where you store your emergency food supplies.

The following suggestions may help you to select an area, or areas, at your current residence where you could hide some of your food (and maybe some firearms and ammunition).

Below Ground: If you have a yard, or some property that belongs to you, then you may wish to bury some of your food. This would be a reasonable option if: (a) you have mild winters, and (b) you could dig a hole in your yard without any of your neighbors seeing what you are doing. However, if you have long winters and the ground freezes to a depth of one-foot or more then burying your food would not work because the food would freeze, and then thaw, and then freeze, and then thaw and the food would be ruined. But if the frost line in your area is six-inches or less, and your neighbors can't see the spot where you intend to bury your food, then this is a very reasonable option.

Before we look at how to bury food pails and cans of food, let's first look at how an "emergency blanket" could be of use in this situation.

Emergency Blanket (52" x 82.5") (also known as a "space blanket" or as a "solar blanket"): For approximately three-dollars you can purchase a thin flexible foil "emergency blanket" in the camping section of many stores, including most Walmarts. The emergency blanket is designed to reflect a person's natural body heat back onto the person. However, it can also be used to help protect your food from freezing during the winter months. If you unfold the emergency blanket and place it directly on top of your food buckets or cans, then the emergency blanket will be an insulator that will help to prevent the freezing cold from penetrating too quickly down into your food. The reason is because the bottom of your food buckets or plywood box will be resting flat on a layer of earth that is at least 50 degrees Fahrenheit (10° C). The bottom of the food buckets, or the plywood box, will be absorbing the natural warmth from the earth and transmitting that warmth up into your food. But heat rises and the emergency blanket will help to keep the natural heat of the earth inside your food buckets or plywood box. The emergency blanket may only make a few degrees of difference during the winter but those few degrees could keep your food from freezing.

Food Pails: If you have the five or six gallon pails of food (food buckets) that have been properly sealed, then you could simply bury the food pails with the top of the pails at least six-inches below the top of the ground. You should line the inside of the hole with a heavy-duty tarp or with a sheet of thick plastic. Then put your buckets into the hole on top of the plastic. Then unfold an emergency blanket and place it over the top of the buckets and push it down around the outside edge of the group of buckets as far as possible. Then cover the tops of the buckets, and the emergency blanket, with the rest of the piece of plastic or tarp. In other words, the original tarp or plastic should be big enough to completely surround your buckets on all sides, and their bottoms, and their tops. The plastic should be at least 4 mil thick (7 mil would be better). Black plastic is better than white plastic because a small piece of black on the ground will not be noticed as quickly as a small piece of white on the ground if a wild animal, or a dog, digs a small hole directly above your food pails. After covering your food pails with the tarp or plastic, shovel the dirt around the outsides of the pails. Then pack the dirt very firmly into the hole using the wood end of your shovel. Then shovel the dirt on top of the plastic above your food pails. Step on the dirt and press it down firmly. Level the ground so the extra dirt is distributed as evenly as possible in the immediate area. For example, if you dig a 36-inch wide hole then spread the dirt out over a 54-inch area to make the ground appear more level in that spot. Depending on your area, you could bury anywhere from four to six food buckets side-by-side in a single large hole. Four buckets could fit in a two-by-two pattern, and six buckets could fit into a two-by-three pattern.

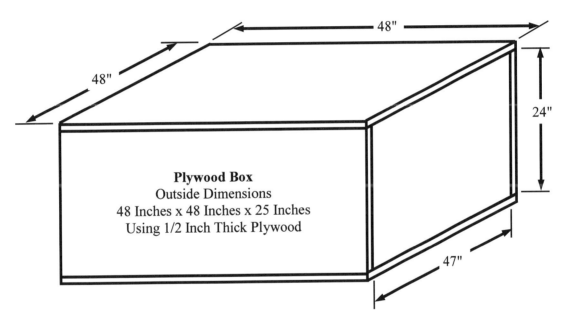

Canned Food: If you have canned food then you could bury several cases of canned food inside a plywood box that you build. You could build a nice plywood box using two sheets of 1/2 inch thick plywood that is 4 feet wide by 8 feet long. The finished plywood box would be large enough to hold approximately 1,200 cans of food (normal 15-ounce cans), or approximately 147 cans of freeze dried or dehydrated food in the big #10 cans (or one-gallon cans). First cut both sheets of plywood in half so you have four pieces of 4 feet by 4 feet plywood (four feet square). Then cut two of those pieces in half so you have four pieces of 2 feet by 4 feet of plywood. Finally, cut one-inch off two of the small pieces of plywood so you have two pieces of 2 feet by 47-inch pieces of plywood. (Note: Most lumber stores, such as Home Depot and Lowe's, will cut the plywood for free, or for approximately 25-cents per cut. I suggest you let them cut the plywood because they will give you an almost perfectly straight and square cut and the cut pieces will be easier to move and to load into your vehicle.) Coat each piece of plywood with a good quality water seal. Coat the inside, the outside, and all the edges with the water seal. Wait at least three-days for it to completely dry. Use 1-5/8 inch long exterior wood screws to assemble your plywood box together. Drill the screw holes using a 7/64" drill bit. Assemble the two 48-inch long by 24-inch high sides to the outside edges of the two 47-inch long by 24-

inch high sides. Remember the plywood is 1/2 inch thick so the 47-inch long side will become 48-inch long when it is attached to the two 1/2 inch thick pieces of plywood. Then screw a 48-inch square piece of 1/2 inch thick plywood onto the bottom of the four sides. The four sides should be flush with the outside edges of the bottom square piece of plywood. Now dig a hole that is at least 30-inches deep and line the inside of the hole with a 9-foot by 12-foot heavy-duty tarp, or with a piece of black plastic that is at least 4 mil thick (7 mil thick would be better).

If you discover that your ground is too hard to dig 30-inches deep then you could dig 18-inches deep and change the depth of the box from 25" tall to 13" tall by cutting each of the side pieces from 24" to 12" tall. (Note: The extra inch is due to the top and bottom of the box.) Then you could purchase one additional sheet of plywood and cut two more tops and then you would have enough pieces to build two separate underground wooden storage boxes.

Place the partially assembled plywood box into the lined hole. Fill the plywood box with cases of canned foods, or plastic tote boxes full of vacuum sealed food, such as white rice. Wrap each case of canned food in a piece of black plastic cut to the proper size, and use two-inch wide clear packaging tape to enclose the case of food in black plastic the same way you would wrap a birthday gift. Also tape a short description of the food item to the outside of the plastic. When the plywood box is full, unfold an emergency blanket over the entire top layer of food cans. Then place the 48-inch square lid on top of the box and screw the lid onto the box. Place a brown, tan, or dark green new shower curtain, or shower curtain liner, on the top of the plywood box. Then cover the shower curtain and the plywood box with the rest of your tarp or piece of plastic. Then shovel the dirt around the sides of the box and then onto the top of the box. Level the remaining dirt on top of the box and on the ground beside the box to make the hole disappear. (Note One: Do not use pressure treated plywood for food storage. Instead use good quality regular plywood, then water seal the plywood, and then protect the outside of the plywood box with a tarp or plastic, and the top of the box with a shower curtain and a tarp or plastic.) (Note Two: The "shower curtain" was not needed on the plastic food pails because the plastic pail lids are naturally waterproof. However, the shower curtain is recommended for the plywood box because you will be burying the box below ground and the shower curtain will help to prevent the rain from making direct contact with the top of the plywood box.)

False Walls: A false wall can be used to hide a secret storage area. Wood paneling is the preferred wall covering because each 4-foot by 8-foot wood panel could be held against the 2x4 lumber studs by using just a few small finishing nails in each panel. Then when you wanted to gain access to your stored food you could temporarily remove the nails and the wood panel directly in front of the food you needed, take out some of your food, and then reinstall the wood panel back in its original position using the original small nails.

A Walk-In Closet or an Oversized Closet: Reduce the size of the closet by building a false wall, or walls, inside the closet to make the closet a little smaller but not so small that it will attract attention. Hide your food behind the false wall. Then give the entire inside of your closet a fresh coat of paint to better disguise the new false wall or walls. Or install cedar paneling on your closet walls.

A Room with Two Closets: Use one closet for your emergency food storage. Then remove the food closet door, install some 2x4's where the door once was, and then put a piece of sheetrock over the old doorway. Paint the new sheetrock and the wall the same color. Or install wood paneling inside the entire room. Unless someone has been inside your home before they will not know that particular room once had two closets.

Hallway Closet: Some hallways have a closet that could disappear. Use the above method to make the hallway food closet disappear.

A Room with a Bare Wall: If you have a room that has a bare wall without any windows or doors, then it might be possible to build a false wall approximately 10 to 12 inches in front of the bare wall. The would provide you with 10 to 12 inches to stack cases of food from the floor to the ceiling the entire length of that wall. You would then need to add sheetrock, or paneling, to that new false wall so it matches the other three walls of the room. When you are finished no one but your family should be able to notice that the room is now just a little smaller than before.

Basement with a Bare Wall: If your home has a basement, and one wall of that basement is a bare wall, then you could use the above method to hide your food.

Large Open Area Basement: If you have a basement that is one large open area then you should consider converting it into three or four separate rooms, and installing a "false wall" in one or more of those rooms to hide your food. Or you could put a hidden closet between two closets between two rooms in the basement. The hidden closet should be between the two visible closets.

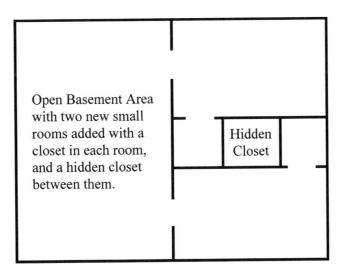

Crawlspace Below Your Home: Some homes have a crawlspace below the first floor. If you enter this crawlspace area you will notice the exposed floor beams of the first floor. If you move to the farthest corner of the crawlspace and install a 1/2 inch thick piece of plywood between the floor beams so the plywood is flush with the bottom of the floor beams, then you could stack some food on that plywood. Do not simply nail the plywood to the bottom of the floor beams because it would be too easily seen. The plywood must be cut so it fits between the floor beams and then nailed into that position. The piece of plywood should be no more than 48 inches long because a person cannot reach more than about 24 inches to get to the food. Both ends of the plywood shelf should be left open so you can reach into the space to get your food. You will probably need to build several of these 48 inch long plywood shelves at the far corner of your crawl space to provide enough space to store a reasonable portion of your emergency food supplies. Store your emergency food in plastic totes or inside some type of thick plastic wrap before putting the food onto the crawlspace shelf. Wear protective clothing and leather gloves when retrieving your food because spiders and other critters will gradually find and decide to use this space. This is a reasonable option if you can get to the crawlway access door without being seen by your neighbors. If your neighbors have a nice view of the entrance to your crawlway space then this option would not work because they could see you transporting lumber and food into the crawlspace and they would have a pretty good idea of exactly what you are doing.

The best way to ensure the success of the above strategy is to put about 95% of your emergency food in two or more of the above locations, and then hide the remaining 5% of your emergency food where it could be found by someone who was doing a very careful search of your home. When your 5% emergency food supply is discovered there is a good chance you will have satisfied the needs of the person or persons doing the search and they will simply take that food and leave. However, you should beg and plead that they please leave some of that food with you in order to create the illusion that they have found all your emergency food.

I realize that some people will consider the above suggestion deceitful. However, please allow me to remind you that you paid for your emergency food and it belongs to you. All you are doing is trying to prevent the theft of your property. There is a big, big difference between voluntary charity and the involuntary confiscation of your possessions by the government or by a criminal.

I Need a Hug

With tears in her eyes the little girl lifts up her arms towards her Daddy,
    and her Daddy picks her up and he speaks softly to her as she cries,

"It's okay. Everything will be all right. The pain will go away real soon."
    And the little girl listens but she continues with her sniffles and sighs.

But gradually the sobs of the little girl become fewer and softer,
    until finally she stops crying and looks at Daddy with love in her eyes.

- - - - - - - - - - - -

Do you feel sad? Are you in pain? Are your cheeks stained with tears?
    Then lift up your hands and say, "Father, I need a hug from above."

And your God with the everlasting arms Who always watches over you,
    will comfort you and strengthen you with His never ending Love.

Scripture References: Deuteronomy 33:27, Isaiah 66:13, Isaiah 51:12, First Timothy 2:8, Psalm 28:2, Psalm 134:2, Psalm 23:4, Jeremiah 31:13, Second Corinthians 1:3-7, Isaiah 41:10, Isaiah 25:8, Jeremiah 31:3, Hebrews 13:5, Isaiah 26:3.

Chapter Thirteen

Some Simple Options for Heating Canned Foods

It is possible to heat some food items while they are still in the can. This would mean no dirty cook pots to wash. However, after heating the can of food you will still need to transfer the food to a bowl or plate so you can stir the food to more evenly blend its ingredients in order to make it a more enjoyable eating experience.

If you decide to heat your food while it is still inside the can then you should first remove the exterior paper label, if the can has a paper label. Then you should remove the top of the can to allow the pressure to escape. Some people recommend simply punching one or two holes in the top of the can with a can opener in order to prevent the ashes from a campfire from getting into the food. However, trying to remove the lid from a can that has been heated to 120 degrees or higher can be a very challenging task.

Following are some options for heating canned foods:

Microwave Oven: If the power is still on then a microwave oven will control the cooking aromas, and it uses very little power, and it is very fast. However, you must remove the food from the can and put it into a microwave safe container before heating the food inside the microwave oven.

Coleman Camp Stove: Another obvious option would be a Coleman Camp Stove. One model uses Coleman fuel and a different model uses the small propane tanks. The major shortcoming is the initial investment in the grill itself and in the fuel, and the fact that they are designed to be used outdoors because they release poisonous gas fumes while in operation. Another disadvantage is that when you run out of fuel the Coleman grill will cease to function. Finally, if you are forced to evacuate your home then which would you rather have in the trunk of your car: (1) a Coleman Grill and some spare fuel, or (2) an extra case or two of canned foods?

Charcoal Grill: A small portable charcoal grill can be used to heat food. You should consider lining the bottom of the grill with a thin layer of sand, or dirt, or small gravel before starting a fire in the charcoal grill. You could use ordinary charcoal briquettes, or you could collect some small sticks from a nearby wooded area and use them to start a very small fire inside your charcoal grill.

If you use sticks then you should consider collecting sticks that have fallen off the trees and are caught in some bushes or that are leaning against something else. These sticks will be extremely dry and they will burn well. If you collect sticks lying flat on the ground then you will probably discover that many of them are damp, or moldy, or rotten and they will not burn well.

The primary shortcoming of both charcoal and sticks is that they must be used outside and as they burn they will release an odor, or smoke, that will attract a lot of attention to your cooking area.

Grill Surface: All you really need is the top metal grill cooking surface off a charcoal grill. You could support this metal grill piece in a variety of different ways and place a heat source below it to heat your food. For example, if you were indoors you could support the metal grill piece on top of four cans of food, and then put a can of "Sterno Cooking Fuel" below the metal grill piece, and you could then heat your food in a skillet on top of the metal grill piece. If you were outdoors you could use four rocks for support and start a fire using some wood sticks from a nearby wooded area.

Fireplace: If you have a wood burning fireplace then you could build a very small fire in your fireplace and heat your meals there. Remember that you only need to heat your food so it would be okay to heat the food over a small flame. In other words, you would not need to wait for the wood sticks to burn down into red hot coals to heat your food. This is one of the differences between simply heating a can of food and cooking from scratch. The major disadvantage of heating food in your fireplace will be the column of chimney smoke that everyone can see. During the cool or cold winter months this would not be an unusual sight. But during the warm summer months a column of chimney smoke will be a "very unusual sight" and almost everyone will notice it and immediately realize you are probably cooking something inside your fireplace. (Note: Additional information about firewood is in the Firewood Chapter in this book.)

Solar Oven: You could purchase a pre-made solar oven or you could build your own "solar oven." Or you could simply line the inside of a small cardboard box with some aluminum foil and then put a piece of heat tempered glass or a "Reynolds Oven Bag" on top of the box. The box should be at least twice as big as your can of food. Place the small solar oven in front of a southern facing window to heat your canned foods. The major shortcoming of this method is that the sun must be shining which may not be the case during a short-term hard times event.

Window and a Dark Cloth: Do not remove the lid from the canned food and do not punch any holes in the lid. Place the can of food under a dark cloth in front of a window in direct sunlight for several hours. You could also use this method by placing the wrapped can of food below the rear window of your car. The dark cloth will achieve two objectives: (1) it will collect and capture more of the sun's energy and do a better job of heating the food, and (2) it will prevent anyone who might pass by from seeing that you are heating a can of food underneath the dark cloth. The major shortcoming of this method is that the sun must be shining which may not be the case during a short-term hard times event.

Sterno Cooking Fuel: The twin packs of Sterno Cooking Fuel may be purchased in the camping section of most sporting goods stores, including most Walmarts. Remove the lid from the can, light the fuel, heat your food, put out the flame, put the top back on the can of fuel, and save the rest of the fuel for your next meal. Since you will only be heating your canned foods, a single can of Sterno Cooking Fuel will last a lot longer as compared to using it to cook a meal from scratch.

Oil Lamp: Remove the glass top from the oil lamp, light the wick, adjust the wick to achieve a very short flame, and then put the flame below a campfire grill and heat the food on top of the campfire grill.

Candle: Place a short round candle inside a candle holder and light it. The short round candles are better because they will last a lot longer inside a candle holder than a long thin candle that will burn down very quickly. You can heat your food above the flame of a candle similar to a "fondue" pot. The glass candle holder in the picture has a long glass stem on its bottom. The long glass stem allows you to move the candle holder to a different location while the candle is still burning. Some candle holders have a flat bottom and the sides of the glass candle holder get extremely hot and it is very challenging to move the lit candle to a different location.

When you stop and think about the above options carefully, the ones that would be the most dependable in the widest variety of short-term hard times events, and which would attract the least amount of attention, would be the last four options above. On the other hand, if the power was still on then the microwave oven would be my first choice.

Note: Several of the above options are only a reasonable choice for heating a can of precooked food. Cooking a food item from scratch will require significantly more heat for a much longer period of time.

Chapter Thirteen: Options for Heating Canned Foods

Chapter Fourteen

Cast Iron Cookware

Cast iron cookware may be used in the kitchen in almost the same way as other cookware, with the major exceptions being as follows:

1. The handles of cast iron cookware get hot so you will need a pair of gloves, or oven mittens, or hot pads, in order to move the cast iron pots after they get hot. Since some of the larger skillets have a front assist handle (see picture on right), you will need 2 gloves, or mittens, or pads. (Note: Handle covers are also available for cast iron but they are not designed to be left on the handle while cooking. And you will still need something that will allow you to grasp the front assist handle. Therefore I personally do not recommend the cast iron handle covers.)

2. Do **not** store food in your cast iron cookware. Use your cast iron for cooking and then immediately remove the food from the pot when it is fully cooked. If you allow your food to remain in your cast iron cookware then the food will gradually begin to acquire a metallic taste, and you will be creating the ideal conditions for the formation of rust. Always remove your food from your cast iron cookware as soon as the food has finished cooking.

3. Wash your cast iron cookware immediately after you have eaten the meal you cooked using the cookware.

4. Do **not** wash your cast iron cookware in an automatic dishwasher.

5. Do **not** use metal spoons, forks, or spatulas with your cast iron cookware. Instead use plastic or wood utensils. Protect your cast iron cookware the same way you would a Teflon coated non-stick cook pot.

6. Do **not** store your cast iron cookware with the lids on the cookware. The lids should be stored off the cookware. This will prevent the possible accumulation of moisture from humid air inside the pot which could eventually lead to a rust problem.

Most foods can be prepared in a cast iron skillet or pot using exactly the same procedures you would use with any other type of kitchen cookware. However, the following suggestions may help improve the quality of your meals:

1. Preheat your cast iron skillet over low heat for about one-minute before you place any food into it.

2. Put a few drops of cooking oil, shortening, or lard in the bottom of the skillet and let it melt. Spread the melted oil over the entire bottom surface of the skillet. The skillet is now ready to receive the food.

3. Do not put frozen or very cold food or cold liquids into your skillet. All foods and liquids should be at room temperature before they are put in the skillet.

The Following Suggestions Apply Specifically to Campfire Cooking

Cast iron cookware may be used when camping. Since cast iron does not have plastic or wood handles you will not have to worry about the cast iron handles melting or burning.

However, the cast iron handles will get very hot so you will need a pair of leather gloves or thick kitchen mittens so you can grasp and move the cast iron cookware when your meal is ready to eat.

1. Use dry wood to build the campfire. Sticks that are off the ground are much dryer than sticks lying on the ground. Look for sticks that are caught in the limbs of shorter trees or bushes.

2. Do not build a campfire bigger than required for your immediate objective.

3. If there is a breeze then you will need to protect your fire with some type of wind break or wind deflector. Even a gentle breeze will cause the fire to burn faster, and hotter, and the breeze will consume your firewood and your red hot coals at a much faster rate. Install your wind break on the incoming wind side of your fire. Or build your campfire beside a natural windbreak, such as a very large rock. Do **not** build a campfire out in the open on an extremely windy day.
4. If you have a camp shovel then dig a shallow pit about 6 inches deep for your campfire. Then dig a cooking trench about 10 inches wide and 6 inches deep on one side of your fire pit. Firmly pack the dirt from your hole into the shape of a dirt wall on the incoming wind side of your fire. (Note: If there is a noticeable breeze blowing then dig your fire pit at least 9 inches deep.)
5. Safely build your fire in the middle of your fire pit. Wait for some of the wood to burn down to red hot coals. Scrape those red hot coals into the cooking trench beside your fire.
6. Do **not** cook over the open flames of your campfire. Instead always cook over the red hot coals that you moved to one side of your fire.
7. If you have a metal grill piece from an old charcoal grill then place it about 2 or 3 inches above the red hot cooking coals. Then put your cast iron cookware on the metal grill piece and cook in the same way you would when cooking on a charcoal grill or a gas grill.
8. If you do not have a camp shovel and you built your campfire on level ground, then support your metal grill on top of three or four flat rocks of the appropriate size. If you do not have a metal grill then support your cast iron skillet on some flat rocks. Never use rocks from a creek or stream because those water saturated rocks may explode or burst when exposed to the heat of a campfire.

How to Use a Cast Iron Dutch Oven When Camping

Always cook a short distance away from the main campfire itself. Measure the diameter of your Dutch oven. This number may be molded into the lid of your oven. You will need some red hot coals from your campfire. To determine the number of coals you will need do the following calculations. The following calculations are based on an internal Dutch oven cooking temperature of 350 degrees Fahrenheit (177 degrees Celsius).

1. Subtract two (2) from the oven diameter and put that many coals **under** the Dutch Oven.
2. Add two (2) to the oven diameter and put that many coals on **top** of the lid of the Dutch Oven.
3. For example, if you have a 12-inch diameter 6-quart Dutch Oven then do the following:

   Place 10 coals (12-2=10) **under** the oven. Arrange the coals in a circle with the coals being about one-inch apart. Do **not** put a coal directly below the center of the oven or you will create a hot spot in the center of the oven and burn any food that may be resting there.

   Place 14 coals (12+2=14) on **top** of the lid of the oven. Place one coal on each side of the lid center handle and then place all the remaining coals equally spaced around the outside raised edge of the lid.

4. To increase the oven temperature by 50°F from 350°F to 400°F, add one more coal below and one more coal onto the lid of the oven. To increase the temperature by another 50°F up to 450°F, then add one more coal below (total of 12 coals below), and one more coal onto the lid of the oven (total of 16 coals on top). (Note: One additional coal above and one additional coal below will increase the internal oven temperature by 27.5 degrees Celsius.)
5. Wear some leather gloves and use some metal **tongs** to pick up, move, and position the red hot coals into the required positions.

Following are some additional suggestions for cooking in a Dutch oven:

Chapter Fourteen: Cast Iron Cookware

1. **Bread:** To bake **bread** in a Dutch oven place a small cooking grate, called a **trivet,** on the bottom of the oven. Then put the bread loaf pan on top of the trivet inside the oven so the bread loaf pan does not rest directly on the cast iron bottom of the Dutch oven. The same procedure should be used for pizzas, cookies, pretzels, crackers, cakes, biscuits, rolls, and any other flour based recipe you wish to bake. A nine-inch diameter non-stick cake pan works exceptionally well with a round loaf of bread. (Note: The picture of the cast iron trivet on the right shows the bottom side of the trivet so you can see the three short legs that keep the trivet supported just a little above the bottom of the cast iron cook pot.)

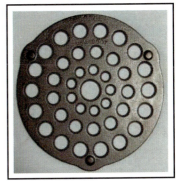

2. **Meat:** To cook **meat** or a roast in a Dutch oven, first melt a little oil, shortening, or lard in the warm oven and spread it over the entire bottom surface of the oven. Then sear or brown both sides of the meat in the oven. This will help to seal the natural flavor and juices into the meat. After the meat has been well seared on both sides you may prepare the meat or roast using any recipe you wish. Depending on the recipe, you may wish to place your trivet in the bottom of the Dutch oven so the meat will rest on the trivet and not make direct contact with the hot bottom surface of your oven.

3. **Stew:** If you wish to make a **stew** then simply add sliced carrots and potatoes and onions to some diced meat cubes. Place your trivet in the bottom of your Dutch oven. The trivet will keep the potatoes and carrots and onions off the bottom of the Dutch oven and prevent them from being scorched. Then prepare the stew according to your favorite recipe.

4. **Vegetables:** If you wish to cook **vegetables** in a sauce then the vegetables should be cooked slightly before adding the sauce. Boil or steam the vegetables for a few minutes (fewer minutes for fewer vegetables and more minutes for a larger portion of vegetables). Then drain off the water, add the sauce, and finish cooking the vegetables for the proper time according to whatever recipe you are following.

5. **Lid:** The **lid** of a Dutch oven may be turned upside down and its smooth curved surface used as a **griddle.** Transfer some red hot coals from your campfire to a position between three flat rocks placed about ten-inches apart. Turn the lid upside down and support it on the rocks so the lid is about 2 or 3 inches above the red hot coals. The inside smooth curved lid surface may then be used to fry bacon, pancakes, or a any other food item you would normally prepare on a griddle.

How to Clean Cast Iron Cookware

Don't let your food stay inside your cast iron cookware after it has been fully cooked. As soon as you are finished cooking you should immediately transfer all the food from inside your cast iron cookware into a large serving bowl or onto your normal eating dishes. Gently scrape off any food that may be stuck to the bottom or sides of the cook pot. Then set the pot aside so it can cool down. (Note: Never put hot cast iron cookware into some water. The rapid temperature change could cause your cast iron cookware to crack or warp.)

After eating your meal carefully check the pot and verify that it has cooled down enough to be handled with your bare hands. Wash the pot with warm or hot water, and some dish soap. You may use a dishcloth or a soft plastic bristle brush, such as the type you would use to clean your fingernails. If you use a soft brush then apply the same amount of pressure you would use if you were scrubbing your fingernails. Do not use a wire bristle brush or a steel wool pad because they will scrape some of the protective coating off your cookware.

After washing thoroughly rinse the pot using warm clean water. Immediately dry all the water off the pot with a dishtowel. Never allow any water to remain on the pot or you will be creating the environment necessary for rust to form. Never allow the pot to soak for an extended period of time in water.

Chapter Fourteen: Cast Iron Cookware

If possible, heat the clean pot briefly before putting it away. You could put the pot into a 350 degree Fahrenheit oven for five minutes. Or you could heat the pot over low heat on one of the burners on top of your stove for two minutes, or over the coals of a campfire. If the sun is shinning you could place the pot in the direct rays of the sun for thirty-minutes, and then turn the pot upside down for another thirty-minutes.

Optional: While the pot is still warm, if you have some cooking oil, bacon grease, pork lard, or beef tallow, then spread a *very, very, very thin coat* over the entire surface of the warm pot, both inside and outside. Carefully wipe the entire pot to remove any excess oil so only a *very, very, very thin coat* is evenly distributed over the entire surface of the pot. Put the pot upside down inside a 350 degree Fahrenheit oven for thirty-minutes. Then turn off the oven and allow the pot to cool down as the oven gradually cools off. After about three-hours, remove the pot from the cool oven, wipe the pot off with a clean dry dish towel, and put the pot into its normal storage area.

Always store your cookware with the lid off. If possible, do not stack your cookware one pot inside the other. These conditions create an environment where the moisture from the humidity in the air can form on the pot and rust can gradually develop.

Never wash cast iron cookware in an automatic dishwasher.

Soap Note: Some people refuse to use soap to clean their cast iron cookware. Following is a direct quote from the Lodge Cast Iron Manufacturing Company General Care Booklet:

> *"Never use harsh detergents to clean iron as it will remove the seasoning." (Lodge Cast Iron Manufacturing Company)*

Ordinary dish soap is **not** a harsh detergent. I always use dish soap, warm water, and a fingernail brush when I wash my cast iron cookware and I have not had any problems with a deterioration in the protective seasoning coating on the surface of the pot. The dish soap helps to remove excess grease, tiny food particles, and it sanitizes the cookware. However, if you prefer not to use soap, then you may follow whatever advice you choose.

Combo Cooker Set

Lodge sells a Combo Cooker cast iron cookware set that contains two skillets. Both skillets have diameters of 10.25-inches and both skillets have front assist handles. The left skillet in the picture has an inside depth of 1.5-inches and it has more gradually rounded sides. The center skillet in the picture has an inside depth of 3-inches and it will hold 3-quarts. When the 3-quart skillet is placed on the bottom, the other skillet can be securely nested on top of it to create a modified style Dutch oven for baking, as illustrated in the right picture.   In this configuration it can also be used as a covered skillet to fry chicken. I suggest that you offset the two handles and front assists when using the skillet in this manner, as illustrated in the right picture. This makes it easier to grasp the top skillet so it can be easily removed to check the food that is cooking in the lower skillet.

If I were on a limited budget then I would only purchase the Combo Cooker cast iron cookware set illustrated above. This would provide me with:
1. a modified style Dutch oven for baking, or
2. a covered skillet for frying foods to lock in their natural flavor, moisture, and steam, or
3. two separate skillets to prepare two different food items.

The above is a very versatile combination and it is a very reasonably priced cast iron cookware set.

Chapter Fourteen: Cast Iron Cookware

Homemade Ventilated Stainless Steel Insert or Trivet (used for baking): If you are baking it is useful if you can bake your food above the bottom of the oven because the bottom of the oven gets very hot. However, the rest of the oven stays at a more even temperature throughout. By placing a ventilated stainless steel insert, which is called a **trivet,** in the bottom of the oven and then putting the item you wish to bake, such as a loaf of bread or a pizza or a few cookies, on another pan on top of the first insert then you will achieve a more delightful end result. The bottom insert (trivet) should go upside down with the outside rim of the insert touching the bottom of the oven. The flat bottom of the ventilated insert will therefore be above the bottom of the oven. The second pan should go right side up and it should contain the item you wish to bake. A 10-inch diameter trivet (insert) fits well in the bottom of a 6-quart Dutch oven, and an 8-inch trivet (insert) fits well in the bottom of the Combo Cooker.

Critical Note: You will need to use a big nail to punch at least twenty big holes in the flat surface of the bottom insert, and at least eight big holes in the side rim of the bottom insert, so the insert can disperse the heat that will be trapped between it and the bottom of the Dutch oven. Drive the nail from the bottom of the insert towards its rim so the nail holes will be facing down towards the bottom of the Dutch oven and you will have a smooth surface on top for the second baking pan. When you make the holes you will need to support the inside of the insert on a flat piece of scrap wood to prevent the insert from being dented with each new hole. Or you can drill the holes in the insert with a hand drill and a 3/16 inch drill bit. Use a hand file to smooth out the inside edges of the holes. Be very careful and use proper safety precautions when using a hammer, a drill, or a file to avoid any unpleasant accidents. After you have added at least 28 big holes to your stainless steel insert then it can then be referred to as a **trivet.**

How to Season Cast Iron Cookware

Until recently cast iron cookware had to be seasoned by the purchaser before it could be used for cooking. Seasoning fills the extremely tiny surface pores in the cast iron cookware. Seasoning has three significant benefits:

1. It provides a slick non-stick cooking surface.
2. It helps to aid in the prevention of rust.
3. It makes the cookware easier to clean.

Newly manufactured Lodge cast iron cookware is already factory seasoned and you may cook in it immediately. Following is a quote from the Lodge Cast Iron Manufacturing Company General Care Booklet:

> *"The oil used to foundry season Lodge Logic and Pro-Logic Cast Iron Cookware is Kosher Certified soy-based vegetable oil. The oil is electrostatically sprayed onto the cookware, then baked at high temperatures. It would take approximately 20 home seasonings to replicate the seasoning process in our South Pittsburg, Tennessee foundry." (Lodge Cast Iron Manufacturing Company)*

However, if you should need to re-season a cast iron pot then the following procedure should be followed:

1. Thoroughly clean the cast iron pot with hot water and dish soap. If there are any rust spots, scrub them vigorously with a steel wool soap pad or a stiff bristle brush. Rinse the pot thoroughly in hot water. Dry all the water off the pot using a dishtowel.
2. Immediately heat the pot in a 350 degree Fahrenheit (177ºC) oven for ten minutes. Or heat the pot on top of your stove on low heat for two minutes. Or heat the pot over the coals of a campfire. Or, if the sun is shinning, then place the pot in the direct rays of the sun for thirty-minutes, and then turn the pot upside down for another thirty-minutes.

3. While the pot is still very warm carefully apply a *very, very thin coat* of cooking oil, bacon grease, pork lard, or beef tallow over the entire surface of the warm pot, both inside and outside. Carefully wipe the entire surface of the pot to more evenly distribute the oil and to remove any excess oil. Only a *very, very thin coat* should be evenly distributed over the entire surface of the pot. (Note: If the pot has a lid it will also need to be seasoned separately.)
4. Place a large sheet of aluminum foil over the bottom shelf inside your oven to catch any oil drippings. Put the pot upside down on the middle shelf in a 350 degree Fahrenheit (177°C) oven for one-hour. Carefully remove the hot pot from the oven and wipe the entire surface of the pot carefully with paper towels to remove any excess oil. Be very careful to avoid burning yourself. Then put the pot right side up in the hot oven for one more hour. Then turn off the oven and allow the pot to remain inside the closed oven so the pot will gradually cool down as the oven gradually cools off. After about three-hours remove the pot from the cool oven, wipe the pot off with a clean dry dishtowel, and put the pot into its normal storage area. Do not store your pot with the lid on it or moisture may develop that could lead to rust problems.

The most common seasoning mistake is to use too much oil or fat in the coating process. The excess oil will form a pool of sticky goo. After the pot cools off the gum pool will have to be scrubbed off and the pot re-seasoned. This problem can be avoided by minimizing the amount of oil used in the seasoning process. It also helps to heat the oven to a temperature that is just below the smoking point of the oil. This higher temperature will result in a darker coating that is less sticky. However, too high an oven temperature will result in a new set of problems. Therefore unless you know the smoking point of the oil or fat you are using, then 350 degree Fahrenheit (177°C) is a safe seasoning temperature. (Note: If you use a lower temperature the oil will not season properly and you will end up with a sticky surface on your cast iron cookware.)

How to Remove Rust From Cast Iron Cookware

You should **not** use rusted cast iron cookware to prepare food because the rust will get into your food and poison your family. If you purchase new cast iron cookware and if you take care of it, then rust should **not** be a problem that you have to deal with. If you inherit some family cast iron cookware and it has been in storage for some time, then it may have some rust issues. If the rust is minor then it may be possible to salvage the cookware. However, if the rust problem is significant then you may not be able to salvage your inheritance. If you find some cast iron cookware for sale at a garage or yard sale then examine it closely before you buy it. If the cast iron contains some rust then my suggestion is to let someone else purchase the bargain.

My personal experience in trying to remove the rust from a cast iron Dutch oven my wife inherited from one of her uncles convinced me that it is generally not practical to believe that you can salvage a piece of rusted cast iron cookware without spending more money than a new replacement piece of cast iron would cost.

Original Rusty Oven	Cleaned with Steel Wool	Right Side Soaked in Vinegar Solution

However, if you wish to experiment with rust removal then try the following:

Step One: Thoroughly clean the cast iron cookware with hot water, soap, and steel wool soap pads. Remove as much surface rust as possible. Replace a used soap pad with a new one when it wears out. Use a stiff bristle wire brush as necessary. Use coarse sandpaper as necessary. When you have removed as much of the rust as you can you are ready for the next step.

Step Two: Completely submerge the cast iron piece in one of the following solutions for 24-hours:

    67% ammonia with 33% water, or a 2 to 1 solution, or
    67% white vinegar with 33% water, or a 2 to 1 solution.

The cast iron piece must be completely submerged in one of the above solutions because the soaking process will change the color of the piece. If the piece is only partially submerged then you will create a permanent line on the piece where the part of the piece that was submerged will always be a different color than the rest of the piece. Be sure to soak the cast iron in an outdoor area because the smell from either of the above solutions is unacceptable to people and it will usually make them sick if they breathe the offensive odors.

Step Three: After you remove the cast iron from the solution, rinse it extremely well with hot water. Then wash the piece with hot water, soap, steel wool soap pads, a wire bristle brush, and some coarse sandpaper. Rinse the piece again in hot water. If you were successful in removing all the rust, then congratulations. You will now need to re-season your cast iron at least three times and then it will be ready to use for cooking.

However, if some rust still remains after Step Three then you will need to repeat the entire process again, from the beginning. And again. And again. At some point you will probably realize you are investing more money in cleaning supplies than the cast iron piece is worth. And when you also consider the time and labor you have invested you will probably wish you had never begun this project, and that you had simply invested your money in a new piece of cast iron cookware instead.

A Humble Birth

It is a 90-mile walk from Nazareth to Bethlehem
    to pay a census tax required by the Caesar of Rome.

There is no room inside the inn so Joseph and Mary
    rent a stall in a stable as a temporary home.

The appointed time arrives for the birth of the child
    but there is no doctor nor midwife nor other caregiver.

Joseph alone is there with his betrothed Mary
    and he helps his future wife her first Child to deliver.

There are no baby clothes available for the newborn Child,
    so the Infant is wrapped in several long strips of cloth.

There are no beds nor cots nor cradles to be found,
    so the Infant sleeps amongst the straw in a feeding trough.

Whose birth merits accommodations such as these?
    Just the First Born and Only Son of our Eternal Majesty.

Scripture References: Luke 2:1-14, John 3:16-18, Isaiah 9:6-7.

Poem: A Humble Birth

Chapter Fifteen

Pure Salt, Iodized Salt, and Sea Salt

Are You Worth Your Salt?

Have you ever heard the expression "Are you worth your salt?" and then wondered what it meant?

In olden days salt had to be transported long distances and it cost a lot of money. Therefore, in addition to a regular wage, a person also received a small ration of salt every day. Without that daily ration of salt a person's health would gradually start to decline. Therefore it became important that a person "earn his salt" every day.

The Importance of Salt

1. Salt is one of the ingredients the human body needs to maintain long-term good health.
2. Most people in the United States don't need any extra salt if they are eating commercially processed foods because those foods already contain salt.
3. On the other hand, fresh vegetables and fresh meat and fresh home baked bread don't contain any salt. And the taste of fresh vegetables and fresh meat and fresh bread won't taste right to the average person if you don't add a little salt.
4. Salt helps to extend the shelf life of foods.
5. Salt helps to prevent the growth of harmful micro-organisms.
6. At the present time salt is very cheap but during a disaster event salt may become very difficult to acquire.

The Shelf Life of Salt

Salt has an indefinite shelf life if properly stored. Salt may be vacuum sealed using an ordinary vacuum food sealer.

The Different Types of Salt

Pure Salt   Iodized Salt   Sea Salt

1. **Pure Salt** may be used to help preserve food.
    a. **Morton Canning and Pickling Salt** is pure salt and it does not contain any extra ingredients. *This pure salt may be used to help preserve food.*
    b. **Morton Salt** is **not** pure salt. It contains salt and calcium silicate.

   At the beginning of the year 2011 you could buy a four-pound box of "Morton Canning and Pickling Salt" for about $1.20 before tax.

2. **Iodized Salt** should **not** be used as a food preservative.

   However, iodized salt is the best salt to use when adding salt to your food just before you eat it. Your body needs a little iodine on a regular basis and a good way to get iodine is by adding a little iodized salt onto your food at the table.

   a. **Morton Iodized Salt** contains salt, calcium silicate, dextrose, and potassium iodide.

   b. **Morton Lite Salt** contains salt, calcium silicate, potassium chloride, magnesium carbonate, dextrose, and potassium iodide.

   For use as a table salt the Morton Lite Salt is recommended because it contains iodide and it can also be used to create an "**electrolyte beverage.**" Therefore, in addition to Pure Salt, it would probably also be a good idea to purchase a few 11-ounce **Morton Lite Salt** containers and add them to your emergency food supply.

3. **Sea Salt** may be used to help preserve food if it is pure salt.

   a. **Morton Sea Salt** contains salt and yellow prussiate of soda as an anticaking agent.

   Commercially processed sea salt is made from sea water by systematically removing the water and the impurities from the sea water until only sea salt remains. This process is carefully controlled and it not the same process that appears on the internet for making sea salt at home. The internet instructions for making sea salt at home usually begin with a comment that you must use very clean sea water, or you must first verify that your sea water does not contain any impurities. Normal sea water contains a wide assortment of impurities and therefore it cannot be used to make pure sea salt following the very simple instructions you read on the internet.

   If you purchase sea salt at the store then you may need a sea salt grinder similar to the one in the picture. This is the same grinder that is used to grind peppercorns and it can be purchased at most Walmarts for approximately $8 in the kitchen section where peppercorn grinders are sold. The sea salt grinder is usually sold with some sea salt inside the grinder as illustrated in the picture.

Chapter Sixteen

Black Pepper, Peppercorns, and Peppercorn Grinders

History of Black Pepper

In today's modern world most people do not give a second thought to many things that were once highly prized but which are relatively cheap today. Black pepper is one of those items. In the distant past wars were fought over black pepper. And the soldiers who fought in those wars were paid by giving them all the pepper they could carry. At that time pepper fetched a handsome price in the marketplace and it was considered to be a commodity that had real value just like silver or gold.

Black pepper is a good source of manganese and iron. It is also a powerful antioxidant. Black pepper helps the body to metabolize and digest food and it can help to prevent gas. It helps the stomach to digest fats and meat proteins, and it aids the body in the absorption of the nutrients and the vitamins in food. However, some people do not like black pepper because of its taste or because it upsets their stomach.

It takes a minimum of three years for a black pepper plant to grow peppercorns. And pepper is not easy to grow everywhere. It is similar to coffee and bananas. If you have the correct soil and environmental conditions then coffee, bananas, or pepper can be grown. But if you try to grow one of these crops in an unsuitable climate then you will not be successful.

Therefore, if your family enjoys the taste of black pepper on their foods, then you will need to store some of it because you will not be able to grow it yourself.

Shelf Life of Black Pepper and Other Spices

Peppercorns, cardamom, cloves, cinnamon sticks, cumin, and nutmeg have a reasonably long shelf life.

However, pepper and most other spices are usually sold with a best-if-used-by date. This date is extremely conservative and the spice will not simply expire when that date is reached. In fact, some of the larger spice companies, such as McCormick, actually recommend that you continue to use a spice as long as that spice still has some of its original flavor. In other words, the potency and the flavor of the spice will gradually decline with the passage of time, but it is still safe to use. However, you would need to use a little more of the spice as it ages to obtain the same flavor results as when the spice was fresh.

Pepper is created by grinding peppercorns into fine, medium, or coarse ground pepper. Ground pepper has a shorter shelf life than whole peppercorns. Whole peppercorns have an indefinite shelf life if stored in their original container in a cool, dark, dry environment. It is also possible to vacuum seal peppercorns using an ordinary food vacuum sealer.

Therefore the most logical way to store pepper is in the form of whole peppercorns. You will also need to purchase and store a pepper grinder.

Pepper Grinders

Pepper grinders may be made of wood, metal, plastic, or glass. But the grinding mechanisms inside these different pepper mills are all very similar. You remove the top of the pepper grinder, put some whole peppercorns inside the grinder, replace the top, and then rotate the grinding mechanism to grind the peppercorns into pepper which falls out the bottom of the pepper grinder.

Some pepper mills have a crank on the top. You hold the bottom of the pepper grinder in one hand above your food and you rotate the top crank with your other hand. Ground pepper falls out the bottom of the grinder onto your food.

Some pepper mills are made in two parts: an upper and lower (see picture on right). You hold the lower half of the grinder in one hand and then rotate the upper half of the grinder with the other hand. Ground pepper falls out the bottom of the grinder onto your food.

Both of the above pepper mills will do a good job of grinding peppercorns into pepper. The major decision is how much you wish to invest in a pepper grinder. The more expensive grinders are usually of a higher quality. But the important part of a pepper grinder is its grinding mechanism. Therefore you should look at the quality of the internal grinding mechanism before you make your final choice of a pepper grinder.

The following three items are shown in the picture:

1. Tone's Whole Black Peppercorns (about $3.64 for 9 ounces at Walmart). At Walmart you can purchase ground black pepper for $1.00 for 2.62 ounces, or approximately $0.382 per ounce. On the other hand, whole black peppercorns can be purchased for almost the same price or about $0.404 per ounce. Therefore, whole peppercorns would definitely be the better value if you are purchasing pepper for a potential future hard times tragedy event.

2. Metal Peppercorn Grinder with a Clear Glass Center (about $8 at Walmart and it is sold with peppercorns inside). This is good pepper mill. It yields a medium grind of pepper and the grind can be increased or decreased a little bit. The glass center area allows you to visually see how many peppercorns are remaining inside the mill so you will easily know when it is time to add more peppercorns.

3. Wood Peppercorn Grinder made by Vic Firth in the State of Maine, USA (about $43 at Amazon.com). This is an excellent pepper mill. The top nut can be turned clockwise to yield a very fine grind of pepper, or it can be rotated counterclockwise to yield a coarser grind of pepper. More information about this pepper mill is available on the manufacturer's web site at: www.vicfirthgourmet.com

I do **not** recommend the small pepper grinders that are sold in the spice racks with a small amount of peppercorns in them. The majority of these little pepper mills are single use items and they cannot be easily opened and refilled.

Chapter Sixteen: Black Pepper, Peppercorns, and Pepper Grinders

Chapter Seventeen

Coffee, Coffee Pots, and Coffee Bean Grinders

If coffee is one of the beverages you enjoy during normal times then you will need to make some plans on how you can continue to enjoy coffee during a long-term hard times event. Unfortunately coffee has a relatively short shelf life compared to most other foods.

There are three basic options for storing coffee:

1. Instant coffee.
2. Ground coffee.
3. Coffee beans.

Let's examine each of the above three types of coffee one-at-a-time.

Instant Coffee

To prepare instant coffee you will need to heat some water to an acceptable temperature and then pour the hot water onto a spoonful of instant coffee inside a coffee mug. Stir with a spoon and you have coffee.

The **advantages** of instant coffee are:

1. It is quick and easy to prepare.
2. It does not require an investment in paper coffee filters.
3. It does not emit the powerful coffee aroma that fresh brewed coffee releases. This may be a significant advantage during a hard times tragedy event because you would not be attracting unwanted attention to your food preparation area. In other words, you could enjoy your cup of coffee in peace.

The **disadvantage** of instant coffee is:

1. Some individuals do not like the taste of instant coffee.

You will need to make your own decision on whether or not you will include some jars of instant coffee in your emergency food reserves.

Ground Coffee

Most people prepare ground coffee using an **electric drip coffee maker**. The ground coffee is placed inside a paper coffee filter and the correct quantity of water is poured into the coffee maker. The coffee maker is then activated, the water is heated, and the water is dispensed on top of the ground coffee. The coffee slowly drips out the bottom of the basket into the coffee pot.

To make coffee **without electricity** you could do the following:

1. Transfer the coffee basket to a secure position above your coffee pot. Some drip coffee makers allow you to swing out the coffee basket while the coffee basket is still attached to the coffee maker. If your coffee maker is made this way then swing out the coffee basket and position the coffee pot on the counter directly below the bottom hole in the coffee basket.
2. Put a paper coffee filter into the basket and add the correct amount of ground coffee.
3. Boil the proper amount of water in a separate cook pot.
4. Slowly and carefully pour the boiling water onto the ground coffee inside the paper coffee filter inside the coffee filter basket.
5. Wait for the coffee to drip into the coffee pot.

The **advantage** of a drip coffee maker is:

1. The taste is acceptable to most people.

The **disadvantages** of a drip coffee maker are:

1. You will need to maintain an inventory of paper coffee filters.
2. It takes longer to brew fresh coffee than to prepare instant coffee.
3. The aroma of fresh brewed coffee will attract every coffee drinker within a half-block radius to your kitchen and they will beg you, and beg you, and beg you to please share some of your fresh brewed coffee with them.

An alternative to the drip coffee maker is an old fashioned **coffee percolator**. This device requires a coarser ground of coffee than the drip coffee makers. You put some water in the bottom of the percolator and then add some ground coffee into the metal basket that fits in the top of the percolator. Then you attach the lid, add heat, and wait for the water to boil which "perks" the hot water up through center spout and the water then flows down over the ground coffee in the metal basket and back into the bottom of the percolator with the rest of the water. This process continues until you have your coffee at the strength you prefer.

Fill the left Basket with Ground Coffee and then put it inside the Coffee Pot on the right.

The **advantages** of a percolator are:

1. The coffee has a taste that is agreeable to most people.
2. You do not need any paper coffee filters.

The **disadvantages** of a percolator are the same as for the drip coffee maker.

Coffee Beans

Finally, you can purchase whole coffee beans and grind them yourself as you need them. This will require that you have a coffee grinder for this specific application. The reason is because you do not want the flavor of your coffee beans to pick up the flavor of something else that may have been ground previously in some type of multipurpose grinder. If you have a coffee grinder that is only used for coffee then you will know that the flavor of your coffee will not pick up any stray unusual flavors that may be offensive to your taste buds. If you grind your own coffee beans then you can set the grind to the coarseness you require, such as a fine grind or a medium grind or a coarse grind.

Coffee beans should be stored in their original bag or container. This bag or container should be placed inside a heavy-duty freezer bag and stored in a dark, dry, cool area. Do not freeze coffee beans because freezing will deplete them of their natural moisture.

Different varieties of green coffee beans have different shelf lives. Before you invest in green coffee beans you should determine the actual remaining shelf life of the beans you are interested in. In other words, you should first determine when the green coffee beans were originally harvested and how long they have already been in storage before you make your purchase.

Green coffee beans that are stored in a dry temperature controlled environment will remain fresh for approximately ten-years. In the coffee industry these are referred to as "aged coffee beans." As the beans are aged they gradually lose some of their bitter taste.

Chapter Seventeen: Coffee, Coffee Pots, and Coffee Bean Grinders

Green coffee beans will need to be roasted before they are used to brew coffee. However, roasted coffee beans have a much shorter shelf life than green coffee beans. Therefore you should not roast your beans until you are ready to use them. Generally you should only roast about one-week's worth of beans at one time to maximize the freshness and flavor of those beans.

There are two basic methods for roasting coffee beans at home. Regardless of which method you use you will need to use some type of fan to ventilate the area because the coffee beans will generate smoke as they are roasted.

1. **Skillet Method:** Place the green coffee beans in a large covered cast iron skillet over high heat. Shake the beans inside the skillet to keep the beans in constant motion. Or you can omit the skillet cover and stir the beans continuously as they are roasting. The beans will gradually turn yellow and then a light brown. After about 5, 6, or 7 minutes the beans will crack and you will hear the first popping sound. If you wish you may stop roasting the beans at this time. Or you may continue to roast the beans for a darker roast. After a total of about 15 or 20 minutes the beans will crack or pop a second time and the beans will have a dark brown color. Now is the time to remove the beans from the heat.

2. **Oven Method:** Preheat the oven to 500°F (260°C). Place a single layer of beans inside a metal colander or a folding metal vegetable steamer. Place the colander or steamer on a metal cookie sheet or a metal pizza pan. Place the coffee beans on the center rack of the oven. You will hear the first crack or pop in about 5, 6, or 7 minutes. You may remove the beans from the oven at this time or you may allow them to continue roasting for a darker roast. However, you must open the oven and stir the beans once per minute after the first pop. When the desired bean color is achieved, or when you hear the second crack or pop, remove the beans from the oven.

Cool the beans as quickly as possible after you remove them from the skillet or from the oven. Shake the roasted beans inside a colander to separate the beans from the tiny particles that are now mixed in with the beans. Discard the tiny particles. Allow the beans to mature for at least four hours before using them. For the optimal coffee flavor wait twenty-four hours before using the beans.

Coffee beans should be ground as you need them to capture their full flavor. When you grind coffee beans they will retain their **maximum** freshness and flavor for about one or two-hours. However, ground roasted coffee beans may still be used for about four-weeks after grinding but after about two-weeks many people will notice a distinctive lose of some of their original flavor.

His Last Day

In the dark of the night with a cheek kiss He is betrayed,
   by one of the twelve closest friends He has made.

He is bound, condemned, spit on, and beaten,
   in a mock trial before the Council of the Sanhedrin.

On Friday morning to the Roman governor He is sent,
   who delivers Him to his soldiers for severe punishment.

He is scourged, spit on, and beaten until He is almost dead,
   and then a thorny crown is pressed deep into His head.

His last chance for freedom is rejected by the crowd
   who scream, "Crucify Him, Crucify Him," extremely loud.

To a heavy wooden cross His hands are nailed with a mallet,
   and everyone watches as His Holy Blood spurts out.

After many hours of pain He takes a deep breath to pray,
   "Father forgive them for they know not what they are doing" this day.

At about the ninth hour He breathes His last and He dies,
   and later blood and water flows out of His spear pierced side.

His dead body is wrapped in linen and then laid to rest
   in a borrowed tomb on Friday evening just before sunset.

Early in the morning on Sunday, the first day of the week,
   Jesus rises from the Realm of the Dead to be King of the Meek.

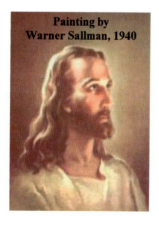

Painting by Warner Sallman, 1940

Scripture References: Luke 22:45-48, Matthew 26:57-60, Mark 14:65, Matthew 27:1-2, John 19:1-5, Matthew 27:22, Luke 23:20-21, Luke 23:32-34, Matthew 27:46, Matthew 27:50, John 19:33-34, Matthew 27:57-60, Luke 23:54, Matthew 27:65 to 28:7, John 20:19-20.

Poem: His Last Day

Chapter Eighteen

A Hand-Cranked Stainless Steel Meat Grinder

Meat grinders can be either electric or manually operated. During a hard times event electricity may not be available when you really need it so I suggest you consider a manually operated meat grinder instead of an electric one. Although it does require some physical energy to grind meat by hand, the amount of effort required is not exhaustive or significantly fatiguing.

Meat grinders are usually made of either plated metal or stainless steel. The plated grinders are made of cheaper metal and the plating will gradually chip off the grinder and rust will attack the grinder. Therefore I recommend that you avoid any type of plated metal meat grinder. Instead I suggest that you invest in a stainless steel meat grinder. A stainless steel meat grinder is the type of equipment you could pass on as a kitchen "heirloom" to one of your children or grandchildren, if you take care of it during your lifetime.

The LEM #10 Stainless Steel Hand Meat Grinder shown in the picture on the right is the meat grinder I recommend for the following reasons:

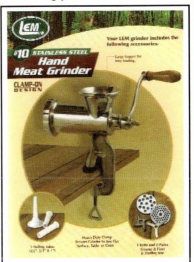

1. In the year 2011 it could be purchased for approximately $83 on "Amazon.com" with an additional $10 shipping fee. Therefore the total delivered cost is approximately $93.

2. It comes with two grinding plates so you can select between a coarse grind or a fine grind.

3. It comes with a plastic stuffing tube flange, three plastic stuffing tubes, and a metal stuffing star.

4. It comes with two white rubber protective feet instead of the two black rubber feet shown in the box illustration.

5. It can quickly and easily be temporarily mounted to the edge of any solid wood surface as shown in the picture. Therefore, after you are finished using it, you can remove it, disassemble it, and wash the entire unit in some hot soapy dish water. Then you can rinse and dry the entire unit and store it out of the way until the next time you need it.

6. Since the handle is made of wood you need to be careful when you clean it. In other words, do not let it soak for an extended period of time in the dish water or you will ruin the wood handle. Wash the wood handle quickly but thoroughly and then immediately rinse and dry the handle to protect the wood from water damage.

Caution: LEM makes a #10 Stainless Steel Meat Grinder and a #10 Plated Metal Meat Grinder. The plated metal grinder sells for about one-half the price of the stainless steel grinder. Please verify that you are getting the stainless steel grinder before you make your purchase.

Advantages of a Meat Grinder

Following are some of the reasons why you might wish to consider making an investment in one of these stainless steel meat grinders.

A hand turned meat grinder has the following advantages:

1. Converts tough cuts of meat and wild game meat into hamburger consistency.

2. All red ground meat looks approximately the same.

3. Ground meat will minimize the number of future complaints you will hear from your family.

4. Ground meat is easier to use in a wider variety of recipes.

5. Ground meat more easily and completely absorbs any seasonings you may have.
6. Ground meat cooks faster and more thoroughly than thicker cuts of meat.
7. Ground meat is easier for most people to chew and it is easier for most people to digest.

You will also need some meat seasoning tenderizer, some chili seasoning, some taco seasoning, some Sloppy Joe seasoning, and any other seasonings that your family normally enjoys.

A Few Tips on How to Grind Meat

1. Chill the meat before grinding. Cold meat is easier to grind than meat at room temperature.
2. Cut the meat into cubes between one-half inch up to one-inch in size.
    a. If the meat does not contain much fat and you are adding fat from another source then cut the meat into one-half inch cubes.
    b. If you are blending two or more different types of meat together then cut the meat into one-half inch cubes.
3. Tender meat should be coarse ground.
4. A coarse grind is preferred for hamburgers because it helps the meat hold together while cooking.
5. Tough meat or meat with lots of sinews should be fine ground.
6. A fine grind helps the meat absorb the meat seasonings and to blend more evenly with other recipe ingredients.
7. If the meat is still too tough after grinding then put the ground meat through the meat grinder a second time.

Chapter Nineteen

Wheat Grinders

Flour is used to make bread, biscuits, rolls, pretzels, donuts, bagels, cakes, pies, cookies, crackers and lots of other things. Therefore flour is one of the foods that most people in the United States of America eat nearly every day. For that reason flour will be one of the foods that will be dearly missed by the average person during a long-term hard times event.

Commercially processed flour that you purchase at the grocery store has a relatively short shelf life. It has also had some of its original nutrients removed and replaced by other stuff so it can be called "enriched flour." Many people in the United States have become so accustomed to eating this type of flour that they find the taste of real flour to be unpleasant and in some cases hard to digest.

If you are storing food for a long-term hard times event then you will need to make a decision about how you are going to provide bread for your family to eat on a regular basis. This is not a simple decision because it will have a significant impact on the well being and happiness of your entire family. Consequently it would probably be a very good idea to purchase a small quantity of wheat berries during good times and grind them into flour, and then use that flour to make some bread for your family to eat. This will give you the opportunity to determine if this type of "bread made from homemade flour" is acceptable to your family. If it is not then you may be forced to include commercially processed flour (not self-rising) in your food storage plans and rotate or replace that flour at least once every two years.

On the other hand, if your family will accept bread made from freshly ground wheat berries then you will need a practical method for grinding your wheat berries. There are three basic options for grinding wheat at home:

1. A clean flat smooth big solid rock and a clean hammer.
2. A hand-operated wheat grinder.
3. An electric wheat grinder.

Rock and Hammer: It is possible to convert wheat berries into a coarse ground flour using a hard flat surface and a clean hammer. This is slow hard work but it will gradually get the job done. This is the traditional method that is still used today by the less fortunate people in the world.

Hand-Operated Wheat Grinder: A **hand-operated wheat grinder** is a much better option. If you try to convert a lot of wheat into flour then your arm will get tired. Therefore this task is usually done by each member of your family for a short period of time to spread the work load and to prevent anyone from getting a sore arm as a result. The grinder in the picture was purchased in 1975 and it uses two grinding stones. You temporarily attach the wheat grinder to the edge of a solid table or a counter. Then you pour some wheat berries into the metal bowl on top of the grinder and you rotate the grinding wheel by hand. The wheat berries are forced between the two grinding stones in front and flour falls out from between these two stones. At the current time grinding stones are not recommended for grinding wheat because they contain some aluminum that will gradually wear off and become mixed in with your flour. Aluminum should **not** be ingested so these stone mills are no longer recommended.

Another option is a hand-operated wheat grinder that does not use grinding stones. One of the most popular of these units is the "Family Grain Mill" which is shown at the top of the next page. When I first bought one of these grain mills many years ago it was very reasonably priced. However, at the current time this unit is about $140. You place the wood block against the edge of a solid flat square surface and lower the clamp below the wood surface and tighten the clamp to temporarily secure the grain mill to the top of the table

	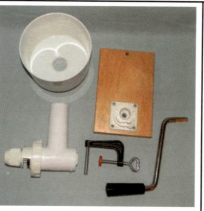	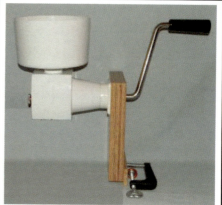
Family Grain Mill Assembled	Family Grain Mill Disassembled	Flaker Attachment Assembled

or counter. Then place a clean bowl below the front of the unit. Then pour some wheat berries into the top plastic bucket and rotate the hand crank. Ground wheat will fall out the front of the unit into the clean bowl. To convert this unit from a manual crank to an electric crank you need to purchase a special electric base that replaces the wood base. The electric base costs about $175 plus shipping in the year 2011 and it is frequently on backorder. There is also a flaker attachment for another $84.

Electric Grinder: An **electric wheat grinder** works exceptionally well if you have electricity. You can adjust the settings on the electric grinder to produce the texture of flour that you prefer, such as a fine grind or a course grind. Since it is electric it will do all the work for you and your arm will not get tired.

In you can afford it then I suggest you invest in a hand-operated wheat grinder and an electric wheat grinder. But if you can only afford one then I strongly recommend the hand-operated wheat grinder because it will work extremely well during serious hardship conditions when there is no power and it will continue to work for many, many years without having to worry about an electronic failure somewhere inside the unit.

Chapter Nineteen: Wheat Grinders

Chapter Twenty

During Hard Times Should You Know Some Basic Gardening Skills?

Occasionally I read advice on the internet from people who do their very best to discourage other people from engaging in any type of gardening activity, or from engaging in a specific type of gardening activity. For example, you may have occasionally read one or more of the following suggestions on the internet:

1. Don't waste your time planting seeds. Always buy your vegetable plants, and fruit trees, and nut trees from a garden supply store.
2. Don't waste your time trying to grow some type of vegetable or fruit tree or nut tree. They will probably all die anyway. Instead you should just buy your vegetables and fruits and nuts at a grocery store.
3. Don't waste your time preparing your meals yourself. Just go to a restaurant and let them do all the work for you.

It is not uncommon for the above advice to be offered by someone who lives inside a big city and who has no place to grow anything, or by someone who does not know how to prepare a tasty meal from scratch.

I personally do not agree with any of the above advice. For example, if you live inside a big city, and if you have a window that gets good sun for several hours every day, then you could still experiment with a few small vegetable plants in some containers in front of that window. All you would need is a small bag or two of "potting soil," and some "Miracle Grow Fertilizer," and some planting pots, or some small plastic containers. Each plastic container should have a hole or a cut in the bottom of the container to allow excess water to escape. Put something under the container, such as a dinner plate, to catch the excess water. You will also need one small package of vegetable seeds, such as radishes.

Radishes are recommended for a small window garden for the following reasons:

1. Radishes are small and they don't require much space.
2. Most radish varieties will grow to full maturity in about 25 days.
3. Radishes may be eaten fresh or added to almost any type of fresh salad. This means there would be no waste, assuming you like radishes.
4. Radishes will produce more radish seeds if you don't harvest all the mature radishes. Simply allow two or three of the mature radishes to continue to grow below the dirt. Each mature radish will eventually send up a seed stalk and when that seed stalk is mature you can harvest it. Inside the pod at the end of each seed stalk you will find a new batch of fresh radish seeds for your next planting.
5. If you make a mistake then you will know about it before one month has passed. This will give you the opportunity to try again and avoid making that same mistake a second time. Therefore the learning curve would be very short and the knowledge you would gain could be significant. Plus you would gain some self-confidence in your gardening skills.
6. If you have children or grandchildren this could be a simple project to help them learn how to grow food from seeds.

Think about this for a minute. One small window pot would allow you to gain some practical hands-on experience with one of the basic fundamental necessities of life -- food. You could learn how to grow vegetables, and how to grow seeds from those vegetables. After you have gained this knowledge then you could repeat this process again, and again, and again for the rest of your life -- if you should ever need to.

Anyone who believes that affordable food will always, always be available whenever they need it at the store, or that their emergency food supply will never, never be exhausted, is betting their life and the lives of their loved ones that the future will never be radically different from the present.

Therefore I strongly recommend that you invest just a little of your time in learning how to grow food from scratch. If you never need this skill then you will not have wasted anything. On the other hand, if your life and the lives of your family members should one day depend on your ability to grow food, then you would already have some practical real world gardening experience that could easily make the difference between whether or not your family survived a serious hard times tragedy event.

Chapter Twenty-One

Vegetable Recommendations for New Gardeners During Hard Times

To grow your own vegetables you will need some seeds, some good rich soil, some water, and lots of sun.

Do **not** buy hybrid vegetable seeds. Most hybrid seeds are only good for one growing season. (Hybrid Seed Note: Some people recommend that you should try to reverse engineer the second generation seeds from a hybrid vegetable to get one of the original parents of the hybrid vegetable. I totally disagree with this recommendation. During a serious hard times event when your family may be desperate for food, and when you have to work hard all summer trying to grow some food, then why would you want to bet your life and the lives of your family members on some random experiment where you are trying to force some second generation hybrid seeds to grow something you can eat. This is a gamble I strongly recommend that you do not participate in.)

Instead please look for and purchase **heirloom** vegetable seeds or open-pollinated seeds, unless you have a very good reason to do otherwise. Many of the heirloom vegetables have been popular with home gardeners since the mid to late 1800s. Heirloom seeds will produce the same exact vegetable year after year after year if you will save the seed that is grown each year and plant it again the next year.

During a serious hard times event I suggest you consider growing mostly root vegetables, such as beets, carrots, onions, potatoes, radishes, turnips, and peanuts. The edible part of a root vegetable grows below ground. Therefore it is invisible unless you know what is growing below the vines or leaves you see on top of the ground.

However, in order to provide some reasonable variety in your meals and to help avoid appetite fatigue, you will also need to grow some vegetables where the edible part of the vegetable is above ground. Anyone who happens to walk by your garden area will see these vegetables and they will know exactly what you are growing and how much you are growing.

Therefore in order to help minimize the complete loss of your entire vegetable crop to looters and thieves during a serious hard times tragedy event, it might be a good idea to have at least two or more vegetable plots. One vegetable plot should contain your above ground vegetables and it should be conveniently located in any area that gets full sun all day. A second or third vegetable plot should be in a more obscure area that also gets full sun and it should contain your below ground vegetables. You should probably allow a few random weeds to grow in this area to help hide your below ground vegetables. Since the vegetables will be growing below ground the only thing visible above ground would be some leaves or vines. And unless a person knew exactly what type of leaf or vine it was then it would be very easy to mistake those leaves and vines as random weeds. In order for this to work you should not plant your underground vegetables in a nice neat straight row. Instead plant them in a random haphazard fashion all over this remote garden area, and whenever possible, mix the different types of vegetables together so you don't have all the leaves of one specific type of vegetable growing close to one another. This means each type of vegetable would be randomly scattered throughout this garden plot and this would help to create the visual illusion of lots of different types of weeds just haphazardly growing together.

The heirloom seed varieties recommended in this chapter are ones I have had previous experience with. There are a lot of other good heirloom varieties in addition to the ones mentioned here. Therefore if you are not able to find the varieties I suggest then it is perfectly okay to buy a different heirloom variety of vegetable seed.

Beans: Pinto, a heirloom bean.

Pinto beans reach full maturity in about 65 to 90 days after planting depending on your climate.

Almost all beans, except green snap beans, contain lots of protein, lots of carbohydrates, and lots of calories. Therefore beans are a very good choice for a hard times garden.

Pinto beans may be eaten as green snap beans when they are first harvested if the bean pod is still soft. Or you can remove the pinto beans from their pods, discard the pods, and dry the beans for future consumption. Pinto beans also make excellent refried beans.

Dry pinto beans may be purchased at your local grocery store in one-pound, or two-pound, or four-pound plastic bags. Dry pinto beans are usually sold very close to the area where white rice is sold. All dry pinto beans are the same and the only difference between the major brand names is how many times the beans are sifted and cleaned to remove tiny dirt particles or tiny twigs.

Planting Instructions: Soak the hard dry pinto beans for one hour in lukewarm water. Place the beans inside a damp towel in a warm dark spot for about 4 days and they will sprout. Plant the sprouted bean 1-inch deep about 6-inches apart in warm soil (60°F or 16°C).

Beets, Regular: Detroit Dark Red, a heirloom variety since 1892.

Detroit Dark Red beets will reach full maturity in 58 to 65 days after planting. Therefore you may be able to harvest two crops of beets in one growing season.

The Detroit Dark Red beet has edible green tops and edible beets. You can usually harvest the green tops several times during the growing season without hurting the beet below ground. This is a significant advantage during hard times because your body will crave fresh green leafy vegetables. The beet leaf greens taste great in a salad. The Detroit Dark Red beet also stores well for winter consumption.

Planting Instructions: Plant the seeds 1/2 inch deep and 6 inches apart. Do **not** plant beets in the same area two years in a row. Rotate beets with either corn or potatoes to maximize the yield from your soil.

Beets, Sugar: Sugar beets will reach full maturity in about 45 days after planting.

Regular beets have about 6% sugar but the special sugar beet has between 14% to 20% sucrose sugar. You can extract the sugar from these beets and make a sweet sugar water or a sugar syrup and you can still eat the beet that remains in the cook pot.

One internet store that sells Sugar Beet Seeds is: http://www.sandmountainherbs.com/beet_sugar.html

Planting Instructions: Plant the seeds 1/4 inch deep and 6 inches apart in the early spring. Keep the ground moist by covering the ground with a layer of mulch. Do not let the ground dry out. Sprouts will appear in about 14 to 21 days. Weed frequently. When the leaves are 12 inches tall they begin storing sucrose sugar in their roots.

Harvesting Instructions: You may harvest the green leaves anytime and eat them as a salad green but be careful to not damage the top of the underground beet when you harvest the green leaves. Dig or pull up the beets when their roots are 2 inches or longer.

Carrots: Danvers Half Long, a heirloom variety since 1871.

Danvers Half Long carrots will reach full maturity in about 75 days after planting. Therefore you may be able to harvest two crops of carrots in one growing season.

The Danvers Half Long carrots are excellent for storing, freezing, or canning.

Planting Instructions: Soak the seeds in water for about 3 hours. Plant each seed 1/2 inch deep. When mature, eat the carrots fresh in a salad, or cook them in stews or soups. Only plant one carrot variety per year, or plant different carrot varieties at least 1,000 feet apart. If you have short mild winters then you may leave the carrots in the ground all winter and harvest them as you need them.

Corn, Sweet: Stowell's Evergreen, a heirloom variety since 1848.

This is a white corn. It will reach full maturity in 80 to 100 days after planting.

One internet store that sells Stowell's Evergreen Corn is:
http://www.seedsavers.org/Items.aspx?search=corn+seeds

Planting Instructions: Soak the seeds in warm water for about 3 hours. Plant 2 inches deep and 12 inches apart in warm soil.

Harvesting Instructions: You can harvest the corn before it fully ripens by pulling up the entire corn stalk with its roots still attached. Then store the entire corn stalk upside down in a cool indoor area. The corn will continue to gradually ripen and you can eat fresh corn on the cob every month for another 3 to 5 months. That is why this corn was named "evergreen."

(Note: If you allow the corn kernels to completely dry out on a few ears of corn then these will become corn seed and they may be planted in the spring to yield a new crop of corn.)

Corn, Dent: Reid's Yellow Dent, a heirloom variety.

This is a yellow corn. It will reach full maturity in about 115 days after planting.

Reid's Yellow Dent corn may be eaten fresh when it is first harvested or it may be dried and then ground into corn meal using a wheat grinder.

Reid's Yellow Dent corn may be purchased at the internet store listed above that sells Stowell's Evergreen Corn.

Planting Instructions: Soak the seeds in warm water for about 3 hours. Plant 2 inches deep and 12 inches apart in warm soil.

Caution: Corn is open pollinated by the wind so plant different corn varieties as far apart as possible. In other words, plant the Reid's dent corn far away from the Stowell's corn.

Harvesting Instructions: Leave the best ears on the stalk. Harvest and eat the other ears as fresh corn. Wait 4 weeks and then pull up the stalks with the corn. Peel back the husks. Hang the corn on their stalks upside down in a well-ventilated area for 4 more weeks. Wait until the kernels are hard and dry. Twist off the full kernels of corn using your hands. Discard the small kernels near the end of the cob. (Note: The dried corn kernels are corn seed and they may be planted in the spring to yield a new crop of corn.) When you need some fresh corn meal you can grind the corn kernels in a wheat grinder. The corn meal may then be used to make a wide variety of tasty things such as corn bread, hush puppies, nacho corn chips, and taco shells.

Onions: Although onions are a root vegetable they have two major shortcomings during a serious hard times event:
1. You can smell the onions from a good distance away while they are growing.
2. I have not been able to find a heirloom onion seed variety that produces an onion that has an acceptable flavor.

Therefore I grow whatever onion seeds I can find at the seed store each spring. I have had good results with white onions and yellow onions. I no longer grow purple onions because they do not store well. If you don't eat purple onions very soon after they mature then they go bad very quickly.

Onion seeds may be planted in the very early spring. If you have mild winters then onion seeds may be planted in the fall for harvesting the next year.

Yellow Sweet Spanish: A hybrid variety that reaches full maturity in about 105 to 130 days.

Plant seeds 1/4 inch deep and about 3 inches apart.

White Lisbon Bunching: A hybrid variety that reaches full maturity in about 40 to 95 days.

Plant seeds 1/4 inch deep and about 1 inch apart.

Peanuts: Buy a bag of raw peanuts (unsalted, unroasted) at your local grocery store and then follow the planting instructions below.

Peanuts will grow in clusters underground to full maturity in 120 to 150 days.

Peanuts are a good choice because you can eat them fresh and you can easily make your own peanut butter using an ordinary food blender if you have a little vegetable oil or olive oil. Only plant one variety of peanut each year.

Planting Instructions: Plant the peanut inside its pink paper thin seed coat for the best germination results. Plant the peanut between 1.5 inches to 2 inches below the top of the ground in soil that you have dug and loosened. You will need a 12 inch diameter wide hole at least 12 inches deep for each peanut so the peanut plant can easily grow underground to its full size. Dig the hole, replace all of the dirt in the hole, step on the dirt to pack it down, and then dig a small hole in the center of the original hole that is no deeper than 2 inches for the peanut. After planting the peanut, cover the peanut with dirt, and step on the dirt above the peanut to drive out any air. Then water the ground and wait.

Harvesting Instructions: When the above ground leaves turn yellow, dig up the entire plant and store indoors for an additional four weeks in a cool, dry area. Leave the peanuts inside their shells until you are ready to eat them or use them for seed. If you shell them for seed then be very careful to not break or tear the pink paper thin seed coat around the peanut.

Potatoes: Red Skin potatoes will reach full maturity in 90 to 100 days after planting.
Remove one red skin potato from your next bag of red potatoes and set it aside and wait for it to grow sprouts about one-inch long. Cut off about 1/2 inch of the potato with the sprout. If there are more than 3 sprouts at one small spot on the potato then break some of the extra sprouts off the potato. Let the cut sprout "harden" in the air for two days. (Note: You can eat the rest of the potato after removing the sprouts.)
Planting Instructions: Place the cut sprout "cut side down" about 4 inches above the bottom of a large deep planting pot and then cover it with about 3 more inches of dirt. When the green vine appears cover it with 2 inches of dirt. When the green vine reappears cover it with another 2 inches of dirt. Continue until you eventually reach the top of your planting pot. Water as necessary. When the top green vine dies wait 2 more weeks and then harvest the potatoes in your pot. Or you can plant potatoes outdoors by following this same procedure.

Radishes: Cherry Belle, a heirloom variety and an "All American Selection" winner in 1949.
Cherry Belle radishes will grow to full maturity in about 20 to 24 days. This has two significant advantages:
1. You have a fresh vegetable to eat in the very early part of spring.
2. You can plant radishes several times during the spring, summer, and fall and continue to harvest fresh vegetables throughout the growing season using the same exact small plot of ground.

The Cherry Belle radish may also be grown as a fall crop.
Most radish varieties will mature in about 20 to 25 days. However, some radish varieties will require about 50 or 55 days to mature so you should read the seed package very carefully before you invest in radishes.
Planting Instructions: Plant the seed 1/2 inch deep about 1.5 inches apart. Radishes do not keep well so each spring you should plant one or two rows of radishes every two weeks. This will provide fresh edible radishes for your family to enjoy throughout the spring, summer, and early fall.

Spinach: Bloomsdale, a heirloom variety since 1908.
Bloomsdale spinach will grow to full maturity in about 45 to 50 days. You can eat **some** of the baby spinach leaves at about 25 days.
Spinach may be eaten fresh, or it can be boiled, or its leaves may be dried and eaten during the winter months. Dried spinach leaves should be boiled in some water before eating.
Planting Instructions: Soak the seeds overnight. Then plant the seeds 1 inch deep about 9 inches apart. Plant spinach every 2 weeks to produce a continuous supply of spinach for fresh eating, or boiling, or drying for the winter. Spinach prefers the cool weather of early spring or late summer.

Tomatoes: Roma, a heirloom variety.
The Roma tomato will reach full maturity in 75 to 80 days.
The Roma tomato is excellent when eaten fresh and it can be made into a tomato paste, or tomato sauce, or it can be one of the major ingredients in a homemade Mexican salsa.
Visit your local grocery store and buy one fresh Roma tomato, slice it, carefully pick out the seeds, and then eat the tomato slices.
Planting Instructions: After you have dried the tomato seeds on a piece of paper you can plant the seeds about 1/4 inch deep and about two feet apart. You will need to support the tomato plant as it grows with wooden stakes beside each tomato vine or with a wire cage around each tomato plant.

Turnips: Purple Top White Globe, a heirloom variety since 1870.
Purple Top turnips will grow to full maturity in about 52 to 55 days. You can plant turnip seeds again in the late summer to yield a fall crop of edible greens and turnips.
The Purple Top turnip produces an edible green top and an edible below ground turnip.
The Purple Top turnip stores extremely well for winter consumption.
Whenever possible select a turnip variety with edible green tops and edible turnips. You can usually harvest the green tops several times during the growing season without hurting the turnip below ground. This is a significant advantage during hard times because your body will crave fresh green leafy vegetables. Turnips are usually grown in southern climates whereas rutabagas are typically grown in northern climates.
Planting Instructions: Plant the seed between 1/4 inch to 1/2 deep and space them about 3 inches apart. You may eat the above ground greens but do not damage the top of the turnip when you harvest some of the greens.

Chapter Twenty-One: Vegetable Recommendations for New Gardeners

One Wish and Not Three

If you had a magic lamp and you were granted one wish and not three,
What would you wish for, if you knew it would be granted for free?

Would you wish for money, or precious jewels, or silver, or gold?
Would you wish for a huge mansion that is beautiful to behold?

Would you wish for perfect health so that life you could enjoy?
Would you wish for true love with a pretty girl or handsome boy?

Or would you wish for something else that is dear to your heart?
Something very special from which you would never ever part?

What would be the **one** best wish considering every possibility?
The answer is simple -- a carefree life to enjoy for all eternity.

But wait! There's good news. This wish can actually come true --
Because God's Son shed His Blood on Calvary to save me and you.

Have faith in Jesus Christ and **all** of these wishes you will receive --
A crown, a heavenly mansion, and a new body to enjoy for eternity.

Scripture References: First Corinthians 15:3-7, Romans 3:22-28, Romans 10:9-10, First Peter 5:4, John 14:2-4, John 3:16, Philippians 3:20-21, First Corinthians 2:9.

Chapter Twenty-Two

How to Grow Each Type of Vegetable and Each Type of Vegetable Seed

The Basic Types of Vegetables

1. **Annual:** They grow from seed to seed in **one** year. New seed must be planted each year.
2. **Biennial:** They grow from seed to seed in **two** years. New seed must be planted each year to produce a crop to eat but it takes two years for the plant to yield seeds for future plantings.
3. **Perennial:** The roots remain in the ground year after year and they continue to produce vegetables to eat each year. Usually after two years seeds can be produced for future plantings, if you need seed at that time.

Vegetables are Listed in Alphabetical Order

Asparagus: Perennial pollinated by insects. Female plants have a fewer number of thick stalks. Male plants have a higher number of thinner stalks. The female plants will yield the red seed berries. The berries are ready to harvest when they turn red and their fern-like top leaves flop over. Cut the tall berry stalk off the plant and hang it inside for ten days to dry. Remove the berries from the stalk and let them soak in a bowl of water for at least an hour to make them easier to open and remove the seed. Dry the seed on a paper towel for ten days and store in a paper envelope or cloth bag in a dry, cool area. Asparagus grown from seed takes **three** years to produce asparagus for the table. It will then produce asparagus each year after that.

Beans: Annual self-pollinating with perfect flowers that have both the male and female parts. Plant different bean varieties at least 150 feet apart. Harvest the beans you wish to eat but leave the bean pods on the best looking, most productive, earliest bearing plants. Later when the bean pods begin to turn brown and the beans rattle inside its pod, the beans are ready to be harvested for seed. Pull up the entire plant with its roots. Hang the plant indoors upside down for 10 days. Then remove the beans from their pods. If you can't dent a bean seed when you bite down on it then it is dry enough for storage. Remove the seeds and store in a paper, cloth, or plastic bag in a dry, cool area. Do **not** store beans in an airtight container. Plant the beans the following spring **after** the last frost and always harvest in the fall **before** the first frost.

Beets: Biennial cross-pollinated by insects. Each flower has both male and female parts. Plant some beets to eat each year and plant some beets to save through the winter to produce seed the second year. Plant the beet seeds you intend to keep through the winter in the early summer (not spring) so the beets don't grow too large the first year. Examine them as they grow and dig up and discard any that have poor above ground leaf quality. The beet will produce a rosette of flowers the first year but no seeds. If a beet produces a seed bolt the first year dig it up and discard it. If you have short mild winters then you may leave the beets in the ground all winter. However, if you have long bitter winter weather then dig up the beets before the first fall frost and save the eight (or more) beets that have the best quality roots. Cut all but one-inch off the top of the beet greens and bury the beets in damp sand or sawdust in a cool humid area for the winter but not below freezing. Inspect the beets the following spring and discard any beets that withered during the winter. Replant the good beets about two-feet apart with their crowns just below the level of the earth. Then wait for them to grow and produce a tall seed stalk. Each stalk will have tiny blossoms. Later multiple corky seed balls will appear that contain five or six seeds each. When the seed balls begin to turn brown they are ready for harvest. Cut off the seed stalk at the ground and hang it upside down indoors in a well ventilated area to dry. Then remove the seeds from the stalk by hand and store in a paper envelope or cloth bag in a dry, cool area. (Note: Do not plant beets in the same exact area two years in a row. Rotate your beet crop with either corn or potatoes to maximize the yield from your soil.)

Broccoli: Annual with perfect flowers that have both the male and female parts. Pollinated by bees. You will need at least three plants of the same type for good cross-pollination. Do **not** plant within 100 feet of Brussels spouts, cabbage, cauliflower, kale, or kohlrabi. When the head of the mature broccoli turns yellow, the seeds will appear within each flower bud inside a mature seed pod. When most of the seed pods have turned brown then harvest the seed pods and store indoors for 10 days. Place the seed pods inside a paper or plastic bag and carefully crush the pods using your hands. Pour the contents of the bag onto a screen and shake the screen to separate the chaff from the seed. Store the seed in a paper or cloth bag in a dry, cool area.

Brussels Sprouts: Biennial with perfect flowers that have both the male and female parts. Pollinated by bees. The seed collection procedure is the same as cabbage (next vegetable below) except Brussels sprouts are very hardy and they may be left in the ground over the winter in all but severe winter climates. They need to be removed from the ground in the northern United States and they have a tendency to dry out during winter storage. There is also no need to slash the top of the Brussels sprouts for the seed stalk to appear.

Cabbage: Biennial with perfect flowers that have both the male and female parts. Pollinated by bees. Easily cross-pollinates with many different vegetables. At the end of the first growing season dig up the **six** best cabbages being careful to **not** damage their root system. Trim off the outer leaves of each cabbage head and store the entire cabbage plant in a well ventilated cool humid area but not below freezing. The cabbage must be kept cool during the winter so it will bolt the following year. Inspect periodically during the winter and immediately discard any heads that begin to rot. The next spring plant the cabbages by themselves at least 200 feet from all other vegetables and all other varieties of cabbage. Plant the cabbages about 30 inches apart and slightly deeper than they were planted the

previous year. Immediately after replanting you will need to cut a one-inch deep "X" into the top center of each cabbage head to provide space for the seed stalk to rise. The leaves grown during the second year will be smaller than the first year. If one of the cabbages shows signs of producing a poor quality seed stalk then dig it up and discard the entire cabbage so it doesn't pass its inferior pollen on to the good cabbages. The cabbage seed stalk will grow about five-feet tall and it will need to be supported between two stakes. Each seed stalk will contain branches of bright yellow flowers which will produce brown seed pods containing as many as 20 seeds each. When the seed pods turn yellow, cut off the entire seed stalk and place it on a large newspaper or cloth sheet. Many of the seeds will fall off onto the sheet. Put the remaining seed pods into a bag and carefully crush them using your hands to separate the seeds from the pods. Shake the seeds on a screen to separate the seeds from the chaff. Store the seeds in a paper envelope or cloth bag in a dry, cool area.

Carrots: Biennial with perfect flowers that have both the male and female parts. Easily cross-pollinated by insects. Therefore only plant one carrot variety per year or plant different varieties at least 1,000 feet apart. If you have short mild winters you may leave the carrots in the ground all winter. However, if you have long bitter winter weather then dig up the carrots before the first fall frost and save the eight (or more) carrots that have the best quality roots. Cut all but one-inch off the top of the carrot greens and place the carrots sideways in a container and bury the carrots beneath damp sand or sawdust in a cool humid area for the winter, but not below freezing. The next spring replant the carrots 18 inches apart with the crown just

below the surface of the earth. Push a shovel into the ground and then lean forward on the shovel handle. Insert the carrot into the ground behind the shovel and remove the shovel. Pack the dirt tightly around the carrot. The seed stalk will grow and produce flowers on a branched stalk. The seeds ripen from the top to the bottom of the stalk. Tie small nylon bags made from old nylon hose around the seed heads so the seeds can breathe and continue to ripen. As the seeds mature they will fall into the nylon bag and not be lost. When the lower seeds begin to fall off, cut off the seed stalk at the top of the carrot and lay it indoors to dry until the rest of the seeds mature and fall into the nylon bag. Shake the seeds on a screen to remove the chaff. Store the seeds in a paper envelope or cloth bag in a dry, cool area.

Cauliflower: Biennial with perfect flowers that have both the male and female parts. Easily cross-pollinated by insects with many other vegetables. Plant at least 200 feet from all other vegetables and other cauliflower varieties. Plant seeds in very late spring or early summer so the cauliflower plants mature in the fall just before the first frost. Dig up your **six** best cauliflower plants at the end of the first growing season and be careful that you do not damage their root system. Store them upside down in a cool area during the winter with their roots facing up. The next spring plant them 30 inches apart. They will yield a tall seed stalk containing yellow flowers and yellow seed pods. When the seed pods turn brown, cut the seed stalk from the top of the cauliflower and lay it on a newspaper or cloth sheet so the seed pods can continue to dry and fall onto the sheet. Put any remaining seed pods in a bag and carefully crush by hand to remove the seeds. Shake the seeds on a screen to separate them from the chaff. Store in a paper envelope or cloth bag in a dry, cool area. (Note: In the extreme northern United States it is difficult to save cauliflower over the winter. In the north start the seeds in individual portable planting pots in early September and then move them into a cool greenhouse for the winter. Move them outdoors in the late spring.)

Celery: Biennial with perfect flowers that have both the male and female parts. Cross-pollinated by insects. Celery requires 120 to 135 days to mature. In the fall dig up the best plants being careful to not damage the roots. Replant the roots in some soil indoors and completely mulch the celery tops with straw or hay. Store in a humid, very cold area above freezing for the winter. After the last spring frost retrieve the celery plants and cut off the leaves and stalks that have rotted, and replant the celery roots outdoors 24 inches apart. The plant will produce a bushy growth about 30 inches tall with white flowers. The seeds will turn brown from the top to the bottom of the bush and they need to be harvested in that sequence. Tie a nylon bag made from nylon hose around the seed heads so you can capture the seeds when the seed head shatters. Then follow the directions for saving carrot seeds (above).

Chives: Perennial pollinated by bees but they will not cross-pollinate with other vegetables. Chives have shallow roots and weeds will kill them if the weeds are allowed to grow and multiply. If you intend to harvest the chive seeds then only harvest the outer leaves of the plant for the table. The chives will produce round pink/purple flowers. When the tiny black seeds appear they are ready to be harvested. Cut off the seed head and dry it indoors for six weeks. Carefully separate the seeds with your hands and store in a paper envelope or cloth bag in a dry, cool area.

Corn: Annual with male tassels and female flowers (ears) on each plant. Cross-pollinated by the wind. The wind can easily carry the pollen 1,000 feet so only plant **one** variety of corn to avoid mixing varieties. Leave the largest most perfect earliest bearing ears of corn on the stalk and harvest the rest for eating. Save the ears from as many **different** stalks as possible to prevent future inbreeding problems. Wait about 4 weeks and then harvest the remaining ears of corn on their stalks but do **not** wait until after the first frost. Peel back the husks and hang the corn on their stalks upside down in a well-ventilated room for another 4 weeks to allow the corn kernels more time

to ripen. Wait until the corn kernels are hard and completely dry. If they are not dry they will not store well. Shelling is the term used for removing the corn from the ears. Twist off the full kernels of corn using your

Chapter Twenty-Two: How to Grow Each Type of Vegetable and Vegetable Seed

hands and discard the kernels near the end of the ear that are small and only partially developed. Store in a paper envelope or cloth bag in a dry, cool area. The following spring soak the seeds in some warm water for three hours before planting to improve their germination ability.

Cucumber: Annual with male and female flowers on the same plant. The male flowers appear in groups but the female flowers do not and a small fruit will be at the base of the female flowers. Cross-pollinated by bees so only plant one variety of cucumber per year. When you stop harvesting cucumbers the cucumber vines will stop producing more fruit. Leave the best looking cucumbers on the vine about five weeks after you have harvested the others for eating. They will become fat and yellow. Harvest them before they start to rot. Cut the cucumber in half and scrape the seedy interior pulp into a bowl of water. Stir the water occasionally to prevent the formation of mold. After about five days the seeds will sink to the bottom of the bowl. Remove them, rinse them off, and place them on a screen to dry for another 10 days. When the seed breaks instead of bends it is dry enough. Store the seeds in a paper envelope or cloth bag in a dry, cool place. The seeds will continue to ripen while in storage.

Eggplant: Annual with perfect flowers that have both the male and female parts. Usually self-pollinated but occasionally cross-pollinated by insects. Therefore only plant one variety per year. Wait for the mature fruit to drop from the plant. However, if there is danger of a frost then cut the eggplant from the plant and bring it inside for another two weeks. Save the fruits from several different plants. Cut the eggplant in half and scrape the seedy interior pulp into a bowl of water. Stir the water until the seeds separate from the pulp and fall to the bottom of the bowl. Remove the seeds from the bottom of the water, rinse, and dry on screens or paper towels. When you can't nick the seed with your fingernail then the seed is dry enough. Store the seeds in a paper envelope or cloth bag in a dry, cool area.

Kohlrabi: Biennial with perfect flowers that have both the male and female parts. Pollinated by bees. Plant the seed in the fall. Mulch the plants during the winter. Inspect the kohlrabi the following spring and dig up and discard any plants that do not have uniform stems of the correct color. Kohlrabi will produce a large spreading seed stalk and the plants should therefore be spaced about 30 inches apart. Harvest the seed using the same procedure as cabbage seed.

Leeks: Biennial. Cross-pollinated by bees so keep different leek varieties separated by at least 200 feet. Remove the smaller plants and leave the larger, higher quality leeks in the ground during the winter. If the winters are long and bitter then cover with a layer of mulch. (Note: When left in the ground leeks will form small bulblets around the base of the plant the following spring. These bulblets can be removed and planted to yield a fresh crop of leeks.) During the second growing season a tall stalk will appear with a ball of tiny flowers at its tip. When the seeds form inside the small paper thin capsules they are ready to be harvested. Cut off the entire seed stalk and place it indoors inside a bag to dry. When completely dry, rub the capsules with your hands to remove the seeds. Store the seeds in a paper envelope or cloth bag in a dry, cool area.

Lettuce: Annual with perfect flowers that have both the male and female parts. Self-pollinating. Separate different varieties by at least one row of some other type of vegetable. Lettuce prefers cool weather and it will go to seed when the days are long and hot. This is called bolting. Lettuce that is allowed to bolt should be separated by 12 inches from one another. The lettuce begins to bolt when its leaves start to taste bitter and a stalk begins to rise from the center of the plant. Leaf lettuce bolts easily but you will need to cut a one-inch deep "X" into the top center of head lettuce to provide space for the seed stalk to rise. As the stalk continues to grow a flower head will form with small yellow flowers which eventually turn into feathery white tufts. Inside the tufts are the tiny black or white seeds. One lettuce plant can produce as many as  30,000 seeds. The seeds do **not** all ripen at the same time. Instead they ripen over a period of 4 to 8 weeks. Watch the stalk and each time you see that some of the seeds have turned dark, shake those dark seeds into a paper bag. Dry indoors for another seven days. Store the seeds in a paper envelope or cloth bag in a dry, cool area. Lettuce seeds need light to germinate so do **not** plant the seeds too deep in the soil the following spring.

Melons: Annual with male and female flowers on the same plant. Melons are cross-pollinated by bees so do **not** plant within 200 feet of any other variety of melon. When the melon is ripe enough to eat then the seeds are also ready for harvesting. Cut the melon and scrape out the seedy interior pulp into a bowl of water. Stir gently and the heavy seeds will settle to the bottom of the bowl. Remove the seeds, rinse, and dry thoroughly on a screen or paper towel. When the seed breaks instead of bending it is dry enough. Store the seeds in a paper envelope or cloth bag in a dry, cool place. In the spring place the seeds between two moist paper towels and then place inside a plastic bag in a warm place. When the seeds germinate, plant the tiny seedlings. (Note: Watermelons are ripe when the side that was touching the ground turns from white to yellow.)

Okra: Annual self-pollinating but only plant one variety per year. Okra have yellow flowers with a red center which is followed by a pod. Before the pod is fully developed it is harvested for eating. However, to yield seed, the pods must be left on the plant until they turn woody in the fall and then they are harvested. Crack open the pods and harvest the seeds.

Onions: Biennial. Onions have the best eating quality and flavor when grown from seed. Cross-pollinated by bees so different varieties should be planted at least 1,000 feet apart during their second year. If an onion bolts to seed the first year then do **not** save the seeds but discard them. Onions with thick necks do not store well over the winter so they should be eaten. Dig up the onions in the fall and save the best quality onions in a well ventilated dry, cool area above freezing for the winter. The next spring cut a shallow "X" in the top of each onion to provide an area for the seed stalk to emerge. Then replant the onions 4 inches apart and cover with 1/2 inch of soil. During the summer a tall seed stalk will appear with a round flower head which will yield black seeds. When the seeds begin to appear cut off the seed stem and dry it indoors for six weeks to allow time for the seeds to mature. Remove the seeds by rubbing with your hand. Store the seeds in a paper envelope or cloth bag in a dry, cool area.

Parsley: Biennial with perfect flowers that have both the male and female parts. Cross-pollinated by insects so do **not** plant different parsley varieties the same year. Don't save the seeds from parsley that bolts to seed the first year. For a continuous supply of parsley plant every two weeks through mid-summer. After the first few frosts in the fall, cover the parsley with leaves, hay, or straw for the winter. Uncover them in the early spring. During the second growing season, parsley will produce tall branching flower stalks that yield lots of seeds. The seed heads ripen slowly so tie a nylon bag made from nylon hose around the seed stalks to catch the seeds when the flower heads burst in the fall. Harvest the seed stalks before the first frost and shake inside a paper bag to remove any additional seeds. Shake on a screen to remove the chaff. Store the seeds in a paper envelope or cloth bag in a dry, cool area. During winter storage the parsley seeds will form a germination-inhibiting coating which should be removed prior to planting. To remove the coating soak the seeds in some warm water for two days the following spring. Change the water every 12 hours and rinse the seeds once more just before planting.

Peanut: Annual self-pollinating but only plant one variety per year. Peanuts grow in clusters underground. When the above ground leaves turn yellow then dig up the entire plant and store indoors for an additional four weeks in a cool, dry area. Leave the peanuts inside their shells until you are ready to eat them or use them for seed. If you shell them for seed then be very careful to not break or tear the pink paper thin seed coat around the peanut. Plant the peanut inside its thin seed coat for the best germination results.

Peas: Annual self-pollinating but occasionally cross-pollinated by bees so plant different varieties at least 100 feet apart. Peas do **not** do well when transplanted so indoor sowing is not effective. Plant peas during the last week of winter or first week of spring as they are hardy plants and can survive spring frosts. When they begin to grow in the spring put a thin layer of mulch close around your plants to help shade the roots and keep the soil cool. Inspect your mature plants and select the strongest, earliest bearing plants with the heaviest set of peas for seed. Allow the peas on those plants to remain inside their seed pods until they are really dry and you can hear them rattle inside their seed pods. This usually occurs about 4 weeks after you have harvested the other peas for eating. If a heavy rain if forecasted, pull up the pea plants, roots and all, and stack the plants indoors in a well ventilated area until the seeds are dry inside their pods. Remove the seeds from their pods by hand. Store in a paper envelope or cloth bag in a dry, cool place. The following spring **before** the last frost, soak the peas in some warm water for three hours before planting outdoors. Poke your finger into the soft earth about 1.5 inches and drop the pea into the hole. Do **not** cover the hole with dirt. Late snows or early spring rains will fill the hole and provide the additional moisture the peas need to germinate.

Pepper: Annual self-pollinating with perfect flowers that have both the male and female parts. However, bees will transport the pollen among plants so different varieties should be planted at least 50 feet apart. Too much nitrogen fertilizer will produce strong healthy bushes but yield minimum fruits. Do not plant where tobacco has grown in the past, or near tobacco that is currently growing. Harvest most of the peppers when they are ready to eat but leave the healthiest best looking peppers on the vine and wait for them to change color and begin to shrivel. Save the peppers from several different plants. If frost is forecast and the peppers have not yet changed color then bring them indoors and wait for the seed to ripen. If pepper seeds are not allowed to fully ripen they will **not** germinate well the 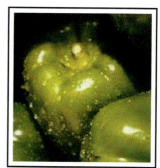 following spring. Cut the fully ripe shriveled peppers and remove the inner cluster of seeds. Place the seeds on a paper towel and allow them to dry for 14 days. When the seed breaks when you apply pressure (instead of bending) it is dry enough. Store in a paper envelope or cloth bag in a dry, cool area. Due to their long growing season pepper seeds need to be started indoors about 8 weeks before the last frost the next spring. Keep the soil very warm and water the soil sparingly during this 8 week period. Pepper seeds germinate best in warm dry soil.

Potato: Annual self-pollinating. Although potatoes can be grown from seed they are typically grown from the eyes (dormant bud) of the potato, or the small, white sprouts that appear on a mature potato as it ages. Potatoes should be stored in a cool area over the winter at a temperature above 45°F (7°C). Short white sprouts on a potato are okay but break off any really long weak sprouts if there are at least three other eyes or sprouts on the potato. Small potatoes the size of an egg or a little larger should be planted whole. Potatoes smaller than an egg should be discarded. Large potatoes with eight or more eyes should be cut into pieces with one to three eyes per piece. Leave as much potato as possible on each piece. Allow the cuts to heal and dry for two days before planting. (Note: Too many eyes on a potato will yield a large above ground plant but very few potatoes below ground.) Plant the cut side facing down about 3 inches deep and about 10 inches apart. When the green tops are about 8 inches high cover them with some more soil. Harvest the potatoes as you need them. (Note: If you wish to experiment with potato seed then very carefully observe your patch of potatoes to see if any of them produce a seed ball along with the above ground leaves. The seed ball will look like a tiny green tomato. Harvest it and save the seeds. Most gardeners who experiment with potato seeds have not experienced good results. You may be the exception.)

Pumpkins: Annual with male and female flowers on the same plant. The female flower has a tiny fruit at its base whereas the male flower does not. Cross-pollinated by bees so plant different varieties at least 500 feet apart. Pumpkins seeds will be ripe at the same time that the pumpkin is ready to be harvested and eaten. Cut the pumpkin open, scrape the seedy pulp into a bowl of water, and separate the seeds from the pulp. Examine the seeds and discard the flat ones. Spread the plump seeds onto a paper towel and allow to dry for 10 days. Store in a paper envelope or cloth bag in a dry, cool area.

Radish: Annual with tiny perfect flowers that have both the male and female parts. Easily cross-pollinated by bees but the tiny flowers are frequently ignored by bees if other larger flowers are nearby. Only plant one variety of radish per year to avoid cross-pollination. The flowers are tiny and will not produce seed during very hot or very dry weather. Harvest **all** the radishes when they are ready to eat. Inspect them and select the most desirable ones to use to produce seed. Cut all but one-inch off the top of the radish green leaves but be careful and do **not** cut the small leaves that are just beginning to develop. Replant the radishes about 8 inches apart with their crowns level with the surrounding dirt. Watch carefully and pull up and discard the first radishes to bolt to seed because they will **not** produce good seed. The radishes that bolt to seed later will produce the best seed. The seed stalk will be two or three feet tall. The green seed pod will first turn yellow and then it will turn brown. Pull up the entire radish plant at that time and hang them in a well ventilated area to dry. Crush the seed pods by hand to remove the seeds. Store the seeds in a paper envelope or cloth bag in a dry, cool area. Radishes do not keep well so the following spring you should plant one or two rows of radishes every two weeks. This will provide fresh edible radishes for the table throughout the summer and early fall.

Rhubarb: Perennial cross-pollinated by insects. Needs a cold climate to do well and is therefore normally only grown in the northern United States. The seeds produced do **not** always result in the parent plant so it is better to propagate by dividing the crown of the rhubarb and replanting them instead. Rhubarb seeds will appear on a tall seed stalk that appears in the summer. When the top of the seed stalk becomes dry and flaky, cut it off and then remove and dry the seeds.

Rutabaga: Biennial with perfect flowers that have both the male and female parts. Pollinated by bees. Typically grown in northern climates whereas turnips are typically grown in southern climates. Rutabagas should be planted earlier than turnips because they grow slower, such as early August. Follow the planting and seed collection directions for turnips.

Spinach: Annual wind pollinated and cross-fertilization is possible with any other variety planted within one mile. Therefore plant only one variety of spinach each spring. Some varieties have either a male or a female flower on each plant but other varieties have both male and female flowers on the same plant. Spinach prefers cool weather and it should be planted in the very early spring or during the late summer. To prevent the spinach from bolting too soon, pick off the largest leaves. The best plants to use for seeds are the ones that are the last to bolt to seed because the plant itself will be a heavier producer of spinach leaves for the table over a longer period of time. When the spinach leaves begin to turn yellow, pull up the plant and remove the seeds by hand. Dry the seeds for 14 days and then store in a paper envelope or cloth bag in a dry, cool area. The following spring plant spinach every two weeks to produce a continuous supply for fresh eating. The seeds may be soaked in a solution of 3 parts bleach to one part water for 10 minutes to help prevent loss to fungus. Then soak the seeds overnight in some clear water before planting them in the soil. Or, instead of soaking in a bleach/water solution, the seeds can be sprouted by placing the seeds between two damp paper towels inside a plastic bag in the refrigerator for 7 to 10 days.

Squash: Annual with male and female flowers on the same plant. The female flower has a tiny fruit at its base whereas the male flower does not. Cross-pollinated by bees so plant different varieties at least 500 feet apart. If two varieties are cross-pollinated the resulting squash will be edible but it will not have the same pleasant taste as the original squash. Winter squash seeds will be ripe at the same time that the winter squash is ready to be harvested and eaten. However, summer squash must remain on the vine for eight weeks after the majority of it has been harvested and eaten. For both winter and summer squash harvest the squash at the proper time and then hang it up indoors for an additional six weeks to dry. Cut the squash open, scrape the seedy pulp into a bowl of water, and separate the seeds from the pulp. Examine the seeds and discard the flat ones. Spread the plump seeds onto a paper towel and allow to dry for 10 days. The seed is dry enough when it breaks instead of bends. Store in a paper envelope or cloth bag in a dry, cool area.

Swish Chard: Biennial with perfect flowers that have both the male and female parts. Cross-pollinated by the wind. The plant is very hardy and may be left in the ground during the first winter with a layer of compost on top. The tall seed stalks will appear the second year and they need to be staked so they can continue to grow to maturity. When the seed stalk becomes dry, remove its seeds and dry them indoors. Store the seeds in a paper envelope or cloth bag in a dry, cool area.

Tomato: Annual with perfect flowers that have both the male and female parts. Self-pollinated but insects can cross-pollinate different varieties so plant different varieties at least 10 feet apart. Select the best looking, earliest bearing, most productive plants for seed collection. Save seeds from a minimum of three different plants to provide for a reasonable gene pool. Harvest tomatoes when they are completely ripe and ready to be eaten. Cut the tomato into quarters and scrape the seedy pulp into a bowl of shallow water at room temperature. Stir the seeds once or twice a day and remove and discard any pulp and seed that floats to the top of the water. After two to four days remove the good seeds that have sunk to the bottom of the bowl. Rinse these good seeds in clean water and place on paper towels or newspapers for 10 days to dry thoroughly. The seeds will stick to the paper and you can save the paper with the seeds attached. Store in a paper envelope or cloth bag in a dry, cool area. In the spring you can peel off a seed with a little paper attached to it and plant them together. The paper will deteriorate quickly after planting and the seed will germinate.

Turnip: Biennial with perfect flowers that have both the male and female parts. Pollinated by bees. Typically grown in southern climates whereas rutabagas are typically grown in northern climates. Plant in the midsummer in the north and in the early fall in the south. Thin the turnips to four inches apart. Leave in the ground during the winter with a covering of mulch to protect them. The second year thin the plants to 18 inches apart. They will produce a seed stalk the second year. When the seed pods turn yellow, cut off the entire seed stalk and place it on a large newspaper or cloth sheet. Many of the seeds will fall off onto the sheet. Put the remaining seed pods into a bag and carefully crush them using your hands to separate the seeds from the pods. Shake the seeds on a screen to separate the seeds from the chaff. Store the seeds in a paper envelope or cloth bag in a dry, cool area.

Chapter Twenty-Three

How to Harvest, Process, and Store Vegetable Seeds

This Information in this Chapter Received the First Place Award of $2,000.00 for the Best Non-Fiction Article Published During April and May of 2007.

A Quick Comparison of Vegetable Seeds to Silver Dollars

The small seed envelopes available for sale at hardware stores and supermarkets are generally priced between $0.97 to $1.69 per package. Each individual package usually contains somewhere between 100 mg to 3.5 g of seed, with an average of 900 mg of seeds per package. 1000 mg equals 1 gram and 1 gram equals 0.035 standard ounces. Therefore 900 mg equals approximately 0.0315 standard ounces or 0.0287 troy ounces. If the average seed package contains 900 mg of seeds and cost $0.97 then that is equivalent to $33.80 per troy ounce and this exceeds the price of $27 for a one-ounce United States Silver Eagle in January of 2011. (Note: $0.97 / 0.0287 troy ounce = $33.80 per troy ounce.)

Therefore at the beginning of the year 2011 seeds cost more per ounce than pure refined silver. And history has repeatedly demonstrated that during serious worldwide famine conditions, food and seeds eventually become more valuable than gold.

Basic Instructions for Saving Vegetable Seeds

Seed Types: When you first purchase seeds you should avoid "Hybrid Seeds." Instead you should buy "Heirloom Seeds" or "Open Pollinated Seeds." Hybrid seeds are "man-made seeds" and they are only good for **one** planting. (Note: If you plant hybrid seeds and then save the seeds from the hybrid plants that are produced, and then plant those seeds the following spring, the results will be unpredictable. The plant that grows will usually resemble one of its parents or grandparents or something in-between. It is also possible that it may produce **no** fruit at all.) Heirloom seeds, on the other hand, will produce crops that yield seeds that will reproduce the same plant year after year after year as God originally intended. (Genesis 1:11 - *Then God said, "Let the earth bring forth grass, the herb that yields seed, and the fruit tree that yields fruit according to its kind, whose seed is in itself, on the earth;" and it was so.*) When you purchase a package of seeds you should **not** plant all the seeds from the original package the first year. Instead you should save some of them for planting in future years in the event your first year's planting efforts are not successful. You should also clearly mark exactly where you plant each type of seed with the name and variety of that seed so you can keep track of which varieties of seed do best in your climate and in your soil.

Disease Avoidance: After you have planted your seeds and the plants appear, do **not** collect seeds from a diseased plant because the disease will have infected that specific plant's genes and all future plants grown from those seeds will be easily susceptible to that same disease.

Seed Selection: Use the very best looking, strongest, and most productive plants in your garden for seeds. Generally you are **not** looking for that **one** special fruit on the vine. Instead you should look for: early bearing of fruit, total fruit yield, fruit size and flavor and aroma, and disease resistance. Also, if applicable, late bolting to seed. Resist the urge to eat your most delectable looking vegetables. Those are the ones you want to duplicate every year in the future. After you have selected the fruits you want to keep for seed, identify them with a special marker such as a wooden stake beside the plant, or a ribbon or string loosely tied to the plant or vine. In most cases (but not all) it is important to save seeds from at least three different plants of the same variety to provide good pollination opportunities the following spring.

Seed Ripeness: Allow seeds to fully ripen before harvesting to achieve the best germination yield the following spring. The seed must be given time to store enough nourishment so it can germinate the following spring and grow into a healthy seedling.

Drying: Seeds must be dried before they are stored (between 5% to 13% moisture content with an average of 8%). Individual seeds should be separated from one another so they can dry more evenly. Larger seeds will require more time to air dry whereas smaller seeds will require less time. Do **not** try to dry the seeds too quickly or they may shrink and crack. And do **not** dry at a temperature higher than 100°F (38°C). Indoor air drying is usually the best. However, if you live in an extremely humid area, then you may dry your seeds by placing them in the sun in front of a southern facing window for about two days. Since there is no easy inexpensive method for measuring the exact moisture content of your seeds, you will need to use your own judgment based on your personal experience. Generally the drier the seed (but **not** below 5%), the longer the seed will remain alive in storage. Based on Dr. James Harrington's research, each additional 1% decrease in the dryness of a vegetable seed from 13% down to 5% will double its storage life. However, below 5% will normally kill the seed and above 13% will usually result in the seed not surviving the first winter. Since the home gardener does not have the expensive equipment to accurately measure the exact moisture content of a batch of seeds, the home gardener may wish to use a trial and error approach. When you first suspect that your seeds are dry enough, put half of them into paper envelopes and label the envelopes with the variety of seed and indicate how many days the seeds were dried. Continue drying the remainder of the seeds for a few more days. Then put half of those seeds into paper envelopes and label them as your second drying with the total number of drying days. After a few more days of drying put the remainder of the seeds into a paper envelope and label them as your third drying with the total number of drying days. When you test each envelope of seeds in future years you can use this trial and error method to estimate the optimal number of drying days for each type of seed based on your climate, and your humidity, and your average normal drying conditions.

Storage: **After** your seeds are dry, store your seeds in a standard small paper envelope, or a paper bag, or a cloth bag in a dry, cool area. Do **not** allow the seeds to remain in direct contact with the air or they will gradually absorb moisture from the humidity in the air with the passage of time. After placing the seeds in a standard small paper envelope or cloth bag, you can store that envelope or bag inside a standard plastic freezer bag. Freezer bags are more expensive and of a higher quality than regular plastic bags. Do **not** seal your seeds inside a vacuum plastic bag without air because seeds are living organisms and they need a **minimum** amount of air to continue their life cycle. The **best** place to store seeds is in a plastic freezer bag inside a refrigerator at a temperature between 35°F to 40°F (or 2°C to 4°C). This will more than double the storage life of your seeds.

Labeling: Clearly label each of your seed envelopes or bags using permanent ink to identify the exact variety of seed and the year the seed was harvested. Also include the number of days the seed was allowed to dry, along with any unusual weather conditions during the drying process, such as unusually humid weather or unusually warm or cold weather during the drying process.

Seed Bank: Most seeds can successfully germinate for three to five years after harvesting, even if they are **not** stored in a refrigerator. Therefore, it is prudent to have your own "Seed Bank" into which you deposit approximately 10% of the seeds you harvest each year. If an unexpected disease attacks your crops one year then you will **not** be able to harvest any seeds from that year's crops, even though you may be able to eat some or most of that year's poor quality marginal vegetables. In this type of situation your "Seed Bank" will permit the re-establishment of the quality of your crops in future years. The seeds in your "Seed Bank" are your insurance against unpredictable future diseases that may sweep through your geographical area. They are also good insurance against an unexpected cross-pollination that produces a seed that is different than you expected. In most cases you will not become aware of this type of problem until harvest time the following fall. Once again, your "Seed Bank" will allow you to re-establish this variety the following spring using seeds saved from previous years **before** the problem appeared.

Emergency Seed Reserve: Each spring you should gradually plant each variety of seed over an extended period of several weeks. You should **not** plant all your seeds of one variety at the same time. This reduces your risk of loss to late frosts and it provides a longer harvest period for fresh vegetables for the table. If you have seeds that are more than one year old which are **not** part of your "Seed Bank" then your first planting the following spring should be one-half of those older seeds. If you do **not** have any two or three year old seeds then do **not** plant more than half your previous year's seed the following spring. Save at least half of the previous year's seed as an "Emergency Seed Reserve" (in addition to your "Seed Bank"). Occasional late snows or an unexpected late frost can kill everything you plant at the beginning of spring. Your "Emergency Seed Reserve" will allow you to plant a second time that same year. Later during the spring or summer other problems may arise, such as heavy rains or no rains or insect damage or tornados or hurricanes, and these disasters could result in no crops to harvest in the fall. In disaster situations like these it provides some comfort to know that you still have a reasonable amount of seed reserved for planting the following year. If you are forced to use your "Emergency Seed Reserve" then only plant half of them and keep the rest of the seeds in reserve. Always keep at least half of your remaining seed as an "Emergency Seed Reserve" for really hard times. This means each future planting will be much smaller but that is much better than having **nothing** to plant at all. Because of unpredictable situations such as the above, each year it would be wise to harvest at least twice the amount of seed you think you will need the following year. This strategy will also provide you with seed to share, sell, or trade and it will bring you one step closer to being an independent, resourceful human being in God's natural order of things.

Preparing Seeds for Planting: (Note: These suggestions are optional.) Place the seeds you wish to plant in the freezer compartment of your refrigerator for three hours. When you remove the seed from the freezer the rush of warm air will help to break its winter dormancy. Then place the individual seeds between two damp paper towels for one day in a warm area. The seed is now in an optimal condition for immediate planting.

Spring Germination Test: (Note: This step is optional.) You can test the viability of your seeds **before** you plant them in the ground in the spring. Use a medium-tip permanent marker to write the name of the seed and the year it was harvested on a **dry** paper towel. Then dampen the paper towel and place ten seeds on one-half of the towel. Fold the towel in half so the seeds are between the two halves of the damp paper towel. Place the damp paper towel inside a plastic trash bag and put it in a warm place. You can put several damp paper towels containing different seed varieties in the same plastic trash bag. Keep the paper towels slightly damp but **not** soaking wet. Periodically check the seeds based on the average germination time for each type of seed. You can determine the "approximate" germination rate by counting the number of seeds that sprout and dividing by the original number of seeds tested. For example, if you tested 10 seeds and 8 of them sprouted, then the germination rate is 80% (8/10 x 100). You can then plant these sprouted seeds in a peat pot indoors if the outdoor weather is too cold, or you can plant them in the ground if warm weather has arrived.

Do You Understand?

Do you understand what makes a bumble bee fly?
Do you understand why God allows people to die?

Can you explain how a tidal wave is formed?
Can you explain how a baby child is born?

With our nose we can smell and with our eyes we can see.
But can you truly explain how these senses came to be?

Our human minds have a limited capacity,
and we cannot comprehend things with God's clarity.

It is not possible to explain the reason behind
the loss of a child, or spouse, or parent, or friend.

Or the loss of your job, or home, or car, or health.
Or car wrecks, or earthquakes, or forest fires, or death.

The first step towards wisdom is accepting the fact that we
will **never** be able to understand many of life's mysteries.

However, everything God created is subject to His command.
And **you** are precious in God's eyes. Now do you understand?

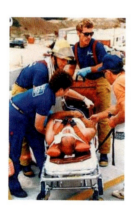 

This Poem is Dedicated to My Grandson **Austin Greg Sisco.**

Scripture References: Genesis 1:1, Hebrews 11:3, Proverbs 20:12, Genesis 7:11-12, Joshua 10:12-14, First Kings 17:2-6, First Kings 19:11-13, Second Kings 2:11-12, Luke 9:42-43, Matthew 8:24-27, Luke 7:11-16, Matthew 26:52-54, Psalm 72:13-14, Psalm 116:15, John 3:16.

Chapter Twenty-Four

How to Grow Fruits, Nuts, Grapes, and Berries

It is very easy to read gardening advice. However, when you actually start to dig that first hole you will quickly discover how much work is really involved. Therefore please be prepared for some really hard work if you decide to plant a small orchard, or a vineyard, or a berry patch.

I planted my first fruit trees, nut trees, grape vines, and berry bushes in the year 1977. Everywhere I have lived since then I have had some type of fruit, nut, grape, or berry bushes growing on my property. Sometimes I was successful and sometimes I was not. The purpose of this chapter is to share what worked for me and what did not work.

Let me begin by mentioning that some climates and some locations are well suited to the growth of certain trees, vines, and bushes due to the number of days of winter weather, and the number of frost-free days, and the average rainfall, and the average wind conditions. Therefore you will probably discover you are very successful with some things and you are a complete failure with other things. This may have nothing to do with your gardening skills. It may simply be that your climate or your specific garden spot is either suitable or not suitable for a particular type of plant. Therefore please try to maintain a balanced perspective and do not take the credit for your successes and do not take the blame for your failures. There are other factors involved that can make your efforts succeed or fail that have absolutely nothing to do with you.

The Big Three

The following three issues are the most important ones for fruit trees, nut trees, grape vines, and berry bushes:

1. Full Sun.
2. Hole Size.
3. Dirt Quality.

Let's examine each of the above three topics one-at-a-time.

Full Sun: Any type of tree, vine, or bush that produces food for human consumption must receive a lot of sun on a regular basis. Therefore the first critical decision that must be made is the location where you will plant your tree, vine, or bush. That location must receive good sun for at least six-hours each day during the spring and summer months. Remember that the position of the sun in the sky in relation to the earth is different during the different seasons of the year. Please keep this in mind as you select your planting site. The planting site you select should be one that receives direct sunlight for at least six-hours each day during the spring and summer months. More sunlight is better than less sunlight. Also please remember that trees will grow very tall and they will eventually cast a shadow behind them. This must be kept in mind as you create your layout for your orchards, vineyards, and berry patches. Plant your vineyards and berry patches on the sun side of your orchard. In the northern hemisphere this will be the south side of your property.

If you plant a tree that is an early bloomer and your area has a history of late spring frosts, then it is better to plant those trees where they do not receive more than six-hours of sun in the early spring. This will help the tree to remain dormant just a little longer and hopeful the tree will not bloom until after the last spring frost. This will prevent the tender young fruit blossoms from being killed every spring by a late frost.

Hole Size: The hole should be at least three times bigger than the root spread of the tree or bush you are planting. By digging a bigger hole you will be providing space for the roots to grow while they are still young and trying to establish themselves. This will increase the odds that your new planting will survive and mature into a healthy tree or bush. The hole should also be at least six-inches deeper than the depth of the roots you are planting for the same reason. Many, many years ago I heard some really good planting advice and I would like to pass that advice along to you at this time: *"It is better to plant a 50-cent tree in a five-dollar hole than to plant a five-dollar tree in a 50-cent hole."* The hole for a tree should be at least a three-feet diameter circle and at least two-feet deep. The hole for a grape vine or berry bush should be at least two-feet in diameter and at least 18-inches deep. If you can dig a bigger hole then do so but please do not dig a hole that is too small for your new tree, vine, or bush. If you dig a hole that is too small then you will regret it later when your new plant dies, or when its growth is stunted, or when it takes a few extra years for it to start producing fruit.

Dirt Quality: Although you may have extremely fertile rich dirt in your new orchard, or vineyard, or berry patch, the vast majority of us will probably have dirt that is not suitable for fruit production. Therefore you will need to shovel the dirt out of the hole into a wheelbarrow and then move that poor quality dirt to another location where it can be strategically used, such as filling in a low spot on your property. Then you will need to put some really good dirt around the roots of the plant in the hole you just dug. I have lived in Maine, and in Florida, and in the mid-west, and in the mid-east. Everywhere I have lived I have had to improve the quality of the dirt on the land I owned. By trial and error I have found the following mixture to be very agreeable for fruit trees, nut trees, grape vines, berry bushes, and vegetable gardens.

Grandpappy's All-Purpose Dirt Mixture:
1 Part Top Soil.
1 Part Humus (or Peat).
1 Part Composted Cow Manure.
1/2 Part Pure Sand (the type used in a child's sand box or when mixing cement).

The above soil enhancers are usually sold in 40-pound bags in the garden departments of many stores in the spring of each year. The top soil is usually good rich soil. The humus or peat will help to hold moisture in the soil. The composted cow manure will provide some nutrients for the roots. The sand will aerate the soil and allow it to breathe. I pour approximately 1/2 bag of each of the first three items into an empty wheelbarrow and then I add about 1/4 bag of sand. Then I use my shovel to thoroughly mix the four ingredients together. When I have finished you cannot tell them apart and the consistency of the dirt inside the wheelbarrow looks uniform. Then I firmly pack that dirt into the bottom of the hole and around the roots of my new fruit tree, or grape vine, or berry bush. Or I pour that dirt into a raised bed vegetable garden area.

"Grandpappy's All-Purpose Dirt Mixture" is a "universal dirt" and I have had very, very good success using it with fruit trees, and nut trees, and grape vines, and berry bushes, and vegetables, and herbs, and flowers, and ornamental plants.

Note: I need to mention that the quality of the top soil, humus, and composted cow manure is not the same at all the different garden stores. When I need to make dirt I will usually buy one bag of each of these items at each of the different garden stores in my area. When I get home I will open each bag and put it beside the bags of the same item from the other stores. When you compare the contents inside the bags side-by-side it is usually easy to see which store has the highest quality product. For example, it is not unusual to find high quality top soil at one store, and high quality humus at a second store, and high quality composted cow manure at a third store. I then buy the highest quality soil enhancers available that year. I do **not** discard the few bags of low quality soil enhancers that I purchased. Instead I mix just a little bit from each low quality bag into each wheelbarrow of dirt I make so they are evenly distributed in my garden area and no single spot gets all the low quality material.

Day of Planting: Do not put any fertilizer on top of the ground on the day you plant your tree, vine, or bush. However, after you have finished planting your fruit tree, or grape vine, or berry bush, you should water the ground thoroughly. This will help to drive out any air in the ground and it will help the new dirt to more firmly pack together. It will also give the roots some water to encourage their acceptance of the new dirt and start their normal growing process.

First Day after Planting: Water the ground again the next day.
Second Day after Planting: Water the new plant again.

Routine Watering: If it doesn't rain then you will need to water your trees, vines, or bushes at least once per week the first year.

Mulch: You should also put a layer of mulch around the bottom of your trees, vines, and bushes to help keep the soil damp, and to prevent the sun from baking the soil, and to make it more difficult for weeds to grow in the fresh rich dirt that surrounds your new planting. However, do not push the mulch up against the trunk of the tree, vine, or bush in order to avoid the potential problems of trunk rot and above ground root growth.

Fertilizer

First Year: There are two schools of thought about using fertilizer the first year:

1. **Don't Use Any Fertilizer:** The first year is important for plant establishment and the most important issue is root growth. If you do not add any fertilizer then the roots will be forced to extend outwards in search of nutrients. This will result in a healthy root system.

2. **Add a Normal Amount of Fertilizer the Second Week After Planting:** The fertilizer will feed the roots and the roots will feed the above ground plant and this is critical the first year. If you don't add any fertilizer then you could starve the roots and the plant will die.

Grandpappy's Compromise: There are good arguments for using and for not using fertilizer the first year. Therefore I have adopted a simple compromise. I mix about 30% composted cow manure (approximately 0.5 - 0.5 - 0.5 in its original bag) into my "dirt" when I make dirt and this adds a very, very small amount of fertilizer into the original hole (approximately 0.15 - 0.15 - 0.15 after mixing). It is enough fertilizer to keep the roots and the above ground plant alive but it is not too much. Therefore it will still encourage the roots to spread out in search of additional nutrients.

How to Add Fertilizer: When you add fertilizer you should sprinkle that fertilizer on the ground above the outside tips of the original roots and just a little bit beyond those roots. This will encourage the roots to stretch out and grow into the richer soil that is just at the tip of their original roots.

Spring Fertilizer: In the early spring of each year add some fertilizer around each of your plants. This will help to feed the plants when they start to produce new growth each year.

Late Summer: Do **not** add any fertilizer in the late summer of each year.

Fall Fertilizer: In the fall of each year after the leaves have died you should put some more fertilizer on the ground around each of your plants. In the spring and summer the above ground portion of a plant thrives and grows. But in the fall and winter the below ground roots of the plant thrive and grow. You need to provide some fertilizer in the fall of each year so the roots will be encouraged to grow and store nutrients for the following spring.

Amount of Fertilizer: Too much fertilizer or too little fertilizer is not good. For each of your plants you will need to determine how much fertilizer to use based on the type of plant and the age of the plant.

Type of Fertilizer: The second year an 8-8-8 fertilizer may be used. After the second year I switch to a 10-10-10 or a 13-13-13 because I want fertilizer and not the inert ingredients. If you have a more powerful fertilizer then you simply use a little less of it. For example, a 10-10-10 is 25% stronger than an 8-8-8 and therefore you would only need to use about 3/4 as much fertilizer. A 13-13-13 is about 62% stronger than an 8-8-8 and you would only need about 2/3 as much fertilizer.

Fertilizer for Nuts, Grapes, and Berries: Beginning in the third year most nut trees, grape vines, and berry bushes will only need a nitrogen fertilizer such as ammonium sulfate or ammonium nitrate. Pecan trees will also benefit from small quantities of zinc.

Other Soil Enhancers: Depending on your geographical area you may need to add lime, or bone meal, or some other soil enhancer to your soil. Check with at least two different garden supply stores in your area and then compare their advice.

Now let's look at each of the different types of trees, vines, and bushes.

Chapter Twenty-Four: How to Grow Fruits, Nuts, Grapes, and Berries

Fruit Trees

The key to being successful with fruit trees is to select a variety that is suited for your specific geographical area. Do not assume that just because a specific variety of fruit tree is available at your local garden shop that it will do well in your area. For example, the Bartlett pear tree is the most popular pear tree in the United States and it is usually available for sale each spring in almost every garden store in the United States. However, the Bartlett pear tree does not do well in some southeastern states. The reason the garden shops in the southeast have it is because each spring people come into the store and ask for it by name. Therefore these garden shops sell their customers what they ask for.

Before you invest in any fruit tree you should consult a gardening book for your area, or do some internet research on the fruit tree varieties that do exceptionally well in your area, and then invest in those specific varieties. A little advance research on your part will yield huge dividends in the future when you harvest your fruits, and it will prevent the disappointment of planting a fruit tree and then watching it slowly die, or waiting years and years and the tree never yields any fruit.

For example, the Bradford Pear Tree and the Purple Leaf Plum Tree will both produce beautiful flower blossoms every spring. But both trees are considered "ornamental" trees and although they will produce a type of fruit, that fruit is not considered to be a good high quality fruit. Every spring many people mistake the Bradford pear for the Bartlett pear and they buy the Bradford pear tree instead. You can avoid a similar mistake by doing just a little research on the varieties available for sale at the garden supply stores in your area before you invest in a specific type of fruit tree.

If the fruit trees are sold as "bare root" trees with their roots packed in sawdust chips then shake off the sawdust chips and soak the roots of the fruit tree in some room temperature water for about six hours. Then immediately plant the fruit tree in its hole. Pack the dirt firmly around the roots but be careful to not damage the root system. (Note: Sawdust chips are actually small wood chips and they are usually dark brown or black in color. This is not the type of sawdust you generate when you use a saw to cut a piece of wood. The reason sawdust chips are used is because they weigh a lot less than real dirt and this minimizes the shipping cost to your location which allows the nursery to sell the trees at the lowest possible price. These sawdust chips should not be mixed with the dirt inside your planting hole. However, after you have firmly packed the dirt into your hole, and watered your new plant, then you could use the sawdust chips as a mulch around the base of your new plant.)

If the fruit trees are sold as "balled root" trees with their roots still encased in their original soil (instead of sawdust chips) then carefully remove the burlap bag, or plastic bag, and then plant the tree with the original soil still in place around the roots of the tree. (Note: Examine the soil and verify that it is soil and not sawdust chips. Soil is heavy. Sawdust chips are not heavy. Soil will crumble between your fingers. Sawdust chips will not crumble between your fingers.) If the tree is inside a plastic or metal pot then carefully remove the tree from the pot and try to keep as much of the original soil as possible around the root system. Then pour the rest of the dirt from the pot into the planting hole. Pack the dirt firmly around the entire root system.

If the fruit tree has been grafted onto a better type of rootstock then plant the tree with the grafting union between two to four-inches above the ground, unless the grafting union is very close to the roots.

Plant your fruit trees a minimum of twenty-feet apart. As they grow they will need this room for their branches to spread out. Do not plant your fruit trees too close to your property border. You do not want to upset your neighbors with "rotten fruit" that falls on their property.

Do **not** purchase dwarf fruit trees. These trees have been grafted onto dwarf root stock and it is the dwarf root stock that keeps these trees small. The dwarf root stock limits the amount of nutrition that travels upwards into the tree. This not only keeps the tree small but it also starves the tree and the tiny fruits will drop off the tree each spring because they cannot get enough nutrients to survive.

Some nurseries are now selling semi-dwarf trees. I have not had any personal experience with these semi-dwarf trees so the following comment is nothing more than an educated opinion on my part. I personally would not invest in the semi-dwarf fruit trees for the same reason I will no longer purchase a dwarf fruit tree.

No fruit set or poor fruit set on a fruit tree is usually due to the absence of a suitable cross-pollinator or to a late frost that kills or weakens the blooms before they are fertilized.

Some fruit trees may be grown from seed and some may not. If you plant a seed it will usually take between eight to twelve years for it to grow into a fruit tree that will begin to bear fruit. On the other hand, if you plant a fruit tree that you purchase from a nursery then it will usually begin to bear fruit in about three or four years. Therefore, if you can afford it, I personally recommend the purchase of fruit trees from your local garden store, or Walmart, or Lowe's, or Home Depot, of hardware store, such as Ace Hardware.

However, if you can't afford the price of a fruit tree, or if a hard times event forces you to relocate to a different area, then you can start an orchard by growing your fruit trees from seed.

Apples: Most apple trees are not self-pollinating and therefore two or more varieties will need to be planted. There are exceptions, such as Golden Delicious, which is self-fruitful. This means it can pollinate itself. However, even the self-fruitful varieties will perform much better if they are planted near a different variety.

The four varieties that are totally non self-fruitful are Jonagold, Mutsu, Stayman, and Winesap, These four varieties produce sterile pollen and therefore they should be avoided, in my opinion.

Golden Delicious is the best choice as a universal pollinator because it is a mid-season bloomer and its blooms will overlap early and late season apple varieties.

Apple Seeds

Apple trees may be grown from seeds. Buy several good brands of apples from the grocery store, such as Golden Delicious, Granny Smith, Jonathan, and Red Delicious. Do not mix the varieties together but keep them separate so you will know which apple is which. When you get home wait for the apple to fully ripen and then very carefully slice each apple and remove its seeds. Do not mix the seeds from different varieties of apples. Eat the apple after you have removed its seeds and make sure you enjoy the taste of that particular type of apple. Instructions for growing apple trees from seed are in the next chapter in this book.

Please don't become discouraged if someone severely criticizes or ridicules you for planting apple seeds. The original settlers of the United States of America brought apples seeds with them from England and they planted those seeds to grow apple trees. John Chapman, born September 26, 1774 in Massachusetts and died March 18, 1845 in Indiana, was nicknamed "Johnny Appleseed" and he was responsible for planting thousands of apple seeds throughout the Midwest. That is one of the reasons apple trees are now grown in almost every state in the United States.

Cherries: Cherry trees are frequently grown from seed, which is the pit at the center of the cherry. If you can find fresh cherries for sale in your area, and if the cherries are named, then you can buy a pint of them, eat the cherries, and save the pits of the cherries and plant them. However, please read the following information because you may need a pollinator.

There are two basic categories of cherries: sweet and sour (tart).

1. All **sour** (tart) cherry trees are self-fertile and they do not need a pollinator. Sour cherries are the typical pie cherry. Montmorency is the most popular sour cherry and it will even pollinate some sweet cherry varieties, such as Bing. Other good sour cherries are Early Richmond and North Star.

2. Most **sweet** cherries are not self-fertile and they will not pollinate themselves or other sweet cherries that

are closely related to them. Sweet cherries need to be pollinated by another sweet cherry that is not similar to itself. Therefore if you plant sweet cherry trees you will need to plant at least two cherry trees and each of those trees should be from a different group. Since one of your trees may die it would probably be a good idea to plant at least one cherry tree from each of the following groups below.

Cherry trees in any one group below will **not** pollinate the other cherry trees in that same group.
Cherry trees in any one group below will pollinate the cherry trees in any other group below.

Sweet Cherry Trees by Group

Group One	Group Two	Group Three
Bing	Sodus	Black Eagle
Lambert	Van	Black Tartarian
Napoleon	Venus	Early Rivers
National	Knights Early Black	
Royal Ann		

A few sweet cherry varieties are considered to be self-fruitful. These include Black Gold, Index, Lapins, Skeena, Sonata, Starkrimson, Stella, Sunburst, Sweetheart, Symphony, and White Gold. These varieties may be used to pollinate any of the varieties in the above table.

Although I have planted approximately 15 different cherry trees during the past 35 years I have never personally been successful with cherry trees. All my cherry trees died within two years after planting with the exception of one Black Tartarian cherry tree. That one cherry tree is still alive and doing well and it flowers every spring but it never produces any cherries because there is no pollinator sweet cherry tree nearby. Every few years I try my luck planting two new pollinator cherry trees but so far none of those trees has survived for more than two years.

Figs: Common fig trees are self-fertile and will pollinate themselves. Fig trees will produce two crops of figs each year: one crop in the Spring on last year's growth, and another crop in the Fall on the current year's growth. Good varieties are Black Mission, Brown Turkey, Celeste, and Desert King.

Peaches: Most peach trees are self-fertile and will pollinate themselves. However, better pollination and a heavier peach crop will usually result from planting two different varieties of peach trees. Peaches can be grown in southern climates. The non self-fruitful varieties are Candoka, Earlihale, Hal-Berta, J.H. Hale, and Mikado and these varieties should be avoided, in my opinion. Some good heirloom varieties are Belle of Georgia, Elberta, and Redhaven. (Note: **Nectarines** are similar to peaches but they are more difficult to grow. Therefore I have never experimented with nectarines and I have always been content to simply grow peaches.)

Pears: Some pear trees are self-fruitful and some are not. Pear trees will usually grow straight up instead of branching out to the sides. It is not unusual for some pear trees to live 40 or 50 years. The most common pear tree in the United States is the Bartlett pear but it will not grow in every geographical area. Anjou (D'Anjou) and Bartlett are partially self-fruitful and they may be used to pollinate other varieties of pear trees. Other good heirloom varieties are Bosc, Comice, and Seckle.

Plums: There are two types of plums: European and Japanese. European and Japanese plums will not cross-pollinate one another.

1. European varieties are Damson and Stanley and both are self-fruitful.

2. Japanese varieties are Abundance, Burbank, Friar, Methley, Redheart, and Santa Rosa. The Methley and Santa Rosa plum trees are partially self-fruitful.

Some plum trees produce a sterile pollen that will not pollinate any other plum tree. If the Methley plum variety will grow in your area then it is a good choice because it is self-fruitful and it will successfully pollinate almost all other Japanese plum varieties.

Nut Trees

Pecan Trees: Pecan trees do well in southern climates. Each tree has a female flower (the pistillate) and a male flower (the staminate). The female flower appears on the new growth each season and the male flower appears on last year's growth. On some trees the female flower matures first and later the male flower matures (called a protogynous variety). On other trees the male flower matures first and later the female flower matures (called a protandrous variety). Therefore it is critical to have at least two different varieties of pecan trees in close proximity to each other and one of those trees should be a protogynous variety and the other tree should be a protandrous variety. This will  ensure good cross fertilization because in the early part of the season the female flower on one tree will be mature when the male flower on the other tree will be mature. A little later in the season the opposite flower on each tree will be mature. Most employees in a garden center are not aware of this information and the only thing they will tell you is that you just need two different varieties of pecan trees. This is not true. If you have two trees and both have the male flowers mature first then cross-pollination will not occur. You need to have the female flowers on one tree mature at the same time the male flower is mature on another tree. The following table lists some of the more common varieties of each type of pecan tree. Please pick at least one variety from each side of the following table if you desire to have a good crop of pecans each year.

Female then Male **Protogynous**	**Male then Female** **Protandrous**
Choctaw *	Caddo **
Curtis ***	Cape Fear
Elliot **	Desirable ***
Harris Super	Farley
Mahan	Hastings *
Mahan-Stuart	Moore
Moneymaker	Success
Schley *	
Stuart	
Wichita **	

The **Barton** pecan variety (**) is the one pecan variety that is considered to be self-fertile because there is a good overlap of its mature male and female flowers each season.

In my opinion the best varieties have an * after their names. Three *** is a higher rating than one *.

I have planted pecan trees in three of the different places I have lived. The vast majority of my pecan trees died the second or third year after planting in all three areas. However, I was very successful with one Desirable pecan tree and one Elliot pecan tree and both trees reached a height of about 30-feet tall and they both produced a big crop of pecans each year. Then I sold that property and moved to a new location. I have tried planting pecan trees at my current location but I have not been successful with them here. The pecan trees I plant here always die either the second or third year after planting. I mention this so you will know that I am not an expert gardener and that I also have failures as well as success stories.

Note: If your local nursery has pecan trees for sale and those pecan trees are simply labeled "Papershell Pecans" then do not buy them. You do not know what variety you are buying and therefore you will probably never get a crop of pecans from those trees. If this is the situation in your area then you may need to mail order your pecan trees from an internet store that sells the exact pecan varieties you will need.

Black Walnut Trees: Black walnut trees will grow in almost every state and in southern Canada and each tree will live about 200 years. Black walnut trees are wind pollinated. To start a new tree I first remove a fresh black walnut from inside its outer slimy protective casing called a husk. I wear kitchen rubber gloves when I do this to keep the stains off my hands. But I do not crack the inner walnut shell. I then plant the entire black walnut inside its shell during the fall about two inches below ground and about twelve inches apart. About one out of every five walnuts I plant will produce a short tree the following year. I normally allow the small trees to grow for between one to three years and then in the late fall I transplant my black walnut trees to their future permanent locations. The black walnut will produce a long tap root so you should not wait more than three years to transplant your trees. Or you can plant your black walnuts in the ground where you want them to grow into a tree. If you do this then plant at least four or five black walnuts in one small area about ten-inches apart in a big circle and wait and see which nuts begin to grow into a tree. Space the walnut trees about 25-feet apart. The tree will start producing nuts in about ten years but it takes about 20 or 30 years to reach a high level of nut production from each tree. (Note: This is the way black walnut trees have reproduced themselves for thousands of years. Please keep this in mind if you are told you shouldn't plant a black walnut but that you should buy a special black walnut tree from a nursery because the nursery trees are disease free or they have been grafted onto special root stocks. There is absolutely nothing wrong with buying a black walnut tree from a nursery and there is also nothing wrong with planting black walnuts yourself and growing your own trees.)

Chestnut Trees: The American Chestnut will not survive due to a blight that will attack it in the United States of America. Several years ago I planted one "Dunstan" Chinese Hybrid Chestnut tree and two "Sweetheart" Chinese Hybrid Chestnut trees. All three trees grew extremely well for about five years. The Dunstan tree grew the tallest. Then one spring a blight appeared on the Dunstan tree and by the end of the summer it was dead. However, both of the Sweetheart trees are still doing fine, they are both about 25-feet tall, and they both produce a nice crop of big chestnuts each fall.

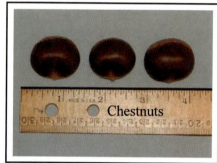
Chestnuts

Almond Trees: Almond trees frequently do well in climates where peach trees do well. I have only planted two "Hall's Hardy" almond trees. They both grew well for about six years. Then one of the trees developed a blight and it died. The other almond tree is still alive but it is a very weak tree and it never produces any almonds. Therefore I cannot offer any good practical advice about almond trees.

Grape Vines

Grapes are highly recommended because:

1. Grapes can be eaten fresh.
2. Grapes can be easily dried into raisins for future consumption.
3. Grapes can be made into a delicious jelly.
4. Grapes can be fermented into a delightful wine.

There are two different major varieties of grapes: bunch grapes and muscadines. In some regions bunch grapes yield superior results and in some regions muscadines yield superior results. At the current time I have both types of grapes planted and they both do well. The bunch grapes mature in late August or early September and the muscadine grapes mature in late September or early October.

When I start a new vineyard I always purchase my grape vines from a nursery in the spring. My personal experience has been that about one grape vine out of every five that I purchase will not survive.

1. **Bunch Grapes:** The grapes grow in clusters with between 40 to 100 grapes per cluster.

2. **Muscadines:** The grapes grow on short stems with between 2 to 5 grapes per stem. A single muscadine grape is usually about twice a big as a single bunch grape.

Grape vines need to be pruned every year. If you decide to grow grapes then you should do some internet research on how to prune the types of grapes you buy, or you should acquire a good book on how to grow grapes.

Berry Bushes

Blackberry Bushes: Blackberries will thrive and spread far beyond their original planting site. Their underground root system grows and grows and new stalks shoot up each spring from these underground roots. The first year the stalk grows between four to six feet tall. The second year the stalk produces blackberries. Then the stalk dies. However, the underground roots continue to grow and spread out and the blackberry patch will continue to get larger and larger with each passing year. The easiest way to start blackberries is to dig up the roots of some wild blackberries and transplant those roots in a very sunny location on your property. However, there is now a "thornless blackberry variety" for sale at some garden shops and if I were starting a blackberry patch from scratch today then that is probably the type of blackberry I would invest in.

Blueberry Bushes: Blueberries require cross-pollination. There are two basic types of blueberries as follows:

1. **Highbush Blueberries:** They were named because they grow taller than wild blueberries, which are called a huckleberry. Huckleberries grow very close to the ground, usually no more than about 12-inches high. The highbush blueberries are usually grown in the northeastern United States. Some good varieties of highbush blueberries are Bluecrop, Bluejay, and Spartan.

2. **Rabbiteye Blueberries:** They were named because the fruit starts off pink, which is the same color as the eyes of a white rabbit. As the berries ripen they gradually turn a bright blue. The rabbiteye blueberry is usually grown in the southeastern United States. Rabbiteye blueberries have almost no diseases, they are easy to grow, and they will live about twenty-years. They will grow to a height of between six to seven feet tall. Some good varieties of rabbiteye blueberries are Climax, Powder Blue, Premier, and Tifblue. I have two plants of each of these four different varieties planted in one long row on my property, with the early varieties at one end of the row and the late varieties at the opposite end of the row. Every year all the varieties produce flowers at almost the same exact time and later the blueberries all mature at almost the same exact time. Some of the blueberries on all the different plants will ripen and turn a bright blue and they will contain enough sugar to be harvested. Therefore I pick the ripe blueberries off all my bushes the same day. Several days later a few more blueberries on each bush will be ripe and I will harvest them. This will continue for about four weeks and at that time I will have harvested all the blueberries on all the bushes. The reason I mention this is because I no longer believe that it makes any difference whether a blueberry variety is named an early, mid-season, or late variety. They will all mature at approximately the same rate over the same approximate time period.

Strawberries: Strawberries grow close to the ground. The strawberries themselves are actually in contact with the ground. This makes it easy for insects and other critters to gnaw on them. I have personally never been satisfied with the performance of strawberries where I have lived so I no longer plant them. However, your area may be more receptive to strawberries and you may have more success with them than I have had.

Conclusion

I have over 30 different gardening books and I have read them all from cover to cover. Many of my books are about one specific topic and a few of them were written as a reference book for a professional grower in order to help him or her maximize the yield from his or her commercial crops. Over the years I have tried many of the strategies recommend in these different books.

Based on my entire collection of gardening books the two gardening books I would recommend today to a new gardener would be the following:

1. **New Illustrated Guide to Gardening,** Reader's Digest, 2000.
2. **Seed Sowing and Saving**, Turner, 1998.

After I post a gardening article on my web site I sometimes receive emails from people who ask me which books I copy my gardening information from. I politely reply that I don't just copy the information from any gardening book.

Instead I simply start writing about a garden topic (or a firearm topic or a economic topic) with which I am familiar and that I have some personal knowledge about. When I am finished typing everything I know into my computer then I check the spelling of some words that I don't have memorized, and I sometimes complete a list with the names of the items I don't have memorized.

For example, in this chapter I did not remember the name of every pecan tree that fell into each of the two categories. I only remembered the names of the pecan trees I have personally planted and that I have had some success with. Therefore I checked my pecan book and filled in the table with the names of the other pecan varieties to make that list as useful as possible to anyone who might be interested in that topic. The same thing applies to the names of the different types of fruit trees. The only ones I have memorized are the ones I have actually grown and I had to look up the names of all the other varieties. I also looked up the birth and death date of "Johnny Appleseed" who I first heard about when I was in the fourth grade.

But at least 95% of this chapter (and almost everything else I write) is nothing more than a "system dump" from the information stored in my brain. There is nothing special in this chapter. This chapter only contains common knowledge information that almost all other older gardeners also know.

Chapter Twenty-Five

How to Grow Fruit Trees from Seed

Genesis 1:11 - *Then God said, "Let the earth bring forth grass, the herb that yields seed, and the fruit tree that yields fruit according to its kind, whose seed is in itself, on the earth;" and it was so.*

Fruit trees may be successfully grown from the seeds of a "heirloom variety" fruit. However, fruit trees will usually not grow from the seeds of a "hybrid variety" fruit. Some people assume that since you can't reliably grow fruit trees from hybrid fruits then it is not possible to grow fruit trees from any type of fruit. Those people would be wrong. Fruit trees may be grown from good quality heirloom variety fruit. However, it will take between four to seven years longer for a fruit tree grown from seed to begin producing fruit when compared to a fruit tree you purchase from a local nursery that is already several years old.

You do **not** have to immediately plant your fruit seeds and pits. It is possible to save the seeds and the pits from your fresh fruit in the refrigerator and then plant those seeds on some future date. This would be practical if you are not currently living in a location where you can grow fruit trees. Instead of throwing your fruit seeds into the trash you could save the seeds and the pits from any heirloom variety fruit you now eat. Then if you relocate to another area at some future time you could take those small fruit seeds and fruit pits with you and start your own orchard. (Note: If you wish to save fruit seeds and fruit pits for the future then after you have dried them you should store them in your refrigerator inside a plastic bag without any holes and do not add any additional moisture to the seeds or pits.)

Instructions for Growing Fruit Trees From Seed

1. **Fruit Varieties:** You must know the exact name (or variety) of the fruit. Most of the fruit sold in a grocery store is sold by its name, such as Golden Delicious Apples, or Bartlett Pears, or Bing Cherries. Knowing the name of the fruit is important for the following reasons:

    a. If the fruit is not named then it may be a hybrid variety and although it may eventually grow into a tree it may never produce any fruit.
    b. Some fruits require a pollinator and you will need to plant compatible varieties if you want your trees to produce any fruit.
    c. Some fruits may not grow in your climate. Therefore you must first verify that a specific type of fruit may be successfully grown in your geographical region.

    Pear Seeds

2. **Fruit Selection:** Select heirloom fruit varieties that can be grown from seed and not hybrid variety fruits. The best fruit for seed and pit collection is fruit that has been allowed to ripen on the fruit tree. Therefore when a specific fruit is in season in your area, if you can find that locally grown fruit at your grocery store or at a road side stand or at a local farmer's market, then it will probably be tree ripened fruit. Another option would be a "pick-it-yourself orchard." Tree ripened fruit is better than fruit that has been shipped from a long distance away and that has gradually ripened while it was in transit. As an example, Ingles Grocery Stores will usually buy their fresh fruit from local fruit growers when that fruit is in season locally. Tree ripened fruit will produce seeds or pits that have stored as many nutrients as possible inside their seeds or pits so their germination rate will be optimal and more of their seedlings will survive. However, it is still okay to plant the seeds from fruit even if that fruit was not ripened on the fruit tree. The only disadvantage is that your germination rate will be a little lower and a few more of your seedlings may not survive. However, all the seedlings that do survive will eventually grow into a healthy fruit tree just like the seedlings grown from tree ripened fruit.

There are hundreds of different heirloom varieties of apples, pears, and peaches but very, very few of them are grown by commercial growers. The following very short list of heirloom fruits are ones you may be able to find at your local grocery store:

Apples, Red: Jonathan, Red Delicious.
Applies, Yellow: Golden Delicious (sweet), Granny Smith (tart).
Cherries, Sweet: Bing, Black Tartarian.
Cherries, Sour: Early Richmond, Montmorency, Stella.
Peaches: Belle of Georgia, Elberta, Redhaven.
Pears: Anjou (or D'Anjou), Bartlett, Bosc, Comice, Seckle.
Plums: Methley (purple-red skin), Santa Rosa (dark reddish purple skin).

Although it was mentioned earlier please let me remind you to first verify that the heirloom variety you are interested in will actually grow in your geographical area.

3. **Final Ripening:** If the fruit is not yet fully ripe then allow it to finish ripening. If the fruit still feels firm then allow it to ripen at room temperature for just a few more days until it feels just a little soft.

4. **Eating:** Eat the fruit. Save the seeds or the center pit. This is an extremely important step because if you don't like the taste of the original fruit then you shouldn't be trying to grow a fruit tree from its seed to produce more of that same exact type of fruit.
   Seeds: Dry the moisture off the seeds using a paper towel.
   Pits: Scrub the pit gently with some warm water and a soft brush to remove any flesh still clinging to the pit.

Peach Pit

5. **Drying:** Dry the seeds or pits at room temperature.
   Seeds: Dry seeds for about three days. The seeds are small and thin and they will normally dry adequately in three days.
   Pits: Dry pits for about ten days. The pits are larger and it takes longer for the larger pits to dry.

6. **Stratification:** Stratification means to chill the seeds or pits at a temperature between 35°F to 40°F (or 2°C to 4°C). Most refrigerators are ideal for this purpose because they consistently control the internal refrigerator temperature within this range of values. Wrap the seeds or pits inside a slightly moist paper towel and then put them inside a ventilated plastic bag in the refrigerator. An ordinary sandwich bag may be used after you punch a few holes in the bag. Write the name of the fruit (such as Granny Smith Apple) and the date on the outside of the plastic bag with a permanent magic marker. Instead of a paper towel you may use a small amount of peat moss inside the plastic bag. Keep the paper towel or the peat moss slightly moist while chilling the seeds or pits.
   Chill the seeds or pits the following number of days:

   Apple Seeds: 60 to 120 days.
   Pear Seeds: 60 to 120 days.
   Cherry Pits: 90 to 105 days.
   Peach Pits: 90 to 105 days.
   Plum Pits: 90 to 105 days.

   If you don't have a refrigerator you can let nature chill your seeds for you. Simply plant your seeds or pits following the "outdoor germination" instructions in step seven but plant your seeds or pits in the late fall of the year.

7. **Germination:** Germination means to sprout the seeds or pits. Do not split or try to break the pits. (Note: The one exception is peach pits. You may carefully crack a peach pit and remove the small almond shaped seed inside.) Only about one seed or one pit in every four will germinate. You can germinate your seeds or pits indoors or outdoors.

Indoors: Transfer the seeds or pits to a shallow planting pot or tray that is at least five inches deep. Cover the seeds or pits with some good quality dirt. Plant apple and pear seeds about one-inch deep and plant pits about two-inches deep. Place in front of a sunny window, or outdoors if the temperature is warm, and then wait. Keep the dirt moist but not soaking wet. If the dirt is too wet then the seeds or pits will rot. Wait for the seedlings to grow. When the seedling is between eight to twelve-inches tall it may be transplanted outdoors if the weather is warm, such as in the late spring. Do not plant seedlings until after the danger of the last spring frost has passed. Mulch the ground around the seedlings but do not put any mulch against the tree trunk to prevent trunk rot and undesirable above ground roots.

Outdoors: You can plant your seeds or pits outdoors in the location where you want your fruit trees to grow. Plant four seeds or four pits about ten-inches apart in a circle. Plant each seed about one-inch deep or plant each pit about three-inches deep. Water the planting hole. Keep the ground moist during the first two weeks after you plant your seeds or pits. After the first two weeks if it doesn't rain at least once per week then water the planting area yourself once per week. Do not over water the planting area to avoid rotting the seeds or pits in the ground. Mulch the area around your planting hole to keep the moisture in the ground and to prevent the sun from overheating the dirt. If more than one seed or pit begins to grow into a seedling in one hole then you can leave the strongest seedling in the original hole and transplant the other seedlings to a hole where nothing is growing.

8. **Orchard Planning:** Keep track of the name of each type of seed or pit you plant in each location so you will know the type of tree that is growing there. The easiest way to do this is to plant a single variety of seeds or pits in one row. For example, if you have four apple varieties then start four long rows. If you have Golden Delicious apple seeds then you should plant those seeds in one of the center rows to provide good cross-pollination to the other varieties of apple trees. Many of your seeds will eventually sprout into a small apple tree. In about twelve years you will have your own apple orchard with a balanced variety of the different types of apples that will ensure good cross-pollination and a heavy crop of apples each year. This same orchard planning concept also applies to cherries, peaches, pears, and plums.

9. **Fertilization and Watering:** The first year you transplant a seeding outdoors you should water that seedling at least once per week if it doesn't rain. It is okay to add just a little bit of liquid fertilizer to your watering pot when you water your seedlings. Beginning in the second year you should fertilize your fruit trees twice per year. Fertilize in the early spring of each year before leaf and bloom set and fertilize again in the fall of each year after the leaves have fallen off the tree.

10. **Staking:** When the fruit tree is about two feet tall it will need to be supported with stakes until its center trunk is strong enough to withstand the wind and rain in your area so your tree will not get bent over. You may use either two or three stakes per tree. If you use two stakes them put them on opposite sides of the tree. If you use three stakes then space them an equal distance apart in a circle around the tree. Drive the stakes down into the ground about twelve-inches from the center trunk of the tree. The tops of the stakes should be about four-feet above ground. Tie the fruit tree trunk to the stakes using thin strips of old cloth or some pieces you cut from some old pantyhose. This will help the fruit tree to grow straight during the early part of its life. You can remove the stakes when the tree is about five feet tall and the tree trunk is strong enough to withstand a strong wind.

11. **Pruning:** Do **not** prune your fruit trees during their early years. Wait until your fruit trees are mature and they are producing fruit before you consider pruning your fruit trees. The best time to prune a fruit tree is when it is dormant during the winter months. The one exception is if you notice any type of disease or blight on a tree limb then you should immediately remove that entire limb from the tree. If the disease or blight reappears on that same tree then you should consider digging that tree out of the ground and burning the tree in a safe area.

12. **Harvesting Fruit:** During the first six years of each tree's life you should pluck off any tiny fruits that set in the early spring. This will allow the tree to grow and mature and not spend its energy on fruit production. If you don't immediately remove those tiny fruits in the early spring during those first six

years then your tree will suffer because it is too young to support a fruit crop. It will normally take at least eight to twelve years for fruit trees that are grown from seed to begin yielding fruit. Please remember to be patient. However, if fifteen or more years have passed and your other fruit trees of the same type are yielding fruit but one tree is not then you may have a sterile fruit tree and you should consider removing it from your orchard and starting a new tree in its spot.

13. **Orchard Management:** If you will strategically replace the poor quality or low producing fruit trees in your orchard every two or three years then you will not have to replace all the fruit trees at approximately the same time when they grow old and die. Instead you will have a healthy orchard that will always bear fruit every year because you are periodically replacing the poor quality fruit trees.

Chapter Twenty-Six

How to Preserve Food for Future Consumption
Using Three Simple Old Fashioned Methods

Basic Food Safety Precautions

1. Wash your hands thoroughly before handling any type of food.
2. Rinse the raw food thoroughly before processing and storing it.
3. Use clean food processing equipment.
4. Always wash the utensils before using them on a different food item to prevent a problem of cross-contamination.
5. Use clean storage containers.
6. Examine the food carefully and discard any food that has mold or bruises or slime or insects or other problems.
7. The shelf life of the food will not be extended forever but it can be increased by a few weeks to a few months (or longer depending on the food item and the preservation method).

The Three Traditional Food Preservation Methods

There are three simple ways to preserve food using traditional old fashioned procedures that do not require any special chemicals, or salt, or equipment:

1. In the ground.
2. In a root cellar.
3. Drying.

Let's examine each of the above three methods one at a time.

In the Ground
(Appropriate for Carrots and Radishes in the Fall)

Leave the vegetables in the original ground where they grew during the summer. This technique works well with carrots and radishes. Mulch the ground above the vegetables with a thick layer of straw. However, if the weather has not yet turned cold and you leave radishes in the ground then they will go to seed.

In a Root Cellar
(Appropriate for Some Vegetables and Some Fruits)

A root cellar is a cool dry dark place underground where the temperature remains between 40°F to 60°F (or 4°C to 15°C).

1. The depth of the root cellar below ground will vary between 1 to 3 feet depending on the frost line in the area where you live. The frost line is how deep the ground freezes in winter.
2. Humidity must be controlled.
3. Insects and rodents must be kept out.

A simple root cellar can be made from a clean empty food grade 55 gallon drum. Plant the drum sideways below ground under at least 12 inches of dirt. Put the food in the drum and then attach the drum lid. Shovel some dirt against the lid to keep it cool inside the drum. The drum will stay cool and it will keep out the air and insects and rodents. Do not place the fruit or vegetables directly against the sides of the drum. Instead store the fruit or vegetables inside wood boxes inside the drum.

Apples, peaches, pears, plums, and tomatoes release ethylene gas while in storage and this gas will cause other foods to ripen and spoil more rapidly. Therefore they should be stored by themselves and not with other foods.

Apples: Store apples in crates no more than three apples high per crate. The crates should be stored on a high shelf in the root cellar.

Cabbage: Remove the roots and the exterior leaves. Store upside down one layer high loosely packed in crates. Cover the crate with a tarp or sheet of plastic.

Carrots: Cut off the crown. Rinse thoroughly. Stack upright in a plastic or wood box and cover with newspaper.

Corn, Stowell's Heirloom Evergreen White Corn: *Before* the corn is fully ripe pull up the stalks with the roots still attached and store them upside down inside your root cellar. The corn will continue to ripen over several months. Therefore you will be able to eat fresh corn-on-the-cob for between three to five more months. That is the reason it is called "evergreen corn." (Note: After the corn has fully ripened, if you will peel back the husks on one ear of corn on three or four different stalks and then allow the corn to dry on the cob you will have "corn seed" to plant in the spring. Twist the corn kernels off the cobs using your hands and discard the small kernels near the end of the ear. Save the bigger corn kernels and plant them to produce another fresh crop of corn.)

Onions: Allow them to dry thoroughly. Then tie them together in small bunches and hang them upside down from a string or a wire. White and yellow onions store well but purple onions do not store well.

Pears: Pears are not ripe enough to eat until after they have been stored for at least a few weeks.

Potatoes: You may dig up the potatoes when the green vine above your potatoes dies or you can leave the potatoes in the ground for a few more weeks. After digging your potatoes allow them to age in a shaded well-ventilated area for about two more weeks. Do not put them in the sun because the sun will turn them green and the green toxin that is created is harmful to pregnant women and nursing women and to babies. Remove any loose dirt clinging to the potatoes but do not wash the potatoes. A very thin layer of dirt will help to greatly extend the shelf life of the potatoes. After two weeks in the shade transfer the potatoes into the root cellar. Store them in a wood crate but not a plastic crate. Cover them with straw. They will stay fresh for up to six months.

Tomatoes: Pick while they are still green and before they are ripe. Wrap each tomato in a piece of paper. They will keep for approximately three months. Before using a tomato, remove it and expose it to some warm air and some light and it will finish ripening.

Drying
(Appropriate for Meats, Fruits, and a few Vegetables)

Introduction to Drying:

1. The food is placed on a tray or a screen and then dried using a good source of heat, such as the heat of the sun, or an oven at very low temperature, or near a wood-burning fireplace. The drying location must be well ventilated and it should not be in direct sunlight. The drying time will vary considerably depending on the outdoor temperature and the humidity in the air at the time of drying. The guidelines below are rough averages and you will need to check your food every day to determine if it is dry enough.
2. Most vegetables cannot be dried because they lose too many nutrients and too much flavor.
3. Dry fruit will feel leathery and it will not contain any moisture pockets. It should feel tough but it should not snap when bent.
4. You must store dried foods in a moisture free and air-tight container such as glass jars, plastic freezer bags, or plastic food saver containers.
5. Store the dried food in a cool dry dark place out of the light between 40°F to 60°F (or 4°C to 15°C).

6. Dried fruit may be eaten as a snack, or it may be used in a granola recipe, or it may be rehydrated by covering it with warm water for one-hour.

Sun Drying: Dry your food on a hot dry day when the humidity is relatively low. Sun drying requires several consecutive days of 100°F (38°C) dry weather. Dry the food in a shaded area and do not place the food in direct sunlight.

Oven Drying: Start at 175°F (80°C) for the first 30 minutes to kill any parasites or pathogens in the fruit. Then reduce the oven drying temperature to between 120°F to 140°F (50°C to 60°C) for fruits. You must frequently turn and rotate the fruit while it is drying.

How to Dry Meat

Trim all the fat off the meat. Then cut the lean meat into strips one-inch wide and 1/4-inch thick. Meat should be dried between 165°F to 185°F (74°C to 85°C) to kill all the potentially harmful microorganisms that might be in the meat. But the temperature should not be so hot that it cooks the meat. The objective is to dry the meat at a safe temperature and not cook it. When the meat snaps or cracks when it is bent then it is dry enough. (Note: Do not discard the fat if the fat is fresh. Instead you should render the fat and then use it strategically in your diet.)

How to Dry Vegetables and Fruit

Vegetables and fruits that are to be used in a recipe can be processed following the instructions below. To eat the dried fruit, put the dried fruit in some boiling water for 1/2 hour or in some warm water for 1 hour.

Apples: Rinse thoroughly and then slice into thin pieces about 1/4-inch thick. Remove the core and the seeds but do not remove the outside peel. Soak the apples in a solution of water and lemon juice before drying. The drying time for thinly sliced apples is about 3 hours. For apples that have been quartered it takes about 2 or 3 days. The apple is dry when it does not feel moist or sticky.

Beans: Most beans, such as kidney beans and pinto beans, do not require any special effort to dry them for future consumption. Pick the bean pod when the beans are fully mature. Leave the beans inside the pods for about two weeks at normal room temperatures to give the beans a chance to harden and to protect them from a multitude of insects. Then remove the beans and discard the pods. The beans will continue to dry at normal room temperatures. (Note: The dried beans may be planted as seed in the spring to produce a fresh crop of beans.) Dried beans will remain fresh and easy to cook for at least two years. If you still have some dried beans left over after three years then they will probably require a really long soaking in a water bath and processing inside a pressure cooker to make them soft enough to eat.

Beets: Rinse thoroughly. Peel the beet and then slice into 1/4-inch thick pieces. Cook the beet pieces. Then drain the beet pieces and dry until they feel leathery.

Blueberries: Sort out any defective blueberries and any twigs or stems. Thoroughly rinse the good blueberries. Place in a single layer on a screen or tray. They will dry in about 5 or 6 days in a warm location or about 4 hours inside an oven at very low temperature (120°F to 140°F or 50°C to 60°C).

Cherries: Rinse thoroughly and then remove the pit. Place on a drying tray in a single layer where the cherries do not touch each other. They will dry in about 4 days outdoors. Or dry in an oven at 140°F (60°C) for about 6 hours. They should feel leathery and slightly sticky. Do not over-dry the cherries. However, it is better to have them a little too dry than not dry enough because if they aren't dry then mold will develop on the cherries. Store the dried cherries in an airtight container.

Corn, Reid's Heirloom Yellow Dent Corn: After this heirloom yellow corn has fully ripened you have two options:

1. You can eat some of the corn fresh, and

2. You can pull up some of the stalks with the corn still attached. Peel back the husks. Hang the corn on their stalks upside down in a well-ventilated area for four more weeks. Wait until the kernels are hard and dry. Twist off the full kernels of corn using your hands. Discard the small kernels near the end of the cob. As you need it you may grind the dried corn into corn meal and use it in a corn meal recipe to make corn bread, hush puppies, nacho chips, taco shells, or corn batter for corn dogs (you can substitute canned Vienna sausages for the hot dogs). (Note: The dried corn kernels are also "corn seed" and you may plant them in the spring to produce another fresh crop of corn.)

Figs: Wash the figs. Boil some water and add two fig leaves. Then quickly dip each fig in the boiling water for three seconds and then immediately remove it. Cut the fig in half. Place them skin side down on a drying tray. Keep the figs separated and dry outdoors. Or dry in a 130ºF (54ºC) oven for about 5 hours.

Grapes: After the dew has dried off them but before midday you should harvest the grapes with about 3 inches of stem attached. The stem enhances the flavor during the drying process. Rinse thoroughly. Dip in boiling water for 30 seconds to crack the skins. Hang the grapes up by their stems and let them dry naturally in a warm room with no extra heat. They will turn into raisins. They are dry when the center of the raison contains no moisture. Seedless grapes are best for making raisins.

Onions: Harvest the onions immediately after the tops die and fall over. Rinse thoroughly and then slice into round slices such as for a hamburger, or dice into small cubes. Place on a tray and dry using the heat of the sun. Or dry at 120ºF (50ºC) for about 24 hours, stirring the onions every 8 hours.

Peaches: Rinse thoroughly and then slice into quarter sections and remove the stone. Place on a drying tray. Turn the peach quarters over every four hours.

Pears: Rinse thoroughly and then slice into halves. Place on a drying tray and cover with a cloth. Dry using the heat of the sun for about six days. Or cut the fresh pears into quarters and they will dry in about three days. Or dry near a wood stove for about two days.

Peppers (Sweet): Rinse thoroughly and then slice into pieces no more than one-inch wide. Remove the seeds. Allow them to dry slowly on a drying tray.

Potatoes: Rinse thoroughly. The skin may be left on or peeled off. Cut into 1/8-inch thick round slices. Put the sliced potatoes in boiling water for 8 minutes. Then transfer the potatoes to cool water or ice water for 15 minutes. Dry the potatoes with a paper towel or a clean cloth towel. Dry the potatoes using the heat of the sun, or an oven, or a wood-burning fireplace, until the potato slices are dry and crisp.

Plums: Rinse thoroughly and then slice into halves and remove the pit. Place on a drying tray and cover with a cloth. Dry using the heat of the sun for about four days.

Spinach: Select clean fresh leaves and do not rinse them. Place them individually on a drying tray in a warm location. The leaf is dry enough when the leaf breaks easily when you bend it. To prepare for eating boil the dried leaves in water.

Strawberries: Rinse thoroughly and then slice into halves. Place the cut side up on a tray and dry using the heat of the sun.

Tomatoes: Plum tomatoes, such as the Roma tomato, dry well. Rinse thoroughly. Dip briefly in boiling water to loosen the skins. Remove the skins. Slice the tomato in half or quarters and remove all the seeds. (Note: Save the seeds and dry them on a piece of paper and then plant the dried seeds the following spring to produce a fresh crop of tomatoes.) Sprinkle some salt on a drying tray and place the tomato halves on the salted tray. Cover and dry in the sun. Turn the tomatoes over every four hours during the day. Bring the tomatoes indoors at night. Store in glass jars when dry. If you wish you may cover the tomatoes in oil inside the jar.

Turnips: Rinse thoroughly and then slice into 1/8-inch thick pieces. Push a thin wire or a string (attached to a needle) through each slice and then hang the slices so the slices cannot touch and dry in a warm area for 10 to 14 days. Then place the turnips on a cookie sheet and heat in a 160ºF (71ºC) oven for five minutes. Allow to cool and then store. This method will preserve the turnips for up to five years.

Special Footnote about Food Vacuum Sealers

Many dry foods, such as sugar, salt, peppercorns, corn starch, baking soda, white rice, oatmeal, grits, instant milk, instant potatoes, and pasta can be protected from insects, oxygen, and humidity by sealing them inside vacuum seal bags. Vacuum sealing will also significantly extend the shelf life of many foods because you eliminate the oxygen and the humidity that can gradually destroy the food.

If you use vacuum sealed storage bags you will not need to purchase any of the "oxygen absorber packets" because the vacuum sealing process will remove all the oxygen from inside the specially designed bags.

Vacuum sealing is also highly, highly recommended for the long-term preservation of individually wrapped hard candies, such as miniature Tootsie Rolls, Caramels, Peppermints, Spearmints, etc. Vacuum sealing hard candies will significantly extend their shelf lives and preserve their original natural smell and their original flavor.

A cheap good quality food vacuum sealer will cost about $40 and a two-roll box of vacuum seal bags will cost about $22.

If you buy the 11-inch wide rolls that are 16-feet long then you can cut individuals bags from the roll to the exact length you need. Therefore there will be very little waste because:

1. You won't need to seal a small item inside a large bag, and
2. You can seal the foods in the quantities you think you will need so you can open one bag at a time and the rest of your food will remain fresh inside its own vacuum sealed bag.

Immediately after you vacuum seal an item inside a vacuum storage bag use a medium tip permanent black magic marker to write a brief description of the contents on the top of the bag and the date you sealed the bag, such as:

16 ounces Pure Salt, Sealed March 2010.

Chapter Twenty-Six: How to Preserve Food for Future Consumption

One Precious Life

"Oh! How precious," are the exclamations
    of the crowd as they stare at the baby girl.

"Oh! How beautiful," are the words heard
    when the baby girl grows up and becomes a new bride.

Time passes and the bride becomes a mother,
    a grandmother, and a very old woman.

Her hair thins and turns white and
    her face withers and wrinkles with age.

"Oh! How precious and beautiful," God exclaims
    as He welcomes His reborn daughter into Heaven.

Scripture References: First John 5:13, Romans 6:23, Titus 1:2, Isaiah 46:4, Philippians 3:20-21, Second Peter 1:11.

Poem: One Precious Life

Chapter Twenty-Seven

How to Convert Human Waste into a Safe Garden Compost Fertilizer

An Updated Modern Scientifically Safe Procedure that Replaces the
Ancient Oriental Unsafe "Night Soil" Method of Recycling Human Waste.

Preface

If any of the following events should occur:

1. a peak oil crisis or a World War that results in a significant reduction in the transportation of food, or
2. commercial fertilizer becomes scarce or extremely expensive, or
3. unemployment increases significantly and many families are forced to grow their own vegetables, or
4. there is a local, national, or worldwide famine,

then the following information would be extremely valuable to everyone who has a vegetable garden. The following information would allow a family to safely and economically enrich their garden soil **every year** in order to provide a continuous harvest of fresh vegetables.

Danger

"Night Soil" is untreated human waste mixed with garden soil. Do **not** use untreated human waste in a garden area. Human waste contains harmful microorganisms that are fatal to humans.

Introduction

All human waste originally came from the earth. And all human waste will eventually be converted back into the earth. If this process is properly controlled then the harmful microorganisms inside human waste will be destroyed and the resulting compost can be safely used to replenish the nutrients in garden soil. Compost is one of nature's best mulches and soil enhancements. It may also be successfully used **instead** of fertilizer. Compost helps to aerate and loosen clays soils. It also helps sandy soils retain their moisture.

The Indoor Toilet Bucket (originally called a "Chamber Pot")

Any 5-gallon or 6-gallon bucket with a tight fitting lid may be used as an indoor toilet bucket. An ordinary toilet stool seat can be attached to the top of this bucket to make it easier to use.

After a person has deposited human waste (poop and urine and toilet paper) into the toilet bucket, sprinkle a little sawdust, or crumbled dry leaves, or dried grass clippings, or chopped brown pine needles, or shredded paper on top of the waste to help control the odor. Then replace the bucket lid to keep the smell inside the bucket.

The Compost Pile

Periodically transfer the contents of the toilet bucket to an outdoor compost pile that is a reasonable distance from your home but close to your garden area. Immediately cover the human waste on the compost pile with a layer of dried leaves, or shredded brown pine straw, or dried grass clippings, or shredded paper. You should use approximately the same amount of covering material as human waste. This will keep the odor under control and it will help keep the heat trapped inside the compost pile. Rinse or clean the toilet bucket and then return the empty toilet bucket to its normal location inside your home. Then immediately wash your hands.

Other Compost Pile Materials

Other desirable items that could be added to the compost pile include crushed egg shells, fruit and vegetable peels, used coffee grounds and filters (2% nitrogen), used tea bags, kitchen scraps, apple cores, fireplace ashes, shredded junk mail, shredded cardboard, garden weeds, and the shredded vines and shredded stalks from garden plants after harvesting the vegetables (such as corn stalks, bean vines, and tomato vines). Always chop or shred any large items into smaller pieces. Farm animal manure from grass eaters is also good if it is at least one-week old.

Do **not** add lime, bones, meat, dairy products, cooking grease, cat or dog droppings, disposable diapers, clothes dryer lint (synthetic fibers), paper with color pictures (potential heavy metals), walnut leaves, diseased plants, or poisonous plants (poison ivy) to your compost pile. (Note: Lime may be added to your garden soil but **not** to your compost pile.)

Alternate your compost covering materials and use a variety of different items. In other words, alternate the use of dried leaves, dried grass clippings, brown pine straw, and shredded paper. Spread each material into a relatively even layer across the top of your pile using a garden rake or hoe that is only used for this one purpose. Try to have approximately the same amount of brown materials (low nitrogen) as green materials (high nitrogen) inside your compost pile. **Green** refers to new or fresh items (freshly cut grass clippings, green pine needles, green leaves, fresh kitchen waste, and all types of fresh manure). **Brown** refers to old or dried items (month old dried out grass clippings, brown pine needles, dry leaves).

Compost Pile Size and Shape

A good size for a single compost pile is 3 feet in diameter and 3 feet deep. Once the pile gets to this size you should start another compost pile nearby.

Carbon/Nitrogen Mixture Ratios

The microorganisms that decompose materials into compost require carbon, nitrogen, water, heat, and oxygen. **Carbon** is used to provide energy. **Nitrogen** is used to form cell structures. As the tiny microorganisms consume these nutrients they produce heat inside the compost pile. The tiny microorganisms need approximately 30 times more carbon than nitrogen (or 30:1). Successful decomposition will take place if the carbon/nitrogen ratio is anywhere in the range between 20 to 40 (or 20:1 to 40:1). Whenever you add a material that has a low ratio you should also add a material that has a high ratio at the same time. Paper, sawdust, and wood ashes should be used in moderation because they have extremely high ratios. Pine straw needles should be chopped or shredded. Tree leaves are one of the best materials you can use to cover human waste because they are widely available and they are easily collected with a ordinary garden rake. However, variety is the key to success because each material brings its own unique blend of other nutrients to the compost pile. For example, grass clippings contain approximately 3.5% Nitrogen, 0.75% Phosphorus, and 2.5% Potassium, and they can be easily collected during the warm months when dried leaves may not be readily available.

Approximate Carbon/Nitrogen Ratios for Different Compost Materials

Ratio	Compost Material	Ratio	Compost Material
15:1	Kitchen Food Scraps	35:1	Fruit Waste
16:1	Human Waste	60:1	Leaves
17:1	Grass Clippings	60:1	Corn Stalks
20:1	Cow Manure	80:1	Straw
25:1	Horse Manure	85:1	Pine Needles
25:1	Vegetable Waste	170:1	Paper
26:1	Oak Leaves	400:1	Sawdust

Water Requirements (and the Top of the Compost Pile)

Do **not** let the compost pile get too dry or too wet. Either extreme is not good for the normal composting process. The moisture level inside the pile should be about the same as a wrung-out sponge. If you wear a rubber glove and you withdraw a handful of compost from inside the pile and you squeeze it tightly then you should be able to extract one or two drops of water.

If you live in a **wet climate** with good rainfall then your compost pile should have a round domed shaped top to help shed rainwater. However, if you live in a **dry climate** with minimum rainfall then your compost pile should have a concave bowl shaped top to capture and diffuse rainwater into the compost pile.

Temperature Requirements

During the **summer months** periodically check the temperature **inside** the compost pile. The easiest way to determine the temperature inside your compost pile is to use a special compost thermometer with a 20-inch stem. Or you could use any thermometer with a stem, such as an instant-read meat thermometer, but you must reserve that thermometer for this one specific application. If your thermometer has a 6-inch stem then dig a small temporary 14-inch deep hole in the compost pile and push the stem of the thermometer into the bottom of the hole to take a reading. Then remove the thermometer and fill in the hole.

The optimal **temperature** range for rapid **decomposition** is between 90°F to 140°F (32°C to 60°C). If the internal pile temperature drops below 90°F (32°C) then the normal decomposition process slows down significantly. If the temperature rises above 140°F (60°C) then **all** the microorganisms in the pile will die, including the beneficial ones.

Fortunately the harmful microorganisms in human waste are destroyed at temperatures between 131°F to 140°F (55°C to 60°C) or slightly higher. But the beneficial microorganisms that facilitate the compost process are not destroyed until the temperature exceeds 140°F (60°C). Therefore the pile should be "turned" if its internal temperature exceeds 140°F (60°C).

After the **final batch of human waste** has been added to the compost pile and the pile is approximately 3 feet in diameter and 3 feet high then pile temperature management becomes extremely important. If the temperature inside the compost pile can be kept at 131°F (55°C) or above for **at least three consecutive days** then all the harmful microorganisms **inside** the pile will die. To kill the microorganisms on the **outside** of the pile, the pile must then be "turned" over with a shovel so the outside of the pile is now on the inside of the pile, and a minimum internal pile temperature of 131°F (55°C) must be maintained for **at least three more days**.

After all the harmful microorganisms have been destroyed then the pile temperature can be allowed to fluctuate anywhere in the range between 90°F to 140°F (32°C to 60°C) and the pile will continue to decompose properly.

Compost Pile Management and Oxygen Requirements

Manage the human waste compost pile just like any other garden compost pile.

Live Earth Worms: Worms are extremely beneficial to have inside your compost pile. Therefore if you find some earth worms in your garden soil then you should carefully transfer them to your compost pile and they will multiply.

Safety: Tools and equipment used on the compost pile should **not** be used anywhere else. As a health safety precaution you should wear rubber gloves and you should wear a face dust mask when turning your compost pile to prevent the inhalation of any fungi or mold spores that may be present in your compost. When you are finished remember to wash your hands thoroughly.

Oxygen and Moisture: Do **not** cover your compost pile with a sheet of plastic because it will deprive your pile of necessary oxygen and moisture and your pile may get so hot it will kill the beneficial microorganisms that are necessary to properly decompose your compost materials.

Turning the Pile: Once a week during the **warm summer months** wear rubber gloves and use a pitchfork or shovel to move (turn) the entire pile a short distance to the side so the previous **top and outside** of the pile are now on the **bottom and inside** of the pile. This will add fresh air into the pile so the aerobic bacteria can more easily facilitate the composting process. It will also help to control the odor of the pile and it will shift any freshly laid insect larvae from the outside of the pile to the inside of the pile where they will be destroyed. If possible, turn the compost pile when the internal pile temperature drops below 90°F (32°C) or rises above 140°F (60°C), or if the pile begins to stink. As the composting process nears completion the internal pile temperature will remain below 90°F (32°C) even after the pile has been turned and it will continue to gradually get cooler and cooler.

Summer Temperatures: Under ideal conditions the internal compost pile temperature can reach 150°F (66°C) or higher during the warm summer months. When the compost pile temperature gets above 140°F (60°C) the beneficial compost microorganisms begin to die. However, any unusual rare exotic harmful microorganisms that might also be present will also be destroyed. Turning the compost pile when its temperature gets too high will bring its temperature back down to an acceptable level.

Winter Temperatures: The compost pile will be relatively inactive during cool and cold weather and if it is simply left alone it will continue to decay slowly and gradually into usable compost.

Waiting Period: Sometime after adding the **final batch of human waste** to a compost pile, the internal pile temperature must be kept at or above 131°F (55°C) for at least six consecutive days. After all the harmful microorganisms have been destroyed the pile should then be allowed to naturally decompose for **at least one-year** before using the compost in a garden area. This means you will need to have at least two or more compost piles so you can add fresh human waste material into a new compost pile while the old compost pile matures. After one-year when the compost process is complete the compost will consist of humus that can be safely used to enrich the soil in a garden plot that can be used to grow vegetables for human consumption.

Finished Compost Characteristics: The compost process will be complete when the compost has a uniform crumbly texture, a dark-brown color, and it has a pleasant slightly sweet aroma like fresh top soil. If you can **easily** recognize large pieces of your original covering materials, or pieces of food scraps, then the composting process is not yet complete.

Final Caution

If the internal compost pile temperature **cannot** be kept at 131°F (55°C) or higher for at least six consecutive days during the summer months then the compost will contain microorganisms that are fatal to humans. Therefore the minimum internal pile temperature is critical to the success of this process. Higher temperatures are better but a temperature lower than 131°F (55°C) is unacceptable.

If you are **not** sure if the temperature inside your compost pile was high enough during the summer to destroy all the harmful microorganisms then fully cook any garden produce from your garden and do not eat any of your garden vegetables raw. Fully cooking their garden produce is the procedure many oriental countries currently use to avoid serious health problems when they use "Night Soil." (Note: In most cases these oriental countries do not follow the above instructions and they simply discard their human waste directly into their garden areas. This is **not** a safe way to utilize human waste and you should **never** be tempted to follow this unsanitary method even if it does has a history that is several centuries old.)

Chapter Twenty-Eight

The Advantages of Mulch in a Garden

Your vegetable plants will produce more vigorously if you place some type of mulch on the ground around the plants (see picture on right).

Most people evaluate the success of their gardening efforts by the size and quantity of the vegetables they grow. However, the size and quantity of your vegetables is directly proportional to the root system of each vegetable plant. If the roots are properly cared for then your vegetable crop should be a good one.

The roots are responsible for transferring moisture and nutrients from the ground to the plant. This is one of the most important principles of successful gardening.

Mulch helps a plant's root system in all the following ways:

1. Mulch protects the ground from the direct rays and heat from the sun. This helps the ground to conserve its moisture for a longer period of time. Moist earth is essential to the transfer of nutrients into the roots that feed the plant.

2. Mulch helps the ground to stay at a more even temperature during the day and during the night. During the day it prevents the earth from baking under the sun. At night it helps the ground to stay warm and not release its warmth into the cool night air. By providing a more consistent ground temperature the root system will be stronger because it will not have to deal with temperature extremes.

3. Mulch minimizes the growth of weeds. Weeds compete with your vegetable roots for moisture and nutrients. Fewer weeds will result in more moisture and nutrients for your vegetables.

4. Mulch encourages healthy root growth. Healthy roots will result in a more productive vegetable garden.

5. There are many different types of mulch including pine straw and wheat straw. Both are organic mulches and as they gradually decay they will add nutrients back into your soil. This is another benefit of using mulch -- it helps to gradually replace the nutrients your vegetable plants remove from the soil.

I personally prefer wheat straw even though it is a little more expensive per bale in my area. A picture of a wheat straw bale is on the right. Each year I purchase my bales of wheat straw from the same store. Some years the bales of wheat straw contain some wheat kernel heads and some years they do not.

One year each bale of wheat straw contained about a dozen wheat kernel heads. I did not bother to remove the wheat kernels and I simply scattered them over my garden area along with the wheat straw. Some of those wheat kernels took root and produced a wheat stalk during the spring. A picture of one of those wheat stalks is on the right. I allowed the wheat stalks to grow beside the corn I planted in the same area and I harvested the wheat later in the year when it was ready. The few wheat stalks did not yield very much wheat but they did provide a little emergency wheat seed for future years if the need should arise.

Are You a Nobody?

Are you a nobody? Are you insignificant, unimportant, and poor?
When you die will you be quickly forgotten and remembered no more?

If you are a nobody then I have some news that will make you very glad.
God loves you and He has some gifts for you because He is also your Dad.

God has created a new body for you that is perfect in every possible way.
Your new body will **never** hunger, or thirst, or grow old day by day.

God has also built a mansion in heaven for you to enjoy for all eternity.
Your new home is more beautiful than any home ever was or ever will be.

And God has sent you this special message so that you will know
that He loves you and you are precious to Him just because He says so.

God loves you so much that He sent His Son Jesus to die on Calvary
to pay the price for your eternal soul if His forgiveness you will receive.

Now that you know that God loves you, will you please love Him too?
God is waiting for your answer. Just say, "Yes God, I also love you."

Scripture References: James 2:5, Romans 5:8, Luke 5:32, First Corinthians 15:40, First Corinthians 15:50-57, First Thessalonians 4:13-18, Revelation 7:16-17, John 14:1-3, Hebrews 11:16, Revelations 21:1-7, Revelation 21:21, Acts 2:22-24, Acts 3:17-21, Romans 10:9-13, Psalm 116:15.

Poem: Are You a Nobody?

Chapter Twenty-Nine

Ant Hills: A Simple Solution

Some General Information About Ants

1. There are over 10,000 different kinds of ants and they live almost everywhere on the surface of the earth.
2. The average life expectancy of an ant varies from 45 to 60 days.
3. Ants live in colonies. The small amount of dirt you see above ground is the entrance to an underground network of ant tunnels and chambers. These chambers are used as resting places, as nurseries, and for food storage.
4. Some ants, such as the red ant, have a sting but black ants and wood ants do not.
5. It is **not** possible to completely eliminate **all** of the ants in an area. Even a professionally trained and equipped pest control expert cannot eliminate all the ants in an area. However, it is possible to minimize the total number of ants and it is also possible to restrict their future population growth opportunities.
6. Ants will usually avoid an area that contains dead ants because this indicates the presence of some type of disease or predator. Ants will also abandon a nest if a significant number of the ants in their colony are destroyed. However, if the colony only suffers minor damage then the ants will simply repair the damaged areas.

Gardening supply stores sell a variety of commercial ant poisons and chemicals that will help you control your ant problems. If you wish you may invest your money in those chemicals and use them as directed on the package. Over the past 30 years I have used a variety of these different chemicals and I have personally discovered that the results I achieved with those professional quality ant control chemicals were **not** any better than the simple method that is explained below.

A Simple Solution to the Ant Problem

As already mentioned above, it is **not** possible to completely eliminate **all** the ants in an area, even if you use a powerful commercial quality ant poison. However, it is possible to control your ant infestation problem using the following simple method.

Pour **one gallon of boiling hot water** directly onto an average size ant hill. Or pour two gallons of boiling water onto a large ant hill. The boiling water will instantly kill the ants.

Due to the large number of dead ants the surviving ants will not try to rebuild in that same exact area. Instead they will invest their time and energy building a new home somewhere close by. Since the surviving ants will be investing a reasonable portion of their time in this new building activity they will have less time available:

1. to gather food, and
2. to care for their young.

Therefore the surviving ants will **not** be significantly multiplying while they are trying to relocate and rebuild their colony. In other words, you will be controlling your ant problem.

There are three methods for pouring the boiling water onto the ant hill:

1. **Method One:** Pour the boiling water over the entire top surface of the ant hill. This method equally distributes the boiling water over the entire upper surface of the ant hill and the boiling water then penetrates several inches down into the ant colony itself.

2. **Method Two:** Quickly push a one-inch diameter stick down into the middle of the ant hill and then quickly remove the stick and toss it aside before the ants climb the stick and attack you. Then immediately pour the boiling water down the hole in the center of the ant hill. This method allows more of the boiling water to penetrate deeper into the chambers below the ground.

3. **Method Three:** Pour one gallon of boiling water over the entire top surface of the ant hill. Then quickly push a one-inch diameter stick into the middle of the ant hill and immediately toss the stick aside. Then immediately pour a second gallon of boiling water down the hole in the center of the ant hill.

You may experiment with the above three methods to determine which technique is most effective against the type of ants that inhabit your area.

It is also possible to mix **one cup of ordinary household laundry bleach** into one gallon of boiling water before you pour it onto the ant hill. The chlorine bleach will interfere with the ants' ability to smell which will cause the following serious problems for the tiny creatures:

1. The ants will have to abandon the immediate area because the chlorine odor will interfere with their ability to follow scent trails and to identify which ants are part of their own colony.

2. If the bleach solution makes contact with the ants' stored food supplies then it will contaminate that food and the ants will have to abandon it.

3. If the bleach solution (or odor) makes contact with the ant larvae and eggs then the adult ants will have to abandon them and start over.

Conclusion

In summary:

1. If you have bleach you should definitely add some bleach to your boiling water before you pour the boiling water onto the ant hill.

2. If you don't have bleach you can still use plain boiling water and achieve very good results. I have personally used plain boiling water on numerous occasions and I have had excellent results every time. (Note: This is the method I always use in my garden area because I do not want the chlorine bleach residue in my garden soil.)

Remember that regardless of what method you use it is **not** possible to completely eliminate **all** the ants. For example, some of the ants will be away from the nest when you pour the boiling water (or commercial ant poison) onto the nest. Therefore be emotionally prepared to repeat the above procedure after the surviving ants reestablish their colony and a new ant hill appears somewhere else in the nearby area. The emergence of the new ant hill will take somewhere between two to eight weeks depending on how many of the original ants survive.

Remember that your primary objective is to control the ant population to the minimum possible level. The above suggestions will enable you to successfully accomplish this objective.

Chapter Thirty

Use Common Sense to Compare
Your Current Location to Another Location

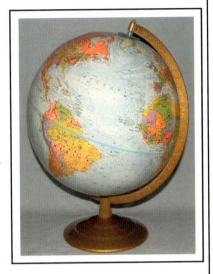

Please apply common sense to any important decision you need to make. This is especially important during hard times because the impact of a poor decision can be devastating to you and to your family. As an example, where would you prefer to live during a serious long-term hard times tragedy event?

Alaska? New York? Arizona? Tennessee? Switzerland?

How would you select the best place to live during hard times?

1. Would you consider the average number of people per square mile?
2. Would you consider the average number of people per square acre of farmland?

There is nothing wrong with either of the above two measures. However, if you only used the above two measures then you would probably arrive at the wrong answer because you would not be using common sense. You would be basing your decision on insufficient information and that would not be wise.

For example, if you believe that low population density is the single most important factor for selecting the best place to live during a serious hard times tragedy event then a logical choice would be to move into the middle of the Arizona desert or to the North Pole. However, the average person would not choose these locations because people can't live there. A really low population density usually means the area is a very difficult place in which to survive and earn a living. During a serious hard times tragedy event do you want to force your family to try to survive in a place where people are just barely able to survive during good times?

Population density is frequently used as a measure for selecting a better area for two reasons:

1. **A high population density** normally indicates more big cities and a big city will not be a safe place to live during a serious hard times tragedy event. (Note: During a serious long-term hard times tragedy event many of the people in every big city will self-destruct due to the absence of fresh water and food. Some of the surviving city dwellers will begin to roam the countryside in search of the things they need to survive and they will kill innocent people in the process.)

2. **A low population density** normally indicates more people living on a farm or homestead and these people are already theoretically surviving off the land. (Note: Many of today's sustenance level farmers receive government aid in one form or another. If that government assistance is stopped then those farmers will not be able to feed their families and they will be forced to make the same types of decisions that city dwellers will be forced to make. Any person who has never lived in one of these poorer farming communities probably does not understand this concept and they have an unrealistic vision of life in these communities that probably resembles a "Little House on the Prairie" television drama. Life today is not like it was during the 1800s or the 1930s. During a serious long-term hard times event farming communities will also begin to self-destruct due to the absence of an adequate supply of food. However, in my opinion, farming communities located in the "Bible Belt" will fare better on the average when compared to farming communities that are located in areas where moral concepts and decisions are based on situational ethics.)

During a serious hard times tragedy event you should probably consider a multitude of different factors if you are considering moving to an area that was better suited for long-term survival. Population density is just **one** of those factors and it is **not** the most important factor. In fact, it is a relatively trivial factor when compared to some other really critical issues.

For example, there is no state where most of the people are evil. There is also no state where most of the people are good. Good people and evil people live in every state. Every state has prisons. Every state has charitable organizations that help the needy people in that state.

During a serious hard times tragedy event the **percentage** of people who will abandon their previous morals in order to survive will not be higher or lower from one state to the next. Every state will contain some people who will steal, rape, and murder. And every state will contain some people who will voluntarily sacrifice their time, money, resources, and even their lives, in order to help others. This will happen inside the big cities and in the farming communities. People are basically the same all over the world. It is only our educational backgrounds and our religious beliefs that creates the illusion that we are different. In the eyes of God our Creator, we are all equal. God did not bestow any special moral or ethical principles on one special group of people who live in one special spot in the world. This isn't based on the teachings of any one religious group -- it is nothing more than simple common sense. And I do not mind if you believe otherwise.

I have lived in Oklahoma, Virginia, Maine, Florida, Michigan, and a few other states. I personally did not notice any difference in the people who lived in those different areas. The majority of the people I came into contact with were intelligent, honest, and kind. I also met a limited number of people in each of those areas who were snobbish, rude, and selfish. But overall I did not notice any significant demographical differences among the people in all the different areas in which I have lived. If the reason you are thinking about moving to a new area is because you think the people there will be nicer than the people where you currently live then you will probably be in for a big surprise. In my opinion it is our own individual personalities that determines how the average person will respond to us and not the personalities of other people.

If you were to use common sense to select a state where the **highest percentage** of its current residents will probably survive a serious hard times tragedy event, then what factors would you consider to be the most important ones in the choice of that state?

In my opinion, if you are thinking about moving to another state then the following factors are just four of the many, many different issues that probably should be considered:

1. **Water Independence:** Does the state currently have enough fresh water to completely satisfy the needs of everyone within the state, or does the state currently have to purchase its water from another state? How important is fresh water to your future survival?

2. **Food Independence:** Does the state export more food than it imports or does the state import more food than it exports? In other words, during a serious hard times tragedy event would it be possible for the state to feed everyone who lived there or would the state need to acquire food from outside its borders? Some farmland is extremely productive and it will generate extremely high crop yields every year. Other farmland is relatively poor and it will only generate low crop yields every year. Therefore it is not the amount of farmland that is important but the quality of that farmland, the number of frost free days per year, the amount of average rainfall each month during the year, and the average wind conditions. During a serious hard times tragedy event every farm will be producing less food than before because there will be less fuel to run the automated farming equipment and there will be less commercial quality fertilizer available. Therefore would you rather be living in a state that cannot feed its people at the current time under optimal farming conditions, or would you prefer to live in a state that currently produces a food surplus? In addition, if you were working the ground yourself by hand, would you rather be working high quality soil or low quality soil? Which type of soil would yield the best return for your hard work?

3. **Religious Freedom:** Is there true religious freedom within the state or does one religious group dominate and control the state? Every state will have more members in one religious group than the other groups. This is not the issue. The issue is whether or not that religious group practices religious tolerance or do they persecute individuals of another faith. Or is the state controlled by a small group of atheists at high levels in government who have passed laws that have stripped away the rights of honest people so that criminals can prosper?

4. **Firearm Freedom:** Does the state allow you the freedom to own and carry firearms to protect yourself and your family members?

Chapter Thirty: Comparing Your Current Location to Another Location

The above are just four of the important factors a person should consider if that person were using common sense to make a decision on which state might be the best one to live in during a serious hard times tragedy event. Trying to make this type of decision based on just one or two "simple statistics" would not be the best way to arrive at the best answer.

Now let's compare a few different states across the United States based on:

1. **Average Annual Rainfall in Inches:** Rain is the source of renewable fresh water. Rain is absolutely necessary for human life, farm livestock, wild animals, farm produce, and timber production.

2. **Year 2009 Dollar Revenue per Acre of Farmland:** This is important because it shows the average agricultural value of all the farmland in each state, assuming the land is used in its most efficient manner by the owners of that land.

3. **Average Number of Frost Free Days per Year:** This directly impacts the number of crops that can be harvested per year. Some areas will allow two crops to be grown each year whereas other areas will only have enough warm weather to grow one crop. If there aren't enough frost free days this also limits the types of crops that can be grown in a region. Finally, if there are **more frost free days** then the **winters will be shorter** which means a family would need **less firewood** to survive the cold weather months.

Data on Fourteen Random States Across the United States

State	Annual Rainfall	Revenue / Acre of Farmland	Average Frost Free Days per Year
Alaska	53.15 inches	$ 45	60 days
Arizona	7.11 inches	$ 135	150 days
Colorado	15.31 inches	$ 210	90 days
Georgia	48.61 inches	$ 802	210 days
Kansas	28.61 inches	$ 299	180 days
Illinois	33.34 inches	$ 608	150 days
Minnesota	26.36 inches	$ 571	120 days
Montana	11.37 inches	$ 54	120 days
New York	39.28 inches	$ 577	120 days
Oklahoma	30.89 inches	$ 168	210 days
Tennessee	48.49 inches	$ 355	180 days
Texas	34.70 inches	$ 156	210 days
Virginia	45.22 inches	$ 434	180 days
Washington	27.66 inches	$ 503	150 days

- - - - Data Sources - - - -

The above annual rainfall data is from: http://www.betweenwaters.com/etc/usrain.html

The above average frost free days data is from: http://www.ncdc.noaa.gov/oa/climate/freezefrost/frostfreemaps.html

The above farmland data is from: http://www.ers.usda.gov/statefacts/us.htm
The above web site contains information for the entire United States of America.
To view the data on one specific state change the ending "us.htm" to the state abbreviation, such as "va.htm" for Virginia or "tx.htm" for Texas.

Chapter Thirty: Comparing Your Current Location to Another Location

The revenue per acre column was found by dividing the year 2009 total "final agricultural sector output" (including livestock and lumber) by the total amount of cropland and pastureland and woodland in production.

----

1. On the average, in the entire United States of America the average revenue was **$ 359 per acre** during the year 2009. Some states did better than this and some states did worse.
2. On the average, all the states **west of the Mississippi River** receive an average of **24.3 inches** of rain per year.
3. On the average, all the states **east of the Mississippi River** receive an average of **42.4 inches** of rain per year.
4. Is average rainfall important to you today? The answer would depend on whether or not you were trying to grow crops, or manage livestock, or if you relied on a water well for your water.
5. Will average rainfall be important to you in the future during a serious long-term hard times tragedy event? Use common sense to answer this question yourself.

The above data are the average statistics for an entire state. No one should make a decision based on the average data for an entire state because this would **not** be using good common sense. Good common sense would tell you that every state has a significant variation in all the above statistics from the west side of the state to the east side of the state, and from the north side of the state to the south side of the state. Any move decision should be based on the average statistics for the exact county within the state you are considering because each county will have either higher or lower statistics than the above state averages. This is because an average converts the high and low values into a composite average.

I am also **not** suggesting that you use the above criteria to select a state to move to. There are many other issues that are also important. The above factors are just three of the issues you should consider in choosing a new location if you are seriously considering a move.

There are a wide variety of other issues you should also consider. For example, do you currently have an extensive network of family members and relatives who live in close proximity to you, and do they have a life history of being hard working ethical individuals? If you have this type of supportive family then a decision to separate yourself from your extended family may not be a very smart thing to do. If you move to a new area then you will be the "outsider" or "immigrant" and you may be treated as one if a serious hard times tragedy event unfolds rather suddenly.

The purpose of this chapter was **not** to list all the different issues you would need to think about before making a move. The purpose of this chapter was to caution you against making an important move decision based on a limited number of statistics and ignoring a wide variety of other statistics that may be of equal or greater significance to your decision. If you will pause and use common sense then you can easily think of many of these other important variables yourself.

In closing, please allow me let to ask one final question. Who do you depend on the most?

1. Do you depend on yourself first and God second?
2. Do you depend on God first and yourself second?

If you were to use common sense which of the above two choices do you think would be the best choice for survival during a serious hard times tragedy event?

Chapter Thirty-One

How to Select the Optimal Retreat Location

If you are thinking about moving to a more lightly populated area then what type of area would maximize your chances for long-term survival during a serious hard times tragedy event? In my opinion all of the following factors should be carefully considered.

Avoid the Following Areas:

1. **Avoid an area that is controlled by a corrupt government that tramples upon the rights of ordinary citizens.**

   There are at least three layers of government that must be taken into consideration for a retreat area:

   a. **The national government** should be relatively stable and it should not be totally corrupt.
   b. **The regional government** should compare favorably to other regional governments. In the United States of America the state governments are the regional governments. Some states are safer to live in than other states because those states still treat their citizens as responsible law-abiding adults. But the citizens in other states have lost many of their original constitutional rights and they are now very easy victims for any criminal that wants to take advantage of them. In those states the government is always happy to take pictures of the dead bodies of its defenseless citizens and then attach those pictures to very detailed reports and then file those reports in a safe place where they can be kept for a very, very long time. (Note: These states have living conditions that are quickly becoming very similar to the unacceptable living conditions that now exist in England.)
   c. **The local government** should not be corrupt. Some small communities are controlled by totally corrupt local law enforcement officials. These areas should be avoided.

2. **Avoid an area that is dominated by a religion that advocates "believe as I do or die."**

   For thousands of years mankind has been periodically devastated by a variety of different religions that have claimed to be the "only true way to worship God" and that "the true worship of God demands that you kill anyone who does not share your faith." The major problem with all of these religions is that there have always been divisions within the religion itself that disagreed with one another. Therefore the "believers" not only killed outsiders but they also killed anyone who didn't agree with their beliefs on specific issues. Any area that is dominated by one of these religious groups is a very unsafe place to live. It doesn't matter if you belong to none of the religious groups or to the most popular religious group. There will always be other people who don't share your beliefs and their only mission in life will be to kill you and your family. Therefore your chances for long-term survival will be very small. In my opinion you would be well advised to avoid living in any area that contains one of these "believe or die" religious groups.

   (Note: Even the Christian religion has frequently been "redefined" into one of these deadly religions. That is the reason many honest God-fearing people migrated to the "New World" and eventually helped to create the "United States of America." Our founding forefathers tried to prevent this type of religious persecution with our "Bill of Rights." But very soon your constitutional religious rights in the United States may be "redefined" and you will be required to accept a government sponsored religion for your own benefit or you will be declared to be an "enemy of the state" and you will be hunted down and executed.)

If you live in an area with a "believe or die religion" then you will be outnumbered by at least three to one. For example, you could quickly and unexpectedly find yourself in the hands of:

    a. a corrupt government, or
    b. a killer religion, or
    c. a criminal who obeys no laws and respects no religion.

Look For an Area That Has All the Following Characteristics

1. **Its residents still have the right to own firearms to protect themselves.**

   There are several levels of firearm freedom as follows:

   a. Any law abiding resident may own and possess firearms. There are no forms to fill out and no fees that must be paid in order to own and carry a firearm. In my opinion this is a correct interpretation and application of the second amendment in the Bill of Rights.
   b. A law abiding resident must file a simple form requesting permission to carry a firearm, pay a small fee, and pass a simple background check.
   c. The laws and regulations for firearm ownership are extensive and very few law abiding citizens are granted the right to carry a firearm.
   d. Only government officials and their police force and law-breaking criminals carry firearms. Honest law abiding citizens are prohibited from having firearms for any reason. In other words, an honest person does not have the right to protect his family from criminals.

   In my opinion either of the first two areas above would be a reasonable place to live. However, anyone living in either one of the last two areas above would have a very small chance of surviving. During a serious long-term hard times tragedy event all the honest hard-working people will either be killed or they will flee for their lives at the first opportunity. They will simply abandon the area to the corrupt individuals who wish to control it (government officials, the police, and the criminals). Without any honest people to do the real work these areas will quickly self-destruct for an overwhelming multitude of reasons, such as no doctors, no utility maintenance repairmen, no farmers, etc.

2. **It is a lightly populated area.**

   There is no single correct way to adequately define how many people constitute a "lightly populated area." The reason is because the answer is a function of how many people the area could successfully support for an extended period of time.

   Let's look at several possibilities:

   a. **A big city:** A big city does not have its own water supply, or its own agricultural land, or its own power generation stations. In other words, the people who live in a big city are dependant on resources that are brought into the city from the outside. If there is any significant disruption in the delivery of those resources then a big city would quickly become a huge graveyard.
   b. **An area with less than one person per square mile:** This type of area is almost always unsuitable for long-term human habitation. In some cases it is also inappropriate for short-term survival. The reason nobody lives there is because nobody can live there. Examples would be the middle of a frozen wasteland, or the middle of a scorching desert, or a small rock covered island, or the top of an extremely high mountain, or a relatively low area that floods every time that it rains.
   c. **An area with an unusually low population density:** There is always at least one very good reason, or several very good reasons, why an area does not have a lot of people living in it. Some of the more common reasons are:

      1. the area lacks critical natural resources, such as a dependable year-round supply of fresh drinking water,

Chapter Thirty-One: How to Select the Optimal Retreat Location

2. the area is unsuitable for the growing of crops or the raising of farm livestock,
3. the area is subject to unpredictable flooding, tornados, hurricanes, earthquakes, or volcanic eruptions,
4. the growing season is too short to grow enough food to last at least two years (to avoid famine conditions during a bad crop year),
5. the winters are severe and they take a terrible toll every year on the health and life-expectancy of everyone who lives there,
6. the distance between farms and ranches is so great that a small gang of ten or twenty criminals could easily subdue and destroy any ranch they wanted to without worrying about the neighbors finding out until it was too late to assist the family being attacked.

d. **A lightly populated area:** Each farm or ranch consists of somewhere between five acres up to about two-hundred acres. The soil and weather conditions in these areas have proven over a long period of time that homesteads of this size can adequately support the people who live on that homestead. The homesteads are relatively close to one another and they are not isolated. If one homestead is attacked then the neighboring homesteads will hear the gunfire and they can immediately come to the aid of the homestead under attack. Because of the small but reasonable number of people in the area there will also be a surplus labor pool that can work in nearby factories. Therefore this type of area would have the potential to be self-sufficient over a long period of time because it has an agricultural base, and it supports farm livestock, and it has small factories that make a variety of useful items for sale to the residents within the immediate area and which permit economic trade for other necessary commodities from more distant communities. This type of area will also usually contain several small towns that are twenty or thirty-miles apart where there are doctors, dentists, repair shops, and a variety of small stores. In my opinion this type of area has the best chance for survival during a serious long-term hard times tragedy event.

3. **It is at least several hundred feet above sea level.**

   Hurricanes have destroyed many coastal areas. Heavy rains have caused flooding in areas that have no previous history of flooding for the past 100 years. Therefore if you want to relocate to a safe area then that area should be at least 300 or 400 feet above sea level. In addition, your home or retreat area should be on high ground compared to the area around you.

4. **It has short mild winters.**

   A short winter means a long growing season. A long growing season usually means you can harvest two crops. When the first crop matures you can harvest it, plow the ground, plant again, and harvest a second crop before the arrival of winter. This is a significant advantage during hard times for two reasons:
   (a) you are able to eat the first harvest sooner which may save you and your family from starvation, and
   (b) you double your food production from the same exact piece of land. For this to be successful you must understand proper crop rotation strategies to prevent the depletion of specific minerals from your soil.

   On the other hand, a long winter means that you have to devote more of your time during good weather getting ready to survive the long winter. In other words, you will be extremely busy cutting and stacking huge amounts of firewood so your family doesn't freeze to death during the winter. This is not the best way to utilize your time during a serious hard times tragedy event. Although cutting firewood is a necessity, it is work that could have been significantly minimized if you had just selected an area with a short mild winter. A long hard winter also means more time trapped inside your home waiting for spring to arrive.

5. **It has a history of good average rainfall (not too much rain or too little rain).**

   Fresh drinking water is an absolute necessity for long term survival. Rain is also necessary to provide good crop yields and to support any type of livestock. Therefore any area that does not constantly replenish its water is not an area that is conducive to long-term hard times survival.

6. **It is surrounded by farm land, dairy cows, and other typical farm livestock such as horses, pigs, sheep, goats, and chickens.**

   Regardless of your primary occupation your family will need to eat. If you have a marketable skill (mechanic, repairman, doctor, nurse, etc.) then you may be able to trade your skills for the necessities your family needs to survive. But if those necessities do not exist in close proximity to where you live, then your family may starve to death.

7. **It has a reasonable supply of trees and forest timber land.**

   Lumber can be used to build a multitude of things. With a reasonable supply of trees a sawmill could produce lumber and a variety of things could be built. This provides jobs and facilitates normal commerce. And lumber is a renewable resource. Just plant new trees after you cut down the mature trees.

8. **It has a few nearby manufacturing facilities of any size.**

   During a serious hard times tragedy event manufacturing facilities can be the lifeblood of a community. They permit the division of labor which improves productivity and achieves economies of scale.

9. **It is not on a major freeway or interstate.**
   During good times being close to a good interstate highway can be a significant advantage. However, during a serious hard times tragedy event the reverse is true. An interstate highway will be the shortest easiest path for everyone to travel who is trying to escape from a dying big city. You need to think about the ramifications of this issue on your own.

Conclusion

Your survival during a serious long-term hard times tragedy event will be directly related to:

1. How prepared you were before the hard times tragedy event begins.
2. Where you are living when the hard times tragedy event begins.
3. Whether or not you believe in prayer.

Chapter Thirty-Two

The Advantages and Disadvantages of Recreational Vehicles (RVs) and Campers

During hard times there is a significant increase in the number of individuals and families who seriously consider living in a Recreational Vehicle (RV) or a camper on a full-time basis. The purpose of this chapter is to provide a balanced perspective on the advantages and disadvantages of RVs and campers.

RV Park Monthly Rental Fee: At the current time the monthly cost to park an RV or a camper in an RV park is somewhere between $350 to $500 per month depending on the park itself. This will normally include a place to park the camper, one additional vehicle, the water, the septic service, and the electricity. It will not include propane but most parks have a propane tank refilling station near the park office where you can refill your empty propane tanks for a reasonable fee. It will also not include cable TV which will be an additional expense.

Camper Living During the 1930s Great Depression

Therefore when you consider the monthly expense of parking a camper at a traditional RV park then it may make more sense for the average family to rent a small apartment instead of buying an RV or a camper. Most small apartments have significantly more space that a big camper. Until you have actually lived in an RV or a camper for an extended period of time you will probably not appreciate the difference a "little extra space" can make in your family's emotional well-being.

Engine or no Engine:

1. **Engine:** If you purchase an RV that has an engine then you will need to add that vehicle to your insurance policy. This is usually a significant extra expense that a family should avoid during hard times. You would also need to keep the RV engine and the transmission serviced and that is another expense you may not be able to afford. When you drive your RV you will also need to tow another vehicle behind your RV so you will have something to drive when your RV is parked. This towed vehicle will significantly reduce the gas mileage of your RV.

2. **No Engine:** Therefore my advice is to not purchase an RV with an engine but to purchase a tow-behind camper instead. You should read your current vehicle insurance policy because a tow-behind camper may be automatically covered under your policy in the same way a tow-behind boat trailer is automatically covered and a tow-behind "U-Haul" trailer is automatically covered.

Standard Tow or Fifth-Wheel Tow: Even if you have the option to pull a fifth-wheel camper you should consider the standard pull behind tow campers instead. A standard tow camper has a better resale value because there are not that many individuals who have the option to pull a fifth-wheel camper.

Quality of Construction and Building Materials: Most new campers have the same general "new" appearance. But a quality built camper will still look really nice after a few years of use. On the other hand, a cheap camper will look like trash in a very short period of time. The upholstery on the sofa will begin to ravel and holes will appear. The carpet will wear down and look terrible. The linoleum floor will have a visible path worn in it. The wall paper will begin to separate from the wall. The wood counter tops and cabinets will begin to look really used. If you take the time to look at several "used" campers before you make your investment you will quickly become very knowledgeable about the differences between good quality and bad quality campers and you will know which "brand names" to avoid. You will also be able to determine if a used camper has been taken care of or if it has been abused.

Plumbing: I suggest you get down on your hands and knees and look at the underside of any camper you are interested in. If there have been plumbing problems or leaks then they should be readily visible on the underside of the camper. One common problem with used campers is when the previous owner did not drain the water lines at the end of a camping season (or install a special RV pink antifreeze in those water lines), and the water lines inside the camper froze and burst in several different places during the winter months.

Sleeping Accommodations: The most important feature of a camper is its bedding. Each person in your family will need a "permanent bed" that is big enough for that individual. No one in your family should have to sleep on a "convertible bed." A convertible bed is a kitchen table or a sofa during the day and a "make shift bed" at night. You would not believe how uncomfortable a "make shift bed" is until you actually try to sleep an entire night on one of them. After one night you will have nothing nice to say about a camper convertible bed. Therefore please don't force someone in your family to sleep on one of those pitiful excuses for a bed. Instead look for a camper that has enough permanent full-time beds for each member of your family.

When you look at those permanent beds think seriously about how a person is going to enter and exit the bed and how a person is going to change the sheets on that bed. You should personally lie down on every bed in the camper to test its comfort yourself. Each mattress should be in one piece and not two or three pieces that you push together to form a "make shift mattress." A bunk twin mattress should be at least three inches thick (four or more inches is preferred). If the camper mattress is unacceptable then you should measure the mattress itself and determine if it could be replaced with a standard twin mattress (38" x 74"), or full mattress (54" x 75"), or queen mattress (60" x 80"). Most camper "twin bunk" mattresses are 28" x 74" or smaller, and most camper "queen" mattress are 60" x 76" (four-inches shorter than a regular queen mattress). Therefore in most situations your only option would be to purchase a "new" camper mattress at a very high price from a RV dealer.

If each person has his or her own permanent full-time bed then that person could lie down at any time for any reason in his or her own bed. If you deprive anyone in your family of this simple basic right then you will have seriously compromised that person's future happiness and well-being.

Extended Slide Space: Some campers have one or more areas that slide out from the camper when it is parked. These slide spaces are pulled into the camper while traveling but extended when parked. If you are going to live full-time inside a camper then one or more of these extended slide areas will make a significant improvement in your overall enjoyment of your camper.

Bath or Shower: Some campers have a small bath tub and some campers only have a stand-up shower. Some campers have the shower above a sit-down toilet. Even if you take a shower 99% of the time, I strongly recommend a camper with a separate small tub. The small tub will also have a shower head so you can still take a shower if you prefer but it will also allow you to take a normal bath. For example, if you need to soak an arm or a leg is some really warm water then being able to sit in a warm tub of water suddenly becomes a necessity and not a luxury. During a serious hard times event the tub could also serve as a convenient place to hand wash your clothes and bed sheets. You could hang a short clothesline above the center of the tub and then you could hang your wet clothes above the tub so they could drip dry into the tub itself.

Laundry: Most campers do not have a washing machine or clothes dryer. Even if you find a camper with a washing machine most RV parks will not allow you to use that washing machine because it will quickly fill up the small septic tank that you attach your camper's flexible drain hose to. Therefore you should be prepared to do your laundry once a week in a nearby coin Laundromat.

Kitchen: Although each camper will have a slightly different kitchen arrangement, almost all of them include a table that will sit four people, a sink with two basins, a propane oven and top burners, a microwave oven, and a refrigerator. Due to space constraints the one thing that is usually missing is kitchen counter space. Therefore if you can find a camper with an open kitchen counter where you can prepare food then this will significantly enhance your enjoyment of your camper. Campers with slides in the center normally have a little more open counter space than campers without slides.

Chapter Thirty-Two: Recreational Vehicles and Campers

Entertainment: Regardless of what type of entertainment sound system your camper has, the chances of your using it very often are pretty slim unless you live by yourself. The sound is normally transmitted to a speaker in each major living area and that means everyone has to listen to the same thing. Therefore, in my opinion, a more reasonable option would be to provide each member of your family with their own individual portable entertainment equipment with ear phones. This would allow each person the opportunity to be entertained in a manner that was most enjoyable to that person without interfering with anyone else. In addition, a flat screen Television and a small DVD player could both be permanently and securely mounted onto a wall across from the sofa. By mounting the Television on the wall you may be able to reclaim a small amount of counter space. (Note: One practical use for this reclaimed counter space would be for a stainless steel gravity fed water filter system, such as the Berkefeld or AquaRain. You could pour water into the top filter compartment and later remove pure drinking water from the lower compartment. This could help to prevent a variety of potential health problems that might be in the water supply at the RV park where you are staying.)

Air Conditioning: The air conditioner will be on the roof. The air conditioning vents will be in the ceiling of each room inside the camper. If possible, you should consider climbing a ladder and looking at the roof of the camper. While you are on the roof you will be able to clearly see the current condition of everything up there, including the roof vents above the bedroom and bathroom, the vent pipes for the water tanks, and the two antenna systems.

While you are on the roof I suggest you gently touch the roof vents and the other plastic pieces to determine their condition. These items sometimes look like they are almost new but they may crumble or crack or fall apart when you give them a very gentle push because they were cheaply made and they could not withstand the sun and the freezing weather. (Note: In my opinion during a hard times event it might make more sense to install several small 12-volt fans inside your camper for comfort instead of using the air conditioner.)

Heat: Most campers are heated with propane. The heat vents are located in the floor of each room inside the camper. Depending on the outside temperature the propane heater may use a significant amount of fuel during the winter months. The reason is because most RVs and campers are not very well insulated. Heat is lost through the windows, through the ceiling, and through the walls. And cold air drifts up from the floor and from around the doorway. One small electric space heater can improve the situation if your camper is properly wired to support the 1,500 watt load of one of these small heaters. However, they do consume a lot of power when in operation. If you try to install two or more of these electric space heaters then you will either overload and flip your camper circuit breakers, or you may catch the wiring inside your camper walls on fire which will quickly burn your camper to the ground. Therefore please resist the temptation to heat your camper with more than one portable electric heater.

On way to reduce your winter heat loss is to install inflatable roof vent spacers inside the interior roof vents in the bedroom and in the bathroom. These inflatable roof vent spacers may be purchased at many RV dealers. The disadvantage of these spacers is that they completely block the roof vent which will eliminate all the exterior light and therefore they will darken any room or bathroom in which they are installed. This may be an advantage in a bedroom but it will probably be a disadvantage in a bathroom.

Height: There are two height considerations as follows:

1. **Inside Ceiling Height:** The inside of the camper should be at least 6.5 feet from the floor to the ceiling. If you can find a camper with 7 feet of clearance from the floor to the ceiling you will probably "feel" more comfortable and less confined than a camper with a lower ceiling. The disadvantage is that it will cost a little more to heat this

extra 6-inch space above your head. The advantage is that you will gain a little more space inside all your wall cabinets and all your closets.

2. **Exterior Height:** Carefully look at the total overall height of the camper. Most campers are constructed very low to the ground and you only have to climb one or two folding steps to enter the camper. However, other campers, such as the one in the picture on the previous page, are built on a frame high off the ground above the wheels and you have to climb three or four steps to enter the camper. These taller campers can be more challenging to park in some RV parks because of low hanging tree branches. They also have a much higher center of gravity which makes them more challenging on a curve at normal highway speeds. Finally, they will not fit under the roofs of some gasoline station refueling areas. Therefore I personally recommend that you do not purchase a tall camper that has its floor frame above the wheels. Instead you should look for a camper where the wheels take up some of the space inside the camper below the sofa, or kitchen table, or kitchen sink.

Conclusion

Before you invest in an RV or a camper you should consider how practical it would be for your specific situation. Please don't entertain "romantic notions" of how you are going to just love a more primitive life style inside a camper. After two or three days all your romantic notions will be replaced with the cold hard facts of reality and at that time you will probably dearly wish you had never invested your money in the camper.

A camper would not be as safe as an apartment or a home during a serious hard times tragedy event. A camper is very easy to break into and the thin walls of the camper will not provide any real protection from someone on the outside who decides to vent his or her rage on your family by shooting your camper full of holes.

Therefore, even though I wrote the above chapter to provide some practical things for you to consider, my personal conviction is that most families would probably be better advised to rent a small apartment during a hard times event.

On the other hand, if you have close relatives who live on a farm in a rural area, and they will allow you to park your camper for free on their property, and you can hook your camper up to their water and electrical systems for a small reasonable monthly fee, then a camper may be a viable option for a small family, or for a single person. However, you would still need to figure out how you are going to properly dispose of your waste water.

Chapter Thirty-Three

How to Build a Safe Temporary Shelter

Introduction

The design of a "temporary shelter" will vary based on the primary reason you are building the shelter.

1. **A shelter from the rain or snow:** If you are hiking and you are a long ways from your normal shelter and you get caught in a sudden severe rain storm or snow storm, then you may be forced to quickly construct some type of temporary shelter to protect yourself from the elements. In most cases you will have to use whatever you can find at hand in the immediate vicinity and fashion it into some type of shelter that will keep the rain, wind, or snow off you until the bad weather has passed and you can travel again.

2. **A shelter for one night:** If you are on a one night camping expedition then a quickly made primitive shelter may be okay. Or if you are on a long hike towards a distant location and it will take several days to complete your journey, then you will probably build a quick lean-to type shelter at the end of each day to protect your sleeping area from becoming wet with the night dew. Most wilderness survival manuals discuss a wide variety of different shelter options that can be constructed for this purpose.

3. **A shelter you will live in for several weeks:** This type of shelter will need to be rain proof, wind proof, and provide safety from wild animals. This is the type of shelter that will be discussed in this chapter. It will probably take an adult male between two to three days to build this type of shelter but when you are finished you will have a safe dry place to sleep at night and you will not have to worry about being killed by wild animals while you are asleep. The type of shelter I recommend will also allow you to stand up so it will be an acceptable place to spend rainy days.

Permanent Shelter versus Temporary Shelter

A cabin cave would be a permanent shelter. Complete instructions for building a cabin cave are in the next chapter in this book. However, since it will take between six to twelve weeks for an adult male to construct a cabin cave, you may need a place to live during its construction.

If you have a mini-van or a regular size van then you could sleep in the rear of the van at night. But if you don't have a van then you will need a "temporary shelter" to help you survive the wilderness environment until your cabin cave is complete.

The reason I cannot recommend a tent as a temporary shelter is because it offers **no protection from wild animals.** A bear could easily collapse a tent on top of you and then kill you while you are trapped inside the canvas. A pack of wolves could easily and quickly tear a tent to pieces and you would become their next meal. Therefore I suggest that you do not depend on a tent for protection from wild animals.

Area Selection

Your temporary shelter should be on higher ground than the surrounding area. This will help to prevent flooding problems inside your shelter during a period of heavy rains.

Your temporary shelter should be in a heavily wooded area with relatively dense bushes close to the ground so the bushes can hide your shelter naturally. People normally will not enter thick underbrush because it is too difficult to walk through.

Your temporary shelter should also be relatively close to the site where you will build your cabin cave (six to twelve weeks of work). Since you will be living in this temporary shelter for several weeks it should be strong enough so you feel safe from wild animals when you are inside it.

Shelter Size

You should be able to stand upright inside your shelter with your back straight. If you are forced to bend over the entire time you are inside your shelter you will be miserable. Therefore the **lowest point** on the inside roof of your shelter should be **at least six-feet** above the ground.

Your temporary shelter needs to be large enough so you can comfortably lie down on your mattress, cot, or sleeping bag. Your bedding should not touch the walls of your shelter to avoid moisture or condensation problems.

The number of people who will be living in your temporary shelter will be a major factor. Each person will need enough space to lie down at night in order to sleep. During the day their cots or mattresses can be stacked to create walking space inside the shelter but the shelter will need to be big enough for each person to stretch out comfortably at night.

The size of your biggest tarp will determine the **maximum possible outside rectangular dimensions** of your shelter. A clear plastic tarp is ideal for this purpose because it will let light into your shelter. Clear plastic tarps are usually sold in the paint department of stores. A clear plastic tarp that is 4 Mil thick and 10 feet by 25 feet would be ideal as a roof tarp. This tarp could be folded in half so the outside dimensions would then be 10 feet by 12.5 feet and the thickness would then be 8 Mil. However, if you don't have a clear tarp then a regular tarp will do fine.

This big tarp will form the roof of your shelter and it should be in one piece to avoid water leakage problems. The roof tarp should overlap each of the four walls by at least six-inches to help keep the inside of the shelter dry. Therefore measure your biggest tarp and deduct at least one foot from each direction to determine the maximum outside rectangular dimensions of your shelter. You do **not** have to build a temporary shelter this big. You can build a smaller shelter if you wish. However, you should not build a temporary shelter bigger than your biggest tarp unless you have a very good reason.

(Note: Tarps are frequently sold based on the cut size of the tarp material before a seam is sewn along all four edges of the tarp. Therefore the finished tarp size may be several inches shorter than the size reported on the tarp label. This is why I recommend that you actually measure the tarp **before** you begin construction on your shelter.)

It is possible to use two overlapping tarps to cover the roof of your shelter. But if the wind is blowing in the direction towards the seam between the two tarps then the wind will blow rain water under the seam and into your shelter. If you duck tape the two tarps together the entire length of this seam then you can minimize this problem. However, you should be prepared for the duck tape to gradually become loose and for the rain to eventually find its way into your shelter. Therefore I recommend one big tarp for your roof instead of two smaller tarps.

A Quick Shelter versus a Better Shelter

For safety and basic survival reasons it would be smart to build a temporary shelter as quickly as possible the first day you are in the wilderness in order to provide a relatively safe dry place to sleep the first night. A quick temporary shelter is something an adult male could construct in one working day. It should provide a safe place of refuge from wild animals and from the elements, such as the wind and the rain.

While you are living inside your quick temporary shelter you could begin construction on a better temporary shelter that would take an adult male two or three days to complete. However, while you were working on this improved shelter you could still sleep safely each night inside your quickly made shelter. And all the building materials you used on your quickly made shelter could be used on your better shelter after you have the four corner posts securely buried in the ground. Therefore none of your efforts would have been wasted because you would be able to use all the sticks and tarps from your quick shelter to complete the construction of your better shelter.

On the other hand, if you are completely satisfied with your quick temporary shelter then you would not need to build a better temporary shelter. Instead you could begin work immediately on your cabin cave.

A Quick Temporary Shelter

A quick temporary shelter could be 70% to 90% completed in one day and therefore it would provide a relatively safe dry place to sleep your first night in the wilderness. The next day you could add some more sticks to the walls and to the roof of the shelter to make it safer and more secure.

There are two minor shortcomings of a quick temporary shelter as follows:

1. A very small amount of water may leak into the shelter at each of the four corners of the shelter during a rain storm. This leakage can be almost completely eliminated by duck taping the tarps together where the tarp corners overlap on the roof.

2. A very small amount of wind may enter the shelter from the corner in which the wind is blowing because it will enter between the two tarps at the overlapping stick area.

The wind and rain problems could be eliminated by hanging tarps on the **inside** of the shelter under the roof and around all four **inside** walls. This would be in addition to the tarps on the outside roof of the shelter and the four outside walls. An outside tarp can be draped over the roof and down the outside of one wall. If the tarp is long enough it may cover two opposite walls.

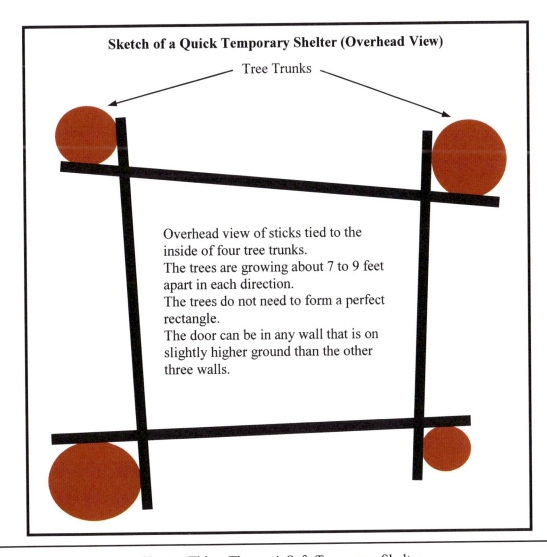

Chapter Thirty-Three: A Safe Temporary Shelter

Instructions for Building a Quick Temporary Shelter

Step One: Find a **relatively flat area** where there are four trees that are growing between seven to nine feet apart with each tree being in the approximate corner of a rectangle. The trees do not need to form a perfect rectangle.

Now follow the instructions for building a "better temporary shelter" which appear below but skip steps two and three in those instructions. Start with step four and continue to follow those instructions all the way through step twenty.

The major differences between a quick shelter and a better shelter are as follows:

1. The **sticks** should be wire tied to the **inside** surface of the four tree trucks for a **quick shelter**. However, for the **better shelter** (discussed below) the sticks should be wire tied to the **outside** surface of the four corner posts.

2. The **tarps** for a **quick shelter** will need to start on the roof and then extend all the way down one of the side walls to the ground. If the tarp is long enough it may extend down two opposite side walls of the quick shelter. In other words, all the tarps for a quick shelter will begin on the roof and then drape over and completely cover either one or two of the side walls. The final tarp for a **quick shelter** will cover the entire roof from the front door wall to the rear wall where rain water will flow off. However, for the **better shelter** the tarps should be wrapped around the outside of the four walls beginning on the left side of the door. You will use several tarps to wrap the four walls and the last tarp should overlap the first tarp by approximately one-foot (beyond the door opening) for rain and wind protection. The **better shelter** will then be completed by putting a tarp over the roof of the shelter with all four edges of that tarp hanging a short distance down each of the four walls to prevent rain from entering the shelter.

Instructions for Building a Better Temporary Shelter

1. Find a **relatively flat area** that forms a ground rectangle with sides of approximately 7.5 or 8 or 8.5 feet to provide a reasonable size temporary shelter that you can stand in, sleep in, and relax in on rainy days. Clear the ground of all vegetation and rocks. Level the ground the best you can but leave a very gentle rear slope. In other words, the front wall of your shelter (with the door) should be on ground that is just a little higher than the rear wall of your shelter to help rain water flow away from the rear of the shelter.

2. Find **four thin pine trees** that are relatively straight and approximately four or five inches in diameter. Saw these trees down at ground level and cover the stumps with dirt. Saw off any side branches. Saw two of these trees to a length of 9 feet long and saw two of the trees to a length of 8 feet long. These four trees will be the corner posts for your future shelter. If the pine tree was originally 16 or more feet tall then you may be able to saw two corner posts from one pine tree if the top of the pine tree was at least 4 inches in diameter at your final saw cut. You may leave the bark on these pine trees.

3. Dig holes **two feet deep** in each of the four corner locations of your future shelter and insert one corner post into each of these four holes. The thick end of the post should go into the ground. The two 9 feet tall posts will support the front wall of your shelter and the two 8 feet tall pots will support the rear wall of your shelter. The two front posts will be 7 feet above ground and the two rear posts will be 6 feet above ground. Securely pack the dirt around the bottom of each corner post.

4. Use **thin wire** to tie long straight thick sticks horizontally to the corner posts with the sticks level with the ground. Thin wire is better than twine because wild animals cannot chew through wire. The sticks should be round and relatively smooth with nothing that could tear a hole in your tarps. The sticks should be between 2 to 3 inches in diameter. Do not cut all the sticks from one area. Gather your sticks from a reasonable distance away from your shelter and from several different areas and then carry them to your shelter site. Cut the sticks off at the ground and then cover the stump with dirt and leaves. It would be best if you sawed the sticks off at the ground. Be sure to bury the sawdust. (It is okay to leave the bark on these sticks.)

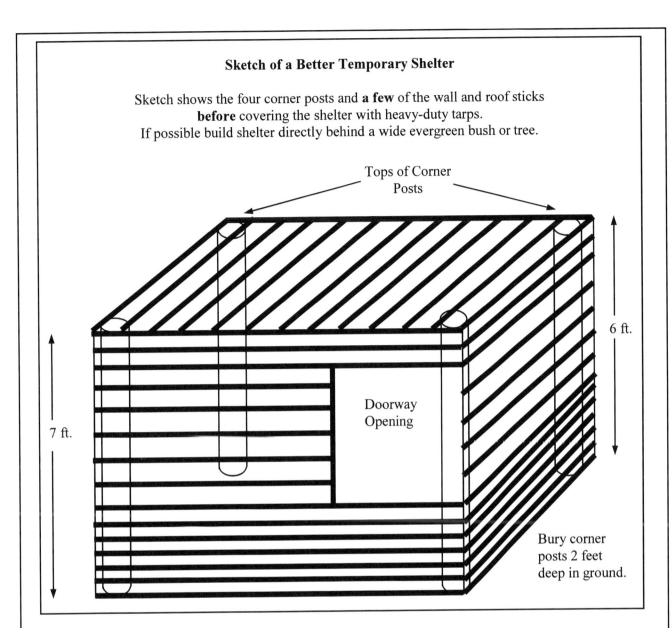

Sketch of a Better Temporary Shelter

Sketch shows the four corner posts and **a few** of the wall and roof sticks **before** covering the shelter with heavy-duty tarps.
If possible build shelter directly behind a wide evergreen bush or tree.

Tops of Corner Posts

6 ft.

7 ft.

Doorway Opening

Bury corner posts 2 feet deep in ground.

5. You will need about **20 good sticks** to begin the construction of the walls and the roof. Use 12 sticks to form the top, middle, and bottom framework of your shelter, or three sticks on each of the four sides equally spaced from the top to the bottom of the shelter. The bottom stick on each wall should make firm contact with the ground to make it more difficult for a wild animal to get into your shelter by crawling under the bottom stick. Use 8 sticks on the roof of your shelter to provide minimal support for your tarps so you can have a place to sleep out of the wind and rain the first night. Continue to add more sticks to the framework until you are satisfied with the safety of your temporary shelter.

6. The **top front stick** should be about 7 feet off the ground at the front entrance to your shelter and level with the tops of the two front corner support posts. The front entrance should be on slightly higher ground than the rear of the shelter for rain water drainage.

7. The **top rear stick** should be about 6 feet off the ground at the rear of the shelter and level with the tops of the two rear corner support posts. You may sleep near the rear wall of the shelter. Or you may sleep in the center of the shelter and move your sleeping cot out of the way during the day.

8. The **top side sticks** on the left and right should slope from the front to the rear at the top of the shelter.

Chapter Thirty-Three: A Safe Temporary Shelter

9. Starting at the ground level secure more sticks to the support posts with a 2 inch space between the sticks until you reach a height of about 4 feet. Then tie the sticks with about 4 inch spaces between them until your reach the top stick. These sticks will form the inside walls of your shelter and they will help to keep the tarps from blowing into your living area. (Note: If you wish to build a stronger shelter then do not leave any space or gap between the sticks. Each stick should touch the stick below it. This will more than double the amount of work and time required to build your temporary shelter but it will result in a stronger shelter.)

10. The reason the sticks should be closer together near the ground is to help protect you from any wild animals that might try to enter your shelter. The sticks should be strong enough to give you plenty of time to grab your gun and shoot the wild animal through the tarp. A tarp with a hole in it is better than a person with teeth bites or claw marks that are bleeding profusely. You can easily patch the tarp hole with some duck tape on both sides of the hole.

11. The front side of the shelter should have sticks from the ground up to a height of about 28 inches and then stop. Start again at the top of the front side of the shelter and tie sticks from the top down to about 72 inches off the ground. Tie a strong straight stick vertically up and down at approximately 3 feet from one of the corners to the top and bottom sticks on the front wall. This will form the doorway opening. Now continue tying shorter sticks to the wall side of the doorway from 28 inches up to the 72 inches to finish building the front wall.

12. Tie some roof support sticks from the front wall to the rear wall at six inch intervals across the top of the shelter to make a roof that will support the roof tarp so it does not sag down when it rains. The sticks need to slope in the direction that the rain will run off the tarp to prevent rain puddles on the roof tarp. In other words, do not tie the sticks across the roof from the left to the right wall. Instead tie the sticks from the front to the rear wall.

13. Arrange and secure the wall tarps so you can enter through the front doorway. The wall tarps should be wrapped around the outside of the four walls in a clockwise direction with the first tarp beginning flush with the left side of the door. The wall tarps should extend about one-inch below the lower side of each wall onto the ground and the opposite side of the wall tarp should be draped over the roof of the shelter. You will need several tarps to complete the rectangle around the outside of the four walls. As you work your way around the walls you should overlap the beginning of each new tarp approximately one-foot across the end of the previous tarp for rain and wind protection. The final wall tarp should overlap the very first tarp by approximately one-foot past the door opening for rain and wind protection. Depending on the size of your last wall tarp it may therefore overlap the previous wall tarp by more than one-foot. When you enter and exit the shelter you will need to be able to temporarily move the wall tarp in front of the door out of your way and then secure it back into position.

14. If you have a clear transparent tarp then hang it over the top roof support sticks to form a shed type roof from front to rear with a one-foot slope to direct rain water off the rear 6 foot tall end of the shelter. The clear tarp will let a lot of light into your shelter even on a rainy day. If you don't have a clear tarp then a regular tarp will be fine. The top roof tarp should be in one piece and it should hang down over the outside of all the wall tarps to keep rain water out of your shelter. Therefore the size of your biggest tarp will determine the maximum size of your shelter. Sprinkle a few leaves and brown pine needles and tiny twigs on top of this tarp to help it blend in with the surrounding environment.

15. Secure the metal grommets on the outside edges of your wall tarps and your roof tarp to the bottom sticks or to stakes driven deep into the ground. The tarps should be snug against the support sticks to prevent a lot of movement during windy weather. Movement will gradually wear holes in your tarps.

16. Also secure the metal grommets to the top sticks and the side supports whenever there is a grommet at that particular location. Use all your grommets to better secure your tarps to your shelter.

17. You should be able to step over the front doorway sticks to enter and exit your shelter after moving the loose doorway tarp out of your way. Tie the doorway tarp to the sticks when you are inside the shelter and when you are away from the shelter.
18. If you wish you can build a small door for your shelter by tying some sticks together and then tying your small door to the top stick on the inside of the shelter. Swing the door up and hold it there to enter and exit. You can tie the door to the bottom of the doorway opening when you are inside the shelter or when you are away from the shelter. Or, if you prefer, you may secure the door to the side of your shelter and then swing the door into the shelter to enter and exit the shelter, similar to a regular door. You should tie the door to the opposite side of the door opening when you are inside your shelter or when you leave your shelter.
19. If you wish you can spread a tarp inside the shelter on the ground to make a floor for your shelter. You can tie the grommets on the outside edges of this tarp to a wall stick a short distance up each wall to make the shelter floor relatively waterproof. However, for this to be effective the floor tarp needs to be at least six-inches longer than the inside floor of your shelter in every direction so you will have at least six-inches to tie to each wall.
20. **Optional:** Transplant several thick evergreen bushes about 7 feet tall close to the outside walls of your shelter to help hide your shelter. Randomly space the bushes to create a natural appearance.

Concluding Comments

A temporary shelter **will not** be acceptable during the cold winter months because you would freeze to death. But during the other months it will provide some safety and a place to sleep at night and a place to rest on rainy days while you are building your cabin cave.

You could put one or more big water buckets or plastic tote containers (black or brown or dark green so it can't easily be seen) at the rear of your shelter to catch rain water when it runs off your shelter roof. However, you must filter the water through a good water filter before drinking it, or cooking with it, or using it to brush your teeth, or washing your dishes. But you can use rain water without filtering to wash your hands, your body, and your clothes. But you should not ingest rain water until after you have filtered it because your roof tarp will gradually collect a few "bird droppings." If you don't have a good water filter then you will need to boil your water to make it safe to drink.

You could store some of your equipment and supplies inside your temporary shelter to keep them safe and dry. Do not store open food containers in your shelter and do not cook inside your shelter or near your shelter. The smell will attract wild animals and insects.

You could put camouflage netting on the roof and sides of the shelter to help disguise its appearance. If you don't have camouflage netting then smear the outside of the tarp walls with dirt to help the walls blend in with nature.

If you use a clear roof tarp then remember to be careful with the use of light inside your shelter after sunset to avoid attracting attention to your shelter. If for some reason you are not exhausted at the end of the work day and you want to stay up after dark, then you could place a regular tarp or some thick blankets across the underside of your roof inside your shelter to block any light from revealing the position of your shelter. You can support this tarp or blankets by weaving the tarp or blankets **up over** every third roof support stick and then **under** two roof support sticks until you reach the wall. Then walk outside briefly after dark to verify that you can't see any light from the inside of your shelter.

Please do not sleep on the ground unless you have to. Some better options would be as follows:

1. **Heavy-Duty Foam Sleeping Pad:** These pads are sold in the camping section of many stores. They are about 3/4-inch thick and they roll out on the ground and then you put a sleeping bag on top of it.
2. **High-Quality Air Mattress:** These air mattresses can be purchased in twin, full, and queen sizes. This means you could use your current fitted sheet sets and your current pillow and your blanket.

3. **Folding Cot:** These cots may have a canvas pad to sleep on or they may have springs and a thin mattress. Normally they are used with a sleeping bag.

4. **Your Current Mattress:** In my opinion this is the best option. Remove the top mattress from your bed and take it with you into the wilderness. You won't need the bottom foundation piece of your mattress set unless you just want to take it with you. Instead of the bottom foundation you could buy a 4-foot by 8-foot sheet of plywood and place the plywood on top of your ground tarp inside your temporary shelter. Then put your mattress on top of the piece of plywood. Now you can use your current fitted bed sheets, and pillow, and blankets and you will be able to get some excellent sleep every night. (Note: The piece of plywood will be too long and you will need to saw a short piece off one end of the plywood so the plywood is about four inches longer than your mattress. This will allow two inches of plywood to extend beyond each end of your mattress. The plywood may also be about one-foot narrower than the width of your mattress. You can use the piece you cut off one end of the plywood below the side of your mattress.)

When your cabin cave is almost done you can remove the tarps from your temporary shelter and use them to make your cabin cave watertight. Then you should take down your temporary shelter and leave no trace it was there. You can live inside your cabin cave as you complete the work on it, such as shoveling the dirt against the tarp side walls and the cabin cave roof.

Chapter Thirty-Four

Grandpappy's Wilderness Cabin Cave

What is a wilderness cabin cave? I have never personally heard or read about anything called *"cabin cave."* However I have thought about this intellectually intriguing concept many, many times during the past thirty-years. After much careful consideration I finally reached the conclusion that this idea was entirely feasible, and I also figured out the most effective way to build a cabin cave. In my opinion it would take one-person between six to twelve weeks to build a cabin cave using a pick, a shovel, an axe, a hand saw, a strong rope, a hammer, a wood chisel, and a bark removal tool (no power tools or chain saw).

Following are some of the **advantages of a cabin cave** when compared to a camping tent, a camping trailer, or a traditional log cabin (such as the cabin under construction in the picture):

1. The exterior of a manmade cabin cave would be of an irregular shape and it would blend in with the surrounding environment. Therefore, unlike a tent, trailer, or cabin that could be easily seen from a distance, a manmade cave would be almost invisible. This would provide its inhabitants with a significant degree of safety. They would also be virtually invisible to modern heat seeking technology.

2. The location of most natural caves and manmade mine shafts are well known to the residents living in the surrounding area and to the government. However, you would be the only one who would know where your cabin cave was located.

3. A carefully hidden cabin cave would be a relatively safe place to store your equipment, supplies, and food.

4. You could snore, sneeze, talk, laugh, or make a little noise and no one outside the cave would hear you.

5. You would not have to worry about a rifle bullet penetrating the walls of your cabin cave.

6. The inside of your cabin cave would remain at approximately 50 to 60 degrees Fahrenheit all year (10 to 16 degrees Celsius). This is a comfortable temperature in the winter, spring, summer, and fall. You wouldn't need to keep a fire burning during freezing winter weather or on very cold nights. You would only need to hang a thick blanket over the inside and outside of your doorway entrance. This would help to block air drafts and it would keep the natural warmth inside your cabin cave. And during the summer months you would be able to stay cool without electrical fans or air conditioners. This means you could get some well-deserved sleep every night regardless of the time of year. (Note: The 55 degree Fahrenheit (13°C) average year-round temperature is the reason bears, groundhogs, and many other animals hibernate inside a cave or a deep hole in the ground. It keeps them from freezing to death during the winter.)

7. You would not have to prepare a huge stack of firewood in order to comfortably survive the winter. You would only need enough wood for a small daily cook fire. And perhaps an occasional small fire after returning to your cabin cave if you went outside for an extended hike during freezing winter weather. If these fires were built from well-seasoned hardwood then these fires could be small and virtually smokeless.

8. Since you would not need to keep a continuous fire burning all winter then there would be no column of chimney smoke to attract attention to the location of your cabin cave.

9. The 55 degree Fahrenheit (13°C) average year-round inside cave temperature would help to extend the shelf life of any food you may already have and it would extend the shelf life of any future wild game meat you convert into smoked meat jerky or pemmican. This temperature would also be appropriate for the winter storage of root vegetables such as potatoes and for whole fruits such as apples and pears.

10. A cabin cave would provide excellent protection from all types of wild animals. A wild animal may be able to dig through the dirt but it could not get through the 4 to 7 inch diameter logs. Any animal trying to attack you by breaking through your doorway entrance log door could be killed by sticking a sharp spear deep into its face, neck, or body.

11. Since a cabin cave is below ground it would be a relatively safe place to be during a tornado, hurricane, or some other type of really bad weather.

12. Finally, a cabin cave may also provide some reasonable degree of protection from nuclear fallout in the event of World War Three.

Instructions for Constructing a Cabin Cave

Location: Look for an area where there are a lot of pine trees. Then look for a relatively steep hill or mountain that is at least 20 feet tall and that is not too far from a reliable source of water (stream, creek, river, lake). Steep hills (45 degree or more slope) usually do not contain animal paths or human trails because it takes too much effort to climb straight up a hill this steep. Look for a natural depression in the side of the hill. This will reduce the amount of manual digging you will need to do. If possible the opening to your new cave should be facing south, southeast, or southwest so the inside of the cave will get as much natural sunlight as possible during the day. To avoid possible future flood waters do not dig your cave at the bottom of a hill. Your cave should be a reasonable distance up the side of the hill based on the terrain. It should be at least 8 feet from the bottom of a short hill or at least 20 feet from the bottom of a very tall hill or mountain.

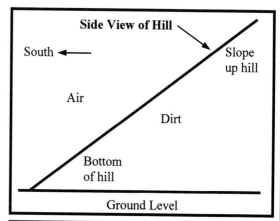

Cabin Cave Size: A one-person manmade cabin cave should have *minimum* inside dimensions of about 9 foot deep, 9 foot wide, and 7 foot tall. This would provide enough space to sleep, and to move around, and to store your equipment and supplies. One-person could move and stack the thin 10 foot long logs needed to build a cabin cave of this size, after the logs have been allowed to dry in the sun. (Note: Two people would require a cabin cave with dimensions of at least 11 foot by 11 foot by 7 foot tall.) Neither a 9 foot nor an 11 foot cave would be subject to the danger of a cave-in or to any special structural problems during construction. However, as a cave gradually gets bigger the risk of a future cave-in also increases.

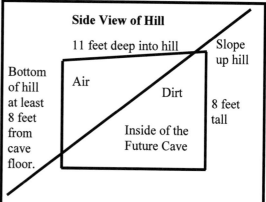

(Note: The following discussion will be based on a cabin cave with inside dimensions of 9 by 9 by 7 feet and with outside dimensions of 10 by 10 by 7.5 feet. This will require a cave hole of 11 by 11 by 8 feet. It will also require a ground tarp of 12 by 12 feet and a cover tarp of 26 by 20 feet. However, the actual cabin cave dimensions may easily be adjusted to more fully utilize whatever size tarps you have available. The cabin cave does not need to be perfectly square. For example, the inside dimensions of the cabin cave

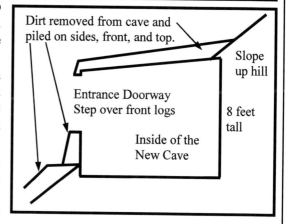

Chapter Thirty-Four: Grandpappy's Wilderness Cabin Cave

could easily be changed to 8 by 10 by 7 feet, or 8 by 12 by 7 feet, or 9 by 10 by 7 feet, or 9 by 12 by 7 feet, or whatever depending on the size of the tarps you actually have available.)

Digging the Cave Hole: You do not want to dig a hole into the side of the mountain. Instead you want to dig a hole straight down into the hill. Therefore the hill should have a steady downward slope from the rear of your new cave towards its front. This will reduce the amount of digging you have to do because the front of the cave will only need to be dug out one or two feet and the back of the cave will be dug out about 8 feet. You will need to dig a cave hole about 11 feet wide by 11 long by 8 feet tall. (Note: The cabin *exterior walls* will be 10 feet square. The cave hole will be 11 feet square and this will give you about 6 inches of working space on each side of your new cabin as you build it. It will also provide enough space to insert an exterior heavy duty waterproof tarp over and around your cabin when you are finished.)

The dirt you remove from the hill can be used to build up the sides of your new cave. This will reduce the amount of digging you have to do by approximately 40% and it will give you a convenient nearby place to toss the dirt from the hole. Shovel as much dirt as possible to your right and left and not down the hill. Your objective will be to create a dirt enclosure around your new manmade cabin cave so it looks as natural as possible. Leave an open space at least 3 feet wide at the front for a cave entrance.

(Note: The doorway entrance should be about 24 to 28 inches above the inside floor of your cabin cave and about three feet wide and four feet tall. Later you can cover the outside doorway entrance with a small camouflage tarp (or waterproof cloth) suspended from the top of the entrance and hanging down. Then transplant a few short evergreen bushes near the front of the outside cave entrance. You can block the inside entrance with a few 2-inch thick pine logs lashed together to make a log door that you can swing to the right so you can enter and exit your cabin cave.)

Cutting the Pine Logs: After you have finished digging your cave hole the inside of your new cabin cave will be constructed with pine tree logs about 10 feet long and between 4 to 7 inches in diameter. A ten-foot long log will yield a nine-foot wide inside room because about seven-inches of each end of the log will be resting on the logs directly below it on each side. You will need a thin piece of string, rope, or rawhide about 10 feet long and one that is 12 feet long so you can cut all your pine wall logs to the proper length. The roof logs and a few of the wall logs will need to be about 12 feet long. Cut the pine tree as close to the ground as possible. Then shovel some dirt onto the tree stump to hide the stump and to help it decay more rapidly. Look for relatively thin straight pine trees with ground diameters of between 7 to 9 inches. This corresponds to outside circumferences of 24 to 30 inches with the bark still on the trees. Do not harvest all the pine trees in one small area. Leave at least half the pine trees alone so you do not create a large empty area which would draw attention to your future cabin cave. You should look for pine trees that are relatively straight and which do not have pronounced curves or odd growth patterns. Leave the poorly shaped pine trees and the really small pine trees and the really big pine trees alone.

(Log Size Note: A traditional log cabin uses pine logs that are between 8 to 12 inches in diameter. This diameter log is needed to support the roof and to provide sufficient thermal mass to keep the heat inside the cabin during the winter. However, the inside of a cabin cave will be much smaller than a traditional log cabin, and it will have a simple flat shed type roof, and the surrounding dirt will provide the insulation needed to keep the cabin cave warm during the winter. Therefore a cabin cave can be built using pine logs that are between 4 to 7 inches in diameter. This size log is much lighter in total weight and each log can be more easily moved by one person, after the log has dried out. However, if you wish to use logs with a larger diameter then you may certainly do so.)

Bark Removal: After you have cut down the pine tree leave the top and branches on the tree for two weeks because they will pull the moisture out of the trunk of the tree. Then cut off the tree top and the limbs. You can usually cut two or three pine logs from one pine tree. Some of the logs will be ten-feet long and some twelve-feet long. Remove the bark from the pine logs using a

Chapter Thirty-Four: Grandpappy's Wilderness Cabin Cave

draw tool which is called a draw knife (picture top right on previous page with wood ... ...de scraping tool (picture bottom right on previous page with red rubber handles). To remove ... pull the tool towards you while applying downward pressure on the tool against the tree. The tool ... slip under the bark and strip the bark off the tree. Gradually work from one end of the log to the other. Then rotate the log 1/4 turn and repeat until you have all the bark off the log. You can now move the 10 and 12-foot logs to your cabin cave location. If possible, let the logs dry in the sun for two more weeks after removing the bark.

Chemical Preservation: After the logs are sufficiently dry they may be chemically treated to extend their useful lives. You may use any exterior wood stain, wood oil, or waterproof clear wood seal ($65 per 5-gallon pail). Use a paint brush to apply a coat completely around each log and let it dry for at least one-day. (Note: Do not paint the cut ends of the logs until later when you notch the log for assembly into your cabin wall.) If possible, use a clear transparent coat or a very light color stain. If you select a dark stain color then the inside of your cabin cave will look dark and depressing. If you use a clear or light color then the inside of your cabin cave will look bright and cheerful.

The Foundation: Find four large rocks with at least one relatively flat surface. Plant each of these rocks into the ground with the flat surface approximately two-inches above the level of the ground. These will be the four corner foundations of your cabin cave. If you have a level then use some string to get these four rocks at the same level height. Smooth out the dirt floor of your new cave and try to get the floor as level as you can. Pack the floor dirt down hard. Jump up and down on it if you need to. Place a 12 foot by 12 foot heavy duty tarp on the dirt floor of the cave and extend it up and over the four rocks. (Note: If you have an extra 12 foot by 12 foot tarp then place it on the ground on top of the first tarp.) Later after carefully positioning your four bottom cabin logs, securely tack or nail or tie the ground tarp at several places to the outside of the four bottom logs.

Building the Cabin Cave: The bigger logs should be used for the walls and the thinner logs on the roof and the interior shelves. (Note: Save your two best logs to put on top of the front and rear walls to support your roof because they will support the weight of your roof.) Alternate the logs by putting the thin end of the next log over the thick end of the previous log. The end of each log should be even with the outside wall and it should not extend past the wall.

Cut a notch in the underside of each log to match the size of the log below it at the corner. Do not cut a notch more than one-fourth through the thickness at the end of the log. See the above notch illustration. You can cut an end notch using a saw by sawing through the log a short distance and then sawing through the log again at 90 degrees to your first saw cut. You will need to notch the bottom and the top of each log so it will fit level with the logs below and above it at each corner.

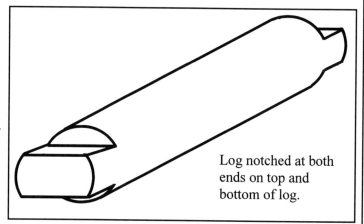
Log notched at both ends on top and bottom of log.

Logs notched in this manner will result in a very stable cabin cave. The notches will allow you to stack each log firmly on the log below it at the corner. Your wall corners will also provide most of the support for your roof. The notches will prevent the log walls from gradually moving or sliding into the cabin. The dirt you pack around the outside of your cabin walls will prevent the walls from falling away from the cabin. Therefore if you use the illustrated notch design your cabin will remain standing for a very long time. (Note: After you cut a notch and you have verified that it fits properly against the other logs then use a paint brush to apply some chemical treatment to the newly exposed cut areas of the log and the outside end of the log.)

To the extent possible each log should make contact along most of its length with the log directly below it on the same wall. There should only be small gaps or spaces between the two logs. This will require some

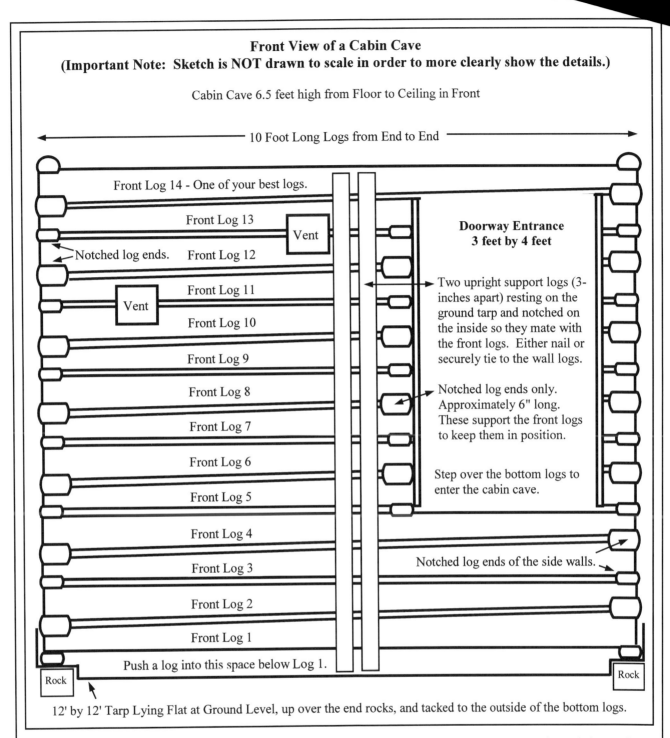

careful fitting and notching of the ends of each log. It would be better to cut each log end notch just a little, and then see if it fits, and do this two or three times until you get a really good fit. This strategy would be better than cutting a deep notch in the beginning and then discovering the notch is too big and you have ruined your log. The roof will be supported by the four corners of your cabin so you should take the time to get a good smooth fit with each log notch in each corner.

You will not need to perfectly match the logs together along their entire length in the same manner as a traditional log cabin because you are going to place a tarp against the outside of each wall and pack dirt against the tarp. Therefore dirt, wind, rain, snow, and insects will not be able to get into the small spaces between your logs.

...d right side walls should have the small end of the first log facing the front of the cave. ...of the first log on the left and right should be at the rear of the cave. Later when you reach ...ately 6.5 feet in height in the front, finish the left and right side walls with another log on each side ...the small end to the front of the cave and the large end to the rear of the cave. Then put one of your best logs across the rear wall of the cave but do not add another log onto the front. This will make the rear wall about 7 feet tall and it will provide at least 6 inches of slope from the rear to the front of the cave. This will be enough for rain water to flow forward.

Optional Interior Wall Shelves (see illustration on the next page): As you build your cabin you may install three log shelves along the entire rear wall of your cabin. The first shelf should be 24-inches off the floor, the second 42-inches off the floor, and the third 60-inches off the floor. See the illustration on the next page.

Doorway Entrance: The doorway entrance will need to be constructed as you build the front wall of the cabin cave. You will need a few short logs to support the front wall on the left side of the door, and the side wall on the right side of the door. When you have finished the front wall you will need to nail or tie some thin logs to the outside front wall on the left side of the doorway to keep the front wall in position so it does not gradually lean over and fall into your cabin.

Small Windows or Air Vents: Install two or three small glass windows with wire screens in the front wall. (Note: If you don't have any windows then install simple air vents.) The windows will let sunlight into your cabin cave and they will let you to see what the weather looks like outside. If you see a deer walk by outside and you have a hunting rifle then you could shoot the deer from inside your cabin through the small window. See the previous illustration for more details about the placement and installation of these windows. For $20 Home Depot sells a 6.25-inch square "Cat Flap" door (picture on right). It has an unbreakable weather resistant clear plastic door that is lockable. The door is in two parts. The swinging transparent door could be mounted on the inside cabin wall. You could then install a wire screen on the other half of the door opening before you mount  it on the exterior front wall. During the hot summer months you could prop the inside door open and the wire screen would let fresh air into your cabin but it would keep the insects out. During the winter you could easily replace the exterior wire screen with a square piece of thick glass to provide additional protection from freezing winter weather. The exterior glass would let sunlight into your cabin cave but it would help to form an air pocket inside the wall of your cabin to help keep the freezing air outside. Some fresh air would still enter your cabin in the winter through the large doorway entrance. (Note: After you have finished the rest of your cabin cave then build an exterior log tunnel using thin logs for each window. However, each window tunnel should gradually get wider as it extends out from the cabin. This will allow more sunlight to enter the cabin and it will provide a downward slope for rain water to flow away from the cabin window. Face one window tunnel directly southwest and one southeast. This will help to direct sunlight into your cabin cave for the greater part of the day.)

(Note: Even if you don't have any glass windows you should still leave a light and air opening in the front of your cabin cave. If you have any screen wire then you could cover the inside and outside of this opening with screen wire to keep insects out of your cabin cave.)

The Roof: Build a shed type cabin roof by installing your logs from rear to front so the spaces between the logs run from the rear to the front of the cave. Alternate the roof logs with a thick end at the rear and then a thin end at the rear. Notch the underside of your roof logs so each one fits over the highest front and rear wall logs. This will help to keep the roof securely in place. Press your roof logs together as tightly as you can and tie them securely to one another. The extra roof log length should extend over the front of your cabin wall (but no more than two-feet).

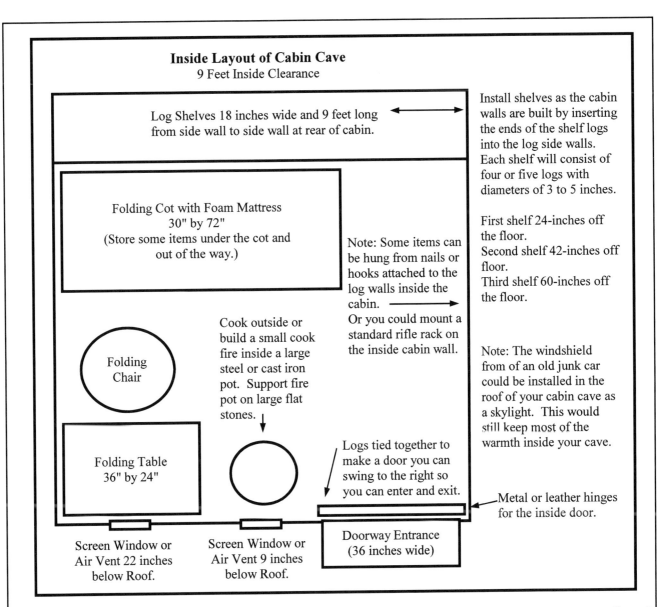

Tarp Covers: Place a heavy duty tarp over the entire cabin so that it covers the roof, the rear wall, and the two side walls. A 26 foot by 20 foot tarp will do the job nicely. (Note: If you have two of these large tarps then use them both to provide more protection.) (Note: If necessary you may use several smaller tarps instead of one big tarp. Place a tarp so that it hangs all the way down each wall to the ground and secure the top of the tarp to the roof. Then place the roof tarp into position so that it covers the four wall tarps. Rain water will now run down the outside of your wall tarps and not into your cabin.)

Use another smaller tarp to cover the front wall. You will need to cut openings in this tarp to match the exact location of your doorway opening and your windows or air vents. Cut each opening down one side, across the bottom, and back up the other side. Do not cut across the top of the opening. Then roll each flap into a tight cylinder and tie them into place just above the door and air vents, after you punch two small holes into the tarp for your flap strings. (Note: You can unroll these flaps later if you need to cover these openings for some reason. For example, you may wish to do this if you leave your cabin cave for several weeks to more completely explore the surrounding wilderness area.)

Packing the Dirt: Fill in the side and back trenches around your cabin cave with dirt so the dirt makes firm contact with your exterior tarps. Use a long pole to pack the dirt firmly down in the trenches outside your walls but be careful you don't tear your tarp walls in the process. You should also put between five to eight

Chapter Thirty-Four: Grandpappy's Wilderness Cabin Cave

inches of dirt on top of the outside roof of your cave. If possible seed this dirt with wild grass seed that is common to the surrounding area. This is called a "sod roof." The inside log roof and the outside dirt roof of the cave should slope down from the rear to the front for water runoff when it rains. Your cabin cave will now be waterproof and when it rains the water will flow forward off the front of your cabin cave.

(Water Note: If you need water then when it rains put another tarp on the outside roof of your cave to direct the rain into some type of water storage container or collect the rain using the tarp itself. Then transfer the rain water into your cave for future use. Rain water is far superior in quality when compared to ground water from a stream or lake.)

Finish your cabin by packing dirt tightly against the front wall of your cabin cave. You should have at least 30 inches of dirt at the bottom of your cabin cave and at least 18 inches of dirt at the roof. This will provide a slope in front. Tightly pack the dirt below your doorway entrance and your windows or air vents. Pack the dirt in a random manner and do not make it look smooth and level. Sow some native grass seed in the dirt to keep it from washing away when it rains.

Transplant some short evergreen bushes (that are common in the surrounding area) in a random fashion several feet in front of your cabin cave. Most of these transplanted bushes will gradually grow and help to more completely hide the location of your new cabin cave. Unfortunately a few of the bushes may die as a result of the transplanting process.

A Few Final Suggestions

After you have selected a good site for your cabin cave and you have tested the ground by digging a few feet deep then you should probably cut down the pine trees before you finish digging out the rest of your cave hole. This will give the pine trees some time to dry in the sun as you work on your cave hole.

Do not store your equipment and supplies directly on top of the ground floor tarp. They may absorb moisture from the earth if you do. Instead lay several 3-inch diameter logs on the ground tarp and stack your items on top of these logs.

Purchase and store at least two good quality hunting knives at your wilderness cabin cave. You will probably discover that you use your hunting knife more frequently than any other item you have at your cabin cave. A hunting knife is one of the tools that is absolutely necessary for wilderness survival. If something should happen to your knife then you will need a replacement. Therefore you should have at least one extra hunting knife at your cabin cave. You should also have an Arkansas Sharpening Stone or a Diamond Sharpening Stone to keep a sharp edge on your knife blade.

Be creative and figure out one or two different ways to secure your cabin log door from the outside to prevent stray animals from pushing the door open and entering your cabin when you are absent. You will need to be able to unlatch your interior door from the outside of your cabin cave. You don't want to get locked out of your own home. You can place a log bar across the entire width of the interior door when you are inside the cabin cave to prevent a wild animal from pushing the interior door open while you are asleep.

Always approach your cabin cave carefully from the outside when you return and use a long stick to move the front tarp away from the doorway entrance to make sure some wild animal has not found this area and decided it would be a great nesting place.

You could build some primitive pine furniture. Or you could use some folding camp furniture inside your cave, such as a folding table and folding chair, a folding cot with a foam mattress (or a high quality air mattress), and a good sleeping bag. (Note: A folding cot would allow you to store things below the cot out of the way.)

Purchase some nice sheets, a good feather pillow, a **thin** blanket, a **thick wool** blanket or down comforter, and a high-quality low-temperature goose-down sleeping bag. Use these assorted sleeping items in your cabin cave at the appropriate times during the year depending on the weather.

Invest in some quality long thermal underwear, some really good wool socks, some cloth gloves, and a soft comfortable ski mask. You may need to wear these items when you go to bed during the winter months.

If you need to build a fire inside your cabin cave then build a **very small fire** inside a large heavy duty steel or cast iron pot that is supported on top of several flat rocks. Cover the inside bottom of the fire pot with two-inches of sand or dirt. The fire pot should be at least 12-inches off the floor and at least 12-inches from the log wall and from anything else that is flammable. Build a smokeless fire using well seasoned hardwood.

Build and learn how to use a solar oven. However, a solar oven will only work when the sun is shinning.

Stock your cabin cave with cast iron cookware and a set of non-stick Teflon coated cookware. Also invest in some good quality plastic food storage containers with snap on lids, some good enamel coated eating dishes, some tableware, and two dish washing pots. If the food storage containers are all the same size they may fit inside one another when they are empty and not require much storage space. You should have both large and medium size food storage containers.

You could hang a rifle rack on one of the interior walls of your cabin. You could also install nails or large hooks in the walls of your cabin and hang things from them, such as your cook pots.

Invest in some commercial quality animal traps, such as the conibear 110, 220, and 330 sizes, and some Duke leg traps, and some aircraft cable snares. These items can currently be purchased on Ebay. Store these items inside your cabin cave. (Note: Traps and snares will allow you to hunt silently 24 hours per day seven days per week in several different locations simultaneously. Your traps will still be working for you even while you are asleep at night.)

Learn how to make meat jerky and how to make pemmican, a native American Indian survival food.

You should also learn how to harvest and process widely available and easily identifiable edible wild foods, such as acorns.

Store all your cabin building tools inside your cabin cave. You may need them to make future repairs on your cabin cave. Your pick and shovel will also be useful for planting a Spring garden.

Store some vegetable seeds at your cabin cave. In the Spring plant your vegetable seeds a reasonable distance away from your cabin cave in a vacant field or other area that gets good sunlight most of the day. Do not plant all your vegetables in one area. Root vegetables that grow below ground, such as carrots, onions, potatoes, and peanuts usually do better in a wilderness environment. Since the edible part of the plant grows below ground they will not attract any special attention to your fresh food supply. Root vegetables also store reasonably well for future consumption during the winter months. Carrots and radishes can actually be left in the ground if your winters are not severe. Tomato seeds are also nice to have because tomato plants are easy to grow and each vine yields a lot of tomatoes. The major shortcoming of tomato plants is they can be easily seen from a distance and their bright color attracts insects and forest wildlife.

You should also have some way to store at least 50 gallons of rain water inside your cabin cave. This could be accomplished using clean empty soft drink bottles with screw on caps or several large plastic storage containers with tight fitting lids. Or you could build a log box inside your cabin cave and then put a waterproof tarp inside the box and then fill the inside of the tarp with rain water.

In addition to a good wilderness survival manual, such as the **SAS Survival Guide** by John "Lofty" Wiseman, you should also have a reasonable supply of paperback novels to read during the winter months. You can normally purchase gently used fiction paperback novels at yard sales and garage sales for between ten cents to twenty-five cents each. In addition to your favorite type of fictional novel you should not overlook novels in areas you may only have minor interest, such as westerns, science fiction, romance, murder mysteries, adventure, etc. In my opinion 200 of these paperback books would not be excessive. You would be surprised at what you will read when you have nothing but time on your hands. Two normal decks of 52 playing cards and a good book on solitaire card games would also allow you to pass away the hours in an entertaining manner.

Although you may not currently read the Holy Bible very often you may discover that your interest in spiritual matters increases significantly when God is the only other Person you have to talk to and He is the only One who can help you to survive a variety of unexpected wilderness survival situations.

Chapter Thirty-Four: Grandpappy's Wilderness Cabin Cave

Materials Estimates for a 9 foot long by 9 foot wide by 7 foot tall Cabin Cave
(Inside Dimensions)
(Note: Tarp Quantities Assume a Double Layer of Tarps on the Roof, Walls, and Ground)

Quantity	Material Description
2	12-foot by 12-foot heavy duty tarps for the floor
2	26-foot by 20-foot heavy duty tarps for the roof and 3 walls
2	12-foot by 8-foot heavy duty tarps for the front wall
1	8-foot by 8-foot camouflage heavy duty tarp. Cut into pieces and hang in front of the doorway entrance and the window tunnels.
1	14 to 18-inch diameter heavy duty steel or cast iron fire pot
2 or 3	6-inch to 12-inch square screen glass windows that swing in and out
2 or 3	Extra glass panes that will fit the windows
1	Tube of waterproof caulk sealant for the two or three windows
4	Metal Hinges for the interior and exterior doors
100	6-inch long nails
100	4-inch long nails
50	Heavy duty wall hooks (shaped like a dish cabinet cup hook -- hang pots and pans and other things on the walls)
5	200-yard rolls of heavy duty nylon cord, or poly cord, or thin wire
10	Gallons of Wood Stain or Waterproof Wood Sealer
1	Rifle rack (plastic type used inside a truck)
Some	Screen wire for the windows
59	Ten-foot long wall logs (4 to 7-inch diameters)
24	Twelve-foot long roof logs (3 to 6-inch diameters)
12	Ten-foot long shelf logs (3 shelves with 4 logs per shelf) (3 to 6-inch diameters)

Minimum Time Estimates for One-Person to Build a Cabin Cave

1.00 Hour = Cut down one thin pine tree. One pine tree will yield two or three logs.
+0.50 Hour = Cut top off tree and remove limbs. Pile the limbs in a safe area for burning.
1.50 Hours = Total time per tree.

0.60 Hours = Total time per log when 1.5 Hours is divided by 2.5 average logs per tree.
0.25 Hours = Cut each log to the proper length.
0.50 Hours = Remove bark from each log.
0.25 Hours = Move each log to the cabin site.
0.25 Hours = Paint each log with chemical treatment.
0.75 Hours = Notch and carefully fit each log into cabin.
2.60 Hours = Total time per log.

2.60 Hours = Total time per log.
X 95 Logs = Total number of logs needed to build the cabin.
247 Hours = Total time required to build the cabin.

31 Days = 247 hours / 8 hours per day = Total estimated time to build the cabin.
4 Days = Dig the cave hole (Note: More time may be required in rocky or hard earth).
1 Day = Pack the dirt around the cabin walls and finish the front of the cabin.
36 Days = Total days to build a cabin cave.

6 Weeks = 36 Total days / 6 working days per week.
6 Weeks = Minimum time estimate for one-person to build a cabin cave.

(Note: If any type of difficulty is encountered at any step in the process then more time may be required to build the cabin cave.)

Chapter Thirty-Five

Clothing

Hats, Caps, and Ski Masks: If you have ever seen a photograph taken of a group of people who were outdoors during the late 1800s you may have noticed that almost everyone in the picture was wearing some type of hat. These individuals were not wearing a hat simply because it was fashionable at that time. They were wearing hats because a hat was considered a necessary article of clothing.

Before there were heated and air-conditioned buildings and heated and air-conditioned vehicles to rapidly transport people between those buildings, people in the 1800s spent a higher percentage of their time outdoors. The purpose of the hat or bonnet was to help keep their heads warm and to protect their face, ears, and the backs of their necks from sunburn (even on a winter day). If you have ever had a serious sunburn on your nose, or the back of your neck, or the top of your ears then you know from personal experience how truly painful this can be. Therefore to protect themselves from this type of injury people in the 1800s used simple common sense (sometimes called horse sense) and they wore a hat or a bonnet.

Today there are all types of head coverings available. Let's look at three of those options: a baseball cap, a hat with a full brim, and a ski mask.

Baseball Cap: One of the most popular head coverings in the United States is the baseball cap. I do not wish to offend anyone who dearly loves these types of hats but a baseball cap only protects the top of your head and your eyes from the sun and in most cases it will not protect your nose or the tops of your ears or the back of your neck. If you are bald, or if you have very little hair remaining on top of your head, then a baseball cap will help to protect your head from sunburn and hide the fact that you don't have very much hair on your head. But a baseball cap is not the best choice for a long-term hard times tragedy event.

Hat with a Full Brim: A hat with a full brim is recommended for a long-term hard times event for the following reasons:

1. It will help to protect a bald head or a head with very little hair from sunburn.
2. It will help to keep any type of head warm.
3. The full brim goes all the way around the hat. Therefore the brim will protect your nose, your ears, and the back of your neck from sunburn, even on a bright sunny freezing cold winter day.
4. If it starts to rain the full brim will catch the rain and direct it away from your head so the rain falls off the rear brim of your hat behind you onto the ground.

Therefore when selecting a hat you should look for a hat that is made from some type of waterproof material and it should have a medium or wide brim that extends all the way around the hat. When you put the hat on your head and you look in the mirror you will probably see that the front brim is higher than the rear brim and therefore it will help to direct rainwater off the back of the hat.

The hat should feel comfortable on your head and it should not feel too tight or too loose. If it is *too tight* then you will be able to feel it pressing against your forehead. If it is *too loose* then it will fall off your head when you bow at the waist. The hat should be a little loose on your head but not so loose that it will be constantly falling off.

Ski Mask: A full face ski mask is also a very useful item to have in cold weather. It will help to keep your entire head warm, including your ears, nose, chin, and part of your neck. On a cold windy day there is nothing that can compare to the comfort of a ski mask to keep your nose and ears from becoming frost bitten.

Depending on the thickness of your ski mask it might be possible to wear your ski mask under your full brim hat if your hat was purchased to be comfortable and your hat does not fit too tightly on your head.

If the wind is not blowing then the bottom half of a ski mask can be lifted up above your eyes and be used to only cover the top half of your head. This will provide a double layer of warmth for your forehead and ears.

If it is extremely cold at night then you may wish to wear a ski mask to bed and sleep with it covering your head, ears, nose, chin, and neck to keep your head and face warm so you can get a decent night's rest. Your eyes, mouth, and nostrils would be uncovered so you could breathe and so you could see when you woke up. In the 1800s many people wore a head covering at night and it was called a "night cap." A night cap had material on each side of the cap that was used to tie the cap under your chin to keep it from working its way off your head during the night. A ski mask does not require these side ties because a ski mask covers your entire head, including your chin, and therefore it will not gradually slip off your head when you turn from side to side during the night, unless you are an extremely restless sleeper.

Therefore it would probably be a good idea to have two ski masks: one to wear during the freezing cold winter days and a clean one to wear to bed at night.

Finally, if you are trying to remain undetected in a rural or wilderness environment then a hat or ski mask will help to cover your head and make it more difficult to see your human facial features at a distance.

Note: Another option for staying warm at night would be to sleep inside a hooded sweatshirt. Place the hood over your head and pull the drawstrings so it fits loosely against your head. If it is really cold where you are sleeping then wear a ski mask under your hooded sweatshirt.

Mosquito Head Net: During hard times the insect population multiplies. All types of flying insects will fly around your head and they will annoy you and distract you and seriously reduce your productivity and your effectiveness in whatever you are trying to accomplish. The simple solution to the flying insect problem is to purchase a mosquito head net for each member of your family. The head net can be worn under a hat or over a hat or with no hat at all. These head nets sell for less than two-dollars in the camping section of many stores. The net will keep the tiny insects out of your ears, eyes, nose, and mouth and you will not experience the unpleasant gagging reflex caused by inhaling a gnat.

Gloves: There are a wide variety of different types of gloves that are designed for a multitude of different purposes. However, for the purpose of this article the only types of gloves that will be discussed will be for work, or for warmth, or for both.

Leather Work Gloves: If you will be using your hands to do hard physical labor then you will probably discover that a good pair of comfortable *flexible* leather work gloves will protect your hands from a variety of injuries and from becoming calloused and blistered. This is of critical importance during a long-term hard times event because if you can't use your hands then your chances of survival significantly decrease.

Warm Gloves: During a cold weather hard times event you will probably discover that you will need to wear warm gloves both indoors and outdoors to keep your hands warm. If the temperature drops really low at night then you will probably discover that you will want to sleep with your warm gloves on your hands. Therefore a comfortable pair of flexible warm gloves is a basic necessity that everyone in your family will need. Wool gloves are usually preferred but wool gloves are normally more difficult to find and they are more expensive than cotton gloves or gloves made from synthetic fibers. (Note: My personal experience has been that a good pair of leather driving gloves perform exceptionally well for keeping my hands warm when I am just sitting around the house and while sleeping during really cold weather.)

Campfire Cooking Gloves with Long Wrists: If you are cooking over a wood burning fire (fireplace or campfire) then a pair of loose fitting leather gloves with long wrists will be extremely useful when you move pots and pans to and from the fire area, and when you stir the food inside the pots near the fire. Campfire cooking gloves should be a little loose so you can quickly shake them off your hands if they accidentally become too hot. Your cooking gloves should only be used for cooking and they should not be used for anything else in order to keep them as sanitary as possible and to help avoid transferring something unpleasant into your food.

The life expectancies of the above gloves are as follows:

1. **Leather Work Gloves:** Gloves that are used for hard physical labor several days each week will usually only last three or four months before you wear holes in them or they start to fall apart. Therefore if you anticipate having to do hard physical labor (gardening or cutting firewood) during a long-term hard times event then you should have several pairs of good leather work gloves for each "worker" in your household.
2. **Warm Gloves:** Gloves that are only worn for warmth will easily last at least five years or a lot longer if they are good quality gloves.
3. **Campfire Cooking Gloves with Long Wrists:** Gloves that are only used when cooking over the coals of a wood burning fire will normally last at least three years. However, do not lay your cooking gloves down too close to the fire when you are not using them or the heat will significantly shorten their useful life.

Finally, I suggest that you try the gloves on before you purchase them. The gloves should feel very comfortable on your hands and they should not be too tight or too loose. During a long-term hard times tragedy event you will be using your gloves a lot and comfort is a very important issue in this type of situation.

Socks: During a long-term hard times tragedy event the one clothing item that will almost always wear out the fastest and which is also the most important to your long-term survival will be your socks. Walking may become critical to your survival during a long-term hard times event and without a good pair of socks between your feet and your boots then walking will become either extremely uncomfortable or impossible.

Most people think socks last a long time because they don't have to replace their socks very often. But these people usually buy their socks in packages of between three to ten pair of socks per package. And most people usually have between six to twelve pair of socks in their sock drawer. Therefore each pair of socks is usually only worn one day each week. And if you only buy new socks once every six months then you think that all socks will last about six months. This is true during normal times but each pair of socks was only used one day each week during those six months so each pair of socks has a life expectancy of about 20 to 30 days of continuous wear. And the reason one pair of socks will last about 25 days is because we don't walk very much during normal times.

However, during a hard times event it would not be unusual for a person to walk two or three times further every day than during normal times. This means a good pair of socks would only last between 10 to 15 days under heavy use, if you were to use the same pair of socks every day. No one would do this if they could put on clean socks each day. But the life expectancy of each pair of socks would still be significantly less than anything a person was accustomed to during normal times.

Therefore when you think about the shortened life expectancy of a good pair of socks and how important socks are to your long term survival then you will probably realize that your current emergency inventory of socks is totally inadequate.

During really cold winter weather you may need to wear two or three pair of socks to keep your feet warm.

The easiest way to extend the useful life of your socks is to keep your toenails trimmed short. During hard times you should seriously consider trimming your toenails once every week. Each time you trim your toenails you should take the time to file each toenail very smooth so it does not have any rough places that can catch and tear a hole in your socks.

You should also learn the proper way to repair your socks. The proper way is called "darning." Instructions for darning socks can be downloaded from the following three web sites:
http://www.ehow.com/how_648_darn-sock.html?ref=fuel
http://www3.telus.net/findNchoose/Darning.html
http://www.wikihow.com/Darn-a-Sock

Lightweight Jacket: A waterproof jacket is necessary for the cool weather months and for cool nights during the warm weather months. The jacket should have an attached hood that will cover your head when it rains or when the wind is blowing. The jacket should have a special pocket or flap below the collar of the jacket to store the hood when it is not needed. Finally, the jacket should be long enough to completely cover your upper body including your groin area.

Winter Coat: Your cold weather coat should be waterproof. If possible it should have a zippered removable lining that will allow you to add more warmth to the coat during the coldest months of winter. The coat should extend down to your knees.

Long Underwear (Thermal Underwear): During cold weather each member of your family should wear long underwear, or thermal underwear, under their regular clothing. This includes wearing a long sleeve upper garment and a long leg lower garment below your normal clothing. The extra layer of clothing will help you to stay warmer and you will lose less of your normal body heat to the surrounding cold air.

There are a lot of different types of long underwear available. You should purchase the best quality you can afford. However, even an inexpensive pair of long underwear is better than no long underwear.

If you can't find any long underwear then you should consider wearing a pair of ladies pantyhose under your jeans, even if you are a male. They make ladies pantyhose in Queen sizes and in Plus sizes that will usually fit an adult male. If you buy black pantyhose then it will not look like you are wearing pantyhose if a temporary small space briefly appears between your jeans and your socks. Read the back of the package to determine the recommended waist, weight, and length of the pantyhose before you make your investment. If you can't find any long underwear you should also consider wearing a long sleeve undershirt below your normal shirt. If you can't find a long sleeve undershirt then try wearing two t-shirts with short sleeves under your normal shirt. Your primary objective is to keep your chest and abdominal area warm because that is where the majority of your vital organs are located and performing their normal functions.

Layers of Clothing: You will stay warmer wearing several thin layers of clothing instead of wearing one or two thick layers of clothing. If you are wearing several thin layers of clothing and it gradually gets colder then you can add another layer of clothing to get warmer. If you gradually get too warm then you can remove a layer of clothing to cool off. But if you are only wearing one or two really heavy layers of clothing then you can't easily add or subtract layers without getting much too warm or much too cool. Therefore several thin layers of clothing are better than one or two thick layers of clothing. You should keep this in mind when you are purchasing your clothing. There is nothing wrong with having a good thick pair of pants and a good thick shirt but you should also have some thinner items that you can wear below those thick items to better control your body temperature and keep yourself more comfortable.

Summer Clothing: During warm weather it is nice to have some type of insect repellant that you can spray or rub on your skin to keep the insects away. But during a serious long-term hard times tragedy event most of us will quickly run out of insect repellant and we will need an alternate solution to the insect problem.

If you are going to remain indoors most of the time during the really warm summer weather then short sleeve shirts and short pants are a good choice. But if you will need to be outdoors for a reasonable portion of the day and there are flying insects, gnats, and mosquitoes that are looking for someone to feed on then you would be providing an easy meal for these insects if a lot of your skin is exposed. However, if you were wearing a very lightweight thin loose-fitting long-sleeve summer shirt, and lightweight thin loose-fitting long summer pants, then you would have less skin area exposed and this could significantly reduce the number of insect bites you receive. If the garments are loose-fitting then they will be sliding around a little bit on your body and this will make it more challenging for an insect to bite through the garment and get to you. If you also wear a mosquito head net then your head will also be protected from insects.

If you are trying to remain undetected in a rural or wilderness environment during the warm summer weather then wearing a thin long sleeve shirt and a thin pair of long pants will help to better conceal your human features and skin.

When I lived in Florida I noticed that the Sporting Goods Stores sold a special type of clothing for hunters that was designed for their hot, humid environment. The clothing had an outer layer of close weave mesh that you could see through and an inner layer of thick weave mesh. The inner mesh pattern was about 1/4 inch square but the mesh material was about 1/8 inch thick. This allowed your skin to breath and it kept the outer close weave mesh far enough off your skin that a mosquito could not feed on you. I tried to find this type of clothing in the Sporting Goods Stores in Georgia and in Alabama but none of them had any idea of what I was talking about. Therefore you may or may not be able to find a store in your area that sells this type of special summer clothing.

Color of Clothing and Boots: During a long-term hard times tragedy event your best chance for survival is to blend in and not attract any unnecessary attention to yourself.

If you are planning to live in the wilderness and never enter a small rural town then camouflage clothing may be a reasonable option for you. The problem with camouflage clothing is that very, very few people inside a rural town wear that type of clothing on a regular basis so you will stand out from everyone else and you will be noticed by anyone who sees you.

On the other hand, if you are wearing solid color dark faded clothing then you will blend it. During a long-term hard times tragedy event there will probably not be too many people wearing new clothes so your best chance of blending in would be to wear something without any type of distinctive pattern or any type of bright color.

In order to strategically choose the best colors for your particular situation you should first very carefully look at your environment and determine which colors are predominate during the different seasons of the year.

1. **White:** If your area is covered in snow for several months each year then you will need some white clothing to blend in during your normal winter weather. But if your area only has snow on the ground for a few days each year then white clothing would probably be a very poor choice. If your area has snow on the ground for several days each month during the winter and you need to blend into a wilderness area, then you should consider purchasing a white rain poncho with a white hood that you can wear over your normal dark color clothing.

2. **Brown:** If your area is surrounded by trees and those trees lose their leaves every fall then brown would be a good choice because the ground probably contains a thick layer of decaying leaves that are different shades of brown. Brown also does not "catch the eye" inside a populated area.

3. **Black:** In my opinion black clothing, black socks, and black footwear would be a good choice for a long-term hard times tragedy event if you do not know exactly where you might eventually be spending most of your time. Each time you wash the black clothing the black color will fade a little bit but it will still be black. At night you will be almost invisible inside a rural town or in the middle of the wilderness. You will also not stand out or attract any attention during the daytime in either one of these two environments. As the black color gradually fades it looks almost like dark navy blue which is a common color inside a populated area. In a wilderness area there are lots and lots of shadows from the trees during the daytime and therefore one more dark object will not attract any special attention.

4. **Dark Navy Blue:** Dark navy blue is a good compromise color if you anticipate spending about half of your time in a populated area and about half your time in a wilderness area. People will generally not notice you if you are wearing navy blue. The dark navy blue color is very close to black so you will disappear at night and blend in reasonably well in the wilderness. On the other hand, medium blue does not blend in well except inside a populated area as blue jeans. The major problem with blue jeans is that they are very noticeable in the wilderness from a long distance away.

5. **Gray:** Medium gray or dark charcoal gray is also a good choice because it does not "catch the eye" like bright colors. Your objective should be to blend in and not be noticed and this is easier to do inside a town or in the wilderness if you are wearing medium gray or dark gray clothing. The trunks of many trees are different shades of gray so you would blend in "naturally" if you were in an area with trees. On the other hand, light gray coloring does not blend in well and therefore light gray should probably be avoided.

I suggest that all your clothing be purchased in dark colors, including your underwear and t-shirts. The quickest and easiest way to attract attention almost anywhere, including a rural town and the wilderness, is to have a temporary small space appear between your shirt and your jeans and a flash of "white" or some other bright color become visible.

You will need to make your own decision about what colors you think would be best suited for whatever situation you think you will encounter during a long-term tragedy event.

Laundry: Ordinary laundry detergent contains "brighteners" which enhance the colors in your clothing. These brighteners add a chemical to your clothing that actually shines when your clothing is viewed through ultra-violet lenses. During a hard times tragedy event you probably will not want clothing that looks great and which can be easily seen at night using night vision equipment.

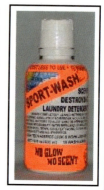

There are two solutions to this brightness problem. The first solution is to wash your clothes in ordinary Ivory brand bar soap. Ivory bar soap does not contain any brighteners. The second solution is to wash your clothes using a special laundry detergent that was designed for sportsmen and hunters and it does not contain any brighteners. One brand is called "Sport-Wash" and it can usually be found in the Sporting and Hunting section of a store that sells sporting and hunting equipment, including many Walmart stores.

Sewing, Spinning, Weaving: Your clothes will eventually need some type of repair. Therefore you should have some hand sewing needles and some thread in a variety of colors. These items may be purchased at a very reasonable price at most WalMarts.

You will also need to know how to make clothes. If you know how to make new clothes then you will be better qualified to repair your old clothes. I therefore suggest the purchase of the following sewing book: **Reader's Digest Complete Guide to Sewing**, 1976 or 2002 Edition.

I do not recommend growing your own cotton. I also do not recommend keeping a small herd of sheep so you can get their wool. Neither of these activities is practical for the realistic self-sufficient individual. In other words, don't invest in a spinning wheel or a weaving loom. I worked six-years in the apparel and textile industries and I have first-hand knowledge and experience making thread and yarn from cotton, wool, and manmade fibers, and then making fabric and socks from those yarns. In my opinion this is not an activity the average self-sufficient individual should be pursuing.

I strongly suggest that you buy a few extra pair of socks and underwear for each member of your family and don't use those items until they are needed during a serious hard times tragedy event.

I also recommend that you invest right now in a small inventory of good quality thread, an assortment of bulk buttons, some bulk elastic, and some good quality denim cloth, some flannel cloth, and some shirt and dress cloth. Then store those items until you need to make your own clothes. When your clothes wear out you can take them apart very carefully and use each piece as a pattern piece to cut your new cloth to the right size and shape. Then sew your new cloth together to make the same item you just wore out.

If the hard times continue for a lot longer than you originally planned then your clothes will wear out and your shoes will wear out. At that time the most practical solution to the clothing and shoe issue would be to make your own from deer skins or cowhide. I suggest you have the following book in your reference library at that time: **Deerskins into Buckskins**, 2nd Edition (not the 1st edition), Richards, 2004.

To make buckskin clothing, or moccasins, you will need some large "craft" sewing needles with big eyes. These craft sewing needles can be found in the sewing section of most Walmarts. Buy hand sewing needles and not machine sewing needles. A hand sewing needle has the eye at one end of the needle and the point at the other end of the needle. A machine sewing needle has the eye and the point at the same end of the needle.

(**Note:** Man's first clothes were animal skins and they were made by God. God showed Adam and Eve how to make clothes from animal skins:

Genesis 3:20-21 - *"And Adam called his wife's name Eve, because she was the mother of all living. Also for Adam and his wife the LORD God made tunics of skin, and clothed them."*)

Eye Protection: Always wear some type of safety glasses everywhere. Always. Everywhere. Wear safety glasses even when you are just relaxing and doing nothing. Your eyes deserve to be protected all the time. Losing one eye during a hard times event will seriously impair your productivity and your chances for long term survival. Losing both eyes would mean that you would become a permanent burden on the rest of your family.

Therefore please visit a hardware store or a Walmart and buy two or three pair of good quality clear safety glasses. Of you could purchase industrial quality safety glasses. If you now wear prescription eyeglasses, then consider investing in a pair of safety glasses made from your current prescription.

Chapter Thirty-Five: Clothing

Chapter Thirty-Six

Shoes and Boots

In the United States of America the vast majority of us have no real appreciation for our footwear. Most of us make our footwear choices based on what looks nice and what blends into our normal work and social environments. Most of our footwear choices are totally inappropriate for a long-term hard times tragedy event where we may have to walk (or bicycle) several miles every day.

Therefore please allow me to make the following suggestions for selecting practical hard-times survival footwear:

1. **Comfort:** Your footwear should be very comfortable. If you could not walk five miles in your shoes or boots then those shoes or boots are not suitable for a long-term hard-times tragedy event.

2. **Size:** To prevent foot blisters you should be able to wear a thin pair of ankle high nylon footies under your existing socks. Or you should be able to wear two pair of thin socks. Therefore your shoes will probably need to be at least one-half size larger than what you have been buying in the past. The average lady will immediately reject this recommendation because in her mind the smaller the shoe size the more attractive she is. However, if on some future day her survival depends on her being able to walk twenty-miles per day for two weeks then she would give anything for a comfortable pair of walking shoes. If she is with a group of people whose lives depend on reaching a specific area in a certain period of time then they will not be able to wait on her. At that time her previous vanity and her current foot blisters will be the reason she won't be able to keep up with the rest of the group and therefore she will be left behind to catch up when and if she can.

3. **Quality:** The footwear you own at the beginning of a hard-times tragedy event will probably need to last each member of your family for several years. Or you will need to purchase several replacement pair of footwear for each family member. Having several pair of shoes is a great idea if you are absolutely certain tyou will never need to abandon you current home. But if events should unfold in an unexpected manner and your survival demands that you abandon your home then you will have a limited amount of space in which to pack all the stuff you want to take with you. In that situation the wisdom of owning and wearing one high-quality set of footwear will become obvious.

4. **Waterproof:** Wet feet cause a multitude of foot problems. Therefore keeping your feet dry and fungus free should be a high priority. There may be times when you must travel in wet weather, or in the snow, or during the early morning hours when the dew is all over the ground vegetation. In those situations waterproof footwear is an absolute necessity.

5. **Slip-Resistant Soles:** Any footwear with smooth soles is a disaster waiting to happen. Ribbed or tread type soles will help you maintain your balance while transversing slippery areas, or areas with loose gravel, or ascending or descending a steep hill. The ability to avoid a potentially disabling accident (sprained ankle or broken leg) is critical to your long-term survival.

6. **Reinforced Toes:** If something really heavy falls on or is dropped on the front part of your feet then your toes could get crushed. If this happens then you will be either temporarily or permanently crippled and this would significantly reduce your chances for long-term survival. Therefore either a steel toe or a reinforced toe is highly desirable in footwear. However, the vast majority of the reinforced toe footwear that is available is extremely uncomfortable to wear. The reinforced toe area rubs against your toes and blisters soon appear. Therefore before you invest in this type of footwear you should try the footwear on while wearing two thin pair of socks and see if the entire shoe and especially the toe area feels really comfortable. In other words, never purchase footwear over the internet or out of a catalog.

7. **Air Cushion Inserts or Soles:** You should probably **avoid** shoes or boots that have "air cushion inserts or soles." I have owned several pair of these "air" shoes in the past and most of them worked fine until they eventually wore out and had to be replaced. But I have had the occasional "air" shoe gradually develop a tiny invisible "leak" and the shoe would squeak whenever I would start walking. You don't need "squeaking" shoes or boots to draw attention to yourself if you are trying to blend in and not be noticed.

8. **Application or Purpose:** Another consideration is how you will normally be using your shoes or boots:
   a. **Work Boots:** You will need heavy-duty boots that meet all the above requirements.
   b. **Walking Shoes:** If you anticipate long distance hikes or walks then the total weight of your footwear becomes a critical issue. In order to minimize fatigue you may wish to purchase shoes that are specially designed for walking. These shoes should have slip resistant soles and they should allow your feet to breathe. You probably will not require reinforced toes because they add additional weight to the shoe and this is a disadvantage is you are just walking from one location to the next location.
   c. **Bicycle Shoes:** To pedal a bicycle you will be raising and lowering your legs continuously. That means you will be raising and lowering whatever you are wearing on your feet. In this situation you should try to minimize the total weight of your footwear. However, a critical issue for bicycle shoes is that they have excellent ribbed or tread types soles that will make positive contact with the bicycle pedals without slipping. A good pair of walking shoes could be used as bicycle shoes if they have the proper type of soles.

9. **Color:** Either brown or black are preferred for a hard times event. Either of these two colors will match your other clothing and they will not attract any unusual attention and either color will help you to quickly and easily blend into a wilderness environment.

10. **Cleaning and Drying:** When your footwear occasionally gets wet you should wipe the moisture off your footwear with an old rag or dry cloth. Do **not** dry your footwear using heat, such as placing your wet footwear near a fireplace. The heat will not only dry off the moisture but it will also deplete the natural oils in the shoe leather and this will significantly reduce the useful life of your footwear. You should occasionally polish your footwear with a good quality shoe polish because the shoe polish will replenish some of the natural oils in the leather. If you need to clean your footwear then you should use saddle soap because it is specifically designed to clean leather.

If the hard-times tragedy event lasts longer than you expected then your footwear will eventually wear out or it will need repairs. If the repair is a relatively simple one then you could fix your footwear if you had the proper repair items. One of the most common repairs is reattaching a loose sole. This can be accomplished using "Shoe Goo" that is sold in the footwear section of most Walmarts near the shoelaces and shoe polish.

However, regardless of the quality of your footwear they will eventually wear out with the passage of time. When that happens you will have three basic options for replacing your footwear:

A. **Cobbler Trade:** You could learn the cobbler trade and then make your own shoes and boots. Over the years I have studied this skill area several times and each time I decided that it was not the type of skill I really needed to learn. However, you may decide otherwise. If there were any good cobbler books on "How to Make Your Own Shoes and Boots" that were still in print then I would recommend one of them here. Unfortunately this is not a trade that has good reference materials for the home craftsman.

B. **Tire Sandals:** You could make tire sandals. Detailed instructions for making tire sandals are at the following web site: http://www.hollowtop.com/sandals.htm

C. **Moccasins:** You could make moccasins using cowhide or buckskins. Two web sites that describe slightly different moccasin construction methods are as follows:
   http://www.i4at.org/surv/mocinstr.htm
   http://jumaka.com/moccasins/MakingMoccasins/MoccasinInstructions.htm

I suggest you locate and then download all the above files and print a hard copy of all three sets of instructions. Then save those instructions inside one of your three-ring binders that you have dedicated to long-term survival literature.

Chapter Thirty-Seven

Personal Hygiene Items

During a hard times tragedy event you will need soap, toothpaste, dental floss, toilet tissue, and feminine pads. You should invest in a small but reasonable supply of these items now while they are still relatively affordable and can be easily purchased.

Soap: Soap is absolutely necessary for your family's long-term good health for all the following reasons:

1. **Personal hygiene:** Good health is maintained by washing your hands before eating and by taking a bath on a regular basis.
2. **Laundry:** If your clothes get really filthy then they will collect lots of germs and those germs will eventually attack your body and you will get sick. During hard times families with small babies quickly revert back to cloth baby diapers that require a really good cleaning before being reapplied to the baby's bottom.
3. **Dish washing:** If your eating utensils are not clean then it won't be long before you get sick from the microscopic organisms that collect and grow on your dishes.
4. **Wound care and other medical situations:** Even small wounds can get infected and become life threatening if they are not properly cleaned with soap and lots of clean water at the earliest possible opportunity.
5. **Disease control:** Soap is extremely valuable in preventing the spread of diseases because you can wash the bed sheets, clothes, and eating utensils of the sick person, and you can also give the sick person a daily bath or cleaning to help neutralize any germs on the sick person's body.

Pure "Ivory" brand bar soap may be used as hand soap, body soap, shampoo, dish soap, laundry soap, and even baby soap. Just shave some soap off the bar with a knife or cheese grater and then put those shavings into some boiling water to make liquid soap. That liquid soap may then be used as dish soap and laundry soap. On the other hand, if you have unlimited financial resources and you have an unlimited amount of space to store your emergency supplies then there is nothing wrong with purchasing some high quality dish soap, laundry soap, and shampoo.

If your family has never used pure Ivory bar soap then I suggest you purchase one bar of pure Ivory soap without any extra ingredients and give each member of your family a chance to take a bath with that bar of soap. If no one in your family has any type of adverse reaction to the Ivory soap then you could consider buying some more of it for a future emergency.

Instructions for making "Homemade Soap" using campfire ashes, rain water, and melted animal fat are in the Homemade Soap Chapter in this book. However, in my opinion, during a serious long-term hard times tragedy event animal fat has more practical applications that using it to make soap. For example, animal fat is one of the three primary ingredients in "Homemade Pemmican." Therefore I strongly recommend that you purchase enough bar soap to last for several years instead of relying on your ability to make homemade soap using nature's free resources.

Solar Shower: A solar shower bag will hold four or five gallons of water. Fill the bag with water in the morning, place the bag in the sun, and in the evening you will have hot or very warm water for a personal shower. Being able to take a simple shower after a hard day of work and cleaning the sweat off your body will allow you to get a really good night's sleep. A good night's rest is critical during hard times. If you can afford it you should buy a solar shower bag for each member of your family. Solar shower bags can be purchased in the camping section of many stores.

Toothbrushes and Toothpaste: You should have one or two spare toothbrushes for each member of your family because toothbrushes do gradually wear out.

Although you can brush your teeth with baking soda, baking soda has so many other extremely practical applications that I would suggest that you do not use your baking soda as tooth powder. Instead you should save it for a true baking soda application. Therefore I recommend that you purchase and store some of the more affordable generic brand toothpastes. During hard times you only need to use a tiny bit of toothpaste on your toothbrush each time you brush your teeth and this will not compromise your dental health. If you are completely out of toothpaste you can still brush your teeth with your toothbrush and some clean water.

Dental Floss: Dental floss is really useful for removing tiny food particles that occasionally become caught between your teeth. Therefore you should have a few spare rolls of dental floss stored for a long-term emergency.

During a long-term hard times tragedy event you will eventually run out of dental floss. It is possible to use very thin fishing line as a substitute for dental floss. You can purchase a 700 yard reel of monofilament fishing line for about $2.50 in the Sporting Goods section of Walmart. One 700 yard reel of fishing line is equal to approximately 12.7 spools of dental floss (55 yards per spool). The monofilament fishing line is sold in 700 yard reels for approximately $2.50 per reel in a variety of sizes. The 4 pound fishing line has a 0.008" diameter and this might be thin enough to serve as dental floss for everyone in your family. Or you could purchase fishing line with a smaller diameter.

During a long-term hard times event another option would be to use synthetic sewing thread as dental floss.

(Note: If you also had a few fish hooks then you could tie about 20 feet of fishing line to the end of a long strong stick and you could make your own homemade fishing pole.)

Razors: Buy a few dozen disposable razors. This will allow you to maintain your appearance so you can appear in public, or at your place of work, and look like a respectable person.

Occasionally you will see the old fashioned "straight razor" recommended as a better investment than disposable razors. If you wish you may purchase one. However, I have purchased and tried three different types of new straight razors during a two year period and I was extremely disappointed with all of them. You may conduct these tests yourself if you wish or you could save yourself some time and money and simply buy a few dozen disposable razors instead.

During hard times there are very, very few jobs. Competition for those jobs is extraordinary. The hiring decision is sometimes made on first impressions. A person who is clean, with clean combed hair, clean shaven, clean breath, and wearing clean clothes will have a superior chance of being selected for any job that is available. In addition that person should have a positive attitude, good manners, good posture, and **not** use offensive words or gestures.

Toilet Tissue: Toilet tissue is a necessity you may not fully appreciate until you don't have any. If you purchase the one-ply toilet tissue then you may need a lot more of it than someone who has two-ply tissue. Most toilet tissue brands are sold in one-ply and two-ply packages, and in regular roll and double roll packages. Therefore you should read the label on the package before you make your purchase. Additional information about toilet tissue appears in the next chapter in this book.

Feminine Pads: The female menstrual cycle will not take time off during a long-term hard times event. Therefore you should have a reasonable supply of feminine pads for all the females in your home. An external feminine pad can be worn by almost any female at any time. On the other hand, the internal versions can not be used by all woman. This choice is a very personal one and each female in your household should be allowed the freedom to make this decision based on her own individual needs and preferences.

Chapter Thirty-Eight

Toilet Tissue

Do not underestimate the value of toilet tissue to your personal health, hygiene, and peace of mind. Toilet tissue is one of the simple comforts of civilization that you will dearly miss if you don't have any. During a serious hard times event you will need to provide for 100% of your normal toilet tissue requirements because you will not occasionally be using the toilet tissue at your place of employment, or at a gas station, or at a restaurant.

A Comparison of Five Leading Brands on January 3, 2011

One double roll of toilet tissue is equal to two regular rolls. The better toilet tissue has two-plys instead of one-ply. (Note: Some brands also have three-plys.) If you purchase the one-ply tissue then you may need a lot more of it than someone who has two-ply tissue. Most toilet tissue brands are sold in one-ply and two-ply packages, and in regular roll and double roll packages. **Therefore you should always read the package label before you make your purchase.**

For example, at the current time one **Angel Soft** Double Roll Two-Ply roll contains 300 sheets of tissue paper. (300 sheets per double roll) x (24 double rolls per package) = 7,200 two-ply sheets of toilet tissue per package. (7,200 sheets) divided by (365 days per year) = 19.7 sheets of toilet tissue per day for one person for one year.

During a hard times event a person in good health would probably discover that 19.7 sheets of two-ply toilet tissue would be more than adequate for one day. Any daily usage that is below 19.7 sheets could be saved and then used during a time when the person was not in good health and needed additional quantities of toilet tissue for a short period of time. You could determine if this estimate of 19.7 sheets per day is reasonable for you by simply counting the number of toilet tissue sheets you use in one day and then adjusting the above values accordingly.

There are three factors that should be considered when investing in toilet tissue:

1. **Softness:** The feel of the tissue paper is a very personal issue. My family cannot detect any significant difference in softness among the major brands. However, some individuals have very sensitive skin or bowel movement issues and a minor difference in softness can make a big difference to these people.

2. **Strength:** The tissue paper should not fall apart when you use it. The thinner lighter tissue paper will require more sheets to do the same job as the thicker heavier tissue paper.

3. **Value:** The price of the package is **not** the most important factor. The value of the toilet tissue is related to the weight of each sheet of paper and the cost of each sheet of paper.

The table on the next page does not consider softness because softness is a personal issue. However, the table does show the weight of a two-ply sheet of toilet paper and the cost of a two-ply sheet of toilet paper for five leading brands of toilet tissue. The table also assumes one 24 Double Roll Package of Toilet Tissue for One Person for One Year.

Comparison of Five Leading Brands of Toilet Tissue
All Packages Contain 24 Double Rolls (or 48 Regular Rolls)
All Packages Contain 2-Ply Toilet Tissue
All Data Collected on January 3, 2011

(Note: The Weight Per Package and the Weight Per Sheet Includes the Weight of the Cardboard Tube and the Plastic Wrap Around the Package.)
(Abbreviations: Pounds = lbs. and Ounces = oz.)

Brand Name	Weight Per Package	Weight Per Sheet	Sheets Per Roll	Sheets Per Day	Cost Per Package	Cost Per Sheet	Cost Per Pound
Angel Soft	6.95 lbs.	0.0154 oz.	300 Sheets	19.7 Sheets	$11.98	$0.00167	$1.72
Charmin	4.56 lbs.	0.0173 oz.	176 Sheets	11.6 Sheets	$14.64	$0.00347	$3.21
Cottonelle	4.75 lbs.	0.0180 oz.	176 Sheets	11.6 Sheets	$14.97	$0.00354	$3.15
Northern	6.95 lbs.	0.0191 oz.	242 Sheets	15.9 Sheets	$13.66	$0.00235	$1.97
White Cloud	5.88 lbs.	0.0127 oz.	308 Sheets	20.3 Sheets	$10.98	$0.00149	$1.87

The following table shows the percent change over a two-year period from February 14, 2009 to January 3, 2011.
A minus sign indicates a decrease and a plus sign indicates an increase.

Brand Name	Weight Per Package	Weight Per Sheet	Sheets Per Roll	Sheets Per Day	Cost Per Package	Cost Per Sheet	Cost Per Pound
Angel Soft	-12%	+3%	-15%	-15%	+3%	+21%	+16%
Charmin	-11%	+1%	-12%	-12%	-4%	+11%	+8%
Cottonelle	-16%	+48%	-43%	-43%	-2%	+71%	+16%
Northern	-18%	+1%	-19%	-19%	Same	+24%	+22%
White Cloud	-11%	-11%	Same	Same	-3%	-3%	+9%

Review of the Data in the Above Tables

1. **Weight per Package:** All five brands reduced the total weight of their package by approximately the same amount from 11% to 18%.
2. **Weight per Sheet:** Three of the brands maintained almost the same weight per sheet. However, Cottenelle significantly **increased** the weight of each sheet of tissue paper by 48% which was a quality improvement but this was accomplished by reducing the number of sheets per roll by 43%. White Cloud significantly **reduced** the weight of their tissue paper by 11% which was a decline in quality.
3. **Sheets per Roll and Sheets per Day:** Four of the brands reduced the number of sheets per roll and the sheets per day (columns mathematically related to one another).
4. **Cost per Package:** Three of the brands **reduced** the selling price of their package by a very, very small percent to create the **illusion** that you are now getting a better value than two years ago.
5. **Cost per Sheet:** Four brands increased their cost per sheet. Only the White Cloud brand decreased the cost per sheet by 3%. They did this by making each sheet 11% lighter than before which means they reduced the quality of their paper. Therefore, this is an **illusionary** price reduction because they decreased the quality of their paper by a higher percent than they reduced the price.
6. **Cost per Pound:** All five brands increased the price per pound of their toilet tissue.

Chapter Thirty-Eight: Toilet Tissue

7. **Summary:** On the average the actual price of toilet tissue has increased by about 14% over the past two years. However, the companies that make toilet tissue were able to obscure this information by reducing the number of sheets per roll and by reducing the total weight of the package while keeping the package selling price almost the same. In other words, we are paying about the same amount of money per package as two years ago but we are getting about 14% less toilet tissue for our money.

Different Ways to Compare the Cost of the Major Brands of Toilet Tissue

Some people like to compare prices based on the cost of the entire package. Some people like to compare prices based on the cost per roll of tissue paper. Both of these measures ignore the number of sheets of toilet tissue per roll and the strength (or weight) of that tissue.

A better way to compare prices is the use the cost per pound of toilet tissue. This includes the price of the entire package, and the price per roll, and the weight (strength) of the tissue paper. The cost per pound is a more reasonable way to evaluate the true value of a package of toilet tissue. The cost per pound (or per ounce) is also the way that most people compare food prices..

The Original Comparison on February 14, 2009
Comparison of Five Leading Brands of Toilet Tissue
All Packages Contain 24 Double Rolls (or 48 Regular Rolls)
All Packages Contain 2-Ply Toilet Tissue

(Note: The Weight Per Package and the Weight Per Sheet Includes the
Weight of the Cardboard Tube and the Plastic Wrap Around the Package.)
(Abbreviations: Pounds = lbs. and Ounces = oz.)

Brand Name	Weight Per Package	Weight Per Sheet	Sheets Per Roll	Sheets Per Day	Cost Per Package	Cost Per Sheet	Cost Per Pound
Angel Soft	7.88 lbs.	0.0149 oz.	352 Sheets	23.1 Sheets	$11.67	$0.00138	$1.48
Charmin	5.13 lbs.	0.0171 oz.	200 Sheets	13.2 Sheets	$15.24	$0.00313	$2.97
Cottenelle	5.63 lbs.	0.0122 oz.	308 Sheets	20.3 Sheets	$15.34	$0.00207	$2.72
Northern	8.50 lbs.	0.0189 oz.	300 Sheets	19.7 Sheets	$13.66	$0.00190	$1.61
White Cloud	6.60 lbs.	0.0143 oz.	308 Sheets	20.3 Sheets	$11.33	$0.00153	$1.72

Conclusion

Over the past few years my family has used four different leading brands of toilet tissue.

1. For about ten years we always used Charmin brand tissue. Then my family became dissatisfied with the quality of that brand. I do not know if the quality of the brand actually decreased. I just know that my family became unhappy with it.
2. For about two years we used the White Cloud brand.
3. For about one year we used the Northern brand.
4. For the past two years we have been using the Angel Soft brand because we cannot detect any quality differences between it and the more expensive brands. Since toilet tissue is a disposable product it just doesn't make sense to pay more for it than necessary.

242 2-PLY SHEETS PER ROLL

You will need to make your own brand choice based on what your family believes is acceptable. Some people have made the decision to not store very much toilet tissue because they believe it takes up too much space. However, based on the above, one 24 Double Roll Package of toilet tissue will probably be adequate for one person for one-year. If you have four people in your family then you would need to store four of these packages and your family would have emergency toilet tissue for an entire year. Or if you wanted to store a two or three year supply then you should store two or three packages per person. In my opinion this is not an unreasonable task. Since toilet tissue does not require a temperature controlled environment you could store your emergency toilet tissue in your attic.

If you decide that it is too much trouble to store some emergency toilet tissue for your family and later a hard times event makes it very difficult to acquire toilet tissue then your entire family will probably not be very happy with you. And you will not be pleased with yourself either. At that time you will probably be willing to pay an extremely high price for a very small quantity of toilet tissue and you will wish you had purchased a reasonable supply of it when it was still relatively affordable and easy to acquire.

How to Wipe Your Rear End After a Bowel Movement When You Don't Have Toilet Tissue

(Note: The following information about an alternative to toilet tissue is being presented for educational purposes only.)

You will need the following items:

1. Latex gloves one size larger than each member of you family would normally wear. Write each family member's name (or initial) on his or her own set of special latex gloves at the wrist area using a black permanent marking pen. Or each family member could have his or her own unique color of latex gloves.
2. At least four soft sponges for each member of your family. Each family member should have his or her own special color sponges.
3. Plastic spray bottle, such as an empty window cleaner spray bottle that has been thoroughly washed and cleaned. Fill the spray bottle with clean water.
4. One small plastic tote container or bucket that is at least 6-inches wide and at least 3 inches deep. Put a few ounces of soapy water in this container.

Wiping Procedure:

1. Put on your own special pair of latex gloves that have your name (or initial) written on the wrist area.
2. Spray a little clean water from the plastic spray bottle on one of your special sponges and use the slightly damp sponge to clean your rear end. If necessary, moisten another one of your special sponges and use it to finish cleaning your rear end.
3. Immediately dip your dirty sponges into the special bucket that contains a few ounces of soapy water. Clean the sponges while you are still wearing your latex gloves. When your sponges are clean, rinse the soapy water off your sponges with some clean water, and then put your sponges in the special sponge drying area near the toilet stool or in a special container on the back of the toilet tank. Pour the dirty soapy water from the sponge cleaning bucket into the toilet stool. Rinse out the sponge cleaning bucket with a little clean water and pour that water into the toilet stool. Then flush the toilet stool. Be considerate. Put some clean soapy water in the sponge cleaning bucket for the next person.
4. Wash your gloves while you are still wearing them the same way you would normally wash your hands with soap and water. You should have one bar of soap that is only used for this one purpose and that bar of soap should always be returned to its own special soap dish.
5. Remove your gloves and put them in the glove drying area near the toilet stool. A plastic towel bar would be a good choice as a glove drying rack. Do not use a towel bar made of wood (germs) or metal (rust).

If you don't have any sponges then you could use old scraps of cloth instead. Just wash the cloths between uses the same way you would wash a dirty cloth baby diaper. If you don't have sponges or cloth then you could simply use water and your latex gloves.

Chapter Thirty-Eight: Toilet Tissue

Chapter Thirty-Nine

Emergency First Aid

The following is not medical advice nor is it a medical recommendation.
Please consult a licensed medical professional to have your medical questions answered.

Emergency First Aid Training

If you have the time and if you can afford it then you could enroll in an American Red Cross First-Aid Training Course. These courses are usually reasonably priced and they can usually be completed in less than one day.

Emergency First Aid Books

The following books describe your options when you don't have immediate access to professional medical care or prescription medicines. The books are listed in the order I would purchase them if I could not afford to buy them all. Some of the material is duplicated in two or more of the following books but the discussion is different and that provides you with a different perspective on the same medical problem.

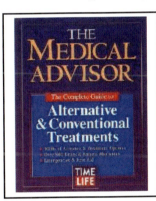 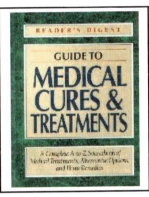 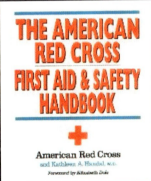 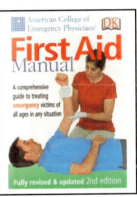

1. **The Medical Advisor - The Complete Guide to Alternative & Conventional Treatments**, by Time/Life Books.
   Hardcover ISBN: 0-8094-6737-2 (1,152 Pages, Size: 10.25" x 8.25" x 2.5").
   (Out-of-Print but you can usually find copies at amazon.com).
   Comment: Has an excellent section on emergency first aid for the most common types of problems. It contains information on about 300 common ailments with detailed information on which symptoms are usually present and what your treatment options are, including both herbal and diet, plus common home remedies and over-the-counter medications. It also describes how to prevent the problem from reoccurring. It has separate sections on medicines, vitamins and minerals, and an illustrated atlas of the human body.

2. **Reader's Digest Guide to Medical Cures & Treatments.**
   Hardcover ISBN: 0-89577-846-7 (480 Pages, Size: 11.125" x 8.5" x 1.25").
   (Out-of-Print but you can usually find copies at amazon.com).
   Comment: Begins with an illustrated anatomy of the human body based on its major functions. It then lists about 500 of the most common health and medical problems, frequently with color pictures. For each medical problem it explains what your options are, including self-treatment and herbal healing when appropriate. It also contains a nice section on medications and a brief summary of the benefits of vitamins and minerals.

3. **American Red Cross First Aid and Safety Handbook**, Kathleen A. Handal, M.D., 1992. Paperback ISBN: 0-316-73646-5 (321 Pages, Size: 9.25" x7.5" x 5/8").
Hardcover ISBN: 0-316-73645-7
Comment: Explains how to handle the most common types of accidents. It also contains a ten page section on childbirth.

4. **DK First Aid Manual**, American College of Emergency Physicians, 2004. Contains simple easy-to-follow instructions with full color pictures for the most common accidents and basic medical problems.

5. **Merck Manual of Medical Information, 2nd Home Edition**, 2004, Paperback, more than 1900 Pages.

6. **Kelley's Textbook of Internal Medicine**, 4th Edition, 2000.

7. **Tooth Extraction, A Practical Guide**, Robinson, 2000.

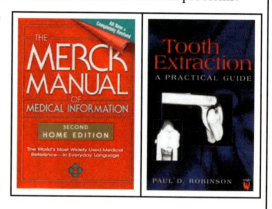

I do not make the above recommendations lightly. Over the past 35 years I have gradually acquired approximately 50 different first-aid books and general reference medical books. In some cases I purchased the book because it received a "glowing" recommendation from someone on the internet. However, in almost every case I was very disappointed with my purchase. At the current time I have a copy of most of the medical reference books that have been recommended at a variety of internet web sites, blogs, and discussion forums, including the "Where There is No Doctor" and "Where There is No Dentist" books. The above seven books are the ones I would buy today. The above seven books are also the ones I would take with me if I had to quickly evacuate my home and I could only take a limited amount of stuff with me.

Where There is No Dentist can now be downloaded for free at the following web site:
http://www.inteldaily.com/news/171/ARTICLE/1426/2007-01-01.html

Where There is No Doctor can now be downloaded for free at the following web site:
http://www.hesperian.org/publications_download_wtnd.php

Emergency First Aid Kit

A simple first aid kit is adequate for most of the minor accidents that can occur around the house. However, if someone is involved in a more serious accident then a more advanced first aid kit could make a big difference. On the other hand, if the person using the kit doesn't know what he or she is doing then the person could do more harm than good. When feasible wait for a medical professional to arrive or take the person to a medical professional if that is possible.

Medic's First Aid Kit: Weight 3.4 pounds, Item Number UZ1-KF-M100
Available from: http://beprepared.com/product.asp_Q_pn_E_kf%20m100
More that 175 medical items and they are of the same quality used by Paramedics & Emergency Technicians. CONTENTS: 25 standard bandages 3/4" x 3", 5 - 7/8" spot pad bandages, 10 iodine prep pads, 3 non adherent sterile 2"x3" pads, 5 surgical micropore 1" tape, 10 antiseptic towelettes, 5 extra large bandages 2"x4.5", 2 ammonia inhalant, 5 bacitracin antibiotic ointment, 10 non-aspiring pain reliever, 20 alcohol prep pads, 3 non adherent sterile pads 3"x4", 5 medium butterfly bandages, 5 large butterfly bandages, 5 fingertip bandages, 5 knuckle bandages, 8 sterile gauze pad 2"x2", 8 sterile gauze pads 3"x3", 8 sterile gauze pads 4"x4", 4 round eye pads, 5 safety pins, 1 oral thermometer, 5 tongue depressors, 1 triangular bandages, 1 - 5 1/2" bandage scissors, 1 EMT Shears, 1 fine point tweezers, 1 small soap bar, 1 porous cloth tape 1"x 10 yards, 1 instant ice pack, 1 sterile eye wash 4 oz., 2 - 2" sterile roller gauze, 2 - 3" sterile roller gauze, 2 - 4" sterile roller gauze, 1 rubber elastic 3" x 5 yards, 2 sterile ABD pads 5" x 9", 1 nylon medic bag, 2 burn free sterile dressings 4"x4", 1 pain relieving gel 4 oz, 2 small vinyl exam gloves, 2 medium vinyl exam gloves, 2 large vinyl exam gloves, 1 wilderness and travel medicine book, 2 mitigator sting and bite treatment.

The above Medic's First Aid Kit contains most of the items you might need for an accident around the home. I suggest you add the following items to that kit: blood pressure cuff and separate stethoscope, ear/nose/throat light and extra batteries, barber scissors, cuticle scissors with curved shank, nose/mouth masks, some extra gauze and tape, a 2 inch wide elastic bandage, a few extra boxes of 3/4 inch and 1 inch non-stick bandages, and an extra box of butterfly closure bandages. You can usually find the 1 inch bandages at a CVS pharmacy. You should also consider purchasing a fever thermometer that you shake down and not one that is battery operated.

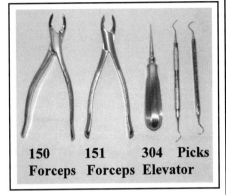

150 Forceps   151 Forceps   304 Elevator   Picks

If you purchase the above **Tooth Extraction** book then you may also want to invest in the most commonly used dental tools for tooth extraction: a 150 Forceps, a 151 Forceps, and a 304 or E304W Elevator. Also some cleaning Picks. These stainless steel dental tools may be purchased on ebay or at amazon.com. However, I strongly recommend that you have all your dental work done by a licensed professional dentist.

Emergency First Aid Over-the-Counter Medicines

Each family has its own unique medical history. For example, one family may have reoccurring constipation issues and they may periodically need some type of laxative. A different family may have migraine headaches and they may periodically need some type of migraine headache remedy. Therefore each family should immediately purchase a reasonable supply of the over-the-counter remedies they have frequently purchased in the past. But each family's choice of these remedies would probably be different from another family's choices.

Walk down the aisle at Walmart, or your local Discount Drug Store, and pick up a least one of each medicine you think you might need. Pick up several of the medicines your family has used in the past on a regular basis. Some over-the-counter remedies you might wish to consider are the following:

1. Anti-Itch Cream (Diphenhydramine Hydrochloidre 2%, Zinc Acetate 0.15%).
2. Zanfel Poison Ivy, Oak, & Sumac Itch Relief (1 ounce tube).
3. Antifungal Cream (Clotrimazole 1%).
4. Triple Antibiotic Ointment (Bacitracin, Neomycin Sulfate, Polymyxin-B Sulfate).
5. Allergy 25mg Tablets (Benadryl or Generic) (for itch relief from poison ivy or multiple insect bites).

The following is **not** medical advice nor is it a medical recommendation nor is it an endorsement for the following companies.

The following is one source where you can purchase pet antibiotics online:

100 Amoxicillin 500 mg Capsules can be purchased online at:
http://www.revivalanimal.com/store/p/2456-Fish-Mox-Forte-500mg.aspx
60 Erythromycin 250 mg Capsules can be purchased online at:
http://www.revivalanimal.com/store/p/2454-Fish-Mycin.aspx
A complete list of pet antibiotics is available at the following link:
http://www.revivalanimal.com/store/p/5922-Fish-and-Bird-Antibiotics.aspx

The following is one source where you can purchase some basic supplies for a reasonable price from India: https://www.alldaychemist.com/

Conclusion

Any medication, including over-the-counter medications, should usually **not** be taken until after you have discussed the medication with your licensed physician and the medication is approved by your medical doctor for your specific medical condition. While you are taking any medication you should be under the supervision of your medical doctor.

Missing Teeth

Have you lost some teeth? Or some hair? Or maybe something else?
Have you ever wished that everything was back in its original place?

If you believe in Jesus you will receive that which you truly cherish.
For God has promised that not one hair on your head will perish.

If God can keep track of every single hair that was once on your head,
Then He can also restore everything of yours, even if it is now dead.

God's power is not limited to our understanding or our puny ways.
God has promised us perfect health for an infinite number of days.

Trust in Jesus and one day a perfect spiritual body you will receive.
An eternal body will be your reward because in Jesus you do believe.

Scripture References: Isaiah 46:4, Mark 10:30, Luke 21:18-19, Matthew 19:26, Matthew 22:31-32, First Corinthians 15:50-57, Romans 6:23, Philippians 3:20-21.

Chapter Forty

Aspirin

This is not medical advice nor is it a medical recommendation.
Please consult a licensed medical professional to have your medical questions answered.

If is always important to consider the risks and the benefits of a specific medication before you take it. However, as you gradually get older you become aware that everything you hear or read is not always the truth. And in many cases it doesn't matter where you hear it or read it, the information is simply not true.

Aspirin is one of those medicines that has been studied extensively over the past few decades. And those studies have shown that aspirin can have a positive impact and a negative impact on the patients in the study groups.

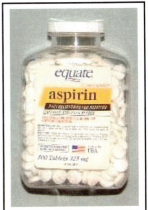

If a qualified medical professional were to review all of the aspirin study test results then he or she would probably find it extremely difficult to draw any type of valid general conclusions because of the differences in the way the tests were conducted. For example, the tests were conducted on aspirin at different strengths, such as 61 mg, or 81 mg, or 100 mg, or 325 mg aspirin tablets. And the test subjects may have ingested the aspirins on a daily basis, or every other day, or only two or three times per week. And the ages and gender of the subjects were not consistent across the studies. And there is no information on whether the aspirins were coated or non-coated. If an impartial person who was qualified in the field of designing experiments were to examine all the different testing methods then that person might conclude that the testing procedures were intentionally designed to make it impossible to consolidate the data and draw any broad general conclusions.

Consequently at the beginning of the year 2011 it is still not possible to draw any firm conclusions about the true risks and the true benefits of aspirin. If a person wants to believe the worst about aspirin then there is some data that will support that opinion. If a person wants to believe the best about aspirin then there is some data that will support that opinion. But if a person wanted to form an unbiased impartial honest opinion about aspirin then that person would not be able to do so. Do you suppose there might be a reason for this?

At the current time the best a person can do is to make a list of the benefits of aspirin and the risks of aspirin and then interpret that data as objectively as possible. Therefore the following information has been summarized from a variety of different sources so you can discuss it intelligently with your physician.

The Following Information is Presented For Fair Use and Information Purposes Only

Caution:
Ask your doctor or other licensed medical professional about whether or not you should take aspirin and whether or not aspirin will interfere with any other medications, vitamins, or herbal remedies you are currently taking or have been advised to take.

What is aspirin?
Aspirin is acetylsalicylic acid.
Aspirin is a mild, non-narcotic medicine that helps relieve headache pain and pain in the joints and muscles.
Aspirin also helps to reduce fever.
Aspirin is classified as a NSAID (non-steroidal anti-inflammatory drug).

How to take aspirin:
Carefully follow the directions on the package label. Take aspirin with a full glass of water.

Different types of aspirin:
There is a difference between an 81 mg low dose aspirin and a 325 mg aspirin. However, there is no research that clearly explains what that difference is.

There is a difference between a coated aspirin and an uncoated aspirin. However, there is no research that clearly explain what that difference is.

At the current time some research appears to indicate that taking a coated 81 mg low dose aspirin once per day has a negligible chance of any harmful side effects and a reasonable chance of several positive health benefits. However, because of the potential negative side effects, all the research indicates that an individual should always discuss the benefits and risks of taking aspirin with his or her physician before taking any type of aspirin for any reason.

History of aspirin:
1. Sometime around 400 B.C. Hippocrates mentioned that a powder made from the leaves and bark of the willow tree would help relieve headaches and pain and reduce fever.
2. In 1829 Johann Buchner discovered that is was the salicin in the willow that actually reduced the pain.
3. In 1853 Charles Frederic Gerhardt created acetylsalicylic acid by buffering salicylic acid with sodium and acetyl chloride.
4. From 1897 to 1899 Felix Hoffmann was responsible for getting Bayer in Germany to produce acetylsalicylic acid. Bayer created the name "aspirin" by using the letter "a" from acetyl chloride, and the "spir" from spiraea ulmaria (where the salicylic acid came from) plus the ending "in." Bayer patented "aspirin" on February 27, 1900.
5. In 1919, after World War One at the Treaty of Versailles, Bayer was forced to give up its rights to aspirin as part of the punishment that Germany received for starting and losing the war.

Risks of taking aspirin:
It may cause stomach upset, heartburn, nausea, and vomiting.
It may cause stomach bleeding, ulcers, and holes in the stomach.
It may cause kidney failure.
It may cause liver damage in people who drink a lot.
It may cause ringing in the ears and hearing loss.
It may cause bleeding in the brain.
It should not be used by someone with anemia, asthma, bleeding problems, chickenpox, the flu, gout, kidney disease, liver disease, low level of vitamin K, lupus, stomach ulcers, or a viral infection.
It should not be used by anyone who has had an allergic reaction to aspirin, tartrazine dye, other medicines, or preservatives.
It should not be taken in conjunction with other medicines.
It should not be taken during the last three months of pregnancy because it may cause problems for the unborn child or it may cause problems during delivery. In fact, all NSAIDs should be avoided during the last three months of pregnancy.
It should not be used by a mother who is breast-feeding an infant because aspirin will enter the mother's breast milk in small quantities.
It should not be used by someone who drinks a lot of alcohol.
It should not be used by someone who smokes tobacco.
It should not be taken while you are having a stroke.
Do not continue to take aspirin if it upsets your stomach.
Do not give aspirin to children age 12 or younger.
It may cause Reye's Syndrome in children who take aspirin to reduce a fever caused by a viral infection, such as chickenpox or the flu. Although this is rare (estimated one case per 100,000 children) it is very serious and it causes brain swelling and fatty deposits on the liver and it can cause permanent brain damage. It can be fatal approximately 30% to 50% of the time.
If given to children with viral diseases it may cause paralysis, brain damage, or death.
Do not lie down for 30 minutes after taking aspirin to prevent throat irritation.
The risk of side effects goes up with the dose of the aspirin. Therefore taking more than 81 mg per day is usually not advisable.

Benefits of aspirin:
Aspirin will relieve mild pains.
Aspirin will reduce fever.
It may be used to help arthritis and reduce inflammation.
It will thin the blood.
It will keep blood from clotting because it makes the blood less sticky.
It slows the clotting action of blood by reducing the clumping of platelets, which are responsible for blood clotting.
It slows the progression of colon cancer.
It might prevent other cancers from occurring.
It will slow or prevent dementia and Alzheimer's disease. Dementia affects about 25% of all individuals age 70 or above.
It will benefit migraine headaches, cataracts, and gum disease.
It will prevent blood clots in veins during long plane trips.
Aspirin can stop heart attacks as they are happening in both men and women by dissolving blood clots that are blocking the flow of blood. Aspirin will also significantly reduce the chance of a future heart attack.
It will help to prevent a future stoke and reduce its severity.
One low dose aspirin per day may help to increase fertility.
One low dose aspirin per day may reduce the chance of pre-eclampsi and fetal growth retardation.
One low dose aspirin per day may help to prevent a miscarriage during the first six-months of pregnancy.
If you need a pain reliever occasionally then ibuprofen or acetaminophen may be okay instead of increasing your daily aspirin dose to deal with the occasional pain. However, you should wait at least 30 minutes after taking aspirin before taking ibuprofen.

A Brief Summary of Aspirin Research Studies:

The following studies do **not** include separate findings for a coated aspirin compared to an uncoated aspirin.

The benefits outweigh the risks of taking a low-dose aspirin for men age 45 or older and women age 55 or older who are at risk for a stroke or heart attack .

A Oxford University study published in the "Lancet" on December 7, 2010 reported that seniors who take one "baby-aspirin" per day (either 75 mg of 81 mg) had a 20% reduction in all cancers. After taking aspirin for five years the subjects had a 34% lower rate of all cancers and a 54% lower rate of gastrointestinal cancers (esophagus, stomach, bowel, pancreas, and liver).

Those taking aspirin for ten years or longer experienced 53% less pancreatic cancer, 50% less colorectal cancer, and 33% less lung cancer.
In a study of 90,000 nurses from 1976 to 1995 who took between 4 to 6 aspirin each week they had a significantly lower rate of colorectal cancer.
A study of 14,000 women who took aspirin three or more times each week for at least six-months were 33% less likely to develop lung cancer.
A study of 28,000 post-menopausal women who took aspirin between 2 to 5 times per week had a 53% lower chance of developing pancreatic cancer.

A ten-year study on 39,876 women age 45 and older showed that a 100 mg aspirin every other day reduces the risk of a stroke by 17% in middle-aged women and it reduces the chance of a stroke and the chance of a heart attack by 34% in women 65 years or older.

In the February 10, 2001 issue of the "British Medical Journal," a review of 39 studies on more than 30,000 pregnant women suggested that taking a low dose aspirin may be beneficial.

In a study of 9,000 women in 16 countries a daily dose of 61 mg aspirin reduced the risk of pre-eclampia by 13%. Pre-eclampsi and fetal growth retardation are due to the blood vessels of the placenta becoming blocked.

A study at the Oxford Institute of Health Sciences reported that taking aspirin reduced the chance of pre-eclampsi by 15%, and it reduced the risk of the death of the fetus or the newborn by 14%, and it reduced the risk of a premature birth by 8%.

The benefits of diabetics taking one aspirin per day are now so widely accepted that further research using a placebo is considered unethical. In a diabetic the aspirin reduces the chance of blindness, coronary artery disease, stroke, and kidney failure, all due to impaired blood circulation in diabetics.

Chapter Forty-One

Herbal Home Remedies

This is not medical advice nor is it a medical recommendation.
Please consult a licensed medical professional to have your medical questions answered.

Many years ago I became extremely interested in herbal home remedies. For about ten years I planted and grew a variety of popular medicinal herbs and I occasionally used those herbs on myself to see if they were as effective as what I had been led to believe in my collection of herbal home remedy books. In almost every case I was seriously disappointed in the results and I eventually purchased an over-the-counter remedy to resolve my minor medical problem. If you wish you may conduct these experiments yourself. However, my suggestion is that you reserve whatever garden space you may have available for edible vegetables and instead purchase a reasonable supply of over-the-counter remedies that you can find at any drug store.

On the other hand, if the hard times continue for an extremely long time then the vast majority of us may eventually have no other options except herbal remedies. Therefore herbal remedy knowledge may become extremely useful at some time in the future. If you are interested in learning more about medicinal herbs then I recommend the following two books:

1. **DK Natural Health Encyclopedia of Herbal Medicine,** by Andrew Chevallier, 2000.
2. **The Complete Medicinal Herbal,** by Penelope Ody, 1993.

The above two books will help you learn the basics on how to grow, harvest, prepare, and use medicinal herbs.

There are two medicinal herbs that my family did find to be useful. They were not as effective as medicines you can purchase with a prescription but they were occasionally effective for some of my family's very minor medical problems. The two herbs were echinacea and barberry. These two herbs proved to be effective about 50% of the time for my family and I if we began using them at the first sign of a problem. However, if one of my family members waited until his or her problem become really painful before letting me know about it then these herbs were not effective and we had to visit a doctor and get a prescription for an antibiotic.

Echinacea (also called purple coneflower) (angustifolia and purpurea)

Echinacea was used by the American Indian Comanche and Sioux and it was quickly adopted by the early American European settlers.

Echinacea may be used against bacterial and some viral infections by stimulating the body's natural immune system. It is also antifungal. Its antibacterial benefits and viral properties have been scientifically documented. It encourages the production of white blood cells. Its antibiotic effect is similar to that of penicillin because it is useful against a wide spectrum of bacteria.

Side Effects: It may cause nausea or dizziness.

Uses: The roots may be used as an immune system enhancement and for general bacteria infections, tonsillitis, sore throat, laryngitis, inflamed gums, gingivitis, and congestion in the nose, sinuses, and lungs. It is an ingredient in some commercially available cough drops and cold remedies. It can be used to help with some allergies, such as asthma. Externally it can be used to treat skin infections, skin ulcers, itching, and stings and insect bites.

How to Grow: This is a perennial flower. About two-weeks after the last flower petals drop off the flower then cut the stems near the ground and harvest the stems with their top center cones. Hang the cones upside down indoors and wait for the center cones to dry out. Then crush the cones with a metal spoon (not your hands) and separate the seeds from the rest of the pieces. If you can't identify the seeds then just save and plant everything the following spring.

Roots: Protect the roots of the original flowering plant with a heavy layer of mulch for the winter. It takes about three or four years for the roots of the original plant to grow large enough for medicinal uses.

Harvesting: High quality root will make your tongue tingle slightly. Harvest the roots after the plant flowers. Wash the root, chop it into small pieces, and allow it to dry.

Preparation: Place one or two teaspoons of the root in one cup of water and bring to a slow boil. Reduce the heat and allow it to simmer for between fifteen to thirty minutes. Allow it to cool and then strain the liquid through a fine sieve or a piece of cloth. Then you may drink it. Drink no more than 3 cups per day. Or it may be applied externally by soaking a small clean cloth with the solution and placing the soaked cloth against the skin.

Barberry

Barberry may be used against bacteria. It may also have antiviral applications. The leaves are a reddish purple color on top and a dull green color on the bottom underside of the leaves (see picture on right). Two of the tiny yellow spring flowers can be seen about half-way down the picture on the underside of the leaves.

Caution: Barberry should not be used for a period longer than one month.

Caution: Barberry should **never** be used by a pregnant woman.

Side Effects: It may cause nausea or vomiting or dizziness or fainting. If you have one of these adverse reactions then stop using it.

Uses: Internally it may be used for cholera, diarrhea, dysentery, hepatitis, urinary track infections, and digestive system aliments. Externally it may be used on eczema and psoriasis. Externally a cold compress soaked in barberry solution may be placed on the closed eyelids to help with pinkeye.

Top Side and Bottom Side

How to Grow: This is a perennial bush. The bush continues to grow a little bit bigger year after year. Although it is better to collect the roots and bark in the early spring or late fall, if you unexpectedly need barberry roots or branch bark then you can harvest them at any time of the year: winter, spring, summer, or fall. In my opinion this is a significant advantage of this herb because it will always be instantly available when you need it and if you don't need it then it just continues to grow all by itself with almost no care on my part. The bush also has thorns and this is an advantage because the bushes can be planted in a long row to form a simple security perimeter. Therefore the bush will not only help you with its roots but the top of the bush will discourage travel through the row of bushes. Travel would have to be around the hedge of bushes and not through the hedge.

Harvesting: Peal off the bark of the stems and the bark of the roots and dry the bark in a warm shady area.

Preparation: Place one teaspoon of the bark in one cup of water and bring to a slow boil. Reduce the heat and allow it to simmer for about fifteen minutes. Allow it to cool and then strain the liquid through a fine sieve or a piece of cloth. Then you may drink it. Drink no more than three cups per day. Or it may be applied externally by soaking a small clean cloth with the solution and placing the soaked cloth against the skin.

Conclusion

Herbal remedies, including echinacea and barberry, should not be taken until after you have discussed the herbal remedy with your licensed physician. Herbal remedies should only be taken if they are approved by your medical doctor for your specific medical condition. While you are taking any herbal remedy you should be under the supervision of your medical doctor.

Chapter Forty-Two

Colloidal Silver

This is not medical advice nor is it a medical recommendation.
Please consult a licensed medical professional to have your medical questions answered.

Until 1938 colloidal silver was the most common antibiotic in use.

It is natural, antiviral, antifungal, and antimicrobial.

Silver attaches itself to pathogens and retards respiration and reproduction. The pathogen then either suffocates or it dies without being able to reproduce and multiply.

It may be used internally or externally.

Bacteria that has become immune to synthetic antibiotics has no immunity against colloidal silver.

Colloidal silver *might* be used to treat E. coli, pink eye, urinary track infections, strep, anthrax, staph, typhoid, gingivitis, athlete's foot itch, ringworm, and skin burns.

Bandages may be saturated with colloidal silver and wrapped around wounds to prevent infections and to help skin burns.

Electrical conductivity cannot be used to determine the concentration of silver in solution.

In sufficient doses silver can cause argyria where the skin turns a blue gray color. This has serious social implications but otherwise it is not dangerous. The amount of silver required to cause argyria is not known at this time.

Never use a product that contains silver for more than one week and always use the silver product with the approval and under the supervision of a licensed medical physician.

At the beginning of the year 2011 there are three different products that are frequently marketed as being "colloidal silver" but only one of them actually is "colloidal silver."

Ionic Silver or Silver Solutions

Produced by the silver generators that are sold for the home production of a silver solution.
It is usually clear or it may have a slight yellow tint.
It is photosensitive and it will react with light and it should be stored in dark glass bottles.
A Simple Test for Ionic Silver: Place one-ounce of solution in a clear glass. Add a pinch of table salt. As the salt dissolves a white cloud of silver chloride will form. If you add a little more salt the white cloud will become more dense. This indicates the product is ionic silver. Discard the test solution because it has now been contaminated.
An ionic silver product should probably not cause argyria if taken sparingly according to the manufacturer's recommended dosage.
One source where you can purchase a silver generator (Dr. Robert C. Beck's Silver Pulsar Model ZBB5) is the following: http://www.energetichealthsecrets.com/beck/silverpulser.php

Silver Protein

Water is added to a silver protein powder. To prevent the silver particles from settling out of solution a protein binder is added, such as gelatin.
The gelatin adds the risk of bacteria formation and this is a serious disadvantage of this product.
The silver is not easily absorbed by the human body and therefore it is the least effective for human use.

Typical concentrations are 30 ppm up to 20,000 ppm and they begin with a light amber color with increasing darkness to almost black.

A Simple Test for Silver Protein: Shake the bottle. If a foam appears on the surface of the liquid and remains there for a minute or two then there is an extremely good chance that it is a silver protein.

A silver protein product can cause argyria.

All silver protein products should be completely avoided.

Colloidal Silver

True colloidal silver is produced by a complex manufacturing process and therefore the cost of its production is high.

True colloidal silver is not clear.

Colloidal silver should probably not cause argyria.

Conclusion

At the beginning of the year 2011 it is currently very difficult to determine if a product that contains silver is actually colloidal silver. Therefore any product that contains silver should **not** be taken without the approval and supervision of a licensed physician.

Chapter Forty-Three

Home Remedies for Insect and Pest Problems

None of the information in this chapter is medical advice nor is it a medical recommendation. Please consult a licensed medical professional to have your medical questions answered.

Bee Stings and Insect Stings (Not Spider Bites)

Inspect the sting area. If the stinger is inside the sting area then scrap the stinger out with your fingernail or the blunt edge of a knife. Do not grasp the stinger to pull it out or you may inject some poison still inside the stinger into the person's body.

Rub some ordinary mud on a bee sting or insect sting and it will help to relieve the pain and minimize the itch. If you don't have any water then you can spit on the ground and make some mud. This may sound disgusting but if you have ever been stung by a bee then you know how painful it can be. If you should get stung again then you now know a simple quick remedy for the bee sting (or other insect sting).

Tick Removal

When a blood sucking tick attaches itself to a person's body the tick buries its mouth under the person's skin. A tick should be removed as soon as possible after it is discovered to minimize the risk of an infection. After removing the tick use some soap and water to wash the area where the tick was attached to the body. There are two methods for removing a tick: the current pull method and the old fashioned heat method.

Current Pull Method: Use some good tweezers. Do not grab the tick around the large part of its body. Instead use the tweezers to grasp the tick as close as possible at its mouth or head where it is attached to the body. Pull gently but pull firmly on the tick. Do not crush the tick with the tweezers. Pull straight out from the body and not at an angle. Do not jerk the tick off the body. Pull gently but pull firmly. Use steady pressure. The tick should release its hold on the body in order to relieve the pressure on its mouth. Destroy the tick after it has detached itself from the body.

Old Fashioned Heat Method: This method is **no** longer recommended. It is presented here for educational purposes only. If the tick is in an area with hair then you be careful not to catch the person's hair on fire. If you use heat then have a gallon of water nearby to quickly put out an accidental fire. Place a small hot object near the rear end of the tick and wait a few seconds. The tick will detach itself and then you can easily and safely remove the tick and destroy it. Some good sources of heat are the lit end of a cigarette, or a long thin metal object that has had one end heated by the flame of a fire, or a **tiny** red hot coal from the fireplace that you pick up with some long tweezers or metal tongs. However, the best way to remove a tick is to pull it off gently with some tweezers as described above.

Chigger Bites

A chigger bite usually appears as a small round reddish circle on the skin and it really, really itches. Most chigger bites are near the ankles, behind the knees, in the groin area, or in the armpits. A chigger is so small it can't be seen by most people without a magnifying glass. The chigger remains on top of the skin and it bites the skin and deposits its saliva into the skin. The saliva begins to destroy the skin tissue and then the chigger begins to feed. When a person scratches a chigger bite the chigger is almost always immediately killed or it is scrapped off the skin and it cannot bite you again and it will die on its own. However the damaged skin tissue will continue to itch for between three to ten days.

When you first notice a chigger bite take a hot shower and use soap and a washcloth and thoroughly rub down your entire body to remove all the chiggers, including the ones that haven't bitten you yet.

No single itch relief treatment works for everyone. Different people respond differently to different treatments for relieving the itch of a chigger bite until the skin heals naturally by itself. You may try any type of anti-itch cream or lotion, or a little Listerine mouthwash dabbed on the bite. Or a little clear nail polish may be dabbed on the bite one time, but nail polish will dry the skin and slow down the natural healing process.

Chapter Forty-Three: Insect Stings, Ticks, Chiggers, Head Lice, and Skunk Deodorizer

How to Get Rid of Head Lice

During serious hard times when the average standard of living declines and sanitary conditions are poor, lice will thrive and multiply. Therefore it would be useful to know how to protect your family from lice and how to deal with lice if they should infest the hair of someone in your family.

Lice Symptoms:

The most common symptom of head lice is itching. The itching normally occurs close to the ears and at the bottom of the neck. But the itching does not have to occur in one of these locations. In addition, approximately half the time the head lice do not cause any itching at all. Therefore the only way to know if someone in your family has head lice is to closely examine the hair on his or her head.

Lice Facts:

1. Eggs are called nits.
2. One adult is called a louse.
3. Two or more adults are called lice.
4. A dead louse is called a good louse (this is a joke).
5. Lice attach themselves to strands of hair using claws on their feet.
6. To stay alive a louse must feed on the human blood that is inside human hair.
7. Head lice do not carry serious diseases. Head lice will only make your head itch. Head lice are a different type of lice than body lice.
8. A louse **cannot** live on a pet, or a rodent, or a mouse, or anything except people.
9. A different type of lice can live on monkeys and apes and they are similar to the type of lice that live on people but they are different and they can't survive on a human.
10. A louse **cannot** fly, or hop, or jump. A louse can only crawl but it can crawl rather quickly for its small size. A louse can crawl up to 9 inches in one minute.
11. In an environment that is shared by several people, such as a home, lice can spread very rapidly from one person to another and from one head to another head.
12. For some reason that is not really understood lice do prefer one person to another person. Therefore it is not unusual for one person to acquire head lice more often than another person even though they do not do anything different to attract the head lice.

Lice Identification:

1. Ordinary dandruff and head lice nits look very similar and both can make your head itch. But dandruff is relatively easy to move up or down on a strand of hair whereas lice and nits will cling to a strand of hair and it is very difficult to move lice or nits along a strand of hair.
2. In order to see a louse and their eggs you will need a very good light that is placed close to the person's scalp.
3. Look very close to where the hair is attached to the scalp to find the lice and their eggs.
4. An adult louse will be either gray or tan in color and it will be about 1/8 to 1/10 of an inch long.
5. Lice feces (poop) will look like tiny black spots.
6. Lice will quickly crawl away from any area of the hair that is disturbed. Therefore you will probably not see an adult louse. Instead you should look for the tiny eggs that are permanently attached near the root of a strand of hair.
7. Lice eggs start their life cycle as a white egg, then the egg turns yellow, and then brown. An egg will be glued to the bottom of a strand of hair approximately 1/2 inch to 1 inch from the scalp.

How Lice Can Get Into Your Hair:

You can acquire head lice in any of the following ways:

Chapter Forty-Three: Insect Stings, Ticks, Chiggers, Head Lice, and Skunk Deodorizer

1. If you give someone a hug and your head or hair touches the head or hair of a person that has head lice then the lice can move onto your hair.
2. If you use the same towel or shower cap as another person then the head lice can move from the towel or shower cap onto your head.
3. If you use the same hair comb or hair brush as a person who has head lice then the head lice can travel from the hair comb or brush onto your hair.
4. If you wear the same scarves, hats, hooded sweatshirts, bicycle helmets, jackets, or coats as another person who does have head lice then the lice can easily move into your hair.
5. If there is a common hat rack or coat closet where everyone stores their hats and coats and those hats or coats are in contact with each other then the lice can travel between the coats and hats. Later when you put on your hat or coat the head lice will crawl into your hair.
6. If you put your head on a pillow that has head lice then the head lice can get into your hair.
7. If you sit down and then lean back and rest your head of a sofa cushion and the sofa cushion contains head lice then the lice can crawl into your hair.

How Lice Reproduce and How Long They Can Live on a Strand of Hair:

1. A louse can live for about one month (or 32 days) under good conditions on a person's head.
2. An adult female louse can lay between 6 to 10 eggs each day. During her entire adult life span a female can lay a total of about 90 eggs.
3. When a female lays an egg she attaches it with some strong glue to a single hair strand at a distance of approximately 1/2 inch from the scalp.
4. The eggs are small and oval shaped and they are only glued to one side of the strand of hair.
5. When an egg is first laid it will be white. But the egg will gradually turn yellow and then it will turn brown and then it will hatch.
6. It takes an egg about 7 to 11 days to hatch after it has been laid.
7. When the louse emerges from the egg it will cling to the strand of hair to which it was originally attached. A baby louse is about the size of the head of a pin. As the hair continues to grow the baby louse will gradually move further away from the scalp since it is still attached to that same strand of hair.
8. After about 7 to 11 days the baby louse will have grown into an adult louse and then it will be able to crawl freely around a person's head. It will also be able to reproduce.

How Long Lice and Nits Can Live After Being Removed From a Person:

1. **Lice:** If a louse crawls off person, or if it is removed from a person, then it will begin to quickly dehydrate. In an ideal environment, such as a cool rainy day, a louse can live for up to 24 hours if it is not attached to a human hair.
2. **Nits:** Lice eggs can survive for about ten to fourteen days after being removed from human hair. The good news is that lice eggs will **not** hatch at normal room temperatures if they are not attached to a live human hair.

Commercially Available Head Lice Chemicals and Products:

All the chemicals currently available for treating head lice, and which are safe to use on a person's hair, are only effective against adult lice. These chemicals usually kill or stun the adult lice. If you examine the lice you comb out of a person's hair you will probably notice that some of the lice are dead and some are the lice are still twitching. None of these chemicals will kill the eggs or nits because the tiny baby louse is protected inside its egg. During the next week after you use these chemicals on a person's hair the eggs will begin to hatch and a new batch of lice will begin to invade the person's hair. Therefore these chemicals recommend that you repeat the entire head washing procedure again sometime between seven to nine days after the first treatment. Consequently there is no advantage to using a commercially available head lice chemical instead of the simple procedure that is discussed next.

How to Get Lice and Nits Out of a Person's Hair:

The most effective method for removing head lice is to use a sturdy comb with teeth that are very close together. Any **strong fine tooth comb** will do the job or you can purchase a special "head lice nit comb" in the pharmacy section of many stores. The RID Lice Comb in the picture on the right can be purchased for about $8 at Walmart and it does have fine metal teeth of two different lengths.

A **fine tooth metal comb** is stronger than a plastic comb. The teeth of a metal comb will not separate as easily as the teeth of a plastic comb and therefore they yield better results as a head lice nit comb. You can purchase a fine tooth metal comb on the internet or in the pet section of many stores or in a specialty pet store.

You will also need a **wide tooth comb** to get the tangles out of person's freshly washed hair.

After you have decided on the two combs you will be using then you should follow this procedure:

1. Shampoo the person's hair with ordinary shampoo to get rid of any dirt or foreign matter that might be in the hair. Rinse the shampoo out of the hair with very warm water.
2. Thoroughly saturate the hair with ordinary hair conditioner. Do not rinse the hair conditioner out of the hair. Let it remain on the hair for about five-minutes. The hair conditioner will not kill or suffocate the lice or nits. The hair conditioner will coat the hair with a very slippery layer of fluid. This will make it very difficult for the lice to retain their grip on the individual strands of hair. The hair conditioner will also shock and confuse the lice for about twenty-minutes. Do not rinse the hair conditioner out of the hair. Leave the hair conditioner in the hair and immediately do the following.
3. Place a good light near the person's head so you can shine the light directly on the person's scalp. This will allow you to see the lice more clearly so you will not accidentally miss any of them as you proceed.
4. Comb the person's hair gently with a **wide tooth comb** to remove any tangles. This is a different comb than the one you will use to remove the lice and their eggs.
5. Begin on either the left side or the right side of the person's head at the hair line and slowly work you way across the top of the person's head to the opposite side.
6. Place your **fine tooth comb** as close as possible to the person's scalp and slowly and gently pull the comb through a few strands of hair. Rinse the comb in some hot water. Pull the comb through those same exact strands of hair a second time. Rinse the comb in some hot water. Pull the comb through those same exact strands of hair a third time. Rinse the comb in some hot water. Now put a hair clip on those hair strands and allow them to hang down the side of the person's head out of the way. Move to the next few strands of hair directly above the strands of hair you just cleaned. You will need to work quickly but you will also need to be thorough.
7. Repeat Step Six until you have worked your way across the top of the person's head and down the opposite side of their head and down the back of their head.
8. When you are finished pour the pot of hot water that contains the hair conditioner, the lice, and the nits into the toilet stool and flush the stool.
9. Thoroughly rinse the person's hair with very warm water.
10. Now carefully inspect the person's hair very slowly from side to side and verify that there are no head lice remaining. If you find a louse or a nit attached to a strand of hair then cut that **one strand of hair** off at the scalp using some barber scissors and put it into a bowl. When you are finished you may have several strands of hair in the bowl that contain either lice or nits. Flush the hair and lice and nits down the toilet stool.
11. It is usually not possible to get every single nit out of a person's hair. Therefore you need to be emotionally prepared when the nits you missed begin to hatch and lice begin to reappear in the person's hair.

12. Every third day for the next six days the person should shampoo their hair and then use hair conditioner on their hair and then comb the hair conditioner out of their hair using a fine tooth comb while still in the shower. Rinse the hair conditioner and the lice and nits down the shower drain after each shampoo and conditioner treatment. This will help to remove any lice that may have hatched from any eggs that were missed the first time.
13. After a total of nine days have passed since the first treatment repeat the above procedure beginning at step one and continuing through step ten. Saturate the person's hair with hair conditioner and comb through it just like you did the first time. If you missed any nits the first time then they should have hatched by now and you will need to remove these baby lice from the person's hair before they become adults and reproduce and lay more eggs.
14. If you want to be absolutely certain you have eliminated all the head lice then repeat steps one through ten after seven more days have passed.

Some Home Remedies That Do Not Work:

Home remedies such as petroleum jelly, mayonnaise, vinegar, and ordinary shampoo do **not** work. Even if you leave one of these home remedies on the person's head for 24 hours inside a plastic shower cap, the lice will not be killed. Never, never put kerosene on a person's hair.

How to Prevent Future Head Lice Problems:

1. Do not share hair combs, hair brushes, towels, or shower caps. Each person in your family should have his or her own personal hygiene items.
2. Do not share clothing until after it has been washed in hot water and dried in a hot-air clothes dryer.
3. When head lice are first detected everyone in your home should be treated for head lice. This means everybody's hair needs to go through the above cleaning procedure.
4. Do not use the same two combs on another person until both combs have been sterilized in very hot water.
5. If everyone in your home is not treated for head lice at the same time then the lice can survive in one person's hair and later migrate to the hair of the other family members and begin multiplying once again.

How to Kill Lice and Nits That Are Not Attached to Human Hair:

1. At a temperature of 125°F (52°C) both lice and nits will die in 10 minutes or less. They will die quicker at higher temperatures.
2. Therefore you should wash all your bed sheets, pillow cases, towels, and clothes using the hot-water cycle on your washing machine. Then you should dry those items in a hot-air clothes dryer for a minimum of twenty-minutes.
3. Stuffed toy animals and small pillows should be put inside an airtight plastic bag for at least one day. Or you could put them inside a two-gallon freezer bag and put them in the freezer for 24-hours to kill the lice.
4. Do not waste your money on commercially available lice sprays because they do not work.
5. If you are concerned that there may be lice in your carpets, or furniture, or anywhere else in your home then there is an easy way to terminate them. After everyone in your family has had the hair conditioner head lice treatment then take your entire family for a two-day visit to the home of one of your close relatives. Spend one night, such as Saturday night, at your relatives home. When you return to your home on Sunday night your home will be lice free. The reason this will work is because a louse cannot survive for more than 24-hours unless it is attached to a human hair. If you remove all the people from your home then any lice that may be present will dehydrate and come to the end of their natural life cycle.

What To Try If the Lice Reappear After You Have Done All the Above:

Instead of hair conditioner pour Listerine mouthwash on the person's hair and follow the above combing procedure just as if you were using hair conditioner. A Florida newspaper reported that Listerine mouthwash will kill the lice and the nits in one treatment. I have not personally tested Listerine mouthwash for this purpose so I do not know if it will actually work. However, I am passing this information on to you so you will have another option to try if the above hair conditioner method doesn't work for you.

If you don't have any hair conditioner or Listerine mouthwash then you may use any kitchen cooking oil or olive oil instead of the hair conditioner. Follow the above combing procedure just as if you were using hair conditioner.

If you do not have any hair conditioner, or cooking oil, or Listerine, or if the lice survive multiple treatments of hair conditioner and combing, then you may have to use the traditional time honored method of getting rid of head lice. Shave all the hair off the person's head and then burn all their hair. This should **never** be done except as a last resort because the reason the lice continue to reappear may be due to your family member coming into contact on a regular basis with another person outside your family and that other person does have head lice.

Please remember that you must also sterilize your bed sheets, towels, and clothing in very hot water, and then dry them at a high temperature inside a clothes dryer.

Skunk Deodorizer
(May be used on people or on pets)

1 cup baking soda
1 quart hydrogen peroxide (neutralizes and breaks down the skunk oil or odor)
2 tablespoons of liquid dish washing soap

Mix all three ingredients together thoroughly. Wear some rubber or plastic gloves to protect your hands and wash your entire body with the above mixture and especially the area that stinks. Allow the soapy solution to remain on your body for about two minutes. Then rinse all the solution completely off using clean water.

Chapter Forty-Three: Insect Stings, Ticks, Chiggers, Head Lice, and Skunk Deodorizer

Chapter Forty-Four

Rechargeable NiMH Batteries (AAA, AA, C, D) and Solar Battery Chargers

Introduction

If you are camping, or if the electricity is off while you are at home, then battery operated radios and flashlights are really nice things to have. If you purchase rechargeable batteries then you could recharge your batteries using the sun if you have a solar battery charger.

1.2 Volt NiMH (Nickel-Metal Hydride) Rechargeable Batteries versus 1.5 Volt Alkaline Batteries

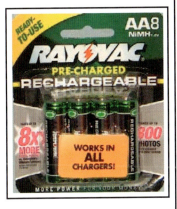

For several years a myth has been circulating around the internet that a 1.2 volt battery will not work in a device that specifies a 1.5 volt battery. The reason given is that the 1.2 volt battery does not have as much power as the 1.5 volt battery. Like many other myths, this myth is not true.

Almost all electronic devices that use 1.5 volt alkaline batteries will also work just as well with 1.2 volt rechargeable batteries **unless** the device specifically states that rechargeable batteries should not be used in it.

The average 1.5 volt alkaline battery will drop to approximately 1.2 volts after approximately 20% to 30% of its useful life. For the remaining 70% to 80% of its useful life it will be below 1.2 volts until it reaches about 0.8 or 0.9 volts and then it will stop working. At this point it will be drained and it will not yield enough volts to operate the electronic device in which it is installed.

The average 1.2 volt NiMH rechargeable battery starts at approximately 1.3 volts and then drops to approximately 1.2 volts and it remains very close to 1.2 volts for approximately 95% of its useful life. For the last 5% of its useful life it begins to rapidly decline down to about 0.8 or 0.9 volts and then it is considered drained and it needs to be recharged.

In addition, 1.5 volt alkaline batteries do not last as long as 1.2 volt NiMH batteries when put into use. And a 1.5 volt alkaline battery only provides about 9 amps of current at the beginning of its fully charged state whereas a 1.2 volt NiMH battery provides about 10 amps of current at the beginning of its fully charged state.

Therefore when you consider all the above information, a 1.2 volt NiMH battery produces more voltage than a 1.5 volt alkaline battery for approximately 90% of the useful life of the NiMH battery. And when it is "drained" the NiMH battery can be recharged again and again for somewhere between 100 to 1000 times depending on the quality of the original battery and the application in which it is used.

I have not done any studies on how many times I have been able to recharge a NiMH battery so I do not know if the **average** manufacturer claim of about 300 to 400 recharges for a NiMH battery is reasonable or if it is overstated.

Whenever possible you should allow your rechargeable batteries to fully discharge inside the device in which they are being used before you recharge those batteries. In other words, wait until the electrical device either stops working or it tells you it is time to replace the batteries. This will mean the batteries are fully discharged and they are now ready to be recharged.

It should also be mentioned that a NiMH battery does **not** have the "memory" problems of a Ni-Cad (Nickel-Cadmium) battery. The original Ni-Cad batteries had to be charged to their peak potential the very first time they were charged or they would remember the first charge level and you would **never** be able to charge that specific battery in the future above that original charge level. NiMH batteries do not work this way and if you don't fully charge a NiMH battery then it only impacts that one usage and it has **no** impact on the future maximum charging potential of that battery.

Most of the time you will probably restore your rechargeable batteries to their maximum power level. However, it is nice to know that if an unexpected emergency occurs and you do **not** have the time to charge your batteries to a full charge, then it is okay to use those partially charged batteries and it will not impact the future charging potential of those batteries. This means if you desperately needed your batteries during a serious hard times event after the sun has gone down or if it is raining, then you could use your batteries in your flashlight or radio even though they were not yet fully charged and you would **not** be damaging those batteries in any way.

Solar Battery Chargers

Solar battery chargers have all the following **advantages**:

1. They are affordable.
2. They are entirely self-contained and the only other thing you will need will be rechargeable batteries.
3. They are easy to use and they do not require a background in electronics.
4. They are small, lightweight, and portable.
5. They may easily be added to an emergency backpack or bug-out-bag. If you also add 12 rechargeable batteries, a L.E.D. flashlight, and a portable world-band radio then you would have light, and entertainment, and access to global news events for many, many years into the future.
6. They will work in a grid-down situation when there is no electricity (as long as the sun is shining).

Solar battery chargers have the following **characteristics**:

1. The sun must be shining for the solar battery charger to work. A solar battery charger will not be useful during a blizzard, or hurricane, or at night. However, sooner or later the sun will shine again and then the solar battery charger will be able to successfully do its job.
2. A solar battery charger will **not** recharge batteries as quickly as a standard 120-volt house current battery charger. However, if the electricity if off, and your batteries are completely drained, then you may not object to waiting a little longer to recharge your radio and flashlight batteries. (Note: Individuals who complain about the time it takes to recharge batteries in a solar charger usually want fully recharged batteries in a few hours. They are not content to wait a little longer for the same results. This time issue can be easily resolved by having a **spare set** of rechargeable batteries that are already charged and ready to use whenever a set of discharged batteries needs to be put into the solar charger.)
3. All batteries are not created equal. That is part of the reason for the price difference between batteries. The more power a battery is able to store the longer it will take to restore the battery to a full charge. Therefore the time required to recharge a battery will increase as the number of mAH of the battery increases. For example:
    a. It will take *approximately* 5 hours of direct sunlight to fully recharge two AA 800 mAH batteries.
    b. It will take *approximately* 10 hours of direct sunlight to fully recharge two AA 1600 mAH batteries.
4. Solar battery chargers are designed to recharge identical batteries of the same exact brand name and of the same exact size at the same time. In other words, you cannot recharge one AA battery at the same time as a AAA battery. Instead you will need to recharge two AA batteries at one time. Or you could recharge two AAA batteries at the same time. Or you could recharge two C batteries at the same time. Or you could recharge two D batteries at the same time. A solar battery charger will recharge all the different size batteries for which it was designed but you can only use it to recharge one size battery at a time.
5. Batteries should be recharged at a temperature between 32°F to 113°F (or between 0°C to 45°C). During the winter this may require that you put your solar charger in front of a window that is facing south. Place your solar charger where it will receive full sun and where a shadow from the frame of the window will not fall across the face of the solar panel.
6. Remove your rechargeable batteries from the solar charger at the end of each day and replace them in the solar charger the next day. Do **not** leave your batteries in the solar charger overnight. (Note: Some solar chargers have a blocking diode that prevents the batteries from discharging during the night.)

This chapter will review two different but similar solar battery chargers. One charger will recharge two batteries at the same time and the other charger will recharge four batteries at the same time. Both chargers share the following characteristics:

1. Each charger will recharge AAA, AA, C, and D batteries.
2. Each charger will recharge Ni-Cad (Nickel-Cadmium) and Ni-MH (Nickel-Metal Hydride) batteries.
3. They will **not** recharge a 9 volt battery.
4. Each charger has a separate rear support bracket that you pull out from the rear of the charger so you can adjust the angle of the solar panel to match the position of the sun in the sky. However, this bracket only has one position so you will need to be creative in propping up the solar battery charger so its solar panel is at approximately a 90-degree angle to the sun.

Solar Battery Charger for Two Batteries

Dimensions: 6.75" by 4.5" by 2.125".
Solar Panel Size: 5.25" by 2.125" or 11.156 square inches.
Weight: 12.2 ounces.
Maximum Charging Rate: 167 mAH into two batteries at the same time.
Price: Approximately $20 plus shipping at amazon.com.

This two battery solar charger was originally called the "Solar Eleven-in-One Battery Charger with Meter." However it is currently being sold simply as a "Solar Battery Charger." Even though the name has been changed this charger has the same exact design as the Eleven-in-One charger. Therefore it will also charge the seven "GUM" size battery that are used in Europe. But the current box label does not mention this fact because it is not important in the United States of America.

This Solar Battery Charger has a meter that shows when you have the solar panel at the optimum angle for recharging your batteries. The meter eliminates the guess work of whether or not you have the solar panel at a good angle. Just keep changing the angle of the solar panel until the meter needle reaches its highest point and then starts going in the opposite direction. The meter will not work until after you have inserted two batteries in the unit. The meter is connected to a circuit from the solar panel through the battery compartment and until you have two batteries inserted inside the unit that circuit is not complete. (Note: If you wish you can check the meter in about two hours when the position of the sun has changed and reposition the solar panel to continue to use the sun in the most efficient manner. However, the solar charger will still continue to recharge your batteries even if you don't adjust the angle of the solar panel.)

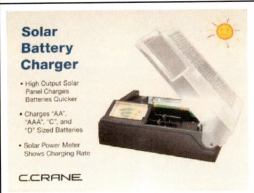

The meter on the Solar Battery Charger will **not** show you how much power you have in each battery. It will only show you how efficiently you are using the sun to recharge your batteries. The meter will show you the estimated amount of time required to recharge two fully discharged batteries based on the angle of the solar panel in relation to the sun and the current intensity of the sun. If your batteries are not fully discharged then it will take less time. And as the position of the sun changes in relation to the angle of the solar panel then it will take more time. And if small clouds occasionally block the sun then it will take more time. Therefore the meter will only give you an approximate amount of time for fully charging each of the different size batteries (AAA, AA, C, and D). The meter is also not calibrated for the different mAH ratings of the batteries that can be purchased so the meter's only practical value is to help you position the attached solar panel at the optimum angle to the sun.

The two-battery charger has the following advantages:

1. It is more affordable than the four-battery charger.
2. It charges two-batteries at one time instead of four. This is an advantage if most of your electronic devices only use two batteries, such as a flashlight or a portable radio. When the batteries are drained you may put them in the charger on the next bright sunny day and you do not have to wait until you have a total of four batteries that need to be recharged.
3. It will recharge the seven standard "GUM" size batteries used in Europe.
4. It has a solar meter to help you learn the best angle to position the solar panel in relationship to the sun to maximize the sun's energy and minimize the total time required to recharge the batteries.

Solar Battery Charger for Four Batteries and for Some Cell Phones

Dimensions: 7" by 6.5" by 2.125".
Solar Panel Size: 4.5" by 4.125" or 18.563 square inches (a seven volt solar panel).
Weight: 13.25 ounces.
Maximum Charging Rate: 167 mAH into four batteries at the same time.
Price: Approximately $28 plus shipping at amazon.com.

This solar battery charger will recharge four batteries at the same time. It also comes with a special cord that plugs into the side of the charger and the opposite end of that cord has five standard plugs for recharging the batteries in some cell phones.

There are at least ten different size plug connectors that are used on cell phones and other rechargeable electronic devices, such as laptop computers. Consequently there is no guarantee that this unit will be compatible with your cell phone or other rechargeable electronic equipment. As an example, one of the five adapters would fit my old Gateway laptop computer but none of them would fit my newer HP laptop computer.

The solar panel on this four-battery charger is approximately 66% bigger than the solar panel on the two-battery charger. Therefore it can recharge four batteries in almost the same amount of time as the two battery charger.

The four-battery charger contains an internal blocking diode to prevent battery discharge after sunset.

Therefore if you live in the United States of America or in any country where "GUM" batteries are not used then the four-battery charger may be a better investment than the two-battery charger even though the four-battery charger does cost about 40% more. The four-battery charger has the following advantages:

1. It will recharge four identical batteries of the same design and of the same size at one time.
2. It contains a blocking diode so you do **not** have to remove the batteries at night.
3. It comes with a cable that has five different size plugs and this may allow you to recharge the batteries in some of your other electrical devices, such as a cell phone.

Suggestions on How to Use a Solar Battery Charger

Batteries are not designed to be left in direct sunlight for an extended period of time. They will overheat and start to leak and you will get some very nasty stuff on the inside of your solar charger. Batteries react to the sun the same way your skin does. If your skin is exposed to direct sunlight for too long you will get a very painful sunburn (or worse). To avoid the sunburn you could sit in the shade. Therefore the simple solution is to put a white cloth over the batteries, between the batteries and the solar panel, which is on a hinge. Then elevate one end of the white cloth with a short stick or piece of plastic to allow the batteries to breathe. (Don't use a piece of metal which could fall into your charger and possibly short it out.) You do not want to create an oven by completely covering the batteries. You only need to provide shade so the batteries do not overheat. This is absolutely necessary in the summer and also in the winter if the sun is exceptionally bright.

The chargers will work on either two or four identical batteries of exactly the same brand name, of the same design, and of the same size, at the same time. You should **not** mix batteries of different brands at exactly the same time. And it is not a good practice to try to recharge batteries that are not equally discharged. Therefore I normally allow my batteries to get very close to a full discharge before I stop using them. Then I can safely place them in the solar charger and each battery will receive an equal charge.

Based on my past experience it would be wise to invest in several rechargeable batteries of the same size. This would allow you to always have spare batteries while your discharged batteries are in the solar charger. And there will probably come a day when some emergency situation demands your complete attention for an extended period of time and you will cook a set of batteries. Therefore it is nice to have spares.

It is also nice to have a spare solar charger in the event the battery chemicals get all over the inside of your charger and it is damaged beyond repair. These solar chargers are probably not outside the budget of most families and most families could probably afford to buy two or more of them. That decision is up to you.

mAH = MilliAmpere Hours

Volt is a measure of electrical force.
All NiMH batteries are rated at approximately 1.2 volts.

Ampere, or amp or amps, is a measure of electrical current.
One milliampere hour, or mAH, is one-thousandth of an amp delivered for one hour.

The number of mAH varies considerably for different NiMH batteries, even from the same manufacturer, such as Energizer, and for the same size battery, such as AA.

The higher the mAH rating the longer the battery will operate an electrical device and the longer it will take to recharge that battery once it is discharged.

Volt - Amp Meter (Multimeter)

If you are interested in an **optional** multimeter that will provide volt and amp readings on your rechargeable batteries then you might wish to consider the GE Digital Multimeter illustrated in the picture on the right (product number 50953). It can be purchased at most Walmart stores for approximately $17 near their electrical extension cord display. Before purchasing this multimeter I visited a Radio Shack Store, an Ace Hardware Store, a True Value Hardware Store, and a Lowe's Home Improvement Store and I carefully examined the different multimeters that were available. The GE Digital Multimeter is the one I selected. Many of the other multimeters did not have a 10A setting so they would not yield a reading for the number of amps in a rechargeable battery. The one disadvantage of this multimeter, and all the other multimeters that have a 10A setting, is that they require a 9-volt battery inside to power the multimeter. However, the 9-volt battery is advertised to power the multimeter for between 100 to 200 hours of continuous use. Since the multimeter has an "OFF" setting you will probably eventually replace the 9-volt battery due to its normal "self-discharge" rate instead of wearing the battery out using it to power the multimeter. Let me remind you that this multimeter is an **optional** piece of equipment and it is **not** needed for any reason other than to satisfy your curiosity about the voltage and amperage of your batteries. This multimeter will **not** measure mAH nor will any other multimeter on the market.

Now let's look at what the volt and amp readings on a rechargeable battery actually tell us.

You will **not** be able to use a battery Volt meter or a "Battery Tester" to determine if your rechargeable batteries are fully charged. Simple "battery testers" are calibrated for alkaline batteries and they only show if the battery is still "good" or if it needs to be "replaced" based on the number of volts remaining in the battery. This is of no value to you when recharging NiMH batteries because the battery will be very close to 1.2 volts the entire time it is reacquiring its total amperage power.

You should know the original mAH rating of your batteries and this is not easy to find anymore. It used to be printed on the front or the rear of the battery package but the battery manufacturers no longer provide this information for their batteries. The battery manufacturers assume you will be recharging your batteries in their 120-volt house current recharging units and they design some special circuits into their recharging units to determine when the battery is fully charged so they can automatically turn off the charger.

You also will **not** be able to use an Amp meter to determine if your rechargeable batteries are fully charged. If you have an Amp meter then you will need to set it on its 10A setting to get a reading on your rechargeable batteries. But all the Amp meter will show you is how much current is currently flowing through the battery at one moment in time. It reports AMPS. The power stored in a battery is measured in mAH, or milliampere hours. An Amp meter will not tell you this value.

Therefore you will **not** be able to use a Volt meter or an Amp meter or a "Battery Tester" to determine if your rechargeable batteries are at their maximum peak potential charge. You will need to use a different method. That different method will be explained next.

How to Determine the Total Time Required to Restore a NiMH Battery to a Full Charge Inside a Solar Charger

Both the two-battery charger and the four-battery charger require approximately the same amount of time to recharge batteries. The two-battery charger will add approximately 167 mAH of current into two batteries in one-hour. The four-battery charger will add approximately 167 mAH of current into four batteries in one-hour. This estimate is based on a bright sunny day with the solar panel aimed directly at the sun at a 90-degree angle to the sun. If the angle is not exactly 90-degrees then the amount of charge declines and the amount of time required to return a battery to a full charge increases. Therefore it is important to have the solar panel pointed directly at the sun. As the position of the sun moves across the sky during the day this means you will need to periodically reposition the solar panel on the charger so that it once again points directly at the sun. If the solar panel is **not** pointed directly at the sun then both chargers will only add about 125 mAH of current per hour into each of the batteries inside the charger. If clouds occasionally block the sun during the day then the charge rate can decline to about 80 mAH of current per hour into each battery and this means it will take approximately twice as long to bring the batteries back to a full charge.

Therefore to determine a reasonable estimate of how long you should leave the batteries inside the charger in direct sunlight you will need to know the mAH rating of the battery. Then divide the mAH rating by 167 to yield the fastest possible recharge time in full sun. Double that value to yield the time required to recharge your batteries on a partly cloudy day.

A few examples of different battery sizes and different mAH ratings are as follows:

Battery	Rating / 167	Minimum Recharging Time
Size AAA	800 mAH / 167 =	4.8 hours of direct sun
Size AAA	850 mAH / 167 =	5.1 hours of direct sun
Size AA	850 mAH / 167 =	5.1 hours of direct sun
Size AA	1300 mAH / 167 =	7.8 hours of direct sun
Size C	1500 mAH / 167 =	9.0 hours of direct sun
Size C	2500 mAH / 167 =	15.0 hours of direct sun
Size D	2500 mAH / 167 =	15.0 hours of direct sun
Size D	3000 mAH / 167 =	18.0 hours of direct sun

The above estimates would apply to the two-battery charger and the four-battery charger because the solar panel on the four-battery charger is bigger and it can recharge four batteries in approximately the same amount of time that the two-battery charger needs to recharge two batteries. The above estimates are the minimum time required. If it is partly cloudy or if the solar panel is not pointed directly at the sun the entire day then the above time estimates will need to be increased.

You will also notice that the size of the battery, such as AAA or C, is not the important issue. The important issue is the mAH rating of the battery. The mAH rating of the battery is what determines the total time the battery needs to remain inside the solar charger in order to return it to a full charge.

If you don't know the mAH rating of your rechargeable batteries then you will need to determine the optimal amount of time to leave those batteries inside your solar charger. In other words, you will need to conduct a simple experiment.

The experimental method I recommend is based on repeated trials and keeping track of your results from each trial. If you will follow this method you will be able to determine how many hours you should leave each of your different types of batteries inside a solar charger.

(Note: Although you may not be too interested in the following information at this time, it may become very important to you at some time in the future if a serious hard time event impacts your family.)

1. Begin by determining how many good hours of direct sunlight you have each day. This may be as many as ten good hours of direct sunlight in the summer. But in the middle of winter you may only have about six good hours of direct sunlight. Where you actually live will also impact this value. The following test procedure may require that you recharge your batteries over a period of two or three consecutive days in order to get enough direct sunlight hours.

2. Place the correct number of fully discharged batteries into the solar charger and put the charger in direct sunlight for five hours following the directions mentioned earlier to avoid "melting" your batteries.

3. After charging the batteries place two or more of those batteries inside a flashlight or radio or other device based on the number of batteries required to operate that device. Then turn the device on and write down the time of day that you activated the device. Check the device every 15 minutes to see if it is still working. Eventually the device will either stop working or it will become too weak to be of practical use. Write down the time of day again. Compute how many hours the device worked on a five-hour sunlight charge.

4. Place the correct number of fully discharged batteries in the solar charger and put the charger in direct sunlight for 7.5 hours following the directions mentioned earlier to avoid "melting" your batteries. After charging remove the batteries and follow the directions in step 3 above and write down how long the device worked on 7.5 hours of sunlight. Since 7.5 hours is 50% more than 5 hours, the actually operating time of the device should be about 50% longer than your first test (or a ratio of approximately 1.50).

    a. If the second time was almost equal to the first time then five hours may have been too long and you will need to experiment with 3 or 4 hours of sunlight.
    b. If the second time was approximately 50% longer than the first time then proceed to step 5 below.
    c. If the second time was a lot less than 50% longer than the first time then do the following math:

    Divide the second time value by the first time value. Then multiply by 5 hours.
    This is the approximate time required for those batteries to receive a full charge.
    For example, if the device worked 12 hours the first time and 15 hours the second time then:

    $(15) / (12) = 1.25$
    $1.25 \times 5 = 6.25$ hours.

    In this situation your rechargeable batteries will be at a full charge in about 6.25 hours.
    This is your final answer and you may stop the test for this type of battery.

5. Place the correct number of fully discharged batteries in the solar charger and put the charger in direct sunlight for 10 hours. After charging remove the batteries and follow the directions in step 3 above and write down how long the device works on 10 hours of sunlight. Since 10 hours is 100% more than 5 hours

the actually operating time of the device should be about 100% longer than your first test, or double the total number of operating hours (or a ratio of approximately 2.00). If the time was 100% longer (approximately 2.00) then proceed to step 6 below. But if the device operating time was a lot less than 100% longer (2.00) then do the following math:

Divide the third time value by the first time value. Then multiply by 5 hours.
This is the approximate time required for those batteries to receive a full charge.
For example, if the device worked 12 hours the first time and 21 hours the third time then:

(21) / (12) = 1.75
1.75 x 5 = 8.75 hours.

In this situation your rechargeable batteries will be at a full charge in about 8.75 hours.
You can verify this value of 8.75 hours by doing the following math:

If the first reading was 12 hours, the second reading was 18 hours, and the third reading was 21 hours, then:

(21) / (18) = 1.167
1.167 x 7.5 = 8.75 hours.

In this situation your rechargeable batteries will be at a full charge in about 8.75 hours.
This is your final answer and you may stop the test for this type of battery.

6. Continue putting fully discharged batteries in your solar charger and continue to increase the time of each test by 2.5 hours and keep track of the results. When the device operating time does not increase by the same multiple as the test time then you have reached a full charge on your batteries. Divide the total number of device operating hours on your last test by the total number of device operating hours on your first test to get the multiplier. Then multiply that number by five hours to get the approximate optimal recharging time for that particular type of battery.

You will need to repeat the above procedure for each different type of battery and brand name of battery you have to determine the optimal full sun recharging time for each type of battery.

The above procedure and math assumes full sun every day. Therefore you should make a note of the average sun conditions on each day of your tests and keep that information with your test results so you can more easily interpret any differences in your results on future tests if the average daily sun conditions are not the same.

I fully realize the above is a lot of work. And I also know that almost nobody will bother to follow the above procedure. However, if one day you are impacted by a serious hard times event and you have a limited number of rechargeable batteries and a solar charger then you will probably be very interested in using the above procedure to get the maximum charge into your batteries each time you recharge them, without damaging those batteries, so you can get the maximum run time out of your flashlights or radios or other battery operated devices.

Recommended Brand of Rechargeable Batteries

The major battery manufacturers are constantly changing and improving the design of their rechargeable batteries. This is referred to as "continuous improvement." Therefore the rechargeable batteries available for sale this month may be replaced by a battery with a different name in a different package next month. Consequently it is not possible to make a specific battery recommendation that would be useful for any reasonable period of time.

However, my personal experience with a variety of different Rayovac brand rechargeable batteries over a period of several years has been more satisfactory than my experience with either the Energizer or Duracell brand rechargeable batteries. But the battery quality from these major manufactures could change at any time so you will need to do your own research on the quality of the different brands of rechargeable batteries that are available for sale at the time you are ready to make your investment.

Chapter Forty-Five

Flashlights

A battery operated flashlight is a critical item everyone should have whenever the lights go out. During normal times a flashlight could help you find the bathroom in the dark of night without having to turn on the electric lights and waking someone else up.

During a power failure when there is no electricity a flashlight has all the following practical uses:

1. It will help you see in the dark.
2. It could help you avoid having an accident or injury by helping you avoid tripping over something in your path.
3. It could help you avoid bumping into something and knocking it over and breaking it.
4. It will help you find the "source" of any strange or unusual noises you might hear.
5. It can provide light so you can perform necessary jobs while the electricity is off, such as finding the paper plates and the plastic forks and spoons so you can fix a simple meal for your family.
6. It will help you locate your emergency battery operated radio so you can listen to the local news to find out how long the power is going to be off.
7. It could be used as a "lantern" or as a "candle" to provide light for your family during a blackout so your family will feel safer and more secure.

A traditional flashlight uses a bulb that has to be replaced on a regular basis. The newer flashlights use a L.E.D. bulb (light emitting diode or LED).

The LED bulbs have the following major advantages:

A. They consume at lot less power than a normal flashlight bulb so your batteries will operate your flashlight for a much longer period of time.
B. The bulb will last for approximately 100,000 hours which means you will not have to replace the bulb during your lifetime (unless the bulb is defective for some reason).

There are three basic types of flashlights that a family should have for emergencies:

1. A flashlight that has a powerful beam that will allow you to see a long ways in front of you.
2. A flashlight that is mounted on a strap you can wear on your head so you can use both your hands to do work.
3. A flashlight that can be used as an area "lantern" or as a "candle" that will allow your entire family to see one another inside one room of your home.

Let's examine each of the above three major functions one-at-a-time.

1. **Brightness:** The brightness of a flashlight beam is directly proportional to the number of batteries used in the flashlight. A flashlight that only uses one battery will provide enough light to see but it will not be as bright as a flashlight that uses two or more batteries. Some flashlights use the C or D size batteries instead of the AA batteries. However, the brightness of the flashlight beam does not depend on the size of the battery, such as AA or D. The brightness of the flashlight beam depends on the number of batteries in the flashlight and the type of bulb or bulbs used in the flashlight.

2. **Head Mount:** Flashlights that use C or D size batteries are too big and too heavy to be comfortably worn on your head. Therefore a flashlight that uses one or more AA or AAA batteries is a better choice for this application.
   a. Some small compact AAA flashlights are specifically designed as head lamps and they are

permanently attached to an adjustable strap that you can wear around your head. The head lamp is mounted on the strap in the front center of your forehead.
   b. Or you could purchase a special head strap that is designed to hold a small flashlight on the side of your head above your right ear (or above your left ear).
   c. Or you could purchase a normal elastic head band strap and use two pieces of "Velcro" to attach your flashlight to the elastic head band. This is easier to do if your flashlight has a nylon carrying pouch because you can put your flashlight in its pouch and then "Velcro" wrap the pouch to the head band.
3. **Lantern or Candle:** Some flashlights allow you to elevate the top of the flashlight so it can be used as an area lantern. Other flashlights allow you to completely remove the top of the flashlight so the flashlight can be used as a candle.

Although it is possible to purchase separate flashlights for each of the above three applications, it is also possible to purchase one flashlight that will do all three of the above tasks.

Recommendation: The flashlight I recommend is the Mini MagLite LED Flashlight that operates on two standard AA batteries. It can be purchased for between $20 to $22 at most Walmart stores in their sporting goods department.

The Mini MagLite LED flashlight has the following advantages:

1. All MagLite flashlights, including this Mini, are extremely well made and they are very high quality flashlights.
2. The top of the flashlight can be twisted so you can see more of the area that is close to you. Or it can be twisted to focus the flashlight beam on a object that is far away from you.
3. The flashlight may be used on "high" power and the batteries will operate the flashlight for about 18 hours. Or the flashlight may be used on "low" power and the batteries will operate the flashlight for about 31 hours.
4. The top of the flashlight may be unscrewed and placed on a flat surface. The bottom of the flashlight can then be placed inside the top piece. This will support the flashlight in an upright position so the LED bulb of the flashlight can be used as an area "candle."
5. The flashlight can be set to blinking mode and it will blink on and off continuously.
6. The flashlight can be set to "SOS" mode and it will transmit the SOS signal continuously.
7. The flashlight comes with a black nylon carrying pouch that can be attached to your belt.

If you purchase a separate flashlight "adjustable head band" (see the picture on the right) then you could wear this flashlight above your ear so you could see where you were walking or looking. This would allow you to work using both your hands at the same time, instead of having to hold the flashlight in one hand.

Chapter Forty-Six

Emerson AM/FM Instant Weather Portable Radio

During a hard times event it would be extremely useful if you could obtain current information about all the following:

1. **Local News:** Being able to quickly find out what was happening within a 25-mile radius of your home.
2. **Regional News:** Having periodic updates of important events within a 100-mile radius of your home.
3. **National News:** Being aware of major political and economic events that could impact your decision making process.
4. **International News:** Staying informed on what is happening in the rest of the world and how it might eventually impact you.
5. **Local Weather Forecast:** Knowing exactly what the current local weather conditions are and how the weather is expected to change over the next few hours and the next few days.

A portable battery operated radio could provide you with all the above information during a hard times event, even if the electricity was not working. Therefore almost any type of battery-operated radio would be better than no radio or an electric radio. In addition, a portable radio could provide some with some entertainment because you would also be able listen to your favorite music.

The Emerson AM/FM Instant Weather Portable Radio

The portable battery operated Emerson AM/FM Weather Radio can be purchased at most Walmart stores for approximately $20 to $22.

The Emerson Radio will operate using any of the following power sources:

1. Ordinary 120-volt AC house current using the power cord that is included inside the rear of the radio, or
2. Two Alkaline or two Lithium AA Flashlight batteries (1.5 volts each), or
3. Two Rechargeable Ni-MH AA Flashlight batteries (1.2 volts each).

I tested the radio using all three of the above power sources and I could not detect any difference in the quality of the sound or the number of radio stations that could be heard when using the different types of batteries versus ordinary house current.

The radio was tested during a severe rain storm at night and the weather channel could be heard faintly but when I turned up the volume I could hear the weather channel clearly. I also tested the radio during good weather during the day and the weather channel could not be heard as clearly as at night. In fact, during the day the weather channel would fade in and then fade out completely. Therefore night reception of the weather channel will probably always be better than daytime reception of that same channel.

If you can afford it then you should also purchase a set of four Energizer Ultimate Lithium AA batteries for approximately $10 and store them for a future emergency. The Ultimate Lithium batteries will last longer in storage than other batteries and they will operate longer once they are put into active use. Therefore they would be a good investment if you can afford them.

If you can afford it you should also purchase eight Rechargeable AA batteries and a Solar Battery Charger. With this combination you would be able to listen to your radio for a very long time even if the electricity were to fail for some unexpected reason.

Electronic devices are no longer being manufactured with life expectancies of ten or twenty years. In some cases the equipment is intentionally engineered to fail after two or three years in order to force us to purchase a new item. Therefore it would probably be a good idea to have more than one type of emergency battery operated radio at your home or retreat location. The Emerson radio would be a good choice as one of these emergency radios. It is affordable, it is reliable, and it easy to operate.

Now let's examine some of the nice features of the Emerson Portable Radio:

1. It provides reasonably good reception on both the AM and FM radio frequencies.
2. It has an internal AM antenna and a 16.5" telescoping FM antenna.
3. It has a weather button on the top of the radio.
    a. The National Oceanic and Atmospheric Administration (NOAA) has more than 750 transmitters in all 50 states, Puerto Rico, the U.S. Virgin Islands, and the U.S. Pacific Territories.
    b. The local weather forecasts are transmitted on frequencies from 162.400 to 162.550 MHz.
    c. In order to receive the weather forecast for your local area you will need to rotate the weather fine tuning knob on the rear of the radio until you can clearly hear the "local" weather forecast.
    d. Once you have this knob adjusted on the rear of your radio you will be able to immediately hear the weather whenever you push the weather button on the top of the radio.
    e. However, the weather channel does broadcast at a lower power level than conventional radio stations so you may need to turn up the volume control on your radio while listening to the weather.
    f. Being able to immediately access the weather could be a significant advantage during serious hazardous weather conditions that could impact your survival.

    Note: To access the weather channel the top weather button must be in the down position and the radio power switch must be in the "on" position. If you only have the weather channel button pressed down and you do not have the power button on then all you will hear will be "static."

    Note: If the weather button is in the down position then all the other functions of the radio will be deactivated and the weather channel will be activated. If the weather button is in the up position then the weather channel will be deactivated and all the other functions of the radio will be available.
4. It has a digital clock with a date and time function.
5. It has an earphone jack on the side of the radio. Therefore, if you have earphones, you can listen to the radio in privacy.
6. It has a convenient carrying handle that allows you to easily move the radio to a different location.
7. The radio measures approximately 8.75" long, 2.5" wide, and 5.6" tall.
8. The radio weighs about 26.5 ounces without any batteries in the radio.

Battery Operation

When you slide the rear battery compartment cover off the back of the radio you will find the permanently attached AC power cord and a space for four AA batteries. One battery is inserted in a small lower battery compartment. Three batteries are inserted in a straight line directly above the first battery. The polarity illustration for the three batteries in the upper battery compartment is clearly labeled and easy to understand.

However, if you look at the illustration for the one battery in the lower battery compartment you might become confused as I first did. The lower battery compartment illustration shows "two" batteries, one on top of the other. The top battery is for the battery in the row of three batteries on the upper level. The partially hidden battery illustration is for the battery in the lower compartment. The one battery in the lower compartment is inserted in the opposite direction from the three batteries in the upper compartment.

When I first put the batteries in the radio I did not notice the "double" battery illustration in the lower compartment and I inserted the lower battery in the wrong direction. The radio would not work. Then I removed all four batteries and very carefully looked at the battery illustration in the lower compartment. That is when I noticed that there were actually two batteries being illustrated and that the clearly visible battery was for the upper battery and that the partially hidden battery that was difficult to see in the illustration was for the lower battery. When I reinserted the one lower battery in the opposite direction to the three upper batteries the radio worked perfectly.

Note: I don't mention the problems I encounter to demonstrate my level of intellectual incompetence. The reason I mention my mistakes to help some people avoid making the same mistakes.

Chapter Forty-Seven

The Grundig "Eton" S350DL Deluxe AM/FM/Shortwave Radio

I suggest you purchase both of the following items:
1. a solar battery charger that will recharge flashlight size batteries, and
2. a battery-operated AM/FM/Shortwave radio.

One of the radios I recommend is the Grundig "Eton" S350DL Deluxe AM/FM/Shortwave Radio (picture on right). Although this is a "battery-operated" radio it is a full size radio. It can be purchased for approximately $100 at your local Radio Shack Store or at amazon.com.

Note 1: The Grundig S350DL and the Eton S350DL are the same exact radio.

Note 2: The Instruction Manual for the S350DL is at this link: http://www.etoncorp.com/upload/contents/307/S350_manual_lowres_GRUN.pdf

Note 3: I rarely mention my background or credentials. However, in this case I think an exception is appropriate. In 1996 I became an FCC licensed amateur radio operator (ham radio). I currently have an Extra Class License, which is the highest license an individual can acquire. Therefore the following comments are not the random babblings of someone who is easily impressed with the latest technological gadget.

The Features of the Grundig S350DL Deluxe AM/FM/Shortwave Radio

Ease of Use: Let me begin by rating this radio based on how easy or difficult it is to operate using a simple scale of 1 to 10 as follows:

a. Rating of 1 = Your car radio with only AM/FM capability.
b. Rating of 2 = Your car radio with AM/FM capability and a CD player.
c. Rating of 3 = The Grundig "Eton" S350DL Deluxe AM/FM/Shortwave Radio.
d. Rating of 10 = An Amateur Ham Radio Station with eight different electronic devices connected together with cables and wires and three different antenna systems.

Size of the Radio: The radio measures approximately 12.25-inches long, 7-inches high (without the carrying strap), and 3.75-inches deep. With the carrying strap the radio is approximately 8.25-inches high.

Listening versus Talking: This radio is only for listening. It cannot be used for two-way communication. In other words, it is not a transmitting radio. This has advantages and disadvantages as follows:

a. **Disadvantages:** During a serious hard times tragedy event you will need a "satellite phone" to communicate with other people anywhere in the world. A satellite phone bounces signals off a space satellite and it does not depend on the local cell phone antenna network. Therefore you would be able to talk to anyone almost anywhere if they also had a satellite phone.

b. **Advantages:** You can listen to this radio and not worry about being located using any type of tracking technology with which I am familiar. The reason is because you are only receiving a signal and you are not transmitting anything. This is the same basic concept as human speech. If a person is speaking then you can easily identify where that person is located based on the sound of their voice. However, if you are only listening to the person then no one will know where you might be because your ears do not make any noise. In fact, hundreds or thousands of people could be listening to one person who is speaking and you would not know how many people were listening or where each of those people was located. This is the same basic concept as listening to a radio broadcast as opposed to transmitting a broadcast.

Features: Now let's take a look of some of the nice features of the Grundig "Eton" S350DL Radio:
1. It has an internal AM antenna.
2. It has a 44-inch long telescoping FM/Shortwave antenna attached to the radio. This significantly improves the radio's ability to pick up weak or distant radio signals.
3. It has a 5.5-inch speaker. This yields better sound clarity from the radio. However, it does not eliminate the static from weak or distant radio signals.
4. It has three separate controls for volume, bass, and tremble.
5. It has a switch for changing from stereo to mono mode.
6. It allows for the reception of AM broadcasts, and FM broadcasts, and Shortwave broadcasts from approximately 3 MHz to approximately 28 MHz.
7. It has two dials for changing the radio frequency. The outer dial allows for the rapid changing of the frequency. The inner dial permits a very slow fine-tuning change of the frequency.
8. It has a digital frequency display so you can read the exact frequency you are receiving, and if you like that radio station then you can make a note of it (along with the time of day) on a separate piece of paper for future reference purposes.
9. It has separate connection ports for attaching optional external speakers, and an optional external FM/Shortwave antenna, and an optional ground wire, and an optional external AM antenna (all these items would need to be purchased separately).
10. It has a digital clock, and an alarm, and a snooze button, and a back-light button. The clock allows you to choose how you want to see the time: as 24 hours, or as 12 hours with AM and PM.
11. It will operate on three power sources as follows:
    a. 120-volt AC house current using the DC adapter included with the radio, or
    b. Four D-Cell Alkaline batteries or four D-Cell Rechargeable batteries, or
    c. Four AA-Cell Alkaline batteries or four AA-Cell Rechargeable batteries.
12. It also has a few other special features that are discussed in the Instruction Manual that can be read at the internet link at the beginning of this chapter on this radio.

AA or D Batteries: Now let's look at the difference between using AA batteries versus D batteries. On the right there is a picture of the back of the radio with its battery compartment cover removed.

The small yellow label on the right side of the bottom of the radio says you must lift the small panel to install either AA or D batteries. If you install D batteries then you leave the panel in the upright position. However, if you install AA batteries then you must lower the panel after you have the AA batteries correctly installed.

The small yellow label on the left side of the radio surrounds a switch you must move to the right or to the left depending on whether you use AA or D batteries. This is **not** explained in the instruction manual.

First I experimented with 4 AA batteries and the radio yielded great reception. Then I removed the AA batteries and inserted 4 D batteries and the radio would not work. I was dumbfounded. I got my separate battery tester to check the D batteries to determine if they were fully charged. They were. I then verified that I had oriented the D batteries plus and minus ends correctly in the radio. Then I read the Instruction Manual. Finally I remembered the small switch inside the battery compartment that I had previously pushed to the AA side. I pushed the switch to the D side and the radio once again yielded great reception using D batteries. I am taking the time to share this with you to help you avoid the same embarrassing mistake I made.

The same clarity and reception was achieved using AA and D batteries. The size of the batteries did not change the performance of the radio.

Both the AA and the D batteries provide approximately 1.5 volts of electricity per battery for a total of 6 volts. However, the D batteries have more amps and therefore they will last longer than the AA batteries. However, it takes longer to recharge a D battery than an AA battery.

Therefore you have a trade-off. The D size batteries work longer inside the radio but they require more time to recharge. The AA batteries have a shorter life inside the radio but they can be recharged more rapidly.

Chapter Forty-Eight

The Grundig "Eton" G6 Aviator Buzz Aldrin
AM/FM/Aircraft/Shortwave Portable Radio with SSB

Introduction

The Grundig "Eton" G6 Aviator AM/FM/Aircraft/Shortwave Portable Radio (picture on right) can be purchased for approximately $100 at your local Radio Shack Store or amazon.com.

The Grundig G6 Aviator AM/FM/Aircraft/Shortwave Portable Radio has the following features:

1. The radio measures approximately 4.9-inches long, 3-inches high, and 1.1-inches deep.

2. The radio weighs approximately 7.3 ounces (207 g).

3. It has an internal AM antenna.

4. It has a 21-inch long telescoping FM/Shortwave antenna attached to the radio. This significantly improves the radio's ability to pick up weak or distant radio signals.

5. It has a 2-inch speaker. This yields reasonably good sound clarity from the radio.

6. It has a switch for changing from music to news (voice) mode.

7. It comes with two small earphones for private listening.

8. It allows for the reception of AM broadcasts, and FM broadcasts, and Aircraft broadcasts (117-137 MHz), and Shortwave broadcasts (150 KHz to 29,999 KHz).

9. It allows for the manual scanning of frequencies using a dial or for the auto scanning of frequencies using a push button. The auto scan function will scan the entire frequency range from beginning to end and then start back over at the beginning. It will automatically stop when it reaches a frequency with sufficient signal strength to be heard.

10. It has a digital frequency display so you can read the exact frequency you are receiving, and if you like that radio station then you can make a note of it (along with the time of day) on a separate piece of paper for future reference purposes, or you can save the frequency to any one of 700 memory locations.

11. It has a digital clock, and an alarm, and a back-light button.

12. It will operate on three power sources as follows (batteries are not included with the radio):

    a. Ordinary 120-volt AC house current using the DC adapter that is included with the radio, or

    b. Two Alkaline or two Lithium AA Flashlight batteries (1.5 volts each), or

    c. Two Rechargeable Ni-MH AA Flashlight batteries (1.2 volts each).

13. The radio will charge two Rechargeable Ni-MH batteries. Insert the two Ni-MH batteries in the radio and then plug the radio into a standard AC outlet. Each 100 mAH in the two batteries will require approximately 1 hour of charging time. For example, two 1100 mAH batteries will require approximately 11 hours of charging time. Two 2300 mAH batteries will require approximately 23 hours of charging time.

Comments about the Grundig G6 Aviator Portable Radio

The small size and the very light weight (7.3 ounces) of this radio make it a truly portable radio that could easily be put into your briefcase, or purse, or bug-out-bag.

The radio will successfully operate of two AA rechargeable Ni-MH batteries. Rechargeable batteries only contain 1.2 volts. (Normal alkaline or lithium batteries contain 1.5 volts.) I tested this radio using the DC adapter that is included with the radio and then I immediately switched to two AA rechargeable Ni-MH batteries. In my opinion there was no difference in the number of stations I could receive or in the quality of the sound from those stations using the rechargeable batteries when compared to the DC adapter.

In the rural area where I live I could not hear any aircraft frequencies. However, if you live near an airport, or in a larger metropolitan area, then the radio may allow you to listen to aircraft frequencies if that is important to you.

During normal daylight listening hours I could not clearly receive any English language shortwave broadcasts. However, after dark I could hear a wide variety of English language shortwave broadcasts, including both music and voice.

The auto scan button on the radio works very well. The auto scan function can be set to stop at any station that has sufficient signal strength to be heard or it can be set to pause for 5 seconds at each station before continuing to the next station. This is a significant advantage in my opinion.

The radio will allow you to save and recall up to 700 different frequencies. This is also a very important advantage of this radio.

The radio has a switch for changing from music to news (voice) mode. This allows you to quickly adjust the radio so it will provide the best possible reception for whichever type of broadcast you wish to listen to.

Although you can recharge your Ni-MH batteries inside this radio while it is plugged into a standard 120 volt outlet, I suggest you purchase a Solar Battery Charger in addition to the radio. This will allow you to recharge your radio batteries even it there is no electricity.

Chapter Forty-Nine

The Basics of Shortwave Radio

Although English is not the most widely spoken language in the world, it is currently an important "second language" in many countries because of the need to communicate with English speaking travelers and investors. Therefore many foreign nations broadcast in their own native language and also on a second frequency in English.

A shortwave radio will allow you to listen to radio stations that are broadcasting from almost anywhere in the world. This is a significant advantage because it allows you to hear a variety of different interpretations of how other major nations perceive significant current world events and news stories. Although every nation will impart its own "bias" to a particular news story, you will have the opportunity to determine how the rest of the world is responding to something that happened in your own country.

Just because you are awake and listening to your shortwave radio please do not assume that the rest of the world is awake and broadcasting. Everyone needs to sleep and different stations go off the air at different times during the day based on where they are located in the world.

Many shortwave broadcasts are from Europe. Therefore if you live in the Eastern half of the United States then you will probably be able to receive those broadcasts using the telescoping antenna attached to your radio. However, if you live in the Western half of the United States then you will probably need to install an external antenna to receive these same European broadcasts.

Shortwave reception during the day is usually poor because of daytime atmospheric conditions and the fact that most European stations are not transmitting their broadcasts in the direction of the United States because they know that most of us are probably at work during the day and therefore we are not listening to our shortwave radios. However, at night reception significantly improves because of the reduced atmospheric interference and the fact that many European stations are now directing their signals toward the United States.

Shortwave radio signals travel extremely long distances by bouncing back and forth off the upper atmosphere and the earth's surface until they reach your radio's antenna. Therefore all of the following factors have an impact on the clarity of a distant radio station:

1. The total distance between your antenna and the broadcasting radio station.
2. The month of the year (seasonal weather fluctuations).
3. The time of day (day or night).
4. Space conditions (solar flares, etc.).
5. Atmospheric conditions close to the Earth (bad weather significantly reduces reception).
6. Nearby tall buildings or mountains (they interfere with reception from radio stations in those directions).

Many people become frustrated with their shortwave radios because they do not know about the above. Their shortwave radio may have more than a thousand frequencies to select from but they can't seem to find a frequency that yields great reception all the time. Therefore they conclude there is something wrong with their specific shortwave radio or they assume they live in an area where shortwave reception is very poor.

The following very brief list of frequencies may help you to get the most enjoyment out of your radio:

Night Frequencies:
Shortwave frequencies between 5,950 to 6,200 KHz are usually pretty good at night.
Shortwave frequencies between 9,200 to 9,900 KHz and between 11,600 to 12,200 KHz are usually average at night.
Shortwave frequencies between 7,100 to 7,600 KHz are usually average at night in the Eastern United States.

Day Frequencies:
Shortwave frequencies between 15,100 to 15,800 KHz are usually pretty good during the day.
Shortwave frequencies between 13,570 to 13,870 KHz and between 17,480 to 17,900 KHz are usually average during the day.

How to Maximize the Reception of a Shortwave Radio

1. Your radio needs to be operating on maximum power. Therefore your radio batteries should be fully charged or you should be using AC power.
2. To avoid electrical interference do not place your radio near electrical equipment such as televisions, stereo equipment, computers, microwave ovens, or any other electrical appliance.
3. Reception is weakest inside steel framed and concrete buildings.
4. Reception is usually best near a window.
5. Try moving your radio to different locations inside your home to improve its reception. If possible put your radio near a southern window, a northern window, an eastern window, or a western window, depending on the location of the foreign country's broadcast you wish to listen to.
6. Change the direction in which you have your telescoping antenna pointed to see if it improves the reception of a weak radio signal. Take your hand off the antenna to test it.
7. If you find a station you wish to listen to but another station's signal is also being received then try changing the length of your telescoping antenna to see if you can isolate the reception of the station you desire. Sometimes increasing or decreasing the length of your telescoping antenna can minimize the interference from a secondary radio signal and improve the reception of a desired radio signal.
8. A longer antenna is usually better than a shorter antenna. A good antenna may be made from a few feet of insulated copper wire. Allow one end of the wire to hang outside of a window. Wrap the other end of the wire to the bottom of your radio's current telescoping antenna.
9. An ear phone or headphone can sometimes improve your ability to hear a signal from a distant station.

Number of Shortwave Radio Stations: At the current time there are not as many shortwave radio stations in operation when compared to a few years ago. This is probably due to the popularity of the internet, and satellite TV, and satellite radio, and iPods, and other hand-held electrical devices. However, there may be a dramatic renewal in the number of shortwave broadcasting stations in the event of a serious worldwide hard times event or in the event of serious censorship of the radio stations within a nation's borders.

Safety Warning: Always disconnect your radio from any outside antenna when you are not listening to it and also during any rain storms to avoid a static electricity shock from traveling down your antenna and destroying your radio. During bad weather you may still listen to your radio using batteries and its internal telescoping antenna but not an outside antenna. Therefore during bad weather you will probably be limited to local radio stations.

A Simple External Outdoor Antenna

You can normally make a significant improvement to your radio's reception of shortwave broadcasts by doing both of the following:

1. **Ground Wire:** Attach one end of an insulated copper wire to the grounding terminal of your radio (after removing about 3/4 inch of insulation) and then attach the other end of that copper wire to a metal object and bury that metal object at least 12 inches below the ground. (Or you may use a standard grounding rod.) The ground wire will normally improve your radio's reception of AM, FM, and Shortwave broadcasts.
2. **Antenna Wire:** Purchase between 30 to 40 feet of insulated stranded 14 gauge (or 16 gauge) copper wire and install that wire in a straight line somewhere outside your residence. Then remove the insulation from approximately 3/4 inch off the end of the wire and attach the bare wire end to the external FM/Shortwave antenna terminal of your radio.

Chapter Fifty

Two-Way Communication:
Cell Phones, Satellite Phones, and Two-Way Radios

During a hard times event your family may or may not need the ability to communicate with one another over extended distances. If you do need the ability to communicate with other family members then you have three basic options as follows:

1. Cell Phones.
2. Satellite Phones.
3. Two-Way Radios.

Let's examine each of the above three options one-at-a-time.

Cell Phones

At the beginning of the year 2011 cell phones are the most popular and the most widely used method of two-way communication for the following reasons:

1. **Size:** Most modern cell phones are relatively small and they frequently measure no larger than 3.5 inches by 2 inches by 3/4 inch. Many cell phones are actually smaller than this.
2. **Weight:** Cell phones are reasonably light at about 3 ounces. The carrying case that you can attach to your belt is about 2 ounces for a total combined weight of about 5 ounces.
3. **Cost:** Depending on your budget you can purchase a cell phone for as low as $0.97 up to about $199. The average cell phone cost is about $40. In most cases the purchase price of the phone requires you to sign a contract for a specific period of time with the cell phone provider. However, there are exceptions, such as the Tracfone.
4. **Range:** When a cell phone is within the operating range of a local cell phone tower, a cell phone may be used to call another phone almost anywhere in the world if that phone is connected to a hard wired network or it is within range of another cell phone tower.
5. **Coverage:** Coverage is almost worldwide with the exception of areas that are not inhabited or in areas with unstable governments.
6. **Portable:** You can easily carry a cell phone with you almost anywhere you go, with certain exceptions, and you can send or receive calls anytime during the day and on any day of the week.
7. **Charging:** The cell phone battery may be recharged using ordinary house current or your automobile battery. Being able to recharge your cell phone battery using your automobile battery is extremely nice because you do not have to worry about a dead cell phone battery in an emergency situation if your vehicle should become disabled and you need emergency roadside assistance (assuming your car battery still works).
8. **Features:** In addition to providing two-way communication most modern cell phones have a multitude of other features, such as text messaging, internet surfing, emailing, and instant weather.
9. **Ease of Use**: Cell phones are extremely easy to use for two-way communication. However, some of the other features on a cell phone may require a diligent review of the instruction manual that comes with the cell phone.
10. **License:** A person does not need a license to purchase and operate a cell phone.

The major **disadvantage of a cell phone** is that it may not work during a serious hard times disaster event. There are two reasons for this:

1. Many of the cell phone towers may be damaged and out of operation.
2. The majority of the people in the disaster area will be trying to use their cell phones at exactly the same time to contact their other family members and this will overload the cell phone network.

Therefore if the major reason you are considering a cell phone is for two-way communication during a serious hard times event then the chances are pretty good that your cell phone will not work at the time you need it the most.

One of the important advantages of a cell phone is that you can use it almost anywhere. This is especially helpful if your vehicle breaks down while you are driving. If you have a cell phone with you inside your vehicle then you can call for assistance and avoid a very long walk and you can avoid the possibility of exposing yourself to harm from criminals who might try to take advantage of you in this type of situation.

At the beginning of the year 2011 the most affordable cell phone is the **Tracfone**. The cost of the cell phone will typically be somewhere between $10 to $20. I recommend the most expensive Tracfone (made by Samsung) because of the superior quality of its microphone and its speaker. It comes with an AC charging adapter. I recommend you purchase the separate DC charging adapter for approximately $10 to $15. You can purchase air time minutes for an entire year, along with double minutes for the life of your phone. At the end of the year any unused minutes will not expire if you extend your contract for another year. The total cost of one year of service which includes 800 minutes of air time is about $100, plus the cost of the cell phone. There are no unexpected fees or charges with the Tracfone. If you unexpectedly need more minutes you can easily purchase them using your Tracfone and a credit card or you can buy extra minutes at any place that sells Tracfones, such as Dollar General or Walmart. The cost of extra minutes for the Tracfone is about $0.125 per minute if you have the free double minutes option on your Tracfone account.

Satellite Phones

A satellite phone has all the advantages of a cell phone with the following three exceptions:

1. **Phone Cost:** The purchase price of a satellite phone is between $500 to $1500.
2. **Monthly Fee:** The **minimum** monthly fee for satellite phone service is about $20 per month for coverage in the United States.
3. **Coverage:** A satellite phone sends its signal up into the air to satellites above the earth. The phone call is then relayed to another satellite phone or to a cell phone or to a hard wired phone anywhere on the earth that currently has phone coverage.

The two major **advantages of a satellite phone** are as follows:

1. It can be used in remote wilderness areas where there are no cell phone towers because the satellite phone sends its signal straight up.
2. It will normally still be operational during a serious hard times disaster event because a satellite phone is not dependent on the local cell phone towers or the hard wired telephone network.

Therefore if your primary concern is reliable emergency two-way communication during a serious hard times disaster event then a satellite phone is the superior choice.

However, if you use a satellite phone during a hard times disaster event and any law enforcement officer or emergency relief worker sees that you have an operating phone then they will immediately confiscate your phone for their own use. When they take your phone they will guarantee you that you will get your phone back and that their organization will pay any and all the extra fees and charges while your phone is in their possession. However, there is a very good chance you will never see your expensive satellite phone again and you will have to pay thousands of dollars in additional air time that you did not authorize but which you are legally responsible to pay under the terms of your contract.

Two-Way Radios

There are a wide assortment of two-way radios but only two will be examined at this time:

1. **Two-Way Hand Held Radios:** These radios may be purchased and used by anyone without a license. Their most significant **disadvantage** is their limited range. Although they may work under optimal conditions at ranges of five or ten miles, most of them have a normal operating range of between one-half mile to one mile. The radio must be turned on to send or receive and this consumes battery power. However, transmitting consumes significantly more power than listening. Many of these radios have multiple channels (such as 22) and each channel may have multiple privacy codes (such as 38) so the total number of privacy combinations may be 836. However, these radios transmit at established frequencies and they are not secure. Anyone with an automatic channel scanner can isolate your frequency and listen in on your conversation. That person can even interrupt your conversation by speaking at the same time you are speaking. Depending on your specific situation these two-way radios may or may not  be of some use to your family in certain circumstances. That is a decision you will need to make on your own.

2. **Amateur Radios (Ham Radios):** To operate one of these radios an individual must pass a test and be granted an operating license. The individual must then invest several hundred dollars (or more) in radio equipment and antennas. Finally, the individual can only communicate with other amateur radio operators and the other operator must be listening to the same exact frequency at the exact time of the transmission. Although an amateur radio may be used at any time of the day and on any day of the week, its transmission effectiveness is impacted by a variety of geographical and atmospheric conditions that will either improve or interfere with its performance. In other words, during severe weather conditions the performance of an amateur radio declines significantly.

Conclusion

During normal times a cell phone is typically the best choice for the vast majority of people. However, during a hard times event in which you become a participant, either a satellite phone or an amateur radio would probably be a much better choice.

The **disadvantage of a satellite phone** is that it requires a functioning satellite network.

The **advantage of an amateur radio** is that each amateur radio is independent of all the other amateur radios in the world. Each amateur radio can function independently from the rest of the amateur radio network. However, during a serious hard times event you may need to use one of the many world-band frequencies and not a short-range local frequency that depends on repeaters. In addition, the exact location of an amateur radio may easily be determined if it is transmitting so these radios are relatively easy to locate. However, if an amateur radio is only used for listening and it is not used for transmitting then it cannot be located using signal tracking technology.

Chapter Fifty: Two-Way Communication

Two-Way Communication

If the voice of God is what you really want to listen to,
then just read your Bible and your wish will come true.

If there is something you would like for God to hear,
then just open your heart in prayer and God will lend an ear.

Each time you read the Bible, God talks and you listen.
Each time you stop to pray, you talk and God listens.

Scripture References: Second Timothy 3:16-17, Second Peter 1:21, Matthew 24:55, Deuteronomy 4:7, James 5:13, Second Chronicles 7:14.

Poem: Two-Way Communication

Chapter Fifty-One

The Basics of Solar Power
and
How to Build a Portable Solar Power Generator

On a camping trip, or during a hard times event, it would be nice to have electricity. For example, your children may still want to play their hand-held electronic games, such as a Game Boy. Or you may occasionally want to use your laptop computer, either to play a game or to watch a DVD movie. If you have a cell phone then you may need to recharge its battery. Therefore a portable solar generator would be a nice item to have on a camping trip or during a hard times event when there was no electricity. However, for this to be a viable option on a camping trip you would need to drive to your campsite in your car or truck because the size and weight of a solar generator exceeds what you could carry in a backpack.

Although a regular generator will produce more power than a solar generator, a regular generator requires a continuous source of fuel, which may not be readily available at your campsite or during a hard time event. And the noise of a regular generator may not be appropriate at a public campground, or it may attract unnecessary attention to your family during a hard times event. On the other hand, a solar generator is able to produce small amounts of power whenever the sun is shining and it is virtually silent. Therefore a solar generator is a more practical item than a conventional gas-operated generator.

Before we look at how to build a simple homemade solar generator we first need to review the basic principles of solar power.

The Basics of Solar Power

Solar Panels: A solar panel converts the sun's energy into Direct Current or DC electricity. Solar panels come in a variety of different sizes and shapes. For the purpose of this discussion we will classify them as either small or large. The solar panel in the picture on the right is a large panel which is rated at 64-watts per hour and its dimensions are approximately 18" wide, 44" long, and 1.5" thick. It weighs approximately 22 pounds.

Small solar panels produce very low DC voltages, such as 1.5 volts for flashlight batteries. Small solar panels are not appropriate for a portable solar generator. (Note: If you are only interested in recharging flashlight size batteries then you should consider the purchase of a Solar Battery Charger which is discussed in the Battery Chapter in this book.)

Large solar panels produce 12-volts DC which is the same as automobile or boat batteries. Larger solar panels are designed and rated for a certain number of peak watts, such as 60W, or 75W, or 100W. If you had a 100-watt solar panel then you could keep a 100-watt light bulb burning for the length of time the sun was shining directly on the solar panel at a 90 degree angle. Since you probably wouldn't want to use the light bulb during the day you would need a battery to store that energy for future use. (Note: In my opinion it would be smarter to buy two 60-watt panels instead of one large 100-watt panel. If one of the 60-watt panels were to become damaged then it could be disconnected and the other panel could still provide some power.)

Batteries: There are many different types and sizes of batteries. They can be used to store the power from a solar panel so that power can be used at some future time. If you are considering the purchase of a 12-volt solar panel, then you should consider the purchase of 12-volt deep-cycle marine or golf cart batteries so you can store the power from your solar panels. Deep-cycle marine and golf cart batteries are of the same approximate size, appearance, and weight as the 12-volt battery in your car. However, the battery in your car is designed for short periods of high energy output. A deep-cycle battery is designed for long periods of continuous power output. The battery will be the heaviest component in your solar system.

Inverters: An inverter changes the DC power from a battery into Alternating Current, or AC electricity, which is what we use in our homes. Although the inverter may be attached to a 12-volt battery it will produce 110-volt electricity which is powerful enough to **kill** you. Therefore you must use the same degree of caution with an inverter that you would for any household appliance. Most inverters have standard three prong electrical outlets for standard household appliances to plug into. Inverters are rated for the number of continuous watts they can produce, such as 100-watts or 1000-watts. They also specify peak watts but the peak watts is for a very short moment of time and therefore you should rely on the rating for continuous watt output. When choosing an inverter you should first determine what equipment you need to operate. Then purchase an inverter that will produce that number of watts. For example, if you want to operate a 700-watt microwave for 90 seconds then you would need at least an 800-watt inverter to provide a small safety margin. The inverter in the above picture is a 1200-watt inverter and its dimensions are approximately 10-inches wide, 13-inches long, and 3-inches high. It weighs approximately 10 pounds. The components on the front panel from left to right are: on/off switch, volt meter, watt meter, and two 110-volt outlets.

Most inexpensive inverters produce low quality AC electricity. For example, if you plug a TV set into an inverter you will normally see wavy lines on the TV screen which are the result of the low quality power. On a TV set it is possible to reduce the wavy line effect by plugging a 25-foot extension cord into the inverter. Then coil the extension cord into a small stack of circles (about 12-inch diameters), one on top of the other, on the floor. Then plug the TV into the opposite end of the extension cord. You should see a noticeable reduction in the wavy line effect on the TV screen.

Before you invest a lot of money in a solar system you should research the costs and benefits very carefully. There are a variety of other components that need to be included in a larger self-maintaining solar system. The power question does not have an easy answer. There are so many variables that there is no one right answer that would be suitable for the needs of all families. Most companies that sell solar equipment have trained professionals that can answer all your questions and help you select exactly what you need for the application you have in mind.

How to Build a Homemade Portable Solar Generator

Now let's look at how to assemble a simple portable solar generator. A portable solar generator consists of the following items:

    One (or more) 12-volt solar panels,
    One (or more) 12-volt deep-cycle batteries (such as marine or golf cart batteries),
    One (or more) 12-volt cigarette lighter adapters,
    One inverter.

In the wiring diagram illustration on the next page I have shown one solar panel and one deep-cycle battery in order to illustrate how to build a basic solar generator.

Inverter Size: When considering the purchase of an inverter I recommend at least a 1,000 or a 1,200-watt inverter (continuous power output) as a minimum. If you wish to purchase a larger inverter then I suggest no more than 2,000-watts. This recommendation applies to a portable solar generator that will be used to supply power to a wide variety of potential applications. If you purchase an inverter that is less than 1,000-watts then you will be limiting the number of potential applications for your solar generator. The larger inverters are also usually of a higher quality and they have a few more features, such as a meter that shows how much power is remaining in your 12-volt batteries, and how much power you are using at the present time. These are really nice meters to have built into your inverter. If your inverter does not have these built-in meters then you will need to purchase a separate DC voltmeter, such as the one discussed later in this chapter.

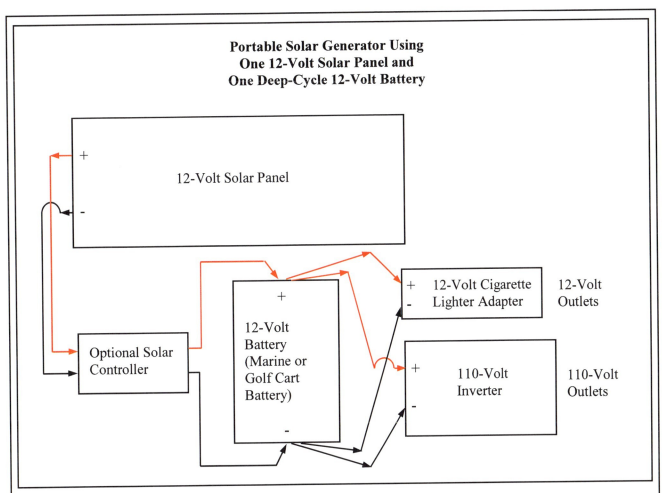

12-Volt Adapter: In addition to the inverter you should also install a 12-volt cigarette lighter adapter on your solar generator system. This will allow you to recharge any battery-operated item that has a cigarette lighter adapter, such as a cell phone, or a Game Boy, or a laptop computer. You can purchase these adapters at most electronic stores including Radio Shack. Radio Shack normally has a one-hole adapter and a three-hole adapter. I recommend the three-hole adapter if you will only be recharging simple items like a cell phone or a Game Boy. The adapter on the right weighs approximately 7 ounces and it measures 3-inches wide by 4-inches long by 1-inch high. If you are going to be recharging batteries that require a higher level of power then you should consider purchasing several single-hole adapters to minimize overheating of the adapter wiring.

The simple solar generator illustrated in the above wiring diagram can be used to recharge your laptop computer battery, the battery in your child's Game Boy, and any rechargeable flashlight batteries you might have (if you also have a 110-volt battery charger for your rechargeable batteries). The solar generator should **not** be used to operate heating (or cooling) appliances because they will drain the power from your batteries very quickly. In other words, no hair dryers or electric heaters or air-conditioners. However, you can operate small fans such as a 12-volt fan plugged into the cigarette lighter adapter or a 110-volt fan plugged into the inverter.

Chapter Fifty-One: Solar Power

Solar Controller: The optional solar controller is recommended to prevent damage to the 12-volt battery, primarily through overcharging. The solar controller in the picture on the right has dimensions of approximately 4.5-inches wide, 6-inches long, and 2-inches high. It weighs approximately 13 ounces.

If you do not have a solar controller then you should disconnect the battery from the solar panel at night. You should also disconnect the battery if you are not going to be present to periodically monitor the charge going into the battery. And you should cover the solar panel with a blanket to prevent it from producing power.

Voltmeter: If you decide to omit the optional solar controller then you will need to purchase a DC voltmeter and periodically check the charge in your 12-volt battery to verify that you are **not** overcharging the battery during daylight hours. The DC voltmeter in the picture on the right has dimensions of approximately 2.5-inches wide, 4-inches long, and 1-inch high. (Note: You will **not** need this additional DC voltmeter if you have a solar controller or if you have an inverter with a built-in voltmeter.)

The wiring-diagram illustration of a portable solar generator can be modified based on your individual requirements. You can add additional solar panels and/or additional 12-volt batteries to your system if you wish. The wiring diagram illustrated on the next page shows three solar panels and three 12-volt batteries. If you wish to use two panels or batteries then just remove the one in the center. If you wish to use four or more panels or batteries then just add them to the center.

You do **not** need to have exactly the same number of solar panels as 12-volt deep cycle batteries.

Since it does rain occasionally, it is usually better to have more 12-volt batteries than solar panels. This gives you the ability to store power for use during bad weather.

If you decide to build your own solar generator then you should utilize the talents of the solar professionals at the company where you purchase your solar panels. You can ask them specific questions about the size of the solar panels in relation to the number of 12-volt deep-cycle batteries you will require. They will also be able to recommend the appropriate solar controller for the type of system you decide to build. They will also be able to provide you with a complete wiring diagram for your entire system that shows the proper gauge of wire to use to connect the specific components within your system.

Normally one of the major cost of the 12-volt deep-cycle batteries is the shipping cost. Therefore it is usually wise to find a battery dealer near your home to purchase your batteries. This not only minimizes your cost but it also simplifies warranty and return issues if your deep-cycle battery does not perform as expected. One source of those batteries is your local Walmart or Sam's Club.

Additional Information: Some additional information about a Solar Generator is included in the last chapter in this book.

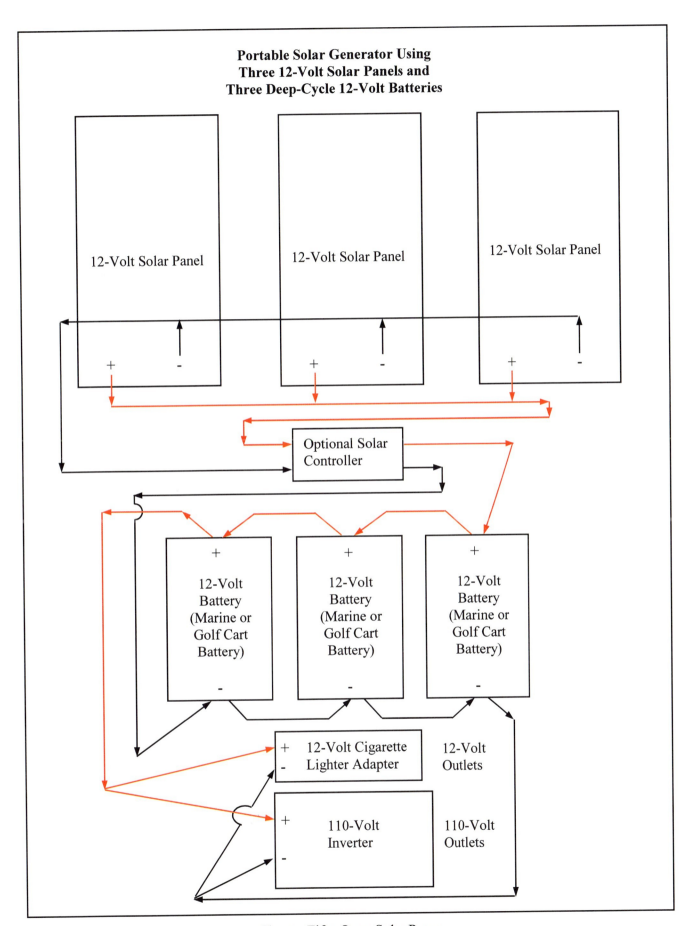

Chapter Fifty-One: Solar Power

The Words of God

Each and every Word spoken by God and recorded by one of His prophets,
will accomplish what God intended and achieve the purpose for which He sent it.

The miracle of God's Words are that He spoke them **once** when they were first needed,
but they continue to transform human hearts one life at a time whenever they are heeded.

God's Words will continue to work miracles day after day and millennium after millennium,
as each one of God's recently born children become aware of His infinite wisdom and compassion.

This Poem is Dedicated to My Grandson **Matthew Scott McClintock, Jr.**

Scripture References: Second Peter 1:21, Second Timothy 3:16-17, Isaiah 55:10-11, Isaiah 59:21, Isaiah 40:8, Psalm 118:89, Matthew 24:55, Proverbs 30:5-6.

Chapter Fifty-Two

How to Build A Safe Fire and Why Fire Is So Important

Fire is an absolute necessity for all the following reasons:

1. Boiling water for one-minute to make it safe to drink.
2. Cooking fish, meat, and some vegetables to make them more palatable and digestible.
3. Providing heat for comfort if the temperature drops below a level that is acceptable to you.

There are a variety of different ways to start a fire, including both modern and primitive methods. Modern methods include matches, butane lighters, magnesium fire starters, and a blast match.

There are also a wide variety of primitive fire starting methods. I suggest you print a copy of all the different primitive fire starting methods that you find and keep them all together in a folder for future reference. One day that information may be useful to you. If you have absolutely nothing else to do you could follow those instructions and learn for yourself how truly challenging a primitive fire starting method really is.

Each primitive fire starting method requires practice and a considerable amount of effort which can quickly exhaust you. Each primitive method is based on the application of either sparks or friction to elevate the temperature of extremely dry tinder material to the point where it will ignite.

The two times when you will desperately need a fire are during:

1. rainy weather when the air is very damp and humid, and
2. freezing weather when the combustible material is either frozen or very, very cold.

Under these types of adverse weather conditions all of the primitive fire starting methods are completely unreliable.

If the air is damp or humid then your sparks will encounter extra moisture in the air and they may not be hot enough to start a fire when they make contact with the tinder material, which is also surrounded by damp, humid air. If you are using friction then it will take a lot more friction to start a fire in a damp environment.

During freezing weather conditions the surrounding cold air quickly saps the heat out of your sparks or from the friction you are trying to create to start a fire. It is extremely difficult during freezing weather to get a fire started using any primitive fire starting method. If you have some really good very dry tinder that you have warmed using your natural body heat then you will increase your chances of getting a fire started but the odds will still be weighted heavily against you.

In addition, during rainy weather and freezing weather it is very easy to quickly become depressed, irritable, and fearful. Primitive fire starting methods are even more difficult to properly execute during these times of emotional stress.

Finally, during adverse weather conditions the sun will not be visible so any fire starting method based on focusing the sun's energy will simply not work.

You will not read about the above shortcomings in any survival manual that teaches and recommends primitive fire starting methods. But the above problems are real and therefore I cannot personally recommend any primitive technique as a primary method for starting a fire.

Besides, during a wilderness survival adventure or a "hard times event" you really don't need to be investing your time and energy in trying to start a fire. You will already have enough stress and pressure in your life from a multitude of other sources. You will also have far more important things you could be doing instead of trying to start a fire using a primitive method.

For all of the above reasons I prefer any modern fire starting method instead of any primitive method. Let's look at four modern methods for starting a fire as follows: matches, butane lighters, a blast match, and a magnesium fire starter.

Matches

1. In the year 2011 you could buy a box of 50 matchbooks (20 matches per matchbook or 1000 paper matches per box) for about $1.20 per box. This works out to approximately 8 matches for a penny.

2. Or you could follow the advice on some survival forums and try to learn how to start a fire using some primitive method, such as rubbing two sticks together. After one or two hours of hard labor your arms will be aching and you will probably still not have a fire going. And when you think about the fact that you could have purchased 8 matches for a penny then you will begin to wonder why you have invested one hour of your time in this unproductive activity.

3. One box of 1,000 matches would yield one fire per day for approximately 3 years.

4. If you practice tearing the match in half from its bottom to its top being very careful when you tear through the match head then you could light two fires per match. This is something you could easily practice right now when there is absolutely no pressure on whether or not you succeed and whether or not you ruin a few paper matches as you learn this simple skill. But if someday you can't buy matches then you could get about 2,000 fires started using your box of 1,000 paper matches or approximately one fire per day for about 5.5 years. (Note: On a scale of 1 to 10, with 1 being extremely easy to learn and 10 being very difficult to learn, the effort required to learn how to tear one match in half and get two fires started from a single match would be a 1 or a 2, in my opinion.)

5. It is also possible to carefully split the half match again by cutting it in half with scissors up through the center of the paper and then through the center of the match head. This is easier to do if you first cut 1/2 way through the match head with a knife before you try cutting through the match head with the scissors. When you are finished each original match would now be in four pieces. This would yield 4,000 fires per box of matches or one fire per day for about 11 years. And your total investment would still only be about $1.20. (Note: On a scale of 1 to 10 this would rate a 2 or a 3, in my opinion.) Since the one-quarter piece of match will be extremely thin it will burn very quickly and you must have your tinder material ready so you can immediately ignite it before the tiny piece of match burns out and before it quickly burns down to your finger tips.

There are a variety of other types of matches including Strike Anywhere Kitchen Wooden Matches and Standard Kitchen Wooden Matches. If you do not have the strike anywhere matches then be sure to include the striking strip off the box in your "necessities bag" or bug-out-bag but wrap it separately inside something waterproof so it cannot accidentally come into contact with the match heads.

If your matches accidentally get damp then they may or may not work after you dry them out.

Butane Lighters

If I were limited to a single fire starting method then I would select a **New Butane Lighter.** New butane lighters can be purchased almost anywhere for one-dollar each or less. A new **small** butane lighter will light about 1,000 fires or one fire a day for about three years. A new $1.00 **standard** size butane lighter will start between 2,000 to 3,000 fires or one fire a day for somewhere between 5.5 years to 8 years. A new **high-capacity** butane lighter will light about 4,000 fires or one fire per day for approximately 11 years.

Purchase at least two different major name brand lighters made by two different companies.

Chapter Fifty-Two: Fire

During a hard times tragedy event you can get the maximum number of fires started from one butane lighter if you will follow this procedure:

1. Do not try to light a fire in windy conditions. Find a safe place to build your fire where there is no wind blowing.

2. Arrange your small fire building sticks above your tinder before you ignite your lighter.

3. Select something that will catch fire very quickly such as a small piece of old newspaper or a small piece of one page torn from an old phone book.

4. Ignite your butane lighter and quickly put the flame below the small piece of old newspaper to get it burning. The instant the newspaper bursts into flames turn off the butane lighter.

5. Immediately put the piece of burning newspaper under your tinder material to start the fire burning.

Why Buy Matches and a Butane Lighter?

The reason I recommend matches and a butane lighter is simple. During freezing weather the striking wheel on a butane lighter can freeze and render the lighter useless for starting a fire. In that situation the matches usually work just fine. However, during really damp humid weather it is possible that the matches may get a little damp and be difficult to strike. In that situation the butane lighter works just fine. If you have a different backup method for starting a fire then you will have a much better chance of starting a fire under a variety of adverse weather conditions.

Other Fire Producing Options

A **Blast Match** is a spark making tool that has Fire Steel inside a plastic protective case. For it to work it does require some really good tinder, such as **clothes dryer lint.** *Extremely dry decayed wood is also very good tinder.* The tiny sparks the blast match creates will start any easily ignitable material burning. However, unless you have some really good tinder that is extremely flammable then the tiny sparks will go out before igniting the tinder. Therefore I prefer a Magnesium Fire Starter instead of a blast match.

A **Magnesium Fire Starter** requires that you shave a little magnesium off the magnesium block and then strike the attached Fire Steel with the blunt edge of your knife to throw some sparks onto the very thin magnesium shavings. The shavings will quickly catch fire and burn extremely well. This is a very reliable way to start a fire and it should work well if both your matches and your butane lighters should fail for some unexpected reason. (Note 1: If all the available tinder is damp or frozen then you could place a few shavings off the magnesium block below some damp tinder. Then ignite the magnesium shavings with an ordinary match to get the tinder burning. Then you could gradually build a normal fire.) (Note 2: There is enough magnesium on the block to reliably start somewhere between 75 to 125 good fires. However, even after you have used all the magnesium the spark making Fire Steel will still be intact and it can be used to start additional fires if you have some really good tinder material.)

Chapter Fifty-Two: Fire

In summary, I recommend that a person have at least **two good butane lighters** manufactured by two different companies, and some **strike anywhere matches** in a waterproof container, and a **magnesium fire starter.** These items are all very small and they do not weigh very much. But with this combination of items you could start a fire under almost any type of adverse weather condition.

How to Build a Fire

1. The secret to successfully building a fire is to select a safe place that is out of the wind and then collect all your fire building materials, including some good tinder.
2. Arrange some very tiny thin dry twigs above your tinder material.
3. When your match or butane lighter is activated you can immediately put the fire to the tinder and start the tinder burning below the very tiny twigs or sticks.
4. Then you should quickly add some slighter bigger sticks to the fire.
5. After they start burning then you can add slightly larger sticks.
6. This does not require much practice but you need to be careful or you could smother the fire and it will go out or you could burn yourself.

How Your Ancestors Started a Fire Without a Match or a Butane Lighter

1. Use a long stick to move the ashes around inside your fireplace. Look for a glowing coal. Use your stick to move the red hot coal to an area where you can easily get to it.
2. Loosely surround the glowing coal with some really good very dry tinder material, such as clothes dryer lint, or shredded newspaper, or extremely dry decayed finely crumbled wood particles.
3. Blow on the glowing coal to provide extra oxygen and the tinder material should burst into flames.
4. Immediately add some very tiny sticks to your burning tinder material and then gradually build the fire the way you normally would.

Note: In the 1800s families heated their homes with a fireplace and they cooked their meals using the fireplace. When they got up each morning their first chore of the day was to get a fresh fire started in the fireplace if it had gone out during the night. If the fire was completely dead and there were no glowing coals then they would use a match to start a new fire. But matches cost money and many families could not afford them. If the fire was completely out and they did not have a match then one of the children would pick up a "coal bucket" and walk two or three miles to the nearest neighbor's house and borrow some red hot coals from the neighbor's wood burning fire. Then the child would return home and someone would start a fresh fire using the live coals in the coal bucket. It was called a "coal bucket" because it could hold the red hot coals from a wood burning fire. (It could also be used to hold the "black coal" from a coal mine). These people were not stupid. In fact, they knew more about hard times survival than any "expert" today because the people in the 1800s lived in what people today would call "hard times" from the day they were born until the day they died. They also knew all the "primitive" ways to build a fire such as rubbing two sticks together. But they also knew from personal experience how much work was involved in those primitive fire starting methods. Since they had a lot of chores to do every day that required hard physical labor, it was considered far more practical to walk a few miles to and from a neighbor's house than to invest the effort required to start a fire using a primitive method. Think about this the next time you read about how "easy" it is to start a fire using some primitive method and how "everyone" should learn how to start a fire using some primitive method. There is nothing wrong with learning how to start a fire using some primitive technique but this is the type of skill that should be very, very, very low on your list of skills that you want to learn. There are simply too many really critical skills you should be learning instead, such as how to grow your own vegetables.

Chapter Fifty-Three

How to Start an Emergency Fire Using the Gunpowder From a Bullet

1. **Before** you try to light a fire begin by collecting a lot of very **tiny** thin dry twigs and sticks, and some **small** dry sticks, and some **average** size dry sticks. Put all of these twigs and sticks close to the location where you intend to build your future fire. Arrange the sticks into three different piles based on the size of the sticks. Dead tree branches caught in shrubs or bushes and that are off the ground are excellent fire starting material. Sticks and branches that have been lying on the ground may be used **after** the fire is burning well.

2. Collect some high quality **dry tinder**. The pile of tinder should be about the size of your closed fist but very loosely arranged so lots of air can get into the stack. If possible, have at least two different types of tinder materials mixed together inside your initial tinder pile. Some examples of good dry tinder would be:
    a. thin strips of paper, or
    b. clothes dryer lint, or
    c. very thin strips of old dry cloth with frayed edges, or
    d. thin shavings off a dry stick (the bark and wood shavings should be thinner than a toothpick), or
    e. very dry decayed wood that has been separated and fluffed up.

3. Carefully remove a bullet from one cartridge shell casing. You will not need the bullet so you may set the bullet aside.

4. Pour the gunpowder from inside the casing onto one side of your small pile of very dry tinder.

5. For safety reasons wear leather gloves and be careful not to burn your hands by having your fingers too close to the gunpowder when it first catches fire.

6 A tiny spark will ignite the gunpowder and start the tinder burning. A spark may be produced using any one of the following methods:
    a. Strike a flint with a piece of steel.
    b. Use a "Blast Match" to produce a spark.
    c. Strike the edge of a "Magnesium Fire Starter" with the back edge of your hunting knife to produce a spark.
    d. If you do not have anything that will produce a spark then you can put the **empty shell** back into the handgun from which it came and fire the **empty shell** directly at the gunpowder. The primer sparks will fly out the end of the gun barrel and ignite the gunpowder on your pile of tinder. This works best with a handgun that has a short barrel. The end of the gun barrel should be about two-inches from the gunpowder but this distance depends on the size (caliber) of your empty bullet shell.

7. Be emotionally prepared for the gunpowder to instantly ignite in the same manner as the head of an ordinary match. The small amount of gunpowder will **not** explode because it is **not** trapped inside a small area inside a bullet shell casing. Instead the gunpowder will ignite and burn because it is surrounded by air. For example, if you have ever watched a movie where someone pours some gunpowder in a straight line across the ground and then puts a match to one end of the gunpowder fuse, then you have seen how gunpowder flares up and gradually burns from one end of the gunpowder fuse to the other end.

8. Quickly add some tiny thin dry twigs and sticks to the small fire. The gunpowder will burn very fast and very hot so you need to have lots of very small sticks already on hand to add to the initial fire because your tinder will burn up very quickly.

9. As the fire begins to increase in size gradually add slightly larger dry sticks. The size of the sticks should be proportional to the size of the fire. In the beginning when the fire is very small use very thin sticks. As the fire gradually gets a little bigger use slightly bigger sticks. When the fire gets to be a normal size then you may add normal size sticks. Do not smother the fire by adding sticks that are too large for the fire in its initial stages of development.

Chapter Fifty-Four

How to Build a Simple Sundial

When the sun is shining a sundial may be used to estimate the approximate time of day. However, because the earth travels around the sun in an elliptical orbit, the position of the sun in the sky will be different during the different seasons. This difference is most noticeable in the middle of the winter when the sun will appear lower in the sky relative to the horizon, and in the middle of the summer when the sun will appear higher in the sky relative to the horizon.

If you push a straight stick into the ground then the shadow cast by that stick will point west at sunrise, north at midday, and east at sunset in the northern hemisphere. (Note: In the southern hemisphere the shadow will point south at midday.) In the northern hemisphere the shadow will move in a clockwise direction around the stick. This is the same direction that the hands of a clock move around the face of the clock.

To make a simple sundial first use a magnetic compass to determine the directions west, north, and east. (Although magnetic north and true north are slightly different, this difference will not have a significant impact on a simple sundial.) Then draw a straight line in the dirt on level ground from due west to due east. In the middle of that east-west line draw another straight line due north. Write the number 6 (or 6:00 am) at the west end of the line, the number 12 (or 12:00 noon) at the tip of the north line, and the number 6 (or 6:00 pm) at the east end of the line.

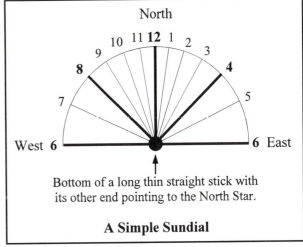

A Simple Sundial

Now draw a line that approximately divides the left side of the sundial in half and write the number 8 (or 8:00 am) at the tip of that line. Draw a line that approximately divides the right side of the sundial in half and write the number 4 (or 4:00 pm) at the tip of that line.

Now draw another line for 7 am on the left side but draw the line a little closer to the number 8 than the number 6 am. Draw a line for 5 pm on the right side but draw it a little closer to the number 4 than then number 6 pm.

Now separate the space from 8 am until 12 noon using three lines with the spacing between the lines becoming a little less as they get closer to the number 12 noon. Separate the space from 12 noon to 4 pm with three lines with the spacing between the lines being a little less as they get closer to the number 12 noon.

Push a long thin straight stick (at least 12 inches long) into the ground at the point where the east-west line and the north line intersect (see the above illustration) and point the opposite end of the stick towards Polaris, or the North Star.

Your exact location on the earth is determined by the intersection of your longitude and your latitude. Your latitude is the angle from level ground at your location to the North Star. For example, if you were at the North Pole then the North Star would be directly above your head and the angle would be 90° straight up which would also be your latitude. If you were at the Equator then the angle from the ground to the North Star would be 0° which would also be your latitude. If you moved from the Equator towards the North Pole then the angle to the North Star (your latitude) would gradually increase to 10°, then 30°, then 50°, then 70°, until you finally reached the North Pole and your latitude would be 90°. You can find your exact latitude on a map that shows latitudes and longitudes. However, for the purpose of constructing a simple compass an estimate will be okay.

In the United States of America if you live in a state that touches the Canadian border then your average latitude is approximately 45°. If you live in a state about halfway between Canada and Mexico then your latitude is approximately 38.5°. If you live in a state that touches the Mexican border or the Gulf of Mexico, then your latitude is approximately 32°. This will be the angle between your straight stick that points to the North Star and the level ground below the stick. Push your long thin straight stick into the ground at the correct angle so it points North towards the North Star. Then use another shorter stick, with a fork at its top, between the ground and your North Star stick to support your North Star stick so it does not begin to gradually lean over closer to the ground.

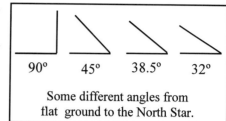

Some different angles from flat ground to the North Star.

This completes your simple sundial. Your simple sundial will allow you to determine the *approximate* time of day. However, during daylight saving time you will need to add one hour to your sundial time to arrive at the current daylight savings time.

Throughout the entire world we now live in designated time zones that are several hundred miles wide. This means the shadow of the stick will be directly below the stick at 12 noon if you live in the center of a time zone. But if you live near the west or east borders of a time zone then the shadow of the stick will be a little to the right or left of the stick at 12 noon and not directly below the stick.

If you live outside the continental United States of America and you wish to construct a sundial, or if you simply wish to improve the accuracy of your sundial, and you have access to a clock and you can determine your exact latitude, then you could easily adjust the angle of the stick to match your latitude, and you could adjust the positions of the numbers around the outside edge of your sundial to match the exact hour of the day the stick's shadow is pointing in a specific direction. Once you have constructed a simple sundial and you have determined the approximate distances between the individual lines for the hours of the day then you could easily duplicate that sundial whenever you wanted to for the rest of your life.

After you have gained a little experience constructing temporary simple sundials in the dirt on the ground you may decide that you want to build a better sundial using a large round block of flat wood. You could then mount your wooden sundial on top of a wooden post that you anchor or bury in the ground. This would put your sundial a little higher than waist level and this would make it easier for everyone to read.

Chapter Fifty-Five

Grandpappy's Homemade Soap Recipe

During hard times sooner or later everyone runs out of soap. To make soap you only need three things:

1. **rainwater,**
2. **cold ashes from any hardwood fire**, and
3. **animal fat** from almost any type of animal, such as a cow, pig, goat, sheep, beaver, raccoon, opossum, groundhog, etc.

All soap consists of the above three ingredients in one form or another and that includes bath soap, dish soap, laundry soap, and hair shampoo.

Soap is not difficult to make and it does not require any special equipment. And soap can be made from things that exist in large quantities in nature and which are typically discarded as being of little value (rainwater, campfire ashes, and animal fat). Therefore, a person who knows how to make good soap could provide his or her family with a small but steady income during hard times by making and selling soap. Soap requires no financial investment in raw materials and therefore it does not require the advance purchase and storage of inventory before the hard times occur.

Soap is a **"perfect consumer product"** for the following five reasons:

1. Soap is a legal product.
2. Everyone everywhere uses soap.
3. Soap is completely used up in a short period of time.
4. When people run out of soap they want to buy more.
5. Soap is relatively low in price so almost everyone can afford it.

In my opinion soap is one of the **basic necessities of life** for the following five reasons:

1. **Personal hygiene:** Good health is maintained by washing your hands before eating and by taking a bath on a regular basis.
2. **Laundry:** If your clothes get really filthy then they will collect lots of germs and those germs will eventually attack your body and you will get sick. During hard times families with small babies quickly revert back to cloth baby diapers that require a really good cleaning before being reapplied to the baby's bottom.
3. **Dish washing:** If your eating utensils are not clean then it won't be long before you get sick from the microscopic organisms that collect and grow on your dishes.
4. **Wound care and other medical situations:** Even small wounds can get infected and become life threatening if they are not properly cleaned with soap at the earliest possible opportunity.
5. **Disease control:** Soap is extremely valuable in preventing the spread of diseases because you can wash the bed sheets, clothes, and eating utensils of the sick person, and you can also give the sick person a daily bath or cleaning to help neutralize any germs on the sick person's body.

In developed countries most people take soap for granted until they don't have any, just like they take water, canning salt, socks, and shoes for granted. When their soap is all gone people suddenly realize how important it really was. Regardless of how much soap you may have stored for an emergency situation it will eventually be used up. At that time it would be useful if you knew how to make really good soap from rainwater, campfire ashes, and animal fat.

There are three major differences between homemade soap and commercial quality soap:

1. Homemade soap does not lather or produce soap bubbles. However, soap bubbles are only for visual appeal. Bubbles do **not** increase the cleaning power of soap. (Note: It is possible to add bubbles to homemade soap and that procedure will be explained below.)

2. Soap made from campfire ashes will not be as hard as soap made from commercial quality lye crystals.

3. Homemade soap has an oilier texture than commercial quality soap. However, homemade soap will still yield very acceptable results for most routine cleaning chores because it will surround and cling to the dirt particles, regardless of their size, and allow them to be more easily washed away.

Soap making lye crystals have been withdrawn from the market because they were being used to make illegal drugs and you can no longer purchase lye crystals at your local grocery store or hardware store. Therefore if you have an existing soap recipe it will probably be of limited value during a long-term hard times event because you can no longer purchase lye crystals at your local grocery store or hardware store.

However, soap making suppliers still sell lye crystals by mail order. But why would you want to purchase an inventory of lye crystals so you can make homemade soap during a long-term hard times event? If you are trying to prepare for a future hard times event wouldn't it make more sense to simply purchase some ordinary soap and put it away for future use. To me this would make far more sense than purchasing some chemicals to make some homemade soap in an emergency.

On the other hand, if the hard times last longer than you expected and you use all the soap you have stored then you could make good soap using lye water made the old fashioned way by using the following soap making procedure that does not depend on commercial quality lye crystals.

Basic Soap Making Equipment

To make soap you will need:

A **cook pot** made of stainless steel, or cast iron, or enamelware, or heat-tempered glass, or a clay-fired cooking pot. Aluminum and tin and Teflon coated pots are **not** acceptable because the soap making lye will adversely react with these materials. The cook pot should be at least twice the size of the batch of soap you intend to make. Generally a one-gallon or four-quart cook pot will be more than adequate as a soap making pot. (Note: You may use the same pot for soap making and cooking. Just wash the pot when you are finished making soap. Some soap recipes suggest having a special pot just for soap making but this is not necessary, in my opinion. You are just making soap in the pot and it will be the same soap you use later to wash the pot after you cook a meal.)

A **long spoon** made of stainless steel or wood. If necessary, an old wood broom handle or a big stick may be used to stir the soap if nothing else is available.

A **glass measuring cup**. You can use a plastic measuring cup but the concentrated brown lye water may permanently discolor the inside of the measuring cup. (Note: If you don't have a measuring cup then use approximately 2.5 times the amount of melted grease as concentrated brown lye water.)

Some type of **mold** to pour the soap mixture into so it can harden into a bar of soap. For example, you could make a soap mold out of a large empty kitchen matchbox by lining it with plastic food wrap. Or you could use the small black plastic serving trays that contain frozen dinner meals, such as a single serving lasagna meal. The soap mold container should be at least 1 to 1.5 inches deep.

A **thermometer** is optional because soap was made for centuries before the thermometer was invented. If you wish to use a thermometer then select a cooking or meat or candy thermometer that will show temperatures from a minimum of 70°F to at least 140°F (21°F to 60°C). An instant-read thermometer works exceptionally well.

Almost anyone can make good soap if he or she has a little patience and is willing to begin on a small scale in order to gain practice and experience.

Grandpappy's Homemade Soap Recipe

Yields two large eleven-ounce bars of soap or a total of 22 ounces of soap by weight.
This is equivalent to approximately four normal bars of store bought soap.

1. **3/4 cup of concentrated brown lye water.** Normal strength brown lye water can be made by pouring rainwater through the cold ashes of any hardwood fire. Detailed instructions for making concentrated brown lye water are near the end of this chapter.

2. **Two cups of melted grease.** Any type of animal fat may be melted into grease, such as beef, pork, lamb, goat, beaver, opossum, raccoon, groundhog, etc. Only use the fat because lean meat will not make soap. Do not use any lean meat. Detailed instructions for melting animal fat into grease are near the end of this chapter. Beef tallow is a hard fat and it makes a hard soap that cleans really well. A soft fat, such as pork lard, may be used in a ratio of up to 50% with a hard fat. (Note: If you do not have access to animal fat then you can ask the employees in the fresh meat section of your local grocery store if they have any beef fat or pork fat for sale.)

(Note: You should reduce the above quantities by one-half when you first attempt to make soap. This will give you the opportunity to gain confidence and experience on a small scale. You may use the above quantities, or any multiple thereof, for future soap making efforts depending on how much soap you wish to make in one batch.)

The Six Soap Making Steps

STEP ONE: Mix the concentrated brown lye water and the grease, stir thoroughly, and give the chemical reaction between 30 minutes to 3 hours to gradually take place. Be patient.

This is the most important step in making soap.

The concentrated brown lye water (or lye crystals) used in soap making can hurt you. Be careful when handling the lye. Wear rubber gloves to protect your skin from the lye. If some lye solution gets on your skin then wash it off immediately with soap and water. Lye is caustic and it will permanently **disfigure** Formica counter tops, kitchen tables, and other nice furniture, even if you wipe it off the surface immediately. Be careful when handling lye and do not let it splash or spill or bubble over onto your kitchen furniture or onto your floor.

Concentrated brown lye water is normally used at room temperature unless the room is unusually cool or cold (below 75°F or 24°C). If necessary heat the concentrated brown lye water to between 80°F to 130°F (27°C to 54°C) in a separate cook pot. The temperature is not critical as long as it is not too hot. The purpose of using warm lye water is to help maintain a warm soap mixing temperature inside the soap mixing pot.

Put the grease into a separate small melting pot and then put the pot on the stove over **very low heat**. Do not heat the grease to the smoking point. If you see smoke then you are burning the grease. Melt all the grease and then allow it to cool back down to 90°F (32°C) for pork lard, or to 130°F (54°C) for beef tallow, or to 110°F (43°C) for a combination of tallow and lard. Do not allow the grease to harden while it is waiting to be added to the soap mixture. The grease must be melted when it is added to the soap mixture and it should be relatively warm. The temperature does not have to be exact but the grease must be warm and fully melted.

Pour one cup of the melted grease into the big soap making pot. Slowly pour 3/8 cup of the concentrated brown lye water into the soap making pot. Stir the mixture for three-minutes. The mixture will look like **brown soup with white streaks in it** (see picture on right). Add another cup of grease and another 3/8 cup of concentrated brown lye water and stir thoroughly and continuously for about 15 minutes. The grease and lye must be completely and thoroughly blended together to make soap. If the mixture is not thoroughly blended then the mixture will separate later and you will not get a good soap.

(Note: You can use a manual hand-cranked blender to speed up the mixing process and reduce the amount of time it takes for the chemical reaction between the grease and the lye to be completed. However, this method does require a little practice and experience because it can also result in what is called a "false trace" which is described in Step Two below.)

(Note: If you increase the original recipe to make larger batches of soap you should still slowly and gradually mix the grease and concentrated brown lye water together at the rate of one cup of grease to 3/8 cup of concentrated brown lye water until all the grease and lye water has been added to the soap making pot. By adding the ingredients gradually and mixing thoroughly each time you can avoid a separation problem later in the process.)

When you are not stirring the soap mixture you should cover the soap mixing pot with a **towel** to help conserve the heat inside the mixing pot. **Remove** the towel if you need to add a **little** heat to the mixing pot and then replace the towel after you turn off the heat.

This part of the soap making process **normally** takes between thirty minutes to three hours if you are using grease made from animal fat. During this time the soap mixture needs to remain slightly warm and just above the temperature at which the grease normally hardens. This is where an instant read thermometer is useful. If the mixture begins to cool too quickly then add just a **little** bit of heat to the soap mixing pot until the temperature of the soap mixture is between 90°F to 130°F (32°C to 54°C), depending on the type of grease you are using and then turn off the heat. Pork lard melts at 85°F (29°C) and beef tallow melts at 125°F (52°C).

(Note: Do **not** cook the soap mixture and do **not** heat it to the boiling point. Although additional heat will speed up the chemical reaction it can also cause potential separation problems later in the process.)

Be patient and wait for the chemical reaction to gradually take place at its **very slow normal speed**. Once every ten or fifteen minutes stir the soap mixture vigorously for one-minute to facilitate a more complete mixing of the lye and the grease. Vigorous stirring means fast and smooth stirring. Do not splash the soap mixture onto the sides of the mixing pot. When you begin stirring the mixture after a ten or fifteen minute rest you will notice that the brown lye water and the grease are still partially separated because you will be able to see streaks of color in the soap mixture as you stir. However, as you stir vigorously for one minute you should attempt to combine the lye and grease into a solid color so there are very few or no streaks in the mixture. Then you may stop stirring and wait for another ten or fifteen minutes.

Each time you make a new batch of soap you may or may not encounter one of the following two problems. These problems may occur because your concentrated brown lye water may be just a little stronger or a little weaker than what you used in your previous batch of soap. You may also encounter one of the following problems if you use a different type of animal fat, or combination of animal fats, than you normally use. The exact amount of concentrated brown lye water that is required will be slightly different depending on the type of animal fat you are using.

Problem One: If a layer of grease forms on top of the mixture then check the temperature of the soap mixture and make sure it is above the temperature that the grease normally solidifies, which is 125°F (52°) for 100% beef tallow, or 85°F (29°) for 100% pork lard, or 110°F (43°) for a 50-50 blend of tallow and lard. If the top layer of grease is simply due to a cold soap mixture then heat the mixture just a little bit and stir the grease back into the mixture. However, if the soap mixture was already at a reasonably warm temperature then heat the soap mixture just a little, then turn off the heat, and then add 5% more of the concentrated brown lye water, and stir the soap mixture thoroughly for ten minutes.

Problem Two: If the mixture does not thicken properly after three hours then heat the soap mixture just a little, then turn off the heat, and then add 10% more melted warm grease, and stir the warm grease thoroughly into the soap mixture for ten minutes.

(Note: It takes time for the concentrated brown lye water and the grease to combine together chemically to make soap. Depending on the type of animal fat or grease you are using it may take as much as twenty-four hours. The most difficult part of Step One is to be patient if the chemical reaction is going slowly and not ruin your batch of soap by adding too much lye water or too much grease in an effort to get the soap mixture to Step Two more quickly. Waiting patiently does not hurt the chemical reaction. Adding too much of the wrong thing can upset the chemical balance.)

When the soap mixture is a **solid cream** or **solid light brown color that displays no streaks when it is first stirred** after a ten-minute rest, **and** it is the consistency of thick gravy or soft pudding (see picture on right), then you can test it using one of the methods in Step Two below. (In the picture on the right the bright white circle is the reflection of my camera flash off the top shinny surface of the stainless steel cook pot.)

STEP TWO: Verify the soap mixture is warm enough and that it is ready to be poured into the molds using one (or both) of the following two test methods.

The grease will gradually thicken if the temperature of the soap mixture gets too low. This will make you think the chemical reaction is complete when in fact it is not. This is called a "false trace." Therefore you must verify the soap mixture is still above the melting point of whatever grease you are using before you test the mixture using either (or both) of the following two methods. The minimum soap mixture temperature is 125°F (52°) for 100% beef tallow, or 85°F (29°) for 100% pork lard, or 110°F (43°) for a 50-50 blend of tallow and lard. If your soap mixture temperature is above the minimum then it is ready to be tested.

(Note: If the soap mixture is **below** the minimum temperature, or if you do **not** have a thermometer, then add a **little** heat to the soap mixture and see if the soap mixture melts back into a fat and lye solution that separates into different colors when stirred gently. If the mixture does show streaks of different colors then continue to add **very low heat** for two minutes, stir the mixture vigorously, and then turn off the heat and cover the pot with a towel and return to the instructions for Step One.)

Test Method One: Use a spoon to lift a little of the soap mixture about one-inch above the top surface of the mixture and then allow one drop to fall back onto the top of the mixture. If the surface of the mixture will support the drop for a moment then the soap is done.

Test Method Two: Try to draw a medium thick line in the top of the soap mixture with the front tip of your spoon. If you can see the line then the soap is done. This is called "tracing."

(Note: When the mixture "traces" the chemical reaction between the lye and the grease is approximately 90% complete. However, the final 10% will happen very, very slowly and it will take another 3 to 7 weeks. The soap will not be ready for use until the chemical reaction has been 100% completed.)

STEP THREE: (Optional Step) - Add Color and Fragrance.

If you wish you may add color and/or fragrance at this time. However, in my opinion, it is generally not worth the effort. Soap is a consumable item and when it is used up it is gone. Investing time and energy to make the soap more colorful or more fragrant has marginal value if you are simply going to use your soap yourself. On the other hand, if are considering the sale of your soap for a profit then color, shape, and smell are important marketing factors. However, do **not** use commercial perfumes or alcohol-based solutions. Adding a fragrance or color that is not compatible with the soap making chemical process may ruin your batch of soap. **Pure** essential oils or herbal solutions are preferred, if you chose to use them. Stir them thoroughly and completely into the soap mixture and then proceed to Step Four.

(Note: Another way to add fragrance is to wait until the end of Step Six when the soap is fully cured after six-weeks. Then place the soap and your fragrance inside an air-tight container and seal the lid. Wait three to six weeks. The soap will gradually become saturated with the smell of your fragrance, regardless of what it might be. Remove the soap and put the lid back on your fragrance bottle or return your fragrance to its own airtight container.)

Chapter Fifty-Five: Homemade Soap

STEP FOUR: Pour the soap into the soap molds and let the soap rest for seven days.

Any container can be used as a soap mold, such as cupcake pans, small boxes, or any other type of container. Lightly grease the inside of the containers. Or place plastic food wrap inside a small cardboard box, such as an empty kitchen matchbox. The small **black plastic serving trays** that contain a frozen dinner meal, such as a single serving lasagna meal, make really nice soap molds if you wash them out first. The soap molds need to be at least 1 to 1.5 inches deep because the soap mixture needs to retain its heat during the initial phase of this step and if the mold is too shallow it will lose its heat too quickly.

Our ancestors would use a thin damp towel to line the inside of whatever container they were using as a soap mold. When the soap finished curing the towel permitted the easy removal of the soap from the mold.

Today the best way to line the inside of a mold is to use plastic food wrap. The plastic food wrap will not react with the soap while the chemical reaction continues to its completion and it provides a very easy way to remove the soap from the mold when the soap is done.

The soap mixture should be above the minimum melting point temperature for the type of grease you are using.

Pour the warm soap mixture into the molds and then put the soap molds in a warm location. **Immediately** cover the soap molds with a thick cloth or blanket to prevent the heat from escaping too quickly. Do not let the cloth or blanket make contact with the soap in the molds. The blanket should simply provide a cover to help keep the molds warm.

Allow the soap to rest in the soap molds for **one day**. Then **remove the towel.**

Let the soap continue to rest in the soap molds uncovered for **six additional days**.

If you peek at your soap during the first day while the soap is covered inside the molds, the soap may look strange depending on what stage of cooling the soap is in. Do not worry. Be patient and wait for the chemical reaction to run its normal course.

During most of this seven-day period the soap may be relatively soft and it will not have the hard consistency you expect from soap. This is normal. Remember to be patient.

STEP FIVE: After a total of seven days remove the soap from the molds.

If you used a hard fat that melts at a higher temperature, such as beef, or goat, or lamb, then the soap will probably be firm enough to be easily removed from the molds. However, if you used some combination of soft fats such as chicken or pork mixed with a hard fat then your soap may not be firm enough for it to be easily extracted from the molds. If your soap feels soft like a firm pudding then put it in the refrigerator for two hours. It should then be firm enough to be removed from the molds.

Turn the soap mold upside down and the soap should fall out if the soap mold was lightly greased or if the mold was lined with plastic food wrap. If the soap does not fall out and you are using flexible plastic molds then flex the sides and bottom of the mold to loosen the soap from the mold so it can release and fall out. If necessary you can use a thin bladed knife to separate the soap from the sides of the mold and then gently help the soap out of the mold. (Note: If you used plastic food wrap to line the inside of your soap mold then you will not encounter this problem.)

If you wish to cut the soap into smaller bars then use a sharp thin knife, such as a serrated steak knife, or use a thin fine wire to saw through the soap. At this time the soap should still be relatively soft, similar to cheese, and it can be divided into smaller sizes if you wish.

If there are any imperfections, lines, or tiny cracks in the exterior surface of the soap you may smooth them out with your fingers at this time.

Chapter Fifty-Five: Homemade Soap

STEP SIX: Air dry the bar soap for 2 to 6 weeks.

After removing the soap from its mold allow the bar soap to dry in a **warm dry dark place** for two to six weeks before using it. If you really need your soap then you could start using it after the second week. But if you want the best possible soap then allow it to air dry for the full six weeks.

Cover a dish or large serving tray with some plastic food wrap and then stack your soap on the dish in a manner that will allow as much air as possible to reach each bar of soap. Do not stack one bar of soap directly on top of another bar of soap. Do **not** put the soap in direct sunlight or in a moist area. The longer the bar soap ages the harder it will become and the better it will perform when used as soap. During this time any remaining water in the soap will gradually evaporate out and any remaining lye will gradually blend in with the surrounding grease. However, if your soap is brown lye water heavy then it will leak out of your soap onto the dish during the first day and you will see a small puddle of brown lye water around your soap. If this happens then drain off the excess brown lye water so it does not have an opportunity to be reabsorbed into your current batch of soap. You should also consider the addition of about 10% more grease to your next batch of soap at the beginning of Step One.

After three weeks turn your bars of soap over so the underside of the soap will have an opportunity to dry in the air for the next three weeks.

After a total of six weeks of air drying put the bars of soap into an air-tight container, or wrap them in plastic wrap, or put them in a plastic food storage bag. Depending on your local climate conditions, this will either prevent the soap from drying out or it will prevent the soap from absorbing moisture from humid air.

When you remove your bar of soap from storage it **may** have a thin layer of white powder on it, which is the result of the air reacting with any lye on the outside surface of the soap. This thin layer of powder will contain some lye and it needs to be removed from the surface of the soap. Just rinse the ash off and forget about it.

You may also discover that the first two or three times you use the soap to wash your hands that it does not work very well. This is because the soap needs a brief adjusting period after making its first initial contact with water. After the soap has been in brief contact with water a few times, and rubbed, and allowed to dry, it will start to behave like normal soap and clean very well, with one exception. Homemade soap does not lather the way ordinary store bought soap lathers. Bubbles are not necessary for a soap to be effective. Bubbles only add visual appeal.

(Note: If you are going to sell your soap for a profit then you should dip the bar of soap in water and allow it to air dry several times to pre-condition the soap for your customers. This will help to reduce the number of customer complaints about your soap not working the way it should.)

You can test the quality of a finished bar of soap by shaving it with a sharp knife. If it crumbles it contains too much lye but it will still be very effective as a good laundry soap. Good all-purpose bar soap will curl slightly when shaved with a sharp knife blade. Keep a written record of your soap making results and make minor adjustments as required on your next batch of soap.

How to Make Special Types of Soap Using Grandpappy's Homemade Soap Recipe

1. **All-Purpose Soap (Bath Soap, Laundry Soap, Dish Soap):** Use 100% beef tallow, or any other hard fat, in "Grandpappy's Homemade Soap Recipe."
2. **Bath Soap:** Use 75% beef tallow and 25% pork lard in "Grandpappy's Homemade Soap Recipe."
3. **Facial Soap (an oily texture):** Use 50% beef tallow and 50% pork lard in "Grandpappy's Homemade Soap Recipe" to make a soft facial soap that has an oily texture that is useful for moisturizing the skin.
4. **Soap Flakes:** To make soap flakes rub a bar of hard soap made from 100% beef tallow (or any other hard fat) over a vegetable or cheese grater (shredder).
5. **Soap Powder:** To make soap powder dry the above **soap flakes** for 10 to 12 minutes in a 160°F (71°C) oven and then pulverize the dry soap flakes.

6. **Liquid Dish Soap or Liquid Laundry Soap or Hair Shampoo:** Add one-pound of **soap flakes** to one-gallon of boiling rainwater and boil for 10 to 12 minutes. Stir frequently. Then turn off the heat and allow the mixture to cool. Pour the liquid soap mixture into a storage container with a lid. The lid will prevent the mixture from drying out. This liquid soap mixture dissolves very quickly in hot water and it makes dish washing and clothes washing much easier. This procedure will also make a good hair shampoo if the original bar of soap was an all-purpose soap that contained an average amount of lye.
7. **Saddle Leather Soap:** Old fashioned "saddle leather soap" is made by using five-parts beef tallow and one-part pork lard in "Grandpappy's Homemade Soap Recipe."
8. **Floating Soap:** Either of the following two methods will yield a bar of soap that floats on top of water:
    Method 1: Just before Step Four fold the soap mixture over onto itself several times and stir really well each time in order to add lots of air bubbles into the soap mixture. Then immediately pour the soap mixture into the soap molds.
    Method 2: After all the grease and lye has been added in Step One and the original mixture has been stirred for at least 15 minutes then add one-teaspoon of ordinary baking soda to the soap mixture and stir really well.
9. **Soap that Lathers and Makes Soap Bubbles:** At the very beginning of Step One replace one-fourth of the grease with either olive oil or coconut oil. (Note: In my opinion olive oil and coconut oil both have better uses than making soap bubbles.)

Other Soap Additives: Kerosene (coal oil), ammonia, vinegar, borax, sugar, milk, honey, and several other chemicals that are occasionally recommended as soap recipe additives provide minimal or no benefit, and may even have a minor negative impact. My suggestion is to **not** use any of them. However, if you wish to experiment with additives such as oatmeal or salt or Vitamin E, then I suggest you do so with a small batch of soap and then verify for yourself that the advertised benefits actually materialize in the soap that you make and they don't introduce other problems into the soap making process.

Volume or Weight: "Grandpappy's Homemade Soap Recipe" is based on volume (cups). In August of 2007 most other good soap making recipes were based on weight because of the variation in the weight to volume ratio of the different types of animal fats that can be used to make soap. These other recipes are based on a very precise concentration of lye water made from commercial lye crystals. If you are working with two variables and you can hold one variable constant then it is not too difficult to predict the amount of the second variable that needs to be used. However, commercial lye crystals are no longer available so it is not possible to easily control the lye variable as a constant in the soap recipe. For this reason I decided to use the easier method of measuring volumes (cups) of lye and grease instead of the more precise scientific method of using weights. When you are working with brown lye water made from campfire ashes, your lye water will be whatever strength it happens to be on the day you make it. If you use "Grandpappy's Homemade Soap Recipe" then you will be **very close** to the correct ratio of water, lye, and grease that is required to make good soap. However, since there will be variations in the strength of your brown lye water, and variations in the type of animal fat you use, you **may** need to make minor adjustments towards the end of Step One depending on what you actually see in your soap making pot at that time. These minor adjustments are discussed as Problem One and Problem Two at the end of Step One near the beginning of this chapter.

Additional Supplementary Information
How to Melt (Render) Animal Fat

Beef fat is called **tallow** and pig fat is called **lard.** Poultry fat is too soft to be used by itself but it may be used in a ratio of about 10% with tallow or a tallow-lard combination. You may also use the fat from farm animals such as sheep or goats, and a variety of wild animals, such as beaver, opossum, raccoon, and groundhog. If there is any lean meat still attached to the fat cut it off and only use the fat to make grease.

Melting animal fat is called **rendering**. Rendering should be done outdoors or in a well ventilated area. The smell of melting animal fat will make most people nauseous. Cut the animal fat into small pieces about one-inch cubed and put them into a pot with about 1/8 inch of rainwater and cook over **low to medium heat**. Gradually add the fat to the pot and stir to keep the hot grease and solid pieces of fat circulating. As you stir be sure to scrape the bottom of the pot to prevent any fat from sticking to the bottom and burning. Do not burn the fat or allow it to smoke. If it starts to smoke then you are applying too much heat and you are burning the fat or grease.

One pound of fat will yield about 2.25 cups of grease. Most of the fat will melt into a liquid but some small solid particles will not melt. These are called **cracklings**. After melting the fat allow it to cool slightly and then strain it through a clean thin cloth and store it in a sealed container until it is needed. The cracklings will be on the top surface of the straining cloth. Save the delicious cracklings for use in other cooking recipes.

(Note: Raw animal fat can quickly become rancid. Therefore raw animal fat should not be saved and then converted into grease at some future date. The best procedure is to render animal fat into grease while the fat is still fresh. Rendered animal fat has a much longer storage life than raw animal fat.)

How to Make Concentrated Brown Lye Water

You will need rainwater (or steam distilled water) and the cold ashes from any hardwood fire, such as oak, hickory, maple, ash, beech, or old fruit trees. Do not use the ashes from a fire that burned pine tree wood.

The cold ashes from any hardwood fire can be converted into lye. Lye made from fire ashes is not as caustic as commercially purchased lye. Any large wooden, plastic, or clay container may be used, such as a huge flower pot. A deep container is better than a wide container. The container should have a **hole in its bottom center** and that is why a flower pot is perfect. Do not use a container made of tin or aluminum because lye is caustic and it will react with these materials. (Note: Or you could use a container with a side-mounted water valve, such as a 5-gallon water jug.)

For example, I use a **clay flower pot** that has a 9 inch outside diameter top, a 5.5 inch outside diameter bottom, and it is 9 inches tall, with sides and a bottom that is 0.25 inch thick. When packed with cold ashes to within 2.5 inches of its top, it holds approximately 145 cubic inches (about 10 cups) of tightly packed cold ashes. **Ten cups of tightly packed cold ashes will yield one-gallon of average strength brown lye water. Tightly packed means the loose ashes were pressed down firmly into the cup.** If you use a different size container then you should do the math to determine how much average strength brown lye water you will get from your container.

Hole in Bottom of Clay Flower Pot

Caution: Lye water is caustic and it will burn your skin. Be extremely careful and wear rubber gloves when handling lye water. If possible lye water should be made outdoors.

Firmly pack a layer of straw, or brown pine needles, or sand about one-inch deep in the bottom of the container to help keep the ashes inside the container. **Firmly pack** the cold ashes from any hardwood fire on top of the bottom layer. Slope the top surface of the ashes slightly from the sides of the container to its center to help direct the water flow to the center of the container. **Tightly pack** the ashes to within two to three inches of the top of the container depending on the size of the container. This empty top space is necessary to receive and hold the hot rainwater when it is first poured into the top of the container.

Place the large container on top of concrete blocks, bricks, or any other type of support so a second smaller container (at least one-gallon or four-quarts) can be placed beneath the center of the upper pot to catch the brown lye water as it drips through the hole in the bottom of the upper pot.

Rainwater is the best water for making brown lye water because it is soft and it contains no minerals or chlorine. (Note: If you do not have access to rainwater then you may use the **steam distilled water** sold at most grocery stores. Steam distilled water is chlorine and mineral free water. Instructions for making steam distilled water are included in the Water Chapter in this book.)

Your objective is to make approximately one-gallon of brown lye water from one fresh batch of cold hardwood fire ashes. Heat about one-half gallon of rainwater to boiling and then slowly pour it over the ashes in the upper container. If the ashes were packed down **firmly** they should not be swimming or floating in water. While the rainwater gradually disappears into the ashes heat another one-half gallon of rainwater and

Chapter Fifty-Five: Homemade Soap

Layer of Pine Needles in Bottom of Flower Pot

Cold Ashes Firmly Packed in Pot

Final Setup

then slowly pour it over the ashes. Wait about one-hour and then heat another one-half gallon of rainwater and slowly pour it over the ashes. Wait about one-half hour. If your brown lye water container has about one-gallon of brown lye water then you may stop. If you do not yet have one-gallon of brown lye water then heat another one-half gallon of rainwater and slowly pour it over the ashes. When you have finished you will have poured a total of approximately 1.5 to 2 gallons of hot rainwater into the pot of ashes. It may take a little while for the water to make its way through the ashes and out the hole in the bottom of the upper container. Be patient. The liquid that drips into the smaller container on the ground will be **brown lye water.** 1.5 to 2 gallons of hot rainwater will yield approximately **one-gallon of brown lye water**. (Note: The ashes will absorb and retain between one-half to one gallon of rainwater depending on the size and shape of your container and how tightly you packed down the ashes in the container. **Discard the used ashes** after you have extracted one-gallon of brown lye water. If you need more brown lye water then use a fresh batch of hardwood fire ashes to extract your next gallon of brown lye water.)

Wear rubber gloves when handling the brown lye water because it is caustic and it will burn your skin if it comes in contact with your skin. If you get some lye water on your skin then wash it off immediately with soap and water.

If necessary the brown lye water can be stored in a safe container, such as a stainless steel pot with a lid or a glass jar with a lid. However, the best procedure is to use the brown lye water immediately to make soap.

(Note: There are several different methods for testing the strength of the brown lye water but **none** of them are necessary. There is **no** reason to complicate the soap making process by attempting to get the brown lye water to a specific strength prior to using it to make soap. If your lye water is at the recommended average strength then you will make a good all-purpose soap. However, if your lye water is a little stronger than average then you will produce a good laundry soap. If your lye water is a little weaker than average then you will produce a good bath soap. Therefore don't be too concerned about the strength of your brown lye water. You will need both laundry soap and bath soap and you will be making soap frequently if you are out of soap. Therefore you can tolerate a little variability in the strength of your brown lye water. Besides, you will be boiling off most of the brown water anyway before you use it to make your soap.)

(Note: Some recipes recommend that you pour the brown lye water through the same batch of ashes several times in order to increase the strength of the lye water. This procedure has marginal value. The first extraction of the lye from the ashes will remove most of the usable lye from the ashes. Trying to squeeze a little more lye out of ashes that have already been seriously depleted of their lye is just not practical. On the other hand, a single extraction of lye from each new set of ashes will yield brown lye water that is of approximately the same strength each time and this will result in a more predictable soap making process that can be replicated over and over again. From a quality control perspective this means the process will have less total variation and therefore it should yield a product that is more consistent from one batch to the next. When you have a consistent stable process it is easier to fine tune the process and improve the quality of your finished product.)

There are **three methods** for making soap from the brown lye water as follows:

Method 1 - Brown Lye Water: Some soap making recipes recommend using the brown lye water in the same strength as it was originally created when the rainwater was poured through the ashes. This method requires a much larger soap making pot and it also adds several hours to the soap stirring process. This is the traditional method that was used in the 1800's and it is the method that is still used today in many third-world countries. If you have a really, really old soap making recipe then this is probably the method it describes. The major difficulty with this method is that it requires considerable skill and experience to consistently produce usable soap. Relatively minor mistakes or poor timing when using this method will result in a batch of nasty stuff that is neither soap nor anything else worth using. That is the reason this method was abandoned by our ancestors when commercial lye crystals became available at the local hardware and general store. Lye crystals significantly reduced the time required to make soap and they also yielded consistent batches of good usable soap.

Method 2 - Lye Crystals: Some modern soap making recipes recommend boiling down the brown lye water until nothing remains except lye crystals and then saving the lye crystals in a safe container for future use. Later, when you want to make soap, you add the lye crystals to a little fresh rainwater and make fresh lye water. This method adds an **unnecessary** step to the soap making process and it does involve some danger when reconstituting the lye crystals into lye water. (Note: These homemade lye crystals are very similar to the lye crystals that were once widely available at most hardware and grocery stores. However, it is no longer possible to purchase lye crystals at the grocery store because they were withdrawn from the market because they were being used to make illegal drugs.)

Method 3 - Concentrated Brown Lye Water: This is the method I developed out of necessity and it is much more practical than either of the above two methods. Boil one gallon of normal strength brown lye water down into 3/8 cup of concentrated brown lye water. If you boil the brown lye water down **before** you use it in a soap recipe then you can reduce the amount of time it takes to stir the soap mixture by several hours. This also simplifies the trial and error method of combining the lye water and the grease and it significantly reduces the possibility of making a failed batch of unusable soap. If you start with one-gallon (16 cups) of original strength brown lye water then it usually takes between 3 to 4 hours to **boil it down to 3/8 cup of concentrated brown lye water**, depending on the amount of heat used. This means you will have reduced the subsequent old fashioned soap stirring procedure by at least 3 to 4 hours. As the water gradually boils away the boiling process begins to proceed faster and faster because there is less water remaining in the pot. By the time the water is down to one-quart or less it boils away very quickly so you will then need to watch it carefully to make sure you don't boil off all your water. (Note: If you make a mistake and you boil the one-gallon of brown lye water down into less than 3/8 cup of concentrated brown lye water then wait until the concentrated brown lye water cools a little bit and then add just enough rainwater to return the concentrated brown lye water to the 3/8 cup mark. Add the rainwater slowly and be careful because the mixture may sputter a little bit.)

(Final Note: The "Grandpappy's Homemade Soap Recipe" that I developed through trial and error specifies the use of the **concentrated brown lye water** made by following Method 3. However, as mentioned previously, most really old soap making recipes recommend putting the brown lye water and grease into a big pot and cooking it over a big fire for several hours and stirring it while it cooked. The reason for the big fire was because they were using original strength brown lye water that contained too much water to make soap. Therefore they had to boil the water off and this frequently resulted in a failed batch of soap, or a batch of soap that was gritty, lye heavy, and of very poor quality. If you follow my "Grandpappy's Homemade Soap Recipe" you will notice that it is **not** necessary to cook the soap mixture. The reason is because the brown lye water has already been boiled down to the correct ratio of water to grease using Method 3. If a person does not know about Method 3 then he or she will probably invest a lot of time and energy in a multitude of unsuccessful attempts to make soap and repeat the very same mistakes our ancestors did in the 1800s before the invention and sale of commercial lye crystals.)

Summary

A brief summary of the most important critical information from "Grandpappy's Homemade Soap Recipe" is as follows:

1. Boiled rainwater poured through ten cups of tightly packed ashes from a hardwood fire will yield one gallon of average strength brown lye water.
2. One gallon of average strength brown lye water should be boiled down to 3/8 cup of concentrated brown lye water.
3. 3/4 cup of concentrated brown lye water should be mixed with 2 cups of warm grease which was made from melting (rendering) almost any type of animal fat.
4. When stirred the lye and grease will combine together in a chemical reaction to make soap. This normally takes between 30 minutes to 3 hours. The soap mixture must be kept above the melting point of the type of animal fat you are using.
5. When the soap mixture traces then pour it into a mold and let it rest for one to seven days, depending on the type of animal fat used. Then remove the soap from the soap mold.
6. Air dry the soap for another 2 to 6 weeks. The chemical reaction will then be 100% complete and all the lye and grease will be gone. The lye and grease will have been converted into homemade soap.

The major contributions my soap recipe adds to the body of knowledge about soap making are items 1, 2, and 3 above. Items 4, 5, and 6 above can be found in any good soap making book and at a variety of internet web sites, with both minor and major variations.

Conclusion

Knowing how to consistently and successfully make soap from rainwater, campfire ashes, and animal fat takes you one step closer to becoming an independent resourceful human being in God's natural order of things.

Chapter Fifty-Six

Other Basic Skills and Information

How to Make Charcoal

There are both simple and sophisticated ways to make charcoal. If you only need a little charcoal for a small forge then the following simple method is a reasonable option.

Any wood you use should be relatively dry. It should have dried in the sun for several months. If you use freshly cut wood then the cooking process will take **much** longer.

Any hardwood may be used, such as oak, hickory, or maple. Charcoal made from hardwoods requires a longer cooking time but the hardwood charcoal will burn longer.

If you use soft wood, such as pine, it will produce soft charcoal that burns quickly. It takes less cooking time to turn soft woods into charcoal. However, soft wood charcoal is the best type for use in a forge. It burns quicker and produces more heat and therefore it is ideal for producing the heat needed for welding and making metals.

Do **not** mix hardwoods and softwoods together when making charcoal. They don't have the same cooking times.

If you cook the wood too long it will burn down into a pile of ashes. The cooking time will vary based on the type of wood, the amount of moisture in the wood, and the size of the wood chunks. Hardwood cooking time will vary from 3 to 6 hours.

Cut some hardwood into small pieces about 2 or 3 inches thick and 3 to 6 inches long. Place inside a cast iron Dutch Oven and cover with a tight fitting lid. Place the Dutch Oven in the hot coals of a campfire and allow the hardwood chunks to cook for several hours. You will need to cover the Dutch Oven and the bed of coals with a thin layer of dirt to keep air from getting into the Dutch Oven.

When the temperature inside the Dutch Oven gets to approximately 480 degrees Fahrenheit (250°C) then the wood begins to decompose and it begins to release gas and vapors. The smoke escaping from around the lid of the Dutch Oven contains poisonous carbon monoxide, carbon dioxide, oxygen, hydrogen, nitrogen, methane, alcohols, tars, and organic compounds. The remaining charcoal is mostly carbon and it is about 1/4 the size of the original wood pieces you started with.

Remove the Dutch Oven from the campfire coals. Allow the oven to completely cool before you remove the lid. If you remove the lid while the oven is still hot then the charcoal on the inside will ignite when it comes into contact with the outside air.

(Note: Activated charcoal is made by letting a very small amount of oxygen into the Dutch Oven while the charcoal is still hot. The oxygen eats many tiny holes into the surface of the charcoal. These tiny holes will trap undesirable molecules from any water that is poured over the charcoal and help to clean the water.)

Large Bodies of Water

An extremely large body of water will retain heat. During the day the water will absorb the heat from the sun. During the night the water will release its heat into the air above the water. This helps to stabilize the temperatures in the immediate area and it minimizes the temperature extremes in those areas. This is extremely important for anyone who lives close to a large body of water. Your daytime temperatures will be a little lower during hot weather and your nighttime temperatures will be a little higher during cold weather. This can help to eliminate the impact of a late freeze in the spring and an early freeze in the fall. In other words, it can have a positive agricultural impact on crops and fruit trees.

How to Make 100% Pure Maple Syrup or Maple Brown Sugar

1. Locate a mature sugar maple tree. A sugar maple tree will yield the highest quality sap for maple syrup. However, all maple trees will produce maple sap but the volume and quality of that sap will not be as good as a sugar maple tree.
2. The best time to collect the maple sap is in the very early spring when the weather is warm during the day but the nights are cold. At this time the sap will be "rising" in the tree.
3. Drill a 7/16 inch diameter hole about four inches deep into the trunk of the tree approximately two to four feet above the ground. Drill the hole so it is pointed slightly upwards into the tree so the sap will flow down out of the tree as a result of gravity. Do not drill a hole in the same spot or at the same height every year. Always drill into a different location in the tree trunk each year.
4. Cut a one-half inch outside diameter hollow plastic pipe about seven inches long. The diameter of the plastic pipe should be just a tiny bit bigger than the hole you just drilled. Carefully wash the plastic pipe and then dry the pipe.
5. Use a clean hammer to drive the clean hollow plastic pipe about one or two inches into the hole with the end of the hollow pipe sticking out about five or six inches beyond the trunk of the tree and directly above a clean bucket on the ground. (Or you can hang a bucket on a nail driven into the tree just above and just a little to the side of the plastic pipe.) Do **not** push the plastic pipe all the way into the tree to the end of the hole you drilled. There should be several inches of clearance inside the tree between the end of the hole and the end of the plastic pipe. This will allow the sap to easily enter the end of the pipe and then begin to flow down the pipe out past the trunk of the tree into the clean bucket.
6. Pour the maple sap every day into another clean bucket and then replace the old bucket under the plastic pipe. Take the sap home with you each day. (Note: When the sap stops flowing you should remove the plastic pipe so the tree can heal itself. Save the plastic pipe for the following year.)
7. Each day, or at least every other day, process the maple sap. Begin by straining the sap through a cheesecloth or a very clean cross weave dish towel. Then put it into a big cook pot with no more than 1.5-inches of sap in the bottom of the pot and bring it to a very gentle boil. Stir the sap while you are boiling off the excess moisture to prevent the sap from sticking to the pot and making a burnt mess. One gallon of maple sap will boil down into about one-third cup of maple syrup.
    a. If you want **maple syrup** then stop the process when the sap has become a thick syrup and the taste is extremely sweet.
    b. If you want **maple brown sugar** then continue to boil the syrup. Watch it continuously because after most of the excess moisture has boiled off it will crystallize into a "brown sugar" very rapidly. When this happens turn off the heat and allow the maple sugar to cool.

    Store the maple syrup or the maple sugar in clean air-tight containers in a cool dark area.
8. For long-term storage process the maple syrup using glass Mason jars and follow the standard instructions for canning food.

How to Make Cloth Mittens

Use any old piece of scrap cloth, such as a worn out shirt, jeans, or dress. Fold the old piece of cloth in half with the inside of the cloth on the outside and pit it together with straight pins. Place the person's left and right hands on the cloth and draw around the outside of each hand with the thumb extended and all four fingers closed together. Draw the wrist straight down on both sides below the bottom of the thumb and the bottom of the little finger to provide enough space for the hand to enter the mitten. Cut out the patterns leaving at least one-inch of extra cloth all the way around the pattern. Place two pattern pieces together so the inside of the cloth is facing out. Sew around the outside of the pattern but do **not** sew the wrist opening closed. Then turn the mittens inside out so the face of the cloth is on the outside and the stitches are on the inside of the mittens. You may hem around the wrist opening of each mitten if you wish.

Chapter Fifty-Seven

Self-Defense

Before discussing some self-defense options let me begin by suggesting the best strategy for winning any type of fight . . . **run away**. Do not engage in a fight just because somebody else is eager to fight with you. If you can run faster than your adversaries then you will have won the fight without losing a lot of blood and maybe even your life. Therefore always consider the option of running away first.

If running away is not possible then you will need to engage your attackers with everything you've got. In other words, you best chance of winning is to use overwhelming force. You did not ask for this fight but you if are forced into it then you should be determined that you are either going to win the fight or you are going to die trying. What you are not going to do is to gracefully stand still and let someone else kill you. And please don't waste one precious second trying to talk your way out of the situation because that will only give your attackers a chance to get into better positions closer to you and all around you so they can bring you down without risking any type of injury to themselves.

Now that running away has been discussed, what are some other options for self-defense? If you have always wanted to learn some form of marital arts (karate, judo, boxing, etc.) then there is nothing wrong with pursuing this course of study. Not only will you benefit from the rigorous exercises but you will also learn how to protect yourself in a hand-to-hand self-defense environment.

However, there are a few shortcomings to these types of training:

1. You will be taught to obey certain rules in order to compete in contests and to avoid seriously injuring your opponent.
2. Although these skills will be with you your entire life (the same as learning how to ride a bicycle), as you gradually age you will become less effective than you were when you were younger.
3. In a life-threatening hand-to-hand self-defense situation your opponent will not be obeying any rules and he or she will be trying to blind you, permanently cripple you, and kill you.
4. In a life-threatening self-defense situation you will probably be attacked by someone who wants the odds in his or her favor and that person will use a loaded firearm or a knife and you will be attacked from the rear without any advance warning.
5. In a life-threatening self-defense situation you will probably be attacked by a least two people and sometimes three or more. The odds will be against you from the very start.

I only mention the above in order to help you make the transition from what you see in the movies to a real life self-defense situation. If you are attacked in real life then you will need to be able to at least equal the odds against you. This means you should also have a loaded firearm and a knife and you should have some basic knowledge of how to use them. If you are attacked from behind and the other person draws first blood then you would at least have the means to inflict some serious damage on your attackers before you die. If your initial wounds are not fatal then you would also have the opportunity to terminate your attackers and maybe even survive your ordeal.

How to Defend Yourself Using a Knife or a Firearm

During a serious hard times tragedy event you should have a permit to carry a concealed firearm. You should select a small firearm that you can carry with you all the time in one of your pockets. Please read and obey the firearm carry rules in your state. If you cross the state line then you will need to comply with the firearm carry rules in that other state. Most states in the United States of America will not recognize a firearm permit issued by another state. You will need to research the firearm carry rules in all the states adjacent to the state that issued your license.

During a serious hard times tragedy event your should also carry a folding pocket knife. Each state has it own laws for what you can legally carry and these laws usually limit the length of the blade. Please read and obey the pocket knife rules in your state.

After you have acquired a firearm and a folding pocket knife for self-defense you should learn how to use them safely and effectively. This can be accomplished by taking a self-defense class in your local area or by purchasing and reading a book on self-defense using knifes and firearms.

With the above thoughts in mind I suggest that you download and print a hard-copy of the following Marine training manual, **Kill or Get Killed**, and that you put that copy inside a three-ring binder. Then I suggest that you read the manual from cover-to-cover. *However, I strongly recommend that you do not share any of this knowledge with anyone else and that especially includes your children.* When children are playing they sometimes don't realize how deadly some of their actions can be and you don't want to teach them something they could use to kill or permanently cripple another child.

Following are two web sites where you may download **Kill or Get Killed**:
http://www.weaponscombat.com/unarmed-combat/kill-or-get-killed.html
http://ebookee.org/Kill-or-Get-Killed-U-S-Marine-Corps-official-training_647122.html

Firearm Maintenance

Firearms are useful for self-defense and for hunting. During a serious long-term tragedy event both of these activities will probably become far more crucial to your survival than they are today.

You will need to occasionally take your firearms apart and clean or repair them. If you are outdoors and you get caught in a sudden thunderstorm then when you get home you will need to be able to take your firearm apart and wipe all the internal parts completely dry. You can find complete disassembly and reassembly instructions for almost every firearm you now own available for free download on the internet. You should locate these instructions, save a digital copy on your computer and on your flash drive, and you should print a hard-copy and put it with your gunsmithing tools. Walmart sells a reasonable set of basic Gunsmith Tools in their Sporting Goods Section for less than $10.

It would also be a very good idea to purchase the following book. It includes disassembly instructions for many of the more popular firearms that are widely available. Even though you may not own all the firearms discussed in the following book, it would be nice to have that information available because nobody knows how the future will unfold and what weapons you may actually be using ten or twenty years from now.

Survival Gunsmithing, J.B. Wood, 1986.

You should have the following minimum inventory of ammunition for each of your firearms:
    1,000 rounds for your handgun.
    1,000 rounds for your hunting rifle.
    5,000 rounds of 22LR ammunition.

If you have a shotgun then you should have 1,000 shotgun shells in a variety of sizes such as the following:
    100 one-ounce sabot slugs.
    200 00-buckshot.
    700 assorted shot sizes such as 4, 6, 7, 7 1/2, or whatever you can find available.

Chapter Fifty-Eight

Should You Own a Firearm?

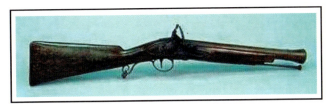

The United States' Constitutional Bill of Rights

Amendment I - Freedom of Religion, Freedom of Speech, Freedom of the Press, Freedom to Peaceably Assemble - December 15, 1791.
Congress shall make no law respecting an establishment of religion, or prohibiting the free exercise thereof; or abridging the freedom of speech, or of the press; or the right of the people peaceably to assemble, and to petition the Government for a redress of grievances.

Amendment II - Right to Bear Arms - December 15, 1791.
A well regulated Militia, being necessary to the security of a free State, the right of the people to keep and bear Arms, shall not be infringed.

A Simple Explanation of the First Two Amendments to the Constitution of the United States

If you do not want to attend church then you do not have to. However, if you do want to go to church then the Constitution of the United States protects your right to attend the church of your choice and no person, or group of persons, or government has the right to prevent you from exercising your freedom of religion.

If you do not want to read a particular magazine or newspaper or internet web site then you do not have to. However, if you do want to read a magazine or newspaper or internet web site then the Constitution of the United States protects your right to read the material of your choice and no person, or group of persons, or government has the right to prevent you from exercising your freedom in this area.

If you do not want to own a firearm then you do not have to. However, if you do want to own a firearm then the Constitution of the United States protects your right to own and carry a firearm and no person, or group of persons, or government has the right to prevent you from exercising your right to bear arms.

A Brief Historical Overview

A government cannot subjugate and persecute its citizens if those citizens have:

1. the right to own and carry firearms, and
2. the right to purchase, store, and/or reload the ammunition necessary for those firearms.

History is replete with examples of entire societies that were destroyed by governments who first disarmed their citizens using the illusion of peace and safety. After peaceably disarming all of its citizens those governments then systematically passed new laws and imposed new taxes. Any citizen who voiced a dissenting opinion was quickly arrested and a public example was made of that person to discourage any further resistance or opposition.

Those government leaders then quickly expanded their power and assumed the same rights and privileges as the kings of olden days. They become the ruling elite and they enjoyed all the power and privileges of their office. Everyone else became an expendable slave. This included the individuals in lower level government positions. If they did not enforce the rules of their leaders then they would be eliminated and replaced with someone who would obey.

The quality of life for those high level government leaders improved for a short period of time as they legally and illegally robbed the citizens under their jurisdiction through taxes, confiscation, imprisonment, and the death sentence. However, their prosperity did not last indefinitely because those leaders didn't produce anything of value. They didn't grow food, they didn't manage a ranch with livestock, they didn't make clothing, they didn't build transportation vehicles, they didn't repair those vehicles, they didn't do anything except steal from the people who did all the honest necessary jobs within that society. But the people who did those jobs quickly realized there was no benefit in working diligently so they only pretended to work and production dropped off dramatically. When that happened there was no surplus being produced. There was not even enough to satisfy all the high level government leaders. Therefore the government eventually collapsed and a new form of government emerged to take its place. But unless that new government was different from its predecessor then it also did not last.

The original authors of the United States Constitution understood the above concepts. They did not want a government similar to the one from which they had just won their freedom. Instead they drafted the Constitution of the United States with its Bill of Rights in an effort to create a lasting government that would be subject to the people it governed. To help guarantee that the new U.S. government did not subjugate its citizens the authors of the Constitution gave all U.S. citizens the right to own firearms without any restrictions ("the right of the people to keep and bear Arms, shall not be infringed.").

The Future of Individual Liberty

Individual human rights will never be protected by any government or by any law. All governments (democracy, republic, socialist, communist) will subjugate and trample upon the rights of the common people if they can get away with it. The only way common people can lead lives of safety and enjoy freedom from tyranny and crime is if the common people have a power that is equal to their leaders and to the criminals who live among them.

Physical combat weapons such as swords and spears and shields do not provide that equality because a stronger taller person has a decisive advantage over a smaller weaker person.

On the other hand, a modern firearm makes all people equal. A five-foot tall 90-pound female can successfully resist an attack from a seven-foot tall 250-pound male if she has a loaded firearm in her hand. (Note: If you are a lady and you are considering the purchase of a firearm then I suggest you purchase and read the following book written by a woman from a woman's point a view: **Effective Defense: the Woman, the Plan, the Gun**, 2nd Edition, by Gila Hayes, 2000.)

A modern firearm helps to make all people truly equal, including:
1. criminals and their potential victims, and
2. government leaders and the people they govern.

If you take away the right of the common people to own and carry firearms, then you place those people at the mercy of unscrupulous government officials, politicians, and criminals. This is why the authors of the Constitution of the United States drafted the first two amendments to the Constitution. The first two amendments guarantee all the other freedoms that the citizens of the United States currently enjoy. If you restrict or modify either of those first two amendments then in a very short period of time the United States will no longer be the land of the free. Instead it will become the land of the wealthy and their slaves. And those slaves will be expendable at the discretion of our government leaders.

If you personally do not want to own a firearm then you do not have to. You may simply depend on someone else to protect your rights.

However, if the only people who have firearms are:
1. government officials and their police force, and
2. the law-breaking criminals within your society,

then you will have no rights at all.

Chapter Fifty-Eight: Should You Own a Firearm?

Conclusion

At the current time in the United States of America each adult has the right to legally purchase and own one or more firearms. You also currently have the right to legally purchase and own a variety of other firearm related items, such as ammunition, scopes, laser sights, holsters, high capacity magazines, and reloading equipment and supplies.

You may choose to exercise your rights in this area or you may choose to ignore them. If you choose to exercise your rights then you can always sell your firearms and other items at some future date if you decide you no longer want them.

But if you choose to ignore your current rights and those rights are taken away from you at some future date then you may end up wishing you had exercised your rights when you could have legally done so.

Chapter Fifty-Eight: Should You Own a Firearm?

Self-Defense

Jesus said, "If someone slaps you turn unto him the other cheek."
Do not let the insult lead to violence -- respond instead by being meek.

Jesus also said, "When you are persecuted in one place flee to another."
Paul descended the Damascus wall with the help of a Christian brother.
Peter fled Jerusalem after being freed from prison by an Angel of grace.
After Stephen was stoned many Christians had to flee to a safer place.

Jesus also said, "If you don't have one, sell your coat and buy a sword."
Several hours later Jesus said to Peter when he tried to defend his Lord,
"Put your sword away. He who draws the sword will die by violence."
Do not use your sword to attack but keep it in reserve for self-defense.

Abraham took the men of his household whom he had trained and
he rescued his captured nephew Lot from an army invading the land.
When Nehemiah supervised the rebuilding of the wall at Jerusalem,
all the workers either wore a sword or they kept one beside them.

"You shall not murder" God commanded from the top of mount Sinai.
It is **not** murder if a person defends himself and his attacker does die.
God explained, "If a thief breaks in at night and he is killed by another,
the defender of the home is innocent and he is **not** guilty of murder."

In summary Jesus said: Be meek but carry a weapon for self-defense.
If you see danger headed your way then flee to avoid its consequence.
If you are attacked and it is not possible to retreat to a place of safety,
then show courage and defend your life and the lives of your family.

Also remember that Jesus said, "Love your enemies and pray for them,"
and whenever possible tell others about Jesus, the only way to heaven.

Scripture References: Romans 12:18-19, Matthew 5:38-45, Matthew 10:23,
Second Corinthians 11:32-33, Acts 12:5-10, Acts 12:16-17, Acts 7:59 to 8:4, Luke 22:36-38,
John 18:10-11, Genesis 14: 11-16, Nehemiah 4:16-18, Exodus 20:13, Exodus 22:2-3, Proverbs 24:10-11.

Poem: Self-Defense

Chapter Fifty-Nine

Should You Have a Concealed Carry Firearms License?

At the current time in many states you may legally acquire a Concealed Carry Firearm License by completing the appropriate paperwork, passing a background check, and paying a small fee.

If you are awarded a Concealed Carry Firearms License then you should study the firearm carry rules for your state and obey them. You should also enroll in a firearms training course and learn the correct safe way to carry and use a firearm.

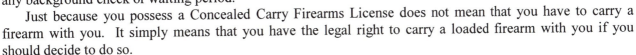

If you have a Concealed Carry Firearms License then you can legally purchase a firearm and immediately take possession of that firearm without any background check or waiting period.

Just because you possess a Concealed Carry Firearms License does not mean that you have to carry a firearm with you. It simply means that you have the legal right to carry a loaded firearm with you if you should decide to do so.

If our society gradually or suddenly collapses then you would be legally licensed to carry a firearm for your own personal self-defense and for the defense of your family members.

f you should ever need to use a firearm in self-defense then you will have demonstrated to the court that you had previously complied with the existing laws for carrying a firearm.

If you are awarded a Concealed Carry Firearms License then you will be one more honest person in your state who has the legal right to carry a firearm and you will be sending a very simple but crystal clear message to your congressmen and other government leaders.

If the government passes new legislation that prohibits non-licensed individuals from owning or using a firearm in self-defense then you may be "exempt" if you already have a Concealed Carry Firearms License.

One Possible Concealed Carry Handgun: If you do not already own a firearm that you could carry on a regular basis then I suggest the Ruger LCP that fires the 380 ammunition. I also suggest that you install a Crimson Trace laser sight on this pistol. The laser sight is automatically activated when you grip the pistol in your hand. If you purchase the Crimson Trace laser it will include a nice carrying pouch that can be used to transport the Ruger LCP in your pocket. The reasons I suggest this specific pistol are: it is an exceptionally high quality very reliable semi-automatic 6-shot pistol, it is relatively flat (less than 3/4-inch) which means it can fit into your pants' pocket without creating the normal silhouette outline of a gun, it is very light weight even when fully loaded (12 ounces), and it fires a 380 caliber bullet which is very similar to the 9mm bullet. I also recommend that you install the finger extension on the bottom of the 6-round magazine to make the pistol more comfortable to grip and to shoot accurately. Also purchase at least 500 rounds of hollow-point ammunition for this pistol.

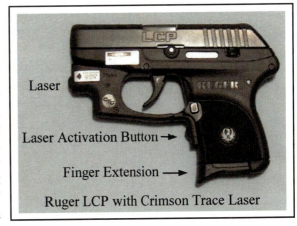

Ruger LCP with Crimson Trace Laser

Conclusion: At the current time you have the legal right to apply for a Concealed Carry Firearms License. It would be sad if you decided that other things were more important and you continue to keep this task at the bottom of your "Future To Do List." One day you may seriously regret that you did not take action on this matter when it was still legally possible for you to do so.

Chapter Sixty

Firearm Safety Rules

Always obey your local, state, and national firearm laws and regulations. These rules and laws do change occasionally so you will need to determine what the current laws are and then you should obey those laws.

Everyone should enroll in a firearms training and safety course and learn the proper safe way to use firearms and then consistently practice those firearm safety rules.

Whenever you are handling a firearm please adhere to the following universally accepted firearm safety rules.

The four universally accepted firearm safety rules:

1. **Always** treat every firearm as if it were loaded and ready to fire.
2. **Never** point a firearm at anyone or anything you do not intend to kill or destroy.
3. **Never** put your finger on the trigger until the sights are aligned on the target.
4. Positively **identify your target** (no guessing) and everything behind your target the bullet might hit.

In addition you should also adhere to the following safety advice:

Grandpappy's safety advice:

1. Always wear safety glasses when shooting any type of firearm.
2. Always wear some type of hearing protection when shooting any type of firearm.
3. Do **not** store or carry your firearm with a live round in the firing position in front of the firing pin. Wait until you are actually ready to use your weapon before you insert a live round into the firing chamber.
4. Do **not** use your rifle scope to look at other hunters. Use binoculars instead.

Chapter Sixty-One

Bolt-Action Rifle or Semi-Auto Rifle?
Revolver or Semi-Auto Pistol?

Introduction

The debate over the advantages and disadvantages of the different types of firearms has been going on for at least one-hundred years.

There is absolutely no way this chapter will in any way influence that debate because the "battle lines" have already been drawn and too many individuals have already taken one side or the other. Once a person has taken a firm position on one of these topics and expressed his or her own firm opinion about the topic then it is almost impossible to get that individual to objectively analyze the subject from a fresh perspective because that person has already made up his or her own mind and therefore the subject is closed as far as he or she is concerned.

On the other hand, if you are flexible in your thinking and you are willing to objectively review all the facts before making a decision then the following information may be of interest to you.

This chapter will review each of the following types of firearms:

1. Bolt Action, Lever Action, and Semi-Automatic Rifles.
2. Revolvers and Semi-Automatic Pistols.

The discussion of the above firearms will be based on accuracy, dependability, ease of use, and suitability for a specific application.

Accuracy

The accuracy of any firearm is directly related to all the following variables:

1. The quality of the firearm or the company that made the weapon.
2. The firearm itself.
3. The condition of the firearm and how well it has been maintained.
4. The type of sighting system used, such as iron sights, scope, or laser.
5. The length of the barrel.
6. The type of ammunition being used.
7. The distance to the target and the prevailing environmental conditions.
8. The skill of the individual shooting the firearm.

Let's examine each of the above topics one-at-a-time.

1. The quality of the firearm or the company that made the weapon.

The quality of a firearm will be directly proportional to its accuracy. Each firearm manufacturer has its own unique manufacturing operations for the production of its firearms. Although these operations may be similar to those used by other companies they are not identical in every way. Therefore there will be differences in the quality of the firearms made by different companies because of the different types of raw materials used, how those raw materials are brought together into the finished firearm, and the quality tolerances and procedures used at each step in the firearm manufacturing process.

In addition, the **same exact company** may also make different models of firearms from a variety of different raw materials using different quality standards for each type of raw material, such as stainless steel or blued steel. Therefore the quality of the firearms made by the **same exact company** will also be different.

However, the firearms made by a reputable high quality firearm manufacturer will normally always be superior to the firearms made by a low quality firearms manufacturer. Therefore if you compared a high quality bolt-action rifle to a low quality semi-auto rifle then you would probably be impressed with the accuracy of the bolt-action rifle. On the other hand, if you compared a high quality semi-auto rifle to a low quality bolt-action rifle then you would probably be impressed with the accuracy of the semi-auto rifle.

Therefore a broad general statement such as "All XXX type firearms are always superior to all YYY type firearms" would simply not be true.

2. The firearm itself.

All the firearms of the same exact model made by the same exact company will **not** have identical accuracies. There will always be **some** accuracy differences between these same exact firearms made by the same exact company. The vast majority of them, or about 96%, will have what is known as the average accuracy for that particular firearm. A small number of them, or about 2%, will have inferior accuracy for that particular firearm (a lemon). And a small number of them, or about 2%, will have superior accuracy for that particular firearm (a cherry). This is based on the bell shaped normal curve which does apply to firearm manufacturing.

Unless you have personally fired more than one of these identical firearms yourself in a side-by-side comparison under identical conditions using exactly the same type of ammunition then you will not be able to determine whether or not the firearm you actually have is average, inferior, or superior in regards to accuracy.

Therefore to make any type of statement about the accuracy of any firearm based on the results of **one** of those firearms would be inappropriate. Unfortunately most of the review articles I have read on the internet and in a variety of firearm magazines are based on the accuracy of one and only one firearm as opposed to a random sample of five or ten of these identical firearms. Most of these articles include a review of the performance of different types of ammunition at different target distances but the conclusions are still based on using one firearm in all the tests.

3. The condition of the firearm and how well it has been maintained.

The bullet travels inside the bore of the firearm until it exits the firearm and then it continues on its way towards the target. Depending on the condition of the inside bore of the firearm the bullet may or may not hit the target where you originally aimed. Therefore the condition of the inside bore of the firearm is extremely important to firearm accuracy.

If the firearm has been properly maintained during its entire life then the inside bore of the firearm should be clean and the internal grooves should be free of any type of powder, lead, or cleaning solvent buildup. If the internal bore is clean and it has not been damaged using the wrong type of cleaning tools or cleaning chemicals, or the improper use of those cleaning tools or chemicals, then the firearm will be as accurate as it can be based on the condition of its bore. But if the bore has been damaged in any way then the firearm will no longer be capable of placing shots in a reasonably accurate manner.

4. The type of sighting system used, such as iron sights, scope, or laser.

Some iron sights are adjustable and some are not. If the iron sights on your firearm are adjustable then you should take the time to learn how to properly adjust them for the type of ammunition you will normally be using at the average distance you will normally be shooting.

However, regardless of the quality of the iron sights on your firearm the accuracy of your firearm can be significantly improved with the addition of either a scope or a laser.

A **scope** is appropriate for a **rifle**. Regardless of whether or not you wear glasses your ability to see details gradually decreases with distance. If you are two feet away from a leaf then you can probably see all the details in the surface of that leaf. But if you are 100 yards away from that leaf then you will probably only be able to identify that it is a leaf and nothing more. A **scope** magnifies objects and makes them easier to see. This is a significant advantage in helping you hold your rifle steady on the center of the target as you gradually squeeze the trigger. Therefore at distances of 100 yards or more a person using a scope on a rifle will be more accurate than that same person shooting that same rifle without a scope at the same distance.

A **laser** is appropriate for a **handgun**. A **laser** allows you to see the approximate spot of bullet impact when you are standing within 50 yards of your target. The laser allows you to hold your handgun steady while you gradually squeeze the trigger. Therefore a person using a handgun laser will be more accurate than that same person shooting the same handgun without a laser at the same distance.

Therefore when discussing firearm accuracy, either a rifle scope or a handgun laser will significantly improve the accuracy of that firearm when compared to its original iron sights.

5. **The length of the barrel.**

On both a handgun and a rifle the longer the barrel the more accurate the weapon will be. However, on both handguns and rifles there is a point of diminishing marginal returns and extra length beyond that point does not significantly improve accuracy and it may even reduce accuracy.

Therefore it is not fair to compare two firearms with different barrel lengths. For example, it would not be fair to compare a rifle with a 20-inch barrel to a rifle with a 28-inch barrel. It would also not be fair to compare a handgun with a 4-inch barrel to a handgun with a 7-inch barrel. A longer barrel gives the longer weapon a decisive advantage in accuracy.

6. **The type of ammunition being used.**

In a handgun a heavier grain bullet is usually more accurate than a lighter grain bullet.

Some ammunition companies produce higher quality ammunition than other companies. Even the same exact ammunition company has different grades of ammunition and their premium ammunition usually costs more than their target ammunition.

Therefore it is not appropriate to compare different firearms if those firearms are shooting different grain weight bullets made by different companies because you are introducing another significant accuracy variable into the equation.

7. **The distance to the target and the prevailing environmental conditions.**

As the **distance** to the target increases the accuracy of the firearm at hitting that target decreases.

As the **environmental conditions** change, such as the speed and direction of the wind, then the accuracy of the firearm will be impacted.

The **trajectory** of the bullet does not remain constant on its way to the target and this also introduces another variable into the accuracy equation.

Therefore distance, environmental conditions, and bullet trajectory all impact the accuracy of a firearm.

8. **The skill of the individual shooting the firearm.**

Some individuals are extremely skilled at shooting firearms and they can accurately hit targets that most of us cannot hit using the same exact firearm and ammunition. Most of us are average marksmen and we can hit targets with an average degree of accuracy but we will never be able to replicate the performance of an expert marksman. Therefore the individual shooting the firearm is another variable in the accuracy equation.

Accuracy Summary:

Based on the above there are many different variables that impact the accuracy of a firearm. If you are interested in an honest comparison between two or more different firearms then you need to keep as many of the above variables as constant as possible to avoid having biased results in your final analysis.

(Note: One additional critical issue in the choice of a firearm is that the firearm should "feel right" when you are holding it. If the handgun feels comfortable in your hand then your average accuracy with that handgun will be better than a handgun that doesn't fit into your hand correctly. The same concept applies to rifles. The rifle should feel comfortable when holding it in a standard shooting position.)

Dependability

Dependability: Does the firearm function correctly every time you use it?

Historical review:

1. Some single-shot firearms have failed in use.
2. Some bolt-action rifles have failed in use.
3. Some lever-action rifles have failed in use.
4. Some semi-auto rifles have failed in use.
5. Some revolvers have failed in use.
6. Some semi-auto pistols have failed in use.

In other words, there is no mass produced firearm in the world that can claim it has never, ever failed in use. If sand or any other type of debris gets into the internal moving parts of a revolver, or a bolt-action rifle, or a lever-action rifle, or a semi-auto then it will **not** function properly.

Disassembling, cleaning, and reassembling most semi-auto firearms and most bolt-action rifles is usually easier than disassembling, cleaning, and reassembling a revolver or a lever-action rifle. Based on my past experience if you have a problem with a revolver then you will probably need to have it serviced by a professional gunsmith. On the other hand, if you have a problem with a bolt-action rifle or a semi-auto firearm then you may be able to correct the problem yourself.

It should also be noted that there are some major differences in the dependability of some specific firearms because of:

1. the design of that specific firearm, or
2. the company that manufactured that firearm.

The published literature on the internet and in a variety of firearm publications contain numerous examples of specific "cheap" firearms that either: (1) have design defects, or (2) were made by a company using poor quality materials and low quality standards. These "cheap" firearms should definitely be avoided.

On the other hand, to say that one entire broad category of firearms is better than all the others is simply not logical. For example, I could not honestly say that either a revolver or a semi-auto pistol is always more dependable than the other one.

In my opinion all the different broad categories of firearms are equal in terms of dependability.

I fully realize that this point of view is offensive to individuals who have already decided that one type of firearm is more dependable than all the others. But that is my opinion based on my real world experience over the past forty years.

You are welcome to form your own opinion on this subject and it may be totally different from mine. And that is okay with me. Each of us is free to have his or her own opinion. However, to claim that our "opinion" is a "fact" is being somewhat presumptuous.

The most important issue is to have a firearm that is clean and that has performed dependably for you in the past.

Chapter Sixty-One: Single-Action or Semi-Automatic Firearms?

If you should need that firearm in the future then it will probably work in the same exact way it has in the past. Trying to predict the odds that your firearm is going to fail when you really need it is an intellectual exercise I do not wish to participate in.

Ease of Use

Most firearms work in basically the same way:

1. Insert a cartridge into the firearm chamber.
2. Aim the firearm at a target.
3. Squeeze the trigger to fire the bullet.

When we talk about being easy to use we usually mean how easy it is to load the weapon and how easy it is to clean the firearm.

Most revolvers, most bolt-action rifles, and most lever-action rifles are easier to load than a semi-auto firearm. You simply insert the cartridge into the firearm in its proper storage location and then use the firearm mechanism to move one of those cartridges into the firing chamber.

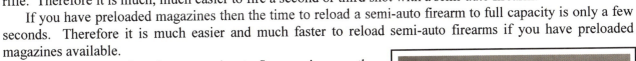

On a semi-auto firearm you must first load the cartridges into a magazine, and then insert that magazine into the firearm, and then use the firearm mechanism to move one of those cartridges into the firing position. Therefore a semi-auto firearm is just a little more complicated to load because the magazine is outside the firearm and after you have the magazine loaded then you must properly insert the magazine into the firearm.

On the other hand, after you fire one round through a semi-auto firearm the next cartridge is automatically moved into the firing position. This is much faster and much easier than using the mechanisms on a revolver, or a bolt-action rifle, or a lever-action rifle. Therefore it is much, much easier to fire a second or third shot with a semi-auto firearm.

If you have preloaded magazines then the time to reload a semi-auto firearm to full capacity is only a few seconds. Therefore it is much easier and much faster to reload semi-auto firearms if you have preloaded magazines available.

Finally, the capacity of most semi-auto firearms is more than the capacity of most revolvers, bolt-action rifles, and lever-action rifles. Therefore once the semi-auto firearm is loaded it will continue to shoot longer before you have to stop and reload it.

It is possible to purchase reloading clips for a bolt-action rifle and reloading wheels for a revolver but their capacities are a lot less than semi-auto magazines. In addition, these devices are not as easy to use or as fast to use as simply ejecting an empty magazine and inserting a full magazine into a semi-auto firearm.

One of the primary arguments that is made against semi-auto firearms is that it takes the average person longer to learn how to use a semi-auto firearm. This issue can be discussed for hours but the simple facts are those stated at the beginning of this section:

Most firearms work in basically the same way:

1. Insert a cartridge into the firearm chamber.
2. Aim the firearm at a target.
3. Squeeze the trigger to fire the bullet.

In my opinion there is almost no difference in how long it takes an average person to learn how to use any type of firearm. Therefore I can not say that one type of firearm has an advantage over any other type of firearm based on how easy it is to learn how to use.

In my opinion it does take a little more time and effort to clean semi-auto firearms when compared to the other types of firearms. However, this is a negligible issue and a person should not make a firearm decision based on the small difference in the time and effort required to clean those firearms.

Therefore based on an impartial review of **all** the above information it would appear that a person would be better advised to purchase a semi-auto firearm instead of a revolver, or bolt-action rifle, or lever-action rifle.

Suitability for a Specific Application

Firearms may be used in all the following situations:

1. Competition shooting events.
2. Casual target practice.
3. Hunting.
4. Combat.
5. Personal self-defense.

There are different categories for **competition shooting events** so if this is what you are interested in then you can find an event that specializes in almost any type of firearm you are personally interested in.

For the average person **casual target practice** is where he will use most of his ammunition. And casual target practice is also the subject of the vast majority of the firearm articles that have been posted on the internet and printed in a variety of firearm magazines. However, most of these articles attempt to extrapolate their target practice results to some other activity, such as hunting or combat or self-defense. The problem is that hunting and combat and self-defense are totally different from casually shooting at a target.

There are two basic types of **hunting** activities:

1. Hunting for sport.
2. Hunting for survival.

When you are hunting for sport the success or failure of your day's adventure does not impact the survival of your family.

But when your family is depending on you to bring something home to eat then the situation is entirely different. When confronted with starvation you do not wish to give the wild game animal a reasonable chance to escape. Therefore you will probably want to fire at least two or three quick shots into the animal's heart/lung chest cavity to seriously weaken it so it can not go very far after being shot. If you only put one round into the chest of the wild game animal then it could run away and die in a place where you will never be able to track it or find it. Therefore in a starvation survival situation you will probably want to put two or three quick shots into any wild game animal that you see. If you have a semi-automatic rifle then this is not too difficult to do. However, if you have a bolt-action or lever-action rifle then this is almost impossible to do.

(Note 1: Some hunting experts discourage firing more than one shot at a wild game animal for a number of reasons. For example, more shots mean more ruined meat. But which would your rather have: most of the meat or none of the meat?)

(Note 2: Please obey all your local, state, and federal hunting laws. These hunting laws normally limit the number of cartridges you can have in your firearm at one time when you are hunting wild game. This will normally require the purchase of **one** specially designed magazine that is blocked on its bottom so that no more than the legal number of cartridges can be inserted into that magazine.)

Combat is a totally different issue. In a combat situation the average soldier will almost always want to have a semi-automatic rifle for normal combat plus a semi-automatic pistol as an emergency backup weapon for close range encounters.

If you are unexpectedly confronted with a life-or-death **personal self-defense** situation then you will not have the time to think carefully and calmly the same way you do when you are shooting at targets. You will need to respond immediately with overwhelming force if you hope to survive. Overwhelming force means lots of ammunition that can be fired very, very quickly, and the ability to reload your firearm in seconds. You will not be able to call for a "time-out" while you try to reload your revolver or your bolt-action rifle or lever-action rifle. The individuals who are trying to kill you will take full advantage of your empty firearm and they will continue shooting at you until you are dead.

Therefore, in a survival hunting scenario, or a combat scenario, or a self-defense scenario the most appropriate choice would be a semi-automatic firearm. And if you can only carry one rifle and one handgun with you all the time, wouldn't it make good sense that those two weapons be semi-automatic firearms?

Conclusion

I have consistently recommended that individuals purchase semi-automatic firearms and learn the correct safe way to use them. However, until now I had not fully explained the reasons why I recommended semi-automatic firearms.

Now it is your turn to make a firearm choice that is appropriate for you and for your family. And please believe me when I say I don't mind if you completely disagree with me and you select a firearm that is not semi-automatic.

Footnote: Some Time-Honored Firearm Myths

The following statements about firearms have been around for at least fifty-years. When I was seriously considering the purchase of my first firearm about forty-years ago I was exposed to all of the following statements. And since these statements were printed in a variety of national firearm magazines and in some of the best firearm books available at that time, I simply accepted them as being true. However, with the passage of time and the opportunity to put these statements to a variety of real-world tests I have been able to gradually conclude that although each one is based on a small element of truth, the statement itself is really nothing more than a time-honored firearm myth.

Myth 1. Bolt-action rifles are more accurate than semi-auto rifles.
On the average this might be true. However, a high quality semi-auto rifle is usually more accurate than an inexpensive bolt-action rifle. A semi-auto rifle with a longer barrel is usually more accurate than a bolt-action rifle with a shorter barrel. Even when comparing two high-quality firearms with the same barrel length and shooting exactly the same ammunition at exactly the same distances, the bolt-action rifle is usually only a little more accurate than a semi-auto rifle. For example, an average shooter may be able to group his shots from a bolt-action rifle into a three-inch circle at 100 yards and into a six-inch circle at 200 yards. Using a semi-auto rifle the same exact average shooter may be able to group his shots into a four-inch circle at 100 yards and into an eight-inch circle at 200 yards. Therefore the bolt-action rifle is indeed a "little bit more accurate" than the semi-auto rifle. However, when you consider that the typical kill zone circle on a deer or larger game animal is approximately an eight-inch circle then this difference is not relevant. It would also not be relevant in a combat situation when shooting at enemy soldiers. Therefore the small difference in accuracy should not be a major factor in the choice of a firearm since both types of firearms will perform reasonably well in a typical hunting or combat situation in regards to accuracy.

Myth 2. A revolver is more accurate than a semi-auto pistol.
As explained at the very beginning of this article, firearm accuracy is dependent on a variety of factors such as barrel length and the quality of the firearm. Based on my own personal shooting experience my accuracy with a revolver and a semi-auto pistol using iron-sights is basically the same. And as the barrel length gets shorter on both firearms then my average accuracy declines accordingly. Fortunately, the accuracy

of both a revolver and a semi-auto pistol can be significantly improved by installing a laser on the handgun. This is especially true for short barrel handguns.

Myth 3. A revolver is more dependable and less subject to misfires than a semi-auto pistol.

On the average this might be true. However, a high quality semi-auto pistol, such as a Glock, will always out-perform an inexpensive revolver when it comes to average life expectancy and dependability. Therefore, just like the overwhelming vast majority of police officers, I would personally prefer to have a high-quality Glock semi-auto pistol instead of any revolver. This is not a "theoretical discussion issue" with a police officer because his or her life may occasionally depend on the handgun he or she is carrying.

Myth 4. One shot one kill.

This is pure Hollywood movie rubbish. Ask any experienced hunter, or police officer, or combat soldier about their opinion on this statement. After they finish laughing they will tell you that "occasionally" a single shot may be deadly but most of the time it takes multiple shots to do the job.

Chapter Sixty-Two

How to Hit the Target Bull's-Eye

What is a Bull's-Eye ?

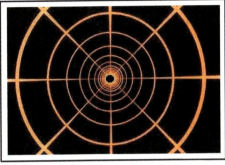

The word "bull's-eye" refers to the small black or red circle in the exact center of a target. It is possible that this term originated because the size of the flat center target circle was the same average size as the round eye of a bull. However, a real bull's-eye is not flat.

On the other hand, according to the "Encyclopedia of Word and Phrase Origins" by Robert Hendrickson (New York, 1997), a more likely origin for the word "bull's-eye" is based on the time and place that modern firearm targets were first introduced into competitive shooting matches. This occurred in England in the early 1800s. At that time in England people frequently placed "bets" on these events, similar to the way people bet on horse races today. The common wager at that time was a flat one crown British coin worth five shillings. This one crown coin was called a bull's-eye. Therefore it is more likely that the word "bull's-eye," when used in reference to a target's center, originated from the name of the British coin that was in common circulation at that time in world history when rifle targets were first used in competitive shooting matches. If the shooter hit the "bull's-eye" of the target then all the people who bet on that shooter won their bets and they received a coin called a bull's-eye.

Individual Abilities

Each one of us has unique talents in a variety of different areas. For example, some of us may be excellent golfers, or excellent musicians, or excellent cooks, or excellent mechanics, or excellent jugglers, or excellent managers. But **no one** is gifted in every possible skill area.

Please keep this in mind if you discover you are an average shooter, or a little below average, or a little above average. Only two or three people out of one-hundred will be truly excellent shooters. And only two or three people out of one-hundred will be very poor shooters. If you discover you are one of the excellent shooters then don't brag about it. If you discover you are one of the poor shooters then don't become upset about it.

However, the vast majority of us will be average shooters, or perhaps a little above or a little below average. We will be able to frequently hit the target bull's-eye but **not** with every single shot. Some of our shots will be a short distance away from the center of the target but those shots will still be close enough to the bull's-eye for most practical hunting scenarios.

Hours of Target Practice and the Learning Curve

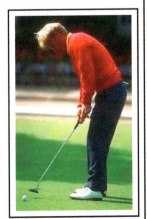

Almost everyone could benefit from training in any area in which they are not already familiar. For example, if you have **never** played golf then a few hours of basic golf lessons could help you to significantly improve your average score on the golf course. However, once you reach your natural "performance plateau" then additional golf lessons will only result in relatively insignificant improvements in your golfing abilities.

On the other hand, if you really enjoy golf then there is nothing wrong with visiting the golf course every Saturday and spending some time hitting several baskets of golf balls down the driving range. But if you believe that hitting more baskets of golf balls will somehow transform you into a "professional golfer" then you need to seriously reevaluate your mental image of yourself.

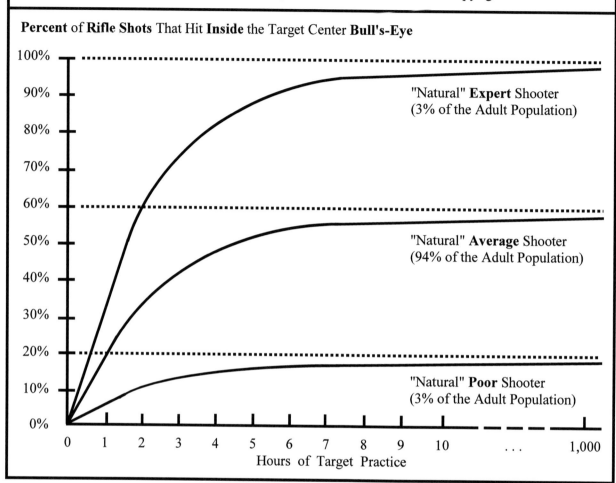

This same basic concept applies to firearms training. At some time during his or her life **everyone** should enroll in a basic firearms training course and learn the proper safe way to handle firearms and the preferred method of shooting at targets. This basic training will significantly improve your "before" and "after" target scores when shooting at paper targets.

But at some point you will reach a level of diminishing marginal returns. The money you invest in more practice ammunition will have very, very little impact on your average shooting performance. When you reach that point you will need to carefully evaluate your priorities. If you can afford more target practice and you really enjoy shooting at targets then you should do so, just like a person who enjoys hitting a basket full of golf balls down the driving range. But do **not** deceive yourself into believing that the additional money you invest in ammunition and training will somehow make a significant difference in your "natural" peak marksmanship ability.

This is illustrated graphical in the three learning curves above:

1. The top curve is for a "natural born **expert** shooter."
2. The middle curve is for a "natural born **average** shooter."
3. The bottom curve is for a "natural born **poor** shooter."

Chapter Sixty-Two: How to Hit the Target Bull's-Eye

Now let's interpret the "learning curve graph" for each of the three hypothetical shooters:

1. **Expert:** If you are a "natural expert shooter" then a few hours of practice may result in your placing 80% to 90% of your shots inside the bull's-eye. And when you miss your bullets will probably be within **one-half inch** around the outside of the bull's-eye. If you continue to practice you could gradually approach 100% shooting accuracy. The question you would have to ask would be as follows: "Is it worth your time and effort to move those very few misses the short one-half inch required to get them all inside the bull's-eye? Or is the one-half inch already close enough for all your shooting purposes?"

2. **Average:** If you are a "natural average shooter" then a few hours of practice could result in your hitting inside the bull's-eye about 50% to 55% of the time. And when you miss your bullets will probably all be grouped within **two or three inches** around the outside of the bull's-eye. If you continue training for a very long time you might improve your performance by a few percent but you will probably never be able to put more than a maximum of 60% of your shots inside the bull's-eye.

3. **Poor:** If you are a "natural poor shooter" then a few hours of practice may improve your shooting performance so you can hit inside the bull's-eye about 10% to 15% of the time. And when you miss your bullets will probably be somewhere within **five or ten inches** of the bull's-eye. Even if you invest a tremendous amount of money and time in more practice your future peak performance will probably never be higher than 20% of your shots inside the bull's-eye.

Note: The learning curves on the previous page were **not** derived from any law enforcement or military data. The learning curves are based on my own personal observations of watching a variety of different people learn how to shoot over the past 45 years -- beginning at Scout Camp in the summers as a teenager. The learning curves also closely correspond to my own shooting performance because I am only an "average shooter." The peak of each of the above learning curves could easily be increased by moving the target closer to the shooter, or the peak could easily be decreased by moving the target further away from the shooter.

When you are evaluating your shooting performance you should compare your **current** performance to your **previous** performance and **not** to someone else's scores. Each of us has our own natural learning curve and as long as we are making noticeable progress along our own learning curve then additional practice is very beneficial. However, everyone eventually reaches his or her own natural learning curve peak (or plateau) and any additional minor improvements will only be achieved after a significant amount of practice. And is most cases that tiny extra performance improvement is not worth the time and money you invest in achieving those marginally better results.

Please keep this in mind if you are told that "practice makes perfect." This is usually the advice of an "expert." The expert remembers how his or her original performance improved with practice and then assumes that all you need to do is practice more so you can achieve the same results. This is an invalid assumption.

However, practice can help you reach your personal "peak" potential. But unless you are a natural born marksman then additional practice will not transform you into an "expert marksman sharpshooter who never misses."

The Four Standard Shooting Positions

When hunting with a rifle there are four standard positions from which you can shoot your rifle. The following descriptions are for a right handed shooter who pulls the trigger with his or her right forefinger.

In each of the following positions you should begin by turning your body so you are facing somewhere between 30 to 45 degrees to the right of the target. You should then turn your head so you are looking straight at the target.

Support the front of your rifle with your left hand, hold the grip of your rifle stock with your right hand but keep your forefinger **off** the trigger, and securely plant the butt of your rifle against your right shoulder.

1. **Standing:** Place your feet directly below your shoulders with your left foot pointed at the target. You will need to support your hunting rifle using the strength in your arms.

2. **Kneeling:** Kneel on your right knee with your right foot behind you on the ground. Your body should be straight from your right knee all the way up to your right shoulder. Bend your left knee at an angle in front of you towards the target and place your left foot flat on the ground and pointed at the target. Support your rifle with your left elbow on your left knee. Your right elbow will have no support.
3. **Sitting:** Sit on your rear end with your knees bent in front of you. Support your rifle with your left elbow on your left knee. Depending on the terrain and the elevation to your target you may also be able to put your right elbow on your right knee. Depending on the terrain you may cross your feet in front of you, or you may place your feet flat on the ground depending on which position feels most comfortable to you. Sitting on an average size rock (about 8 inches round) is usually more comfortable than sitting on the ground and it elevates your shooting height the same distance as the height of the rock.
4. **Prone (Lying Down):** Lie on the ground on your stomach with the centerline of your body at a 30 to 45 degree angle to the target. Support your rifle with your elbows which should be firmly planted on the ground in front of you.

**Shooting Accuracy and
Difficultly Getting into the Shooting Position and
Approximate Height Visibility Over Objects Between You and the Target**

Position	Accuracy	Ease to Assume	Visibility
Prone	Best	Slowest	15 Inches
Sitting	Good	Slow	30 Inches
Kneeling	Okay	Fast	42 Inches
Standing	Worst	Fastest	64 Inches

If you can hold your rifle steady then your accuracy will improve.

1. If your rifle has a sling then put your left forearm through the sling and wrap it one complete turn around your left forearm so you can use the tension of the sling on the front of the rifle to help hold the rifle steady with your forearm.
2. It is easier to hold your rifle steady if you can support it with something, such as supporting your elbows on your knees or your elbows on the ground. In most cases the ground is more stable than your knees so the prone position yields the best shot placement accuracy. Sitting allows you to use both knees for support so it is the second best position. Kneeling only uses one knee for support so it is the third best. Standing provides no rifle support so it is the least preferred in terms of accuracy of shot placement.
3. To improve your shooting results while standing try to find some type of temporary stationary support for your rifle or for your elbows, such as a really huge rock or the side of a tree trunk.
4. A rifle support tripod or a bipod is also nice but if you have the time to set one of these items up then you could just as easily have assumed a sitting or kneeling firing position, or found a nearby tree to help steady your rifle while aiming at the target.

Dry Fire Practice

The term "dry fire" means that you pull the trigger **without** any ammunition inside the firearm. Do **not** dry fire any type of **rimfire** rifle or handgun. Rimfire means the gun powder inside the cartridge is ignited by striking the outside rim of the case. The 22 caliber bullet is a rimfire bullet. This includes the 22 short (22S), 22 long (22L), 22 long rifle (22LR), and 22 Winchester Magnum Rimfire (22 WMR).

Do **not** dry fire any really old or antique firearm. Some of the older weapons have firing mechanisms that could be damaged if you dry fire them. Therefore the best strategy is to **never** dry fire a really old firearm.

It is okay to dry fire modern **centerfire** rifles and handguns. Centerfire means the gun powder inside the cartridge is ignited by striking the primer in the bottom center of the case.

Chapter Sixty-Two: How to Hit the Target Bull's-Eye

The Army Marksmanship Training Unit begins with three weeks of dry firing before they issue any ammunition.

Dry firing has all the following advantages:

1. It does not cost anything. It requires no investment in ammunition or "target practice range" fees.
2. It can be done indoors or outdoors. You do not need to be at a safe "target practice range" to dry fire your weapon.
3. It eliminates a lot of psychological stress because you know the weapon is empty and that you are just practicing.
4. It allows you to get to know the feel of the trigger so you can safely practice "squeezing" the trigger in the proper manner.
5. It allows you to practice keeping the scope cross hairs (or iron sights) on the target as you squeeze the trigger.
6. It allows you to more rapidly learn proper shooting habits so your initial real target range results using live ammunition will be much better.

After you are really comfortable with your weapon and the way it feels when you "dry fire" it then you can go to the Shooting Range and practice with live ammunition. However, by that time you should have mastered the basic firearm shooting procedures so the only new variables you will need to master will be the feel and sound of your rifle as it releases its bullet towards the target, and how to gradually improve your accuracy as you fire your weapon at targets placed at different distances.

Breathing and Squeezing the Trigger

The average individual can significantly improve his or her shooting performance by properly mastering the following two variables:

1. **Breathing (Elevation Error):** If you breathe while you are shooting then you will be increasing and decreasing the elevation at which your bullets hit the target.
2. **Trigger Pull (Windage Error):** If you pull (jerk) the trigger instead of squeezing it then you will pull the firearm to the right (if you are right handed) and your bullets will hit the right side of the target area.

Breathing: As you breathe your lungs and your chest area expands and contracts. If you have your rifle butt against your shoulder then your normal breathing will cause the front muzzle of your rifle to rise and fall. In other words, you will not be able to keep your scope cross hairs properly centered on the target bull's-eye.

There are three schools of thought on the proper time at which to stop breathing and hold your breath while you squeeze the trigger:

1. Take a breath and then hold it with your lungs full of air.
2. Take a breath and release half of it and then hold the rest of it inside your lungs.
3. Take a breath and release all of it and then hold your breath.

If you think about your normal breathing cycle then you will realize that you breathe in and then you almost immediately breathe out to relax the pressure inside your lungs and expel carbon dioxide. Then your lungs pause for just a moment and then you repeat your normal breathing cycle. You do this 24-hours a day without even thinking about it.

If you practice the first technique above then you will be interrupting your normal breathing cycle and you will feel uncomfortable and you will want to expel the carbon dioxide trapped inside your lungs.

If you practice the second technique above then you will also be interrupting your normal breathing cycle and this forces you to think about the air still trapped inside your lungs when you should be thinking about your target.

Chapter Sixty-Two: How to Hit the Target Bull's-Eye

If you practice the third technique above then your body will have completed its normal breathing cycle and it will be at the natural short break that it always takes before it begins another cycle. This is the best time to temporarily interrupt your normal breathing cycle because your body will remain calmer longer as you squeeze the trigger.

Therefore, of the three breathing techniques, the third one is best for maximizing your shooting performance. Take a normal breath, let it all out, and then hold your breath for the three, four, or five seconds required to squeeze the trigger of your rifle. This will help to minimize the elevation error in your shooting performance.

Trigger Pull: Instead of pulling or jerking the trigger quickly it is better to firmly squeeze the trigger in a slow continuous smooth motion. This will minimize the windage error in your shooting performance.

Some modern firearms have a single-stage trigger pull and some have a two-stage trigger pull.

1. **Single-Stage Trigger Pull:** The resistance is uniform over the entire distance required to complete the trigger pull. On some firearms this distance is relatively short but on other firearms it is much longer.

2. **Two-Stage Trigger Pull:** The first stage is relatively longer in length and it overcomes less resistance. The second stage is relatively shorter in length and it overcomes more resistance. If you will practice dry firing your weapon you will gradually be able to detect the end of stage one and the beginning of stage two. This will psychologically prepare you for the moment when your weapon fires.

Do not worry about holding your breath while you first learn the feel of your weapon's trigger pull. If you will practice dry firing your weapon you will gradually learn the total distance the trigger needs to be pulled before the firing pin is activated. You should continue to practice dry firing your weapon until you can successfully squeeze the trigger and dry fire your weapon in three or four seconds or less.

Then you should practice dry firing your weapon while holding your scope cross hairs (or iron sights) steady on a target, and holding your breath, and completing the trigger sequence in three or four seconds or less.

If more that four or five seconds pass and you have not completed your trigger pull and you begin to feel uncomfortable holding your breath then you should stop and relax the pressure on your trigger finger and stop the firing sequence. Do not take your sights off the target. Wait a few seconds, take a few normal breaths, relax, and then begin the trigger pull sequence again. If you have done a sufficient amount of dry fire practice then this should only happen to you on rare occasions at the target practice range.

In summary, the following steps will help you maximize your shooting performance:

1. Wear hearing and eye protection whenever you are shooting a firearm.

2. Aim the rifle at the target. Acquire the bull's-eye. Relax but do not allow your weapon to drift too far from the bull's-eye.

3. Take three normal slow breaths.

4. At the end of the third breath, after you have expelled the air in your lungs, begin to hold your breath and once again quickly center the scope cross hairs on the target bull's-eye.

5. Slowly but firmly squeeze the trigger with the tip of your finger in a smooth continuous motion. Do not move the rest of your body.

6. The bullet explosion should come as a "surprise" even though you were expecting it.

If possible, limit your target practice using live ammunition to one-hour or less per day. This will help to minimize shooting fatigue.

If possible, skip at least one-day between practice sessions. This will give you time to properly reflect on and think about your most recent range results. Simple minor things that you could do that may improve your performance will occur to you during this interval between range visits. This will help you maximize your progress along your own natural learning curve.

Target Practice, Hunting, and Self-Defense

The above **target practice** strategy is very effective for improving your accuracy when shooting at paper targets. Being able to accurately shoot at paper targets will also improve your shooting results in other situations.

If you are **hunting** from a "stationary hunting blind" then the above procedure would allow you to properly and accurately place your shot in the animal's kill zone so you could bring some meat home for the family to eat. However, if you are walking and looking for wild game animals then it is possible that you will see the animal at approximately the same time it sees you. In that situation you will need to be able to quickly acquire your target and fire a round at the animal's kill zone before it disappears out of range of your hunting rifle.

The above target shooting instructions are **not** appropriate for a **combat or self-defense** scenario when the enemy is shooting back at you. You will need to consult a military or law enforcement training manual to learn the proper way to protect yourself and return fire when engaging a hostile enemy force. However, even in this situation you would still need a rifle scope that has been properly centered so you could hit the enemy soldier in his "kill zone."

Single-Shot or Semi-Automatic Firearms

Rifles - Bolt Action, Lever Action, or Semi-Automatic: The difference in accuracy between bolt action, lever action, and semi-automatic rifles is very small. Therefore I would always select a semi-automatic rifle so I could quickly fire a follow-up shot if the current situation required it. The time required to cycle another cartridge into the rifle chamber using either a bolt-action or a lever-action rifle will allow whatever wild game animal you are hunting enough time to completely disappear: (1) into the woods, or (2) over the horizon, or (3) out-of-range of your rifle.

Handguns - Revolver or Semi-Automatic Pistol: For this same reason I would also prefer a semi-automatic pistol instead of a revolver.

Self-Defense: In a self-defense survival situation you will not have the calm rational emotional composure that you now have as you read this paragraph. If you are being shot at and your life is in danger then you really need a weapon that **automatically** loads another cartridge into the firing chamber so you can continue to shoot back at your adversary until your weapon is empty. You will **not** be happy with the slow response time of a bolt-action rifle or a lever-action rifle or a revolver in a self-defense situation

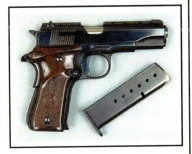

when your life, or the lives of your family, depends on your ability to neutralize the attacking party. If you have extra magazines then you could also quickly reload a semi-automatic weapon.

Safety: Do **not** insert a cartridge into the firing chamber of your rifle or handgun until you are actually ready to fire your weapon. In other words, do not store or carry your firearm with a live round in the firing position in front of the firing pin. I know that many firearms are advertised as 7+1, or 11+1, or 15+1, and that the "plus one" means one round in the firing position. But this is a very hazardous way to store or carry your firearm. Everyone who has accidentally shot either themselves or someone else will testify that this is a stupid habit to get into. None of these individuals ever believed that they would make the mistake of accidentally discharging their firearm. Every single one of them honestly and truthfully believed they were going to be extra careful and therefore they would not have an accident. This type of thinking is similar to running with a sharp knife in your hand and somehow believing that you will never, ever stumble or fall and accidentally injure yourself with that knife. Almost everyone can see the stupidity of running with a sharp knife in your hands and a smart person will simply not do it. Therefore do **not** load a live round into the firing position inside your weapon until you are actually ready to use your firearm at the target practice range, or you actually need your weapon for emergency self-defense in a life-threatening situation.

Chapter Sixty-Two: How to Hit the Target Bull's-Eye

Handguns

A handgun is only accurate at a very short distance, usually within 25 feet or less to your target (or much closer if you are shooting a relatively large caliber such as the 44 Magnum). If you are an average shooter and you are shooting a handgun in a caliber that you can control then you should be able to hit somewhere on the paper target with most of your shots if you are within twenty-feet of the target. However, do not expect to see a lot of bull's-eyes. Any shots inside the bull's-eye are probably due to random chance unless you are shooting a very low caliber bullet with negligible recoil.

The primary purpose of a handgun is for personal self-defense at close ranges. Handguns are not designed for normal hunting or combat situations.

Handgun Hunting: Only the other hand, if you are simply squirrel hunting, then a 22LR handgun will do the job if you can get close enough to the squirrels to accurately shoot them in the head. My personal experience is that I can usually walk to within pistol distance of squirrels that are on the ground when I am walking in the woods.

Handgun Laser: It is okay to put a laser under the barrel of a handgun to help you more quickly and accurately aim your handgun at the target. Some individuals recommend against the installation of a laser on a self-defense handgun because it may reveal your location to armed robbers who are invading your home in the middle of the night. However, if you will think about this for a moment, the first time you fire your handgun at night the muzzle blast will instantly show everyone exactly where you are. If you are using your handgun for emergency self-defense in a highly stressful life-threatening situation when criminals are shooting at you then my opinion is that it would be advantageous to have a laser to quickly assist you in realigning your handgun on the "kill zone" of each attacker so you could end the conflict as quickly as possible with your being the only surviving participant.  A laser would allow you to hold your handgun slightly to one side as you fire it. This means you would **not** need to keep your handgun directly in front of you so you could "aim" down the barrel of your handgun at your assailants. If your attackers were firing at the muzzle blast from your handgun then it is possible that their bullets will miss you out to the side that you are holding your handgun. However, this is just my opinion and you may follow whatever advice you choose. If you install a laser under the barrel of your handgun then you will need to follow the instructions that come with that laser and adjust it so that it points to the approximate location your handgun bullets hit when you fire your handgun at a target. It would probably also be a good idea to practice shooting your handgun while holding it in one hand out to one side of your body so you can develop some skill in this type of shooting using your handgun and your laser to place your bullets in the "kill zone" of the paper target.

Handgun Self-Defense: If the primary purpose of your handgun will be for emergency self-defense then after you have your handgun sighted on the target you should practice firing "two" rapid shots at the target in the same way that law enforcement officers train. This is referred to as a "**double tap**." Unfortunately some target practice ranges will not let you rapid fire any type of firearm.

Handgun Scope: Do **not** install a scope on the top of your handgun even if your handgun came with special scope mounts, such as some 44 Magnum revolvers. A handgun does **not** have the accuracy repeatability of a rifle.

Rifles

A rifle is accurate based on the normal range of the caliber of ammunition that it shoots. The closer you are to the target the easier it is to group your shots very close to the bull's-eye. As you move further away from your target you will notice more variability in where your shots hit the target in relationship to the center of the target.

Do not try to replicate your accuracy with a rifle when you are using your handgun. If you are aware of this from the beginning then you will be less likely to become emotionally upset when you compare the holes in your handgun targets to your rifle targets.

Shotguns

I am not going to discuss shotguns in this chapter because:

1. This article is about hitting the bull's-eye and this is relatively easy to do with a shotgun at its normal effective range.
2. I believe the average person would be better off with a rifle and a handgun instead of a shotgun.

A shotgun does have valid useful applications in a variety of situations. However, a rifle is more versatile in a wider variety of situations. If I could only carry one firearm then that firearm would be a rifle. If I could carry two firearms then I would carry a rifle and a handgun.

Barrel Length

A longer barrel will generally provide better accuracy at greater distances than a shorter barrel. If you are purchasing firearms then this may be an important consideration depending on the options actually available in the type of weapon you desire.

If you live and hunt in an area with relatively flat land where the visibility is easily one-mile in almost every direction then a longer barrel is an absolute necessity.

However, if you will be hunting inside a heavily wooded area most of the time, then a longer barrel will make it more difficult to maneuver your rifle into a firing position when you are surrounded by trees, limbs, bushes, or other shrubbery. In that situation a shorter barrel that has the necessary accuracy at your maximum shooting distance would be preferred.

Bullet Caliber (or Bullet Size)

Firearm caliber is an important consideration. You will need a bullet that is big enough to terminate whatever type of wild game you may be hunting. But a really big caliber is not appropriate for smaller game animals, such as raccoons and opossums. The amount of information currently available on each of the different calibers is truly overwhelming.

Therefore instead of discussing the advantages and disadvantages of every possible caliber please allow me to simply recommend that you avoid any "special" caliber that can only be fired in a limited number of weapons and which may not be available at many locations that sell common caliber ammunition.

Instead, if it is possible, you should consider a rifle or handgun in one of the following "common" calibers:

Common Rifle Calibers: 22LR, 223 (5.56x45), 30-30, 7.62x39, 308 (7.62x51), 30-06.
Common Handgun Calibers: 22LR, 38, 357 Magnum, 9mm, 40 S&W, 45 ACP, 44 Magnum.

If you are going to use a semi-automatic firearm then you need to select a caliber that can be fired in a semi-automatic firearm. Some calibers are very common calibers but there are no semi-automatic weapons that fire them.

The rifle caliber should be big enough to be effective against the largest wild game animal in your geographical area. Your local gun shop or gunsmith will be able to assist you in this decision.

If you are in the market for a new rifle then you should make the caliber and rifle decision simultaneously. The rifle should be capable of semi-automatic fire and it should fire a caliber that is lethal against the largest wild game animals in your geographical area.

Recommended Rifle Caliber: If I could only carry one rifle, and if I intended to use that rifle for hunting and self-defense, then I would carry an original design AK-47 that shoots the 7.62x39 ammunition. That

Chapter Sixty-Two: How to Hit the Target Bull's-Eye

caliber is adequate for the largest wild game animal where I live and it is lethal for self-defense purposes at the range at which I can accurately shoot the rifle.

However, if I lived in an area with larger wild game animals, or if I lived in an area where the visibility was normally one-half mile or more in almost every direction, then I would definitely upgrade to a 308 (7.62x51) semi-automatic rifle. However, the reason I personally prefer the smaller AK-47 is because:

1. it is lethal at the average maximum visibility distance in my geographical area, and
2. the AK-47 rifle is more affordable, and
3. the AK-47 weighs less and is it less fatiguing to carry on your back, and
4. 7.62x39 ammunition is a lot cheaper than 308 (7.62x51) ammunition, and
5. the total weight of fully loaded 7.62x39 magazines is a lot less, and
6. 7.62x39 ammunition is not regulated in the same manner as 308 ammunition (no 308 steel-core armor-piercing bullets for civilians).

Recommended Handgun Caliber: My first choice of a handgun would be a 40 S&W semi-automatic pistol. Most adults can comfortably grasp this weapon and shoot it accurately because it has an average recoil. It also has a law-enforcement history of being an effective single-shot man stopper.

If my hand were larger and if I could comfortably grip and control the recoil of a larger caliber handgun then I would select the 45 ACP semi-automatic pistol. The reason this would **not** be my first choice is because I may have a spouse, or teenage or older children, who may not be able to shoot this weapon effectively. If I were incapacitated and someone else in my family had to take my place and defend the family with my handgun then it would be sad if that handgun fired a bullet that person could not shoot accurately.

Distance to the Target

All firearms have a **maximum possible distance** if the bullet is fired at an angle up into the air and it covers an arched trajectory until it eventually falls to the ground. This distance is an interesting statistic but it is of little practical value because the bullet has lost almost all of its power and energy when it finally makes contact with the ground.

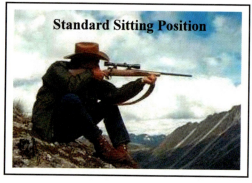

All firearms also have a **maximum accurate distance** at which they can be consistently relied upon to accurately hit a target. This distance will vary depending on the length of the barrel and the type of ammunition used. When the bullet arrives at the target it will punch a pretty hole in a paper target. However, it should be noted that punching a hole in the center of a piece of paper is not as difficult as penetrating the hide of a wild game animal.

All firearms also have a **maximum lethal distance**. This is the distance at which the bullet will still have enough remaining lethal force to penetrate and terminate the intended target, such as a deer. This is the distance you need to know for whatever firearms you may possess. This topic will be discussed in more detail later in this chapter.

Finally, the maximum lethal distance may be reduced depending on the terrain in which you intend to use your firearm. If you are a competition shooter and all your shooting will be at prescribed distances over clear terrain then this will not be an issue. But if you are a hunter then you will need to consider how far a bullet will normally travel before it makes contact with the deer, or a tree trunk, or a limb, or a bush, or anything else that may be between you and your target, such as the deer. In most heavily wooded areas 75 to 100 yards is the normal maximum shooting distance when the leaves are on the trees. However, during the autumn and winter months it is not uncommon for this distance to increase by an additional 25 to 50 yards when all the trees loose their leaves and the visibility significantly improves.

After selecting the appropriate distance for your particular application then that is the maximum distance at which you should shoot your rifle when hunting wild game animals.

How to Select the Optimum Distance for Your Rifle Scope "Zero" Setting

There are four factors that will help you determine the best distance to "zero" or set your rifle scope cross hairs:

1. The average line-of-sight **visibility** distance in the area you will normally be hunting.
2. The maximum **lethal** distance of the ammunition you will be using.
3. The normal **trajectory** of the ammunition you will be using.
4. The average **accuracy** of your hunting rifle.

Visibility: You need to determine the average visible distance over which you will be shooting your rifle. If you will be shooting across a watermelon field and the visibility is one-half mile in every direction then you can set your scope for the maximum lethal distance of the ammunition you will be using.

On the other hand, if you normally hunt inside a heavily wooded area then it would be very unusual to have a clear shot at a target that is more than 100 yards away. According to the available statistics provided by deer hunters each hunting season, in heavily wooded areas the vast majority of all deer are shot at distances of 100 yards or less.

Lethal Distance: A bullet begins to lose its power (or energy) the instant it emerges from the end of the rifle barrel. The bullet continues to loose energy the further it travels until it eventually hits the ground and comes to a complete stop. When the bullet stops it has lost all of its power or energy. However, long before it comes to a complete stop the bullet will have lost so much of its energy that it will no longer be lethal. In other words, it will no longer have the ability to penetrate an object such as the hide of an animal. The bullet may still have enough energy to sting or bruise the hide of the animal but if it can't penetrate the animal's hide and then continue to penetrate deep enough to kill the animal, then for all practical purposes the bullet has become ineffective even though it may still be in high-speed motion.

To **effectively** kill a deer, or any other average size game animal, a bullet should have **at least 800 foot pounds (ft. lbs.)** of remaining kinetic energy when it makes contact with the deer. A 7.62x39 bullet has an average muzzle exit energy of about 1,500 foot pounds and it has about 875 foot pounds of remaining energy at 200 yards, and about 800 foot pounds of energy at 240 yards. Therefore a 7.62x39 bullet would still be considered "lethal" at a distance of approximately 240 yards.

For a quick comparison a 223 (NATO 5.56x45) bullet has a muzzle energy of about 1,200 foot pounds. At 100 yards the 223 still has about 930 foot pounds of remaining energy, and at 150 yards it has about 800 foot pounds of remaining energy. Therefore if you limited your deer hunting with the 223 to 150 yards or less you would still have a lethal hunting rifle.

The 308 (NATO 7.62x51) has a muzzle energy of about 2,500 foot pounds. At 300 yards it still has about 1,400 foot pounds, and at 600 yards it has about 800 foot pounds of remaining energy. Therefore a 308 has a lethal range of about 600 yards. However most of us are average marksmen and we have trouble hitting **anywhere** inside a 12-inch diameter circle at 300 yards. Therefore most of us would have to limit our hunting shots to a distance that is considerably less than the maximum lethal range of the 308.

Note 1 - Minimum Energy: Some references quote 900 foot pounds as the minimum required kinetic energy. Other references quote 1,000 foot pounds. In each case the answer is correct for the type of hunting bullet being recommended. A round nose bullet, or a flat nose bullet, or a wider bullet will require **more** energy to penetrate an object to the same depth when compared to a pointed bullet. A pointed bullet, or a thinner bullet, will require less energy to penetrate to the same depth. Therefore there is no single correct answer in this debate since the answer is a function of the design of the bullet. A pointed bullet, such as a 223 or a 7.62x39, only requires about 800 foot pounds for it to be lethal against medium size game animals such as a deer. This entire minimum energy debate also assumes that you hit the deer in its "kill zone."

Note 2 - Maximum Energy: Rarely will the topic of too much energy be discussed. However, to be successful a hunting bullet needs to penetrate the hide of the animal and expand inside the animal. It should do as much damage as possible inside the animal or while passing completely through the animal. If the bullet hits the animal's heart then the animal is dead. Period. End of discussion. But an animal's heart is **not** a big target. And if the bullet just misses the heart then it will destroy lung tissue. The more lung tissue destroyed the quicker the animal will die. But if the bullet still has a tremendous amount of remaining kinetic energy when it makes contact with the animal then it will quickly pass straight through the animal without expanding and exit the opposite side of the animal. If this happens then very little internal damage will be done and the animal can easily escape and you will never find it. The animal will probably die a slow death but there is also a small chance that it may gradually heal and survive. Too much energy is the one disadvantage of the 308 and the 30-06 when hunting medium size game animals at distances of 200 yards or less. For example, the 308 has about 2,100 foot-pounds at 100 yards and about 1,700 foot-pounds at 200 yards. With this much power the pointed bullet could quickly pass completely through a deer, or smaller animal, without stopping and without expanding. Therefore when you select your rifle caliber you should seriously consider both its maximum and minimum energy at the distances over which you will be hunting. This is one of the reasons the round nose 30-30 is a great deer cartridge for distances of 100 yards or less which is the typical hunting distance in heavily wooded areas.

You will need to consult a rifle ballistics table to determine the energy of your hunting ammunition at different distances. When you consult a ballistics table make sure you look for the "energy" data in foot-pounds (ft. lbs.) and not the column that has "velocity" data in feet-per-second (fps). Those columns are sometimes side-by-side in the table.

As you consult the different ballistics tables you will notice that they do **not** all agree because of differences in the bullet weights, the initial powder charge, the type of powder, the rifle barrel length, and a variety of other factors. If you are certain you will always be using the same exact hunting bullet all the time then you could simply look that bullet up in one of the ballistic tables. However, if there is a chance that you may use different bullets of the same caliber then it would probably be a good idea to copy the ballistic data from several different tables and then use the table that has the lowest numbers to give yourself a margin of safety when hunting. If you are hunting for meat then it doesn't do anyone any good unless you can find the deer after you shoot it so you can bring it home to the food freezer.

After you have determined the distance that your rifle caliber bullet still has at least 800 foot-pounds of remaining energy (for a pointed bullet), then that will be the **maximum** distance at which you should shoot at wild game animals.

Trajectory: Immediately after the bullet leaves the front muzzle of your rifle the bullet will gradually slow down and begin to make its way towards the ground due to wind resistance and gravity.

If your rifle is perfectly level to the ground then the bullet will travel in a straight line for a short distance and then it will gradually begin its decline towards the ground. This is illustrated in the **dotted line trajectory** in the illustration at the top of the next page. Since the center line of the rifle bore is perfectly level with the ground, the bullet will **not** travel above the center line of the rifle after it leaves the rifle barrel.

If you have your rifle pointed at a very slight angle up into the air then the bullet will travel up into the air for a short distance before it begins to descend towards the ground. In this case the bullet will also **not** travel above the center line of the bore of your rifle. But if you have your rifle pointed at a slight upward angle then the bullet will travel slightly upwards but **not** above the center line of your rifle bore. (Remember that you have the center line of your rifle bore pointed slightly upwards into the air.) You could observe this event if you could watch the bullet's trajectory from the side. This would be possible if someone else fired your rifle using "tracer ammunition" and you were standing a safe distance away at a 90-degree angle far off to one side. This is illustrated as the **solid line trajectory** in the illustration on the next page.

Or you could place a series of targets (or large flip chart pages) at 25 yard intervals in a straight line along the bullet's estimated future path and you could then document the trajectory path of your bullet as it passed through each of these thin paper targets on its way to the earth.

Chapter Sixty-Two: How to Hit the Target Bull's-Eye

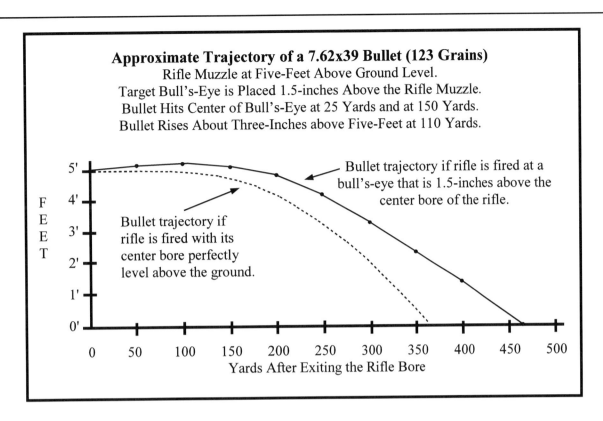

Since the bullet is initially traveling upwards for a short distance **before** it begins its normal descent to the earth, the bullet will in fact pass through the bull's-eye of two targets. It will pass through one bull's-eye while the bullet is rising and it will pass through another target bull's-eye while the bullet is falling. In the illustration for 7.62x39 ammunition this would occur at 25 yards and 150 yards respectively. The bullet would reach a maximum height of about three inches above the rifle barrel at its highest point along its trajectory. But if your targets are placed 1.5 inches above the front muzzle of the rifle then the bullet will only be about 1.5 inches above the target bull's-eye at its maximum trajectory. For a 7.62x39 bullet the maximum bullet trajectory height will occur at a distance of approximately 110 yards from the rifle muzzle. At 175 yards the bullet would be about 1.5 inches below the bull's-eye. By the time the 7.62x39 bullet has reached a distance of 200 yards the bullet will pass through the target at a distance of about 4 inches below the target bull's-eye.

If you had your rifle scope set to the above parameters and you were shooting 7.62x39 ammunition then you could accurately shoot and kill a deer at any distance out to a maximum of 175 yards away without having to worry about estimating the distance to your target or making any elevation corrections on your scope. You could simply line up the scope cross hairs on the center of the proper heart/lung circle of the deer and slowly squeeze the trigger. Regardless of how far away the deer may be your bullet would never travel more than 1.5 inches above or below the cross hairs of your rifle scope. For deer hunting this would be an almost certain kill if you used the proper ammunition that was still lethal at 175 yards and there were no other factors, such as a significant cross wind and whether you are shooting up or down a hill at the deer (these topics will be discussed later in this chapter).

Hunting Rifle Accuracy: Shoot three (or four) shots at a variety of targets placed at 25 yard or 50 yard intervals. In other words, shoot at targets at the following distances: 25 yards, 50 yards, 75 yards, 100 yards, 125 yards, 150 yards, 175 yards, and 200 yards. As you move further away from your target the average circle that you draw around your three or four shot groups on each individual target will gradually increase due to a number of different factors. When the circle reaches a maximum diameter of about four-inches then you should consider that distance to be the normal reliable accuracy of your hunting rifle. In the future you should confine your hunting shots to this distance (or less) whenever possible. You should also record the distance information and the date on each of these practice targets and save them for future reference purposes.

In summary, to determine your **maximum** effective hunting distance use the **minimum** of the following distances:

1. The maximum average visibility in your normal hunting area.
2. The lethal range of your ammunition at which it still has at least 800 foot pounds of remaining kinetic energy (for pointed bullets).
3. The trajectory of your bullet so that it does not rise or fall more than two-inches during its flight path until it hits your target.
4. The distance at which your hunting rifle can still group at least three shots into a four-inch diameter circle.

- - - - - - -

Example One: As an example assume you are hunting deer using 7.62x39 ammunition in a forest area and you have determined the following values:

1. Maximum visibility is 110 yards in the forest.
2. The lethal range of 7.62x39 ammunition is 240 yards.
3. Your rifle has a plus or minus two-inch trajectory out to 175 yards.
4. You can accurately group three shots within a four-inch circle at a maximum distance of 150 yards.

Based on the above numbers you should limit your shots to 150 yards or less over open terrain, or out to the maximum visible distance in the forest which will probably be 110 yards or less. You would leave your scope exactly the way you now have it set up even though you probably will not be using it out to its maximum trajectory range of 175 yards.

- - - - - - -

Example Two: As a second example assume you are hunting deer using 7.62x39 ammunition in a very lightly populated rural farming area:

1. Maximum visibility is 800 yards in most areas.
2. The lethal range of 7.62x39 ammunition is 240 yards.
3. Your rifle has a plus or minus two-inch trajectory out to 175 yards.
4. You can accurately group three shots within a four-inch circle at a maximum distance of 225 yards.

Based on the above numbers you should limit your shots to 175 yards or less. However, if you memorize the amount of your bullet's drop for distances out past 175 yards then you could shoot out to 225 yards but you would need to aim a little **higher** for any shots out past 175 yards based on the estimated trajectory for your bullet at that distance.

- - - - - - -

Summary of "Average" Ballistics Data for Three Common Rifle Calibers
When the Rifle Bullet Passes Through the Target Bull's-Eye at a Distance of 25 Yards
and the Target Bull's-eye is 0.5 inches Above the Rifle Muzzle
at 25 Yards for the 223 (5.56x45)
and the Target Bull's-eye is 1.5 inches Above the Rifle Muzzle
at 25 Yards for the 7.62x39 and 308 (7.62x51).

Rifle Caliber	First Bull's-eye	Second Bull's-eye	Maximum Trajectory	Minimum Trajectory	800 Ft. Lbs.
223 or 5.56x45	25 Yards	175 Yards	+ 1.0" at 95 Yards	- 1.0" at 200 Yards	150 Yards
7.62x39	25 Yards	150 Yards	+ 1.5" at 110 Yards	- 1.5" at 175 Yards	240 Yards
308 or 7.62x51	25 Yards	220 Yards	+ 3.0" at 125 Yards	- 3.0" at 260 Yards	600 Yards

Chapter Sixty-Two: How to Hit the Target Bull's-Eye

Note 1: Depending on which references you consult you will see that the effective "kill zone" on a deer is an imaginary circle that may vary from 8-inches to 12-inches in diameter around the heart/lung area of the deer. Therefore using this data your bullet could rise and fall a maximum of between four to six inches from center and it would still hit inside the lethal kill zone of a deer. However, smaller game animals, such as a beaver, do not have a "kill zone" this big. Therefore I personally prefer to use the smaller rise and fall of plus and minus two-inches for the trajectory of my hunting bullets. However, the ammunition you use in your hunting rifle may have more ballistic variability than plus and minus two-inches and that may dictate a different logical decision for your particular hunting rifle. This is a personal judgment decision and you may follow whatever advice you prefer.

Note 2: You should also consult any good hunting book that shows the cross-section of the insides of a variety of different game animals so you can determine the correct point at which to aim for a quick kill of each animal. This is called **shot placement**. Shot placement, or hitting the animal in its kill zone, is just as important as selecting a large enough bullet for that particular animal, and hitting the animal with that bullet while the bullet still has enough remaining lethal force to quickly and humanely kill the animal.

Rifle Scopes: The Top and Side Adjustment Controls

Safety Precaution: Larger caliber rifles generally have more recoil than smaller caliber rifles. If you place your eye too close to the scope then when the rifle fires it will recoil backwards and the scope will move backwards with the rifle and you will get a serious "black eye" or something worse. Therefore always:

1. make sure that the butt of your rifle is firmly seated against your shoulder, and
2. make sure your eye is a "safe" distance away from the scope.

If your rifle is not **firmly** seated against your shoulder, and if you don't hold that shoulder steady, then your shoulder will travel backwards with your rifle recoil while your eye stays in the same approximate location and you will get hit in the eye with your rifle scope. Most of us have to get one serious "black eye" before we appreciate the wisdom of this advice. Perhaps you can be one of those rare individuals who does not have to repeat this particular mistake yourself.

There are two adjustment controls on a rifle scope as follows:

1. **The Top Adjustment Control Dial (Elevation):** Moves the horizontal cross hair that extends from the left to the right side inside your scope. To move the point of bullet impact "Up" rotate the dial counter-clockwise. To move the point of bullet impact "Down" rotate the dial clockwise.

2. **The Side Adjustment Control Dial (Windage):** Moves the vertical cross hair that extends from the top to the bottom inside your scope. To move the point of bullet impact "Right" turn the dial counter-clockwise. To move the point of bullet impact "Left" turn the dial clockwise.

Depending on the type of scope you may first have to remove a cap that covers and protects each of the adjustment dials. If the protective cap is screw mounted then you can remove it by turning it in a counter-clockwise direction. If you rotate the protective cap and nothing happens then the protective cap is simply pressure mounted and it will snap on and off the control dial. Some scopes do **not** have any protective cap and

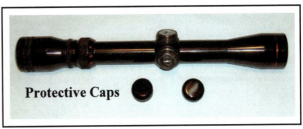

you can adjust the dial control by simply rotating the control dial immediately without having to first remove any type of protective cap.

Some of the control dials are designed to be moved with your fingers. Other control dials must be moved with some type of tool, or with a coin from your pocket such as a dime.

Chapter Sixty-Two: How to Hit the Target Bull's-Eye

Read the instructions that came with your scope to learn the proper way to care for your scope and the proper way to adjust your particular scope. Most centerfire rifle scopes are set so that each click on the adjustment dial will move the point of bullet impact 1/4 inch at 100 yards (Type C Scope), or 1/2 inch at 100 yards (Type D Scope). If you are initially adjusting your scope at the recommended range of 25 yards then you will need to keep that in mind. And if you are trying to adjust the point of impact at any distance other than 100 yards then the one-click ratio will not be correct. The following table may help you to better estimate the number of clicks required to move the point of bullet impact on the target.

Bullet Impact Adjustment Per One Click on the Dial

Distance to Target =	25 Yards	50 Yards	100 Yards	200 Yards
Type C Scope =	1/16 Inch	1/8 Inch	1/4 Inch	1/2 Inch
Type D Scope =	1/8 Inch	1/4 Inch	1/2 Inch	1 Inch

If you are closer to the target you will need more clicks to move the point of impact one-inch on the target. But if you are further away from your target you will need fewer clicks to move the point of impact one-inch on the target.

Based on my personal experience I have discovered that it is usually easier to get the point of impact correct in one direction at a time. In other words, I will first get the horizontal point of impact correct so the bullets hit at the correct center height on the target halfway between the top and the bottom of the target. Then I will adjust the left or right vertical point of impact so the bullets hit in the center of the target halfway between the two sides of the paper. However some people prefer to do both adjustments at the same time. Therefore you may follow whichever procedure you prefer.

(**Safety Note:** Remember the first and second firearm safety rules which are: (1) **Always** treat every firearm as if it were loaded and ready to fire, and (2) **Never** point a firearm at anyone or anything you do not intend to kill or destroy. Therefore **never** use your rifle scope instead of binoculars to look at other hunters. If your rifle were to accidentally discharge then you would be guilty of murder. Even though you might claim that your firearm went off accidentally you could not claim that you were only "accidentally" looking at the other hunter through your rifle scope. You need to remember that what you see through your rifle scope is exactly what your rifle is pointed at. Would you want other hunters pointing their rifles and their rifle scopes at you? I think not. Therefore don't do it to other hunters.)

How to Properly Center the Cross Hairs Inside Your Rifle Scope

Use proper safety precautions and make sure that your bullets have a proper range backstop and that your bullets will not exit the "shooting range" and injure someone or damage any type of property. Always wear **hearing** and **eye protection** whenever you are shooting a firearm.

Zeroing a rifle scope is best done on a very calm day when there is **no noticeable** wind. If your scope is properly centered for "no wind" conditions then you can later adjust your point of aim for different wind conditions as appropriate. "Wind drift" will be discussed later in this chapter.

Allow the barrel of your rifle to cool down between shots so that you will not be introducing another variable into the sight adjustment process. In other words, wait at least one-minute before you fire another shot through your rifle barrel.

Adjustments to your rifle scope should be based on the **average of three shots**. Fire three bullets at the target and then draw a circle that surrounds all three of the holes in your target. Compute the distance from the center of the circle you just drew to the center of the target bull's-eye in order to determine the average correction necessary to center your shots on the bull's-eye. Do **not** measure the straight line distance from your circle to the center of the target bull's-eye. Instead you will need to measure **two** distances. You will need to measure the distance from the center of your circle to the center of the page (from left to right) on a horizontal straight line for your windage adjustment. You will also need to measure the distance from the center of your circle to the center of the page (from top to bottom) on a vertical straight line for your elevation adjustment.

Generally it is much easier to initially center your rifle scope at a target that is only 25-yards away. After you can successfully hit the bull's-eye on a target that is 25 yards away then you can gradually move the target out to any distance you prefer and you will only need to make minor adjustments to the cross hairs inside your scope. However, if you start at 100-yards then your original shots may not even be on the paper target and therefore you will have no idea how to make the correct adjustments to your scope cross hairs.

As already discussed above you should place your paper target so its bull's-eye is approximately one or two inches above the front muzzle of your rifle. For a 223 the bull's-eye should be about 1/2 inch above the rifle muzzle. For a 7.62x39 and a 308 the bull's-eye should be about 1.5 inches above the rifle muzzle. This will allow you to impart a slight upward trajectory to your bullet before it begins its downward descent and it will help you to increase the effective distance at which your rifle will be "accurate." Depending on your "shooting range" this may require you to shoot your rifle from a sitting or prone (lying down) position. If you shoot at a target bull's-eye that is exactly level with the center bore of your rifle (or a little lower) then you will not achieve the optimal zero settings for your rifle scope and you will be disappointed with your future shooting results when hunting any wild game animal that is **not** at the same exact distance from your scope as your original paper target.

If you are at a "professional target range" and your targets must be attached to a pulley wire to move them out into the firing range, and the bull's-eye of the target will always be approximately level with the center bore of your rifle, then aim for a spot about one or two-inches above the original target's bull's-eye to set your rifle scope. You can create a new higher bull's-eye on your target using a black felt tip marking pen. Just draw a new bull's-eye the same diameter as the one on your target but about one or two-inches above the original bull's-eye.

If you are not at a "professional target range" then you can establish a level target range for shooting by stretching a piece of string tightly between two sticks or poles driven into the ground (or between two trees) and then verifying the level of the string using a carpenter's level. This will not yield "surveyor accuracy" but it will be adequate for our simple shooting tests. Place the center of the bull's-eye of each target level with the string and then make sure the front muzzle of your rifle is about one or two inches below the string or below the target bull's-eye.

After properly securing your rifle scope to your rifle there are three methods of centering the cross hairs inside your rifle scope:

1. Trial and error.
2. Bore sighting.
3. Using your rifle iron sights (if you have see-through scope mounts).

Trial and error: Simply shoot your rifle three times at the bull's-eye on a really big target that is about 25 yards away. Based on the average position of those three shots on the target you can then adjust the cross hairs inside your scope accordingly. This method is relatively simple and easy to do if you have a really big sheet of paper or a really big cardboard box. However, this method normally does require a slightly higher investment in ammunition because your first few shots may be a really long distance away from the target bull's-eye.

Bore sighting: If your rifle bolt is removable then remove the bolt from your rifle. Properly secure your rifle to some type of bench rest or between two sand bags so your rifle will not move. Then look through the inside rifle bore and mentally remember exactly where on the target the bore is pointed. Then look through your scope and adjust the cross hairs to that approximate position on the target. Then look through the rifle bore and verify that your rifle has not shifted position. If it has then note the new position that it is pointing to on the target and adjust the scope cross hairs to match. Continue this procedure until the image you see when looking through the inside bore of your rifle is in the center of the cross hairs of your scope. If your rifle does not have a removable bolt then you could invest in a special "bore sighting tool" (collimator) that is placed inside the front muzzle of the rifle and then you adjust the scope cross hairs to match the center of the optical

Chapter Sixty-Two: How to Hit the Target Bull's-Eye

target that extends above the tool in front of your scope. This will put you somewhere on the paper target when you first shoot the rifle. However, in my opinion the first method above is just as good and therefore I suggest that you **not** invest in a special "bore sighting tool" unless you intend to zero new rifle scopes to earn a living.

Iron Sights: Most rifles have iron sights permanently attached to the top of the rifle. The design of those iron sights vary somewhat but the most common design is shown in the illustration on the right. Point the rifle at the target and align the top of the front sight so that it is level with the right and left tops of the rear sight as shown in the illustration. Depending on the size of the target bull's-eye and your distance from the target, it may be necessary to align the very **bottom** of the target bull's-eye with the straight line formed by your front and rear sights. This is necessary because the bull's-eye may appear so small at 100 yards that it is difficult to see and it may be completely covered by your front and rear sights if you try to center those sights on the center of the bull's-eye.

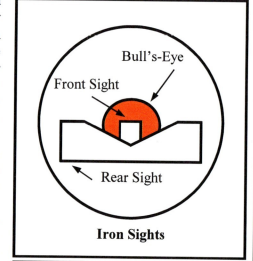
Iron Sights

Shoot your rifle three times at a target using your iron sights to determine where the bullet actually makes contact with the target (on the average). If your rifle has adjustable iron sights (either front, or rear, or both) then make the appropriate adjustments following the instructions that came with your rifle until your shots hit the approximate center of the bull's-eye. Make sure your iron sights are properly tightened to your rifle before you continue. Record the date, the yardage, and the words "iron sights" on your paper target along with the make of rifle and the type of ammunition you are using. Save this target for future reference purposes.

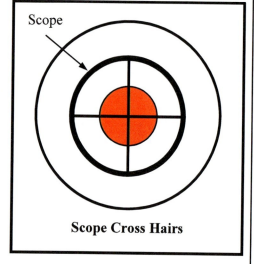
Scope Cross Hairs

If you have "see-through" scope mounts then you can use either your iron sights or your scope depending on the current hunting situation. For example, sometimes there is a light fog early in the morning and some scopes will not provide as good a sight picture as your iron sights.

If you will be purchasing new scope mounts then I personally suggest that you invest in good quality see-through scope mounts. See-through scope mounts will elevate your rifle scope approximately one-inch higher than regular scope mounts and therefore you will need to raise your head and your eye about one-inch higher than normal. Individuals who are accustomed to the lower mounts find this uncomfortable and therefore they will try to discourage you from using these types of mounts. You will need to make your own decision about the type of scope mounts that you prefer.

However, almost everyone agrees that higher quality scope mounts are preferred to the cheaper mounts. Price is not the only issue. Look at the number of screw holes in the top surface of one of the scope mounts. If each side of the scope mount has two screw holes then you will have two screws on each side of each mount locking your scope to your scope mount. However, if each side of the scope mount only has a single screw hole then you will only have one screw on each side of each mount locking your scope to your scope mount. If possible, always buy scope mounts with two screw holes on each side of each scope mount. In other words, you would have a total of eight screws locking your scope to your scope mounts instead of four.

See-Through Scope Mounts: Look down your iron sights at the bull's-eye of a target that is 25 yards away and without moving your rifle immediately look through your scope to see where the scope cross hairs are centered. Make a mental note of the image you see. Repeat this process three times (look down your iron sights and then through your scope). Then adjust your scope control knobs the appropriate number of "clicks"

Chapter Sixty-Two: How to Hit the Target Bull's-Eye

to put the scope cross hairs on the center of the target. After you have your scope cross hairs adjusted to match the original sight picture that you see through your iron sights then you will **stop** using your iron sights and you will only use your scope. Test fire three shots using your scope. Look at the target and draw a circle around the three holes in the target. Compute the horizontal distance and the vertical distance from the center of the circle you just drew to the center of the target bull's-eye. Adjust your scope cross hairs accordingly.

Fire three more shots and verify the results. Repeat this process until your three shots are reasonably well centered around the bull's-eye using your scope. Then place a new target at 50 yards and fire three shots. Do not worry about the point of impact **above** the bull's-eye. **Only** adjust the windage left/right dial to better align the bullet in the center of the target halfway between the left and right edges of the target. Then place a new target at 75 yards and repeat. Record the data for the three shots and **only** adjust the left/right cross hairs as necessary. Repeat at 100 yards, 125 yards, and 150 yards (if possible). If feasible and possible on your "shooting range" then repeat at 175 yards, 200 yards, 225 yards, and 250 yards. (Note: For most of us distances beyond 100 yards may not be possible on our "shooting range.") Record all the data. Make sure you write the date, the yardage, the make of rifle and scope, and the type of ammunition on each paper target and keep those targets for future reference.

You will probably discover that your bullets hit all the targets at each of the different distances at approximately the same right/left center of the target (assuming a calm day with no noticeable wind). Depending on the ammunition, you may also notice that the bullets were less than three or four inches above the bull's-eye when the targets were closer and less than three or four inches below the bull's-eye when the targets were further out. At some distance the bullets may have dropped 4-inches below the bull's-eye. This is the maximum range for your rifle with the scope originally centered at 25 yards. It will also now be centered at some other distance further out. And you can now successfully hunt medium size wild game animals without having to estimate the exact distance to the target, as long as the animal is anywhere within the lethal accurate range of your rifle. Your shots will hit the animal in its kill zone which is usually an eight-inch circle on medium size game animals, such as deer.

As an example, your hunting rifle may be bull's-eye centered at 25 yards and at 125 yards. It may rise four-inches above the bull's-eye at 85 yards. And it may drop four inches below the bull's-eye at 150 yards. Therefore your effective eight-inch kill zone would be anywhere out to a maximum distance of 150 yards.

A high-power hunting rifle will not work on really small game animals such as rabbits or squirrels. If you are going to hunt rabbits or squirrels with a **rifle** then I suggest that you use 22LR ammunition and that you get within **25 yards** of the animal and shoot it in its head (if your 22LR rifle is that accurate at 25 yards). If you are using a 22LR **pistol** then you should probably get within **25 feet** of the squirrel.

Impact of a Cross Wind

Depending on the direction from which the wind is blowing the wind will have one of the following three impacts:

1. **Front or Head Wind:** A wind blowing directly into your face will **decrease** the normal trajectory range of your rifle. Generally it will **not** blow your bullet off course by a significant amount.

2. **Rear or Tail Wind:** A wind blowing directly from your rear will **increase** the normal trajectory range of your rifle. Generally it will **not** blow your bullet off course by a significant amount.

3. **Side or Cross Wind:** A wind blowing from your side will blow your bullet off course. It may also have a minor impact on the trajectory of your bullet.
Therefore you will need to understand the impact of a cross wind on your bullet.

Cross Wind: When you are hunting and your shooting distance will be at 100 yards or less then a 10 mile-per-hour cross wind will drive your bullet off its straight line flight path by one-inch or less. Even if you are shooting at a small game animal with a four-inch kill zone, this amount of drift should not result in your missing the "kill zone" on your target.

Chapter Sixty-Two: How to Hit the Target Bull's-Eye

If your shot will be more than 100 yards then you may need to estimate the current wind speed and the wind direction and determine the wind's probable impact on your hunting bullet. The wind will not only blow your bullet sideways but it may also change your bullet's normal trajectory by lifting the bullet up or pushing the bullet down a little bit. As an example, at 200 yards the wind could push your bullet three-inches (or more) off its original center line to the target. This might cause you to miss your target's kill zone and the animal may then escape and die by itself in some lonely place.

Approximate Impact of a 10 mile per hour 90-degree Cross Wind

Bullet Caliber	100 Yards	200 Yards	300 Yards
223 (5.56x45)	0.9 Inch	3.6 Inch	8.5 Inch
7.62x39	0.8 Inch	3.4 Inch	8.0 Inch
308 (7.62x51)	0.7 Inch	3.2 Inch	7.5 Inch
30-06	0.7 Inch	3.0 Inch	7.0 Inch
Average "Rounded"	1.0 Inch	3.0 Inch	8.0 Inch

Note 1: The wind drift data values for each caliber in the above table are the *average* wind drift numbers from several different ballistic tables from several different sources. There is a lot of variability in wind drift data depending on which ballistics table you consult. For the same caliber these wind drift differences are caused by differences in bullet weight (grains), bullet composition, and bullet shape. However, at 100 yards these differences have a minor impact on wind drift, usually plus or minus 0.2 inches or less for different weight bullets of the same caliber. But at 300 yards the difference can be plus or minus two or three inches for the same caliber. If you will always be shooting the same exact bullet, with the same number of grains, of the same shape, from the same manufacturer, then you should use the wind drift numbers for your bullet instead of the above average table values.

Note 2: If your rifle caliber is not in the above table then consult any good wind ballistics table to determine the wind drift for your bullet based on a ten-mile per hour cross wind blowing at a 90-degree angle to your shot.

Note 3: I realize there are slight ballistic differences between a 223 and a NATO 5.56x45 bullet, and also between a 308 and a NATO 7.62x51 bullet. But for most hunters those differences are not significant. However, if you wish you may consult a ballistics table that has your exact caliber listed and use that data instead of the "average" approximations that are listed above.

The wind drift table contains very little data because most of us can't remember all the necessary statistics required to compensate for shot accuracy under normal hunting conditions when we frequently only have a few seconds to align our rifle on the target and slowly squeeze the trigger. However, most of us can remember two or three numbers and then make adjustments to those numbers as the situation requires. If your hunting rifle has a lethal "kill zone" trajectory of 200 yards or less then you would only need to memorize the 100-yard and 200-yard numbers in the above table for the caliber of bullet you shoot in your hunting rifle.

On the other hand, if you wish to exactly determine the impact of the wind on your bullet then the first thing you would need to know would be an accurate determination of the true wind speed at the exact time you intend to fire your rifle. The second issue would be an accurate measure of the exact angle from which the wind is blowing. The third factor would be that the wind normally does not blow at a constant steady speed but it slows down and speeds up over a very short period of time. The fourth factor would be that trees or other objects on the wind side of the bullet's flight path will change the wind turbulence as the bullet passes those points. These four factors are very difficult to simultaneously correlate accurately when you only have a few seconds in which to make your shot and your adrenalin level is also quite high.

Therefore if the above factors could be simplified into an easy method for quickly "estimating" the impact of the current wind conditions then you could make a quick decision about your point of aim on the animal's "kill zone circle."

Simple Wind Drift Mathematics: If the wind is blowing from a 45-degree angle instead of a 90-degree angle then it will result in 75% of the above wind drift values and **not** 50% even though a 45-degree angle is one-half a 90-degree angle. Therefore, for "practical rough estimates" we can ignore the exact angle at which the wind is blowing and simply use the original 90-degree wind data.

Therefore memorize the 10 mile per hour wind drift numbers for your rifle at 100 yards, 200 yards, and maybe also at 300 yards. If you believe the wind is about 10 miles per hour then use the table values for your caliber of ammunition exactly the way you have the numbers memorized. But if you believe the wind speed is only about 5 miles per hour then divide those values in half. If you believe the wind speed is 20 miles per hour then multiply those values by two. If you believe the wind speed is 30 miles per hour then multiply those values by three.

After you quickly do the appropriate mental multiplication then you should align your scope cross hairs that distance away from the center of the animal's "kill zone" into the direction that the wind is blowing from and slowly squeeze the trigger. In other words, if the wind is blowing from your right then aim that distance to the right of the animal's kill zone. If the wind is blowing from your left then aim that distance to the left of the animal's kill zone.

If you will use this simple technique then you can leave your scope "windage" adjustment dial alone and not move it to compensate for a cross wind. It is really nice to be able to always know exactly where your bullet will hit at different distances under no wind conditions. But if you are constantly changing your scope windage and elevation settings then after a short period of time you will have to stop and reset your rifle scope back to its original zero. But if you follow the above suggestions then there will be **no** need to adjust your windage or elevation scope controls and your scope will remain centered the way you originally aligned it.

Grandpappy's Average Wind Drift Values

In the real world there are several problems when you try to be extremely precise with wind drift data:

1. The wind does **not** always blow at exactly 90-degrees to your line of fire. A 45-degree cross wind results in a 75% wind drift effect.
2. It is extremely difficult to accurately estimate fractions of an inch at 100 yards, or 200 yards, or 300 yards.
3. It is extremely difficult to accurately estimate the exact distance to the target when the target is a wild game animal (because all deer are not the same exact size).

Therefore it would be useful if we could make the intellectual transition from a perfectly controlled wind drift experiment to a practical real world hunting situation. In other words, instead of trying to be precise to within 1/10 of an inch, let's be satisfied if we can get our shot to within approximately one-inch of where it needs to be.

The above wind drift table begins with one of the smallest hunting calibers (.223 caliber) and it continues up to one of the larger calibers (30-06 caliber). From the smallest to the largest caliber the average wind drift distance at 300 yards varies by only 1.5 inches. If you compute the approximate average of the above table values and then round that average to the nearest whole number, then you could easily compute a single wind drift number for each distance and use it for all calibers. Those are the average rounded values on the bottom line of the above table.

Therefore when I am hunting and there is a 10 mph cross wind, and the target is at 100 yards then I use one-inch, at 200 yards I use three-inches, and at 300-yards I use eight-inches, regardless of the caliber of firearm that I might be using at the time. I then try to roughly guess the wind speed and the distance to the target. Then I quickly adjust my wind drift numbers accordingly. Then I adjust my point of aim to match my quick calculations. This simple quick easy estimate usually works for me. It might also work for you depending on your firearm, the caliber of bullet you hunt with, your ability to estimate distances, and your ability to guess approximate wind speeds.

You should also remember that if you exceed the normal trajectory range of your hunting rifle then you will also need to compensate for the additional trajectory drop of your hunting bullet. When you only have a few seconds to make a decision about your point of aim this can easily cause you to completely miss the target, or to simple wound the animal and it will die later in a remote lonely area. Therefore even though there is a lot of literature dedicated to "long range" hunting, my advice is that you should seriously consider limiting your hunting shots to the normal lethal trajectory range of your hunting rifle.

I realize the above "wind drift" simplification is inadequate for anyone who wishes "perfect" shot placement. But most of us only want to be able to reliably hit the game animal in its "kill zone" so we can bring some fresh meat home to the family to enjoy for supper.

Shooting Up or Down a Hill

Only a few of your hunting shots will be on perfectly level ground. Most of your shots will be fired at a game animal that is a little above or a little below the center bore of your rifle. If the animal is only five or ten feet above or below you then you can ignore the difference in elevation and simply align your scope cross hairs in the center of the animal's "kill zone" the same as if you were shooting over level ground.

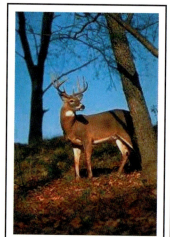

If you are shooting inside the normal trajectory range of your rifle then you can also ignore the difference in elevation. In other words, for a 7.62x39 bullet that is fired at a game animal that is a maximum of 175 yards away, then you can **ignore any difference in elevation** and align your scope cross hairs as if the animal were on perfectly level ground.

However, if the game animal is more than 10 feet above or below you, and your shot will be further away than the normal plus or minus two-inch (or three-inch) trajectory of your hunting rifle, then aim a little "**lower**" than normal.

In other words, to compensate for shooting at extended distances either up or down a hill, aim a little "**lower**" than normal.

To determine approximately how much lower you will need to remember the trajectory data for your rifle cartridge at approximately three-fourths of the visual distance to the animal. This will be a simple quick approximation but you will probably not have the time to do research on the data or consult any type of ballistics chart.

Simple Elevation Mathematics: If you are shooting **inside** the normal trajectory range of your rifle then you can **ignore any difference in elevation** and align your scope cross hairs as if the animal were on perfectly level ground. However, to compensate for shooting at extended distances either up or down a hill **outside** the normal trajectory range of your rifle then aim a little "**lower**" than normal.

Finally, if the animal is beyond the lethal kill zone of your hunting rifle then you need to ask yourself why you are attempting this shot? If the reason is because the animal is not a "meat" animal but it is a "pest" animal that is killing your livestock or eating your crops, then take the shot and hope for the best. Even if you don't get a quick kill, if you can mortally wound the animal then it will probably eventually die due to the loss of blood or other reasons.

Gun Cleaning Kit and Gun Tool Kit

If you can afford it then you should consider investing in a **Multiple Purpose Gun Cleaning Kit** that could be used to clean almost any type of handgun, rifle, or shotgun, including the smallest BB or pellet rifle up to the 50 caliber BMG (Browning Machine Gun). Although you may not currently have an application for all the gun cleaning accessories in this kit you may discover that you will eventually need many of them if you continue to acquire more firearms during your lifetime. The Universal 61-Piece Gun Cleaning Kit in the picture on the right is available at some Walmarts in their Sporting Goods section for approximately $40.

Chapter Sixty-Two: How to Hit the Target Bull's-Eye

In addition to a gun cleaning kit you will also need additional gun cleaning patches, gun cleaning solvent, and gun cleaning oil. If you wish you may purchase specially formulated gun cleaning chemicals. Or you may use Automatic Transmission Fluid (ATF) to clean your firearms and 20 weight (synthetic) motor oil to lubricate your firearms.

You should keep all the special hex wrenches and other firearm adjustment tools that you gradually acquire in a special portable **Gun Tool Kit** reserved just for your firearms. This gun tool kit could be a cloth bag or a plastic box or a small metal tool box. You can add to this tool kit yourself as you gradually acquire more tools, such as the tools that come with any scope mounts, scopes, or lasers that you mount on your firearms. If you will keep all your special firearm tools together then they will be easy to locate at some future date when you again need them to make an adjustment to your firearm or one of its accessories.

The one additional tool kit that you should seriously consider buying is a special **Gunsmith Screwdriver Set** (picture on right) that contains all the special screwdrivers you will normally need to properly disassemble and reassemble your firearms without damaging them.

"Lemons" and "Cherries"

Your average shooting performance will be directly related to the average accuracy of the firearm you are using.

Several years ago I had the following two rifles and they were both chambered for 22LR ammunition:

1. A Marlin Model 39AS Lever Action 22LR. It would consistently group three-shots into a **five-inch** circle at 50 yards.

2. A Ruger Model 10/22 Semi-Automatic 22LR. It would consistently group three-shots into a **one-inch** circle at 50 yards.

In both of the shooting tests I was the only shooter (please remember I am only an "average shooter"). In both cases I was in a standard sitting position without any type of bench rest. The ammunition was exactly the same. The distance and other conditions were also the same because the targets were in the same exact location. I paused, relaxed, and intentionally took my time to aim carefully before firing each shot. The only significant variable was that I was using two different firearms.

I also tried a different brand of 22LR ammunition. The above results did not change.

I do **not** mean to imply by this that all Ruger Model 10/22 rifles are more accurate than all Marlin Model 39AS rifles. That simply is not true.

What I do mean to imply is that some Ruger Model 10/22 rifles shoot significantly better (or worse) than other Ruger Model 10/22 rifles. And some Marlin Model 39AS rifles shoot significantly better (or worse) than other Marlin Model 39AS rifles. If you find a rifle that has remarkable accuracy then I suggest you never sell it.

The above concept is important because you may be evaluating your average shooting performance based on the results of **one rifle**. If you have an "average accuracy" rifle then your results will be directly related to your true average shooting ability. But if you have a "poor accuracy" rifle then your poor performance may be due to your rifle and **not** to your natural born ability as a marksman. The only way you can test this theory is to shoot the same type of ammunition at the same distance in a similar rifle to see if your average accuracy remains approximately the same.

This concept also applies to other things such as trucks. Occasionally someone will buy a brand new truck and it will be a "lemon" and it will break down during the first 1,000 miles of driving. And someone else will buy the same exact model of truck and it will be a "cherry" and it will last 500,000 miles. Most people understand this concept when it comes to vehicles. But this same exact concept also applies to firearms and to

Chapter Sixty-Two: How to Hit the Target Bull's-Eye

almost every other item that you might purchase, such as DVD players and washing machines. Most of these units will be normal average quality items but a very small number of them will be either lemons or cherries.

In my opinion my particular Marlin was a "lemon" and my particular Ruger was a "cherry."

In most cases when a person discovers that he has a firearm that is not reliable or that it has some other type of problem then he becomes very anxious to sell it or trade it. You should keep this in mind if you see an unbelievable bargain on a firearm. There may be something seriously wrong with that weapon. Before you make a decision to purchase that firearm I strongly suggest that you first have it examined by a professional gunsmith and then you should test fire it to determine its potential accuracy.

In my opinion you should purchase "new" firearms whenever possible. "Used" firearms do have certain advantages but they also have the potential to be very inaccurate or they may need a major repair that is not obvious until after you have fired a few shots through the firearm. However, one important exception would be antique firearms that you purchase for their rarity or investment value or because they are "pre-1899" federal regulation exempt firearms.

Summary and Conclusions

The four universally accepted firearm safety rules:

1. **Always** treat every firearm as if it were loaded and ready to fire.
2. **Never** point a firearm at anyone or anything you do not intend to kill or destroy.
3. **Never** put your finger on the trigger until the sights are aligned on the target.
4. Positively **identify your target** (no guessing) and everything behind your target the bullet might hit.

Grandpappy's safety advice:

1. Always wear safety glasses when shooting any type of firearm.
2. Always wear some type of hearing protection when shooting any type of firearm.
3. Do **not** store or carry your firearm with a live round in the firing position in front of the firing pin. Wait until you are actually ready to use your weapon before you insert a live round into the firing chamber.
4. Do **not** use your rifle scope to look at other hunters. Use binoculars instead.

To improve your accuracy when shooting at paper targets:

1. Dry fire your weapon without any ammunition in it until you are comfortable with your breathing cycle and your trigger pull.
2. Wear hearing and eye protection whenever you shoot a firearm.
3. Aim the rifle at the target. Acquire the bull's-eye. Relax but do not allow your weapon to drift too far from the bull's-eye.
4. Take three normal slow breaths.
5. At the end of the third breath, after you have expelled the air in your lungs, begin to hold your breath and once again quickly center the scope cross hairs on the target bull's-eye.
6. Slowly but firmly squeeze the trigger with the tip of your finger in a smooth continuous motion. Do not move the rest of your body.
7. The bullet explosion should come as a "surprise" even though you were expecting it.
8. If possible, limit your target practice using live ammunition to one-hour or less per day to minimize shooting fatigue.
9. If possible, skip at least one-day between practice sessions to maximize your progress along your own natural learning curve.

To determine the *maximum* effective hunting distance for your rifle use the *minimum* of the following distances:

1. The maximum average **visibility** in your normal hunting area.
2. The **lethal range** of your ammunition at which it still has at least 800 foot pounds of remaining kinetic energy (for a pointed bullet).
3. The **trajectory** of your bullet so that it does not rise or fall more than two-inches (7.62x39) during its

flight path until it hits your target. If you have a rifle caliber other than 7.62x39 then you may use plus or minus four-inches if necessary.

4. The distance at which your hunting rifle can still **accurately** group at least three shots into a four-inch diameter circle.

To center the cross hairs on your rifle scope:

1. Place the bull's-eye of all your targets approximately 1.5 inches about the front muzzle of your rifle (use 1/2 inch for a 223).
2. Wait at least one-minute between shots to allow your rifle barrel time to cool off.
3. Adjust the cross hairs inside your rifle scope so your rifle is zeroed on the bull's-eye at 25 yards.
4. Only adjust your scope windage dial to center your shots between the left and right edges of the target at 50, 75, and 100 yards.
5. Continue to move the targets out 25 yards at a time until your shots fall four-inches below the bull's-eye. This is the maximum accurate range of your rifle.
6. Look at your collection of targets and determine which target, in addition to the one at 25 yards, has your shots grouped equally around the center bull's-eye of your target. Your rifle will also be zeroed at this yardage in addition to 25 yards.
7. Verify that the maximum trajectory of your bullets did not exceed four inches above or below the bull's-eye over the entire lethal trajectory range of your rifle. (Note: I use plus or minus two-inches for a 7.62x39 bullet but your rifle caliber may require plus or minus four inches.)

Simple wind drift mathematics:

1. **Front or Head Wind:** A wind blowing directly into your face will **decrease** the normal trajectory range of your rifle. Generally it will **not** blow your bullet off course by a significant amount.
2. **Rear or Tail Wind:** A wind blowing directly from your rear will **increase** the normal trajectory range of your rifle. Generally it will **not** blow your bullet off course by a significant amount.
3. **Side or Cross Wind:** Memorize the 10 mile per hour wind drift numbers for your rifle caliber at 100 yards, 200 yards, and maybe also at 300 yards. Or you could use Grandpappy's Universal Average Wind Drift Values as shown in the table below.

Grandpappy's Universal Average Wind Drift Values
for a 10 mile per hour 90-degree Cross Wind

Distance =	100 Yards	200 Yards	300 Yards
Wind Drift =	1 Inch	3 Inches	8 Inches

Multiplication Factors for Different Wind Speeds
(mph = Miles Per Hour)

Wind Speed =	5 mph	10 mph	15 mph	20 mph	25 mph	30 mph
Multiply By =	0.5	1.0	1.5	2.0	2.5	3.0

If you believe the wind is about 10 miles per hour then use the appropriate table values exactly the way you have the numbers memorized. But if you believe the wind speed is only about 5 miles per hour then divide those values in half (or multiply by 0.5). If you believe the wind speed is 20 miles per hour then multiply those values by two. If you believe the wind speed is 30 miles per hour then multiply those values by three. After you quickly do the appropriate mental multiplication then align your scope cross hairs that distance away from the center of the animal's "kill zone" **into** the direction that the wind is blowing from and slowly squeeze the trigger. In other words, if the wind is blowing from your right then aim that distance to the right of the animal's kill zone. If the wind is blowing from your left then aim that distance to the left of the animal's kill zone.

Simple elevation mathematics:

If you are shooting **inside** the normal trajectory range of your rifle then you can **ignore any difference in elevation** and align your scope cross hairs as if the animal were on perfectly level ground. However, to compensate for shooting at extended distances either up or down a hill **outside** the normal trajectory range of your rifle then aim a little "**lower**" than normal based on the trajectory data for your hunting bullet.

Distance, Trajectory, and Lethal Energy:

Summary of "Average" Ballistics Data for Three Common Rifle Calibers
When the Rifle Bullet Passes Through the Target Bull's-Eye at a Distance of 25 Yards
and the Target Bull's-eye is 0.5 inches Above the Rifle Muzzle
at 25 Yards for the 223 (5.56x45)
and the Target Bull's-eye is 1.5 inches Above the Rifle Muzzle
at 25 Yards for the 7.62x39 and 308 (7.62x51).

Rifle Caliber	First Bull's-eye	Second Bull's-eye	Maximum Trajectory	Minimum Trajectory	800 Ft. Lbs.
223 or 5.56x45	25 Yards	175 Yards	+ 1.0" at 95 Yards	- 1.0" at 200 Yards	150 Yards
7.62x39	25 Yards	150 Yards	+ 1.5" at 110 Yards	- 1.5" at 175 Yards	240 Yards
308 or 7.62x51	25 Yards	220 Yards	+ 3.0" at 125 Yards	- 3.0" at 260 Yards	600 Yards

As the distance increases the number of variables also **increases** and the chance of your hitting the animal in its kill zone significantly **decreases**. Therefore please limit your shots to the maximum accuracy range of your hunting rifle to avoid simply wounding an animal. A wounded animal will almost always escape to its den or bedding area and there it will die a slow and unpleasant death. This is not a quick humane kill and it benefits no one, unless the animal is a "pest" and it needs to be dispatched to protect your livestock or your crops.

Therefore regardless of your centerfire rifle caliber, if you are shooting at a distance of 150 yards or less then you can probably ignore the trajectory of your bullet, and the differences in elevation to your target, and only make minor adjustments to your point of aim if a cross wind is blowing. Some of the larger centerfire rifle calibers can extend this distance out to approximately 250 yards, more or less. However, unless you are a truly skilled marksman who has a significant amount of practice shooting under a wide variety of elevation and wind conditions at extended ranges beyond 250 yards, then you should probably not attempt shots past 250 yards with your hunting rifle. There are too many variables to compensate for and the probability of your hitting the target in its kill zone at that extended distance is relatively small.

Lemons and Cherries:

Your average shooting performance will be directly related to the average accuracy of the firearm you are using.

Chapter Sixty-Three

Should You Install a Laser Sight on Your Firearm?

Introduction

The Holy Bible tells how a simple shepherd boy defeated a nine-foot tall heavily-armed battle-hardened soldier using a smooth round stone and a sling. While Goliath was lying stunned on the ground David ran forward and removed Goliath's sword from its sheath and then David immediately cut off Goliath's head with Goliath's own sword. According to the Bible that is the last recorded incident of David using his sling. From that day forward David slew thousands of enemy soldiers using a sword. David had the wisdom to upgrade his self-defense weapon when the opportunity presented itself. (1 Samuel 17:40-51)

It should be noted that David's smooth round stone was a primitive projectile and David's sling was a primitive projectile delivery device. David was successful because he was able to quickly and accurately hit exactly where he was aiming with his projectile.

Today's modern projectile weapons are firearms and bullets. If you already own a firearm then you will need to decide whether or not you should upgrade your firearm with the most advanced technology currently available. In other words, should you add a laser sight to your existing firearm? In order to help you make this decision this chapter will review the advantages and shortcomings of laser sights.

Advantages of a Laser Sight

1. Helps you quickly and accurately align your firearm on the center of the target.
2. Permits a more rapid **accurate** follow-up shot on the same target if the situation requires it (a double tap).
3. Helps you to more quickly realign your firearm on a target if you move to a different location behind some more effective cover.
4. Allows you to accurately shoot around or over some type of cover without having to physically sight down the barrel of your firearm. You only need to be able to see where your laser dot appears on the target before you squeeze the trigger.
5. Allows you to focus on the target instead of trying to focus on your front sight and on the target at the same time. Only having to focus on one object is much easier to do.
6. Permits a wider field of peripheral vision because you are focusing on a more distant object instead of a closer object (your front sight). You can see more things off to each side of the original target. In other words, if you are being attacked by multiple individuals it gives you the opportunity to see more of those people at the same time and not become distracted by the one person you are currently shooting at. This allows your brain time to subconsciously plan your future shots at those other targets.
7. Allows you to more rapidly acquire and successfully hit multiple targets in different locations at different distances.
8. During practice training sessions it results in more accurate results in less time using less ammunition. You will be pleasantly surprised at how quickly your average accuracy will significantly improve as you practice shooting at paper targets.

9. Allows you to practice dry firing your weapon at a target and visually seeing how the point of bullet impact changes as you squeeze the trigger. This is a significant training aid because it helps you learn how to hold your weapon steadier as you squeeze the trigger. This will improve your future average accuracy with your firearm even when you are not using your laser sight.
10. It will **significantly** improve your average accuracy with a short barrel handgun (2 or 3 inch barrel). The iron sights on short barrel handguns are very close together and this introduces more variability in the accuracy of the weapon. However, a laser sight allows you to concentrate on holding the laser dot on the center of the target and you will become a better shot with a short barrel handgun. I had to personally experience this significant accuracy improvement with a short barrel handgun before I would change my opinion about the average accuracy of a short barrel weapon. (Note: Due to a shortage of 380 ammunition I only fired six-rounds with a Ruger LCP but I was astonished at how close those shots were to the center of the target bull's-eye when I used the Crimson Trace Laser Sight as an aiming tool.)

Shortcomings of a Laser Sight

1. A laser dot is extremely difficult and sometimes impossible to see in bright sunlight during the middle of the day. This is especially true when the sun is shining directly on a white or brown or red object.
   (**Note:** In artificial light a laser dot is very easy to see. Even during the middle of the day if you are indoors the laser dot will be easy to see against any background, including white, brown, or red.)
2. On a bright sunny day if you can't see your laser dot on the target then you need to be intellectually prepared to fire when see that your front sight is properly aligned on the target and the target is in a direct line with the barrel of your weapon and your forearm. If you hesitate on a bright sunny day during a stressful gunfight then you may get shot.
3. Your laser batteries may expire at a time of critical need. Therefore you should continue to practice without your laser sight each time you practice with your laser sight. This will enable you to remain reasonably proficient with and without a laser sight.
4. Laser sights are relatively expensive. A handgun laser sight will usually cost somewhere between $180 to $290 (more or less).

Proper Handgun Grip

Your handgun should fit into your hand so the barrel is in an almost straight line with your forearm. In other words, your handgun barrel should line up with whatever you are pointing your forearm at. This will minimize the time required to align the laser dot on the center of your target. This will also allow you to more accurately shoot your handgun in the middle of a bright sunny day when your laser sight is ineffective.

Practical Laser Sight Applications

1. **Handguns:** Yes, a laser sight is an excellent addition to a handgun.
   Most handguns are accurate at a maximum of 50 feet (usually a lot less) and this is an ideal application for a laser sight.
2. **Shotguns:** Yes, a laser sight may be installed on a **semi-automatic shotgun** but **not a pump action shotgun**.
   a. The major problem with mounting a laser sight on a shotgun is that you will need to periodically realign the laser sight because the recoil of a shotgun will gradually change the point of laser dot aim until it no longer corresponds to the average center of shotgun shell impact.
   b. However, the laser dot can be easily re-aligned on a shotgun by adjusting the windage and elevation laser sight settings until the laser dot appears on the target in the same spot as the top front sight of the shotgun.
   c. A laser can be installed below the front barrel of a semi-automatic shotgun and it will allow you to more quickly and accurately align the shotgun when hunting or when using the shotgun for self-

defense in a stressful situation. The first laser I installed in 1998 was under the barrel of a semi-automatic shotgun and I was very pleased with its performance. The laser activation cord extended down under the barrel of the shotgun and the laser activation button was installed on the left front hand grip of the shotgun. Since it was a semi-automatic shotgun the front hand grip was stationary and it was not used to load a shell into the shotgun chamber.
   d. This is the reason a laser sight would be significantly more difficult to install on a pump action shotgun. The pump moves back and forth under the barrel and therefore you could not mount the laser activation switch on the pump. The pump may also interfere with the laser cord if you try to mount the laser switch near the shotgun trigger. It may be possible to work out these technical issues with a pump action shotgun but I do not have a reliable solution to these issues at this time. Therefore I do **not** recommend the addition of a laser sight to a pump action shotgun.

3. **Rifles:** No, a laser sight is **not** appropriate for a rifle.
   The range of a rifle is significantly greater than either a handgun or a shotgun and you really need a good rifle scope so you can clearly see your target and properly align your shot on the center of the target while taking elevation and wind drift into consideration. A rifle scope will also allow you to zero your rifle from point-blank range out to the accurate trajectory range of your rifle which is usually at least 150 yards. Your rifle bullet will rise and fall over this distance but if your scope was properly zeroed then you should still be able to hit inside the kill zone of your target. Suggestions on a very reliable method of sighting in a rifle scope are discussed in the "How to Hit the Bull's-eye" chapter in this book.

Installation of a Laser Sight

1. You can install a laser sight yourself. You do **not** need a gunsmith to successfully install a laser sight.
2. Most laser sights can be installed in thirty-minutes or less by following the simple instructions that come with the laser sight.
3. Laser sights can be installed without making any permanent modifications to your firearm. This means you can remove the laser sight at a future date and restore your firearm to its original factory condition and appearance, and no one would know that the firearm was once equipped with a laser sight.

Types of Laser Sight Mounting Systems

1. **Under Barrel Mount:** Appropriate for some handguns and some shotguns. The laser sight is mounted under the firearm barrel. You then adjust the windage and elevation settings of the laser sight so the point of laser dot aim matches the average point of bullet impact on the target.
2. **Inside Barrel Mount:** Superior for semi-automatic handguns because the laser sight replaces the internal guide rod and spring. Therefore the laser is always aligned with the bore of the pistol. And the laser is completely hidden from view and completely enclosed inside the pistol. Therefore you can still use your current holster, grips, and other handgun accessories. The laser can be removed at any time and your original guide rod reinstalled to convert the weapon back into its original factory condition.

Laser Activation Switches

1. **Pressure Activated Switch:** The switch is mounted on the outside of the weapon. When you grasp the weapon in a normal manner the activation button is depressed. In this situation the laser will automatically come on whenever you are properly holding your firearm.
2. **On/Off Switch:** You must intentionally activate the laser sight and the laser sight will remain on until you deactivate it. This type of switch allows you the opportunity to easily practice with or without your laser sight. This is an advantage because you need to be reasonably proficient with your firearm without the use of a laser sight.

Types of Laser Beams

1. **Steady Beam:** The laser beam is a constant round dot.
2. **Pulsating Beam:** The laser beam produces a blinking on/off round dot. However, the round laser dot is "on" for more time than it is "off." Field tests have shown that this type of laser dot is more quickly seen (even on red objects) because it flashes on and off. The human eye can more easily and quickly detect an object in motion (flashing).

Laser Dot Size

The size of the laser dot gradually gets larger the further the target is away from the laser sight. Since everything appears smaller at further distances you will not notice the increase in the size of the laser dot unless you have a point of reference of a standard size with which you can compare the laser dot image.

Laser Batteries

1. Laser batteries will discharge at a very, very slow rate when they are not being used.
2. Most laser batteries may be stored for 3 to 4 years before being installed inside a laser sight.
3. Laser batteries will discharge rather quickly when in continuous use. Most laser documentation quotes an average battery life of between 2 to 4 hours of continuous use. Continuous use means the laser sight had been activated and the laser beam dot is visible. Continuous use does **not** occur if the laser has been turned off and the batteries are simply residing inside the laser unit. (Note: Laser sight batteries discharge in approximately the same fashion as ordinary batteries inside an ordinary flashlight.)
4. If possible, select a laser sight that uses a standard size battery that can be purchased at any place that sells watch batteries or hearing aid batteries.
5. Buy at least two extra sets of laser batteries. When you use those batteries buy some more.
6. At least once each year, such as on your birthday, always buy at least one extra set of fresh laser batteries and replace the batteries inside your laser sight even if you have not used your laser all year. This will help to ensure that your laser sight will be operational if you should need it in an emergency self-defense situation.

Specific Laser Sight Recommendations

1. **LaserMax Brand:** LaserMax produces internal guide rod laser sights (with an **on/off switch**) for semi-automatic pistols made by Beretta, Glock, ParaOrdinance, SigArms, Springfield, and the Model 1911 Colt 45.
   a. **Activation:** Whether you are left or right handed, if you are holding your pistol in its normal firing position the on/off switch can be activated with your trigger finger before you place your finger on the trigger.

   b. **Installation on a Glock** (see picture on the next page): Make sure the pistol is unloaded. Remove the magazine. Disassemble the upper slide from the lower part of the pistol. Remove the original Glock Slide Lock Switch and Slide Lock Spring. (Note: The slide lock spring is silver colored and a black circle has been drawn around it in the picture on the next page.) Install the new LaserMax Slide Lock Spring and Slide Lock Switch. Remove the Glock Spring Guide and insert the LaserMax Laser Sight into the original Glock Spring Guide position. Reassemble the pistol. Pull the slide back. Pull the trigger (pistol still unloaded). Peel and then apply the small "Laser Warning Label" on the front barrel of the Glock. The LaserMax Laser Sight is now installed. Save the original three Glock parts so you can return the pistol to its original factory condition at some future date if you decide to remove the LaserMax Laser Sight. (Note: The LaserMax Laser Sight for the Glock Model 22 uses three Energizer 393 or Rayovac 393 or Walmart 393 watch batteries.)

c. **Accidental Activation:** On some pistols the laser on/off switch may be accidentally activated when inserting the pistol into a holster, or when adjusting the pistol inside the holster. If your holster has an open bottom then you will be able to see the laser dot pointing towards the ground. Never look into the open end of your holster when you have your firearm in the holster. You will not only be looking directly into the laser beam (if it is on) but you will also be looking into the barrel of your firearm. This would be stupid so resist the temptation to do it.
d. **Recoil Spring:** If you are a high-volume shooter then you may need to replace the recoil spring based on the recommendations of your pistol manufacturer. (Note: According to the LaserMax Manual that accompanies the Glock Laser, the new LaserMax Spring that comes with the LaserMax Laser Sight is good for 5,000 rounds.)

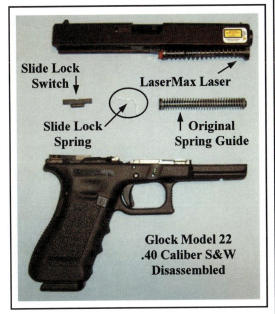

2. **Crimson Trace Brand:** Crimson Trace produces external and internal laser sights with **external button activation switches** for Glock, Kel-tec, Ruger, Sig Sauer, and Smith & Wesson.

Safety

1. **Never** look into the beam of any type of laser and **never** point a laser beam at someone's face or eyes. Permanent eye damage could result.
2. **Never** store your laser sight where a child may find it and play with it. This could result in permanent eye damage to the child and/or to the child's playmates.
3. Attach the laser "Danger Warning Label" that comes with your laser sight onto your firearm. This will keep you in compliance with federal laws and this may help to avoid a potential future legal technicality problem.

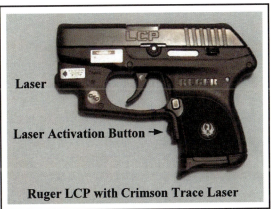

Conclusion

At the current time in the United States an adult may legally purchase firearms, and high-capacity magazines, and laser sights. However, new laws can be passed at any time and without any advance warning and without asking you for your opinion. If new firearm laws are passed then those laws may restrict the future sale of some items, such as high-capacity magazines and laser sights, to law enforcement personnel only. The window of opportunity is now. It would be sad if you let this opportunity to upgrade your firearm pass you by.

Victory

Do you want to know how to win an important victory,
in the game of life where the rewards last for eternity?

Many believe, "An eye for an eye, and a tooth for a tooth."
Perfect justice is their guide in their quest for the truth.

But Jesus said, "If someone hits you, let him hit you again.
If someone wants to take your coat, do not try to stop him.

"Love your enemies, and pray for those who persecute you.
Do good to them, and earn a reward for the things you do."

The night before Jesus was nailed to the cross by his hands,
all the Powers of Creation were ready to obey His commands.

But Jesus chose to obey the will of His Heavenly Father,
and He let Himself be led like a Lamb to the slaughter.

He let others beat, humiliate, and torture Him to death,
and as it was happening He prayed for their forgiveness.

Many have the power to force others to do their will,
but few have the Strength to be meek, loving, and humble.

Meekness and Love are the rules Jesus taught us to obey.
Be Meek and win an Eternal Crown you can wear every day.

This Poem is Dedicated to My Grandson **Stefan Cree Johnson.**

Scripture References: Matthew 5:38-45, Matthew 5:34, Luke 6:35-36, Matthew 26:36-39, Matthew 26:50-54, Matthew 27:1-2, John 19:1-3, Luke 23:32-34, James 1:12, Revelation 2:10, Titus 4:6-8, First Peter 5:4, Revelation 3:11.

Chapter Sixty-Four

Cost Comparison Between
Factory-Loaded Ammunition and Hand-Reloaded Ammunition

There are some significant cost differences between reloading shotgun shells and reloading pistol and rifle ammunition. The following cost summaries illustrate these differences (all cost data collected in June 2009):

Pistol Ammunition Summary:
$0.270 = Total Cost of one **New** Factory-Loaded 40 S&W 165 Grain Pistol Cartridge.
$0.206 = Total Material Cost to Reload one **Used** 40 S&W 165 Grain Pistol Cartridge.
$0.064 = Cost **Savings** of Reloading one **Used** 40 S&W 165 Grain Pistol Cartridge.

Rifle Ammunition Summary:
$0.800 = Total Cost of one **New** Factory-Loaded 308 Caliber 165 Grain Rifle Cartridge.
$0.480 = Total Material Cost to Reload one **Used** 308 Caliber 165 Grain Rifle Cartridge.
$0.320 = Cost **Savings** of Reloading one **Used** 308 Caliber 165 Grain Rifle Cartridge.

Shotgun Shell Summary:
$0.240 = Total Cost of one **New** Factory-Loaded 12 Gauge 2.75-inch #7.5 Shot Shotgun Shell.
$0.410 = Total Material Cost to Reload one **Used** 12 Gauge 2.75-inch #7.5 Shot Shotgun Shell.
-$0.170 = **Additional** Cost to Reload one **Used** 12 Gauge 2.75-inch #7.5 Shot Shotgun Shell.

Shotgun Slug Summary:
$0.631 = Total Cost of one **New** Factory-Loaded 12 Gauge 2.75-inch One-Ounce Shotgun Slug.
$0.738 = Total Material Cost to Reload one **Used** 12 Gauge 2.75-inch One-Oz. Shotgun Slug.
-$0.107 = **Additional** Cost to Reload one **Used** 12 Gauge 2.75-inch One-Ounce Shotgun Slug.

A more detailed cost analysis that supports the above numbers appears at the end of this chapter.

The above data is based on average costs as of June 2009. I did **not** select the lowest possible cost nor the highest possible cost for each item. Instead I used the average cost.

If a person wanted to prove a specific point then he or she could easily select a set of extreme cost data that would support his or her point of view. For example, a person could compare the cheapest reloading materials to the most expensive factory-loaded ammunition and show a large savings. Or a person could compare the most expensive reloading materials to the cheapest factory-loaded ammunition and show a loss.

Since I am not trying to encourage or discourage reloading I used the average cost numbers for each material to provide a more balanced perspective.

This data suggests that the average person could save a little money by **reloading pistol and rifle ammunition.** On the other hand, the average person would save money by purchasing **new factory-loaded shotgun shells** instead of reloading empty shotgun shells.

The above conclusion is the same one I reached in 1974 when I first investigated the costs of reloading ammunition. In 1974 I could save money reloading both pistol and rifle ammunition but I would have paid a premium if I had tried to reload shotgun shells.

The previous analysis does not take into consideration the cost of the reloading equipment. If a person were to invest $290 in reloading equipment plus $40 in one set of reloading dies in a specific caliber, then that person would need to reload the following number of empty cartridges to recover the cost of the total investment of $330:

      5,156 Pistol Cartridges = $330 divided by $0.064 savings per pistol cartridge, or
      1,031 Rifle Cartridges = $330 divided by $0.320 savings per rifle cartridge.

This clearly illustrates that a person would need to reload a lot of ammunition in order to breakeven on his or her investment of $330 in reloading equipment that includes one set of reloading dies. Therefore the average person would probably be better advised to invest in new factory-loaded ammunition if he or she can still find it available for sale.

However, if factory-loaded ammunition becomes increasingly difficult to find, or if its price continues to increase, then a person might want to consider the reloading option as a viable alternative.

Some additional information about the reloading process is in the next chapter in this book. That chapter also discusses the art of bullet casting and how to reduce your lead bullet cost to approximately $0.05 per bullet using clip-on lead wheel weights and ordinary solder that contains tin.

The cost information below is being provided to support the cost data at the beginning of this chapter. The following cost data is based on the average costs for each material as of June 2009:

Pistol Cartridge (40 S&W 165 Grain FMJ):
$0.030 = Primer Cost ($29.99 per box of 1,000 divided by 1,000).
$0.016 = Average Powder Cost ($15.79 per pound divided by 959 cartridges per pound).
$0.160 = Average Bullet Cost ($15.99 per box of 100 divided by 100).
$0.206 = Total Cost to **Reload** one Used 40 S&W Pistol Cartridge.
$0.270 = Average Cost of one **New** Factory-Loaded 40 S&W Cartridge ($13.49 per box divided by 50 rounds per box).

Rifle Cartridge (308 Caliber 165 Grain):
$0.030 = Primer Cost ($29.99 per box of 1,000 divided by 1,000).
$0.120 = Average Powder Cost ($21.99 per pound divided by 184 cartridges per pound).
$0.330 = Average Bullet Cost ($16.49 per box of 50 divided by 50).
$0.480 = Total Cost to **Reload** one Used 308 Rifle Cartridge.
$0.800 = Average Cost of one **New** Factory-Loaded 308 Cartridge ($15.99 per box divided by 20 rounds per box).

Shotgun Shell (12 Gauge 2.75-Inch #7.5 Shot):
$0.039 = Primer Cost ($38.99 per box of 1,000 primers divided by 1,000).
$0.049 = Average Powder Cost ($18.49 per pound divided by 378 Shells per pound).
$0.290 = Average Shot Shell Cost ($50.99 per 11-pound bag divided by 176 Shells per bag).
$0.032 = Average Wad Cost ($7.89 per bag of 250 Wads divided by 250).
$0.410 = Total Cost to **Reload** one Used 12 Gauge Shotgun Shell.
$0.240 = Average Cost of one **New** Factory-Loaded 12 Gauge Shotgun Shell ($23.97 per case of 100 shells divided by 100 shells per case).

Shotgun Slug (12 Gauge 2.75-inch One-Ounce Slug):
$0.039 = Primer Cost ($38.99 per box of 1,000 primers divided by 1,000).
$0.107 = Average Powder Cost ($18.79 per pound divided by 175 Shells per pound).
$0.560 = Average One-Ounce Slug Cost ($13.99 per 25 Slugs divided by 25).
$0.032 = Average Wad Cost ($7.89 per bag of 250 Wads divided by 250).
$0.738 = Total Cost to **Reload** one Used 12 Gauge Shotgun Slug.
$0.631 = Average Cost of one **New** Factory-Loaded 12 Gauge Shotgun Slug ($9.47 per box of 15 slugs divided by 15 slugs per box).

The cost of the empty metallic brass shell case and the empty plastic shotgun shell is not included in the above figures because those items are being reused and therefore they may be considered a "sunk cost." A sunk cost is an expense that was incurred in the past and it is not relevant for future purchase decisions. In other words, after you have paid for the factory-loaded ammunition, and you have fired that ammunition, then you have the choice to either: (1) discard your empty shell cases, or (2) reuse those cases. If you decide to reuse your empty shell cases then you do not incur any new additional expense.

Sales tax and/or shipping expenses were not included in the above data. These costs would be unique to your geographical location and they would equally impact all the above costs by the same ratio.

The above costs for **new factory-loaded ammunition** are based on the cost of that ammunition at a Walmart in the southeastern United States during June of 2009.

Chapter Sixty-Five

How to Make Your Own Ammunition

For Fair Use and Educational Purposes Only.

Warning: The failure to follow standard safety precautions when working with any type of explosive, or any type of molten metal, could result in a potentially devastating accident. Lead has documented dangerous health consequences and all safety precautions should always be followed whenever lead is being used in any manner. Therefore the information in this chapter is provided for information purposes only and the author disclaims any liability for any damage or injury as a direct or indirect result of the use of this information. If you use any of the information contained in this chapter then you do so at your own risk.

Introduction

The reason I am taking the time to write this chapter is due to the current worldwide ammunition shortage that has existed for several years now. There are three possible future scenarios regarding the supply of factory-loaded ammunition:

1. The demand-supply relationship may change and ammunition may once again become widely available the way it was prior to the year 2009.
2. The current situation may become the new status quo. What we are seeing today may continue for many years into the future. In other words, we may see the occasional restocking of some calibers of ammunition in small quantities at some stores on a random basis. However, that ammunition will quickly disappear from the store shelves even if the store limits the number of boxes that may be purchased by each customer.
3. The situation may get much, much worse and ammunition may eventually become extremely scarce or simply not available.

Therefore it would probably be useful if you knew how to replenish your ammunition without having to rely on the current ammunition supply chain. This chapter will provide some practical information to help you achieve this objective.

The Three Basic Types of Ammunition

| Shotgun Shells | Rimfire Ammunition | Centerfire Ammunition |

Shotgun Shells: Shotgun shells cost too much to reload. It is cheaper to buy new shotgun shells than to purchase all the individual components needed to reload an empty shotgun shell. The reason is because the only part of the shotgun shell that can be reused is the plastic shell case. But the plastic shell case does not cost very much. When purchased separately the other three components of a shotgun shell are significantly more expensive than a brand new factory fresh shotgun shell. Therefore a person would spend more money reloading used shotgun shells then he or she would spend on the purchase of brand new factory-loaded shotgun shells. At the current time shotgun shells are not in short supply in the United States and you can buy as many as you wish at almost any store that sells ammunition, including most local Walmart stores. However, this situation could change at any time so you should purchase as many shotgun shells as you think you will need right now while they are still relatively easy to obtain.

Rimfire Ammunition: Rimfire ammo, such as the 22LR, is activated by striking the outside rim of the shell case. Rimfire ammo is not reloadable. Rimfire cases are single use applications and they cannot be reused. Therefore if you need 22LR ammunition then you should purchase an adequate supply of it while it is still available for sale.

Centerfire Handgun and Rifle Ammunition: Centerfire ammo is activated by striking a primer in the bottom center of the shell case. Centerfire ammo may be reloaded if it is made of brass and if it contains a Boxer primer. The balance of this chapter will be devoted to centerfire ammunition.

The Four Basic Components of Centerfire Ammunition Cartridges

All metallic centerfire ammunition cartridges have the following four standard components:

1. **Brass Case:** After you have fired some of your existing ammunition then you can save and reuse the empty brass cases from that ammunition. The brass cases may be reused several times if you keep your powder loads to a reasonable level.

2. **Primer:** Centerfire primers may only be used once. They can't be recycled. You must replace the used primer with a new primer. You can buy boxes of new primers (if you can find them available), or you can remove the primers from new factory-loaded ammunition (preferably from a caliber you personally do not need).

3. **Gunpowder:** You can buy canisters of gunpowder from a gun shop that sells reloading equipment, or you can remove the gunpowder from new factory-loaded ammunition (preferably from a caliber that you personally do not need).

4. **Bullet:** You can cast your own lead bullets using a bullet mold. You can make these cast lead bullets using scrap used lead wheel weights from any automobile junk yard or any tire store.

If you have all four of the above components, and you have a standard universal reloading press, and reloading dies in the caliber you need, and a bullet mold of the correct caliber, then you could reload your own ammunition.

Individuals who are not familiar with the reloading process sometimes criticize hand-loaded ammo as being inferior to factory-loaded ammo. In response to this it should be noted that on July 25, 1993 Robert Fray set a new world's record for the smallest shot group at 1,000 yards using ammunition he loaded himself. This implies that it is not the reloading process but the diligence of the individual who is doing the reloading that determines the reliability and accuracy of the reloaded ammunition.

With this in mind let's now examine each one of the above four components of ammunition.

The Brass Shell Case

The Shell Case:

1. Holds the primer firmly in its correct position.
2. Contains the powder charge between the primer and the bullet.
3. Holds the bullet firmly in place above the powder charge.
4. Keeps everything in its correct position.
5. Protects the primer and the powder from moisture (humidity) damage.

Case

However, the case can't protect the cartridge from high heat. Therefore always store your ammunition, primers, and powder in a cool dry area at normal room temperatures (or below if you have air-conditioning). Never store them in an attic, garage, inside a vehicle, or in direct sunlight.

After you have fired an existing cartridge save the empty used brass shell case. The empty brass shell can be reloaded several times depending on the quality of the original brass case and how much powder you use when you reload the case.

If your ammunition is sold in boxes and each box contains a plastic tray that holds each cartridge in its own separate individual area then put your empty brass shells back inside their original storage tray.

If your ammo is loose packed then save your empty brass shells in an ordinary plastic sandwich bag. Use a permanent black marker to write the brand of original ammunition, the caliber, and the date on the outside of the plastic bag. If you don't have a permanent black marker then write this information on a small piece of paper and place it inside the plastic bag with your empty shell cases.

Brass consists of approximately 70% copper and 30% zinc. All factory-loaded ammunition does **not** have a brass shell case. Some of the factory shell cases are made from mild steel, or aluminum, or copper. Brass cases can be reloaded. Steel, aluminum, or copper cases cannot be reloaded. Steel cases are sometimes coated with a lacquer finish to protect and seal them and this finish can make the steel case look like it might be brass. Brass is non-magnetic. A simple magnet will help you identify the steel cases.

Most ammunition made **outside** the United States has:

1. A shell case that is **not** made of brass and it is therefore not reloadable, or
2. It does **not** have a Boxer primer and therefore it is not reloadable.

However, most ammunition made **inside** the United States (and some European ammo) are made of brass and they are also Boxer primed. Therefore they are reloadable. Primers will be discussed in the next section.

In summary, in order to use standard reloading equipment to reload your own ammunition that ammunition must have:

1. a metallic brass shell case, and
2. a Boxer primer.

Primers

Ammunition may be either rimfire or centerfire:

1. **Rimfire ammo,** such as 22LR, is activated by striking the outside rim of the shell case. Rimfire ammo cannot be reloaded. Rimfire cases are single use applications and they cannot be reused.

2. **Centerfire ammo** is activated by striking a primer in the bottom center of the shell case. Centerfire ammo may be reloaded if it is made of brass and if it contains a Boxer primer.

The primer ignites the powder inside the cartridge case. Primers are single use disposable items. They cannot be recycled. Used primers must be discarded and replaced with new primers.

There are two different types of centerfire primers:

1. **Berdan Primers:** Originally invented in the mid-1800s by Hiram Berdan, an American ordinance officer. It has two (or sometimes three) flash holes that are off-center around the edges of the primer. Berdan

Chapter Sixty-Five: How to Make Your Own Ammunition

primers are used in Europe and in the communist countries. (Note: Berdan primed cartridge cases can be recycled but you need special equipment and the primer must be replaced with a new Berdan primer. This process is not as simple as replacing a Boxer primer. Therefore unless you have a really good reason for reloading Berdan primed cases then you should not consider reusing them.)

2. **Boxer Primers**: Originally invented in the mid-1800s by Edward M. Boxer, a British ordinance officer. It contains a cup, an anvil, some detonation compound, and a single flash hole. A used Boxer primer is easy to extract from an empty cartridge shell case using a simple punch tool that is a little smaller in diameter than the primer itself. The primer is pushed out of its pocket from inside the cartridge so the primer exits the bottom of the case in the same direction from which it was activated by the firing pin of the firearm. Boxer primers were adopted for use in the United States. Boxer primed ammunition is reloadable if the shell casing is made of brass.

Boxer Primer

Boxer primers are **not** interchangeable with Berdan primers. You will occasionally read internet stories about someone who did this, but you will also read that the process was extremely complicated, and it resulted in lots of failures, and the end result was **not** a consistently safe cartridge that could be used in a handgun or rifle. Therefore, for safety's sake, do **not** try to substitute a Boxer primer for a Berdan primer. You do **not** want to create a cartridge that could explode inside a firearm being held in your hand and which will be in close proximity to your face.

There are four basic types of Boxer primers as follows:

Diameter	Pistol	Rifle
0.175 inches	Small Pistol	Small Rifle
0.210 inches	Large Pistol	Large Rifle

Each company that makes primers uses their own numbering system to designate the different size primers. However, in addition to printing their unique primer number of the box, each company also clearly labels the box of primers for its specific application, such as Small Pistol Primers or Large Rifle Primers.

For reference purposes the following table shows the primer number used by each primer company for each type of primer:

Primer Size	CCI Number	Federal	Magtech	Remington	Winchester
Small Pistol	500	100	1 1/2	1 1/2	1 1/2
Large Pistol	300	150	2 1/2	2 1/2	7
Small Rifle	400	205	7 1/2	6 1/2	6 1/2
Large Rifle	200	210	9 1/2	9 1/2	8 1/2

The above primers are used in the following firearm calibers:

Primer Size	Firearm Calibers
Small Pistol	25 Auto, 32 Auto, 380 Auto, 9 mm Luger, 38 Special, 357 Sig, 357 Magnum, 40 S&W, 45 GAP
Large Pistol	10 mm Auto, 41 Remington Magnum, 44 Magnum, 45 Auto
Small Rifle	222, 223 (NATO 5.56x45), 25-20, 30 M1, 32-20
Large Rifle	243, 250, 25-06, 270, 284, 30-30, 300, 303, 307, 308 (NATO 7.62x51), 30-06, 356, 358, 375, 444, 45-70, 450, 6 mm, 7 mm, 7.62x39 mm, 8 mm, 9.3x62 mm

Chapter Sixty-Five: How to Make Your Own Ammunition

If you look at the primer list it becomes obvious that the two most widely used primers are Small Pistol primers and Large Rifle primers. If you can find these primers for sale then you should consider making an investment in them.

However, if you need the Large Pistol primers or the Small Rifle primers then you should also buy some of them (if you can find them).

Rifle primers should **not** be interchanged with pistol primers. Rifle primers are designed to receive a more powerful hit from the firing pin and they contain more detonation compound because they are designed to ignite more gunpowder inside the rifle cartridge.

Magnum primers are also available but they are primarily for slow burning powders or for use in extremely cold shooting environments (sub-zero temperatures). Magnum primers should **not** be interchanged with non-magnum primers because they will raise the detonation pressure inside the cartridge. A serious accident could result if you try to use a magnum primer in an application for which it was not designed. The best strategy is to **not** interchange magnum and non-magnum primers.

Whenever possible it is advisable to seat primers just a tiny bit below the flush level of the cartridge bottom (but no more than 0.005 inches). Feel the bottom of the empty case immediately after the new primer has been seated and if you can feel the primer extending up from the bottom of the case then you have not seated the primer far enough into its pocket. Adjust your reloading equipment just a little bit and try again. If you are using a Reloading Press then you will probably not be able to withdraw the empty brass case from its shell holder if the primer is not adequately seated in the brass case.

Static electricity may ignite a primer. Therefore take the appropriate safety precautions to eliminate any source of static electricity from the area where you store or use your primers.

At the current time primers (and smokeless powder) are becoming extremely difficult to find. However, without a primer you cannot reload your used ammunition cases.

Fortunately there is a simple solution to this primer (and powder) shortage. It is possible to transfer the primer and the powder from a new factory-loaded cartridge to one of your used brass shell cases. Obviously you would not want to make this exchange for a caliber you currently need. However, if you can find factory-loaded ammunition in a caliber that you personally do not need, and if it contains the size primer that you do need, then you could purchase that ammunition and salvage the primer and the powder inside the new factory-loaded cartridge.

For example, if you needed 380 pistol ammunition and you could find some 9 mm Luger ammunition but you did not need the 9 mm ammunition then you could purchase the 9 mm ammo and disassemble it and transfer the primers and powder to your empty 380 shell casings. This is just one example.

Generally if you are buying cartridges so you can salvage their component parts then the following issues should be considered:

1. The cartridge must use a Boxer primer of the same exact size as the one in your existing used shell cases. If you need a small pistol primer then the ammunition must contain a small pistol primer. If you need a large rifle primer then the ammunition must contain a large rifle primer. And so forth.

2. If possible try to purchase new factory-loaded ammunition that is a little larger than the shell casing you need to reload. For example, if you need to reload 380 ammunition then you could buy 9 mm or 38 Special or 40 S&W, if you can find them available. This would provide a little extra powder over and above what you would need to reload your 380 ammunition. However, if the only ammo you can find is a box of 50 cartridges for a 32 Auto then you could buy it. Although you would now have 50 new primers of the correct size you would not have enough powder to reload 50 of your 380 shell cases because the 32 Auto cartridges are smaller than your 380 cartridges.

3. If possible purchase new factory-loaded ammunition that has the same size bullet that you need. For example, some 357 magnum bullets may be used in some 38 Special shell cases (and vice-versa).

Information on how to remove a primer from a factory-loaded cartridge is at the end of this chapter.

Chapter Sixty-Five: How to Make Your Own Ammunition

For the past ten-years a "primer myth" has been circulating around the internet. The "myth" is that primer companies are now adding something to their primers so those primers will have a "much shorter shelf life." This is not true. The companies that make primers do not add anything to their primers that will cause their primers to expire after a certain period of time, such as two years. If new primers are stored in a cool dry environment then they will still be okay to use many decades from now.

Gunpowder

There are two basic types of gunpowder:

1. **Black powder** is a combination of 75% saltpeter (or potassium nitrate), 15% charcoal, and 10% sulfur by weight (which is a 15:3:2 ratio). When ignited it produces a lot of smoke. It is relatively inefficient since it only converts about half of its original mass into a gas that can be used as the projectile propellant. Black powder can also explode even when it is not restricted inside a confined space.

2. **Smokeless powder** is a nitrated cellulose (or nitrocellulose) based propellant. Smokeless powders are non-corrosive and they produce almost no smoke when used. All smokeless powders provide their own oxygen for combustion and they will quickly burn up. Therefore they leave almost no residue. And they generate less recoil. Smokeless powders will not explode if they are not confined but they will burn very rapidly.

Smokeless powder is used inside modern centerfire ammunition cartridges.

In some "black powder rifles" smokeless powder may be substituted for black powder. However, the reverse is not true. Black powder may **not** be used in place of smokeless powder.

Although there are instructions for making black powder and smokeless powder on the internet, none of these powders are easy to make and they all require the use of a variety of commercial quality chemicals. If you have access to those commercial quality chemicals then you would probably also have access to gunpowder. Therefore why would you want to make gunpowder? In my opinion, trying to make homemade gunpowder isn't practical for a self-sufficient individual who wishes to avoid potentially devastating accidents. Therefore after carefully studying a wide assortment of gunpowder recipes I decided it was impractical to believe that I could make gunpowder at home in a safe and relatively easy cost-effective way. Therefore the only logical alternative was to acquire commercially available gunpowder.

Prior to the year 2009 canisters of smokeless powder were widely available for sale at any gun shop that also sold reloading supplies. Most gun shops still have a very small quantity of smokeless powder for sale.

Canisters of smokeless powder are already packaged for safe handling and for long-term storage by the manufacturer. Do not open the container until you are ready to use the powder. Store the powder in its original container in a cool dry area. Write the date you purchased the powder on the powder container before you put it into storage.

Never store gunpowder in a glass container.

Check your local fire codes for any special regulations for storing gunpowder. In most areas you must exceed a specific quantity of gunpowder before these codes take effect.

At the current time canisters of smokeless powder are becoming more difficult to find and their price has increased substantially. If smokeless powder disappears from the marketplace then a reasonable second source would be the smokeless powder that is inside new factory-loaded ammunition (in a caliber you don't need).

Handgun powders, rifle powders, and shotgun powders are usually **not** interchangeable (although is some special cases they may be).

Therefore for safety's sake:

1. Do **not** use a rifle powder to load a handgun cartridge.
2. Do **not** use a handgun powder to load a rifle cartridge.
3. Do **not** use a shotgun powder to reload either a handgun or a rifle cartridge.

It is **not** possible to identify the type of powder used in factory-loaded ammo. Ammunition factories use powders that are not available to the reloader. There is no data on these powders available to reloaders.

However, even though it is not possible to identify the type of powder used in a factory-loaded cartridge, it is still possible to safely use that powder in another cartridge that uses the same type of primer and is of the same generic class of firearms (either handguns or rifles). The following example shows how this can be safely accomplished.

One Example of Reloading a 380 Brass Case with Smokeless Powder
(Starting Minimum Safe Load Data from the
Speer Reloading Handbook #14, 2007 Edition)

Caliber = Bullet Type =	**380 Auto** 95 Gr. RN	**9 mm Luger** 115 Gr. RN	**38 Special** 158 Gr. LRN	**357 Magnum** 125 Gr. TMJFN	**40 S&W** 155 TMJFN
AA No. 5 Powder =	4.6 Gr.	6.0 Gr. (4.6/6.0) (77%)	5.6 Gr. (4.6/5.6) (82%)	No Data x x	7.9 Gr. (4.6/ 7.9) (58%)
AA No. 7 Powder =	5.9 Gr.	8.6 Gr. (5.9/8.6) (69%)	No Data x x	12.0 Gr. (5.9/12.0) (49%)	10.0 Gr. (5.9/10.0) (59%)
Bullseye Powder =	3.0 Gr.	4.2 Gr. (3.0/4.2) (71%)	3.1 Gr. (3.0/3.1) (97%)	No Data x x	5.4 Gr. (3.0/5.4) (56%)
H. Universal P. =	3.6 Gr.	4.7 Gr. (3.6/4.7) (77%)	4.2 Gr. (3.6/4.2) (86%)	7.5 Gr. (3.6/7.5) (48%)	6.2 Gr. (3.6/6.2) (58%)
Unique Powder =	3.8 Gr.	5.6 Gr. (3.8/5.6) (68%)	4.0 Gr. (3.8/4.0) (95%)	8.6 Gr. (3.8/8.6) (44%)	7.2 Gr. (3.8/7.2) (53%)
Average % =	-	(72%)	(90%)	(47%)	(57%)

Explanation of the above Table Data

Example 1: Assume that you wish to reload an empty 380 Auto brass case with a 95 Grain Round Nose (RN) 380 Auto Bullet and you have a factory-loaded 9 mm Luger cartridge that contains a 115 Grain 9 mm Round Nose (RN) Bullet. But you do not know what type of smokeless powder is in the 9 mm cartridge.

However, if you remove the powder from several 9 mm cartridges, and weigh and record the amount of powder inside each 9 mm cartridge, and then calculate the average powder grain weight in all the 9 mm cartridges, you will know the average grain weight of the powder used in your factory-loaded 9 mm cartridges. If you use the average percentage from the bottom of the above table then you could then use approximately 72% of that average powder weight in each of your 380 brass shells that will contain a 95 Grain Round Nose 380 Auto bullet.

Example 2: We will use the same empty 380 Auto brass case but now we have a factory-loaded 38 Special cartridge with a 158 Grain LRN Bullet. Once again we do not know what type of powder is in the 38 Special cartridge. But we can still empty the powder from several cartridges and compute the average grain weight of powder in each cartridge. Then we consult the bottom of the above table and use approximately 90% of that average powder weight in each of our 380 brass shells.

Chapter Sixty-Five: How to Make Your Own Ammunition

Example 3: Use 47% of the average powder weight from the 357 Magnum factory-loaded cartridge to load a 380 brass case.

Example 4: Use 57% of the average powder weight from the 40 S&W factory-loaded cartridge to load a 380 brass case.

Note: In each of the above examples you will have some smokeless powder left over after you have transferred the proper amount of smokeless powder from a factory-loaded cartridge to an empty 380 brass case. However, if you have a supply of small pistol primers then you would only need to unload enough of the factory-loaded cartridges until you had the right amount of powder to fill your empty 380 cases. For example, if you had fifty empty 380 brass shell cases then you would only need to disassemble thirty-six 9 mm factory-loaded cartridges (50 times 0.72 = 36). This would provide enough smokeless powder for fifty 380 brass cases and it would provide 36 small pistol primers. You would need to supply the other 14 small pistol primers from your inventory of small pistol primers. However, if you do not have any small pistol primers then you will need to disassemble fifty 9 mm cartridges in order to have enough primers for your fifty 380 shell cases. But you would now have the extra powder from fourteen 9 mm cartridges that you could add to your smokeless powder inventory.

Why will this work? A factory-loaded cartridge is filled with the correct amount of smokeless powder for the bullet it shoots. The amount of powder used in that cartridge will provide for safe, consistent, and accurate shooting performance with that cartridge. The above table shows the percentage of that powder grain weight that will be needed for the exact type of bullet you wish to load in your empty brass shell case. Since we are working with percentages it does not matter what type of smokeless powder is used in the original factory-loaded cartridge as long as we are careful and use just the right amount of it in our hand-loaded cartridge. The **percentage** will be correct regardless of the actual grain weight of the powder used in the factory-loaded ammunition.

The reason we use the average percent at the bottom of the table is to help avoid using too much powder or too little powder. That is the reason we don't select the lowest percent in each column or the highest percent in each column. Either the lowest percent or the highest percent may result in a powder load that is a little too low or a little too high. By using the average we get closer to the middle of the values and we will have a powder load that should provide good average shooting accuracy and reliability.

Caution: The primers must be of the same exact type. In other words, if you wish to reload an empty brass case from a handgun that has a **small pistol primer** then you must select a factory-loaded handgun cartridge that contains a **small pistol primer.** If you wish to reload an empty brass case from a rifle that has a **large rifle primer** then you must select a factory-loaded rifle cartridge that contains a **large rifle primer.** The powder is custom matched to the type of primer used in the factory-loaded cartridge and it will not perform in a predictable manner with a different size primer.

Caution: Do **not** use the powder from a +P or other high performance cartridge. These cartridges may be loaded with a special powder and/or maximum amounts of powder and you should not use them to reload your normal ammunition cartridges.

Caution: Do **not** use the powder from a rifle cartridge to reload a handgun cartridge.

Caution: Do **not** use the powder from a handgun cartridge to reload a rifle cartridge.

Caution: The above table is only **one example.** You must do the math yourself for whatever caliber and grain weight bullet you need to reload and compare it to the caliber and grain weight of the cartridge you have available for salvaging its powder. The actual percentages will change based on those factors.

Caution: If you do not understand the above math then do **not** attempt to reload your ammunition using the smokeless powder that you salvage from a factory-loaded cartridge.

Caution: The smokeless powder you purchase in canisters at a gun shop is 100% powder and it does not contain any filler material. If you use this type of powder in your handgun or rifle brass shell cases then there will almost always be a little extra unused space between the bottom of the shell case and the base of the bullet after the bullet has been seated to its proper depth in the case. If you shake a hand-loaded cartridge you can hear the powder moving about on the inside of the cartridge in this empty space. However, a factory-loaded cartridge typically fills the entire space inside the cartridge. The factory accomplishes this by mixing a compatible type of filler material with the smokeless powder. Therefore when you try to transfer the powder from a larger caliber factory-loaded cartridge to one of your smaller caliber hand-loaded brass shells, you may discover that the factory smokeless powder will not fit in the available space inside your smaller shell. If you encounter this problem then you will not be able to use that particular type of factory-loaded ammunition in your particular reloading application and you will need to experiment with a different caliber of factory-loaded ammunition that uses less filler material.

Caution: If you need to salvage the smokeless powder from a rifle cartridge then you should select a rifle cartridge in a caliber as close as possible to the one you need to reload. For example, if you need to reload a 243 then you may use the powder from a 250, or 25-06, or 270 cartridge. However, you should **not** use the powder from a 444 or 450. The reason is that all rifle powders are not the same. Even though the cartridge may use the same exact size primer, the powder used in larger caliber rifle ammunition is usually different from the powder used in smaller caliber rifle ammunition. This fact will become obvious to you when you look up both calibers in a reloading manual and you discover that the same brands of powder are **not** listed for both rifle calibers.

The following **minimum safety precautions** should be observed whenever you are working with any type of gunpowder:

1. Do **not** smoke when working with gunpowder.
2. Do **not** work with gunpowder near a wood-burning fireplace where a stray ember might accidentally float over to your workbench.
3. Do **not** work with gunpowder in the direct sun or in a very hot environment.
4. Store gunpowder in a cool, dry place.
5. Store powder in the same container in which it was purchased. Those containers are designed to come apart if the powder accidentally ignites. The powder will burn up very rapidly and not explode. Do not store powder inside containers where the pressure can build up or you will be creating the conditions for a potential explosion.
6. Never store or work with large volumes of gunpowder in one area. Always store and work with small volumes of gunpowder to limit the potential damage that might be done by an accident.
7. Do **not** work with more than one type of gunpowder at a time. This will help to prevent the accidental use of the wrong powder. When you have finished the current job, and it is time to start another job that uses a different powder, then put the current powder back in its normal storage location away from your work area, and then bring the new powder container to your work area.
8. Never mix gunpowders or primers from different ammunition or from different ammo companies even if the ammunition itself appears to be exactly the same. The internal components can be significantly different.
9. If you have several boxes of factory-loaded ammunition of the same caliber and bullet grain weight from the same ammunition manufacturer, then look for the production lot number on the ammunition box. The lot number will either be on the outside of the flap, or on the inside of the flap, or somewhere else on the outside of the box. Verify the production lot numbers are the same. If they are the same then the smokeless powder will be the same. If the lot numbers do **not** match then the powders may be different and you should keep those lots separate and not mix the powders together for any reason.

Chapter Sixty-Five: How to Make Your Own Ammunition

Lead Safety Hazards

Some substances are absorbed into your body and they are not gradually eliminated over time. Some examples are sun poisoning, radiation poisoning, and lead poisoning.

The potential hazards of working with lead are real and they are not exaggerated. Lead has the same impact on the human body whether it is inhaled or swallowed. It may cause cancer. Lead can damage brain cells, kidney cells, and the reproductive glands. It can cause birth defects. It can cause a miscarriage in a pregnant woman.

Lead fumes can be created when melting lead, stirring lead, or pouring lead.

The Minimum Safety Precautions When Working With Lead

1. Always melt your lead in an outdoor location. If you melt lead indoors, regardless of what type of ventilation system you use, some of the lead fumes will settle on your ceilings, walls, floors, cabinets, and furniture. These tiny lead dust particles will eventually make their way back into your breathing air and gradually and systematically poison you. Therefore, for safety's sake, melt your lead outdoors in a naturally well-ventilated area.
2. When melting lead always wear the proper safety equipment including safety glasses (or a full face shield would be even better), fire-resistant gloves, long heavy pants, a thick long-sleeve shirt, and shoes. A welder's apron would also be appropriate.
3. Wear a breathing mask to prevent the inhalation of tiny microscopic lead particles that may be floating in the air.
4. Do not allow any liquids (water, soda, sweat, etc.) to make contact with the molten lead or you will have a splatter explosion that will spew hot load a long ways in many directions simultaneously. When you are working with molten lead you will have your attention focused primarily on the hot lead while melting, stirring, and pouring the lead. You will not notice the small drop of sweat that gradually forms on your face and which may eventually drop into the melting pot. If this happens then a dangerous splatter will result. Therefore always wear the appropriate safety equipment when working with molten lead.
5. Never add a freshly cast bullet directly back into the molten lead. Set any defective bullets aside and allow them to cool. You may melt them and reuse them on another day when you make your next batch of bullets.
6. The dross spooned off the top of the molten lead contains lead oxide which can be harmful if inhaled. Therefore dispose of it promptly and in a safe manner. Do not save it and allow it to accumulate in a container.
7. Do not smoke, eat, or drink while working with lead.
8, Carefully wash your hands after working with lead or with any type of ammunition.

Bullets

The bullet is the projectile in the top of the ammunition cartridge. Although all four components in the cartridge are necessary and each makes its own contribution to reliability and accuracy, it is the bullet that actually does the work. The bullet leaves the cartridge shell casing behind and travels towards its target to accomplish its objective.

Bullet

Some bullets are used in more than one caliber firearm. In other words, the same exact bullet may be used in two or more different firearms. Although the bullet may be the same the brass cases will be of a different size. Therefore the only cartridge you can load into your firearm will be the one specifically designed for your firearm. However, when you are buying bulk bullets, or when you are salvaging factory-loaded ammunition, it is helpful to know which caliber bullets may be used in more than one type of brass shell case.

The following list of handgun calibers may be useful in this regards:

0.355" Diameter = 380 Auto, 38 Super Auto, 9 mm Luger, 357 Sig.
0.357" to 0.358" Diameter = 38 Special, 38 S&W, 38 New Colt Police, 357 Magnum.
0.400" Diameter = 40 S&W, 10 mm (but the 10 mm uses a large pistol primer).
0.428" to 0.430" Diameter = 44 S&W Special, 44 Magnum, 44/40.
0.451" to 0.452" Diameter = 45 Auto, 45 Auto Rim, 45 GAP (but the 45 GAP uses a small pistol primer).

Although the above bullets will have the same **diameter** they may not work in your firearm. In addition to the proper **diameter**, the bullets must also be of a proper **grain weight** and **shape** as the bullets used in your firearm. If all three of these variables match then you could salvage the primer, the gunpowder, and the bullet from the factory-loaded cartridges and transfer them to your empty brass shell cases.

Bullets are single use items. After it has been fired then the bullet cannot be reused. It must be replaced. At the current time some gun shops have a very small supply of a very limited selection of some bullet calibers. However, this selection is decreasing all the time and the price is increasing. Therefore now might be a good time to consider homemade cast bullets.

There are a variety of different ways to classify bullets but for the purposes of this chapter we will use two categories: jacketed and non-jacketed.

A **jacketed bullet** has a soft lead core that is surrounded by a thin hard covering material such as copper alloy, cupronickel, or steel. Jacketed bullets are known by a variety of different names such as Full Metal Jacket (FMJ), Jacketed Hollow Point (JHP), and Ball. Jacketed bullets are very nice and they do have some advantages over non-jacketed bullets. For example, they are harder and therefore they more easily penetrate metal targets.

However, **non-jacketed** lead bullets do have some advantages over jacketed bullets as follows:

1. They cost less.
2. They expand more easily after making contact with a game animal.
3. They are not as hard as a jacketed bullet and therefore they can help to extend the life of a firearm barrel.

Homemade cast lead bullets can be made inside bullet molds.

Bullet molds may be classified based on the following variables:

1. **The metal from which the mold is made:** The bullet mold itself may be made from cast iron, steel, or aluminum. Aluminum will heat up more quickly and it will not rust. Other metals require more time to heat up and if not properly cared for they will gradually begin to rust.

2. **The number of mold cavities:** Bullet molds may have one, two, or six individual bullet cavities. My personal preference is the two cavity mold. It heats up more evenly and it allows you to make two bullets at the same time. (Note: The Lee Brand 2-Cavity Aluminum Molds come with their own wooden mold handles.)

3. **The caliber of bullet:** Each bullet mold is designed to produce a bullet of a specific caliber (diameter).

4. **The shape of the bullet:** For a particular caliber the shape of the nose of the bullet should be matched to the purpose of the bullet.

5. **The grain weight of the bullet:** In most situations a heavier grain bullet is preferred to a lighter grain bullet. Heavier grain bullets require a smaller powder charge and they produce less recoil. Therefore if you have the option to purchase different grain weights for the same caliber and design of bullet then the heavier bullet is usually a better choice.

6. **Whether or not a gas check is required:** A gas check is a small metal disc that is placed on the bottom of a soft lead bullet to keep the powder gases from leaking around the outside of the bullet as it moves through the inside of the

Gas Check

firearm barrel. It also helps to protect the base of the bullet from the hot gases. Gas checks are **not** required on most handgun bullets. Gas checks are required on some magnum handgun bullets and most rifle bullets. The diameter of the metal gas check is the same as the diameter of the bottom of the cast bullet. If you make rifle bullets (or some magnum handgun bullets) then a box of gas checks must be purchased separately and one gas check installed on the base of each cast bullet. (Note: Gas checks are not needed on jacketed bullets because of the metal jacket that covers the lead portion of the bullet.)

If the same caliber bullet could be used in two different firearms, such as 38 Special and 357 Magnum, and you intend to use both firearms then you have two options. If you can afford it then you should consider a separate bullet mold for each caliber. But if funds are limited then you may need to select one bullet mold that would make bullets that will function reasonably well in both firearms.

Note on Micro-Bands: Some bullet designs have micro-bands. Micro-band bullets require a special lubricating compound (Liquid Alox) that may not be available during a long-term hard times event. Therefore unless you have a valid application for the micro-band bullets and you can afford to purchase a reasonable inventory of the micro-band lubricant then a different design of bullet should be selected for a long-term hard times event.

How to Make Lead Bullets

The art of casting lead bullets has a history that is over 200-years old. Several good books have been written on bullet casting. And a number of good articles have been published in a variety of reputable firearm magazines over the past fifty-years. These books and articles contained state-of-the-art information when they were originally published. But the technology used in bullet casting has changed over the years. Therefore if you decide to cast your own bullets then I strongly suggest that you study the most recent literature on this topic and not rely on books and articles that were published ten, twenty, or thirty years ago.

This same caution applies to following the advice of an "experienced bullet caster" who has been casting bullets for twenty or thirty years using the same equipment and technique. The mold casting equipment that is available today has been improved. Therefore what works reasonably well for an "old-timer" may not be appropriate for you and your new equipment.

Of all the topics I have had the opportunity to study during my lifetime, the art of bullet casting probably has the highest number of different opinions about each step in the bullet casting process. The problem is that each of these different opinions is "true" when it is applied to the exact parameters on which it is based. But if you change any one of the basic parameters then the outcome also changes. You need to be aware of this if you decide to delve deeper into the topic of bullet casting.

The information presented below is current and it is based on what will actually work today with the equipment and materials you can purchase today.

Cast lead bullets may contain a mixture of the following elements:

1. **Lead (Pb):** Lead is the primary component of cast bullets. The lead content of a cast bullet may vary from approximately 84% to 96%.

2. **Antimony (Sb):** Antimony increases the hardness of the bullet. Approximately 3% to 4% antimony is optimal. This will result in a bullet of sufficient hardness but the bullet will also not be too brittle or prone to fragmentation.

3. **Arsenic (As):** Arsenic significantly enhances the heat treating process. A very small amount of arsenic (0.2%) will act as a catalyst and it will help to significantly increase the final hardness of a cast bullet.

4. **Tin (Sn):** Although the maximum amount of tin can be 4%, a tin ratio of between 2% to 3% is optimal in a finished bullet for the following reasons:

    a. Tin improves the fluidity of the metal by decreasing its surface tension. This helps the molten lead to more easily and completely fill all the groves inside the bullet mold cavity. Therefore the addition of tin significantly increases the percentage of good quality bullets and it results in fewer bullets being rejected due to groove or surface imperfections.

b. Tin improves the solubility of antimony by creating a compound of SnSb.
c. Tin improves the performance of the bullet by helping it to expand more easily when the bullet makes target contact.
d. Tin helps to minimize the chance of bullet fragmentation.
e. If the tin ratio is kept below 4% then it will not adversely impact the bullet's response to heat treatment.
f. Tin can also be used to modify the **diameter** and the **weight** of the final bullet. Using the same exact bullet mold cavity the addition of tin will result in the following impact:

1/2 percent tin will yield the smallest diameter bullet with the highest weight (wheel weights with no extra tin added).

2 percent tin will **increase** the final bullet diameter by approximately 0.001-inches and **decrease** the total bullet weight by about 3%.

4 percent tin will **increase** the final bullet diameter by approximately 0.0015-inches and **decrease** the total bullet weight by about 6%.

Adding more tin quickly reaches a point of diminishing returns. In quantities greater than 4% tin will create more problems than it will solve. Therefore 4% tin is considered to be the maximum tin ratio for cast bullets. (Note: Some references quote a maximum tin ratio of 5% but the majority of the current literature recommends a tin ratio no higher than 4% when using ordinary lead clip-on wheel weights.)

If you do not have any tin then that is okay. A bullet made from nothing but clip-on wheel weights will still be a very good bullet. However, if you can acquire some tin then the tin will improve the casting process and give you a little more quality control over your final results.

Bullet Hardness

Hardness: The hardness of lead and lead alloys is most commonly measured using the Brinell Hardness Number (BHN). A higher number means a harder alloy.

A harder bullet is less prone to **gas cutting**. When smokeless powder ignites it is converted into a gas that pushes the bullet through the firearm barrel. This gas can force its way around the outside edge of a soft bullet. This is called a gas cut. Gas cutting results in a less accurate shot and it can leave lead deposits inside the firearm barrel. However, a hard bullet will not be prone to gas cutting. Therefore a harder bullet is superior to a softer bullet.

Hardness and Heat Treatment: Hardness depends on how the molecules in an alloy bond together.

1. When an alloy is in a molten state most of the molecules are dissolved and they move about freely.
2. After the molten alloy is cast into the shape of a bullet and the bullet begins to cool then the molecules have a chance to separate.
3. The slower the cooling process, the more the molecules can separate.
4. However, if a hot bullet is immediately quenched in a cool water bath then the molecules do not have a chance to separate and a harder bullet is the result.
5. Cool water quenching helps to trap the molecules together before they can separate.
6. After removing the heat treated bullet from the cool water bath the hardness of the final bullet will continue to increase for a period of between one to three days. At that time the bullet will have reached its maximum hardness.
7. Ice cubes added to the quenching water will keep the water cooler. After you remove the bullets from the water the bullets will fully harden in about one day.
8. If you use room temperature water it will take between 2 to 3 days for the bullets to fully harden.

Cool water heat treating **immediately** after casting can increase the "approximate" BHN of different alloys as shown in the following table:

Approximate "Average" Characteristics of Some Common Lead Alloys Used to Make Cast Lead Bullets
(Note: For reference purposes Pure Lead has a BHN=5 and the average Jacketed Bullet has a BHN=100.)
(BHN = Brinell Hardness Number)

Metal	Lead	Antimony	Tin	Arsenic	No Heat Treat	After Heat Treat
Linotype	84%	12%	4%	0%	22 BHN	24 to 25 BHN
Wheel Weights (Clip-On Type)	95.3%	4%	0.5%	0.2%	7 to 9 BHN	18 to 30 BHN
Wheel Weights (Plus Extra Tin)	93.8%	4%	2%	0.2%	7 to 9 BHN	18 to 30 BHN

Wheel weights are the small pieces of metal that are attached to the rim of your wheels when you have your tires balanced. The exact metal composition of wheel weights varies from one manufacturer to another. The composition has also gradually changed over the years. Therefore it is not possible to precisely predict the exact ratios of the different metals in a used clip-on wheel weight. Because of this variation there will be some differences in the actual BHN of bullets made from wheel weights before and after heat treating. However, the averages shown in the above table are a reasonable approximation for the average clip-on wheel weight.

Recycled Lead Wheel Weights:

There are two basic types of lead wheel weights as follows:

1. **Stick-on wheel weights** are almost pure lead. Therefore they are **not** a good choice for casting lead bullets.
2. **Clip-on wheel weights** are **excellent** for casting bullets. They contain lead, antimony, tin, and a trace amount of arsenic.

Used wheel weights can be found at almost any automobile junk yard or tire store. A simple common magnet may be used to separate iron, steel, and lead wheel weights. Iron and steel are magnetic. Lead is not magnetic. A lead wheel weight will not stick to the magnet (but the metal clip at the top of the lead wheel weight will adhere to the magnet).

Clean the old wheel weights before you melt them. If necessary scrub them with hot soapy water and a wire bristle brush to remove dirt and other materials from the surface of the wheel weights. Carefully and thoroughly rinse the wheel weights and then thoroughly dry the wheel weights in the sun. The wheel weights **must** be completely dry before adding them to the melting pot.

Do not be concerned about the metal clips attached to the top of the wheel weights. They have a significantly higher melting point and they will float to the top of the melting pot where they can be removed with a slotted spoon.

Clip-on Lead Wheel Weights

One-pound is equivalent to 7,000 grains. Therefore one-pound of used wheel weights could be used to produce the following number of bullets based on the grain weight of the bullet:

Number of Bullets per One-Pound of Used Clip-On Wheel Weights

Bullet Grain Weight	Number of Bullets Made
110 Grain Bullet	63 Bullets per Pound
170 Grain Bullet	41 Bullets per Pound
230 Grain Bullet	30 Bullets per Pound

Sources of Tin:

The most common source of tin is from commercial solder. There are three basic types of solder as follows:

1. **Resin Core Solder** is primarily for electrical applications.
2. **Acid Core Solder** is primarily for plumbing applications.
3. **Solid Wire Solder** is for a variety of applications. Solid Wire Solder may be used to make lead bullets.

Solder can be made from a variety of different materials. The solder package will usually specify what the solder is made of. However, this is not always the case. Sometimes the package will direct you to an 800 number or a web site for a list of the materials used in the solder. If the materials are not clearly stated on the package then that solder is not appropriate for the production of lead bullets.

The two types of solder that are useful in the bullet casting process are as follows:

Solid Wire Solder

1. 95/5 Solid Wire Solder which contains 95% tin and 5% antimony.
2. 60/40 (or 50/50) Solid Wire Solder which contains 60% Tin and 40% lead (or 50% tin and 50% lead).

The 95/5 Solid Wire Solder is the best choice for casting lead bullets. The 60/40 (or 50/50) Solid Wire Solder is the next best choice. Each type of solder contains an adequate ratio of tin plus at least one other metal used in the casting process. None of these solders contains any extra metals or any type of additional compounds in its core.

However, these solders are **not** as easy to find as they once were (June 2009). One store that usually sells at least one of these solders will be your local Ace Hardware Store (or the Ace Internet Store). If you can't find one of these solders locally then you can always do an internet search and locate a plumbing supply store that sells these solders over the internet.

How to Add Tin:

1. If you are using a 95/5 solder then multiply the weight of the lead wheel weights by **0.017** (1.7%) and add approximately that much solder to your melting pot.
2. If you are using a 60/40 solder then multiply the weight of the lead wheel weights by **0.026** (2.6%) and add approximately that much solder to your melting pot.
3. If you are using a 50/50 solder then multiply the weight of the lead wheel weights by **0.033** (3.3%) and add approximately that much solder to your melting pot.
4. Remember that the wheel weights already contain approximately 1/2% tin.
5. The tin (solder) should be added to your melting pot at the same time you add the wheel weights.

Mathematical explanation of why the above percentages are correct:

Let's assume you have five-pounds of used clip-on wheel weights.
Five-pounds of wheel weights is equal to 80-ounces (5 pounds x 16 ounces/pound).
The wheel weights are assorted sizes but each one contains a metal clip that will be discarded.
Assume that the average weight of the metal clip is approximately 4% of the total weight of the wheel weight. After removing the metal clip (4%) the net weight of the wheel weights (96%) is therefore 76.8 ounces (80 ounces x 0.96).

Chapter Sixty-Five: How to Make Your Own Ammunition

Assume that the 76.8-ounces of wheel weights contain about 1/2 percent tin or **0.38 ounces of tin** (76.8 ounces x 0.005).

For 95/5 Solder add 1.7% solder:
The amount of 95/5 solder to add will be approximately 1.3 ounces (76.8 ounces x 0.017).
1.3 ounces of 95/5 solder will contain approximately **1.24 ounces of tin** (1.3 ounces x 0.95).
The total weight of tin will therefore be approximately **1.62 ounces of tin** (0.38 ounces + 1.24 ounces).
The total weight of all the metal (wheel weights and solder) will be **78.1 ounces** (76.8 ounces wheel weights + 1.3 ounces solder).
The percent of total tin in the alloy will now be approximately **2 percent** (1.62 ounces divided by 78.1 ounces).

For 60/40 Solder add 2.6% solder:
The amount of 60/40 solder to add will be approximately 2.0 ounces (76.8 ounces x 0.026).
2.0 ounces of 60/40 solder will contain approximately **1.2 ounces of tin** (2.0 ounces x 0.6).
The total weight of tin will therefore be approximately **1.58 ounces of tin** (0.38 ounces + 1.2 ounces).
The total weight of all the metal (wheel weights and solder) will be **78.8 ounces** (76.8 ounces wheel weights + 2.0 ounces solder).
The percent of total tin in the alloy will now be approximately **2 percent** (1.58 ounces divided by 78.8 ounces).

For 50/50 Solder add 3.3% solder:
The amount of 50/50 solder to add will be approximately 2.5 ounces (76.8 ounces x 0.033).
2.5 ounces of 50/50 solder will contain approximately **1.25 ounces of tin** (2.5 ounces x 0.5).
The total weight of tin will therefore be approximately **1.63 ounces of tin** (0.38 ounces + 1.25 ounces).
The total weight of all the metal (wheel weights and solder) will be **79.3 ounces** (76.8 ounces wheel weights + 2.5 ounces solder).
The percent of total tin in the alloy will now be approximately **2 percent** (1.63 ounces divided by 79.3 ounces).

A postal weight scale or a kitchen weight scale may be used to weigh the metals that will be added to the melting pot. This scale should be reserved for use only in the bullet casting process and this scale should **not** be used for any other application due to the danger of lead poisoning.

Bullet Casting Equipment

In order to make good bullets using lead wheel weights you will need a few pieces of equipment and a few other materials as follows:

1. **Melting Pot:** A basic 4.5-inch diameter cast iron melting pot can be used to melt the lead wheel weights. (Note: This item is still manufactured today by Lodge and it is already factory seasoned so it can be used immediately.) This is the way our ancestors made bullets. They would start a small fire, wait for it to burn down to red hot coals, and then put the small cast iron pot over the red hot coals. Then they would immediately add their lead to the pot and wait for it to melt. The pot has pouring spouts on both sides at the top so the molten lead could be poured directly into the bullet molds. Or a cast iron ladle (picture far right) could be used to transfer the molten lead from the pot to the bullet molds. The small cast iron pot was only used to melt lead. It was never used for anything else. That same rule applies today. If you purchase a cast iron melting pot then you should **never** use it for anything except to melt lead to avoid the dangers of lead poisoning.

Or, if you wish, you can spend a little more money and purchase an electric melting pot. There are a variety of these electric melting pots for sale from bullet casting companies, such as the one made by Lee called the Production Pot IV (picture on previous page). The Lee pot has a variable heat control, a ten-pound melting capacity, a twenty-minute melting time, and a bottom pour spout that is under the front edge of the pot so the molten lead can be easily distributed directly into a bullet mold without having to use a cast iron ladle.

When the wheel weights (and solder) have completely melted you will see a gray layer of molten residue on top of the molten lead. This is the tin and it should **not** be skimmed off the top. Now is the time for fluxing.

2. **Fluxing the molten lead:** The best time to add flux is **immediately** after the metal has reached its liquid molten stage and before the molten metal has a chance to heat up another 100 degrees or so. Our ancestors used paraffin, or beeswax, or candle wax, or beef tallow as flux. If you wish you may still use any one of these materials today. Or you can purchase a special bullet casting flux from any company that sells bullet molds. **Immediately** after the metal has reached its liquid molten stage, add a small amount of the flux to the pot. About a teaspoon of flux will do but the amount of flux depends on the amount of metal in the pot and the amount of impurities in the metal. If you are melting more lead and it has a higher percentage of impurities then you will need to add more flux. The flux will smoke and it may even catch fire. However, continue to stir the flux into the molten metal until the solution is well mixed. Fluxing helps to keep the tin and the antimony mixed with the molten lead but it causes any other impurities to separate out and float to the top surface where they can be scooped off with an old tablespoon with a wood handle (or a cast iron ladle). These impurities will look like a dark gray powder. If you are using wheel weights the metal clips will also be floating on top of the molten lead at this time. Use a slotted spoon with a wood handle to skim the metal clips off the top of the molten metal. You may need to flux the molten metal more than once if it contains a lot of impurities.

The impurities and foreign matter on top of the molten metal is called "dross." The dross needs to be scooped off the top of the molten lead and set aside. Later, after the dross cools down, it should be safely discarded because it contains lead particle residue.

3. **Bullet molds:** Now is the time to fill the cavity (or cavities) in your bullet mold. Complete detailed instructions on how to prepare and use your bullet molds will be contained inside the box with your new molds. Follow those instructions carefully.

Lee 2-Cavity Aluminum Mold

4. **Pouring the lead:** The molten metal should be carefully poured into the small opening in the sprue plate on the top of your bullet mold. This can be accomplished using a cast iron ladle. Or, if you have an electric melting pot with a bottom pour spout, then you can distribute the molten lead out the bottom of the pot through the special front spout. If you have a new electric melting pot then it will come with detailed instructions on how to use and care for your new equipment.

5. **Allow the lead to harden into a "soft" bullet:** After a little practice with your new mold you will learn how long to wait before you knock the sprue plate open, and then how much longer to wait before you open the mold and gently "knock-out" the new lead bullet(s) onto a dry clean soft towel (folded at least two layers thick). If you are wearing heat resistant gloves (such as welder's gloves) then immediately pick up the hot bullet from the dry folded towel and transfer it onto a wet towel in a cool water bath. The cool water quenching bath should be at least four-feet away from your lead melting pot. You should then immediately fill the bullet mold cavity with fresh molten metal. The bullet mold needs to be kept hot and the easiest way to do this is to not pause and inspect your bullets as you make them but to keep the bullet casting process going

Lyman Single Cavity Hollow-Point Steel Mold

Chapter Sixty-Five: How to Make Your Own Ammunition

continuously. This is especially true if you are casting hollow-point bullets because the hollow-point tip "or pin" needs to be kept very hot for it to form a proper cavity in the top of the hollow-point bullet.

6. **Cool Water Quenching Tray:** The cool water quenching tray should have been prepared before you cast your first bullet. A shallow plastic pan or metal pan about two-inches deep may be used for quenching. (This pan should **never** be used for anything except bullet quenching to avoid lead poisoning.) Fold another towel and place the folded towel in the bottom of the quenching pan (or use two smaller hand towels). Then fill the quenching pan with cool water and a few ice cubes. The folded towel (or two small hand towels) should be at least one-inch below the top surface of the cool water. Cool water quenching needs to be  started as soon as possible after you remove the hot bullet from the bullet mold. However, you should **never** drop a hot bullet from the mold directly into the quenching water. If any water splashes onto your hot mold it could damage the mold. Or the water may later drop off the wood mold handle into the molten metal inside the melting pot and this would be dangerous. Therefore if you are wearing heat resistant gloves, or if you have an assistant, then transfer the hot bullets from the dry towel onto the wet towel inside the cool water bath as soon as possible after removing them from the bullet mold to maximize the heat treating process. Be careful to not let any water splash onto your gloves or you will be transferring the water to your melting pot area and this would be dangerous.

After your bullets have cooled down inside the cool water bath for about ten-minutes (or at the end of your bullet casting session), you may remove the bullets from the cool water bath, dry them off completely with a clean dry towel, and then set them aside at room temperature. The bullets will gradually continue to get harder for a period of between one to three days. At that time the bullets will have reached their maximum hardness and the next step in the bullet making process may be followed.

Do not wash the above towels with your ordinary laundry. The above towels may contain tiny particles of lead. Keep these towels separate from your other towels and only use these towels in the bullet casting process.

Optional Oven Heat Treating Method: If you feel that you may not be able to follow the above quenching procedure without having some type of accident then you could heat treat your bullets on another day using the "oven method" and a baking pan that will fit inside that oven. However, since you are working with lead bullets whatever oven and baking pan you use for heat treating lead bullets must **never** be used for anything else to avoid lead poisoning. A small portable electric oven with an accurate reliable thermostat will do the job. Preheat the oven to 450°F (232°C). Line the bottom of the baking pan with a piece of aluminum foil. Stand the bullets upright on the aluminum foil so there is a small space between each of the bullets. Place the pan of bullets inside the 450°F (232°C) oven. Wait one-hour. Remove the pan of bullets and immediately transfer the bullets into a cool water quenching bath. Then follow the above cool water quenching tray instructions. (Note: Do not exceed an oven temperature of 450°F (232°C). The average bullet made from clip-on wheel weights will begin to deform at a temperature of about 465°F (240°C). If deformation begins then you will have to completely remelt the bullets and recast them a second time.)

7. **Lube:** There are a variety of ways to lubricate a cast bullet. Most web sites and most of the older literature recommends the old way which is to simply lube the bottom grooves of a cast lead bullet. However, if you follow the above bullet casting procedure then you should lube your newly made bullets the new way as follows:

Place your hardened bullets in a bowl (only used for bullet casting) and then add a little Liquid Alox bullet lube (picture on right). Shake the bullets around inside the bowl until they are covered with the lube. Pour the bullets onto wax paper and let them dry

Chapter Sixty-Five: How to Make Your Own Ammunition

for at least 12 hours. (Note: If you size your bullets then lubing will probably need to be done before and after sizing.)

Sizing was once necessary because the original bullet molds were made of cast iron. Most of the older bullet casting literature discusses sizing in great depth. Today's modern aluminum bullet molds and steel bullets molds will generally produce high quality bullets that do not need sizing. If you have a micrometer then you can determine this yourself. It should be noted that different alloys will yield slightly different finished bullet diameters and bullet weights using the same exact bullet mold.

8. **Sizing Decision:** To determine if your bullets need to be sized, seat one lubed bullet the proper depth into a brass case. Then insert that cartridge into your firearm chamber. If the bullet does not freely enter the chamber then this batch of bullets needs to be sized (or the bullets need to be remelted and some of the tin scooped off the top of the molten lead before fluxing so the finished bullet diameter will be smaller after casting). Sizing must be done before seating the bullets into brass cases. Lubing must be done again after sizing. There are a variety of web sites that describe how to size a bullet using a special sizing die that exactly matches the caliber of bullet you are making. You will need a special sizing die for each caliber bullet that you make.

9. **How to Size Before Casting:** It is possible to adjust the diameter of a bullet prior to casting by changing the tin percentage. If you use clip-on wheel weights without any extra tin added to the melting pot then the final hardened bullet will have its minimum possible diameter. If you increase the percentage of tin you can increase the diameter of the bullet as follows:

1/2 percent tin will yield the smallest diameter bullet with the highest weight (wheel weights with no extra tin added).

2 percent tin will **increase** the final bullet diameter by approximately 0.001-inches and **decrease** the total bullet weight by about 3%.

4 percent tin will **increase** the final bullet diameter by approximately 0.0015-inches and **decrease** the total bullet weight by about 6%.

The older cast iron bullet dies also took more time to heat up and therefore the first five, ten, or fifty bullets were of poor quality and they had to be set aside so they could be remelted at a later date and reused in the casting process. Today's modern aluminum bullet molds and steel bullet molds will usually produce good quality bullets immediately, or after only one or two poor quality bullets have been cast and set aside.

Smokeless Powder Footnote for Cast Lead Bullets: For many years most references recommended a fast-burning powder for jacketed bullets and a slow-burning powder for cast lead bullets. However, at the current time the Speer Reloading Manual # 14 (2007 edition) recommends a medium-burning powder for cast lead bullets. This is important because it means that a fast-burning powder inside a factory-loaded cartridge is now much closer in performance to the medium-burning powder currently recommended for cast lead bullets.

Historical Criticisms of Cast Lead Bullets

The fact that cast lead bullets are not jacketed has resulted in a lot of bad publicity for these bullets. The reason is because of "lead fouling" inside the firearm barrel.

When lead fouls the inside of the firearm bore it gets deep down into the rifling grooves. And as it gradually builds up it interferes with the accuracy of the shot. And lead fouling can be difficult and time consuming to remove.

There are several things that can be done to minimize the problem of lead fouling:

1. **Clean the Bore Before Using Lead Bullets:** Thoroughly clean your firearm barrel before you start using lead bullets. Make sure you remove all traces of your "jacketed bullets." If necessary use a gun cleaning solvent to remove all the residue inside the barrel. Then push a few clean dry patches through the barrel to make sure it is both clean and dry. If you start with a clean barrel that contains no traces of your previous "jacketed bullets" then you will have significantly reduced the possibility of a future lead fouling problem.

2. **Bullet Size (Diameter):** The diameter of the cast lead bullet should be between 0.001-inch to 0.003-inch **larger** than the diameter of the inside bore of the firearm. This keeps the powder gases behind the bullet so the gases can push the bullet forward out the front end of the barrel. You can increase the diameter of a bullet from an existing bullet mold by adding between 1% to 4% tin to the metal mixture prior to casting.

3. **Bullet Softness:** If the lead bullet is too soft it will not pick up the rifling inside the barrel and it will exit the barrel without having any spin imparted to it. Without spin the bullet quickly looses its accuracy. This problem can be resolved by heat treating the cast lead bullets.

4. **Heat Treating:** Heat treating must be done **before** you lube the bullet and before you seat the bullet into a brass shell case. Heat treating ordinary lead wheel weight cast bullets will significantly increase their hardness. A harder bullet will shoot more accurately and it will leave significantly less lead behind in the firearm barrel.

5. **Bullet Lubrication:** Most of the old literature only recommends lubing the bottom grooves of a cast lead bullet. This meant that the nose of the bullet was bare lead and therefore it could easily deposit lead particles inside the firearm barrel as it made its way through the barrel. However, the current literature recommends lubing the entire surface of the bullet. This puts a hard finish over the entire lead surface of the bullet and therefore it helps to minimize potential lead deposits inside the firearm barrel.

6. **Clean the Bore After Shooting Lead Bullets:** There is no solvent that will dissolve and remove lead deposits. If you try to use a chemical strong enough to dissolve lead it will also attack the inside of the firearm barrel. To remove any tiny lead deposits inside the firearm barrel you will need to use the stiff bristle cleaning brush that came with your cleaning rods. This stiff bristle brush will loosen the lead and break it free from the inside of the barrel. Then you can remove the tiny lead particles with a clean patch that has been very lightly moistened with solvent or gun oil. After all the lead has been removed you should finish cleaning the barrel using whatever cleaning procedure you normally follow.

How to Reload Ammunition

You now have all four ammunition components: the brass case, a Boxer primer, some smokeless powder, and a bullet. You now need to be able to safely and correctly assemble these four items together into an ammunition cartridge. To accomplish this task you will need the following minimum reloading equipment:

1. **A Single Stage Reloading Press:** A reloading press holds the reloading dies (one at a time). The reloading process includes removing the used primer (decapping), resizing the brass case to its original dimensions, expanding the case mouth slightly to facilitate the installation of a new bullet, installing a new primer, and seating a new bullet at the proper depth in the cartridge (and sometimes crimping the case mouth around the new bullet). A good press provides the mechanical leverage so these tasks may be easily accomplished manually. The sequence of activities is usually done in batches. For example, if you are reloading 20 cases then you would perform the first operation on all 20 cases. You would then change dies and perform the second operation on all 20 cases. And so on.

   Note: A new reloading press will come with an instruction manual and it will contain all the information you will need so that you can properly and safely use and take care of your new equipment. Therefore I am not going to include that information in this chapter.

   Note: The green RCBS Reloading Press in the above picture was purchased new in 1974 and it is still in excellent condition in the year 2010 and it still functions flawlessly.

Chapter Sixty-Five: How to Make Your Own Ammunition

2. **Reloading Dies for each caliber:**

   2 Piece Die Set for Rifle Ammo: Contains a decapping/resizing/expanding die, and a bullet seating die. (Note: Some rifle sets include 3 dies.)

   3 Piece Die Set for Handgun Ammo: Contains a decapping/resizing die, and an expanding die, and a bullet seating die. (Note: Some handgun sets include 4 dies.)

   Note: All reloading dies must be adjusted to work properly with the caliber and case you are using. However, all new die sets come with a very detailed set of instructions for using and adjusting the dies in that set. Therefore I am not going to include that information in this chapter.

   Note: Pistol **Carbide** Die Sets do **not** require case lube. This is a significant advantage during a long-term hard times event when case lube may not be available. The Lee Brand **Carbide** Die Sets also come with the Shell Holder and a powder measure as part of the die set. Therefore if you are purchasing new dies then pay the small extra premium for the **carbide** pistol dies. If the die set does not specifically say "carbide" then it is not a carbide die set.

   Note: Rifle dies do require case lube. Therefore if you will be reloading rifle ammunition you will still need a Lube Pad.

3. **Shell Holder:** The shell holder keeps the empty brass case in the exact center position of the reloading press. Since different calibers have different shell case diameters there is no universal one-size shell holder that works for all calibers. However, some shell holders will accommodate more than one caliber. For example, the 38 Special and the 357 magnum both use the same size shell holder.

   Some die sets include the shell holder but some do not. If the die set you purchase does not specifically say that it includes the shell holder then you will need to purchase this small item for the caliber you need. Each company that makes reloading dies also makes shell holders and the part numbers they assign to their shell holders are different than the part numbers a competitor will assign to their shell holders. Therefore do not rely on a shell holder part number unless you are buying the same exact brand shell holder as your reloading dies. Instead read the back of the shell holder package and select the correct size shell holder for the caliber you are reloading.

4. **Deburring Tool (or case trimmer):** This small tool has two cutting ends. It allows you to remove any tiny burrs on the mouth of the case. The pointed end of the tool fits **inside** the case mouth and when you rotate it you will trim off any tiny burrs on the inside mouth of the shell case. The opposite end of the tool fits around the **outside** of the case mouth and when you rotate it you will trim off any tiny burrs on the outside of the shell case.

5. **Plastic Block for Holding Brass Shell Cases:** This plastic block holds the empty cases upright while you are working on them. It holds the empty case primer side down. This allows you to fill each individual case with gunpowder. Since the case is upright the powder will stay inside the shell case. The trays are designed so the shell case extends a reasonable distance above the top of the plastic block so you can pick up each shell case. The illustrated red block is an universal block and it may be used with pistol and rifle cases because it has both shallow holes and deep holes. Make sure the block you purchase is designed for the caliber of ammo you will be reloading. (Note: The plastic case that comes with some brands of new factory-loaded ammo holds the ammunition with the bullet side down and the primer side up. This will not hold the empty shell case in the correct position for reloading that caliber of ammunition.)

Chapter Sixty-Five: How to Make Your Own Ammunition

6. **Case Lube Pad:** Lubricate the pad with some special case lube (not bullet lube) and then roll your clean empty brass cases back and forth on top of the lube pad to lube the outside of the brass cases. After you have lubed the cases they will enter and withdraw more easily from the reloading dies without damaging the brass cases or the dies. The case lube pad in the illustration is an old pad and it has seen a lot of use.

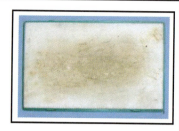

7. **Primer Tray:** This relatively flat 8-sided green tray will hold several primers in a loose random manner. This makes it easier to pick up and use the primers one-at-a-time.

8. **Powder Weight Scale and Powder Measure:**
A Powder Weight Scale will allow you to precisely measure the exact weight of powder required. A Powder Measure dispenses the same exact amount of powder into each empty brass shell. You could purchase both pieces of equipment. But if your finances are limited then you really only need the Powder Weight Scale. It allows you to measure the weight of the powder in the small metal tray and then you can pour the powder from that tray directly into an empty brass shell case.

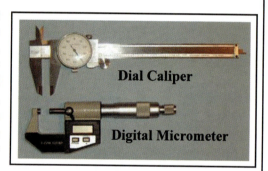

9. **Measurement Gage:** You may need a measurement gage (caliper or micrometer) to verify specific critical dimensions of your cast iron bullets and your hand-loaded ammunition. You have two options. A simple dial gage is manually operated and it does not use any batteries. A digital gage will also do the job but it will not work unless you have a battery. If you are anticipating the use of this gage during a hard times tragedy event when replacement batteries may not be available then the manual dial gage would be the better choice even though it relies on the "old technology."

Dial Caliper

Digital Micrometer

10. **Universal Case Expanding Die:** If you will be casting your own lead bullets and loading them into your brass shell cases then you will also need to flare the case mouth slightly to accept your new lead bullets. Lee makes a Universal Case Expanding Die (Lee part number 90798) that will work with all calibers from 22 to 45 caliber. It cost about $12.00 and since it can be used with almost any caliber bullet it is a great value, in my opinion. One of the places where this item can be purchased on the internet is from MidwayUSA.com (Midway part number 140461). It might also be available at your local gun store.

11. **Reloading Manual:** You will need a relatively recent edition of a reloading manual. It will list the exact powder weight to use with each grain weight bullet for each caliber. At the current time the industry standard is the Speer Reloading Manual, Number 14, 2007 Edition.

Frequently you will see older reloading manuals for sale at a deep discount. I suggest that you not buy a really old manual for two reasons: (1) the powder brand names change over time, and (2) new caliber bullets are designed and introduced into the marketplace. Old reloading manuals will not contain information on these new calibers (such as the Glock 45 GAP), and they may not have any data on the powders currently being sold at gun shops.

If you can afford it you should purchase reloading manuals from two different publishers. For example, the 49th Edition of the Lyman Reloading Handbook was published in the year 2008. Although both the Lyman and the Speer manuals will have some data on the same exact grain weights of bullets in a specific caliber, each manual will also have some grain weights listed that are not included in the other manual. In most cases the Lyman manual has more data on more different grain weight bullets in each caliber than the Speer manual. The Lyman manual also has a six-page article on cast bullets. Therefore, although the Lyman manual is not the most recommended one in the reloading industry, it is the manual I personally prefer. Even though the Lyman manual has fewer pages, each of those pages is almost twice the size as one page in the Speer manual. Finally, neither manual has color pictures, if that is important to you.

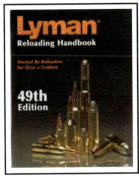

If you are looking for a reliable good quality reloading press that will last at least one lifetime then you should seriously consider the RCBS Rock Chucker Supreme Single Stage Master Reloading Set. This set contains all the basic reloading components you will need except for the appropriate reloading dies and shell holder (which are unique for each caliber bullet).

Your local gun shop may have this Reloading Press Set in stock. They may not sell the Entire Set as a single item but they may have each of its components for sale on an individual basis. Therefore you should visit your local dealers first. Or look in your local yellow page phone book and call your local gun shops on the telephone. If you can't find the reloading equipment you want locally then you can check to see if you can find the equipment available at an internet store.

How to Remove a Bullet and a Primer from a Live Cartridge

Always wear safety glasses when using any type of bullet puller. Bullet pullers are only designed for centerfire cartridges.

Never insert a rimfire cartridge or a black powder cartridge into a bullet puller. You may accidentally fire these cartridge using a bullet puller.

Kinetic Inertial Bullet Puller: To safely remove a bullet from a live cartridge you will need a kinetic inertial bullet puller. A bullet pullet looks like a hammer. The bullet puller illustrated in the picture on the right is a universal puller and it will work with most handgun and rifle calibers.

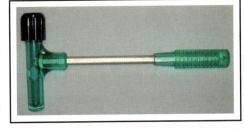

To use a kinetic bullet puller, a new factory-loaded centerfire cartridge is inserted bullet end first into the large top end of the puller. The cap is then tightened around the base of the cartridge case. The opposite plastic end of the puller is manually hit against a hard solid surface. The cap holds the shell case in position but the bullet still contains downward kinetic energy and it will try to pull free from its case. Several short medium strength blows are preferred to one or two heavy blows. After several medium blows the bullet will separate from its case and the bullet and the gunpowder will fall into the hollow cavity end of the puller. You can see through the green plastic and you will be able to see the bullet and the powder mixed together in the bottom of the bullet puller. You can then pour the powder and the bullet out the small hole in the side of the puller. You can then remove the cap and salvage the brass shell case with its primer intact.

If you use a solid wood block as your striking surface then the bullet should pull free from its case after about 5 or 10 medium strength blows. If you exceed twenty blows and the bullet is still inside its original shell case then you are not using enough downward force. Increase the amount of pressure a little bit and keep striking the solid wood block. After you have successfully removed two or three bullets from their cartridges then you will have a pretty good feel for how much strength to use to loosen the bullet in somewhere between 5 to 10 blows.

After you remove the bullet from its case then you will have some gunpowder and a live primer (the primer will still be in the bottom of the brass case). The bullet might also be of use to you. After you remove the primer you will also have the empty brass case that might be of value to someone else. Therefore save the empty cases and the bullets in addition to the gunpowder and the primers.

RCBS Bullet Pullet with Collet Purchased Separately: Bullets can also be removed using a standard reloading press and a special collet die holder and a collet die of the correct diameter that matches the diameter of the jacketed bullet you wish to remove. RCBS makes this special collet die holder (Midway part number 680804, price $21.49) and the individual collet dies for each bullet caliber (price $12.49 each). Using your reloading press to remove a jacketed bullet is easier than using the above kinetic inertial bullet puller. In the picture the bullet puller is on the left side of the green box. The collet which was purchased separately is shown in the middle of the green box.

However, the kinetic inertial hammer-like bullet puller will work with almost all caliber bullets whereas the RCBS bullet puller die requires a special collet die for each individual caliber.

There are also some other special tools that could be used to remove a bullet from a brass shell case. However, to keep this chapter to a reasonable length I will not discuss those other special tools.

There are also a variety of **dangerous unsafe ways** to remove a bullet from a live cartridge. Do not attempt to remove a bullet from a live cartridge using a pair of vise-grip pliers or a bench vise. If you crimp, dent, or crush the rim of a live cartridge you could ignite the primer and the bullet will fire out the end of the case, or the case may rupture and explode. Therefore do not attempt to remove a bullet from a live cartridge using pliers or a bench vise, even if you read somewhere on the internet that a person claims to have done this safely. This is *not* a safe way to remove a bullet from a live cartridge.

Primer Removal: The live primer may be removed using a standard reloading press by inserting the brass shell into the correct size shell holder and then slowly and gently pushing out the primer using the correct size die punch. Almost everyone who has any experience with reloading has had to occasionally remove a live primer that didn't fit into the empty shell case correctly. Since we work with these tiny primers all the time we don't give it much thought. However, removing a live primer may ignite the primer. Therefore if you are going to remove a live primer you should take all the appropriate safety precautions, such as wearing safety eyeglasses, a long-sleeve shirt, and leather gloves. If the primer is accidentally ignited then it will fire its small denotation charge up and out the open top end of the empty shell case. However, since the brass case is empty there will be no gunpowder to explode (or bullet to be fired).

Lee makes a Universal Depriming and Decapping Die (Lee part number 90292) that can be used on all caliber brass shell cases (price about $10.00). The inside of the die is larger than the outside of the biggest brass shell case. And the decapping pin is in the exact center of the die. Therefore if you have a shell holder of the correct size then this die can be used to remove the primer from any size brass case. One of the places on the internet where this item can be purchased is MidwayUSA.com (Midway part number 136543). Or you may be able to find this special die at your local gun shop.

Note: If a live primer is accidentally ignited then the detonation compound inside the primer will flare up through the top of the empty brass shell case and enter the inside of the oversized decapping die and then be forced back down around the outside edges of the die towards the bottom of the press. This has not yet happened to me so I can't describe what damage might be done to the decapping die. It is possible that the die decapping pin may become bent or damaged.

Note: Primers are factory matched to the exact powder used inside the cartridge. Do not try to use a different primer with a different powder. A potential disaster may result. Therefore carefully label your primers and your powder so you will know which ones may be safely used together. The powders used at ammunition factories can vary from one production lot to the next. Even in the same exact bullet the powder may be different from one box of bullets to the next box. The factory is able to precisely determine exactly how much powder is required to produce the required accuracy for that type of bullet. If the production quality of the powder varies then the factory can easily adjust the powder charge so the cartridge still delivers the required accuracy for the final consumer. Therefore treat each individual box of factory loaded bullets as being unique, unless the box has a stamped production lot number on it and all the lot numbers match.

Final Summary and Conclusion

For many years I have recommended that an individual would be better advised to invest in factory-loaded ammunition instead of reloading equipment. I still believe that if you can find enough factory-loaded ammunition for each of your firearms then you should invest in that factory-loaded ammunition instead of reloading equipment.

In my opinion the **minimum** investment in factory-loaded ammunition would be the following:
1,000 rounds for your handgun.
1,000 rounds for your hunting rifle.
5,000 rounds of 22LR ammunition.

If you have a shotgun then buy 1,000 shotgun shells in a variety of sizes such as the following:
100 one-ounce sabot slugs.
200 00-buckshot.
700 assorted shot sizes such as 4, 6, 7, 7 1/2, or whatever you can find available.

However, if you are **not** able to obtain a reasonable inventory of factory-loaded ammunition for your firearms then now would be a good time to seriously consider reloading your existing centerfire brass shells yourself. That is the reason I wrote this chapter.

Following is a very brief summary of **some** of the more important topics that apply to reloading ammunition and casting lead bullets:

1. You should always save your empty brass shell cases because you may be able to reload and reuse them in the future. It is relatively easy to save the empty brass shell cases from a revolver or bolt-action rifle or lever-action rifle. However, you may discover that it is more challenging to recover all the empty shell cases from a semi-automatic weapon, especially if you are shooting in an outdoor area where the normal ground vegetation can hide the empty brass shell case.

2. Trying to make smokeless powder at home is **not** practical for a number of good reasons. Therefore some other source of smokeless powder needs to be found, such as the canisters of smokeless powder for sale at some gun shops or some gun shows.

3. The primers and the smokeless powder from factory-loaded ammunition in a caliber you do not need may be safely removed and then transferred to your empty brass shell cases that you do need to reload. The bullet may also be used if the bullet diameter, grain weight, and shape matches your requirements.

4. Factory-loaded ammunition may be safely disassembled using a kinetic inertial bullet powder. This type of bullet puller will work on most calibers of centerfire handgun and rifle ammunition.

5. A live primer may be removed from its brass shell case using the Lee Universal Depriming and Decapping Die (Lee part number 90292) and a universal reloading press, such as the RCBS Rock Chucker.

6. Ordinary clip-on lead wheel weights can be converted into good quality bullets if you have the proper knowledge and some basic minimum equipment.

7. Modern bullet dies will generally produce bullets that do **not** need to be sized. However, if your firearm requires a slightly different diameter bullet than the one currently produced by the die then the bullet diameter can be changed by adding or subtracting tin (solder) from the wheel weight alloy.

Chapter Sixty-Five: How to Make Your Own Ammunition

8. Heat treating your lead bullets **immediately** after casting in a cool water quenching bath will significantly increase their hardness. This will significantly reduce the potential problems of gas cutting and lead fouling inside the firearm barrel. It will also improve the accuracy of your new bullets.

9. Lubricating the entire surface of the bullet with Liquid Alox will put a hard smooth coating around the entire exterior surface of the bullet. This will also help to significantly reduce the potential problems of gas cutting and lead fouling inside the firearm barrel. It will also improve the accuracy of your new bullets.

10. Slightly expanding the mouth of an empty brass shell case before you seat your new cast bullet will help to achieve a better fit of the bullet inside the brass case (Lee Universal Case Expanding Die, Lee part number 90798).

This chapter does **not** discuss everything you will need to know to make your own bullets and to reload your empty brass shell cases. This chapter also does **not** discuss every possible safety precaution in the bullet casting and ammunition reloading process. This chapter is only a brief summary of some of the more important topics in those areas.

However, if you purchase a new Reloading Press, and new Reloading Dies, and new Bullet Casting Molds, then those items will contain instruction manuals and detailed instruction pages that will more fully educate you in the reloading and bullet casting process. In addition, the Speer Reloading Manual (or the Lyman Reloading Handbook) contains almost everything else you might need to know.

Target Practice: In closing please allow me to suggest that you carefully ration whatever ammunition you may currently have in your possession. Although practice is important it is **not** as critical as having ammunition available when you really truly desperately need it, such as for emergency self-defense or for hunting to put some meat into the cook pot. For example, if you consume a box of 50 cartridges each month shooting at paper targets then in just one-year you will have consumed 600 rounds of your ammunition (50x12=600). On the other hand, if you limit your target practice each month to 5 rounds of ammunition then after one-year you will have only consumed 60 rounds of ammunition. If you only practice once every three months then you will only consume 20 rounds per year but you will still be able to maintain your current marksmanship skill level (5 rounds of ammunition multiplied by four times per year = 20 rounds).

Chapter Sixty-Six

Pellet Air Rifles:
.22 Caliber and .177 Caliber

Let me begin by listing the advantages and the disadvantages of a pellet rifle.

First, the **disadvantages** of pellet rifles in general:

1. A pellet rifle is a single-shot rifle. Unlike a bolt-action rifle, you must fold the barrel forward on the rifle, insert a pellet, and then return the barrel to its original position. This is a slow time-consuming process. It is much slower than a bolt-action rifle where you can usually load about five cartridges into the magazine and then eject and insert a new cartridge by simply operating the bolt.

2. It requires a moderate degree of effort to fold the barrel forward to load a pellet (this is called breaking the barrel). Some women, and some teenagers, may not have the strength to do this. If you will grasp the end of the barrel as close as possible to the front sight then it will be easier to break the barrel to insert a pellet.

3. A pellet rifle would be useless against predatory animals. Therefore I would never carry a pellet rifle into the woods as my only method of firearm protection.

4. A pellet rifle would be almost useless as a self-defense weapon. A pellet could penetrate a thin shirt and the skin of a person and theoretically it could kill a person. However, if a person were wearing several layers of clothing then the pellet may not do anything more than make the person angry. On the other hand, a pellet shot to the neck, eye, or ear could be deadly so this is not a toy for a younger child.

5. The range of a pellet rifle is significantly less than a 22-caliber rimfire long-rifle cartridge.

6. A pellet rifle should never, never be dry fired. Always have a pellet in the chamber before pulling the trigger on a pellet rifle. (Note: You should also never dry fire any type of 22 rimfire firearm.)

7. Pellets are single use items and each pellet may only be fired one time. The same pellet may not be fired a second time because it may damage the inside of the rifle barrel.

Now for the **advantages** of pellet rifles in general:

1. Although a pellet rifle does have a serial number, it does not need to be registered as a firearm. However, each nation has its own laws so please check the laws where you live.

2. A pellet rifle may be purchased in many states within the United States without any type of paperwork. Once again, each state and each county can have its own pellet gun laws so you will need to verify the laws in the area where you live.

3. The ammunition for a pellet rifle is relatively inexpensive at approximately $2.00 per 250 pellets, or about $0.008 each. The Premium Hunting Hollow Point pellets cost about $6.97 for 500 pellets, or about $0.014 each.

4. A pellet rifle makes a muffled "twang" sound when fired. In my opinion it sounds very similar to the "make-believe sound of a handgun with a silencer when fired in a movie." A real silencer, or sound suppressor, does not muffle the sound the way the movies would lead you to believe.

5. A pellet rifle may be a reasonable option for anyone who lives in an area where firearm laws prevent honest law-abiding citizens from owning firearms.

6. Depending on the hunting laws in your area a pellet rifle could be a reasonable option for hunting small game, such as squirrels or rabbits. However, as I have mentioned in several of my other chapters, I strongly recommend steel traps and snares for collecting wild game instead of any type of hunting rifle.

The Beeman Dual Caliber Pellet Air Rifle

1. At the beginning of the year 2011 a Beeman Dual Caliber Pellet Air Rifle could be purchased in the sporting goods section of many Walmart stores for about $98.

2. The rifle comes with two interchangeable barrels: a 22 caliber barrel and a 177 caliber barrel. To swap the barrels you remove a single set screw on the underside of the barrel at the front of the wood forearm grip, slide the barrel out of the rifle, insert the other barrel into the rifle, and replace the set screw. This is all done with an allen wrench that is provided with the rifle. In addition, an additional spare set screw is included with the rifle. (Note: In the picture of the rifle on the Beeman box the entire length of the second barrel is not shown. Each rifle barrel extends down inside the wood stock so that it is directly below the rear end of the upper rear iron sight.)

3. The rifle will fire a 177 caliber pellet at approximately 1,000 feet per second (fps) and it will fire a 22 caliber pellet at approximately 800 fps. (Note: An object needs to be traveling faster than approximately 1100 fps to break the sound barrier, or 1128 fps at sea level at 70°F or 21°C.)

4. The rifle has iron sights and the rear iron sight is easily adjustable for both windage and elevation. Both the front and rear iron sights are permanently attached to the front half of the barrel.

5. A 4x32 scope and scope mounts are included with the rifle. However, the scope is mounted onto the rear half of the barrel. The front half of the barrel must be folded forward to load a pellet and then returned to its original position. If the front barrel is not 100% perfectly realigned with the rear half of the barrel then the point of pellet impact will not be consist when using the scope.

6. The safety is automatically engaged each time you fold the rifle barrel and insert a new pellet. I like this. The safety is directly in front of the trigger and it is easily disengaged by pushing it forward with the end of your finger before pulling the trigger to the rear.

7. It is equipped with a quality European hardwood stock that has a solid rubber butt piece at the end of the stock to cushion the rifle against your shoulder.

8. Since the barrel can be completely removed, the pellet rifle may be stored in a space 32.5 inches long by 6.5 inches wide by 2.0 inches thick if the scope is removed.

Pellet Information

If you invest in a pellet rifle then I also strongly recommend that you invest in at least 5,000 pellets. If possible, buy the 22 caliber pellets. If the 22 caliber pellets are not available then the 177 caliber pointed pellets are about 1/2 the price of the premium 177 caliber hollow point pellets and therefore you could acquire a lot more of them for the same amount of money. I do not recommend the flat nose target pellets for anything so please don't buy them if anything else is available for sale.

The 22 caliber pellet is approximately 65% heavier than the 177 caliber pellet. This could make a significant difference when hunting wild game animals that are a little bigger than a rabbit, such as an opossum, or a groundhog, or a raccoon. However, before hunting any type of animal please verify and obey the hunting laws in your area. At the beginning of the year 2011 Walmart is selling the 22 caliber and the 177 caliber hollow point hunting pellets for the same exact price. Therefore I suggest you invest in the 22 caliber pellets if you can find then available.

| 22 Caliber Hollow Points | 177 Caliber Hollow Points | 177 Caliber Pointed Pellets |

I tested the penetration power of the 177 caliber pointed pellet on some old scrap pieces of plywood that I had. The results are as follows:

1/8 inch thick plywood: A 177 caliber pointed pellet completely penetrated and exited the rear of the plywood at 25 feet, 50 feet, 75 feet, and 100 feet.

5/8 inch thick plywood: A 177 caliber pointed pellet completely penetrated and exited the rear of the plywood at 25 feet, 50 feet, 75 feet, and 100 feet.

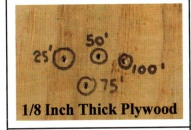

1/8 Inch Thick Plywood

The reason I conducted the above simple tests was to determine for myself if the pellet rifle could be used to kill small game animals. I know that small game animals have fur and skin and that their hides are not made of wood. However, I also know that skin and fur is not as hard as wood and if a pointed pellet will go completely through a small piece of plywood then that pellet has a good chance of penetrating the hide of a small wild game animal and killing that animal.

If I were using a pellet rifle to hunt small game then I would get close enough to shoot the animal in the brain.

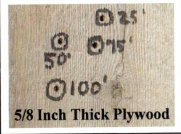

5/8 Inch Thick Plywood

I did not conduct tests out further than 100 feet because when you are in the woods you normally won't see a small game animal until you are relatively close to it. In addition, there are shrubs, and bushes, and other types of vegetation in the woods that will prevent a clear shot at a long distance. Finally, a small game animal is a relatively small target and you will need to be within the repeatability accuracy of your pellet rifle.

The above shooting tests were conducted with the iron sights on the rifle from a standing position without any type of additional support below the front rifle barrel. I was not aiming at a specific spot on the plywood. I was just aiming at the plywood in order to determine if the pellet would penetrate the plywood. Therefore the grouping of the four shots on each piece of plywood is nothing more than random chance. (Note: I drew black circles around each of the small pellet holes and I labeled each hole with the distance to the target.)

The next day I exchanged the 177 caliber barrel for the 22 caliber barrel. I did not bother to test the 22 caliber barrel on the 1/8 inch thick plywood. Instead I simply tested it on the 5/8 inch thick plywood at a distance of 100 feet. The 22 caliber hollow point pellets easily penetrated the 5/8 inch thick plywood at 100 feet. However, since I had exchanged barrels the average point of pellet impact was about six inches to the left and about three inches higher than the grouping with the 177 pellets. I did not expect the rear iron sights to provide the same average point of pellet impact because of the difference in the size and weight of the two pellets (177 caliber and 22 caliber) and the fact that a reasonable wind was blowing from the right to the left on the second day of the test.

Even though a pellet rifle will not accumulate gunpowder deposits inside the barrel it will still gradually accumulate lead deposits inside the barrel from the lead pellets. Therefore at the end of each shooting session you will need to swab the inside of the barrel using a cleaning rod, a cleaning patch, and a tiny bit of lubricant.

Chapter Sixty-Six: Pellet Rifles

Note: If I did not already own a 22 caliber long-rifle "LR" rimfire semi-automatic rifle then I would invest in a rimfire rifle instead of a pellet rifle. Walmart has the "Savage Arms, Inc. 64F 22LR" semi-automatic rifle with a 10-round detachable magazine for approximately $137. Walmart has the "Marlin Model 60 22LR" semi-automatic rifle with a tubular magazine for about $148. If money is not an issue then you should consider the "Ruger Model 10/22" semi-automatic rifle with a 10-round detachable magazine. If you can find the Ruger Model 10/22 semi-automatic Stainless Steel rifle then this would be even better. In my opinion you should have a semi-automatic rifle and not a "bolt-action" rifle or a "lever-action" rifle.

Chapter Sixty-Seven

Emergency Backpack or a Suitcase on Wheels (Bug-Out-Bag or B.O.B.)

If you were told that you had five-minutes to evacuate your current home or you and your family would perish, what would you do?

If you already had an emergency backpack or suitcase packed for each member of your family then you could spend those five minutes collecting any food, medicine, and clothing that you should take with you, along with any jewelry or other valuables, and your family photograph album, and your fireproof metal box that already contains the original copies of all your birth certificates, marriage licenses, diplomas, school transcripts, business certifications or licenses, deeds, wills, and other important documents.

If you had taken the time to think about this ahead of time then you should have already made a list of the items you absolutely wish to take with you along with where those items are usually stored. This list will help you to quickly collect everything you really need without overlooking something critical due to the pressure of the current evacuation situation.

The emergency backpack or suitcase is usually referred to as a bug-out-bag of "B.O.B." for short.

Some people recommend packing a "B.O.B." for a 72-hour or 3-day emergency. I do not agree with this advice. My personal opinion is that your "B.O.B." should give you the option to survive for at least six-months if you are forced to evacuate your home. Obviously you could not store a six-month food supply in one backpack but you could store enough of everything else to last each member of your family for at least six-months. If an unexpected hard times event forces you to quickly abandon your home then after you put everyone's emergency "B.O.B." into your escape vehicle then you could put as much food as possible into your vehicle and then you could abandon your home.

The items you store inside your "B.O.B." should be high-quality new items instead of used items in poor condition. The reason is simple. If a hard times tragedy event occurs and you are forced to use the stuff in your "B.O.B." then those items may be all that you have for many, many years into the future. Wouldn't it be nice to have high-quality new equipment and clothes instead of things that are almost ready to fall apart?

The average family will need a separate "B.O.B." for each member of the family plus a special family "master" backpack that contains items that will be shared by everyone in the family. Some minimum suggestions for a "B.O.B." are as follows:

A **master backpack** for the entire family should contain the following:

1. A really big detailed map of your state that shows all the major roads and all the secondary roads.
2. Separate individual maps of all the states that adjoin your state.
3. Good maps of each of the National Forests in your state and the nearby states that show all highways, dirt roads, hiking trails, camp sites, and rivers.
4. A "Coghlan's Six Function Whistle Compass" with a thermometer, a whistle, a mirror, a magnifying glass, and an LED flashlight (cost about $10 at most Army/Navy Surplus Stores).
5. A portable Katadyn Pocket Water Filter (cost about $230).
6. A solar shower bag that can be used to heat water in the sun to take a warm shower (cost about $7).
7. A magnesium fire starter (contains magnesium and "fire steel") (cost about $8).
8. A stainless steel camping mess kit with cook pots and enough stainless steel plates and tableware for each member of your family (cost about $25).

9. Pair of large loose-fitting leather gloves with long wrists (wear them when you need to cook over a wood burning fire) (cost about $5).
10. Dish towel and a dish cloth and a reusable pot scrubber pad.
11. A variety of vegetable seed packets, such as sugar beets, carrots, radishes, corn, spinach, and tomatoes. Each spring replace last year's seed packets with fresh seed packets (long-term food) (total cost between $1 to $6).
12. Twelve professional quality wild game snares (short-term and long-term food) (total cost about $15).
13. At least one monofilament gill net for fishing (short-term and long-term food) (cost about $40).
14. At least one big spool of monofilament fishing line (short-term and long-term food) (cost about $3).
15. Approximately 100 fish hooks in a variety of different sizes, and some swivels, and some lead sinkers (short-term and long-term food) (cost about $3).
16. Merck Manual of Medical Information, 2nd Home Edition, 2004, paperback, not the most recent edition (cost about $14).
17. A high quality first aid kit and some anti-itch cream and some triple antibiotic ointment.
18. A box of 100 additional one-inch wide bandages (you can cut a big bandage down into a smaller one if necessary) (cost about $3).
19. A reasonable supply of antibiotics your family is not allergic to, such as Amoxicillin or Erythromycin.
20. One-half ounce bottle of cheap clear fingernail polish to put on chigger bites to help relieve the itch (cost about $1).
21. A small sewing repair kit with thread, needles, a needle threader, a thimble, and a few extra buttons (cost about $2).
22. Stainless steel barber scissors, fingernail clippers, toenail clippers, nail file (buy good quality items - total cost about $15).
23. A Leatherman Wave Multitool (cost about $75).
24. A stainless steel hatchet with a leather sheath (cost about $40 for a good hatchet).
25. A folding "Sierra Saw" for sawing wood at a campsite (cost about $9).
26. A folding shovel (cost about $12).
27. A heavy-duty tarp (size from 9'x12' up to 20'x30') (emergency shelter and rainwater collection) (cost between $10 to $20).
28. One roll of duck tape (cost about $3).
29. 12 or more heavy-duty one-gallon zipper freezer bags for the temporary storage of rainwater at your camp site.
30. 12 or more heavy-duty one-gallon zipper freezer bags for the temporary storage of food at your camp site, such as dried meat jerky, or fresh fruit and fresh vegetables, or dried fruit and dried vegetables.
31. At least 200 feet of strong thin nylon or polypropylene twine (minimum breaking strength of at least 100 pounds) (cost about $3).
32. 115 feet of 20 gauge wire (buy in hardware section) or 22 gauge floral wire (cost about $3).
33. A portable world-band shortwave radio that can operate on normal AA batteries (cost about $100).
34. A solar battery charger that will recharge the four basic standard sizes of rechargeable flashlight batteries: AAA, AA, C, and D (cost about $30).
35. Twelve rechargeable AA batteries manufactured by at least two different companies, such as Duracell, Energizer, or Rayovac. Separate them and store them two per small package to prevent the loss of the entire set of batteries if one of them starts to leak (cost about $20).
36. SAS Survival Guide by John "Lofty" Wiseman, or the Boy Scouts Handbook, First Edition, 1911, Dover printing (cost between $8 to $12).
37. A flash drive with digital copies of all the important legal documents for your entire family, such as birth certificates, marriage licenses, deeds, titles, retirement account records, diplomas, school records and transcripts, immunization records, medical insurance cards, insurance policies, family photographs, and anything else your family would like to preserve and take with you in digital form. A digital copy can be of great assistance in helping you to get a replacement original copy if you are not able to take the originals with you.

Each member of your family should have his or her own **personal backpack** that contains the following:

1. Personal hygiene items such as: large bar of soap, toothbrush, big tube of toothpaste, dental floss, hand mirror, hair comb or brush, a few bandages, and a razor if the person shaves. A female backpack should also contain feminine pads.
2. If appropriate, an extra spare pair of prescription eyeglasses or reading glasses.
3. 20 paper towels (emergency toilet tissue).
4. One pair of latex gloves one size larger than the person would normally wear.
5. Four soft sponges.
6. Your normal daily prescription medicines plus whatever pain relief tablets you prefer.
7. Food that does not need to be cooked but has a long shelf life (some 2400 or 3600 Mainstay lifeboat food ration bars, plus some miniature tootsie rolls or caramels that are vacuum sealed, plus some multivitamins that are vacuum sealed).
8. Water container such as a clean empty Gatorade bottle in an outside pocket of the backpack (fill the empty bottle with fresh water just before leaving).
9. 6 clean heavy-duty one-gallon zipper freezer bags for the temporary storage of rainwater (or food) at your camp site.
10. Good quality rain poncho with attached hood (may also be used as the roof of an emergency shelter, or for rainwater collection, or as a wind breaker during bad weather).
11. Hand towel and a wash cloth.
12. Thin lightweight blanket and an empty pillowcase (may be filled with clothing to make a pillow).
13. Clothing (t-shirt, shirt, pants, lightweight jacket).
14. Four pair of socks.
15. Two pair of underwear.
16. Mosquito head net.
17. Ski mask.
18. One pair of soft warm gloves.
19. An adult and a teenager should also have a pair of good flexible leather work gloves.
20. Safety eye glasses.
21. Folding blade pocket knife with no more than four blades (not a Swiss Army Knife).
22. An adult and a teenager should also have a fixed blade hunting knife (without a gut hook) and a belt sheath, such as the Buck Model 119.
23. Sixteen books of paper matches, 20 matches per matchbook (total of 320 paper matches that are vacuum sealed).
24. Butane lighter.
25. High quality LED flashlight that operates on 2 AA batteries, such as the "MiniMag Lite" that works on high power (100%) and low power (25%) and can be used as a "candle" by twisting off the top of the flashlight (cost about $22). An LED flashlight consumes significantly less battery power than a traditional flashlight and the LED bulb never needs to be replaced (100,000 hours).
26. Two Energizer "Ultimate Lithium" AA batteries stored outside the flashlight.
27. A paperback novel that the person has not yet read but would find entertaining, or a comic book, or a coloring book and some crayons or colored pencils.
28. A deck of 52 playing cards, or a deck of "Uno" cards, or five "Yacht" six-sided dice, or some other small travel game that could keep an adult or a child entertained. A game that can be played by two or more people or by one person as a solitaire game is recommended.
29. A small pad of ruled paper (50 sheets, 5" x 7"), a wood pencil, and a small pencil sharpener.
30. Photocopies of important documents, such as a birth certificate, immunization records, school records, driver's license, medical insurance cards, daily medicine prescriptions, etc. (not digital copies).

An adult male backpack should not exceed approximately 30 pounds.
An adult female backpack should not exceed approximately 25 pounds.
Teenager and children backpacks should not weigh more than the individual can carry comfortably.

One of the common mistakes that people make is to load a backpack and then see if they can lift it. If they can lift it they think it is okay. They are wrong. The weight of the backpack should be something you could carry for many miles and not just across the room. In the 1800s when people traveled in covered wagons on their way west they would frequently start with a wagon loaded to its capacity and which could be pulled by their team of mules or oxen. But their team would quickly become exhausted and they would have to stop and rest and they would continue to fall further and further behind the rest of the wagon train. Then they would start throwing stuff out of their wagon beside the trail so they could catch up with the rest of the wagon train. Before they began their trip these people had been advised to lighten their wagon load but their were hard-headed and they would not listen to good advice. A smart person is able to learn from the mistakes of others without having to repeat those same mistakes himself.

If possible you should also have at least one heavy-duty folding luggage carrier with large wheels. The luggage carrier could be used to carry several backpacks or suitcases at one time by one strong healthy person. In an emergency a small child could sit on top of a backpack on the luggage carrier and be pulled along behind an adult. If you have two small children then you should consider purchasing two heavy-duty folding luggage carriers. Carrying a small child in your arms will quickly exhaust you.

If you have a growing child then you should consider purchasing clothes one size larger than your child currently wears and putting those clothes into your child's B.O.B. For example, if your child currently wears a size 6 then buy some size 7 clothes and put those clothes in the child's B.O.B. After your child grows a little bit and can wear a size 7 then remove those clothes from the backpack and give them to your child and immediately replace them with the next larger size, such as a size 8. This way the clothes in your child's backpack will always be new. And your child can gradually grow into that clothes size if a hard times event occurs. And if a hard times event doesn't occur then you will not have wasted any money because your child will always be wearing the clothes you purchased last year at last year's more affordable prices.

You can avoid mold and mildew problems by vacuum sealing each item before putting it into your backpack. For example, you could vacuum seal the soap, the paper towels, the clothes, the hand towels, the blankets, the feminine pads, the knives, the medicines (if appropriate), the candy, and the matches. Vacuum sealing will remove all the air trapped between the clothes, the towels, and the blankets and this will reduce their size to approximately one-half their original folded size and this will provide more storage space inside each of the backpacks.

Store the butane lighter inside two heavy-duty zipper freezer bags (one-pint size) but do **not** vacuum seal the butane lighter. (**Note:** You should also **not** vacuum seal ammunition inside a vacuum bag. The vacuum may gradually and slowly begin to pull the primer and/or the bullet slightly loose from their brass shell casing and if that happens then you will have a dangerous round of ammunition that may not fit into your firearm, or it may result in an disastrous accident when you try to shoot it.)

One very common problem with an emergency backpack is when a member of your family needs something and decides to "temporarily" borrow that item from his or her backpack. Later when a real emergency occurs you discover to your horror that everyone's backpack has been vandalized by the members of your own family.

Chapter Sixty-Seven: Emergency Backpacks

Chapter Sixty-Eight

Bicycles for Emergency Transportation

Introduction

Unlike horses and other farm animals, bicycles do not require any food, or water, or pasture, or daily care. They also don't generate any garden manure and that could be either a plus or a minus depending on your situation. Most people find bicycles more comfortable to ride than a horse because they don't create saddle sores.

And a bicycle is ready to go the instant you need it, even if an EMP (Electro Magnetic Pulse) blast disables other modes of transportation. During natural disasters such as approaching hurricanes, the streets and bridges quickly become grid-locked due to unusually heavy traffic, stalled cars, and accidents. In these situations a bicycle may be the most reliable way to escape the disaster area.

A person could purchase a bicycle and then store it for decades with just a little oil on its chain and on its other moving parts. At some future date, if a serious catastrophe were to occur then your bicycle may become extremely useful in two important ways: (1) transportation between locations, and (2) as a pack mule.

First, however, let's consider walking as an alternative to a bicycle.

Walking: The average adult male or female can walk between 3 to 3.6 miles per hour if they are in average physical condition and if they are not carrying a load or pushing a cart or buggy. If the person is carrying a weight in excess of 5 pounds then the distance taken with each step decreases in order to maintain body balance and minimize fatigue. Depending on the person, the average adult pace varies between 27 to 34 inches if the person is unencumbered (not transporting a load). If the person is carrying a load between 5 to 35 pounds then each step is approximately 4 inches less. Between 35 to 50 pounds each step is an additional 6 inches less (or a total of 10 inches less than unencumbered). Fatigue also becomes a significant factor when the load exceeds 35 pounds. Therefore the average person carrying a 35-pound load will walk between 2.6 to 3.1 miles per hour, which will result in a 12 percent reduction in the total distance traveled. A person carrying a 50-pound load will walk between 2.0 to 2.4 miles per hour, which is a 32 percent reduction in the total distance traveled. Therefore, although walking is an alternative, it is a relatively slow option and it does significantly limit the amount of weight a person can carry for any reasonable distance.

Transportation: Depending on the type of catastrophe, transportation may or may not be necessary or even desirable. However, if it is necessary and automobiles are not available for some reason then a bicycle would enable a person to cover distances easier and faster than walking. As previously mentioned, a person can walk about 3 miles per hour but a bicycle can easily cover between 10 to 30 miles per hour, depending on the road conditions (hills, etc.) and the physical fitness of the rider. Therefore a person riding a bicycle could travel the same distance in one hour that he or she could walk in one day. The actual total distance traveled will obviously depend on the physical fitness of the rider. For example, if a person could only walk four miles in one day then he or she could ride a bike four miles in one hour. If the person could walk 15 miles in one day then he or she could ride the bike 15 miles in one hour. In each case the person would then probably be physically exhausted and he or she would need to rest the balance of the day. However, the advantage of riding the bicycle is that it would permit the individual more time to focus on other duties once the day's journey has ended.

Pack Mule: When forced into service as a pack mule an adult human male can carry about 30 to 35 pounds and still be able to walk 2 or 3 miles per hour. However, most bicycles will allow the rider to add about 20 pounds to the front wheel and about 30 pounds to the rear wheel for a total of about 50 pounds plus the rider. It is extremely fatiguing to ride a bike with a backpack strapped to your back. If you let the bike carry your load then you can invest your energy more productively in pedaling the bike. If the rider is willing to walk beside the bicycle and push the bicycle then a typical adult bicycle could be loaded with 200 to 250 pounds of supplies and equipment strapped to the metal frame of the bike.

Or a bicycle trailer could be attached to the rear of the bicycle and the rider could add between 100 to 250 pounds of supplies onto the bicycle trailer. You could purchase a special bike trailer or you could convert a two-seat child trailer (see picture on right) into an equipment trailer by removing the children's compartment and replacing it with a large lockable waterproof plastic storage box securely mounted between the two trailer wheels. If you use a rear mounted bike trailer to transport supplies and it is not lockable then you need to be very careful when you travel through an area where there are other people. People will steal things off your rear bike trailer when you aren't looking or while you are being intentionally distracted by one of their associates. This type of theft can be prevented by using a locking waterproof plastic storage box bolted to your trailer instead of just strapping things down to a basic flatbed trailer. The lock could be built into the storage box itself or it could be a standard padlock placed through the top and bottom of the heavy duty plastic storage box.

Even if you are walking and pushing a fully loaded bike, you can still occasionally stand with your right foot on the left pedal and lean the bike gently away from you at a slight angle to maintain its balance, and then coast down a hill or incline while operating your hand brakes to keep the bike at a safe speed.

A bicycle will allow you to travel faster, further, with more supplies and equipment, and with less effort, and this could make a significant difference in your chances of survival. Even if you do not anticipate the need for transportation during a catastrophe, a bicycle would still be a good investment in the event you were forced to become a refugee for some unexpected reason and your automobile was not available. Anyone could be forced into the life of a refugee due to events beyond his or her control, such as forest fires, or floods, or drought that results in dry wells and dry lakes and therefore dry cities, or enemy soldiers with heavy artillery who are destroying all the homes they find.

Two or three-hundred pounds of supplies and equipment is not a lot but it could keep one person alive for one-year (or longer) depending on how wisely you selected your items and how successful you were at supplementing your food supplies with hunting, trapping, fishing, foraging, and growing simple vegetables from seeds such as corn and beans and tomatoes. Growing pinto beans or kidney beans is a lot easier than searching for wild edible plants.

Note: If a bicycle is not available then an individual could move a load, such as a backpack, between locations using a standard folding luggage carrier. The luggage carrier should be a heavy-duty unit with the largest possible wheels. Larger wheels make it easier to pull or push the load on smooth surfaces and they also permit easier travel over uneven surfaces, such as grass or fields. An adult can pull or push a luggage carrier loaded with 70 pounds and travel further in one day than if they were carrying half that much weight in a backpack on his or her back. Another less desirable option would be a backpack or suitcase with small plastic wheels permanently attached to the unit. This option is better than carrying the load on your back or in your hand but the small plastic wheels are not designed for long-distance travel over paved areas and they will quickly wear out and your mobile unit will become disabled. Therefore a good quality luggage carrier would be a much better alternative because it will last significantly longer than the little wheels permanently mounted to a backpack or suitcase. However, if I didn't have a luggage carrier then I would use the suitcase or backpack with the attached wheels.

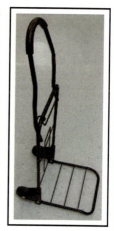

Chapter Sixty-Eight: Bicycles

Bicycle Construction

Bike Style: Any style adult bicycle is acceptable. This includes mountain bikes and road bikes. Some mountain bikes and some road bikes are extremely well designed and they are well built and they can easily handle a wide assortment of road conditions, including the occasional holes in a paved road. On the other hand, some mountain bikes and some road bikes are very poorly designed and they are cheaply built and they will become disabled the first time they encounter an adverse road condition. Therefore carefully examine the construction quality of the bike and do not select a bike based only on the visual appeal of its paint job and decals. Also, do not buy a mountain bike simply because you think all mountain bikes are superior to all road bikes. They are not. It is the quality of the individual bicycle that is the most important factor.

I recommend a bike with a fixed rigid rear wheel as opposed to a spring mounted rear wheel. The advantage of a spring mounted rear wheel is that it helps to absorb road shocks and not transmit their full force to the saddle. The advantage of a fixed rear wheel is that you can install a more substantial rear luggage rack over the rear wheel. This will be discussed in more detail later.

Folding bikes are also nice and ebay sometimes sells them for $200 or less. However, unless you really need a folding bike then a normal fixed frame bike is probably a better investment and it will probably last longer before needing repairs.

All bicycles need roads or paths or trails or some other relatively smooth unobstructed surface to ride on. Therefore don't buy a mountain bike simply because you think you will be riding through wilderness areas. If you are in a thick forest then you will be walking beside your bike and picking it up and carrying it over obstacles, such as fallen trees. Almost any type of bike works fine when you are walking beside it.

Price: You can purchase a bike at a specialty bike shop or at a store such as Walmart. If you make your purchase at a bike shop you may discover you are paying a premium for the bike because bikes, bike accessories, and bike repairs are the only source of revenue for the bike shop. However, a store such as Walmart has a standard markup on most of its items and their profit on bicycles is not that much different from anything else in the store. At Walmart you can usually find a really nice selection of good bikes for under $200. If you look carefully you can also find several below $100 and a few below $75. If you go to a bike shop then the bikes usually start at $200 and quickly jump to $300 or $400 and some are even priced at $800 and $1200 and $2000. The final decision on how much you wish to spend on a bike is up to you but I think you could get a very, very nice bicycle for less than $200. (Note: I have a $59 ten-speed bike that I purchased 12 years ago from Walmart and I am still very happy with it.) Many, but not all, of the accessories mentioned below can also be purchased at a very reasonable price at stores such as Walmart. However, some items must be purchased or ordered through a specialty bike shop or purchased over the internet.

Gears or Speeds: A bicycle with three or more speeds is highly desirable. A bicycle operates the same way an automobile does. If you only had one gear in your car then you would not be very happy with the performance of your car. With three or more gears in your car, the car can shift gears as you gain speed and improve the performance of your car. If you encounter a really steep hill, the car can shift into a lower gear. The same principle applies to bikes. Many, many years ago there were only single-speed bikes. To demonstrate the advantage of the newly invented three-speed bike a simple road test was conducted. An adult male racing champion was allowed to ride his favorite one-speed bike but a petite female was given a three-speed bike. The race was over a typical course involving some hills and some decent stretches of level ground. The young lady literally beat the socks off the professional male bike racer because she had three gears to pick from. She could pick the best gear for climbing a hill and a different gear for maximum speed on level ground. The professional bike racer only had one gear and he couldn't keep up with the lady even though he had substantially more strength in his leg muscles. That simple two-person race resulted in the end of single-speed bicycles in professional bicycle races.

The Optimum Number of Speeds: Any number of speeds between 3 to 21 will yield good performance. The total number of speeds is not as important as a person might expect.

A three-speed bike has one front gear and three rear gears. All three speeds work just fine.

A ten-speed bike has two front gears and five rear gears for a total of ten combinations. However, each front gear works best with the three (or four) gears closest to it on the rear. So the right front gear works best with the three right gears on the rear wheel. And the left front gear works best with the three left gears on the rear wheel. Therefore, even though the bike has ten possible speeds, somewhere between six to eight speeds are used most often. The reason is chain crossover. If you use a front gear on the far right with a rear gear on the far left then the chain is at a bad angle and the chain undergoes excessive tension and chain wear and other chain problems are more likely, such as chain breakage. Therefore most bike riders use the three or four rear gears that are most closely aligned with the front gear currently in use.

A 21-speed bike has three front gears and seven rear gears for a total of 21 options. However, based on the previous discussion, somewhere between 9 to 12 of those options are high quality combinations that minimize chain wear.

Therefore a three-speed bike has three good gear combinations, a ten-speed bike has about six really good gear combinations, and a 21-speed bike has about nine really good gear combinations. In my opinion, there is nothing wrong with a good ten-speed bike. I have a ten-speed bike and I really like it. I also have a 21-speed bike and I like it too. I suggest that you select a bicycle based on factors other than the number of "total" possible speed combinations.

Brakes: Hand operated braking systems are really nice. Rubber brake pads and disk brakes both work well in my opinion. Don't let a bike salesperson talk you into a bike with disk brakes unless that bike also has all the other features you really need. You should also purchase a spare set of brake pads for your front and rear wheels. There are two basic sizes so look at the ones on your bike before you purchase your spare brake pads. Bicycle brakes will wear out before the other parts on your bicycle, just like the brakes on your car will wear out and need to be replaced several times during the life of your car. Spare brake pads cost between $4 to $6 for a set of two rubber pads.

Tire Size: A 26-inch tire is a very good choice for adults. Some individuals prefer a 24-inch tire and that is also a very popular tire size. A 27-inch tire is also an option but in a disaster situation it may be very difficult to find replacement parts for a 27-inch tire.

Tire Design: Any standard tire design will be okay. Smooth tires and knobby tires each have certain advantages but your choice of a good bike should probably be based on factors other than the design of the tire tread. All the different tire designs work reasonably well in most situations, although some are superior for specific applications.

Bike Comfort and Riding Fatigue: When selecting a new bike there are two related issues that should be considered: (1) comfort, and (2) riding fatigue.

1. **Comfort:** Most of us grew up riding a bike and we already know what feels right and what doesn't. To evaluate a new bike you should sit on the seat and then lean forward slightly and put your hands and some of your weight on the front handlebars, with your arms slightly bent at the elbows. If you feel comfortable in this position then the bike is worthy of further consideration. Remember that the seat height is adjustable and if you need to move the seat up or down to improve your comfort then that is really easy to do on today's modern bicycles.

Don't let a thin skinny bike seat influence your decision about comfort because you can easily replace the seat for about $20. It is the rest of the bike that can't be easily modified. The seat design issue will be discussed in more detail later in this chapter.

Some individuals, such as professional racers, prefer a really low set of handlebars so they can lean forward to an almost horizontal position to minimize wind resistance. However, in this position you must tilt your head and neck backwards so you can see ahead. This position is not comfortable for many people.

When you are standing upright astride your bicycle with both feet on the ground the center bar should not make contact with your groin area.

Most new bikes have the adjustable seat in a low position so the prospective customer can sit on the seat and put both feet on the ground to stabilize the bike. This is the seat position from which most of us learned to ride and it is the way we teach our children to ride. It is very easy to start and stop a bike if both of your feet can touch the ground when you are stopped. There is nothing wrong with this seat position and it works well for short riding distances when there are frequent stops. However, this low seat position will result in your becoming tired more quickly if you are riding a long distance.

2. **Riding Fatigue:** To find the best seat height to minimize long distance riding fatigue you will need to sit on the bicycle seat and extend one leg straight down to one of the pedals in its lowest position. When you are sitting on the seat the pedal in the down position should allow you to fully straighten your leg. This means you will have to get off the seat when you stop so you can put your feet on the ground and keep your bike upright. To minimize fatigue and maximize power while riding your legs need to be straight when each pedal is in the full down position. Adjust the height of the seat by trial and error until you find the optimum seat height that is just right for you. However, unless you anticipate long distance bike rides, there is no need to raise the seat and you can leave the seat in a low position so both your feet can touch the ground when you are stopped.

Seat or Saddle ($20): If your bike comes with a standard slim style racing seat then I suggest you consider replacing it with a Wide Bottom Gel Seat. Your rear end will be spending a lot of time on this seat and those thin seats are not comfortable for an extended ride, in my opinion.

Kickstand: The kickstand should be long enough to support the bicycle in an almost vertical position when on level ground. If the kickstand is too short then the bicycle will fall over when a front wheel luggage rack and saddlebags are added as an accessory.

Pedals: Most bikes have good pedals and you will probably not need to replace them. This is one area where an upgrade is definitely not recommended.

Gasoline Engine or Battery Power: I have looked at adding either a gasoline engine or a battery powered motor to my bicycle many, many times during the past few years. Each time I decided not to invest in either option. Their range is usually 30 miles or less and their speed is usually 30 mph or less. Both types of motors take up space and weight behind your seat that could be used to store other more useful items. Instead of motorizing your bicycle I suggest that you use the power in your legs unless: (1) you are unable to do so, or (2) you intend to use your bike for daily commuting back and forth to your current place of employment to save a little gas money.

Bicycle Accessories

Bike Tool ($13): The bike mega ultra-tool is a special bike tool that includes all the tools and accessories needed to perform minor (or major) repairs to your bike if it should require service while you are on the road. At a retail price of about $13 this tool is a real bargain.

Tire Patches ($2): For emergency repair of a flat tire.

Air Gauge ($3 to $25): A dial gauge is usually more accurate than a stick gauge. However, they are also more expensive. If money is an issue then a simple automobile tire gauge will do the job. A bicycle tire requires a lot more air pressure than an automobile tire because the surface area of the tire that actually makes contact with the road is very small.

Chapter Sixty-Eight: Bicycles

Small Storage Bag That Fits Under the Seat (or attach it to the front handlebar) ($7): Use it to store your special bike tool, a Leatherman type tool, a 6-inch adjustable crescent wrench, an air gauge, tire patches, a small can of Three-in-One oil inside a small plastic freezer bag, a small LED flashlight, a good folding stainless steel pocket knife, a butane lighter, a small good quality first aid kit, and any special tools such as the little hex wrenches that come with any accessories you install on your bicycle.

Air Pump ($8 to $25): A necessity, in my opinion. The hand pump model that attaches to the side of the bike frame is really nice. I also have a smaller more compact air pump but it does not work as well as the mid-size air pump that attaches to the side of the bike frame. Some bikes have predrilled threaded holes for attaching the special air pump holder and some bikes do not. If your bike doesn't have the predrilled threaded holes you can attach the air pump holder to your bike using two Velcro straps.

Rear Luggage Rack ($20 to $35): My suggestion is to avoid the rear luggage rack that mounts only to the seat post. However, if you have a spring mounted rear wheel bike then this may be your only option. My preference is a rear luggage rack with two downward metal supports on each side that attach to the frame of the bicycle just above your rear axle. It will support more weight than a seat post mounted luggage rack. These luggage racks can be mounted to the rear frame of most bikes using the pre-threaded holes just above the rear axle. The holes are generally either 5mm or 6mm and when you add a lock washer they eliminate the need for an inside nut to hold the luggage rack to the rear frame. An inside nut could get in the way of the chain when it tries to make contact with the outside rear gear. If your bike has a rear hole that it is not threaded then you can add threads by purchasing one or two extra bolts of the correct diameter and screwing them into the opening to thread the hole. This may damage the threads on those bolts but if they are extra bolts then you can simply toss them in the trash when you are done. Or you could use a tap and die set to thread the holes. Luggage racks can be purchased at your local bicycle shop or they can be purchased over the internet.

Front Luggage Rack ($15 to $30): Adds about 20 pounds of extra storage capacity to the front of your bike. It can be used for any item but it is best suited for bulky light weight items such as extra clothing and a blanket or a sleeping bag and a small pillow. Do not put too much weight over your front wheel or you may find your bicycle difficult to steer. Some bikes have mounting holes just above the front axle. Neither of my bikes had those holes so I used 3-inch long predrilled braces to mount the rack on the front of each bike. (Necessity is the mother of invention.) If you are looking for a new bike then I suggest that you examine the front fork to see if it has the predrilled holes just above the front axle for installing a front luggage rack. After you mount your front luggage rack  and put a few things onto it, you may discover that your bicycle falls over. This is because the kickstand that came with your bike is too short. Install a longer kickstand and you will solve this problem.

Luggage Rack Design: The front and rear luggage racks are each uniquely designed for their specific application and you should not buy two of the same type in the belief that you can simply turn it end to end and make it fit on the opposite end of your bike. It won't work. Each rack has it own special mounting hardware designed specifically for one end of the bike. You will need one rack for the rear and a different but similar design for the front.

Saddlebags or Panniers ($30 to $200 per pair): Bicycle side saddlebags are called panniers. I have three different brands, including Jandd and Ortlieb. Ortlieb was the most expensive of the three brands and I bought a pair of them due to their most excellent reviews on the internet. However, they are not my favorite panniers. My personal preference is the Jandd Economy Panniers. The Jandd Economy Panniers have good quality workmanship and materials, they are rain proof, they attach quickly, easily, and securely to either the front or the rear luggage racks, they have a zipper closure, they are really easy to open and close, and their design makes it easy to store and remove items from the panniers. If I purchase any more panniers they will all be the Jandd Economy Panniers. Panniers can be special ordered through your local bicycle shop or they can be purchased over the internet. The Jandd Economy Panniers can be purchased at this web site: http://www.jandd.com/detail.asp?PRODUCT_ID=FEP

Bungee Cords and Cargo Nets ($2 to $6): Saddlebags can be used to store items on both sides of your luggage racks. You can also secure items to the top flat surface of each luggage rack using elastic bungee cords and/or cargo nets. They also make specially designed panniers for use on top of these racks but I prefer the flexibility of being able to secure my own personal survival backpack onto the top of the rear luggage rack and my sleeping bag on top of the front luggage rack.

Speedometer: I prefer a non-electric speedometer. However, the one I purchased would only fit on one of my bikes. Although a battery-operated speedometer would have worked on my other bike, I decided I really didn't want one of those. You need to make your own decision on whether or not you need a speedometer.

Water Bottle (Optional): Attaches to the frame in the center of the bike. I bought one out of curiosity but I only bought one. In a refugee situation the small amount of water in the bottle would not last very long. A person would be far better off with a quality water filter such as the Swiss Katadyn Pocket Water Filter. It will process up to 13,000 gallons of water for drinking purposes and it is about the same size as the water bottle designed for bicycle mounting. If you should become a refugee then one of your most important priorities every day will be a fresh supply of safe drinking water. The Katadyn Pocket Water Filter will easily solve this problem for several years. There are lots of other cheaper water filters available that are advocated by a wide variety of individuals but they will only process a few hundred gallons of water before they wear out. If you should become a refugee, then your family will be depending on you for everything and water should not be one of your daily problems. In my opinion everyone should become as educated as possible about water and its importance.

Shoes: Most bike shops sell special bicycle shoes. You may buy a pair if you wish. However, your normal walking shoes will do just fine if they do not have a flat smooth sole. Your normal walking shoes should have ribbed or tread type soles for traction while walking. This type of sole will also make positive contact with the pedals on your bike and prevent your foot from slipping off the pedal when in motion. Since you will not be riding all the time, a quality set of footwear will need to function as walking shoes in addition to riding shoes. Your shoes are a very important consideration because the shoes you are wearing when you first become a refugee will probably be the only pair of shoes you possess for several years. I suggest you read the Shoe Chapter in this book and then purchase a really good pair of quality walking shoes instead of an expensive pair of high performance bicycle shoes.

Helmet: If you like the bicycle style helmets then buy the one that appeals to you. However, a motorcycle helmet is a better investment, in my opinion. Just walk over to the automotive section and they usually have nice motorcycle helmets for $90 or less. During the past 50 years I have had occasional rare accidents with bicycles and motorcycles and, in my opinion, a helmet is an absolutely necessary piece of safety equipment.

Other Safety Equipment: You may invest in other typical bicycle safety items, such as elbow pads, knee pads, and gloves as you believe appropriate.

Rain Gear: A good rain suit is a nice thing to have. It consists of a waterproof upper, usually with an attached hood, and a waterproof pair of pants. You will need waterproof pants if you intend to ride your bike in the rain. If you already have some type of waterproof jacket then waterproof pants will complete your outfit.

Bicycle Lock: Always take your bike inside wherever you happen to be and lock it securely so it can't be stolen. If you leave your bike outside, even locked to a bike stand, you will eventually discover there are some people who will intentionally disable your bike or steal stuff off your bike. You really don't need those kinds of problems.

Headlight: I have a battery-operated halogen headlight on one of my bikes. It uses two standard C cell batteries. I was not impressed with the headlight so I did not install one on my other bike. (Note: For about $90 you can buy a nice six-volt headlight with a rechargeable battery.)

Oil: I normally use whatever type of oil I have available, such as motor oil or Three-in-One oil. I put a little oil on the chain, the gears, and the axles before I put the bike in storage. This consists of hanging the bike on a bike hook from the ceiling of the garage. This may not be the best way to store a bike but it has not caused me or my bike any problems for more than twelve years.

Child Carrier Seats: There are several different types of child carrier seats. Let's look at three different models.

| Rear Mount | Front Mount | Rear Trailer |

1. The first child seat mounts behind the rider's seat and it replaces the rear luggage rack. Therefore I don't recommend this type unless you have two small children and for some reason you must install two child seats on one bike. If you have two children then the rear trailer option is a better choice.
2. The second option is a child seat that mounts between the front handlebar stem and the rider's seat post. This puts the child where you can see the child at all times and it positions the child so the child can see where you are going, regardless of whether you are riding or walking beside the bicycle.
3. The third option is a two-seat child carrier that attaches to the rear of the bike.

If you are forced into a refugee situation and you have small children then a bicycle would allow you to travel relatively quickly with your young children. Young children cannot walk very far before they become tired and they need to be either carried or transported. Carrying children is not a good option if it can be avoided.

The best solution would be to have one front mount child seat per adult or teenager bicycle. However, in an emergency, one adult could transport up to four small children on one bicycle and the adult could either ride or walk beside the bike. One child could go in the forward child's seat (mounted between the handlebars and the rider's seat), one child could go in a child's seat mounted behind the rider's seat, and two small children could fit in a child trailer attached to the rear of the bicycle. If one person had to transport four small children using one bicycle then there would be very little space left over for food, supplies, and equipment, but your primary responsibility in this type of emergency situation would be the immediate safety of your children.

If you perceive a situation where you would need to transport several children on one bicycle then you should also consider installing a quality set of heavy duty children's rear training wheels on each side of your bicycle to help keep your bicycle upright at all times.

Quick Summary of Important Bicycle Features
(Listed in order of importance.)

1. Fixed rear wheel instead of a spring loaded rear wheel.

2. Between 3 to 21 speeds. A ten-speed bike is a good compromise but a 21-speed bike also works really well. Regardless of the total number of speeds, if you are riding a heavily loaded bicycle then you will probably discover that you can't ride your bike up a steep hill and that pushing it up the hill is the only alternative.

3. A 26-inch tire is preferred but a 24-inch tire is a good second choice. (Note: The center bar should not make contact with your groin area when you are standing on both feet.)

4. You should feel comfortable sitting on the bicycle.

5. Predrilled mounting holes above the front and rear axles for easy mounting of luggage racks. (Note: A handlebar basket will not fit on most bikes with hand operated brakes and gear shift controls.)

6. Two predrilled holes in the middle of the bike frame for mounting a "water bottle holder" which can also be used to attach the "air pump holder." However, two velcro straps can be used to attach the air pump holder to the bike frame if necessary.

7. Finally, a long kickstand and a wide bottom seat. However, these two items can be easily replaced if necessary.

Conclusion

Different bike enthusiasts have different opinions about the advantages and disadvantages of every possible type of bicycle and bicycle accessory. I am not a bike enthusiast. I am just an ordinary person who has ridden bicycles for more than 50 years, beginning with a single-speed bike, and then a three-speed, and then a ten-speed, and then a 21-speed. The information in this chapter is just my opinion and it is nothing more than my opinion. Before you invest in a bicycle you should research this topic very carefully and collect a variety of different opinions and then make your own decision based on what is best for your particular situation and your anticipated riding conditions.

Before you spend any money on a bicycle you should first make a list of the different bicycles that are available along with their prices, and a list of the different options and accessories you wish to purchase for your bike. Then add up the total cost and determine whether or not you can afford it. If not, then reconsider the bike, the options, and the accessories based on need and not simply desire.

Finally, I strongly recommend the purchase of the following book: **"Bicycle Maintenance & Repair,"** 5th Edition, by Todd Downs. I suggest you place this book inside a two-gallon plastic freezer bag and store it inside one of the rear saddlebags on your bicycle. Bicycle maintenance and repair is not complicated if you know what to do. A typical bicycle has a variety of different simple adjustments that can be made and knowing the correct sequence of adjustments is very important. This book, plus your bicycle multi-tool and your Leatherman type tool and your 6-inch adjustable wrench, will help you keep your bicycle operational until it eventually wears out from old age.

One place where you can begin to acquire additional knowledge about bicycles is Sheldon Brown's web site at: http://sheldonbrown.com/home.html

His web site contains a lot of information and you should read the articles that are of interest to you. When you are finished reading you will be able to make a superior choice about the type of bicycle that is just right for you.

I truly hope you will never need your bicycle except for recreational purposes. However, if world events should unfold in an unexpected fashion then your bicycle would allow you to take your most important survival possessions with you if you were suddenly forced into becoming a refugee and your car was not available for some unexpected reason. *In my opinion the best option would be to avoid becoming a refugee, if that is possible.* However, if the choice were between certain death or life as a refugee, then I would select the life of a refugee. A good bicycle would significantly improve a person's chances of survival in a refugee situation.

Chapter Sixty-Nine

Basic Hand Tools

Hatchets and Saws

Hatchets and saws were common household items in the 1800s and they still have many practical uses today. In my opinion they will become indispensable during a long-term hard times tragedy event.

Hatchets: A good quality stainless steel hatchet in a leather belt sheath can be easily attached to your belt and it would therefore be with you whenever you might need it. It has a flat rectangular end that can be used to drive nails or to crack hickory nuts. It can also be used in an emergency to crush/grind corn or wheat into flour. The sharp end can be used for a variety of simple chopping tasks or it can be used as a self-defense weapon similar to the American Indian tomahawk. (Note: A modern hatchet with a stainless steel head and a stainless steel handle would be a better investment than an old-fashioned hatchet with a standard steel head and a wood handle.)

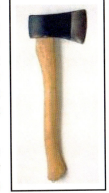

Saws: There are a variety of different types of saws available but the most useful one for the average person would be a wood saw. If you don't already have a good wood saw then I recommend the Stanley Sharptooth Saw with a 15-inch blade. It can be purchased as most Walmarts and Lowe's and Home Depots. It will cut wood on both the pull and push strokes and it will cut through the wood in the shortest amount of time with the least amount of effort. But that is just my opinion and you may purchase any type and name brand of saw you wish.

Home Repairs

Regardless of whether you rent an apartment or you own your own home, you should have the basic tools and knowledge required to make simple home repairs, such as tightening a loose screw in a cabinet hinge, or installing a substantial sliding bolt lock on your front door, or adding a new heavier nail (or long screw) to a door frame to make it more secure.

If you were forced to abandon your current dwelling then you may need to build a new dwelling from scratch at your new location, or you may need to make some significant repairs to an existing dwelling at your new location.

In all of these situations it would be helpful if you had some knowledge of basic building techniques and proper construction methods. Therefore I suggest the addition of the following book to your reference library:

Fundamentals of Building Construction, 4th Ed., Allen & Iano, 2004.

The advantage of the above book is that it discusses almost everything you might someday need to know. Most of the books that are sold at home improvement stores discuss one specific construction concept and they are not a comprehensive reference manual.

Basic Complete Portable Tool Set

If you already own a reasonable set of hand tools then you should also own a portable hand-held tool box so you can easily transport all your tools to wherever you might need them. The portable tool box would also allow you to quickly put all your tools into your escape vehicle if you had to abandon your home in an unexpected emergency situation.

If you do not already own a reasonable selection of hand tools then you should seriously consider investing in a good set of quality hand tools that are already pre-assembled inside a convenient plastic tool box that can be easily transported between locations.

A picture of a portable tool set is shown above. Similar sets can be purchased at most hardware stores, and at home improvement stores, and at most Walmarts.

The above tool set only contains the most common hand tools required for basic repairs. If you know you will need a specialty tool for a specific application then you should also purchase that specialty tool. Some examples might be: a metal file, a hand saw with a 15-Inch Sharp Tooth saw blade, and a stainless steel hatchet with a belt sheath.

The fastener collection shown on the right only contains the most common small fasteners that would be necessary for simple basic repair tasks. It would also probably be a good idea to buy some heavy duty nails, some heavy duty screws, and some larger bolts, washers, and nuts.

Leatherman Wave Multi-Tool

Another extremely useful tool is the Leatherman Wave Multi-Tool shown in the picture on the right. It is a small multi-purpose high quality hand tool that comes in a belt sheath. It can be purchased in the sporting goods section of most Walmarts at their knife case display area.

Chapter Seventy

Firewood, Fireplaces, and Cast Iron Stoves

The two primary reasons for building a fire are:
1. To provide heat for your home.
2. To provide a convenient place to cook food from scratch or to heat food from a can.

Firewood

To build a fire you will need firewood. You have two options for acquiring your firewood as follows:

1. **Purchase Your Firewood From Someone Else:** If you purchase your firewood and only split firewood is available then you will have to purchase what is available. But you might ask your firewood supplier if there is a price difference between split and unsplit logs. If there is a big price difference then the next question would be the average size of the unsplit logs. If the average size is what you can burn in the Texas Fireframe (discussed later in this chapter), then you could save some money by purchasing the unsplit logs instead.

2. **Cut Your Own Firewood:** If you decide to cut your own firewood then may I please offer the following advice. After you have the tree **safely** on the ground, leave it alone for at least six to eight weeks. Most people want to start cutting on the tree immediately but that is not the best way to cut firewood. If you will leave **all** the limbs on the tree, and the top on the tree, then they will suck the moisture (sap) to the tips of the branches and this will help to quickly dry out your recently downed tree. After waiting about two months you will discover that the wood is reasonably dry and it doesn't weigh very much because most of the moisture in the wood is now gone. However, if you start cutting the tree into firewood size lengths immediately after you cut the tree down, then the moisture will be trapped in each piece of firewood and it will take a lot longer for those pieces to dry in the sun.

Chainsaw Safety: A chainsaw is an excellent tool that can be used to cut down trees and to cut firewood to the proper length. However, it can also cripple or kill you if you are not extremely careful with it. Before you begin cutting your own firewood you should receive proper instructions on the safe way to cut down a tree and the safe way to use a chainsaw to cut firewood.

Gas or Electric Chainsaw: There are advantages and disadvantages of both gas and electric chainsaws. If you have solar panels and some deep-cycle batteries and a 120-volt inverter and some 100-foot long electrical extension cords, then I recommend the electric chain saw with a 16-inch long blade. You simply push the button to start the saw and release the button to stop the saw. At my age this is a significant advantage. You will need to make your own decision about which type of chain saw would be best for your specific application.

Splitting Firewood: In my opinion it is much easier to split firewood with a steel wedge and a sledgehammer than with an axe. Place the tapered end of the steel wedge against the upright end of the log and tap it into place with the head of the sledgehammer. Then continue striking the steel wedge with the head of the sledgehammer to split the log into firewood. Extremely wide logs may need to be split into quarters or sixths or eights.

Stacking Firewood: Do not stack your firewood directly on top of the ground. The moisture in the ground will attack your firewood and your stack of firewood will gradually begin to rot. Before you begin stacking your firewood put two long sticks on the ground from side to side in the spot where you wish to stack your firewood. The sticks can be about one or two inches in diameter and the length of your intended stack of firewood. If you don't have any sticks then you can use pressure treated 2x4 lumber instead. Then stack your firewood on top of the two long sticks or 2x4s. By elevating your firewood a short distance off the ground the air will be able to circulate below your firewood and help to keep it dry, and the ground moisture will only attack the two sticks that are making direct contact with the ground.

Protecting Firewood from the Rain: Stack your firewood under a shed or porch, or cover your firewood with a tarp or an old shower curtain. Then buy a new shower curtain for your bathroom.

Type of Wood: Any hardwood may be used for firewood. However, soft woods such as pine should not be used because they will gradually deposit a thick layer of pitch inside your chimney and that pitch could eventually catch fire and burn your house down.

Length of Firewood Logs

The maximum length of your firewood logs will depend on the size of your fireplace or the size of your cast iron stove. The maximum log length should allow air to properly circulate around the outside of your logs while they are burning. The burning logs should not make direct contact with the inside walls of your fireplace or the inside walls of your cast iron stove.

A firewood log that is too short can still be successfully used. However, a log that is too long will not fit in your fireplace or stove. Therefore it is better to have firewood that is shorter than to have firewood that is too long to be used.

On the other hand, if you are cutting your own firewood and you cut your firewood a lot shorter than it needs to be then you will be investing more time and energy in cutting your firewood than necessary. Therefore you should determine the correct log length you will need and then cut your firewood to that length or an inch or two shorter.

Fireplace: The **maximum** log length should be at least four-inches shorter than the interior width of your fireplace at its rear. In addition, the cut firewood should not extend more than two-inches off each end of your cast iron grate or Texas Fireframe. In other woods, measure the length of your grate or Fireframe from left to right and add four-inches to that value to arrive at the **maximum** firewood log length. However, if you will be using your fireplace to cook your meals then the **maximum** length of the firewood logs should **not exceed** the length of your grate or Fireframe from left to right. The reason for this will be explained later in this chapter when cooking with firewood is discussed in detail.

Cast Iron Stove: The **maximum** log length should be at least eight-inches shorter than the inside length of your cast iron stove from front to rear. You do not want to have part of your fire burning directly below the stove pipe vent at the rear of your stove because that heat will rise directly up the vent and disappear outside your home. This would be wasteful. If you follow my recommendation later in this chapter and you install a cast iron grate on the inside bottom of your cast iron stove then the **maximum** length of your logs should be the length of your cast iron grate. In general, the logs should not be longer than the distance from end to end of the burners directly above the fire area.

Cast Iron Stove and a Cast Iron Grate

Curing a New Stove or a Used Stove: Wipe the cast iron stove clean of dust and dirt. If necessary use a little soap and water to remove any surface stains. Completely rinse the soap off the stove and then carefully dry the stove. Cover the entire outside of the stove and attached stovepipe with a very, very thin layer of extra virgin olive oil or cooking oil or melted shortening or melted animal fat. Then start a very small fire inside the stove and allow the fire to heat the cast iron so the excess oil melts off the oven and what remains is cured into the cast iron itself. Allow the stove to cool and then inspect the exterior surface carefully to make sure you didn't miss any spots. If you missed one or more spots the first time then repeat the process and make sure you cover any spots you originally missed.

Cast Iron Grate: I recommend that you purchase and install a cast iron fireplace grate in the bottom of your cast iron stove. This would be the same type of grate you would use in a conventional wood burning fireplace. Before you invest in one of these cast iron grates you should measure the diagonal opening at the front of your cook stove to determine the maximum clearance available for inserting a cast iron grate. Place your logs on this grate and start your fire. The grate will allow air to circulate below and around the outsides of your logs to produce a superior fire inside your cast iron stove.

Wood Burning Fireplace and a Cast Iron Grate

You will need a cast iron grate or a Texas Fireframe (discussed later in this chapter) if you are using a wood burning fireplace. The grate elevates the firewood off the bottom of the fireplace and it allows air to circulate around the logs as they are burning to yield a better fire. A grate or Fireframe should be placed about one-inch from the rear of the fireplace and at least one-inch from the side of the fireplace. The side clearance will depend on the size of the grate in relation to the length of the firewood you will be using. Whenever possible the grate should be centered below your firewood so an equal amount of each log extends off the left and right sides of the grate. The ends of the firewood logs should be at least one-inch or more from the sides of the fireplace.

You have two options for selecting the optimal size of cast iron grate as follows:

1. Purchase the largest cast iron grate you can find but which still leaves at least one-inch of clearance from the grate to the rear of the fireplace, and at least one-inch of clearance on both the left and right sides of the grate and the walls of the fireplace. This grate should then be positioned in the center of your fireplace and left there when heating your home with firewood or when cooking a meal inside your fireplace.

2. Purchase a cast iron grate that is approximately one-half the width of the inside of your fireplace from left to right and which still leaves one-inch of clearance from the rear of the grate to the rear of the fireplace. Place the grate on the left side of the fireplace about one-inch from the left wall of the fireplace. Build a normal fire on the grate and wait for the wood to burn down into red hot coals. The red hot coals should fall through the openings in the grate onto the floor of your fireplace. Then use a steel fireplace poker to slide the cast iron grate from the left side of your fireplace to the right side of your fireplace. Leave about one-inch of clearance from the right side of the grate to the right wall of the fireplace. Then place a folding campfire grill inside your fireplace on the left side above the red hot coals. You can then use cast iron cookware to cook your meals on top of the campfire grill on the left side of your fireplace. While your meal is cooking you can start a new small fire on the cast iron grate on the right side of the fireplace. This method will allow you to shift the cast iron grate back and forth from left to right and from right to left inside your fireplace whenever you need red hot coals to prepare a meal. If you don't need to cook then you can leave the cast iron grate in its current position to support your firewood while you heat your home with a normal fire.

Texas Fireframe
(May be purchased at: www.texasfireframe.com)

The Texas Fireframe was invented by Lawrence Cranberg, Ph.D. for use in a wood burning fireplace. It is made of heavy-duty steel. The bottom part of the Fireframe looks very similar to a standard cast iron grate that you would use in a conventional wood burning fireplace. However, the Fireframe has two vertical steel front supports, one on the left side of the lower grate and one on the right side of the lower grate. Attached to each of these two vertical steel supports is another piece of steel that extends horizontally about 1/4 of the way across the front of the grate and then they turn at a 90-degree angle and continue about 1/2 of the distance above the lower grate. These two horizontal pieces can slide up and down the vertical steel supports.

The Texas Fireframe is 25" long from left to right, 13.5" wide from front to rear, and 15" high from bottom to top. The lower log grate is 20.5" long by 13" wide and it is 6" high off the ground at the front and rear, 5" off the ground on the left and right, and it has 4" of clearance below the grate. The upper support arms are 7.25" long from front to rear, with a open gap space of 11" between the upper left and right support arms. If you will measure the opening inside your current fireplace then you should be able to determine if the Texas Fireframe will fit inside your existing fireplace.

To build a fire on the Texas Fireframe you put your biggest log (about 6 inches in diameter) on the rear of the Fireframe. You then put two or three smaller diameter logs (2" or 3" diameters) on the lower grate. Then you finish with one or two logs (3" to 5" diameters) on the upper support arms. The result is that you have created a "C" shaped pattern using your logs with the open part of the "C" facing into your home. You then put a few sheets of crumbled newspaper into the open area between the upper and lower logs and light the newspaper. A few minutes later the upper logs will start burning and then the other logs will start burning and you will have a nice fire in your fireplace. But because of the "C" shape of your fire a significant amount of the heat generated by the fire will be directed out of the fireplace into your home.

I purchased a Texas Fireframe Grate in 1999 and I have used it in my home every winter since then. The Fireframe uses **no** electricity and it will fit into almost any standard size fireplace. And it really does significantly increase the amount of heat that is actually transmitted into my home from the burning logs.

When the fire has completely burned itself out then there will be a pile of ashes in the bottom of the fireplace. That pile of ashes looks **exactly** the same regardless of whether you are using **unsplit** logs or split firewood.

When the significance of this sinks in then you quickly realize that unless there is a good reason to split your firewood then you are simply investing extra labor that yields no positive return. (Unless you need the exercise and you have absolutely no other manual chores to do.) Therefore any system that can provide a good fire using **unsplit** logs is a real time and energy saver.

Texas Fireframe

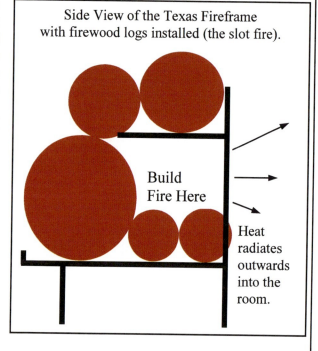

Side View of the Texas Fireframe with firewood logs installed (the slot fire).

Build Fire Here

Heat radiates outwards into the room.

In my opinion there are four major **advantages** to the Texas Fireframe:

1. **Heat:** You get a **lot** more heat into your home from the burning logs and it doesn't require any electricity or a fan.

2. **Unsplit Logs:** You can use **unsplit logs**. This is a major factor for me. Cutting down a tree and then cutting it into firewood lengths is only part of the job. If you then have to split each of the logs, you expend a lot more effort. And if you are trying to conserve your energy then splitting logs is not the way you want to spend your time.

Chapter Seventy: Firewood, Fireplaces, and Cast Iron Stoves

3. **Easy Fire Starting:** The **unsplit logs** can easily be lit with a few sheets of newspaper rolled up and placed in the center cavity between the logs. Until you actually do it you probably will not believe this is possible. With a regular fireplace grate you need newspaper and lots of small tiny sticks or kindling to start the fire. Then you gradually add slightly bigger sticks until the fire is burning well enough so that you can start putting your split firewood on the fire. None of this kindling is necessary with the Texas Fireframe. And a really good fire is heating your home in about 15 minutes instead of 30 minutes (or longer).

4. **Low Risk of a Chimney Fire:** The risk of a chimney fire is very close to zero with a Texas Fireframe grate. If you are forced to use a wood burning fireplace as a primary source of heat for an extended period of time then it would be nice to feel safe that your home isn't going to burn down as a result of a chimney fire.

The major **disadvantage** of the Texas Fireframe is its initial cost. However, the Texas Fireframe is made of very sturdy material, as opposed to the normal fireplace grates you typically find in the hardware stores. Over the years I have burned up and replaced several of those cast iron grates. After twelve years of using my Texas Fireframe on an intermittent basis each winter I can't see any damage anywhere on the entire unit (a picture of my Texas Fireframe appears earlier in this chapter). My guess is that my Fireframe will easily last another 10 or 15 years or maybe longer. Therefore, if you consider the replacement cost of a cast iron grate every five to seven years then the cost of the Texas Fireframe grate is probably about the same as several cast iron grates over a 20 to 25 year time period. And when you factor in the difference in price (or labor savings) from unsplit logs then the Texas Fireframe is clearly a lower cost option over the long run.

I can personally verify that the statements made by Dr. Lawrence Cranberg regarding the operation and efficiency of the Texas Fireframe Grate are not overstated. A very comfortable fire can be started on the Texas Fireframe Grate using **unsplit logs** and a few sheets of newspaper. The resulting fire burns well and a significant amount of the heat from the fire enters the room and does not disappear up the chimney.

Normally I use the approximate size logs that are recommended for the grate. I always place the biggest log I have available on the rear of the grate. However, as I burn through my firewood each winter, I sometimes use two medium logs on top (instead of one), and three smaller logs on the bottom (instead of two). Even with these minor changes the grate still provides a significant amount of heat for my home. I have occasionally used split firewood and that also does exceptionally well on the grate.

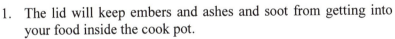

Cast Iron Cookware

Cast iron cookware is the recommended cookware for use on a cast iron stove or inside a wood burning fireplace. Cast iron cookware is 100% cast iron and it does not contain any parts that are made of plastic or aluminum or wood that could melt or catch fire when exposed to the intense heat of a wood burning fire.

I suggest you purchase cast iron cookware with a lid for two reasons:

1. The lid will keep embers and ashes and soot from getting into your food inside the cook pot.

2. The lid will keep more of the heat and the flavor of the food inside the cook pot which will minimize the amount of firewood needed, reduce the total time required to cook the food, and maximize the flavor of the finished food.

Some cast iron cookware, such as a Dutch Oven, is sold with the lid as part of the unit. However, most of the other cast iron pieces are **not** sold with a lid. Instead a lid must be purchased separately. I strongly recommend that you purchase a lid for each piece of cast iron cookware that you acquire.

For additional information about cast iron cookware please read the Cast Iron Cookware Chapter in this book in order to learn how to cook with cast iron and how to take care of cast iron cookware.

Stainless Steel Cookware and Teflon Coated Cookware

If you can find 100% stainless steel cookware without any plastic parts then it could be used to cook over a wood burning fire.

A stainless steel skillet cover may be used to cover your pots and skillets and it can be safely used with a wood burning fire.

Some stainless steel cookware if very cheaply made and it will **not** last very long in any type of cooking application.

The advantage of cast iron cookware over stainless steel cookware is that food will usually not stick to the inside of the cast iron cookware.

Cookware that has a Teflon coating on its interior cooking surface can be used with a wood burning fire if the rest of the cookware is made of heavy-duty metal and it does not contain any aluminum or have any plastic or wood handles. This type of cookware can sometimes be found in the camping section of a sporting goods store, or a hardware store, or an Army-Navy store, or a Walmart.

Suggestions for Cooking on a Cast Iron Stove, and in a Conventional Fireplace, and using the Texas Fireframe

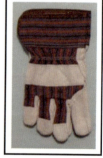

You will need a pair of heavy-duty leather gloves with loose fitting wrists to cook inside a fireplace or over a cast iron oven. The loose fitting wrists will allow you to quickly shake the gloves off your hands if the gloves accidentally become too hot from the fire or a cast iron skillet.

Do **not** cook over the flames of a wood fire. Instead wait for the wood to burn down into red hot coals and then cook over the red hot coals. This is the same basic principle as cooking over charcoal.

Cast Iron Stove: Cast iron cookware is easy to use on a **cast iron stove**. Simply place the cookware on the top burners to cook your food. Or use lid lifters to remove the burner covers and place your skillet directly above the fire inside the stove.

Cast Iron Stove Burner Lids: If you put your skillet on top of the burner lids then the lid itself will capture and retain some of the heat and less heat will be transferred to the bottom of the skillet and it will take longer to cook your meal. However, sometimes you only want to keep food or water "warm" and the best way to do this is to leave the lid on the stove between the fire and the bottom of the skillet or cook pot. On the other hand, if you remove the burner covers with a lid lifter and then place your skillet directly above the opening into the stove, then more of the heat from inside the stove will make contact with the bottom of your cast iron skillet. This will result in less time being required to cook whatever you have in your skillet. However, for this to work the diameter of the bottom of your skillet needs to be at least one-inch wider than the diameter of the round opening on top of the stove.

Wood Burning Fireplace: In a **conventional fireplace** you should wait for your firewood to burn down into red hot coals. Then you have several options as follows:

1. **Cast Iron Dutch Oven:** Place a Dutch Oven directly on top of your cast iron grate above the red hot coals, or move the grate and place the Dutch Oven on top of the red hot coals.

2. **Charcoal Flat Metal Grill Surface:** Place a charcoal metal grill surface across the top of your cast iron grate inside your fireplace. Then you can cook with a cast iron skillet on top of this flat metal grill surface.

3. **Folding Campfire Grill:** If you purchased a cast iron grate that is about one-half the width of your fireplace, then you could move the cast iron grate to the other side of the fireplace as described earlier in this chapter. Then put a folding campfire grill over the red hot coals and then you can cook on the surface of the campfire grill.

4. **Pot Hook:** You can hang a pot with a wire handle from a hook that swings into and out of the fireplace.

Texas Fireframe: If you are using a **Texas Fireframe** then after the logs have burned down into red hot coals you have two options as follows:

1. **Cast Iron Dutch Oven:** Place your food inside a cast iron Dutch Oven with a lid and place the Dutch Oven on top of the lower part of the Texas Fireframe directly above the red hot coals.

2. **Cast Iron Skillet:** Place your skillet directly on top of the lower cooking grate and cook your meal inside your skillet. Or place a charcoal metal grill surface across the lower part of the Texas Fireframe. After you have positioned your metal grill in its most advantageous position then you can place a skillet on the metal grill surface and cook your meal.

Chapter Seventy: Firewood, Fireplaces, and Cast Iron Stoves

Ordinary People

A destitute childless widow named Ruth
    became the great-grandmother of a King.

A teenage shepherd boy named David
    killed a giant with a stone and a sling.

An orphaned Jewish slave girl named Esther
    saved her people from death with just one plea.

A hot-tempered fisherman named Peter
    walked on the waters of a wind tossed sea.

A woman ashamed of her life of sin
    used her tears and her hair to wash our Lord's feet.

A boy with five loaves and two small fish
    gave his food to Jesus so 5,000 could eat.

Who does God use for deeds both great and small?
    Just ordinary people like you and me, and that's all.

Scripture References: Ruth 1:4-5, 1:16-18, 2:2, 4:13, 4:17,
First Samuel 17:4, 17:32-33, 17:45, 17:48-50,
Esther 2:5-7, 8:5-6, 8:11,
John 18:10, Mark 14:70-71, Matthew 14:29,
Luke 7:37-48, John 6:9-13, Acts 4:13.

Poem: Ordinary People

Chapter Seventy-One

Charity During Hard Times

The Basic Problem

Hard times usually result in an overwhelming number of people:

1. who do not have a job of any kind, and
2. who have no steady income from any source, and
3. who are either homeless or are living with close relatives.

During hard times these individuals need almost everything, including food, shelter, clothing, and basic medical care.

During really hard times the large and growing number of homeless individuals greatly exceeds the carrying capacity of their local community in terms of voluntary charitable donations. There are just not enough homeless shelters and free food/soup kitchens that provide one meal per day to accommodate everyone. To survive during hard times these homeless individuals must choose between becoming thieves or beggars or both.

Therefore during hard times the crime rate increases significantly. Since God was expelled from our school systems and our work places many decades ago, there are now a large number of people who have little or no respect for any type of authority, or for the rights of anyone other than themselves. These individuals do not evaluate their actions on any moral or ethical principles other than whether or not their action results in an improvement in their own personal welfare.

Therefore as our current hard times tragedy continues to unfold, any family that still has a home that contains a wage earner will quickly learn that if they are going to continue to survive they must not make themselves an obvious or easy target for thieves or a target for a continuous stream of beggars.

Each individual family will need to make their own decision on whether or not they can afford to be charitable. Some families are already in such serious financial difficulty that they are barely able to meet their own basic survival needs and charity is simply not an option. Other families may be a little better off and they may be able to afford a little charity every now and then. The difficulty is that homeless families do not need help every now and then -- they need it continuously.

If a person or family makes the decision to dispense charity directly from their home or apartment then they may experience the following problems:

1. Having anyone and everyone knocking on your door at any time of the day or night.
2. Receiving verbal abuse, or something worse, when you honestly have no charity to give away at the current time.
3. Experiencing the occasional angry face-to-face confrontation with an individual or family that is not grateful for what you do offer to give to them and they accuse you of being able to give more and they demand that you do so or suffer the consequences.

For these reasons, among others, a prudent family will need to determine how they can be charitable without putting the safety of their own family at risk.

One Possible Solution

Fortunately there is a simple solution to this charity dilemma. After determining what they can afford to give away, each family can give money, food, and/or clothing to a local food pantry, homeless shelter, orphanage, or church with the stipulation that the gift be used to help the needy families in the local area.

This giving strategy is not new. In was recommended by Jesus Christ in Matthew 6:3-4: *"But when you do a charitable deed, do not let you left hand know what your right hand is doing, that your charitable deed may be in secret; and your Father who sees in secret will Himself reward you openly."*

Charitable donations may be made to an organization that is near the donating family or to one that is a reasonable distance away if anonymity is desired. The advantage of donating to a nearby establishment is that the donating family can direct any beggars to its location. The family would not have to mention whether or not they personally donated anything of value to the charitable organization -- they could simply say they heard that food was available there.

During hard times the beggar (hobo) information network works extremely well and everyone knows which homes always say "no" and which ones sometimes say "yes" and which ones always "give directions to the nearest charitable organization." You can put a simple note and a directions map on your front door (or gate) to help reduce the number of beggars who actually knock on your door. The note could be written in both English and Spanish. Without opening the door you could ask who is knocking and what their business is, and then give directions through the closed door. Remember that an innocent looking beggar could also be a very skilled thief and/or killer. Always keep your doors closed and bolted during hard times and ask and answer questions through the door. Do not open your door even to those who actually have or pretend to have hearing deficiencies. The note on your front door should be adequate to answer any question the hard of hearing may have.

To the extent possible, try to be polite to everyone who knocks on your door. Just remember that at some point in the future it could be you and your family on the outside knocking on someone else's door. However, after you have given directions to the charitable organization, if the person or family continues to be persistent and they will not leave then you may need to call 911 and report them. (Note: If this problem repeats itself too often then you may need to add a sentence to the note on your door or gate that says you will immediately call 911 and report anyone who knocks on your door to ask for any type of donation.)

During serious hard times the local churches and their leaders will be confronted with an increasing and overwhelming number of requests for help. Many churches will respond by setting up committees to oversee the collection, storing, and distribution of food, clothing, and other supplies to needy families. Some churches already perform this function in their communities on an ongoing basis and they distribute food to needy families once a week, or every other week, or once a month. (Note: During serious hard times a once-per-week distribution would be preferred so the families that are newly added to the distribution list do not have to wait too long before receiving assistance.)

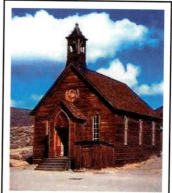

The advantage of making your charitable donations to a church or other charitable organization is that they can more equally distribute the available charity to everyone who is in need. And when the charity is all gone then those who received it will know that more will not be available until some future time, whether it is a free hot meal the following day, or a few more free groceries one week or one month from now.

A nearby local church or other charitable organization is a superior method for equitably distributing charity to everyone who is in need for all the following reasons:

1. They will receive charitable donations from anyone regardless of whether or not the individual is a member of the organization or church.
2. They are usually located within a reasonable distance of the families who are donating the charity.
3. They are usually within walking distance or bicycle distance of the needy families.
4. They distribute charity to local residents and individuals passing through their community and therefore they help to relieve local suffering and reduce the local crime rate.
5. They minimize the chance of one family receiving more charitable assistance than another family.
6. The local charitable organization usually knows if any work is available locally and they will pass that information on to the welfare recipients. This helps those in charge of dispensing charity to identify the families who have members who could work but chose not to. Families who accept work assignments and

faithfully discharge those work duties will also usually be told where they can rent a meager but simple room to live in.

7. The recipients of the charity do not have to be members of the church or charitable organization.
8. The recipients of the charity will quickly learn where and when the charity is being distributed and this will help to minimize their investment in time and energy in searching for assistance.
9. The recipients of the charity will quickly learn that it is fruitless to beg door-to-door in a local area because anyone who has anything to give has already donated it to the local charitable organization.
10. The recipients of the charity will be able to maintain some of their dignity because they will not be forced to beg door-to-door and humble themselves before anyone and everyone who opens the door.
11. It provides everyone in the local area with an immediate and helpful answer to anyone who is in need of assistance. No one ever has to say, "No, I can't help you." Instead everyone can provide directions to the nearest charitable organization.
12. When the total amount of available charity in an area is not adequate to sustain all the families in that area that need charity assistance then some of those families will realize it is time to move on to another area where the overall economic conditions might be more favorable.

If you chose to make your charitable donations to a local church or other charitable organization then you will need to be consistent. Except for close family members it would be unwise to make exceptions for anyone, including your close friends and neighbors. You do not want to be put into a position where you have to chose which of your friends or neighbors are worthy of your assistance and which ones are not. Those that you are not able to help will quickly turn on you and they will hate you and this could eventually result in a disaster for you and your family.

It would be much better to say to everyone, whether it is one person or a small family or a large group of people, that food and other assistance is being freely distributed at a local charitable organization and then give directions to that organization. You should not tell anyone whether or not you actually contributed anything to that organization because if you do then it could result in resentment against you for not giving your donation directly to your friend or neighbor. These individuals will also remember that you had extra resources to share at a time when they did not and as the hard times continue they will reflect on that fact over and over and it may eventually lead to an attack on your home or apartment.

Nobody has the resources to feed, shelter, and clothe all their friends and neighbors for an unknown period of time. The current hard times we are experiencing will probably continue to get worse for many years. If you make an exception for anyone in the early phase of the hard times tragedy then that person or family will expect you to continuously assist them for the duration of the event, even if you tell them that the original donation is a one-time gift when you first give it to them. It would be much better to not start a dependency relationship than to start one and then have to stop it. After the initial gift of resources has been consumed that family will return to beg at your doorstep every day, and each day you don't give them something their hatred and suspicions about you will grow and this could eventually lead to a disaster for you and your family.

Conclusion

If our economy continues to weaken, then more and more people will lose their jobs and their homes. The government will not be able to help them in any meaningful way because the true unemployment rate will be extremely high and the government's tax revenues will be seriously reduced. The government will not have the money or the resources to help all the homeless families survive. (Note: If the government simply issues more money then this will only result in hyperinflation and it will not solve the original problem. Instead it will create a variety of new problems and it will actually make the hard times much worse.)

As the number of homeless families gradually increases there will eventually come a time when their combined needs will exceed the available supply of charitable donations and government assistance. When that happens each homeless family will not receive enough assistance to sustain itself. If our economy degenerates to the point where a large number of us cannot meet our minimum needs for survival then the events that will follow are not pleasant ones to contemplate.

The Book

Adam and Eve, Abraham and Sarah,
David and Bathsheba, Joseph and Mary.

Famous names from distant ages past,
all written in a Book we know is most Holy.

Even a poor unnamed widow who gave her two mites,
has a place in Scripture and a home in Glory.

Wouldn't it be grand if your name was inside the Book
and not just on its cover or on its first page?

Be not dismayed. God has another Book and
He wrote **your** name in it when you were just a babe.

And if you claim Jesus Christ as
your personal Savior while you still breathe,

Then your name will **never** be erased
from the Lamb's Book of Life for all eternity.

This Poem is Dedicated to My Granddaughter **Olivia Ryan Atkins.**

Scripture References: Psalm 139:13-18, Daniel 12:2-3, John 3:16-18, Luke 10:20, Revelation 3:4-5, Revelation 20:11-15, Revelation 21:27, Matthew 24:55, John 3:36, Acts 4:12, Acts 2:21, John 5:24-29.

Chapter Seventy-Two

Pets and Livestock

While my brother Randy was alive (picture on right) he occasionally said he would willingly die if it became necessary to protect his dog. And he meant it.

Although my brother was married several times during the course of his life, he never had any children of his own. But my brother did have several dogs during the course of his lifetime. When each one of his pet dogs passed away due to old age, it would not be long before he would have another dog to take its place. My brother eventually passed away at the age of 60. He had been in poor health for several years and he did not have a dog when he died. However, if my brother were still alive today then he would be in complete disagreement with everything that I am about to write about pets.

During the course of my own life I have had several pets and I have had children and eventually grandchildren. Therefore my perspective on the value of human life in comparison to the life of a family pet is based on a different set of life experiences than my brother.

During normal times there are a variety of good reasons to have a pet, such as loneliness, companionship, or the need for a seeing-eye dog if you are blind. There are also two other common reasons that people give for having a dog:

1. Almost everyone says their dog is a good guard dog because the dog barks when anyone or anything approaches their home or apartment. However, during a hard times event this barking will attract attention to you and your resources and it will probably result in your demise as opposed to your salvation. On the other hand, if you have a dog that has been trained not to bark but to alert you of approaching danger in some other way, then your dog may be of some value during the coming hard times.

2. Even if you have a "hunting breed dog" that dog will not know how to hunt unless it has been trained. Training a hunting dog takes a lot of time and patience. If your dog is already a very successful hunting companion then it may have some value during the hard times ahead. However, in my opinion, a good set of steel traps would be a more effective way to catch wild game than to go hunting with a rifle and a dog. A good set of steel traps will cost about the same amount of money as a good dog. However, unlike a dog, you will not have to feed the traps every day. The traps will feed you.

During really hard times there may still be some valid reasons to have a pet but there will also be some equally valid reasons not to have one.

At the very beginning of a hard times tragedy event no one will consider it unusual to see a person or a family with a pet. However, as the hard times gradually continue to get worse then fewer and fewer pets will be seen for the following two reasons:

1. Starving people have a different perspective about dogs and cats than non-starving people. A starving person sees the animal as a meal and if the animal is alone and unattended then the animal quickly becomes a meal. Although a starving person may have been repulsed at the idea of eating a dog or a cat during normal times, after prolonged and acute starvation the starving person's perspective gradually becomes more practical. During the Great Depression of the 1930s household pets became a rare sight and they were usually only seen in the homes of wealthy families.

2. People who are experiencing hard times eventually run out of money and food. When that happens they take their pet to the Humane Society or they simply take their pet several miles away and turn it loose to fend for itself. Of these two options, the Humane Society is the better choice during hard times. A pet

that is simply turned loose to fend for itself will eventually become someone's meal, or that pet will become a member of a "wild dog pack" that will surround and kill anyone and anything they can in order to survive.

Several weeks after the onset of a serious hard times tragedy event, most pets will be gone. The only pets that will remain will be the pets that are living with individuals and families who are not experiencing the hard times. These will be the people who not only have enough food to feed themselves but they will also have enough extra food to keep their pet alive.

Pets make noise. That noise will attract attention to your family. It will not be possible to keep a low profile and remain out of harm's way if your family has a pet. Eventually not only will your family be attacked and killed but your pet will be eaten by someone. People who have already decided they are going to keep and protect their pet during the coming hard times need to think very carefully about the eventual consequences of their decision.

For example, during a serious hard times tragedy event many people will die, including many children who will starve to death. How do you think someone who has lost a child due to starvation will feel if he happens to look out his window and he sees you walking your dog and your dog stops to take a really well-deserved bowel movement. He will instantly realize that you have enough food to not only keep yourself alive but also to feed your pet. He will also realize that you did not consider the life of his little child to be as important as the life of your pet. If you didn't care about the life of his child, why should he feel guilty about rounding up several of his starving friends and then attacking you and killing everyone in your household and taking everything that you own?

I have already told each of my children that they may bring their spouses and their children and come live with me in our small 1,800 square foot home if really hard times make it necessary. However, I have also told them that they absolutely could not bring any of their friends, or any of their in-laws, or any pets with them. I don't have the space or the resources to provide for the number of potential individuals that would entail. And I do not wish to be put into a position where I have to decide which friends and/or in-laws are welcome and which ones are not. I am also not going to put the safety and well-being of my wife, my other children, and all my grandchildren at risk for the sake of one or more pets. If any of my children believes that their pet is more important than the lives of people (similar to my brother's opinion), then I do not intend to try to convince them otherwise. They may simply go somewhere else to live with their pets but not here. I fully realize that many of you who are reading this paragraph will call me hard-hearted and cruel. May I suggest that you wait until two or three months after the onset of a serious hard times tragedy event and then call me names.

Farm Livestock

The second topic in this chapter is about farm livestock, such as chickens, rabbits, dairy cows, pigs, sheep, and goats. If you already live on a farm and you are responsible for the care of these animals then you probably already know what I am about to write.

The purchase price of the farm animal is only the beginning of the story. You will also need to provide space to keep the animals, feed to supplement the animals' diet, and medicine when the animals get sick. You will also need to clean up the manure that the animals drop every day inside their stalls, and you will need to protect the animals from their natural predators and from thieves. Finally, neighborhood dogs love to attack and kill chickens and to chase the other farm animals around.

Farm animals also require care every day. Each time you interact with the animal there is a chance the animal will injure you, even when you are attempting to be very careful.

During a serious hard times tragedy event you really don't need to be on the receiving end of any type of "accident." Therefore I strongly recommend against trying to become completely "self-sufficient." A better strategy, in my opinion, would be to maintain a low profile until the worst part of the hard times event has passed. At that time it may then be prudent to gradually learn how to manage one or two small farm animals. After you have been "pecked" or "scratched" by a chicken, or seriously scratched by the nails of a rabbit, or bitten deeply by the teeth of a rabbit then you will be better prepared for the more serious injuries that are customary with the larger farm animals.

All types of livestock make noise. That noise will attract attention to your place. During hard times the starving people who live all around you will hear your livestock. Do you think you can defend your place and all your livestock from hundreds of starving desperate people? Perhaps you can. I know I could not. I live in an area where a few of my neighbors have chickens, and some have horses, and some have dairy cows, and some have goats. But the vast majority of my neighbors do not have any type of livestock. When the hard times tragedy really begins to unfold then one of two things will probably happen:

1. The families without livestock will steal and eat the livestock of their neighbors, or
2. The families without livestock will try to purchase or barter for some livestock from their neighbors in order to improve the future food production potential of their own little homesteads.

I hope that most of my neighbors select option two above. However, I live in the real world and I suspect that at least a few of my neighbors will select option one instead.

Therefore my recommendation is to not invest in any livestock at this time unless you live in a very, very secluded area. You would be much better off investing your money in pre-packaged foods, such as non-fat powdered dry milk, canned beef, chicken, and tuna, and an assortment of canned vegetables and fruits.

Pre-packaged foods are advantageous for all the following reasons:

1. They are already packaged for long-term food storage.
2. They will be available for your immediate consumption.
3. They will not make any noise that would attract attention to you.
4. They will not require any daily care and therefore you will not have to worry about any type of "accidental injury."

However, sooner or later everyone will run out of stored food. Before that happens you should reevaluate the costs and the benefits of the different types of farm livestock. Depending on the area where you live, and the situation in your area at that time, it may then make good sense to acquire and manage a few farm animals. In order to have a reasonable chance of success at that time, I suggest the immediate purchase of the following book: **Backyard Livestock**, by Thomas and Looby, any printing from 2007 or before.

Read the above book from cover to cover but wait to make your investment in livestock until the worst part of the hard times tragedy event has passed.

(Note: Rabbits do not make any noise. However, I spent two-years raising rabbits before I quit. Based on my own personal first-hand experience, the amount of meat I got from my rabbits was not worth the time and effort and money I invested in them. During a two-year period I invested at least ten times more money in those rabbits than I received back in return in the form of rabbit meat. I would have been far, far better off if I had just invested my money in some canned beef, chicken, ham, and fish. If anyone asks my opinion about raising rabbits then I reply that it is much easier and cheaper to use steel traps to catch the wild rabbits in my area. Wild rabbits do not require an investment in rabbit cages, or rabbit feed, or cleaning up rabbit poop.)

You should also purchase and store some vegetable seeds. However, it would probably be prudent to plant just a few of those seeds each year in order to replenish your seed stock each year and to gain some first-hand experience with the specific gardening problems normally encountered in your geographical area. After the worst part of the hard times tragedy event has passed then you would have a better chance of planting your seeds and harvesting your crops without attracting unnecessary attention to your family and your home.

Illusion versus Reality

Just imagine -- a rustic log cabin with a small barn and the family milk cow. What a truly romantic mental image. But the image has no realistic estimate of the amount of work involved. About once per year you will have to pay to breed your cow with a bull to keep her milk "fresh." And you will get no milk for about two months each year. And every day at approximately 6 in the morning and 6 in the evening you must milk the cow. Whether you want to or not. Regardless of what you may be doing at those two times during the day you must stop and milk the cow. You can't sleep late. And you have to lead the cow out to the pasture in the morning and bring the cow into the barn in the evening. Even in the pouring rain. And you must provide some type of feed or hay for the cow during the winter months. And cows are just like people. Some are easy to get along with and some have very disagreeable dispositions. Guess which type of cow the dairy farmer is trying to get rid of? After you have the cow for one-week you will probably be willing to pay someone to take the cow off your hands. This isn't conjecture. I spent six-months on a small dairy farm when I was in my early twenties.

For each $100 that you invest in a cow (or a milk goat) you could have purchased approximately 14 boxes of instant powdered milk. A 64-ounce box of powdered milk will make 20 quarts or five-gallons of milk. Fourteen boxes of instant milk would therefore equal 70-gallons of reserve milk inside your home that is just waiting for you to consume it. If you spent $400 then that would equal 280-gallons of instant powdered milk. And you would not have to get up every morning at 5:30 to milk a cow. And you wouldn't have to worry about being kicked by a cow and then being laid up in bed for a few days while your body heals. And you would not have to protect the cow from your starving neighbors or from vicious predatory animals. You should think about it very carefully before you make an investment in a milk cow or a milk goat (usually a few milk goats).

Footnote About Objectivity

The number of individuals who strongly recommend that you invest in some type of livestock is overwhelming. Please believe me when I say I don't mind if you have pets or if you invest in farm livestock. You have a right to make your own decisions in this matter just like you do in all the other matters that pertain to your life.

Most of the questions I receive about pets and livestock are from individuals who:
1. Are trying to convince themselves that their opinion is correct.
2. Repeat the same information that can be found almost anywhere on the internet or in any good book on animals.
3. Do not present a balanced perspective on the topic but focus exclusively on the positive issues and neglect to mention any of the negative issues.

For the better part of the past 100 years people have been leaving their farms and accepting jobs in nearby towns, cities, and factories for all the following reasons:
1. Farm work is very hard work. It is hard work every day, seven days per week. Farm animals require a farmer's attention every day.
2. Jobs in town or in factories are usually much easier than farm jobs.
3. Jobs in town or in factories usually pay much better than farm jobs.
4. A town job usually means a dependable paycheck on a regular basis.
5. On the other hand, a farmer doesn't get a paycheck on a regular basis.
6. And sometimes the farmer doesn't get a paycheck at all due to crop failures or because of the loss of his livestock for one reason or another.

If you speak to an experienced farmer or rancher then he or she will be able to show you all of his or her scars that were acquired while working on the farm.

I find it amazing that the people who strongly recommend farm animals always neglect to mention their scars. If they don't have any scars then they either have no real experience or very limited farm animal experience and they are simply repeating what they read somewhere else.

If they do have scars then they aren't telling you everything you need to know about farm animals and they are intentionally omitting their heart-breaking tragic stories.

Chapter Seventy-Three

The Three Most Important Wilderness Survival Items

If you were unexpectedly stranded in a wilderness environment then your chances of survival would be significantly enhanced if you had three common items in your possession. This assumes you are not stranded in a barren wasteland, or in a frozen snow covered wilderness, or in a hot barren desert. Each of these situations would require a unique set of additional items.

However, assuming you are simply in a dense forest, or in a jungle, or on a tropical island, then the following three items would significantly improve your chances of survival:

1. a knife,
2. a new butane lighter, and
3. a compass.

The above three items are listed in the order of their importance to your survival. Let's examine each of the above three items one-at-a-time.

A Knife

Other than the will to live, the most important survival necessity is a **basic hunting knife**. A knife **cannot** be made from scratch in the middle of the wilderness. And there is no backup primitive tool that can perform all the functions of a modern steel knife. Therefore everyone should have a knife in his or her "possibilities bag." If you have a good knife then your chances of survival skyrocket even if you only have a little survival knowledge. However, if you don't have a knife then your chances of survival are greatly reduced regardless of how much survival knowledge you may have.

A knife has a multitude of practical uses such as providing you with:

1. Immediate protection and self-defense while you construct more suitable weapons.
2. The ability to quickly sharpen a strong stick to make a spear for hunting and for protection.
3. The ability to gradually and carefully build a handmade bow and arrows.
4. The ability to cut vines and/or animal hides into thin strips to use as cord so you can make or build things.
5. The ability to cut and build a variety of primitive traps and snares to capture wild game.
6. The ability to properly skin an animal and slice the meat into thin strips to make meat jerky.
7. The ability to properly scrap and prepare a deer skin so it can be brain tanned into a useful buckskin.
8. The ability to convert a buckskin into a nice pair of moccasins.

Either a fixed blade hunting knife or a high quality folding knife will work exceptionally well. I prefer a fixed blade knife in a sheath. However, if space is limited then a good folding knife is an excellent second choice. Since a knife is an absolutely critical necessity in a wilderness survival situation, I personally recommend that you have **two different brands and types of knives** in your "possibilities bag" in the event you lose or damage your primary hunting knife.

There are several companies that make good hunting knives, including Buck, Gerber, and Winchester.

| Buck with Gut Hook | Gerber with Gut Hook | Winchester Fixed | Winchester Folding |

The **Buck Knife** in the left picture is a typical hunter's knife because of the shape of its blade and the fact that it has a "gut hook" that makes opening and skinning a dead animal relatively easy. The steel blade is in one piece and it extends all the way to the end of the handle which makes the knife very strong. The handle is riveted to the blade in three places. The knife has a composite handle that is easy to hold onto if it gets wet. The knife also has a "lanyard" hole at the handle end of the blade so you can tie the end of the knife to your belt, if you believe this would be appropriate. This knife is an excellent hunter's knife because of the short four-inch blade and the "gut hook." However it is not a good self-defense knife for these same two reasons.

The **Gerber Knife** in the center left picture is similar to the Buck Knife but it has a composite handle that completely surrounds the lower portion of the blade. This makes the knife very easy to control even if it gets wet while you are skinning an animal.

The **Winchester Knife** in the center right picture is a basic fixed blade knife that is useful for a variety of tasks, including emergency self-defense. It has a solid steel blade that extends all the way to the far end of the handle and it has a "lanyard" hole.

The **Winchester Folding Knife** in the right picture has three blades -- a standard knife blade, a gut hook, and a saw blade. Each blade locks into position when it is fully extended. This prevents the blade from accidentally closing onto your fingers while you are using the knife. To unlock the blade you must press the blade release lever at the handle end of the knife. This knife also comes with a belt sheath which is not visible in the above picture because it is behind the cardboard insert in the back of the plastic package.

There is a huge body of knowledge on knives and I do not intend to summarize all of that knowledge into this one chapter. However, I would like to make the following four comments:

1. A fixed blade knife that has a steel blade that extends all the way to the far end of the handle is a very strong knife. Some knives have blades that only extend about half-way down inside the handle. This is a cheaper production technique and it results in a weaker knife.
2. A "stainless steel blade" will never rust. A stainless steel blade is more difficult to sharpen but it will hold its edge longer than a non-stainless steel knife.
3. A belt sheath designed specifically for the knife will allow you to conveniently carry the knife on your belt so it will always be within easy reach.
4. To keep your knife sharp you will need an Arkansas Sharpening Stone or a Diamond Sharpening Stone. You will also need to learn the proper way to sharpen your knife.

As you gradually learn more about knives you will discover that different companies make specialty knives for every conceivable purpose. Because of the wide variety of applications it is very easy to become confused about the best knife choice for your particular situation. Therefore, please allow me to make the following recommendations:

1. Buy two knives.
2. Buy a name brand fixed blade knife without a gut hook for maximum flexibility and for self-defense, such as the Winchester Basic for about $16 (picture above), or the Buck Model 119 for approximately $39 (picture on next page). The Buck Model 119 is 10.25 inches long from end to end with a 5.75 inch steel

blade that is approximately one-inch wide. The Buck knife in the picture on the right is a new knife but I have personally had one of these knives since 1972. I used my Buck Model 119 extensively during my Maine adventure in 1975. My old Buck knife is still in excellent condition. The only noticeable thing that Buck has changed over the years is the sheath design.

3. Also buy a name brand folding blade knife with a gut hook for skinning game, such as the Winchester Folding Knife pictured above. Your primary folding knife should have a maximum of no more than three or four blades.
4. Do **not** buy a Swiss Army Knife. If you want a "tool knife" then I suggest you consider the "Leatherman Wave Multi-Tool."

A New Butane Lighter

Fire is an absolute necessity for all the following reasons:

1. Boiling water to make it safe to drink.
2. Cooking fish, wild game, and wild plants to make them more palatable and digestible.
3. Providing heat for comfort if the temperature drops below a reasonable level at night.
4. Quickly lighting a brush fire that will create a lot of smoke to alert and guide rescue search parties, planes, helicopters, or boats to your exact location.

There are a variety of different ways to start a fire, including both modern and primitive methods. **Modern methods** include matches, butane lighters, magnesium fire starters, and a blast match. A complete discussion of these different fire starting methods is in the Fire Chapter of this book.

A Compass

A compass is useful on overcast days, on rainy days, and at night. It will help to keep you from traveling in the wrong direction so you don't waste time and precious energy needlessly. Regardless of where you are, if you can travel consistently in one direction you should eventually reach a road that you can follow. However, without a compass the chances of your traveling in a straight line are greatly reduced.

The **"Coghlan's Six Function Whistle Compass"** shown in the picture on the right can be purchased at some Army Navy Surplus Stores for approximately ten dollars. It contains all of the following items:

1. Compass on front (see bottom of green package - direction finding).
2. Thermometer on back (see top of green package - weather changes).
3. Small mirror in center (partially extending right side of compass - light signaling and face/eye inspection).
4. Magnifying glass in center (partially extending left side of compass).
5. Whistle on bottom (noise signaling for help).
6. LED Flashlight on top (see top of green package - emergency light).

A variety of other ways to determine direction in addition to a compass are discussed in the Compass Chapter in this book.

Conclusion

If you have the above three items and you know how to use them then your chances of survival in the wilderness will be very good. However, if you need some additional practical guidance in the use of these items then I recommend that you include the following book in your "possibilities bag":

SAS Survival Guide, by John "Lofty" Wiseman.

The First Commandment

In five days God created the heavens and the earth,
the sun and the moon, and the birds in the sky.

On the sixth day God formed man from the dust,
and God breathed Life into the man with a sigh.

On the sixth day God blessed man and God said,
"Be fruitful and multiply."

Before God told man that if he ate the fruit from
the Tree of Knowledge he would surely die,

Before God gave man the Ten Commandments
on Tablets of Stone at Mount Sinai,

God first spoke to man on the sixth day and said,
"Be fruitful and multiply."

This Poem is Dedicated to My Granddaughter **Trinity Renee Atkins.**

Scripture References: Genesis 1:1, Genesis 1:26-31, Genesis 2:7, Genesis 2:15-17, Genesis 9:1, Exodus 19:23-25, Exodus 20:1-17, Exodus 24:12.

Chapter Seventy-Four

Compass Instructions and Alternatives
(or How to Find Your Way With or Without a Compass)

A good compass has been a valuable asset to explorers, travelers, and hunters for many centuries. However, as technology advances the traditional compass is gradually being replaced by GPS units (Global Positioning System). The purpose of this chapter is to discuss some alternatives to a compass other than the GPS.

Let's begin be examining the primary function of a compass. The magnetic needle of a compass points to magnetic north. Magnetic north and true north may be slightly different depending on your exact location but they are usually close enough for normal decision making purposes. Looking at the picture of the blue compass on the right, North is on top of the compass, East is on the right, South is on the bottom, and West is on the left. The needle in the center of the compass rotates on a pivot and points to magnetic north (the red side of the needle). If you wish you can rotate the entire compass in your hand until the "N" on the display lines up at the red end of the needle in the center of the compass. The letters **N, E, S,** and **W** on the compass are printed on the fixed display but the needle rotates freely above the display in a protected glass area. To function properly the compass must be held level in a horizontal position.

On some compasses the letters are on a dial on the outside border of the compass. The dial can be moved by hand so you can manually rotate the outside dial until the letter "N" lines up with the magnetic needle inside the compass.

In the picture of the black compass below, the **N, E, S,** and **W** are printed on a floating dial inside the compass. As the dial rotates to magnetic north, the letters automatically line up correctly.

Regardless of which type of compass you have, the relative position of **N, E, S,** and **W** in relation to one another is always the same. Therefore, if you can correctly determine any **one** major compass direction (north, east, south, or west) then you automatically know all **four** compass directions.

Many camping supply stores, including Walmart, sometimes carry a small compass that is part of a multi-function unit that usually includes a miniature thermometer and a whistle (and sometimes a folding magnifying glass). The design of these units vary from one store to the next. In the above picture of the blue compass the thermometer is on top, the compass is in the center, and the whistle is on the bottom of the unit. In the picture of the black compass on the right the compass is on the front side, the whistle is on the bottom, and the thermometer is on the back side of the unit. A small magnifying glass folds into the center of the unit out of the way until it is needed. The thermometer will help you determine the actual temperature (no more guessing). The whistle has a variety of uses such as helping rescue teams determine your location in the event you get really lost.

If you plan on exploring a new area, then it is usually a good idea to carry two compasses with you. The reason is simple -- accidents happen. If your primary compass should become damaged in any way then you would still have a back-up compass to guide you to your destination. A small spare compass is relatively light and you won't notice it unless you need it in an unexpected emergency. Then it could quickly become one of your most valuable assets.

If you should decide to carry two compasses then may I suggest that they be made by different companies. If you should ever **really** need your compass then you can compare the readings on both compasses and if they agree then you can be reasonably comfortable basing your decision on that information. But if both compasses are made by the same company then you may start wondering if some type of manufacturing defect is causing the compasses to malfunction, particularly if your gut instincts tell you that North is in a different direction.

Regardless of how careful you are there is still a possibility you might find yourself in a unexpected situation without a compass. If that happens then it would be advantageous if you knew how to determine the basic compass directions without the aid of a traditional compass.

Let's look at the following six methods for determining basic compass directions:

1. the Sun,
2. the Moon,
3. the Stars,
4. a Straight Stick,
5. a Wrist Watch, and
6. a Simple Homemade Compass.

The Sun

Although this is an obvious method for determining directions, it is included here for completeness. The sun rises in the east and sets in the west. The best time to determine east or west is in the early morning and late evening when the sun is near the horizon. During the middle of the day it is more challenging to accurately determine east and west by simply looking at the sun.

The Moon

Except for the few nights each month when the moon is full or almost full (or the dark new moon), the bright side of the moon always points in the direction of the sun. Between sunset and midnight it will point west towards the setting sun. After midnight it will point east towards the rising sun.

The Stars

In the northern hemisphere the stars appear to rotate around the **North Star** (or **Polaris**) as the Earth spins. It is relatively easy to look at a star chart with all the stars and constellations neatly identified and think that

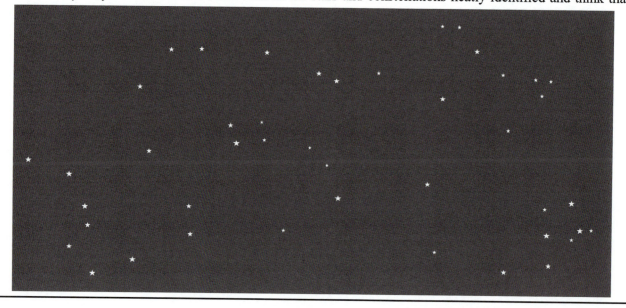

Chapter Seventy-Four: Compass Instructions and Alternatives

finding the North Star is no big deal. However, it is an entirely different challenge to walk outside at night and find the North Star in the sky. For example, look at the illustration on the previous page. Only a **very small** portion of the sky is shown. In addition, only a few of the larger stars in that part of the sky are shown. Can you find the North Star just by looking at the illustration on the previous page?

Identification of the North Star is easier if you can first find the **Big Dipper** or **Cassiopeia**. The **North Star** is approximately half-way between the Big Dipper and Cassiopeia. The North Star is at the handle end of the **Little Dipper**.

The **Big Dipper** may be above, or below, or to the right, or to the left of the North Star. If it is below the North Star then it may be below the horizon and therefore not visible at the current time. The two stars at the cup end of the Big Dipper point towards the North Star. The distance between those two stars when multiplied by five is the approximate distance to the North Star.

Cassiopeia, or the **W**, is on the opposite side of the North Star from the Big Dipper. In my opinion it is much harder to identify by itself. Once again, the **W** may be above, or below, or to the right, or to the left of the North Star. If it is below the North Star then it may be below the horizon and therefore not visible at the current time. The center of the W is about the same distance from the North Star as the Big Dipper.

Although the **Little Dipper** contains the North Star as part of its constellation, the entire Little Dipper may **not** be visible. If it is below the North Star then a good part of the Little Dipper may be below the horizon. The Earth is constantly rotating and the stars will appear to be rotating around the North Star with the passage of time. But it is not the stars that are moving -- it is the Earth. For example, just after dusk the Big Dipper may be clearly visible. But as the Earth rotates then the Big Dipper could disappear below the horizon.

Academic knowledge, such as the above, is only of practical value when you become proficient in its application. When you can walk outside at night and look into the sky and easily find the North Star then you will have mastered this concept.

While you are practicing, you can use the moon to orient yourself. Once you know which way is east and west, then you can determine which way is north. Then you can look in the northern part of the sky and continue your search for the North Star. (Why do you need the North Star if you have the moon? Because sometimes the moon is full, and sometimes there is no visible moon in the sky, and sometimes the moon is behind some heavy clouds but the stars in the northern sky may still be visible.)

In the southern hemisphere the stars appear to rotate around the **Southern Cross**, which is relative easy to find by itself (compared to the North Star by itself). The longer bar of the Southern Cross points south.

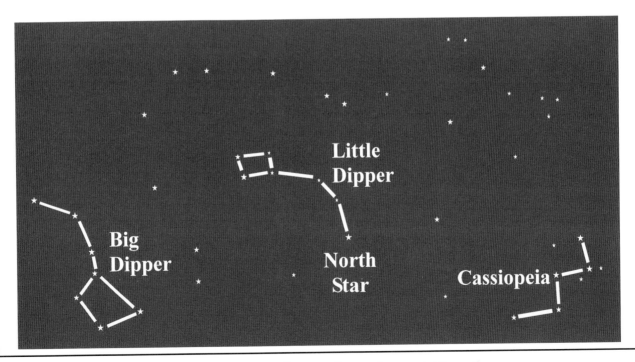

Chapter Seventy-Four: Compass Instructions and Alternatives

A Straight Stick

Method One: Find a relatively straight stick that is about two-feet long. Push one end of the stick far enough into the ground to hold it stationary. Point the opposite end of the stick directly at the sun so the stick **does not cast any shadow**. Wait 30-minutes for the sun to change its position in the sky. The stick will now be casting a very short shadow which will be pointing east.

Method Two: Find a relatively straight stick that is about two-feet long. Push one end of the stick far enough into the ground to hold it stationary. Point the opposite end of the stick straight up into the air so it **does cast a shadow**. Place a small rock at the tip of the stick's original shadow. Wait 30-minutes for the sun to change its position in the sky. Place a second small rock at the tip of the stick's new shadow. A straight line between these two rocks will be pointing from the west to the east, with the position of the first rock indicating west and the position of the last rock indicating east.

In the picture the short stick lying on the ground directly above the compass is aligned west to east with west being on the left side of the picture. The slanted stick in the ground at the top of the picture has a white rock placed at the east end of its shadow (after 30-minutes elapsed). The upright stick in the ground at the bottom of the picture has a white rock at the tip of its shadow (after 30-minutes elapsed). The white rock on the far left was the position of the upright stick's original shadow. The white rocks between the two end rocks were placed on the ground at the end of the 30-minutes so the direction west to east would be clearly visible in the picture.

A Wrist Watch (or Pocket Watch)

If you have an ordinary wrist watch (or pocket watch) with an hour-hand and a minute-hand (or any non-digital clock), then you can determine South by using the sun. This is especially useful during the middle part of the day. If the sun is visible then point the short hour-hand at the sun and **South** will be half-way between the short hour-hand and the number 12 on the watch. This works consistently on standard time. If you are on daylight saving time then use the number 1 instead of the 12. You also need to be north of the equator.

If you are south of the equator then point the number 12 at the sun and **North** will be half-way between the number 12 and the short hour-hand on the watch.

A Simple Homemade Compass

Magnets come in a variety of shapes, such as horseshoe and rectangular. All magnets have north and south poles. If you have a rectangular magnet then tie a thin string or thread to the center of the magnet and tie the opposite end of the string to any stationary object (chair, tree limb, whatever). Adjust the string on the center of the magnet until it is evenly balanced and then wait for the magnet to stop moving. It will be aligned with the north and south poles of the earth. If you know which direction is north then you can mark the ends of the magnet for future reference. However, remember that opposites attract. The south end of the magnet will be pointing to the north pole. The north end of the magnet will be pointing to the south pole.

If you have a magnet and a sewing needle (any size needle or a small nail), then stroke the north end of the magnet along the surface of the sewing needle from its eye to its point. Remove the magnet from the point of the needle, lift it up, and put it on the eye of the needle again. Stroke the needle 30 times from its eye to its point, always in the same direction. Then put a small cork, or chip of wood, or piece of styrofoam in a bowl of still water. Put the needle on top of the cork, wood, or styrofoam. Wait until the needle stops moving and the head of the needle will be pointing north. (Make sure there are no large metal objects nearby or the needle will point to them instead.)

Conclusion

In today's modern world, knowing which direction is north is not necessary very often. If a person wants to go somewhere then a good road map and the ability to decipher that map is usually adequate. However, if a person unexpectedly found himself or herself in a potentially hostile or dangerous environment, or in an unfamiliar environment, then the ability to positively identify compass directions could make the difference between that person's life or death.

Footnote About Bad Advice

You may occasionally see incorrect information on the internet. For example, I once read a very elaborate post about how you could tell if the moon was getting closer to being a full moon or whether it was getting further away from being a full moon. Someone had looked at a new digital clock and had noticed that the illustration on the clock had the quarter-moon facing in one direction before the full moon, and the quarter-moon was facing in the opposite direction after the full moon. The individual immediately leaped to the conclusion that this was a fact of nature and posted his new knowledge on the internet. I watched as about thirty different people added their comments to his original observation but not one of them was aware that his observation was 100% wrong. The bright side of the moon always points towards the sun and this has absolutely nothing to do with whether or not the moon is getting closer to being a full moon or if the full moon has passed. Every night the bright side of the moon will point west towards the setting sun until about midnight, and then after midnight on that same night the bright side of the moon will point east towards the rising sun.

Star Travel

One-million = 1,000,000.
One-billion = 1,000,000,000.
One-trillion = 1,000,000,000,000.

Our Sun is the closest star to Earth and it is 93-million miles away.
Alpha Centauri is the next closest star and it is 26-trillion miles away.

If we had a spaceship that could travel at a speed of one-million miles per hour,
Then we could travel to Alpha Centauri in 2,968 years if we had enough power.

The next time you look up and see all the beautiful stars in the sky at night,
Remember it would take about 3,000 years to travel to just one of those lights.

- - - - - - -

In the beginning God said, "Let there be light." And what God said was instantly done.
On the fourth day God created over 100-billion stars and He named every single one.

It was **easy** for God to create 100-billion stars just like the Bible says that He did.
God spoke and the stars appeared because all creation had to do whatever God said.

- - - - - - -

Are you in a situation or facing a task over which you have no control at all?
Then pray, and have faith, and remember that with God **nothing is impossible**.

Scripture References: Genesis 1:3-5, Genesis 1:14-19, Psalm 147:4, Isaiah 40:26, Matthew 19:26, Luke 18:27, Ephesians 6:18, James 5:12.

Chapter Seventy-Five

Homemade Bow and Arrows

The primary purpose of a primitive homemade bow is to hunt wild game. However, a better way to hunt wild game is with a modern rifle. Even a simple 22-caliber rifle is more accurate at a greater distance that the highest quality factory-made precision bow and arrows.

However, none of us can predict the future. Therefore it is a good idea to have a back-up plan if your hunting rifle is not available or if it can't be used for some totally unexpected reason.

The purpose of this chapter is to provide information on how to make a primitive handmade bow and arrows. However, a good hunter will **not** rely on one single method of putting meat on the table. There is nothing wrong with a handmade spear (a sharpened stick), or hand-set snares, or other animal traps. Your objective is to obtain food and not to impress anyone with how you did it.

With that said let's focus our attention for the duration of this chapter on the topic of a primitive handmade bow and arrows.

A bow increases the range at which you can successfully hunt and put meat into the cook pot. However, the purpose of the bow is to deliver the arrow. The arrow does the job of bringing down the game. The bow is just the delivery device.

A great bow with a lousy arrow has a very small chance of putting meat on the table. However, a poor bow with a great arrow has a much better chance of putting meat in the cook pot. Therefore the arrow is more important than the bow.

In a survival situation you may need meat immediately. Therefore a quickly made bow will be required. While you are using your quickly made bow each day to hunt wild game, you can still be working on a more advanced bow for future hunting expeditions. The same concept applies to the arrows. A quickly made arrow will do in the short term but a better arrow will be preferred in the future.

Let's begin by looking at how to make a primitive handmade bow and arrows very quickly. Then we will look at how to make a better quality homemade bow and arrows.

A Quick Homemade Bow
Accuracy Range: 10 to 20 feet

Wood: Yew, willow, locust, cedar, hickory, ash, oak, elm, birch, or maple (never use pine or a dead tree with its roots still in ground). Select branches, saplings, suckers, or shoots near a creek or stream (their growth rings will be closer together). Your future bow should be as straight as possible with no knots or side branches. Select and cut 2 or 3 potential bow shafts.

Length: 50 inches to 60 inches (from ground to between chest and chin). Cut or saw the wood to length. Do **not** break the wood.

Diameter: At least 1 inch at its center and 3/4 inch at its top end. Never more than 2 inches in diameter at its center.

Test: Step on the center of the bow and grip the two ends in your hands. Bend both ends of the bow 3 or 4 inches. If it breaks then discard it and start over.

Bark: Peel off the bark by hand. Do **not** whittle on the wood. Allow the wood to dry for 24 hours in the shade (not in the sun).

Handle: (Right picture.) Wrap the center of the bow with leather or tape. Wrap the top center of the bow several times to form an arrow rest.

Notches: (Left picture.) Cut string notches at both ends of the bow on each side in a "V" shape towards the inside. Do **not** cut the outside of the bow. Reinforce both ends with a wrap of tape.

Bow String: The string should be 12 inches longer than the bow. Use nylon twine, or string, or a leather strip, or shoe laces tied together. If your string is extremely thin, then twist 3 or more strings together to form a strong bow string.

Attach String: Tie the string securely to the bottom thick end of the bow. Make a loop or slip knot in the other end of the string about 6 inches shorter than the bow. Place the thick end of the bow on the ground on the outside of your left foot. Hold the top end of your bow in your right hand. Lower the bow and step beyond the bow with your right foot and place the back side of your right knee against the inside of the bow. Hold the string slip knot in your left hand and bend the bow across the back of your right knee towards your left hand. Slide the string slip knot over the narrow end of the bow.

Practice: Hold the center of your bow in your left hand with the large end down. Extend your left arm to shoulder level and straight out to your left side (slight bend at elbow). Put an arrow on the left side of your bow on the arrow rest and fit the notched end of the arrow into the string. Pull the notched end back with your right forefinger and thumb (or pull the string back with the top two fingers of your right hand above and below the arrow notch). Sight down the arrow with your right eye. Then move your head out of the way. Release the string and the notched end of the arrow. If necessary, unstring and adjust the bow string slip knot.

Optional Items: Wear a glove on your left hand and a long sleeve shirt. The glove will help protect your left hand from the arrow shaft (and its feathers) as the arrow exits the bow at high speed. The long sleeve shirt will help protect your left forearm from a potential bow string burn. (Note: Most archery supply stores sell a leather forearm pad that straps onto your left forearm to protect it from a bow string burn. Or you could tie a hand towel around your left forearm using some string or shoelaces.)

Storage: Always unstring the bow when it is not in use.

Quick Arrows

Number of Arrows: Start 20 potential arrows. You will probably end up with 5 or 6 good arrows.

Wood: Any straight sapling, shoot, or sucker without branches or knots. They should be between 24 to 30 inches long and between 1/4 to 1/2 inch in diameter. Shorter arrows remain straighter, fly better, and don't break as easily. Remove the bark. Tie all the arrows together into a bunch to help to preserve their straightness. Cure the arrows for one to ten days (but not in the sun) and hand straighten each day as necessary.

Point: Whittle the narrow end of the arrow to a point. Harden the point of a green arrow by charring it over the hot coals from a campfire.

String Notch: Notch the thick end of the arrow for the bow string. Wrap twine around the notch end to strengthen it and to prevent it from splitting.

Practice: Shoot each arrow at a very soft target (a pile of leaves or a pile of some very loose dirt). Keep the arrows that fly straight on a regular basis. Discard the unpredictable arrows.

Chapter Seventy-Five: Homemade Bow and Arrows

A Better Homemade Bow
Accuracy Range: Up to 50 feet
Always have one spare bow ready to replace your primary bow when it wears out.

Wood: Same as the Quick Bow.

Length: Same as the Quick Bow.

Diameter: 1 to 2 inches at center with 1.5 inches the best.

Test: Same as the Quick Bow.

Bark: Same as the Quick Bow.

Bend: Place the thick end of the bow against the toe of your left boot and hold the thin end of the bow loosely with your left hand. Grasp the bow loosely by its center with your right hand and pull it gently towards you. The bow will rotate in your left and right hands until it bends with the natural curve of the wood. Mark or scratch the side of the wood facing you. Later you will string the bow against its natural bend to maximize its power. Do **not** bend the bow again until it is finished.

Removing Wood: Do **not** whittle on the wood. Hold the edge of your knife straight up and down against the wood (at a 90 degree angle) and scrape off a tiny amount of wood with each motion. Do **not** tilt the blade so it can cut into the wood. Always remove wood from the center towards the end of the bow. Don't remove any wood from the outside of the bow. Remove wood from the inside (the string side) and the two sides only. Be patient. Work slowly. Be patient.

Shaping: Leave the center round so it fits your hand comfortably. Start a little above the center of the bow and shape towards the narrow end. There is less wood there and it will determine the shape of the opposite end. Taper the wood from the center to a 3/4 inch diameter at the top end. The bow shape can be round over its entire length but it should gradually get smaller in diameter from center to top. (Note: If you wish to gradually flatten and taper the bow from the center to its ends in an oval shape you will have a superior shape but you will also invest a lot more effort.) When you finish the top end then shape the bottom thick end of the bow so it matches the top end.

Seasoning: Lay the bow down in a warm dry spot (but not in the sun) and let it dry for two days. After two days warm the bow near a fire and rub it down with oil or animal fat. Rub the bow with a cloth for an hour. Then let it dry near the fire and then rub it down with more oil or animal fat. Continue drying and rubbing oil into the bow until the wood is saturated. The bow is now ready for use. In the future, about once a week, rub the bow down with oil (or animal fat) and let it dry. The oil (or fat) will make the wood more flexible and keep it from cracking.

Handle, Notches, String: Same as the Quick Bow.

Attach String: Same as the Quick Bow **except** bend the bow against its natural curve when you attach the string.

Better Arrows

Arrowheads: Split the thick end of the arrow and insert the arrowhead. Tie the arrowhead to the thick end inside the split. Arrowheads are useful for hunting larger animals, such as deer, but they are **not** needed for smaller animals, such as squirrels and rabbits.

String Notch: Notch the thin end of the shaft for the bow string.

Feathers: Cut wing or tail feathers in half down the quill. (Or use thin plastic cut into a right-triangular shape, about 4 inches long and 1/2 inch high.) Cut a very thin scratch at the notch end of the arrow the same length as the feather to help hold the feather quill stationary. Use dental floss, fishing line, or thread to tie 3 feathers equally spaced at the end of the arrow near the string notch. (Note: If you have some glue then glue the feather to the thin scratch and then tie the feathers to the arrow.)

Spiral or Spin: If you would like for your arrow to spiral while it is in flight (like a football or a bullet from a rifled barrel), then attach the feathers to the rear of the arrow shaft so each feather twists 1/3 of the way around the shaft. The back of the feather should twist 1/3 of the way around the shaft from the front of the feather. This will sometimes improve the ability of the arrow to fly straighter towards its target.

Chapter Seventy-Six

How to Catch Wild Game
Using Professional Quality Snares and Steel Traps

Always Consult and Obey Your Local and State Hunting and Trapping Laws.

This chapter will briefly discuss professional quality snares and the different types of steel traps. These devices are used to catch wild game and therefore they can seriously injure you if you are not careful while you are handling them. If you are careless then there is a good chance you could hurt yourself. Therefore you should proceed at your own risk.

There are three different devices that can be used to catch wild game as follows:

1. Professional Quality Snares.
2. Conibear Steel Traps.
3. Pan Steel Traps.

Each of the above devices will be discussed in this chapter.

Professional Quality Snares

The snare in the picture below is a professional quality snare made for professional trappers. The parts of the snare are indicated in the picture.

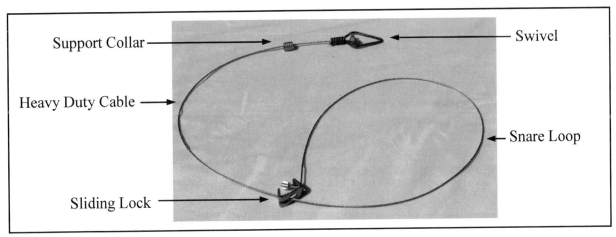

Snare Setting Options

There are three basic ways to set snares:

1. **Spring Snare:** On the ground but tied to a bent branch to lift the animal off the ground when snared.
2. **Ground Snare:** On the ground or on a slanted tree and secured to a tree trunk or stake driven into the ground.
3. **Water Snare:** In the water and secured to a stake driven into the ground.

Wire Size: 20 gauge to 28 gauge wire might work for the first option above but it will **not** work for the other two. If the animal is on the ground when it is caught then it will fight the snare and within two minutes it will either twist the wire so badly it will break, or the animal will chew through the wire with its teeth. It does not matter if the wire is galvanized, or coated, or copper -- it is too thin and it will **not** work. You must use heavy duty wire with a swivel if you intend to set the last two types of snares above. However, if you set the first type of snare then the animal will be hanging by its neck and the light weight wire will strangle the animal because it will not be able to gain any leverage in the air.

How to Repair a Professional Quality Snare

An animal will fight the snare when it is caught. Sometimes the snare cable will become twisted and chewed on and the snare wire will become severely damaged. If you were using a **long** snare cable for larger animals then you may be able to salvage part of the wire cable and convert it into a **shorter** snare for snaring smaller animals.

Even if the entire wire cable is ruined, all the other parts of the snare are still fine and they should be saved and attached to a new piece of heavy duty cable (save the lock, the swivel, and all the other parts on the snare). Only the snare cable itself should be discarded (or used for some other purpose).

How to Season Professional Quality Snares

A new snare is made from bright shiny heavy-duty airline cable. The shiny surface of the cable must be converted into a dull finish in order to help it blend into the natural forest environment. Shiny cables are very easy to see and animals will notice and avoid them. Dull cables are not easy to see and therefore they will not be avoided by the animals you are trying to catch.

Separate each individual cable from all the others so each cable is by itself. Open and close the snare end of the cable about 20 times to remove any tiny burrs on the aircraft cable. This will allow the snare to close quickly and smoothly around the animal at the proper time.

Fill a large **metal** pot about half full of water and bring it to a boil. (Do not use a Teflon coated pot or you may scratch the interior surface with the metal snares). Place all of your snares in the boiling water so each snare is completely under water. Very slowly add one cup of baking soda to the boiling water. The boiling water will foam up when you add the baking soda so add it very slowly to keep the pot from foaming over onto the stove. Reduce the heat to medium so the water is just barely bubbling. Boil for about 15 minutes. Turn off the heat and pour the soda water solution down the drain of a nearby stainless steel kitchen sink. The snares will fall into the bottom of the stainless steel sink. Let the snares cool for a few minutes and then thoroughly rinse them using warm or cool water to remove all the baking soda residue. The snares are now seasoned and they may now be used to catch wild animals.

How to Form a Professional Quality Snare Loop

When you first examine the snare opening you will see that it forms a tear drop shape. This is **not** the desired shape. Use your hands to bend the snare wire cable so that it looks more like a circle instead of a tear drop. The size of the circle should match the size you intend to use when you actually set your snares. Open and close the snare about 10 times to remove any new burrs that may have appeared after the baking soda seasoning process.

How to Store Professional Quality Snares

Form the snare opening into the size loop that you intend to use when you set the snare. Then wrap the other end of the snare cable in and out of the circle several times until you reach the end of the cable. The snare can now be stored and the circle you just created will gradually become the natural size circle that the snare will "remember" when you later use your snare.

How to Set a Professional Quality Snare

A snare is of no value if you can't find it the next day. Lost snares mean lost equipment. You must be able to find your snares **after** you set them. Look for nearby landmarks that will help you remember exactly where you set your snares. Before you risk loosing your snares you should put something of little value, such as a penny or a nail, at the spot where you plan to put your snare and then see if you can find it the next day. Take some notes on how you got to that location and then see if you can find that same exact location the next day by referring to your notes and the landmarks you identified. If you will practice first then you can avoid the loss of your equipment.

Chapter Seventy-Six: Snares and Traps

Look for a well used animal trail. Then follow the trail and look for a place where the trail becomes relatively narrow due to natural obstacles (trees, bushes, large rocks, gully, steep hill bank, etc.).

Use 14 gauge wire to secure the swivel end of the snare to a nearby narrow tree trunk. Or attach it to a heavy short log (called a drag). If necessary, drive a stake deep into the ground and attach the snare to the stake.

Form the snare loop into a circle of the proper size and place the snare circle in the very center of the path. If possible, the snare slide should be at the top of the snare circle loop. The snare should not be touching the ground. Attach some spare 14 gauge wire to a nearby tree trunk or a tree branch (or a stick you force into the ground) and use the 14 gauge wire to support the snare circle at the correct height off the ground.

Push a few 2-foot to 3-foot long sticks into the ground at random spots to narrow the trail so the animal must pass through the exact spot where you placed your snare. This is called "blocking" or "fencing." Lean or wedge a stick or branch against the tree and above the snare so the animal will not be tempted to try to jump over the snare. This is called a "duck stick" because it forces the animal to duck its head into the snare loop.

Muskrat: 3" circle with entire snare below water and 1/2 inch above bottom of pond.

Rabbit: 4" to 5" circle 2 inches off ground.

Raccoons: 8" circle 3 inches off ground (tree snare = 5" or 6" circle 2 inches off tree).

Coyote: 12" circle 10 inches off ground.

Beaver: 12" circle with 1/2 of the circle under water.

Deer: 14" circle 16 inches off ground with a "Duck Stick" just above the top of the loop.

Squirrels and raccoons and possums like to climb trees. If you see a tree growing at a 30 to 45 degree angle then it will probably be used by animals to gain access to the tree canopy above the forest floor. Set a snare at waist level on the top side of the slanted tree so the bottom of the snare loop is 2 inches above the tree trunk and the snare circle is perfectly centered above the tree trunk.

Another option is to lean a pole or thick tree branch against a tree and then set your professional quality snare (or a series of cheap loop wires) along your improvised tree run.

Steel Traps

There are two basic types of steel traps:

1. **Conibear traps** that have side springs and a dual wire trigger with a latch (called a dog) that hooks over the trigger. The 110 size has one side spring and the 220 and 330 have two side springs.

2. **Pan traps** that have two jaws and a pan between the open jaws and a latch (called a dog) that hooks onto the pan.

New traps should be seasoned and adjusted prior to use. Some of the companies that sell steel traps will also season those traps for you if you are willing to pay a small additional fee. My recommendation is that if you find a supplier who offers to do this then you should take advantage of this service. These suppliers sometimes sell their traps on ebay.

If you season your traps yourself then look through the supplier's web site and purchase some trap dye at the same time you order your traps.

Finally, regardless of how your traps are seasoned, your traps will gradually acquire some rust when they are put into actual use. If you are aware of this ahead of time then you will not be shocked when you first notice the rust when you check on your traps after they have been set.

Seasoning traps: Place the new traps in some hot soapy water and wash off the protective oily factory coating. Place the traps outside on the ground for two weeks to allow them to weather and acquire a little rust. Then use some trap dye (purchased from the same company where you bought your traps) to dye the traps a more natural color so the trap will blend in with the normal forest environment.

Pan Traps - How to Adjust the Pan Height: Open the trap and set the hook (called the dog) onto the pan so the trap is ready to be used. The pan is in the center of the trap and when an animal steps on it, it releases the dog and the trap jaws close on the animal's leg or paw. For the trap to work correctly, the pan of the trap must be level with the two surrounding jaws of the trap. Look at the trap from the side and adjust the height of the pan accordingly. **Be careful not to hurt yourself.** Some traps have a pan screw adjustment that lets you elevate or lower the pan by twisting the screw. Some pans do not have a screw adjustment and you must use a heavy duty screwdriver or pliers where the pan is attached to bend it up or down so the pan is level with the jaws of the trap.

Pan Traps - How to Adjust the Chain Length: The chain on most pan traps is too long. A long chain gives the animal more maneuverability and a better chance to escape from the trap. A short chain keeps the animal in a very small area and makes it more difficult for the animal to get loose. Examine the chain and remove a few links so the chain is about 8 inches long. Save the links in case you wish to increase the chain length later. Reattach the swivel to the end of the shortened chain.

Where to Set the Traps

In freezing weather conditions put a "tiny amount" of antifreeze on the hinges of the trap so the trap can close and not freeze into an open position.

Look for a well used animal trail. Then follow the trail and look for a place where the trail becomes relatively narrow due to natural obstacles (trees, bushes, large rocks, gully, steep hill bank, etc.).

How to Set Steel Traps

Pan Traps - Use 14 gauge wire to secure the trap swivel to a nearby tree or to a stake driven deep into the ground. Dig a shallow depression in the forest floor at a narrow spot in the trail. The trap needs to sit in the depression so the top of the trap, including the pan, is just a tiny bit below the forest floor. Pack the dirt around the outside jaws of the trap to secure the trap in position. Sprinkle the dirt on the inside of the jaws of the trap but do not fill the area below the pan. Sprinkle a little dirt on the pan so it is hidden. Place some small leaves or pine needles over the entire trap area. Place a "step stick" directly in front of and behind the trap on the trail so an animal coming in either direction will need to step over the stick and place its paw in the middle of the trap on the pan. Each step stick should be about 1 inch in diameter and at least as wide as the trail. A step stick should be placed flat on the trail about one inch away from both sides of the trap.

Pan

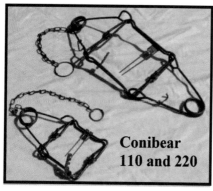
Conibear 110 and 220

Conibear Traps: Ground or Trail Set - Open the trap (use a special spreading tool on the size 220 and 330). On the size 220 and 330 traps set the safety on each of the two springs. Use 14 gauge wire to secure the swivel end of the conibear trap to a nearby tree or to a stake driven into the ground. Find a good size stick that will fit tightly between the two metal pieces that form the outsides of the square trap. Wedge the stick tightly between the two sides of the trap and then fasten the latch (dog) to the two-wire trigger. On the small 110 trap use the middle latch (dog) notch. On the medium and large traps (220 and 330) use the inside notch for the tightest fit. Do **not** remove the two spring safeties until **after** the trap is completely set into position. The conibear trap should not fall off the stick when you shake the stick gently. Push the stick into the ground so the conibear trap is in the center of the trail. The two trip wires should be on the top of the trap pointing down towards the ground. (Note: The ends of the two trip wires can be bent slightly so they form a small U" shape towards the outside of the trap.) Lean a "duck stick" above the trap against a tree or bush so the animal will have to duck and go through the trap instead of trying to jump over the trap. If the weather is freezing then place two small sticks on the ground under the conibear trap to keep it off the freezing ground. Place some leaves and sticks on and around the trap itself to break up its outline and disguise it. If necessary, push some sticks into the ground to narrow the path and force the animal into the trap. After the trap is completely set then remove the two safety catches from the two side springs.

Conibear Traps: Tree Set - Look for a tree that is growing at a 30 to 45 degree angle from the ground. Set the trap at waist height. Drive two nails into the tree trunk and bend them at a slight outward angle to hold the two jaws of the conibear trap in position. Then put the conibear trap on the outside of the two nails so the nails hold the trap upright on the tree trunk.

Wire the swivel end of the trap to the tree trunk using 14 gauge wire. Place leafy sticks around the trap to help disguise it. The final step is to remove the two safety catches from the two springs. If you use bait then place a very small amount near the base of the tree and place most of the bait past the trap higher up on the tree. Put leaves over the bait so it can not be seen by the birds. However, the bait can still be smelled by passing animals.

Types of Bait

Conibear traps should have the bait placed just beyond the trap in order to encourage an animal to stick its head through the trap to get to the bait.

Pan traps should have the bait tied to a piece of vine and then suspended from a tree branch above the pan trap so the bait is between 18-inches to 24-inches above the pan trap. The animal will be looking at the bait and trying to smell the bait and the animal will usually not notice the pan trap until after stepping into it and getting caught by the leg. If you have enough extra traps then it is a good idea to put two or three pan traps on the outside of an 18-inch diameter circle on the ground below the bait.

1. Put a little **peanut butter** before or beyond a conibear trap, or suspended above a pan trap.

2. **Fish heads** should be placed beyond a conibear trap in a small hole with the trap in front of the hole, or suspended above a pan trap.

3. Push the center of a cut two-inch long **corn cob containing dried or fresh corn** onto the two trip wires of the conibear trap.

4. Remove **acorns** from their shells and place them in a row leading into and though the trap to the other side of the trap where most of the acorns are piled. Leave the broken shells beside the acorns so it looks natural.

How to Butcher an Animal

All animals are easier to skin immediately after they have been killed. Always use plastic or rubber gloves when handling animals to prevent the spreading of any disease. Gut the animal and remove its internal organs and then skin the animal if you wish to preserve its furry pelt. If you do not want the fur then cut the meat away from the bones and put the meat into a plastic zipper freezer bag for transport. Remove all the fat because it will go rancid very quickly.

Additional Trapping Information Online

Additional information from two of the ten Bushcraft Books can be viewed at the following two links:

Snares and Traps (Part 1):
http://tions.net/CA256EA900408BD5/vwWWW/outdoor~03~081

Tracks and Lures (Part 1):
http://tions.net/CA256EA900408BD5/vwWWW/outdoor~03~071

A Comprehensive 157 Page State of Michigan Trapper Instruction Manual (pdf file = 8.13 MB) is at the following link:
http://www.michigan.gov/documents/dnr/MI_Trapper_Education_Manual_82307_206561_7.pdf

Tips for Hunting Wild Game using Firearms, Traps, and Snares

1. Animals are more nutritious than most wild plants. But they are more difficult and time consuming to obtain.
2. Animals remain alive by being constantly alert. Their senses are superior to ours. Their physical attributes are superior for flight, fight, and hiding. The only advantage humans have is their brain.
3. A firearm is better than a bow and arrows for putting meat in the pot. Snares and traps are better than a firearm because they will work 24 hours per day seven days per week after they have been properly set.
4. Sunrise and sunset are the best hunting times.
5. The best way to hunt with a firearm or a bow is to sit quietly out-of-sight downwind along a trail leading to a water source.
6. If you have a semi-automatic hunting rifle then put two quick shots into the heart/lung chest area of a medium to large game animal.
7. If a wounded animal runs away then wait 5 minutes and then follow the blood trail. It will lie down if not pursued and become too weak to move.
8. Any wounded animal is dangerous. Approach it cautiously and kill it quickly and safely. Gut and bleed all animals immediately after the kill.
9. If you see a rabbit during the day then it can be temporarily frozen by emitting a sharp whistle.
10. When you skin and gut an animal, leave its entrails on the ground as bait. Set a series of snares along paths leading to the butchering area.
11. Observe birds. Their flight pattern may reveal their nest and their eggs. Efforts to obtain small birds far exceed any nourishment they provide.
12. A weighted net may be used as a casting snare. Throw the weighted net over the animal, or over the small bush in which the animal or bird is hiding.
13. Thin flexible wire is better than string for setting snares because animals can't chew through it to free themselves. 20 or 22 gauge wire is preferred for small and medium size game animals. However, 26 or 28 gauge may be used for very small game animals, such as squirrels. 20 to 28 gauge wire should be used in a "spring snare" which is tied to a bent tree branch that is under pressure so that it will lift the animal up off the ground so it hangs by its neck when it trips the snare trigger. If you set "ground snares" without a "spring" then a professional quality 14 gauge snare wire with a swivel will be required.
14. Don't set traps or snares on well used trails. Animals know their territory and avoid the unusual. Set traps on side trails.
15. Do not use whittled wood for traps. Leave the bark on snare sticks. Carved notches should be darkened by rubbing dirt on the carved area.
16. Check your traps every morning and every evening.
17. Snares and traps should be moved to a new location every four or five days.
18. Do not set traps that could hurt people.

Chapter Seventy-Seven

Gill Nets:
The Easy, Efficient Way to Catch Fish for the Frying Pan
(Check Your State and Local Laws for any Restrictions on the Use of Gill Nets.)

Introduction

Generally any type of fish net is an offense to the average recreational sport fisherman. For these individuals fishing is only a hobby or a sport and his fishing success or failure each day does not impact the future survival of his family.

On the other hand, if his family's survival depended not only on his ability to catch fish but also on his ability to do a wide variety of other chores every day, then the average sport fisherman would probably change his opinion about fish nets.

In defense of fish nets it should be noted that:

1. At least eight of Jesus' disciples used nets to catch fish: Simon Peter and his brother Andrew, James and John the sons of Zebedee, Thomas (called Didymus), Nathanael from Cana in Galilee, and two other disciples not specifically named (Matthew 4:15-22 and John 21:1-3).

2. Jesus approved of the use of fish nets (Matthew 15:35-39, John 6:10-13, and John 21:8-13).

3. Jesus gave His disciples specific instructions on how to use fish nets to catch the maximum number of fish (Luke 5:4-7 and John 21:4-6).

Therefore if Jesus approved of the use of fish nets, then perhaps we should not be too quick to criticize them.

Gill Net Basics

There are a lot of different types and designs of fish nets. This chapter will only discuss one type of fish net that is called a "Gill Net."

Gill Nets have been the subject of several different research studies in a variety of states including Florida, Georgia, Kentucky, Louisiana, Michigan, Mississippi, Oklahoma, Texas, Virginia, Washington, and Canada. These studies date back to the 1970s. These studies include tests using both monofilament nets and nylon nets, in a variety of different mesh sizes, and in side-by-side comparisons that were conducted during all twelve months of the year. The average results from these different studies have been consolidated and included in the test result summaries that appear in this chapter.

Applications: Gill nets may be used in either fresh water or salt water.

Mesh Size: Nets are classified based on the size of the mesh. The mesh opening is formed into a square and the length of any one side of the square is referred to as the size of the mesh.

The size of the mesh will determine the size of the fish caught in the net. For example, an average size mesh will allow smaller fish to swim through the net. Larger fish will not be able to enter the mesh. A fish of the proper average size will be able to push its head through the net but it fins will prevent it from swimming through the net. When it tries to back out of the net the fish will get caught by its gills and the fish will be trapped.

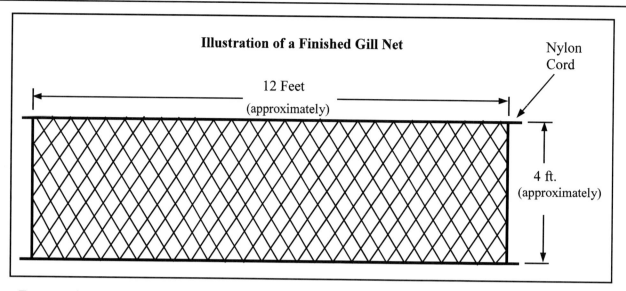

Tests conducted on different mesh sizes yielded the following results:

1. Mesh sizes of one inch or less capture too many small fish that are not big enough to eat. This is wasteful because these small fish will not have the opportunity to grow into a size that would provide a "good meal."

2. Mesh sizes of two inches or more allow too many average size good quality edible fish to escape. However, if you are **only** interested in the larger, longer, heavier fish then this larger mesh size is more effective for capturing these bigger fish.

3. For the average fish, the most efficient mesh size is between 1 1/2 inches to 1 5/8 inches (3.8 cm to 4.1 cm). This size mesh will catch the maximum number of fish of average edible size, plus a reasonable number of larger fish. It will also catch more total pounds of edible fish each day.

Gill Net Dimensions: The length and width of your Gill Net should be based on where you intend to use your net. If you will be using your net in a gentle flowing river or stream, and the stream is only 15 feet across and only three feet deep, then a 12-foot by 4-foot Gill Net would work well. But if you are using your net in a huge lake (or other body of water) that is 15 or more feet deep then a 50-foot by 10-foot Gill Net would be a better choice.

Harvesting: Several fish can be caught during one day with a Gill Net. Therefore you should check your Gill Net at least once per day and remove the fish and then reset the net. If you catch more fish than your family can eat in one day, then you should not reset your net until your family has consumed all the fish you have already caught. However, if you have the means to preserve your catch of fresh fish for future consumption then you may reset your net immediately.

Cleaning: Nets cleaned of debris once each day are twice as efficient as nets that are only cleaned once every two days.

Location: Fish are somewhat territorial. Therefore when your daily catch starts to decline then it is time to move your net to a new location.

Storage: When you are not using your Gill Net you should store it inside a plastic bucket, or a plastic container, or a Ziploc Freezer bag. Punch several small holes in the storage device so moisture can gradually drain out and evaporate, and the net can gradually dry out.

Gill Net Material

Gill Nets may be made from two basic types of fishing line: **monofilament** or **nylon**. Some commercial fishermen will only use nets made from one or the other of these materials. Their choice is based on their past experience in their specific fishing region and the type of fish in that region. If you know any of these experienced commercial fishermen then you should ask them for their advice on this topic. Most of these fishermen will probably be happy to share their knowledge with you. However, I suggest that you speak to at least two or three different fishermen to get a better idea of what works best for the average fishermen in your area.

If you do not know any commercial fishermen then the following advantages and disadvantages of the different types of fishing nets may help you to make the best choice for your particular future application:

Monofilament nets have the following **advantages:**
1. They can be set and retrieved faster.
2. They experience fewer tangle problems.
3. On the average they incur less damage than a nylon net.
4. They do not adhere to twigs, sticks, or weeds and therefore these items may be more easily removed from the net.
5. A monofilament net is much easier to clean than a nylon net.
6. Fish may be removed faster and easier from a monofilament net.
7. They are clear and they can't be seen by the fish. Therefore they catch more fish during the day and at twilight.
8. They catch more different types of fish.
9. They catch more total fish of the same type.
10. On the average a monofilament net will catch twice as many pounds of fish as a nylon net.

Monofilament nets have the following **disadvantages:**
1. They are more expensive than nylon nets.
2. They are not as flexible as nylon nets.
4. The mesh does not stick to the fish as easily as nylon nets. Therefore it is possible for a fish to more easily escape from the net if it is not entangled in some other way in the net.
4. In the dark of night a monofilament net has the same efficiency as a nylon net.

Nylon nets have the following **advantages:**
1. They are usually less expensive than monofilament nets.
2. They are more flexible and therefore they more easily cling to the fish.
3. They will gradually become stained the same color as the water in which they are set. This will gradually make them more difficult to see. Therefore do not try to wash the water stains off a nylon net.

Nylon nets have the following **disadvantages:**
1. In addition to fish nylon nets also more easily cling to everything else, including all types of sticks, twigs, and weeds. Therefore nylon nets are very difficult to clean.
2. It is more difficult to remove fish from a nylon net.
3. Nylon nets tangle up more easily and they are more difficult to untangle.

The State of Louisiana conducted a two-year test on Gill Nets that ended in 1981. They tested both monofilament nets and nylon nets in a variety of different mesh sizes. The different nets were sewn together side-by-side and they were used in the same waters at exactly the same time. Most species of fish could be caught by either net. However, thirteen different species of fish could only be caught in the monofilament webbing. And four species of fish could only be caught in the nylon webbing. Overall the most efficient mesh size for both monofilament nets and nylon nets was 1 5/8 inch (approximately 4 cm).

Therefore, unless I had a very good reason to use a nylon net, then I would personally prefer to have a Gill Net made from monofilament line instead of nylon line. The reason is because monofilament line is more versatile, and it will capture more different types of fish, and it will capture more total pounds of fish each day.

Gill Net Construction

1. Use braided nylon cord or braided polypropylene cord or parachute cord for the top support line of the Gill Net. This "Top Cord" should be between 1/8-inch to 3/16-inch in diameter. The length will depend on how big a Gill Net you wish to construct. The Gill Net in the illustration earlier in this chapter has a 13-foot long "Top Cord."

2. Use medium or heavy weight fishing line for the mesh. The weight of the fishing line should be based on:
   a. The maximum size fish normally caught in your area (the weight of one fish).
   b. The size or total square footage of your Gill Net (the total number of fish that will be captured each day).

   10-pound to 15-pound fishing line is adequate for smaller nets (12-feet by 4-feet) and average size fish (one or two-pound fish).

   20-pound to 30-pound fishing line will be needed for larger nets (25 feet by 8-feet) and larger size fish (three pound or larger fish).

   If you will be using your Gill Net in a variety of different areas to catch a variety of different types of fish then a 25-pound line is a good choice.

3. For a 12-foot long net, cut a 30-foot long piece of fishing line. This will be used to tie your top row of Gill Net diagonals.

4. Tie the fishing line into a mesh pattern going from left-to-right to the thin nylon top cord at 1.5-inch intervals (4 cm) with a 60-degree angle going down to a temporary support stick and a 60-degree angle going back up to the thin nylon top cord with an up and down length of approximately 1.5-inch in each direction. (Note: Some sources recommend tying the line from right-to-left instead of left-to-right. Depending on whether you are right-handed or left-handed, you may do it the way that is most comfortable for you.) The long wood stick or piece of wire will keep the fishing line from becoming tangled.

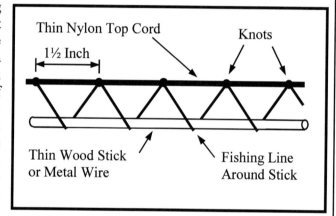

Tie the fishing line to the thin nylon top cord. Continue looping the fishing line around the wood stick and tying the fishing line to the thin nylon top cord until you reach the right end of your Gill Net. Then tie the fishing line to a straight piece of nylon cord that will run from the top to the bottom of the Gill Net (see the illustration of a finished Gill Net earlier in this chapter).

Note: Instead of two thin wood sticks you could use two plastic water pipes. The Top Cord should be lying flat against the pipe. The equation for the circumference of a circle is $C = (3.1416) \times (diameter)$. A one-inch outside diameter pipe will have a circumference of approximately 3.14-inches which will yield a finished square mesh size of approximately 1.57 inches or a little less than 1 5/8 inches. A 1.25-inch outside diameter pipe will yield a square mesh of approximately 2-inches. A 1.5-inch outside diameter pipe will yield a square mesh of approximately 2 3/8 inches. One side of the square mesh will be approximately equal to one-half the circumference around the outside of the pipe.

5. Cut another 30-foot long piece of fishing line. This will form your second row of Gill Net diagonals. You will need a second wood stick or piece of wire to hold the bottom of this piece of fishing line stable just like you did on the top row of fishing line diagonals. Tie the fishing line to the bottom of each loop of the top fishing line with a knot, then loop around the bottom stick, and repeat until you reach the end of your Gill Net. At this time you can remove the upper stick and use it for your next row of diagonals.

6. The interior mesh diagonals will be two sizes. The shorter diagonal (side to side) will be approximately 1.5-inches (4 cm) wide, and the longer diagonal (top to bottom) will be approximately 2.5-inches (6.3 cm)

long. However, this net would be called a 1.5-inch mesh (4 cm) because the mesh could be stretched into a 1.5-inch square. To create this finished pattern, tie a knot every 1.5-inches. The size of the opening should be based on the average size of the head of the fish in your area. The head of the fish should be able to enter the net up to a point past its gills. However, the body of the fish should **not** be able to pass completely through the opening in the net. If the fish in your area are larger than normal then you should increase the size of the diagonals by tying the individual knots further apart than 1.5-inches, such as 1.75-inches, or 2-inches, or 2.25 inches, or 2.5-inches (4.4 cm to 6.3 cm).

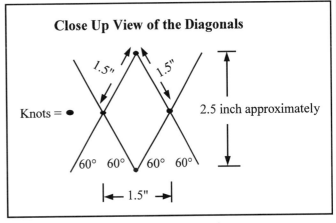

7. Cut a second long piece of thin nylon cord about 13-foot long and tie it to bottom of the mesh diagonals so it can be used to anchor the Gill Net to the bottom of the river after it is placed in the water. Remove and discard the two wood sticks that were used to keep the fishing line from becoming tangled during construction. Your finished Gill Net should look like the illustration earlier in this chapter. (Note: The length and width of your net may be bigger or a little smaller than the illustration.)

How to Use a Gill Net

Gill Nets are generally **not** used like a conventional fish net. A conventional fish net is cast into the water in the hope that it will fall over the fish and capture the fish inside the net. A Gill Net is typically **not** used this way. A Gill Net also does **not** use any fish hooks.

The correct way to use a Gill Net is to tie a long rope to each of the top corners of the Gill Net. Later you will use these ropes to pull the net of fish from the water.

There are two basic types of Gill Nets:

1. **Tie-Down (TD) Nets:** Used in flowing water (rivers and streams). A Tie-Down Net has a bottom line and weights are attached to the bottom line to hold the net in position in the moving water.

2. **Flag Nets:** Used in still waters (ponds and lakes). A Flag Net has a top line but it usually does not have a bottom line. It is supported by the top line in a manner similar to a cloth flag that is hung on a flag pole by one side of the cloth flag. However, a flag net is hung straight down into the water and not out to the side like a cloth flag blowing in the wind.

Floats may or may not be attached along the top line of either a Tie-Down Net or a Flag Net depending on your specific application.

There are a variety of different ways to use the above two different types of Gill Nets:

1. **Moving Water Tie-Down Net (Gentle Stream or Gentle River):** Secure the end of each rope to a tree or other stationary object near the water so the net can be stretched straight across the water. Tie several weights (rocks) to the bottom of the Gill Net. Drop the weighted bottom of the net into a stream or river. If possible, the entire net should be under water. The fish will not see the thin mesh of the net and the fish will swim into it. Small fish will swim through. But the head of a larger fish will enter the net but its body will not pass through the net. The front gills of the fish will become caught in the net as it tries to free itself. (**Note:** Do not attempt to use a Gill Net in a fast moving stream because any large foreign objects floating down the stream will rip the Gill Net to pieces.)

2. **Still Water Flag Net (Lake or Pond):** Secure the end of each rope to a tree branch near the water so the net can be stretched straight across the curved bank of a lake. The tree branch should have some flexibility in it so the Gill Net can move one or two-feet with the swimming action of a fish. Do not attach

any weights to the lower edge of the Gill Net. Lower the net into the lake or pond.

Side, Middle, and Top Net Catch: The fish will swim into the net and the net will move forward with the fish for a short distance. When the net begins to slow the fish down and the fish feels the net against its body then the fish will try to turn and get out of the net. But the sides of the net will cling to the fish and the fish will get tangled up inside the net.

Bottom Net Catch: Lower the net until about six to twelve-inches of the net is lying on the bottom of the pond. If a fish swims towards the lower part of the net and turns away from the net then the turning action of the fish will cause the bottom of the net to rise up and surround the fish. As the fish tries to escape it will become entangled in the bottom of the net.

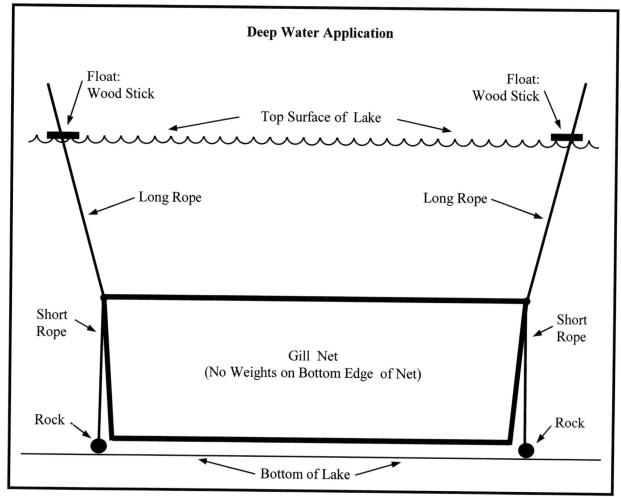

3. **Deep Water Flag Net:** Determine the depth of the water by tying a heavy rock to a long nylon rope and then lower the rope until the rock touches the bottom of the lake. When your raise the rope you can determine how deep the water is at that location. Tie a nylon rope that is one-foot wider than the net to each of the **top** two corners of the net. For example, if you have a 12-foot long by 4-foot wide net then tie a 5-foot rope to each **top** end of the 12-foot long net. Tie a weight to the bottom end of each of these 5-foot short ropes. Then tie two more long ropes to the top edge of the 12-foot long net. These two long ropes will need to be long enough so they can be tied to two trees on the bank of the lake. Tie some type of float (piece of wood) to these ropes at the exact depth that you want the net to be under water. Lower the net down into the water and then secure the ends of the long ropes to some trees on the bank of the lake.

Rope Note: Instead of cutting your nylon rope to the desired lengths it is better to simply tie one really long rope to the top edge of the Gill Net so that approximately 5-feet of the rope extends down the side of the net. Tie a rock to this short end of the rope. Then tie the long end of the rope to a tree on the bank of the lake. Any rope that is left over can be coiled around the tree trunk or it can be coiled onto the ground beside the tree. This will allow you to keep your ropes at their maximum length for use in a variety of different deep water applications.

In deep waters you should experiment and determine if the Gill Net is more effective in one of the following two situations:

   a. When its lower edge is about one-foot above the bottom of the lake (see illustration on the previous page), or
   b. When it has one-foot of its lower edge lying on the bottom of the lake (tie rocks higher on the short ropes).

4. **Shallow Water Flag Net:** In shallow water the Gill Net may be used like a conventional fish net. If you have a partner then your partner should hold one side of the net and you should hold the other side. If you don't have a partner then you could hold one side of the net in each hand, or you could secure one side of the net to a tree that is growing close to the water. Lower the bottom of the Gill Net down into the water so that the bottom of the net touches the bottom of the stream bed. Pull the net through the water and towards the bank of the stream. Remove any fish that are caught inside the net. This technique is extremely effective when you can actually see the fish swimming in the shallow waters of the stream.

5. **Emergency Survival Tie-Down Net:** In a true survival situation a Gill Net may also be used as a Weighted Net to capture birds or small animals. Tie several small rocks to various locations around the outside edge of your net and then toss the weighted net so that it falls over the bird or the animal on the ground, or over the small bush in which the bird has nested. Please consult any good wilderness survival manual to learn more about how to use a Weighted Net in this manner.

One Source of Gill Nets: It is possible to purchase high quality factory made Gill Nets from the following internet company: http://www.texastastes.com/p129.htm

What Does God Look Like?

"What does God look like?" asked the two little girls named Isabelle and Gracie.
Grandmother thought about it for a moment and then she replied lovingly,
"That is a question the two of you will need to ask your Grandpappy."

Grandpappy's Answer:

God made us in His image. We look like God and God looks like us.
One day many years ago God had a Son. His Son's name was Jesus of Nazareth.
Jesus was just a baby boy but He looked like God. Jesus also looked like us.

But God is not a person. God is an invisible Spirit and God is everywhere.
Invisible means you can see through it just like you can see through the air.
And just like the air, God is beside you, and above you, and everywhere.

When God chooses to be seen He looks just like us because we are His children.
God made us and He loves every one of us. We are all His precious children.
Children look like their parents. We look like God. God looks like His children.

Isabelle Age 4   Gracie Age 3

Scripture References: Genesis 1:26-27, Genesis 2:7, Luke 1:30-35,
John 14:9, John 3:16, First John 4:16.

Poem: What Does God Look Like?

Chapter Seventy-Eight

Are You Prepared for a Worst Case Breakdown in Society?

Introduction

A worst case breakdown of society may **not** happen during your lifetime. However, to believe that it could never happen would be to ignore history. Every major nation on the face of the earth has experienced one or more breakdowns in its society during the past two-hundred years.

For example, in the United States of America:

1. During the last year of the American Civil War living conditions in the southern states became life threatening on a daily basis. There was no food to eat, there were no crops growing in the fields, and there was no place a family could stay where they could truly feel "safe."

2. During the flu epidemic of 1918, thousands of normal, healthy people across the entire United States suddenly got sick and a few days later they died. People became terrified and they didn't want to leave their homes because they were afraid they would catch the flu and die.

The above are just two examples of a worst case breakdown in society. If you live in a nation somewhere else on the globe then you could easily add at least one or two examples from your own nation's history books.

Bullies

During a long-term worst case breakdown in society the bullies in each local geographical area will try to dominate that area. Bullies can be defined in a variety of different ways but for the purposes of this discussion we will use the following definition.

A bully is anyone who:

1. Is significantly stronger than almost everyone else, or
2. Is significantly more intelligent than almost everyone else, or
3. Has the most powerful and deadliest weapons at his or her disposal, or
4. Has some type of government or law enforcement job and they quickly enact some new laws that they enforce using martial law or deadly force, or
5. Is the head of an existing "Homeowner's Association" and he or she convinces the majority of the other homeowners that they have the right to search everyone's home and confiscate whatever would be of use to their entire community.

Right and wrong has nothing to do with being a bully. A bully is simply someone who doesn't have what he or she wants and he or she decides that it is perfectly okay to simply take it from someone else. A bully has no respect for any type of law, either civil or moral, unless those laws support the bully's current objective.

Food Production and Food Distribution and Food Storage
During a Worst Case Breakdown in Society

During a worst case breakdown in society food production and food distribution will come to an immediate standstill. Any agricultural crops in a geographical area will be immediately stolen (or confiscated or requisitioned) by the local bullies, and by the local criminals, and by anyone else who is lucky enough to successfully steal the food without losing his or her life in the process.

There is not enough food stored in the entire world to keep everyone alive for more than three months if all food production comes to a complete halt. This assumes an effort would be made to distribute the food to all the starving people in the world. Every bully in every geographical region will claim that he or she is doing his or her best to get the necessary food supplies to everyone and everyone should be patient until the food can actually be delivered to them. However, this will be a lie. The bullies intend to keep all the food for themselves and for the individuals who are loyal to them and they will simply wait for everyone else to starve to death.

The long-term problem is that the bullies don't know how to produce food, and even if they do know how, they will not actually do the work themselves. In fact, most bullies don't know how to do any type of truly productive activity that would be necessary during a worst case hard times event. Therefore when the bullies in one geographical area run out of food they will try to take over an adjoining geographical area and the bullies will gradually and systematically kill one another off, or they will starve to death.

It is not reasonable to believe that the bullies will get all the food. Normal, average people will also get a small percentage of the food. The reason is because people will not simply sit down and wait until they starve to death. They will venture out and go looking for food in the most logical places. They will begin at grocery stores, and then they will think of food distribution warehouses, and then they will consider nearby farm land and the barns and silos on those farms. They will kill the families on those farms, and take everything they can find, and slaughter every farm animal and butcher it crudely on the spot leaving at least 50% of the edible meat to rot or to be eaten by wild animals and birds. These starving people will also search the homes of their neighbors. If a neighbor doesn't have any food then the neighbor should not object. But if the neighbor does object then all the hungry families in the neighborhood will organize and attack that household and take their food and anything and everything else they want. During a worst case breakdown in society there will be no respect for private property, or for the lives of anyone including very small children and infants. This is not a theory -- this is a fact. *This is what has actually happened during every documented breakdown in society for the past two-thousand years.* And there is absolutely nothing you can do to prevent it from happening again.

When it is all over there will only be a few survivors. These survivors will fall into one of the following three general categories:

1. People who made detailed and extensive plans ahead of time to survive a worst case scenario, and they purchased and stored supplies, and they successfully executed their plans at the proper time.

2. People who survived by killing a family that was prepared and they stole everything that family had. This second group will be a very small group when compared to the first group because most of the people in the first group will be prepared to defend themselves against the people in this second group. Therefore very, very few people in this second category will actually survive. The plan of this second group of people is flawed in a multitude of different ways but they can't see the flaws and that will be the reason they will fail. Their plans will usually be based on either deception or on overwhelming numbers. The problem with deception is that they underestimate the intelligence of the people in the first group. The problem with overwhelming numbers is that a three-month supply of food for four people will only last a gang of thirty people for approximately two-weeks. Therefore the gang of thirty people will need to be constantly on the move. And some of the places they attack may only have two-weeks of food. And each time they stage an attack some of the gang members will be killed or wounded. In this type of situation, at least 50% of the time a wound will eventually prove to be fatal for a variety of different reasons.

3. A few of the bullies and their supporters will survive. The only way a bully can survive is by taking that which belongs to someone else, just like the people in group two above. The bully will not work to produce the food or any other item that is desperately needed. Therefore, the bullies will gradually be reduced to an insignificant number but this can take several years. However, a bully can be eliminated in a matter of hours if the people decide to revolt.

How Will the Bullies Succeed in Dominating Your Area?

Starving people will believe almost anyone, or anything, if it gives them hope. All you have to do is to promise them something like, "A chicken in every cook pot." This was a famous slogan during the Great Depression of the 1930s. However, this slogan was nothing more than an empty promise that gave people hope. You can't eat hope but you can focus your thoughts on it. And hope will frequently keep people from doing something about their situation as they gradually starve to death.

Therefore the bullies will convince the vast majority of the starving people in a geographical area that they are truly saddened by the lack of food and they would appreciate it if the starving people would please allow them the freedom to collect all the "surplus" food in the area so it can be equally and freely distributed to everyone. Obviously the starving people have nothing to eat and therefore nothing to "give up" and "everything to gain" so they will unanimously say "Yes, please help us."

Then the bullies will explain that they will be sending out **"Special Humanitarian Teams"** to search everyone's home, business, and real estate to locate the surplus food, collect it, and then bring the food to a central distribution site where it can be more easily distributed equally to everyone in the area. Unfortunately, these Special Humanitarian Teams will need to be heavily armed for two reasons: (1) to protect the food while it is in transport back to the special distribution site, and (2) to force those greedy, unethical, selfish, wicked, evil hoarders who have some food to share it with all the starving people who desperately need it.

Any person or family who does not voluntarily allow the Special Humanitarian Teams the complete freedom to thoroughly search their entire home, business, and real estate will be considered to be an "enemy of the free people" and their homes or business will be burned to the ground and everyone inside will be shot. This will not be a military battle. The Special Humanitarian Teams will not risk their lives to fight these "enemies of the free people." They will simply burn their homes to the ground and shoot everyone as they try to escape the burning building. Therefore please don't say "no" to our Special Humanitarian Teams because you will die if you do. There will be no exceptions.

As the Special Humanitarian Teams carefully search every home, business, and piece of real estate each Team Leader will make a very detailed list of everything of potential value at each location. However, during the first search the only thing that will be taken will be food. For example, the bullies may say that all food in excess of three cans of food per person, or two pounds of food per person, will be requisitioned for the good of the people. (Or the bullies may simply take all the food.)

Therefore the bullies will gain complete control of a geographical area by using the following simple plan. But they will not announce their "entire plan" at the beginning. Instead, after the first search is over, each new search will come as a complete surprise to the people in that geographical area.

1. **First Search:** An extensive careful search will be conducted of every building and home. The Special Humanitarian Teams will compile a very detailed inventory that lists everything in every home and building that might be of potential future value to the bullies. However, during this first search only food will be confiscated (stolen) and the food will be taken to the bully's headquarters.

2. **Second Search:** The bullies will explain that no food has been distributed yet because of attacks on the food distributions trucks. (Note: This could be the truth or a complete lie and it really doesn't matter because the end result will be the same.) Therefore the Special Humanitarian Teams will now conduct another smaller search based on the inventory from the first search. All extra ammunition and firearms will be requisitioned for the use of the Special Humanitarian Teams to help them protect the food and to prevent the theft of that food while it is being freely distributed to the starving people. The Special Humanitarian Teams will decide which firearms you will be allowed to keep when they visit you. You will not be left completely defenseless. The Team will leave you some type of firearm, such as a single-shot pistol or bolt-action rifle, and up to a maximum of ten rounds of ammunition for that firearm depending on the number of people in your household. However, if a Special Humanitarian Team is not able to find enough firearms and ammunition to adequately protect itself, then the Team may take all your firearms and ammunition and the Team may not leave you anything except some instructions on how to build a very effective spear by tying a kitchen knife to a broom handle. If you will please just cooperate

then we can start delivering the free food to you very soon. However, please remember that anyone who resists will be shot.

3. **Third Search:** We apologize that no food has been delivered to you yet. Our Special Humanitarian Teams have used up all their fuel during the first two searches. Therefore all extra fuel, equipment and supplies will now be requisitioned. This will include gasoline, diesel fuel, propane, solar power systems, wind turbines, water filtration systems, and anything else us bullies decide to take at this time.

4. **Fourth Search:** We realize that some of you have not yet received any free food. (Note: The truth will be that at least 99% of the people will have received nothing to eat from the bullies.) Therefore all items of value, such as silver, gold, and jewelry will now be collected. This will also include family heirlooms, such as a small sterling silver candlestick that has been in your family for 120 years. A married person may keep his or her wedding ring if the spouse is still alive and if the wedding ring weighs less than a specified amount and the wedding ring does not contain a precious stone. This is absolutely necessary so us bullies can purchase additional food supplies for all you starving people who have not yet received any free food. Anyone who resists will be shot.

5. **Fifth Search:** Any item still on the original inventory list that us bullies want will now be collected. For example, we may decide that we want that new Hummer vehicle that only has 3,000 miles on it because it would be really useful in helping us distribute the free food to all you starving people.

6. **Sixth Search:** The food distribution effort has been going slowly and you haven't received any food yet because we need more volunteers. Therefore the Special Humanitarian Teams will now be collecting all the individuals who would be useful to our community's humanitarian effort. This will include all extremely attractive teenage girls and all very strong teenage boys. It may also include some exceptionally attractive married women in their twenties or thirties and all able bodied men who can do forced labor. (This will also include men who might eventually decide to resist and fight back because of all the injustices done to their families.)

Please remember that a careful search and a detailed inventory was made of your possessions during Stage One so you will not be able to lie to the Special Humanitarian Teams at any subsequent stage in the requisition (theft) process.

Anyone resisting at any stage will be immediately shot, along with everyone in their home, and their home will be burned to the ground.

Note One: The leading bully or bullies will not leave their fortress of safety. They will convince others to do the dirty work for them. At first the overwhelming vast majority of the individuals on the "Special Humanitarian Teams" will truly believe they are performing a valuable and necessary service for their community. However, as time passes, most of them will gradually realize the truth. But by that time they will be committed because the community will know who they are and they will no longer be trusted because they shot and killed too many people who initially resisted. From that time forward their only hope for long-term survival will be to remain loyal to the bullies. This was the plan of the bullies to begin with and everything is working exactly the way the bullies originally intended.

Note Two: The only way to stop this type of "organized crime" would be to decapitate the head of the snake. However, the head bully will usually be an extremely brilliant person and the vast majority of the people who will be working for him or her may not actually know who he or she is because he or she will be working through a "spokesperson." Even the spokesperson will frequently not realize that he or she is not really in control but that he or she is actually being controlled by a significantly more intelligent bully. When things eventually fall apart and the bully system is destroyed the spokesperson will receive the blame and the punishment of the "free people," and the real bully will usually escape, which was the real bully's plan to begin with. Therefore, to quote and paraphrase one of the famous Star Trek movies, "Resistance will be futile."

How Long Will the Food Last?

Now let's do a little math.

1. Let's assume that a prepared family has a three-month emergency food supply.
2. Let's also assume that for each prepared family there are 99 other families with one-week or less of food in their homes.
3. If all the food of the one prepared family is distributed equally to all the other 99 families then each of the other 99 families will receive an additional one-day's worth of food.
4. Therefore after about one-week all 100 families will begin to starve to death.
5. After about three more weeks, or a total of four-weeks, all 100 families will have died of starvation (if you do not consider cannibalism).

Don't like the above math? Well let's change the numbers and be more optimistic as follows:

1. Let's assume that a prepared family has a one-year emergency food supply.
2. Let's also assume that for each prepared family there are only 49 other families with one-week or less of food in their homes.
3. If the food is distributed equally (due to voluntary charity, or requisition, or confiscation, or theft) then each of the 49 other families will receive an additional one-week's worth or food.
4. Therefore after about two-weeks all 50 families will begin to starve to death.
5. After about three more weeks, or a total of five-weeks, all 50 families will have died of starvation.

Still don't like the above math? Well let's change the numbers and include all the food stored in every local grocery store and every local food warehouse. Current estimates are that each geographical area has about three-days worth of food within its geographical boundaries. That means there is enough stored food to feed everyone in each geographical area for approximately three-days. If the food distribution network comes to a standstill then there will be no more food. On your own please add three-days of food for every family to both of the two above math examples and see what the revised answer is with all the stored food added into the original equation. (Note: Some people may not believe the math in this example because they look at all the food in a big grocery store and they know that if they had all that food then their family could survive for several years. What these people don't realize is that they are not the only family that depends on that grocery store. There are usually thousands of families shopping at that store every week and the food supplies in that store would not feed thousands of families for very long. The truth is that the food would only last about three-days if every family got an equal share of that food. This is the reason the bullies will attempt to take control of the food. The bullies do not want to share that food with anyone because then the bullies would also starve to death in a very short period of time. Therefore, to make sure that they live as long as possible, the bullies will keep the vast majority of the food for themselves and for the individuals who help them to defend the food once they have it under their control.)

Still don't like the above math? Then let's include all the stored food in the entire world. According to a variety of different estimates there is about a three-month worldwide food supply if the food was shared equally with everyone in the world. Even if you assume that each government allows half of its citizens to starve to death then there would still only be a six-month food supply for the remaining one-half of each country's citizens.

The above math is the reason that bullies will attempt to confiscate, requisition, or steal all the food within a geographical area. And once they have the food in their possession they will not be distributing it for free to anyone for any reason, even though they solemnly promised to do so before they got control of the food. The bullies aren't stupid and they completely understand the above math but they have no intention of sharing this basic knowledge with you because then you wouldn't voluntarily go along with their plans.

Therefore if you are one of those individuals who has decided not to prepare because you expect your charitable neighbors to feed you, or you expect the local bullies to feed you, then the chances are very high that you will starve to death during a worst case breakdown in society.

Chapter Seventy-Eight: A Worst Case Breakdown in Society

If the bullies succeed in gaining control of all the food in a geographical area then nobody is going to take any of that food away from them except through the use of deadly force, or if a person agrees to become a willing slave and do whatever the bullies command. Unfortunately, the bullies will not need too many slaves so please don't expect to get one of these highly sought after and very desirable "starvation wages only" slave positions.

The bullies will also realize that their days are numbered unless they can somehow grow more food. Therefore, except for a few doctors and repairmen, almost everyone who hasn't starved to death and who can still do a day's work will be put to work by the bullies in one way or another in growing food. The wages will be one day of food for one day of work. If you don't work then you don't eat. If you don't like the job assigned to you then there are 10 other people who do want your job. If you try to steal some of the food you are growing then you will receive the death penalty. If you try to work outside the established bully system to grow your own food then you will become an easy target for anyone and everyone who wants your food and the bullies will not do anything to protect you. And you won't be able to protect yourself because the bullies now have all your firearms and anyone using a firearm will be reported to the bullies for not complying with their original demand to surrender all weapons and ammunition.

Starvation, Plague, and Death
During a Worst Case Breakdown in Society

During a worst case breakdown in society all charity will quickly come to a complete halt. This will have nothing to do with anyone's good intentions. It will be the simple mathematical result that there will not be enough food for everyone.

The overwhelming vast majority of the people in every geographical area will starve to death, or they will kill one another over scarce food resources. And there will be absolutely nothing a family, or a government, or a religious organization can do to prevent it.

However, at the beginning of a worst case breakdown in society all of these groups will attempt to relieve the suffering of their neighbors but they will quickly run out of resources. When those resources are exhausted then the people who were receiving the "free food" will become an uncontrollable mob that will destroy (burn down) the homes of the families who originally gave them some free food, and the government distribution centers that gave them some free food, and the religious organizations that gave them some free food. They will sincerely believe that these groups are holding back on them and therefore they deserve the punishment that is inflicted on them. It will never occur to this mob of people that the food supplies have actually been completely consumed and that there is simply no more food to give away.

After the mob grows tired of burning down buildings and other peoples' houses, the mob will break up and everyone will go home. They will not go home because they want to. They will go home because they will be exhausted and they will be too hungry to continue destroying the property of others.

Starvation is a slow process but in the early stages it weakens a person's mind and body. A person quickly loses the ability to think clearly and rationally and he starts doing things he would never do if he weren't starving to death. For example, a well-fed person would never think of killing and eating a rat. But a starving person will eat almost anything, including things he knows he should never eat. This will lead to a variety of illnesses and plagues that will sweep through and devastate every geographical area.

After about three or four months the death toll due to people killing one another over a can of food, and through starvation, and through plague will drastically reduce the population within every geographical area.

When that happens there will be two major groups of survivors:
1. individuals who are just barely alive (skin and bones), and
2. individuals in reasonably good health.

Most of the people who are preparing for hard times have not seriously considered the above and they will not be intellectually prepared for it. However, now that you have read this short chapter, if the above does happen during your lifetime, then at least you will not be completely shocked by the events as they unfold.

Who Will Survive?

Most people are familiar with the medical decisions that must be made on a battlefield. There are only a limited number of medics and medical supplies, and those medics have been trained to always help the wounded soldiers who have a very high chance of survival if their wounds are simply cleaned and properly bandaged. But those same medics are also trained not to invest time in trying to help a wounded soldier who has no chance of survival because his wounds are too extensive. By doing what they were trained to do, the battlefield medics are able to save the maximum number of lives based on the time and resources they have at their disposal.

A worst case breakdown in society will be very similar to the above battlefield analogy. Since food production and food distribution will come to a complete halt for several months (or several years), there will simply not be enough food to keep everyone alive. Decisions will therefore need to be made on who gets the available food and who does not. These types of decisions will be made by the bullies in each geographical area. If a person has a skill the bullies think is very desirable, such as a medical doctor, then the bullies may allow one or two medical doctors into their small group as slaves.

However, the vast majority of us don't have any special skills that would be of any immediate value to these bullies. Therefore if we desire for our families to survive then we must take matters into our own hands and we should make plans right now to purchase and store a reasonable level of supplies to get our family through a worst case breakdown of society.

Or we can simply say that we would not want to live in that type of world and we would prefer to starve to death. This is an easy statement for a healthy person to make. However, if you are one of those individuals who believes this way then may I humbly suggest that you put your convictions to a simple test. Don't eat anything for three-days. However, please drink lots of water during this time or you will die. At the end of a three-day fast without any type of food, or any type of calories, or caffeine, then honestly evaluate how you feel and then decide whether or not you would be content to gradually and slowly continue to die of starvation. If you decide this is not the way you would like to die then perhaps you should start making preparations right now so your family at least has the chance to survive.

Just like the battlefield medic, any family that is prepared will need to make decisions on who they can help and who they will not be able to help. This type of decision is one that is best made by each individual family and it is not something that should be forced on or dictated to a family.

Therefore you should have made a decision about this issue long before an actual decision needs to be made during a worst case breakdown in society. If you have family members who have worked hard all their lives, and they would be an asset in helping to rebuild society, then this is the type of person who more closely resembles the wounded battlefield soldier who only needs to have his or her wounds cleaned and bandaged in order to survive. But if you also have some family members who have rarely worked at a steady job, and who have spent most of their lives on welfare, then this type of person may more closely resemble the soldier who has wounds that are too extensive to survive even if you invested a significant amount of your time and a significant amount of your limited resources trying to help him or her.

Conclusion

The reason I have taken the time to write this chapter is because I suspect most people have never done the above math and therefore they have an unrealistic vision of how things will unfold in the event of a worst case breakdown in society.

In closing please allow me to repeat what I mentioned at the very beginning of this chapter -- there is a chance that a worst case breakdown in society may **not** happen during your lifetime.

Chapter Seventy-Eight: A Worst Case Breakdown in Society

However, if it does happen, then all the planning and supplies in the world will not help you survive unless God is on your side.

Therefore, in my opinion, the most important preparation step is to get right with God before anything drastic happens. Then pray on a regular basis that God will watch over you and your entire family.

Also please remember that God is interactive and He expects us to do our part, just like Noah and Joseph did their parts.

Chapter Seventy-Nine

The Basic Rules of Survival During Hard Times

Introduction

Whenever a significant number of people are devastated by hard times then the basic rules that govern that society always change. If you are not aware of these changing rules then you may quickly become a victim instead of a survivor. The purpose of this chapter is to briefly discuss how a person can survive in a rapidly changing hard times environment.

Ordinary People

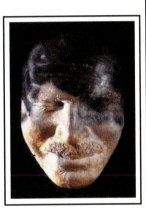

First, you should be *emotionally prepared* to see the **dark side** of ordinary people. This may eventually include people you have known for a very long time.

There is no place in the entire world where human beings do not have a dark side to their character. During normal times most of us keep our dark side under control because of the social consequences that would result if our dark side became visible to others.

However, a person's dark side may quickly assert itself in either one of the following two situations:

1. When a person believes there is no chance (or almost no chance) of being caught or punished.
2. When a person has nothing to lose if he is caught and everything to gain if he is not caught.

During serious hard times either one of the above two situations could result in the dark side of a person taking control of his or her actions. And this dark side can emerge in a large percentage of the population in less than one-day.

For example, consider the following three events that occurred in the United States, where each event was the result of a different set of circumstances but where the consequences were almost identical:

1. The New York City Blackout that began on July 13, 1977 and lasted for one 24-hour period:
   a. 1,037 fires were started,
   b. 1,616 stores were looted and damaged,
   c. 3,776 people were arrested.

2. The Rodney King Rioting in Los Angeles, California that started on April 29, 1992 and continued for six days:
   a. 3,600 fires were started,
   b. 1,100 buildings were looted and destroyed,
   c. over 10,000 people were arrested,
   d. 53 people died violently.

3. The Hurricane Katrina Disaster in New Orleans on August 29, 2005 included:
   a. an undocumented number of carjackings, murders, rapes, and looting.

Each of the above events was the result of a different set of circumstances. However, in each situation the dark side quickly emerged in a large percentage of the people in the affected geographical area, and the resulting chaos and destruction was similar in all three situations.

Therefore if our world continues to slide further and further down into a devastating hard times economy then you should be emotionally prepared to personally witness the dark side of people. And if you want to survive then you should make preparations right now to properly and adequately protect yourself, and the ones you love, and the place you call home.

Criminals

Second, the people who will hurt you will not look like criminals. The reason is because criminals intentionally dress and act like ordinary people whenever they are planning to engage in a criminal activity. A criminal will do his or her best to look and act like a normal average person so he or she can catch his or her victims by surprise.

A criminal can be either a man or a woman, attractive or unattractive, short or tall, thin or heavy, weak or strong, of any age (6 years to 96 years), of any race, of any ethnic background, and either well-dressed or poorly attired. I have personally visited prisons and taught Bible Study Classes in the evenings and the people inside the prison look exactly like the people on the outside except for their prison uniforms. If you try to stereotype criminals then you will quickly become an unsuspecting, unprepared victim for every criminal who does not fit your personal vision of what a criminal should look like.

Children

Third, during a serious hard times tragedy event kidnappings will increase exponentially. Children are the easiest people to kidnap and even if you pay the full ransom promptly and exactly as instructed there is still the chance you will never see your child again. At the beginning of a serious hard times tragedy event you must explain the seriousness of this to your children and make sure they don't go anywhere without you. Your children are too precious to gamble with their lives. Even your own yard will not be a safe place for your children to play. During a hard times tragedy event you will need to keep your children indoors with you. And you will need to keep them relatively quiet in order to avoid attracting unnecessary attention to your home. If your children are playing and laughing loudly then anyone who passes your home will hear them and they will instantly realize that the people inside your home are not experiencing the hard times. This will make your home a target for a surprise attack and that attack will probably occur in the middle of the night.

Dogs

Fourth, during hard times be extremely cautious around dogs. A large number of dogs will be abandoned at the beginning of a serious hard times tragedy event. Since these dogs will have been domesticated they will have little or no fear of people. When confronted with starvation dogs join together to form packs and a pack of dogs will attack, kill, and eat any animal or any person they can bring down. The size of the dog is not as important as the number of dogs in the pack. A pack of just six dogs can quickly surround and overpower even a strong adult male. A person only has two hands and two feet and it is very difficult to properly coordinate all four extremities at exactly the same time against a multitude of attackers. After the dogs get you bleeding in several different places it will be just a matter of time before you become too weak to fight due to the loss of blood. Therefore, if possible, do not travel alone and

always become immediately alert the instant you see a dog. If you believe this would be difficult for you to do then during a hard times event when you see a dog think "bear." The best strategy for dealing with a stray dog or dogs is the same strategy that works with a bear -- avoid it by putting as much distance as possible between it and you. If this is not possible and you are attacked by the dogs then terminate the dogs as quickly as possible.

In summary, most dogs and most people will probably not hurt you. However, you only have to misjudge one time and you could forfeit your life. Therefore during a hard times tragedy event you should be more careful because the basic rules of society will have changed.

Survival Strategies for Hard Times

Let me begin by defining three different types of hard times:

1. **Normal Hard Times:** This is what most of us would call an economic recession. This is not what the government calls a recession because the government is constantly manipulating their statistics to give the illusion of a healthy economy. Normal hard times occur when many different types of businesses have significantly decreasing sales revenues that force them to layoff large numbers of their employees, and they close some of their branches, and this results in a lot of personal bankruptcies. As long as you personally still have a job and a place to call home then you can refer to this period as a "recession."

2. **Serious Hard Times:** This is what most of us would call an economic depression. There are huge reductions in sales revenues and massive layoffs nationwide. A lot of different businesses and financial institutions declare bankruptcy. *You personally lose your job and your home.* If you are lucky you can move in with someone else in your family who still has a job. If you aren't lucky then you may have to live in your car, if you still have a car, or you may be forced to live in some type of tent in a "temporary tent city." Regardless of who you are, or what you did in the past, or how many college degrees you have, as soon as you are forced to become a part of the "temporary tent city crowd" you will be perceived as one of the unproductive members of society and the local city and county officials will make your life far more difficult than it already is. You will also be feared by most of the local residents who still have some form of income and some type of home or apartment. This level of resentment and harassment is the trigger that unleashes the "dark side" of these ordinary people.

3. **Extreme Hard Times:** This occurs when government and financial institutions work together to save themselves and the savings, pensions, and lives of most of the remaining ordinary people are sacrificed. Utility services become intermittent and unreliable. Necessary goods and services become scarce. Inflation rapidly escalates. In order to create the illusion that the government cares about you and that the government is trying to help you, official price controls are implemented and those prices are set at "pre-inflation price levels" which is below the current actual cost of the goods. Therefore most items are only available on the "gray or black markets" where their selling price at least covers the cost of the product. The government and the financial institutions blame everyone else for these problems -- especially anyone or any group that voices a dissenting opinion. During this period there will be widespread starvation, epidemics, lootings, murders, rapes, and general lawlessness. Each person and family will be individually responsible for their own safety and survival. (Note: The current "spot" price of gold and silver is an example of government price controls in action. Almost anyone, including the government, would be more than happy to buy gold or silver at the official "spot" price which is significantly below the current true market price. However almost everyone, including the government, will not sell any gold or silver at the current "spot" price unless they are forced to do so. Therefore there are almost no sales of silver or gold at the current official "spot" prices.)

How to Protect Yourself

During **normal hard times,** which began for many of us in the spring of the year 2007, it would be a good idea for every adult in your household to always carry a folding pocket knife all the time, even when you are at home. (Note: Please verify and then comply with your local and state laws.)

This folding pocket knife should have all the following features:

1. The knife should only have one blade.
2. The knife should be very easy to open.
3. The blade should have a strong sharp point.
4. The blade should have a very sharp cutting edge.
5. The blade should be between 2 to 3.5-inches long (check your local and state laws for the maximum legal blade length).
6. The knife should have a locking blade.

The only purpose of this folding pocket knife will be for personal self-defense and it should be selected based on that single objective. The knife should not be used for anything except an emergency self-defense situation. Don't gradually dull the blade or the point on this knife by using it for a variety of daily cutting tasks.

If you use a knife for self-defense then I suggest that you use it like a rapier and not like a cutlass. The original swashbuckling pirates used great strength to slash and chop their adversaries with a heavy cutlass that had a sharp edge. These strong, husky pirates were easily defeated by smaller more agile men who used a thin light weight rapier with a deadly point and no cutting edge. The rapier was used in a quick thrusting in and out motion. A skilled swordsman could execute two or three quick in and out thrusts in the time it took a stronger man to swing a heavy sword from side to side and then regain control of the sword at the end of its stroke. The purpose of the rapier was to penetrate quickly and deeply and then be quickly withdrawn so the swordsmen could step backwards to safety. A self-defense knife should be used in the same manner as a rapier. Do not try to imitate the fancy knife fights you see in the movies where the men are swinging their arms and their knives from side to side. Those types of movie knife fights are performed for the camera and they have no relationship to real world survival.

During **serious hard times** every adult in your household should always carry a fixed blade hunting knife inside a knife sheath attached to his or her waist belt. This is in addition to the folding pocket knife that is inside his or her pocket. This means each adult would always have two knives -- one knife readily visible at their side and the other knife inside one of their pockets. (Note: Please verify and then comply with your local and state laws.) Criminals simply cannot afford to get injured so they will almost always avoid a person who is visibly armed and they will wait until they see someone who looks like an easy target. The fixed blade hunting knife in the picture on the right is a Buck Model 119 and it can be purchased at most Walmarts for about $40. If you are already living in your car or in a "temporary tent city" then you should now have some type of fixed blade hunting knife for self-defense purposes. This knife can also be used for a variety of necessary daily tasks, such as skinning squirrels and rabbits for the cook pot. Always wipe the blade of your knife clean before you return it to its sheath. Use a sharpening stone at the end of each day to keep the knife edge extremely sharp. (Note: If someone politely asks to see your knife you should always politely say "No, my knife is very important to me and I never let anyone handle my knife." This should also be your standard reply if anyone asks to see your firearm.)

During **extreme hard times** every adult in your household should always "open carry" a semi-automatic high-capacity pistol in a holster on his or her belt in addition to a folding pocket knife and a fixed-blade hunting knife, even when he or she is at home. (Note: Please verify and then comply with your local and state laws.)

If you do not already own a high-capacity semi-automatic pistol then the following suggestions may help you make a good choice:

1. A 40-caliber S&W bullet is normally considered the minimum caliber for effective self-defense.
2. Most people, including females, can handle the recoil of a 40-caliber pistol.
3. The pistol should be a "full-size" pistol as opposed to a "compact" model.

4. The pistol should feel comfortable when holding it in your hand.
5. The pistol magazine should hold at least 10 rounds. 15 rounds would be even better.
6. The pistol should come with two high-capacity magazines.
7. Hollow point ammunition is preferred for self-defense purposes.
8. A heavier grain bullet is preferred to a lighter grain bullet.
9. The pistol holster (purchased separately) should have a special pocket attached that carries the extra magazine.
10. If the pistol does not have a non-slip grip then either replace it or add a non-slip grip.

The above information is a very brief summary of the most important sidearm criteria that I have seen during the last twenty-years. However, just like any other topic there are individuals who have very strong opinions about every possible aspect of firearm ownership, including whether or not a revolver is better than a semi-automatic pistol. I do not wish to become involved in that debate. You may consult whomever you wish and make whatever purchase you feel comfortable with. However, if you want a specific recommendation for a weapon that simultaneously meets all the above criteria then that weapon would be a Glock Model Number 22 with two 15-round magazines. The Glock 22 shoots the 40-caliber S&W. Buy new if possible because the used pistols have generally seen extensive use at the target practice range.

Walmart sells the 50 round and the 100 round value packages of Remington 40-caliber S&W 180 Grain Hollow Points. If you can afford it you should seriously consider purchasing at least ten boxes of this ammunition for your new pistol. Whenever possible, always practice with the same exact ammunition you will be using later for self-defense. If you are going to invest in new pistols for each adult in your household then you should consider buying exactly the same weapon for each person for a variety of good reasons. The exception would be if a person has a small hand and cannot comfortably hold a "full size" pistol. In that situation comfort and pistol control take precedence over standardization of weapons and ammunition. Also enroll in a firearms training course and learn the correct safe way to use your new weapon.

Model 1911
45-Caliber

45-Caliber Note: The 45-caliber Model 1911 ACP (Automatic Colt Pistol) usually comes with a seven-round magazine. The 45 ACP (not to be confused with the 45 GAP or Glock Automatic Pistol) is also a good choice for self-defense but for different reasons. The Glock Model 21 ACP is a standard 45-caliber pistol that comes with two 13-round magazines. The Glock Model 21 is also an excellent pistol. However, a 45-caliber pistol has more recoil than a 40-caliber pistol and therefore some people find it more difficult to shoot accurately. The Glock Model 21 ACP also has a slightly bigger grip from front to rear which makes it more challenging for individuals with smaller hands to grasp because they can't comfortably wrap their fingers around the grip and gain comfortable control of the trigger with their index finger.

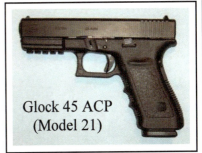

Glock 45 ACP
(Model 21)

1. The **standard** Glock Model 21 (45 ACP) has a total grip circumference of 6.00-inches just below the trigger.
2. The **slim** Glock Model 21 (45 ACP) has a total grip circumference of 5.75-inches just below the trigger.
3. The **standard** Glock Model 22 (40 S&W) has a total grip circumference of 5.50-inches just below the trigger.

(Note: The bigger grip circumference on the Glock Model 21 is necessary because of the extra length of a 45 ACP round when compared to a 40 S&W round.)

Chapter Seventy-Nine: The Basic Rules of Survival

If you are going to invest in firearms then you will also probably need a rifle. A discussion of the advantages and disadvantages of the different types of rifles is discussed in the Firearm Chapter of this book. However I will briefly state my opinion about rifles here. If I were going to select only one rifle and if I were going to buy one of these rifles for each adult in my household then I would buy the original model AK-47 that shoots 7.62x39 ammunition because it can be effectively used for self-defense and for hunting, and the ammunition is a pointed bullet, reasonably priced, not too heavy, very accurate, and a single shot is very deadly.

Whenever you are handling a firearm please adhere to the following universally accepted firearm safety rules:

1. Always treat every firearm as if it were loaded and ready to fire.
2. Never point a firearm at anyone or anything you do not intend to kill or destroy.
3. Never put your finger on the trigger until the sights are aligned on the target.
4. Positively identify your target (no guessing) and everything behind your target the bullet might hit.

(Note: Resist the temptation to invest in ammunition reloading equipment. Instead invest whatever funds you would have spent on reloading equipment and reloading supplies on ready-to-use ammunition that has already been professionally loaded and sealed at the factory. However, if you wish to know more about the reloading process then please read the Ammunition Chapter in this book.)

Personal Self-Defense
How to Survive an Attack During Extreme Hard Times

As previously mentioned, during extreme hard times each person and family will be individually responsible for their own safety and survival. Although the government and its various law enforcement agencies will still exist they will be overwhelmed by the widespread lawlessness that will exist nationwide. Therefore the chance they will be able to protect you or your home will be close to zero. During an extreme hard times event you will have to protect yourself, your family, and your home.

If you doubt the truth of the above statement then do a simple internet search on the current situation in Mexico (or almost any other South American nation). The Mexican government and the Mexican police are losing the battle every day against the nation's drug dealers and criminals. Innocent people, including little children, are dying every day in the mayhem that exists in that country. This is the situation that exists right now in Mexico. And it may not be very long before this type of widespread lawlessness begins to run rampant in the neighborhood where you live.

During normal times there is unemployment, and there are robberies, rapes, and murders. As our current hard times continue to get worse, more and more people will lose their jobs and their homes, and they will become a part of the gradually increasing population of homeless people. During normal times these homeless individuals can usually survive on the charity and goodwill of the people in the area where they live. However, as the number of homeless people gradually increases there will eventually come a time when there will not be enough charity or government assistance to meet everyone's minimum needs for survival. When that happens then these individuals will have nothing to lose by trying to steal what they need. And as the hard times continue to get worse and worse and worse, these crimes of necessity that began as simple robberies will evolve into the more serious crimes of rape and murder. The "dark side" of these people will take control and what would have been a simple robbery during "normal hard times" will now end in murder in order to eliminate all the possible witnesses and any chance of being punished. If you don't believe this will happen then do an internet search on either Argentina or Venezuela. The people in both of those countries are currently living in extreme hard times that actually began several years ago.

With the above perspective in mind, the following information may help you successfully defend yourself and your home during an extreme hard times tragedy event. This information is divided into three sections as follows:

1. How will the attack begin?
2. What should you do if you are attacked?
3. What should you do after the attack is over?

1. How will the attack begin?

You will receive no advance warning. You will not be given any time to prepare. You will be outnumbered. The odds will be against you from the very start. You will receive no mercy. Your only chance is to have thought about this ahead of time and to have already made a decision about what you are going to do.

2. What should you do if you are attacked?

If you are away from home when you are attacked, and running away is an option, then run away. If you can run faster than your adversary then you will have won the victory without losing a lot of blood.

Don't waste one second trying to negotiate or beg for mercy. Either immediately run away or immediately engage your attackers with everything you've got.

The reason honest law-abiding people almost always lose street fights, and frequently their lives, is because they don't want to seriously or permanently injure the person who is attacking them. Think about that for a moment. And then make a decision right now about what you will do if you are attacked. You need to make that decision now so you do not waste precious time at the beginning of a fight trying to figure out some strategy to defend yourself. Simply defending yourself will not win the fight. To survive you must *temporarily* become as brutal and ruthless as your attackers. Your attackers will be trying to permanently cripple you, permanently blind you, and kill you as quickly as they can. Pause right now and think about that. Should you be trying to do anything less to your attackers?

If you are fatally wounded during the fight then do not simply give up and lay down and wait to die. Even a fatally wounded person will usually live for at least 30 seconds or longer after being wounded. You now have nothing to lose by trying to fatally injure or permanently disfigure or cripple all your attackers before you die. If you succeed then you will have prevented some or all of them from harming another innocent human being (such as a member of your own family). After all your attackers are dead it is still possible that you may survive your injury. But you will have no chance to survive if you simply give up. And don't try acting like you are dead. Your attackers aren't stupid and they will make sure you are dead before they leave the crime scene.

You should decide right now that if you are attacked during an extreme hard times tragedy event that you will not stop fighting until you are either victorious or you are unconscious, completely incapacitated, or dead. If you will make this intellectual decision right now then your mind and your body will automatically take over if you are attacked. And it is entirely possible that if you do not hesitate, and if you reciprocate with everything you've got, then you may actually live to see another day.

If you respond immediately with overwhelming force then you will probably take your attackers by surprise and for a few seconds you may actually have the advantage. The reason is because most of your attackers' previous victims probably didn't put up much resistance before they were terminated. Therefore, based on their past experience, your attackers will probably be expecting you to do one of two things: (1) to try to talk your way out of the situation, or (2) to wait until you know how serious the situation is before you actually try to defend yourself. Therefore your attackers will probably be anticipating another easy kill and they will not be expecting you to immediately defend yourself with everything you've got.

3. What should you do after the attack is over?

If you are away from home and you survive an attack and you are physically able to leave, then put as much distance between yourself and the fight scene as quickly as you can. Do not wait for the attacker's friends to show up and finish you off. After you have retreated to a safe place then immediately bandage your wounds and try to stop the bleeding. Then immediately seek medical assistance from a trained medical professional.

Chapter Seventy-Nine: The Basic Rules of Survival

If you survive an attack then do not criticize yourself about the way you behaved during the attack. Do not intellectually punish yourself by trying to think of ways you could have won the fight without hurting any of your attackers. You did not initiate the aggression and therefore you are not morally responsible for the fate of your attackers. Instead you should take some comfort in the fact that you have reduced the number of criminals who will be attacking innocent people in the future. And you will have probably saved one or more innocent lives. However, the people who will not get attacked in the future by those particular criminals will never know what you have done for them.

Community Defense

Regardless of where you live you are part of a larger social community. This is true if you live in an apartment building, or in a suburb on 1/2 acre lots, or in the country on 10 acre lots. Everyone has neighbors. During extreme hard times it would be a good idea if everyone worked together to help defend their community.

Effective community defense can be based on this very simple principle: *If you can hear gunfire, or the cries of someone who needs help, then you should respond appropriately.* If you do not assist your neighbors in their hour of need, then the violence will gradually move in your direction and you could be the next family that is in serious trouble. Therefore a smart person will try to stop the violence before it reaches his or her family.

Resist the temptation to establish community defense based on natural geographical boundaries, such as an apartment building, or all the homes on one block. The family that lives in a corner house will be a neighbor to all the families that live in the corner homes on the other three corners. And the family that lives in the last house on this side of the county line will be a neighbor to the family that lives in the house just across the county line. Therefore, in most cases, geographical boundaries would not be the best way to establish an effective community defense.

A better way to establish an effective community defense would be to use sound. *If you can hear gunfire, or the cries of someone who needs help, then you should respond appropriately.*

During an extreme hard times tragedy event if a group of criminals is attacking one house (or a subdivision of homes), then the surrounding community that is not under immediate attack would be in an ideal position to help stop the invasion. The criminals cannot defend themselves from every possible direction. Therefore while most of their attention is focused on their current primary objective, the individuals in the surrounding community could carefully move into a position where they could safely pick off the criminals one-at-a-time. This would not need to be a coordinated military campaign. The families that live extremely close to the current violence may be able to see the criminals from their own windows and therefore they would be able to help without leaving the safety of their own homes. Individuals that live a little further away would need to carefully exit their own homes, and then carefully move into a safe position behind some effective cover, and then positively determine who is shooting at whom. If a person is firing shots at innocent people trapped inside a home then that person needs to be stopped. On the other hand, if a person is shooting at a criminal who is shooting at the house, then you should not shoot at that person because he or she is one of your neighbors. If each person will positively identify the criminals before he or she pulls the trigger then everyone can avoid making the mistake of accidentally killing one of their own neighbors.

The above strategy does involve some personal risk. However, waiting for the criminals to gradually make their way to your home during an extreme hard times tragedy event involves far more risk in the long-term.

Conclusion

In summary, during extreme hard times each one of use will be personally responsible for our own survival, and for helping our community to survive. Remember the motto of our nation's founding fathers: "United We Stand. Divided We Fall."

The best strategy for personal self-defense would be to avoid the fight. This can be achieved by intentionally maintaining a very low profile at your home. Do not do anything that would attract attention to your house or to your community. If possible do not leave your home during extreme hard times. If you absolutely must leave your house then do not travel alone if possible. And always carry some type of weapon for self-defense regardless of where you are.

The best strategy for effective community defense would be based on sound. *If you can hear gunfire, or the cries of someone who needs help, then you should respond appropriately.*

If you will follow these suggestions then you will significantly reduce the chance that you, or your home, or your community will be attacked. And if you are attacked then you will have a much better chance of surviving the ordeal.

Also remember that the ultimate outcome of any situation is always in the Lord's Hands. Therefore, in addition to becoming better prepared to survive hard times, you should also pray every day that He will watch over you, your family, your home, and your community.

Finally, please accept my most heartfelt apology for upsetting you with the information in this chapter. I know these topics are not pleasant ones to think about. However I sincerely believe the above information may save your life and the lives of your loved ones.

The Good Old Days

It seems there are fewer people now engaged in honest labors.
It is getting so bad you can't even trust some of your neighbors.

People skillfully cheat one another whenever they can.
Those in power are quick to defraud a widow or orphan.

Evil doers make careful plans how to shed innocent blood,
and then deny any wrongdoing as their victims are buried.

Everywhere bribes have been accepted by rulers and judges.
Even our most trusted leaders have passed laws to enslave us.

Within our own families there are some who bear our own name,
who will turn on us and betray us if it brings them worldly gain.

What kind of godless age is this that we now live in,
when behavior like the above is really quite common?

That was the question asked long ago by the prophet Micah,
about 700 years before the birth of the Messiah.

Sometimes we think the good old days must have been better.
But people have not changed; they have only gotten smarter.

In every age we must each choose between good and evil.
Who will you follow: a righteous God or a wicked devil?

Scripture References: Micah 6:11, Micah 7:2-6, Ecclesiastes 7:10.

Chapter Eighty

During Hard Times Will You Accept God's Help?

During a serious hard times tragedy event you will probably discover that you need God a lot more than you ever realized. The reason is because you will be exposed on a daily basis to all the following:

1. **Shortages:** Basic human necessities will become scarce and they will become extremely difficult to obtain. This includes things that many people now take for granted, such as safe drinking water, and food, and a safe place to sleep each night. Anything can happen to your reserve water, and your reserve food, and your place of shelter and you could quickly become a homeless helpless refugee. Wouldn't it make good sense to pray to the "One Who Provides All" and ask Him to protect your home and your supplies and your family from loss and harm.

2. **Crime:** All types of crime will increase. Almost everyone will need almost everything. An overwhelming number of people will be forced to make the following very simple decision, "Should I sit down and wait to die a slow agonizing death due to dehydration, or starvation, or exposure, or should I 'temporarily' set my morals aside and confiscate (steal) the things I need for survival?" After a person intellectually justifies that first theft then each new theft becomes much easier. And sooner or later it will become necessary to kill someone during a theft and then each new murder will become much easier. In this type of high crime environment some people will believe they can successfully defend themselves from these thieves and murderers. But a smart person will realize that there is no way you can defend yourself from a unexpected bullet in the back of the head. However, you can pray that "He Who Sees All" will protect you and your family from harm on an ongoing basis.

3. **Food:** If you decide to grow your own food and to hunt, trap, and fish, then you will quickly discover that nature can defeat your very best efforts. And there is no way you can control nature. However, you can pray to the "One Who Does Control Nature" and improve your chances of being successful at gardening, hunting, trapping, and fishing.

4. **Natural Disasters:** Nobody is safe from a natural disaster. Without warning an earthquake could happen anywhere. Without warning a gentle rain could turn into a deluge and your entire area could be flooded. Without warning a tornado could completely devastate an area. There is no way a person can protect his family from a natural disaster. But there is One who can protect your family and He is only a prayer away 24 hours per day 7 days per week.

5. **Death:** If an unexpected accident were to instantly claim your life (or the life of someone you love) then you (or your loved one) would be immediately transported to either heaven or hell. The only way to avoid hell and be guaranteed eternal life in glory is to know Jesus Christ as your personal Savior.

Therefore, I suggest you own at least one good reference study Bible and that you read it on a regular basis with your family. My personal choice is the following Bible:

Nelson's New King James Version (NKJV) Study Bible.

I strongly recommend the above Bible because:

1. Each book of the Bible has a really good introduction that includes the historical background about that book.
2. Each page contains excellent detailed footnotes and simple explanations of specific scripture verses on that page.

3. It has good word definitions on the exact page the word is actually used in the Bible.
4. It has a great subject index.
5. It has a few full color maps in the back of the Bible.

The above Bible would be a good choice for someone who does not already own a good Bible.

However, if you already have a good Bible then instead of buying another one it may be a better idea if you simply read the Bible you already have. May I suggest that you start on the first page of the book of Genesis and continue to read, as time permits, until you finish the last page of the book of Revelation. Then do it again. And again. And again for the rest of your life.

2 Chronicles 7:13-14
When I shut up heaven and there is no rain, or command the locust to devour the land, or send pestilence among My people, if My people who are called by My name will humble themselves, and pray and seek My face, and turn from their wicked ways, then I will hear from heaven, and will forgive their sin and heal their land.

Matthew 6:31-33
Therefore do not worry, saying, 'What shall we eat? or What shall we drink? or What shall we wear?' For after all these things the Gentiles seek. For your heavenly Father knows that you need these things. But seek first the kingdom of God and His righteousness, and all these things will be added to you.

Chapter Eighty-One

The Reasons I Decided to Become a Christian

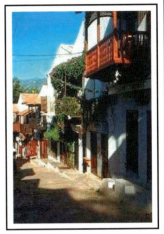

In 1976 I had a job as an Engineer and I spent approximately one-half of my time working on the island of Puerto Rico.

After work in the evenings there was very little to do. Almost every radio and television station broadcasted their programs in Spanish. Even the John Wayne movies had John Wayne speaking in Spanish (not Spanish sub-titles but actual Spanish sentences instead of English sentences). Since my knowledge of Spanish was very elementary the only way to pass the time was to read. As the weeks stretched into months I started reading a wide variety of paperback books.

I would buy the paperback books at the Miami airport bookstores and I would take the books with me on the airplane. That way I had something to read in the evenings at my motel in Puerto Rico. I read a variety of books, including fiction, westerns, mysteries, science-fiction, and several "How To" books.

One day in February I noticed a small book for sale with the title "An Explanation of the UFO Phenomena From a Christian Perspective." I was mildly interested in UFO's so I bought the book. As an Engineer I had a pretty solid background in science because my Engineering degree had required me to take many, many college courses in chemistry, physics, thermodynamics, and advanced calculus. Therefore I read the book with the critical eye of someone who has a reasonable background in science and who could not be easily persuaded by inaccurate information. As I read the book it made me stop and think carefully about many things I had only casually thought about in the past. When I finished the book I had a very strong desire to learn more about God. Therefore over the next several months I read a variety of religious literature written by a lot of different people who had totally different opinions about some very basic religious concepts.

One evening while reading inside my motel room in Puerto Rico the answer about "God" finally dawned on me. I was devastated that the answer hadn't occurred to me earlier in life.

Following is a very brief summary of some of the more important concepts that led me to my understanding about "God."

Is There Really a God?

1. **Is the Earth a Simple Cosmic Coincidence or Was the Earth Created?**

   My academic education from the first grade through four-years of college had consistently taught me that the earth was a cosmic coincidence. My former textbooks had presented two basic options for how the earth was formed:

   A. **The Big Bang Theory:** There was some type of huge cosmic explosion and the entire world was created as a result of this magnificent historic event.

   B. **Evolution:** The earth gradually formed in space over a period of trillions and trillions of years.

   The first thing I did was carefully examine both of the above theories to determine if one of them was superior to the other one. Based on my meager knowledge of the universe I knew that outer space was a huge lifeless freezing cold vacuum where life, as we know it, could not exist. There is no oxygen or hydrogen or water in outer space. But if the elements that make water don't exist in space, then how did the vast majority of the earth's surface become covered with water? I knew for a "fact" there was a **tremendous amount of water** on the earth. But where did all that water come from? And where did the air that we breathe come from? Neither of the above two theories had any answers to these two simple questions except to ridicule anyone who would ask such questions and not simply accept the scientific explanation that "it just happened" on faith. That was unacceptable to me so I had to personally reject both of the above scientific explanations about how the earth was formed.

2. **Did Man Evolve or Was Man Created?**

    The next question I needed to answer was how did people, and animals in general, get on the earth? I had three basic theories to evaluate as follows:

    A. **Evolution:** Animal life gradually evolved over trillions and trillions of years. But this theory assumes the existence of a single cell organism to begin with. There is no explanation of how life entered that first cell that eventually became a man. And there is no explanation of how a simple single cell organism somehow figured out that it needed to "see." Or "hear." How did a blind deaf cell know that it needed these senses. And these senses are extremely complex in their basic functions and in the way they relay their data to the brain. To believe in evolution requires that a person simply believe that "it just happened" because there is no valid scientific explanation of how or where animal life came from. In addition, all our current scientific data is actually in opposition to the theory of evolution since we know that instead of evolving that more and more species are actually becoming extinct each year. Therefore I had to personally reject the theory of evolution.

    B. **Space Travel and Colonization:** The next theory is that the earth was seeded with people by transporting them by spaceship from some distant world and colonizing the earth. Once again, based on my scientific background, I knew that Alpha Centauri, the closest star, was approximately a **3,000 year journey** away if you could travel at the speed of **one-million miles per hour.** And even if that were possible, I still had to explain how mankind got on that distant planet to begin with. If evolution was scientifically impossible on earth, then I could not force myself to believe that it was somehow possible on some distant planet. Therefore I had to reject the theory of colonization.

    C. **Creation:** The earth and mankind were intentionally created by God. This requires that a person believe in a supreme being. However, unlike the above two theories, this one did not require me to abandon any of the scientific principles that I currently understood based on my formal education of 16 years in school. To accept this theory I simply had to believe in God and in science. At the tender age of 27 this seemed like the most logical choice if I was going to be true to my own conscience.

3. **Are There Many Gods, or No God, or One God?**

    A. **Multiple Gods:** In grade school I learned about the different gods of the Romans, and the Greeks, and a variety of other civilizations. When I went to grade school these gods were taught as part of our study of mythology. We were never taught to believe in these gods. We were just being educated in what some primitive people believed in. And, according to mythology, these gods were always arguing and fighting with one another about something. Therefore, as an adult, it was relatively easy for me to reject the idea of multiple gods.

    B. **No God:** When I was attending college this was the "unspoken" opinion of most of the faculty and many of the students. But if I accepted this theory then I would be left with no explanation for where the earth came from. Therefore, unless I could come up with a least some plausible explanation for the existence of the earth, I had to rule out the possibility of there being No God.

    C. **One God:** This is the foundation of many of the most popular religions on the earth at this time. Therefore this theory needed to be examined in more depth.

4. **If There is One God Then What is His Name?**

    If God created the earth and mankind then God also created the thousands of different languages that exist all across the globe. Since God perfectly understands all these different languages, is it reasonable to believe that the name of God is correct only when it is spoken in one specific language? This was an intellectual dilemma for which I did not have an answer.

    If God only has one correct name that can only be correctly pronounced in one language, then are the people who speak that language the only people who are important to God? If that is true, then why did

God allow so many different languages since He knew that the vast majority of the people on the earth would never learn any language except the language spoken by their parents in the land in which they were born?

I could not answer this question to my own satisfaction. Instead, I chose to believe that God understands the motives within a person's heart, and if that person truly believes in Him and truly wishes to honor and worship Him, then God would accept that person even if that person only spoke the language of his or her birth.

5. **Does God want everyone to know about Him or just a few very select special people?**

A careful study into the question about whether or not there is a God will eventually result in having to answer the question about whether or not God can be found by anyone who diligently searches for Him, or whether He can only be found by following the guidance of a small group of people who claim that they have special information about God that is only available to them and the people who join their group.

   A. **Is there secret hidden knowledge about God available only to a select few?** The number of groups that claim that they have some type of special secret knowledge about God is truly overwhelming. If you will just become a member of their group for the rest of your life, and if you will make a vow of secrecy to never tell anyone outside the group what you have learned, then they will gradually reveal their knowledge to you based on your willingness to serve God and do His will as defined by the leaders within the group. The more you serve the group the higher in rank you will rise within the group. Unfortunately there is no way to honestly know if any one of these secret groups actually has a "special revelation from God." There is also no way to evaluate the advantages and disadvantages of each of these different groups prior to joining them because their activities are kept secret. Therefore I made the personal decision not to join any of these groups because my original objective was to find out if there really was a God, and it did not seem logical to me to believe that God would hide himself from everyone except one very small group of people.

   B. **Does God reveal himself to anyone and everyone who diligently seeks Him?** There is an overwhelming amount of information about God available to anyone who wishes to study religion in great depth. This knowledge is freely available to anyone who looks for it. However, I also discovered that very few people actually go looking for this type of information. The vast majority of people simply are not interested in learning about God by searching for Him on their own. Therefore I eventually reached the simple conclusion that God was easy to find by yourself if you will just take the time to look for Him. This is the path I chose to follow and it has consistently proven to be the right choice for me.

6. **Is one religion or faith the best way to learn about God?**

After reaching the conclusion that there is one God, and that He can be found by anyone, the next question that needs to be answered is which religion or faith most closely teaches the truths about God. There are two basic options to choose from:

   A. **God does not care which religion you practice as long as you practice some religion:** This point of view has been around for a very long time. However, it is difficult for an intelligent person to accept this point of view because each of the major religions claims that it is the only way to worship God and that all the other religions are false religions. If a person accepts the statement that all religions are basically equal before God then that person must immediately reject the basic premise of each religion that it is the only way to God. This creates a paradox and therefore it can't be true.

   B. **There is only one true religion just like there is only one true God:** If God can be found by man then there must be some way that man can worship God in a manner that would be pleasing to God. Once this conclusion is reached the next major decision has to be which religion is the one that God wants you to participate in?

7. **Which religion is correct?**

A correct answer to this question is the key to finding God and worshiping Him in a manner that is pleasing to Him. However, the correct answer can only be reached by simultaneously answering several different but related questions:

A. **Does God always tell the truth? Does God expect His followers to always be truthful to everyone?**

The answer to these two questions was intuitively obvious to me.

>Yes, God is always truthful.
>Yes, God expects us to always tell the truth.

However, some religions only expect their people to tell the truth to each another and they have permission to lie to everyone else if they believe it is appropriate. Since I have a very high opinion about the integrity of Almighty God, it was impossible for me to believe that God would approve of lying. Therefore I could not seriously consider any religion that provides conditions under which its people can tell lies.

B. **Does God tolerate differences among His people or must everyone do everything exactly the same way at exactly the same time?**

Some religions have very strict formal procedures for doing everything, and other religions have less formal procedures. I was not able to determine if more or less formality was preferred by God. However, I do know that God made each one of us different from everyone else. If God intentionally created so much diversity among his children, then it seemed logical to me that God might accept a **little** variation in the way that we individually chose to honor and worship Him as long as we don't do something that is offensive to Him. But that is just my opinion. You will need to make your own decision in this matter.

C. **Does God want His people to live in peace or in constant fear?**

1. Some religions actively promote peace and harmony within their own religious community and with everyone outside their religious community.

2. Some religions believe that they alone have a right to live here on this earth and that God expects them to exterminate anyone who does not share their faith.

Since each one of us achieves religious insight at a unique time within our own lives, it did not seem appropriate to me to force a person to make that decision based on when another person decides that the time is right to make the decision. Given a little more time and access to a little more information a person may chose the right religious path on his or her own. But if that person is forced to make a religious decision or face death then I personally do not believe that God accepts that person's decision because it was forced on him or her. However, some religious faiths believe that God honors a decision whether it is voluntary or forced. However, my personal opinion is that God only accepts religious decisions that are voluntary. You will need to make your own decision about this issue.

D. **Does God need your help to achieve His will?**

1. Some religions believe that God needs your help to achieve His will here on this earth.
2. Some religions believe that God's will on this earth will be done regardless of what you do.

I do not know the answer to this question but I have personally chosen to believe that God's will on this earth will be done regardless of what I do or don't do. You will need to make your own decision in this matter.

E. **Does God want you to make a personal decision to follow Him or can someone else make that decision for you?**

Some religions believe that a child's parents can make the decision about a child's eternal destiny by performing some religious ritual for the child while the child is still an infant, or at some time before the child achieves the status of adulthood. In other words, once a child's eternal destiny has been decided for the child, the child can do anything he or she wishes during his or her entire life and that child would still go to heaven at the time of death.

I do not know if this is God's plan or not, but it did not seem to be consistent with God being a true and just God who says that He will judge each and every one of us based on our own actions instead of the actions of someone else. Therefore I could not personally accept this religious concept. Instead I chose to believe that each person must individually make a decision to accept or reject God.

F. **Is suicide acceptable to God?**
   1. Some religions believe that any type of suicide is a one-way ticket to an eternal hell.
   2. Some religions believe that religious suicide is a one-way ticket to an eternal heaven.

There is no scientific way to prove or disprove either one of the above two opinions.
Therefore I had to answer this question for myself using common sense. Suicide is murder. Murder is wrong. Therefore, if God always tells the truth, and if God is always consistent and He does not change, and if God does not want us to commit murder, then God would not be pleased with anyone who commits suicide. Based on this simple reasoning I had to conclude that suicide is not acceptable to God and therefore it should be avoided.

G. **Does God want you to sacrifice the lives of your children to please Him?**

Some religions believe in child sacrifice. If God demands the lives of little children then how did you get to be an adult? This ancient religious practice is totally offensive to me and therefore I could not seriously consider any religion that currently practices it or that has a history of practicing it. Unfortunately this religious practice periodically reappears during serious hard times. Therefore I needed to mention it here in the hope that you will not personally choose to follow any religion that advocates child sacrifice as the way to appease God so that God will bless you.

H. **Do you get one lifetime to find God or do you get reincarnated many times?**

If you don't find God while you are here on this earth do you get multiple chances to come back to the earth until you eventually find God? If this is true then nobody ever needs to find God and you can do anything you want and you will keep coming back again and again and again. Therefore I had to personally reject the theory of reincarnation.

I. **Where does your spirit go when you die?**

There are three predominant views about what happens to you when you die:

   1. **You simply die and that is the end of you.** Nobody has an eternal spirit and therefore there is no such thing as life after death. (Note: This is the perspective of an atheist. An atheist is an individual who does not believe in God or in life after death.)
   2. **Your spirit becomes part of a huge universal spirit.** Everyone has an eternal spirit and regardless of what you do while you are alive, when you die your spirit simply becomes part of some large spiritual body. This belief is very popular with people who are basically good people and who do not want to be restricted in any way by any type of religion. These people have chosen to become their own God and decide what they should do and shouldn't do. Since they don't intend to do anything really bad it becomes intellectually easy for them to believe that their eternal spirit will simply mingle with other eternal spirits. The major problem with this perspective is that these people have replaced God with their own beliefs. Therefore I could not personally adopt this philosophy.

3. **There is a place of eternal joy called heaven and a place of eternal punishment called hell.** Although there is nothing that can support this belief while we are here on this earth, this teaching is the only one that appeals to my personal understanding of what a true and just God would do. However, many people choose to reject this belief because they don't personally wish to believe in a place called hell and therefore they make all types of excuses why hell cannot exist.

J. **What are the most important principles or rules of the religion?**

Each major religion has one or more primary religious principles upon which it is founded. To be a member in good standing in that religion the person should adhere to these major principles.

The Christian religion has two basic principles upon which all the other Christian principles are derived:

1. **Love God with all your heart, mind, and spirit.** Heaven is a place for people who love God and who truly want to please God. Heaven is not a place for rebellious spirits. Therefore the first rule of Christianity is that you must love God above everything else. It is still okay to love others but God must come first.

2. **Love your neighbor as yourself.** When asked to define the concept of a neighbor Jesus told the parable of the Good Samaritan. A Samaritan was the most despised person on the face of the earth at that time. Therefore Jesus told us to love everybody, including our worst enemies. We are not only commanded to love them but also to pray for them and to forgive them. When I first became a Christian I did not fully appreciate the importance of this commandment. But as I grew in the Christian faith the fundamental truth that underlies this command has gradually become obvious to me. Perhaps it will also eventually become obvious to you.

K. **If you make a mistake does God reject you and cast you into Hell?**

In the Christian religion there is a difference between eternal salvation and eternal rewards:

1. **Eternal Salvation:** The moment a person accepts Jesus Christ as his or her Savior then that person's soul is forever safe in the hands of Jesus Christ. Jesus' death on the cross was the full and final payment for the eternal souls of everyone who voluntarily chooses to put their trust in Him. After a person is saved through faith in Jesus Christ that person does not have to do anything else to go to heaven. And if a person does something really bad then that does not cancel out Jesus' death on the cross because Jesus' death paid for all the person's sins: past, present, and future.

2. **Eternal Rewards:** If a person does good works that deserve a reward then that reward will be waiting for that person in heaven. If a person doesn't do anything that deserves a reward then there will be no rewards for that person in heaven. The "saved" person's soul will still go to heaven but that person will be one of the "least in the kingdom of heaven." However, being one of the least in the kingdom of heaven would still be infinitely better than being cast into an eternal Hell.

Conclusion

After carefully thinking about all of the above issues I reached the following conclusions:

1. There is only One God.
2. God created the earth and everything on the earth and everything in outer space and everything in heaven and in hell.
3. Anyone can find God. There is no small group of people who know some spiritual secret about God.
4. God always tells the truth and he expects us to always tell the truth.
5. God desires for His followers to live in peace with everyone.

6. God is not pleased with someone who commits suicide or someone who sacrifices the lives of little children.
7. A decision to believe in God must be voluntary.
8. A person who believes in God must also love God.
9. If a person loves God then he or she will want to worship God in the way that God says He is to be worshiped.
10. A person who pleases God will go to heaven. A person who rejects God will go to hell.
11. The only way to please God is to become a Christian. A person can become a Christian by accepting God's Son Jesus Christ as Savior.
12. The Holy Bible tells the truth about God and about His Only Son Jesus Christ.

After a person decides to accept the Christian faith then that person will need to find and attend a local Christian church on a regular basis. However, a person needs to be very careful about which "Christian" church to join because all churches are not the same.

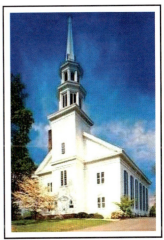

1. Some churches supplement the Holy Bible with one or more additional "holy books" which are considered equal to or better than the Bible. In my opinion it is very easy to deviate away from the teachings of the Holy Bible if you are following the teachings in some other book.
2. Some churches select a few passages from the Holy Bible and base their entire faith on those few verses. They basically ignore all the other teachings in the Holy Bible.
3. Some churches teach that certain parts of the Holy Bible are true but other parts aren't true, or those other parts are no longer valid and can therefore be safely ignored.
4. Some churches teach from the Holy Bible and from nothing else. They believe every word in the Bible and they teach the entire Bible from cover to cover. And they encourage their members to read the Holy Bible for themselves and to practice what it teaches. This is the type of Christian church that pleases God.

So Many Religions

Mormon, Catholic, Adventist, Christian, Islam, and Hindu.
So many faiths and so many religions from which to choose.

Muhammad, Buddha, Confucius, Gandhi, and Jesus, too.
Are they all about the same or is one just right for me and you.

Each religion claims it is the best way to worship God in Heaven above.
Just do things their way and it will result in blessings and love.

Since these claims contradict each other, they cannot all be true.
Therefore we should carefully select the right religion to pursue.

This subject can be debated until you are blue in the face,
but the final answer must ultimately lead to the Throne of Grace.

The path to that Throne is Jesus Christ, God's only begotten Son.
The Christian faith offers God's gift of forgiveness to everyone.

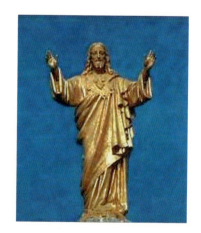

Scripture References: Hebrews 4:16, Mark 4:11, First Corinthians 2:13-14, John 1:1, John 1:14, Luke 2:11, John 14:1, John 10:30, John 11:25-26, John 8:24, Ecclesiastes 7:20, Romans 3:23, James 2:10, Matthew 16:26, Romans 6:23, Romans 5:8-9, Leviticus 17:11, John 3:16, Romans 10:9-10, Acts 16:31, Joel 2:32, Mark 1:15, Second Corinthians 6:2.

Poem: So Many Religions

Chapter Eighty-Two

How to Become a Christian

Let's look at what the New King James Version of the Holy Bible says about how you can become a Christian.

The Secret Mystery

Mark 4:11
"To you it has been given to know the mystery of the kingdom of God;"

You are about to learn the secret of life after death.

Spiritual Truth or Foolishness

1 Corinthians 2:13-14
"These things we also speak, not in words which man's wisdom teaches but which the Holy Spirit teaches, comparing spiritual things with spiritual. But the natural man does not receive the things of the Spirit of God, for they are foolishness to him; nor can he know them, because they are spiritually discerned."

The things you are about to learn are common knowledge among Christians. Once they have been explained to you then you will understand the most important truth about life and death. And you will probably want to share your new knowledge with others. But the Bible tells us that not everyone has the ability to understand these truths because they are spiritual truths. These spiritual truths will appear as foolishness to many people.

Now let's look now at the first of these spiritual truths.

The One and Only True God

John 1:1
"In the beginning was the Word, and the Word was with God, and the Word was God."

God was alive in the beginning. He is alive now. And He will live forever.

The Son of God

John 1:14
"And the Word became flesh, and dwelt among us,"

Luke 2:11
"For there is born to you this day in the city of David a Savior, who is Christ the Lord."

One day about 2000 years ago, God visited this earth in human form. He was born as the baby Jesus in the town of Bethlehem (the city of David).

The Father and the Son

John 14:1
"Let not your heart be troubled; you believe in God, believe also in me."

John 10:30
"I and My Father are one."

In the above two scriptures Jesus tells us that He and God are the same. God (the Father) stayed in heaven while Jesus (the Son) visited the earth to tell us about the Father.

The Promise of Eternal Life

John 11:25-26
"I am the resurrection and the life. He who believes in Me, though he may die, he shall live. And whoever lives and believes in Me shall never die. Do you believe this?"

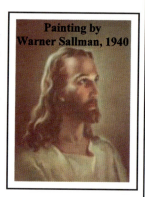

Jesus said that anyone who believes in Him will not die but will live forever. And then Jesus asked this question, "Do you believe this?"

The Penalty of Sin

John 8:24
"if you do not believe that I am He, you shall die in your sins."

Ecclesiastes 7:20
"For there is not a just man on earth who does good and does not sin."

Romans 3:23
"for all have sinned and fall short of the glory of God,"

James 2:10
"For whoever shall keep the whole law, and yet stumble in one point, he is guilty of all."

Matthew 16:26
"For what profit is it to a man if he gains the whole world, and loses his own soul? Or what will a man give in exchange for his soul?"

The Bible clearly tells us that no one can live his or her entire life without committing some type of sin. (If the truth were known, all of us commit many different types of sins over the course of our lives.) However, it only takes one sin to make us a sinner. And the penalty for sin is the condemnation of our eternal soul. The Bible mentions Hell more often than it does Heaven. Hell is a real place where condemned souls spend eternity in agony. The Bible also asks this question: "What can you offer God to redeem your soul from an eternity in hell?"

The Gift of God

Romans 6:23
"For the wages of sin is death, but the gift of God is eternal life in Christ Jesus our Lord."

God has provided a way for us to avoid Hell so we can spend eternity in Heaven. That way is through faith in God's Son, the Lord Jesus Christ.

Forgiveness of Sin

Romans 5:8-9
"But God demonstrates His own love toward us, in that while we were still sinners, Christ died for us. Much more then, having now been justified by His blood, we shall be saved from wrath through Him."

Leviticus 17:11
"for it is the blood that makes atonement for the soul."

John 3:16
"For God so loved the world that He gave His only begotten Son, that whoever believes in Him should not perish but have everlasting life."

Christ was crucified and He shed His life's blood on the cross at Calvary. God accepted the death of His only Son as full payment for your sins and mine. Three days later, Jesus returned from the dead and took possession of His dead body. The grave

Chapter Eighty-Two: How to Become a Christian

could not hold Him. The grave won't be able to hold us either if we believe that Jesus Christ is God's only Son, and that He died that we might have eternal life in Heaven.

Accepting Jesus Christ into Your Life

Romans 10:9-10
"if you confess with your mouth the Lord Jesus and believe in your heart that God has raised Him from the dead, you will be saved. For with the heart one believes unto righteousness, and with the mouth confession is made unto salvation."

Acts 16:31
"Believe on the Lord Jesus Christ, and you will be saved, you and your household."

How do you become a Christian? By telling someone, anyone, that you believe that Jesus Christ was God's only Son, that He died on the cross in payment for your sins, and that He rose from the dead and He is alive in Heaven right now waiting on you. Can you do that? If you can then you will spend eternity in Heaven instead of Hell.

When is the Best Time to Become a Christian?

Mark 1:15
"The time is fulfilled, and the kingdom of God is at hand. Repent, and believe in the gospel."

2 Corinthians 6:2
"Behold, now is the accepted time; behold, now is the day of salvation."

When should you become a Christian? Today. Right now. Don't put it off another minute. Unlock the doors to heaven with the only key that will fit -- faith in Jesus Christ, the one and only Son of the Living God.

Concluding Comments

God only grants forgiveness to sinners. It doesn't matter what you have done in the past, God will forgive you (unless you have accepted the mark of the beast on your right hand during the end times). You don't have to clean up your life to become a Christian. I am a Christian and I still make mistakes and I still occasionally yield to sin. But God forgives me and He will forgive you too. But you must take the next step toward God. God has already taken a giant step toward you. He has allowed His only Son to die on the Cross to pay for all of your sins: your past sins, your current sins, and all the sins you will commit after you become a Christian. But you have to accept God's forgiveness by believing in His Son. Please do it now. Go tell someone, anyone, that you have accepted Jesus Christ as your Savior.

The Tree of Life

Adam and Eve ate from the Tree of Knowledge of Good and Evil,
instead of the Tree of Life which would have made them Immortal.

Since that day when our first parents followed the advice of Satan,
we have all been trapped in a world filled with death and destruction.

We must each decide if we will continue in our first parents' direction,
or choose a new path that leads away from the pit of eternal damnation.

The good news is that God has provided a method for our redemption.
His Son Jesus died on the cross and paid the ransom for our salvation.

When Jesus ate His Last Supper with His eleven friends and one enemy,
He broke a loaf of Bread and He said it represented His broken Body.

Jesus Christ, the Only Son of God, is The Bread of Life for you and me.
Jesus Christ is our second chance to partake of that Life Giving Tree.

However, we still have the freedom to choose just like Adam and Eve.
But if you accept Jesus as Savior, then Eternal Life you will receive.

This Poem is Dedicated to My Granddaughter **Isabelle Claire McClintock**.

Scripture References: Genesis 2:9, Genesis 2:16-17, Genesis 3:4-7, Genesis 3:22-24, John 6:35, Luke 22:19-20, John 6:32-35, John 6:47-51, John 3:16-18, John 1:29, Revelation 2:7, Revelation 22:1-5.

Poem: The Tree of Life

Chapter Eighty-Three

Is Salvation by Faith Alone or is Something More Required?

Introduction

God will make the final decision on who is saved and who is not saved. God looks at our hearts and God will judge each one of us based on His Perfect Will and His Perfect Wisdom. God will **never** by restricted by anything man writes or says.

Please keep this in mind as you read the following words. The following words are nothing more than my words, with a few scriptures added. The scriptures are Holy. But my words are nothing more than the words of a man.

My primary objective in writing this chapter was to help me more clearly understand the role of water baptism in the Christian faith so I could explain it to anyone whom might be interested in this topic. Water baptism is one of those topics that has divided churches, and it has frequently brought one Christian into conflict with another Christian. I do not wish to create additional divisions or conflicts within the Christian faith. However, these divisions existed long before I was born and they will continue to exist long after I am dead.

Salvation and Water Baptism

Let me begin by clearly stating the issue. The issue is **not** "Should a Christian be water baptized?" All Christians who wish to follow the teachings of Jesus Christ should be water baptized as an act of obedience and submission before God.

The fundamental question is whether or not water baptism is a necessary part of the salvation process, or if it is simply the outward public act of a repentant sinner to the will of Jesus.

The answer to this question must be based on what the Holy Bible says about baptism.

1. Jesus was water baptized and we should follow His example. But Jesus did not personally water baptize anyone. (John 4:2 - "it was not Jesus who baptized, but his disciples.")

2. The apostle Paul only water baptized two different individuals plus one household of people. Paul spent most of his time preaching the gospel but he did not water baptize the people he led to a saving faith in Jesus Christ. (1 Corinthians 1:14-16.)

3. One of the two thieves who were crucified beside Jesus did confess Jesus with his mouth but he was not water baptized. The thief died on his cross a short time after Jesus died. However, Jesus still granted that thief access into paradise. (Luke 23:39-46.)

4. Cornelius and his household believed the Gospel message about Jesus Christ and immediately they all received the gift of the Holy Spirit. At that point it would be difficult to argue that they were not saved. Then they were water baptized. (Acts 10:30-48.)

How can a person be saved?

1. Many, many scriptures say if a person will only believe then he or she will be saved.
(Luke 7:44-50, John 3:3-21, John 3:36, John 5:24-29, John 11:25, John 20:30-31, Acts 10:38-43, Acts 16:31, Romans 3:22-28, Romans 10:8-13, Ephesians 2:4-10, 1 John 5:12-13.)

2. Three scriptures say a person must believe and be baptized in order to be saved.
(Mark 16:15-20, Acts 2:38-39, Acts 22:12-16.)

3. The first part of one scripture verse might be interpreted as saying that water baptism will wash away your sins. However, if you read to the end of that verse you will notice that it clearly says that calling on the name of the Lord is critical to the forgiveness of sins.
(Acts 22:16 - "Arise and be baptized, and wash away your sins, calling on the name of the Lord.")

In whose Name should we be baptized?

1. Several scriptures say be baptized in the name of Jesus Christ. (Acts 2:38, Acts 8:15-16, Acts 10:48, Acts 19:5.)
2. One scripture says be baptized in the name of the Father, the Son, and the Holy Spirit. (Matthew 28:18-20.)

Since there is only One God, and since the Father, the Son, and the Holy Spirit are One, then it appears that if you are baptized in the name of Jesus or in the name of the Father, the Son, and the Holy Spirit then you are being baptized into one of God's many different but perfectly correct names.

Is water baptism the complete submersion of the body under water, or is water baptism the pouring of water on a person's head?

1. **Submersion:** The Holy Bible says that Jesus was baptized in the Jordan River and that when He came up out of the water the Holy Spirit descended on Him. This could be legitimately interpreted in either of the following two ways:
   a. Jesus was completely submerged below the water and then He came up out of the water.
   b. Jesus walked down into the Jordan River and He was baptized by John the Baptist and then He walked up out of the Jordan River.

   There are also several other scriptures that indicate that people were baptized in a large body of water. (Matthew 3:4-17, Mark 1:4-11, Acts 8:34-40.)

2. **Pouring:** Some people may have been water baptized inside a person's home. If this was the case then water was probably poured on those people to baptize them. (Acts 9:17-19, Acts 22:12-16, Acts 16:29-34.)
   In the Old Testament a small quantity of oil was poured on a person to sanctify that person for a specific task.

If the New Testament contained very clear instructions on how water baptism was actually done then we should be obedient and we should water baptize people in exactly that way. However, since God intentionally decided to not give us specific instructions for water baptism, then it may be that God simply desires for a person to be water baptized and God is not concerned with exactly how that ritual is performed. But that is just my opinion and it is nothing more than one man's opinion. Each Christian Church will need to make their own decision on how they will practice water baptism.

There is more than one type of baptism:

1. There is baptism by water. (Matthew 3:11-12, Mark 1:8, Luke 3:16, Acts 1:5, Acts 8:38, Acts 10:47, Acts 11:16.)
2. There is baptism by the Holy Spirit. (Matthew 3:11-12, Mark 1:8, Luke 3:16, John 1:33, Acts 1:5, Acts 11:16, 1 Corinthians 12:13.)
3. There is baptism by fire. (Matthew 3:11-12, Luke 3:16.)

Which comes first: baptism with water or baptism with the Holy Spirit?

1. Some people were water baptized and later they received the Holy Spirit. (Acts 2:38-39, Acts 8:14-17, Acts 19:4-7.)
2. Some people received the Holy Spirit and later they were water baptized. (Acts 10:30-48.)

Chapter Eighty-Three: Is Salvation by Faith Alone?

A Few Holy Scriptures:

Mark 16:15-16
He said to them, "Go into all the world and preach the good news to all creation. Whoever believes and is baptized will be saved, but whoever does not believe will be condemned."

The above scripture says believe and be baptized and you will be saved. But it also says if you do not believe you will be condemned. It does **not** say if you are not water baptized you will be condemned. In fact the above scripture does not clearly indicate whether the baptism reference is to water baptism or to baptism by the Holy Spirit. However, in Titus 3:4-7 the Bible says that washing by the Holy Spirit is what saves us.

If you read the entire Holy Bible from cover to cover you will find many, many scriptures that clearly say that any person who will not believe will be condemned.

However, I could **not** find one scripture anywhere in the entire Bible that clearly says that any person who is not water baptized will be condemned.

Proverbs 30:5-6
Every word of God is flawless; he is a shield to those who take refuge in him. Do not add to his words, or he will rebuke you and prove you a liar.

Jesus Christ personally spoke the following words about Himself:

John 3:16-18
"For God so loved the world that he gave his one and only Son, that whoever believes in him shall not perish but have eternal life. For God did not send his Son into the world to condemn the world, but to save the world through him. Whoever believes in him is not condemned, but whoever does not believe stands condemned already because he has not believed in the name of God's one and only Son."

The above words are a "direct quote" spoken by Jesus Christ about Himself. Jesus did **not** mention water baptism. Jesus said that anyone who simply believes in Him will be saved.

There is no simple straightforward answer to the question about the role of water baptism in the Christian faith. The Holy Bible is not an easy to read "how to" book that clearly explains everything in a simple step-by-step order. The Holy Bible requires diligent study to more clearly understand its teachings and the Will of God Almighty.

However, God intended for His "Plan of Salvation" to be so simple that even a child could understand it. Anyone who believes that only a really, really smart person will be able to understand the Holy Bible has a serious problem with personal pride. Please remember that God resists the proud but God will honor the humble believer. Which are you?

A Few More Scriptures:

Luke 10:21
At that time Jesus, full of joy through the Holy Spirit, said, "I praise you, Father, Lord of heaven and earth, because you have hidden these things from the wise and learned, and revealed them to little children. Yes, Father, for this was your good pleasure."

Proverbs 3:5
Trust in the LORD with all your heart and lean not on your own understanding;

Ephesians 2:8-9
For it is by grace you have been saved, through faith -- and this not from yourselves, it is the gift of God -- not by works, so that no one can boast.

1 Corinthians 1:17
For Christ did not send me to baptize, but to preach the gospel --
not with words of human wisdom, lest the cross of Christ be emptied of its power.

Chapter Eighty-Three: Is Salvation by Faith Alone?

A Quick Summary

In the Old Testament when something was important to God then He would give very detailed instructions on how to do what He expected. I have found it interesting that the New Testament does not contain any clear specific instructions about water baptism. For example, the New Testament does **not** contain answers to any of the following questions:

1. **How should water baptism be done:** complete submersion of the body, or pouring water on the head, or sprinkling a few drops of water on the head?
2. **How old should a person be before he or she can be baptized:** 7 days, 3 years, 7 years, 12 years, 16 years, 20 years, 25 years, or is the person's maturity more important than the person's age?
3. **When should a person be baptized:** immediately upon confessing Jesus as Savior, or anytime the same day, or sometime within a week, or just whenever it is convenient?
4. **Where should a person be baptized:** indoors, outdoors, only in a river, or in any pool of water?
5. **Who should perform the baptism:** anyone who has been previously baptized, or any elder of the church, or only an ordained minister?

If water baptism is absolutely necessary for salvation then is any baptism method okay as long as the person is water baptized? Or do specific conditions have to be met or else the water baptism doesn't count and the person is doomed to an eternal hell?

Since water baptism is part of the Christian faith, this means that at some time in the past every Christian Church or Denomination had to make a decision on how they would water baptize new believers. The original founders of each Christian denomination had to use their own judgment in making their baptism decisions as they felt led by the Holy Spirit. Then these baptism procedures were passed down as tradition from one generation to the next.

Unfortunately most Christian denominations today now believe that the way they water baptize new believers is the only way that is acceptable to God. I personally do not know if the water baptism method that is currently practiced by any one Christian denomination is more acceptable to God than the baptism methods practiced by other Christian denominations. The reason I don't know is because all the different baptism methods now being used are based on the interpretations of the founders of each Christian denomination and all of these baptism methods can be supported in one way or another using different scriptures from the Holy Bible.

Consequently I cannot tell you exactly how water baptism should be done because I have not been able to find a clear description of water baptism anywhere in the Holy Bible. Therefore I suggest you be content with whatever water baptism method that is currently being used at the Christian Church you regularly attend.

Now that I have been honest and I have explained what I don't know, please allow me to tell you my current opinion about salvation. But please, please remember that the following is just the opinion of a man and God will **never** be restricted by anyone's opinion on this topic, and that includes my opinion.

Salvation

If you believe that Jesus Christ is the one and only Son of God, and that He died on the Cross as the full and final payment for all your sins, and that God raised His Son from the dead, and you accept Jesus' death on the cross and the shedding of His Holy Blood as the full ransom payment for your eternal soul, and you confess Jesus Christ as your Savior, then you will be saved. The moment you believe you are saved and you immediately receive the gift of eternal life and you will spend eternity with God in Glory.

Chapter Eighty-Three: Is Salvation by Faith Alone?

Obedience and Growth in the Christian Faith

1. As soon as possible after you are saved you should be water baptized in the name of the Father, and the Son, and the Holy Spirit.
2. Then you should try to gradually understand and follow more of the teachings of your Savior Jesus Christ.
3. You should never be ashamed of your Savior Jesus Christ and you should be willing to tell anyone who asks you about your faith in Jesus.
4. You should understand and practice the two great commandments: (1) Love God with all your heart, soul, and mind; and (2) love your neighbor as yourself.
5. You should remember the Sabbath day and you should attend a Christian Church every week that teaches from the Holy Bible and not from some other "inspired document."
6. You should have a desire to read the Holy Bible on a regular basis and you should allow God to speak to you through His Holy Words to help you better understand His Ways.
7. You should pray every day for more of God's wisdom and guidance and you should ask God to help your life unfold according to His Perfect Will.

Conclusion

For the **Scribes and Pharisees** among us I believe the above is a reasonable summary of most of the relevant scriptures that mention salvation. If we believe in Jesus Christ then our sins will be forgiven and we will go to Heaven. If we want to have some rewards when we get to Heaven then we need to be obedient to the teachings of Jesus Christ.

For the **Children** among us I believe that God does not desire for anyone to perish and He will evaluate each one of us based on whatever standard He selects. For many of us that standard might be the following:

Romans 10:13
"Everyone who calls on the name of the Lord will be saved."

A Closing Footnote

I don't mind if you have a completely different opinion on the above topics. You are entitled to your beliefs just as I am entitled to my beliefs. Based on my beliefs, if I was standing at the gate into Heaven and God asked me for a reason why I should be allowed to enter then I would probably say something similar to the following:

I know I deserve to be cast into Hell.
I am a sinner and I have never, never done anything that would make me worthy of spending eternity with You.
However, when Your Son Jesus died on the cross for the sins of the entire world, I was one of those wicked sinners that He died for.
And I have always told anyone who would listen about my faith in Your Son Jesus and my adoration for His Holy Name.
And I have never had any hope of receiving Your gift of eternal life other than my faith in what Your Son did for me on Calvary.

That's probably what I would say, assuming I was able to speak without choking on the words. What would you say?

Respectfully,
Grandpappy.

The Rapture

About 2,000 years ago Jesus' disciples asked Him, "What signs will appear before you return again?"
Jesus' answer is recorded in the 24th Chapter of Matthew so we can recognize these signs when they begin.

- - - - - -

Several years later Jesus told His disciple John to record his vision of these events in the Book of Revelation.
Satan will persecute Christians for a time but God will punish Satan's followers with death and destruction.

- - - - - -

Jesus, The Lamb of God will open the First Seal:
Matthew 24:5: There will be wars and there will be rumors that the wars are getting worse day by day.
Revelation 6:1-2: A man wearing a crown will have a weapon that can be fired from very far away.

Jesus, The Lamb of God will open the Second Seal:
Matthew 24:6-7: Nations will fight one another and many kingdoms will declare war on foreign lands.
Revelation 6:3-4: The entire earth will be at war and men will kill each other with the weapons in their hands.

Jesus, The Lamb of God will open the Third Seal:
Matthew 24:7: Food will become so scarce that there will be severe famines across the face of the earth.
Revelation 6:5-6: A day's wages will only buy food for one day because that is what the food is now worth.

Jesus, The Lamb of God will open the Fourth Seal:
Matthew 24:7-8: There will be pestilences, and earthquakes will also occur at any time and in any place.
Revelation 6:7-8: Plagues, hunger, war, and wild animals will kill one-fourth of the entire human race.

Jesus, The Lamb of God will open the Fifth Seal:
Matthew 24:9-28: Many Christians will be slain. But 3½ years after the first seal of the tribulation,
Christian persecution will greatly escalate when in the Holy Place stands the abomination of desolation.
Revelation 6:9-11: Christians everywhere on the face of the earth will be marked for termination,
and many will be slain but their souls will receive a white robe when they reach their heavenly destination.

Jesus, The Lamb of God will open the Sixth Seal (the Rapture of the Saints):
Matthew 24:29-42: The sun will be darkened, the moon will not shine, and the stars will fall from the sky.
Jesus will return with the sound of a trumpet and will gather His elect from the earth to be with Him on high.
Revelation 6:12-7:14: The sun will turn dark, the moon will turn red, and the stars will fall from the sky.
The sky will roll up like a scroll. Later a multitude of Christians appear in heaven although they did **not** die.

Jesus, The Lamb of God will open the Seventh Seal:
Revelation 8:1: There will be a profound silence in heaven for the space of about half an hour.
With every Christian now safe in heaven, the earth will soon begin to witness God's wrath and His power.

Poem: The Rapture

Chapter Eighty-Four

The Rapture

Introduction

There is a debate going on among Christians over the timing of the Rapture of the saints. The Rapture is that instant in time when the Lord Jesus Christ appears in the clouds of the heavens and He calls all His followers to come up to heaven to be with Him. According to scripture, the dead in Christ will be raised first, and then we who are alive and remain will join them in the clouds to be forevermore with the Lord.

> **1 Thessalonians 4:16-17** - "For the Lord himself shall descend from heaven with a shout, with the voice of the archangel, and with the trump of God: and the dead in Christ shall rise first: Then we which are alive and remain shall be caught up together with them in the clouds, to meet the Lord in the air: and so shall we ever be with the Lord."

The fact of the Rapture is not in question (at least not among Christians). However, there is a question about when the Rapture will occur. Some Christians believe it will occur immediately before the tribulation period begins. Other Christians believe it will occur either during the tribulation period, or near the very end of the tribulation period. (The tribulation is a seven year period of time preceding the thousand year reign of Christ on earth.)

The most logical way to address this issue is to see what the Holy Bible has to say about this event. Christians believe the entire Bible is the true and accurate Word of God and it is without error. Therefore it should be used to answer the question of when the Rapture will occur. One word of caution, however. Do not rely on footnotes added to your Bible. A biblical footnote is not the inspired Word of God even though it is printed in your Bible. It is simply one person's interpretation of scripture. With that caution in mind, let's take a look at the 24th chapter of Matthew and the book of Revelation.

In the 24th chapter of Matthew, Matthew recorded the words of Jesus when He replied to the question His disciples asked Him, "What shall be the sign of thy coming, and of the end of the world?" The book of Revelation records the words of Jesus when He revealed unto John the events of the end times. By comparing these two books we can uncover some important clues as to the timing of the Rapture.

> **Matthew 24:3**
> "And as he sat upon the mount of Olives, the disciples came unto him privately, saying, Tell us, when shall these things be? and what shall be the sign of thy coming, and of the end of the world."

The above verse establishes the context of the following verses of scripture within the 24th chapter of the book of Matthew.

First Seal (Appearance of the AntiChrist)

> **Revelation 6:1-2**
> "And I saw when the Lamb opened one of the seals, and I heard, as it were the noise of thunder, one of the four beasts saying, Come and see. And I saw, and behold a white horse: and he that sat on him had a bow; and a crown was given unto him: and he went forth conquering, and to conquer."

> **Matthew 24:4-5**
> "And Jesus answered and said unto them, Take heed that no man deceive you. For many shall come in my name, saying, I am Christ; and shall deceive many."

The opening of the first seal is normally interpreted to be the beginning of the tribulation period when the AntiChrist appears on the scene in his full glory. In the book of Matthew, Jesus warns His followers to be on the lookout for this person.

Second Seal (War)

Revelation 6:3-4
"And when he had opened the second seal, I heard the second beast say, Come and see. And there went out another horse that was red: and power was given to him that sat thereon to take peace from the earth, and that they should kill one another, and there was given unto him a great sword."

Matthew 24:6-7a
"And ye shall hear of wars and rumors of wars: see that ye be not troubled: for all these things must come to pass, but the end is not yet. For nation shall rise against nation, and kingdom against kingdom:"

In both Revelation and Matthew, Jesus says that immediately after the appearance of the AntiChrist there will be a period of war.

Third Seal (Famine)

Revelation 6:5-6
"And when he had opened the third seal, I heard the third beast say, Come and see. And I beheld, and lo a black horse; and he that sat on him had a pair of balances in his hand. And I heard a voice in the midst of the four beasts say, A measure of wheat for a penny, and three measures of barley for a penny, and see thou hurt not the oil and the wine."

Matthew 24:7b
"and there shall be famines,"

In both books, Jesus tells His followers that a severe famine will follow the war, and a day's supply of food will sell for a full day's pay (a penny was a day's wage in those days).

Fourth Seal (Disease)

Revelation 6:7-8
"And when he had opened the fourth seal, I heard the voice of the fourth beast say, Come and see. And I looked, and behold a pale horse, and his name that sat on him was Death, and Hell followed with him. And power was given unto them over the fourth part of the earth, to kill with sword, and with hunger, and with death, and with the beasts of the earth."

Matthew 24:7c-8
"and pestilences, and earthquakes, in divers places. All these are the beginning of sorrows."

Anyone who has studied history and the events that follow a major war knows that a period of famine normally occurs after the war, and a period of disease and death follows next. When people become weak due to the lack of food, diseases their bodies could have easily withstood when they were healthy are now able to kill them. This is precisely what Jesus says will happen in both books of the Bible.

Fifth Seal (Christians Slain in Large Numbers)

Revelation 6:9-11
"And when he had opened the fifth seal, I saw under the altar the souls of them that were slain for the word of God, and for the testimony which they held: And they cried with a loud voice, saying, How long, O Lord, holy and true, dost thou not judge and avenge our blood on them that dwell on the earth? And white robes were given unto every one of them, and it was said unto them, that they should rest yet for a little season, until their fellow servants also and their brethren, that should be killed as they were, should be fulfilled."

Matthew 24:9,14-15,21-22
"Then shall they deliver you up to be afflicted, and shall kill you: and ye shall be hated of all nations for my name's sake. ... And this gospel of the kingdom shall be preached in all the world for a witness unto all nations; and then shall the end come. When ye therefore shall see

the abomination of desolation, spoken of by Daniel the prophet, stand in the holy place, (whoso readeth, let him understand:) ... For then shall be great tribulation, such as was not since the beginning of the world to this time, no, nor ever shall be. And except those days be shortened, there should no flesh be saved: but for the elect's sake those days shall be shortened."

Daniel 9:27
"And he shall confirm the covenant with many for one week: and in the midst of the week he shall cause the sacrifice and the oblation to cease, and for the overspreading of abominations he shall make it desolate, even until the consummation, and that determined shall be poured upon the desolate."

Revelation 2:10
"be thou faithful unto death, and I will give thee a crown of life."

The book of Daniel gives us a clue as to the timing of the fifth seal. Daniel mentions that in the middle of the seven year period the AntiChrist will try to establish himself as God upon the earth. At that time Christians will be slain in large numbers. This passage of scripture makes it very difficult to hold the view that the Rapture will occur before the opening of the first seal. If there are no Christians left on earth then where do all these new converts come from? Who, of their own accord, without the witness of a fellow Christian, would be willing to accept the Christian faith if that meant they would be immediately slain? If all the Christians are Raptured before the first seal is opened then there would be no Christians around at this time to lead the unsaved to Christ. How then could we explain the presence of a large number of Christians at this point in time?

The most logical way to account for them is if the Rapture hasn't happened yet. All the preceding events (war, famine, disease, and Christian persecution) are things that Christians have faced many times during the past 2,000 years. There is no logical reason why we should be spared from facing them again today.

Sixth Seal (Sun, Moon, and Star Signs)

Revelation 6:12-13, 7:1-4
"And I beheld when he had opened the sixth seal, and, lo, there was a great earthquake; and the sun became black as sackcloth of hair, and the moon became as blood; And the stars of heaven fell unto the earth, even as a fig tree casteth her untimely figs, when she is shaken of a mighty wind. ... And after these things I saw four angels standing on the four corners of the earth, ... Saying, Hurt not the earth, neither the sea, nor the trees, till we have sealed the servants of our God in their foreheads. And I heard the number of them which were sealed a hundred and forty and four thousand of all the tribes of the children of Israel."

Matthew 24:29-33
"Immediately after the tribulation of those days shall the sun be darkened, and the moon shall not give her light, and the stars shall fall from heaven, and the powers of the heavens shall be shaken.
And then shall appear the sign of the Son of man in heaven; and then shall all the tribes of the earth mourn, and they shall see the Son of man coming in the clouds of heaven with power and great glory. And he shall send his angels with a great sound of a trumpet, and they shall gather together his elect from the four winds, from one end of heaven to the other.
Now learn a parable of the fig tree; When his branch is yet tender, and putteth forth leaves, ye know that summer is nigh: So likewise ye, when ye shall see all these things, know that it is near, even at the doors."

In both Revelation and Matthew the sun, moon, and star signs are the same. Notice also the parable of the fig tree in both books. Remember that Jesus is the one who is revealing these events to both John and Matthew, and He uses almost the same terminology even though these two revelations are separated in time by at least forty years. Notice also that this is the first appearance of the 144,000 witnesses. They were not present prior to this time to convert others to the Christian faith.

Notice also the appearance of the Son of Man (Jesus), the angels, and the trumpet call that collects the elect (Christians) from all over the earth.

Matthew 24:40-42
"Then shall two be in the field; the one shall be taken, and the other left. Two women shall be grinding at the mill; the one shall be taken, and the other left. Watch therefore: for ye know not the hour your Lord doth come."

Revelation 7:9
"After this I beheld, and lo, a great multitude, which no man could number, of all nations, and kindreds, and people, and tongues, stood before the throne, and before the Lamb, clothed with white robes, and palms in their hands:"

In the book of Matthew, after the sun and moon are darkened, the Lord returns for His followers. In the book of Revelation, a great multitude of Christians, from all over the world, suddenly appear in heaven. For someone with an open mind, these two descriptions are almost identical to what we Christians call the Rapture of the saints. Notice also that this reference to the Rapture in the book of Revelation occurs right after the 144,000 Jews are ordained to spread the Gospel. God does not want anyone to perish and he has provided a way for the Gospel to be carried forth after all the New Testament Christians are Raptured.

1 Thessalonians 4:16-17
"For the Lord himself shall descend from heaven with a shout, with the voice of the archangel, and with the trump of God: and the dead in Christ shall rise first: Then we which are alive and remain shall be caught up together with them in the clouds, to meet the Lord in the air: and so shall we ever be with the Lord."

The above verse adequately describes the event that we Christians commonly call the Rapture.

1 Thessalonians 5:2-4
"For yourselves know perfectly that the day of the Lord so cometh as a thief in the night. For when they shall say, Peace and safety, then sudden destruction cometh upon them, as travail upon a woman with child; and they shall not escape. But ye, brethren, are not in darkness, that day should overtake you as a thief."

The disciples asked Jesus for signs of His coming. Why would Jesus give them specific details about His return if none of His followers were going to be alive when those signs came to pass? In the above verse Paul tells us the Rapture should not overtake us as a thief in the night. He is confirming what Jesus told His disciples. When we see the signs that Jesus spoke of come to pass, then we should be prepared to either be slain for our Christian faith, or to be Raptured into heaven, if we survive the time of Christian persecution.

Seventh Seal (Trumpet Judgments)

Revelation 8:1-2
"And when he had opened the seventh seal, there was silence in heaven about the space of half an hour. And I saw the seven angels which stood before God; and to them were given seven trumpets."

The seventh seal begins God's wrath on an unbelieving world. Christians will be spared from that wrath because they will be Raptured after the opening of the 6th seal and before the opening of the 7th seal.

The entire 70th week of Daniel is commonly referred to as "The Tribulation" by many Christians. This is a poor choice of terms for Daniel's 70th week because it easily leads to a misunderstanding of other passages of scripture. The first six seals deal with Satan's persecution of mankind. The opening of the seventh seal begins God's Wrath on an unbelieving world (from which Christians are spared).

Conclusion

I encourage you to purchase and read Marvin Rosenthal's book, **The Pre-Wrath Rapture of the Church**. He does an excellent job of explaining many other scriptures that help to clarify when the Rapture will occur.

Chapter Eighty-Five

What Does the Bible Say About Alcohol?
(Note: Alcohol includes Wine, Beer, and Fermented Drinks.)

Introduction

One of the issues that periodically divides Christian Churches is the subject of alcoholic beverages. The two extreme positions about alcoholic beverages are as follows:

1. Anyone who is a true Christian will not drink any type of alcoholic beverage and that person will criticize anyone who does drink any type of alcoholic beverage.
2. It is okay for a Christian to drink any type of alcoholic beverage.

The above two positions are in direct opposition to one another. Therefore, if a person desires to be the type of Christian who is approved by God as being someone who correctly interprets God's Words and God's Laws, then that Christian should base his or her beliefs on what the Holy Bible says about alcoholic beverages and not on what he or she personally wants to believe, or on the "tradition" of his or her Church.

With this in mind let's examine the subject of alcoholic beverages using the Holy Bible as our guide. The Holy Bible has both good things and bad things to say about alcoholic beverages. To ignore either side of this subject would be inappropriate.

Negative Comments about Alcoholic Beverages

Let's begin by examining the "negative" comments about alcoholic beverages:

> **Proverbs 20:1** - Wine is a mocker and beer a brawler; whoever is led astray by them is not wise.
>
> **Proverbs 21:17** - He who loves pleasure will become poor; whoever loves wine and oil will never be rich.
>
> **Proverbs 23:19-21** - Listen, my son, and be wise, and keep your heart on the right path. Do not join those who drink too much wine or gorge themselves on meat, for drunkards and gluttons become poor, and drowsiness clothes them in rags.
>
> **Proverbs 23:31-35** - Do not gaze at wine when it is red, when it sparkles in the cup, when it goes down smoothly! In the end it bites like a snake and poisons like a viper. Your eyes will see strange sights and your mind imagine confusing things. You will be like one sleeping on the high seas, lying on top of the rigging. "They hit me," you will say, "but I'm not hurt! They beat me, but I don't feel it! When will I wake up so I can find another drink?
>
> **Proverbs 31:4** - It is not for kings, O Lemuel -- not for kings to drink wine, not for rulers to crave beer,
>
> **Ephesians 5:18** - Do not get drunk on wine, which leads to debauchery.
>
> **1 Corinthians 6:9-10** - Do you not know that the wicked will not inherit the kingdom of God? Do not be deceived: Neither the sexually immoral nor idolaters nor adulterers nor male prostitutes nor homosexual offenders nor thieves nor the greedy nor drunkards nor slanderers nor swindlers will inherit the kingdom of God.

The bible contains two stories of men who became drunk with wine and who had an unfortunate experience while they were unconscious:

1. **Noah** planted a vineyard and he drank some of its wine and became drunk. (Genesis 9:20-27.)
2. **Lot** was encouraged to overindulge in wine by his two daughters and while he was under its influence each of his daughters got into bed with him and each of his daughters became pregnant by her own father. The oldest daughter gave birth to Moab the father of the Moabites, and the youngest daughter gave birth to Ben-Ammi the father of the Ammonites. (Genesis 19:32-38.) It should be noted that Ruth was a Moabitess (Ruth 1:22) and she became the great-grandmother of King David and she was therefore also an ancestor of our Lord Jesus Christ.

Positive Comments about Alcoholic Beverages

Now let's examine the "positive" comments about alcoholic beverages.

Psalm 104:14-15 - He makes grass grow for the cattle, and plants for man to cultivate -- bringing forth food from the earth: wine that gladdens the heart of man, oil to make his face shine, and bread that sustains his heart.

Deuteronomy 7:12-13 - If you pay attention to these laws and are careful to follow them, then the LORD your God will keep his covenant of love with you, as he swore to your forefathers. He will love you and bless you and increase your numbers. He will bless the fruit of your womb, the crops of your land -- your grain, new wine and oil -- the calves of your herds and the lambs of your flocks in the land that he swore to your forefathers to give you.

Deuteronomy 14:26 - Use the silver to buy whatever you like: cattle, sheep, wine or other fermented drink, or anything you wish. Then you and your household shall eat there in the presence of the LORD your God and rejoice.

Wine as a Drink Offering to God

God commanded that wine be offered to Him twice every day:

Exodus 29:38-42 - This is what you are to offer on the altar regularly each day: two lambs a year old. Offer one in the morning and the other at twilight. With the first lamb offer a tenth of an ephah of fine flour mixed with a quarter of a hin of oil from pressed olives, and a quarter of a hin of wine as a drink offering. Sacrifice the other lamb at twilight with the same grain offering and its drink offering as in the morning -- a pleasing aroma, an offering made to the LORD by fire. For the generations to come this burnt offering is to be made regularly at the entrance to the Tent of Meeting before the LORD.

God commanded that wine be offered to Him as part of the following regular sacrifices:

1. Leviticus 23:9-14 - Wave offering.
2. Numbers 15:1-7 - Freewill offering.
3. Numbers 15:8-12 - Fellowship offering.
4. Numbers 28:9-10 - Every Sabbath day.
5. Numbers 28:11-15 - First day of each month.
6. Numbers 28:26-31 - Feast of Weeks.
7. Numbers 29:1-6 - Feast of Trumpets.

Ezra 6:9-10 - Whatever is needed -- young bulls, rams, male lambs for burnt offerings to the God of heaven, and wheat, salt, wine and oil, as requested by the priests in Jerusalem -- must be given them daily without fail, so that they may offer sacrifices pleasing to the God of heaven and pray for the well-being of the king and his sons.

God commanded that wine be offered to Him on a regular basis. Therefore anyone who believes that wine is a sinful thing does not share God's perspective on wine.

Melchizedek, both a King and a Priest

The priest king Melchizedek furnished both **bread and wine** for the people to enjoy:

> **Genesis 14:18-19** - Then Melchizedek king of Salem brought out bread and wine. He was priest of God Most High, and he blessed Abram, saying, "Blessed be Abram by God Most High, Creator of heaven and earth.

Jesus Christ is a priest forever in the order of Melchizedek:

> **Psalm 110:4** - The LORD has sworn and will not change his mind: "You are a priest forever, in the order of Melchizedek."
>
> **Hebrews 5:5-10** - So Christ also did not take upon himself the glory of becoming a high priest. But God said to him, "You are my Son; today I have become your Father."
> And he says in another place, "You are a priest forever, in the order of Melchizedek."
> During the days of Jesus' life on earth, he offered up prayers and petitions with loud cries and tears to the one who could save him from death, and he was heard because of his reverent submission. Although he was a son, he learned obedience from what he suffered and, once made perfect, he became the source of eternal salvation for all who obey him and was designated by God to be high priest in the order of Melchizedek.
>
> **Hebrews 6:19-20** - We have this hope as an anchor for the soul, firm and secure. It enters the inner sanctuary behind the curtain, where Jesus, who went before us, has entered on our behalf. He has become a high priest forever, in the order of Melchizedek.

The Holy Bible clearly says that Jesus Christ is a priest forever, in the order of Melchizedek. And the Holy Bible clearly says that Melchizedek provided both bread and wine for the people to enjoy. Therefore, Jesus Christ will provide both bread and wine for the people to enjoy.

On two different occasions Jesus multiplied the bread that was given to Him and He fed the multitude of people who followed him. The first time Jesus fed 5,000 men with five loaves of bread and two fish (Matthew 14:13-21, Mark 6:35-44, Luke 9:12-17, John 6:5-13). The second time Jesus fed 4,000 men with seven loaves of bread and a few small fish (Matthew 15:32-38, Mark 8:1-9).

The First Miracle of Jesus Christ

The very first miracle that Jesus performed was to turn plain ordinary water into the finest quality wine for the people at a wedding feast to enjoy:

> **John 2:1-11** - On the third day a wedding took place at Cana in Galilee. Jesus' mother was there, and Jesus and his disciples had also been invited to the wedding. When the wine was gone, Jesus' mother said to him, "They have no more wine."
> "Dear woman, why do you involve me?" Jesus replied. "My time has not yet come."
> His mother said to the servants, "Do whatever he tells you."
> Nearby stood six stone water jars, the kind used by the Jews for ceremonial washing, each holding from twenty to thirty gallons.
> Jesus said to the servants, "Fill the jars with water"; so they filled them to the brim.
> Then he told them, "Now draw some out and take it to the master of the banquet."
> They did so, and the master of the banquet tasted the water that had been turned into wine. He did not realize where it had come from, though the servants who had drawn the water knew. Then he called the bridegroom aside and said, "Everyone brings out the choice wine first and then the cheaper wine after the guests have had too much to drink; but you have saved the best till now."
> This, the first of his miraculous signs, Jesus performed at Cana in Galilee. He thus revealed his glory, and his disciples put their faith in him.

Chapter Eighty-Five: What Does the Bible Say About Alcohol?

God accepted Jesus' death on the cross as the full payment for the sins of the entire world because Jesus was sinless. Since Jesus was sinless then Jesus' turning the water into wine was not a sin from God's point of view. Anyone who tries to portray turning water into wine as being a sin does not share God's perspective on this issue. (Note: The normal procedure for making wine is to add some water to the juice squeezed out of some grapes and then letting that juice and water mixture slowly ferment into wine.)

Nazirite and Nazareth

Now let's take a look at the difference between the two words "Nazirite" and "Nazareth."

Nazirite: A special vow of separation to the Lord.
Nazareth: A town in Judea about 90 miles north of Bethlehem.

> **Numbers 6:1-4** - The LORD said to Moses, "Speak to the Israelites and say to them: 'If a man or woman wants to make a special vow, a vow of separation to the LORD as a Nazirite, he must abstain from wine and other fermented drink and must not drink vinegar made from wine or from other fermented drink. He must not drink grape juice or eat grapes or raisins. As long as he is a Nazirite, he must not eat anything that comes from the grapevine, not even the seeds or skins.' "

> **Numbers 6:19-20** - " 'After the Nazirite has shaved off the hair of his dedication, the priest is to place in his hands a boiled shoulder of the ram, and a cake and a wafer from the basket, both made without yeast. The priest shall then wave them before the LORD as a wave offering; they are holy and belong to the priest, together with the breast that was waved and the thigh that was presented. After that, the Nazirite may drink wine.' "

During the time that a person was under the Nazirite vow he or she could not drink wine, or grape juice, or eat grapes, or raisins, or even the seeds or the skins. It should be noticed that the word "wine" and the word "grape juice" are different words and that the translators of the Holy Bible knew the difference and they were careful in correctly translating these words.

Please also note that when the Nazirite vow had been fulfilled then the person could once again drink wine.

Two individuals in the Holy Bible were to be Nazirites for life:

1. **Samson** - Judges 13:2-7.
2. **John the Baptist** - Luke 1:11-15.

Although Jesus was born in Bethlehem, Jesus' parents were from Nazareth and Jesus grew up in town of Nazareth. Nowhere in the entire Bible does it say that Jesus was a Nazarite. However, Jesus was sometimes referred to as Jesus of Nazareth.

> **Acts 3:6** - Then Peter said, "Silver or gold I do not have, but what I have I give you. In the name of Jesus Christ of Nazareth, walk."

Restrictions on the Consumption of Alcoholic Beverages

The Holy Bible does have some restrictions on the consumption of alcoholic beverages. These restrictions applied to the priests whenever they entered the Tent of Meeting or the inner court of the temple.

> **Leviticus 10:8-9** - Then the LORD said to Aaron, "You and your sons are not to drink wine or other fermented drink whenever you go into the Tent of Meeting, or you will die. This is a lasting ordinance for the generations to come."

> **Ezekiel 44:21** - No priest is to drink wine when he enters the inner court.

Permission to Drink Alcoholic Beverages

However, the Holy Bible clearly says in the New Testament that Deacons, and Preachers such as Timothy, are permitted to drink wine in moderation:

1 Timothy 3:8 - Deacons, likewise, are to be men worthy of respect, sincere, not indulging in much wine, and not pursuing dishonest gain.

1 Timothy 5:23 - Stop drinking only water, and use a little wine because of your stomach and your frequent illnesses.

One scripture that could be used to condemn the drinking of wine is the following. Please note that the following scripture only suggests that wine should not be consumed in front of an immature Christian. The following verse does **not** forbid the drinking of wine.

Romans 14:21 - It is better not to eat meat or drink wine or to do anything else that will cause your brother to fall.

If a Christian were to **blindly practice** the above verse then he or she would have to stop eating meat and drinking wine. The reason is simple. Some Christians and some non-believers are vegetarians and they do not eat meat. Some of these vegetarians are offended by anyone who does eat meat. Therefore if a Christian did not want to offend one of these vegetarians then he or she should refrain from eating meat. In addition, some people are overweight and they cannot successfully control their appetite for food. Therefore a Christian should not eat meat because it might tempt these overweight people into becoming even more overweight. (Note: We will examine the meat issue in more detail later in this chapter.)

The above paragraph is an example of the type of **invalid** reasoning that could be used by someone to suggest that a Christian should not drink any type of alcoholic beverage because it might offend a non-drinker, or because it might set the wrong example for a non-believer or for an alcoholic. An alcoholic is a person who cannot control his or her appetite for alcoholic beverages and who cannot practice restraint and who cannot consume alcohol in moderation as the Holy Bible recommends.

The following scripture clearly addresses the meat issue for Christians:

Acts 10:9-16 - About noon the following day as they were on their journey and approaching the city, Peter went up on the roof to pray. He became hungry and wanted something to eat, and while the meal was being prepared, he fell into a trance. He saw heaven opened and something like a large sheet being let down to earth by its four corners. It contained all kinds of four-footed animals, as well as reptiles of the earth and birds of the air. Then a voice told him, "Get up, Peter. Kill and eat."
"Surely not, Lord!" Peter replied. "I have never eaten anything impure or unclean."
The voice spoke to him a second time, "Do not call anything impure that God has made clean."
This happened three times, and immediately the sheet was taken back to heaven.

Based on the above scripture a New Testament Christian has the freedom to eat any type of meat and he or she is not bound by the Old Testament regulations about which animals are considered to be clean (may be eaten) and unclean (may not be eaten). Remember also that when Jesus multiplied the loaves of bread He also multiplied the fish and gave then to the people to eat.

1 Timothy 4:3-5 - They forbid people to marry and order them to abstain from certain foods, which God created to be received with thanksgiving by those who believe and who know the truth. For everything God created is good, and nothing is to be rejected if it is received with thanksgiving, because it is consecrated by the word of God and prayer.

Colossians 2:16 - Therefore do not let anyone judge you by what you eat or drink, or with regard to a religious festival, a New Moon celebration or a Sabbath day.

Summary

Based on the above scripture verses from the Holy Bible the following general statements can be made:

1. God created grapes and God created the fermentation process. Therefore God created wine.
2. God commanded that wine be offered to Him on a regular basis.
3. The priest king Melchizedek provided both bread and wine for the people to enjoy.
4. Jesus Christ is a priest king forever in the order of Melchizedek.
5. The first miracle of Jesus Christ was to turn plain ordinary water into the finest quality wine for the guests at a wedding feast to enjoy.
6. The apostle Paul said it is okay for Deacons and Preachers to consume wine in moderation.
7. There is **no** commandment anywhere in the entire Bible that says "Thou shall not drink alcohol."
8. The Bible does say that drinking too much alcohol will make you drunk. This is a bad condition to be in. If you drink alcohol then you should drink in moderation. If you are not able to control your appetite for alcohol then you should consider abstaining.
9. A person may voluntarily refrain from drinking alcohol or from eating meat if he or she wishes. However, that person should not criticize another person who voluntarily chooses to drink alcohol or to eat meat.
10. The Bible recommends the moderate consumption of wine for health reasons (1 Timothy 5:23). This is supported by several modern medical research studies that report a variety of positive health benefits from consuming a small quantity of wine on a regular basis.

The above statements are all 100% supported by the Holy Scriptures quoted in this chapter. The only reference to a source other than the Bible are the medical research studies mentioned in item 10 above and those studies support the information in the Bible and they do not contradict that information.

No effort was made to change what the Bible says by quoting cultural differences, or society expectations, or history, or geographical considerations, or traditions, or the writings of some famous Bible scholar. Anyone who wanted to modify the Words of God to support a different viewpoint about alcoholic beverages could easily do so by adding material from other sources that supported his or her own personal opinion on this topic. The above summary is **not** based on personal opinion. It is based 100% on the Word of God.

Conclusion

1. A sincere honest Christian will base his or her beliefs on Holy Scriptures.
    2 Timothy 2:15 - Do your best to present yourself to God as one approved, a workman who does not need to be ashamed and who correctly handles the word of truth.
2. Anyone who knows the truth but does not share it with others is **not** doing the will of God.
    2 Timothy 4:2-4 - Preach the Word; be prepared in season and out of season; correct, rebuke and encourage -- with great patience and careful instruction. For the time will come when men will not put up with sound doctrine. Instead, to suit their own desires, they will gather around them a great number of teachers to say what their itching ears want to hear. They will turn their ears away from the truth and turn aside to myths.
3. Anyone who knows the truth but says something different is a liar.
    Mark 7:6-9 - He replied, "Isaiah was right when he prophesied about you hypocrites; as it is written: " 'These people honor me with their lips, but their hearts are far from me. They worship me in vain; their teachings are but rules taught by men.'
    "You have let go of the commands of God and are holding on to the traditions of men."
    And he said to them: "You have a fine way of setting aside the commands of God in order to observe your own traditions!"
    Matthew 7:21-23 - "Not everyone who says to me, 'Lord, Lord,' will enter the kingdom of heaven, but only he who does the will of my Father who is in heaven. Many will say to me on that day, 'Lord, Lord, did we not prophesy in your name, and in your name drive out demons and perform many miracles?' Then I will tell them plainly, 'I never knew you. Away from me, you evildoers!' "

Chapter Eight-Six

What Does the Bible Say About Giving?

The following questions are ones that should be answered using the Holy Bible:

1. What is a tithe?
2. What is a gift?
3. Are Christians expected to tithe, or give, or both?
4. What are treasures in heaven?

Let's begin with a formal definition of the word "tithe" from **Webster's New Collegiate Dictionary:**

tithe: verb, 1: to pay or give a tenth part especially for the support of the church; 2: to give a tenth of one's income as a tithe.

tithe: noun, a tenth part of something paid as a voluntary contribution or as a tax especially for the support of a religious establishment.

Now let's look at what the Holy Bible says about the concept of a "tithe."

When was tithing first mentioned in the Bible?

Genesis 14:18-20
Then Melchizedek king of Salem brought out bread and wine. He was priest of God Most High, and he blessed Abram, saying, "Blessed be Abram by God Most High, Creator of heaven and earth. And blessed be God Most High, who delivered your enemies into your hand." Then Abram gave him a tenth of everything.

Genesis 17:3-5
Abram fell face down, and God said to him, "As for me, this is my covenant with you: You will be the father of many nations. No longer will you be called Abram; your name will be Abraham, for I have made you a father of many nations."

Genesis 28:20-22
Then Jacob made a vow, saying, "If God will be with me and will watch over me on this journey I am taking and will give me food to eat and clothes to wear so that I return safely to my father's house, then the LORD will be my God and this stone that I have set up as a pillar will be God's house, and of all that you give me I will give you a tenth."

Genesis 32:28
Then the man said, "Your name will no longer be Jacob, but Israel, because you have struggled with God and with men and have overcome."

Abraham was the father of the entire Hebrew nation. He and his wife Sarah had one son named Isaac. Isaac and his wife Rebekah had two sons named Esau and Jacob. Therefore Jacob was the grandson of Abraham. Jacob's name was changed to Israel and he had twelve sons who became the twelve tribes of Israel. One of those twelve sons was named Judah and one was named Levi. The descendants of Levi were called Levites. The Levites were selected by God to be Priests and workers in the Tabernacle. However, Jesus Christ was born to Mary and Mary was descended from Judah.

What is a tithe?

Leviticus 27:30
A tithe of everything from the land, whether grain from the soil or fruit from the trees, belongs to the LORD; it is holy to the LORD.

Leviticus 27:32
The entire tithe of the herd and flock -- every tenth animal that passes under the shepherd's rod -- will be holy to the LORD.

During Old Testament times a tithe consisted of a portion of everything that a person received and it specifically included grain, fruit, and livestock.

How much is a tithe?

Abraham gave a tenth of everything to Melchizedek. His grandson Jacob promised to give a tenth of everything he received to God.

Therefore a tithe was a tenth, or ten-percent, of **everything** a person received and it was not just limited to grain, fruit, and livestock, but it also included clothing, silver, and gold.

Where was the tithe to be brought?
Who was to receive the benefit of the tithe?

Deuteronomy 14:22-27
Be sure to set aside a tenth of all that your fields produce each year. Eat the tithe of your grain, new wine and oil, and the firstborn of your herds and flocks in the presence of the LORD your God at the place he will choose as a dwelling for his Name, so that you may learn to revere the LORD your God always. But if that place is too distant and you have been blessed by the LORD your God and cannot carry your tithe (because the place where the LORD will choose to put his Name is so far away), then exchange your tithe for silver, and take the silver with you and go to the place the LORD your God will choose. Use the silver to buy whatever you like: cattle, sheep, wine or other fermented drink, or anything you wish. Then you and your household shall eat there in the presence of the LORD your God and rejoice. And do not neglect the Levites living in your towns, for they have no allotment or inheritance of their own.

Joshua 18:1
The whole assembly of the Israelites gathered at Shiloh and set up the Tent of Meeting there.

A tithe was to be set aside each year based on what was received that year. The tithe was to be taken to the dwelling place of the LORD. During Old Testament days this was originally the Tabernacle Tent at Shiloh and later it was Solomon's Temple in Jerusalem. The family who gave the tithe was to consume the tithe but they were commanded to share a part of the tithe with the Levites who served God.

How often was a special tithe to be given?

Deuteronomy 14:28-29
At the end of every three years, bring all the tithes of that year's produce and store it in your towns, so that the Levites (who have no allotment or inheritance of their own) and the aliens, the fatherless and the widows who live in your towns may come and eat and be satisfied, and so that the LORD your God may bless you in all the work of your hands.

Deuteronomy 26:12
When you have finished setting aside a tenth of all your produce in the third year, the year of the tithe, you shall give it to the Levite, the alien, the fatherless and the widow, so that they may eat in your towns and be satisfied.

Chapter 86: What Does the Bible Say About Giving?

Amos 4:4
Bring your sacrifices every morning, your tithes every three years.

A tithe was brought to the Temple every year.

However, every third year the entire tithe was to be given to the Levites and **none** of it was to be consumed by the family that gave the tithe. The tithe of the third year was to be enjoyed by the Levites and by foreigners, orphans, and widows.

Who was to tithe?

Malachi 3:8-12
"Will a man rob God? Yet you rob me.
"But you ask, 'How do we rob you?'
"In tithes and offerings. You are under a curse -- the whole nation of you -- because you are robbing me. Bring the whole tithe into the storehouse, that there may be food in my house. Test me in this," says the LORD Almighty, "and see if I will not throw open the floodgates of heaven and pour out so much blessing that you will not have room enough for it. I will prevent pests from devouring your crops, and the vines in your fields will not cast their fruit," says the LORD Almighty. "Then all the nations will call you blessed, for yours will be a delightful land," says the LORD Almighty.

Number 18:25-26
The LORD said to Moses, "Speak to the Levites and say to them: 'When you receive from the Israelites the tithe I give you as your inheritance, you must present a tenth of that tithe as the LORD's offering.'"

Everyone was required to tithe. This included the Levites who were commanded to give a tenth of what they received to the LORD.

In Malachi 3:8-12 God condemned the Israelites for not bringing the entire tithe in the third year to the temple and giving the entire third year tithe to the Levites.

Summary of Tithing Scriptures

In summary:
1. A tithe is one-tenth of everything a person received.
2. Everyone was to tithe including the Levites. The Levites were a tribe of Israel set aside by God as Priests and workers in the Temple.
3. Every year the tithe was to be taken to the Tabernacle Tent or to Solomon's Temple.
4. For two consecutive years the tithe was to be consumed by the family that gave the tithe but the family had to share their tithe with the Levites.
5. Every third year the entire tithe was to be given to the Levites and none of it was to be eaten by the family that gave the tithe. The tithe of the third year was to be enjoyed by the Levites and by foreigners, orphans, and widows.

Since I prefer to base my Christian beliefs 100% on what the Holy Bible says I do not feel comfortable adding to what the Bible says or subtracting from what the Bible says. Therefore the above summary on tithing is 100% based on Holy Scriptures. Nothing was added to the scriptures and nothing was omitted.

It would be relatively easy for anyone to modify the above summary by adding information extracted from other historical documents, or from Jewish traditions, or from the writings of different Christian leaders down through the ages. If a person wanted to prove or disprove a specific interpretation about tithing it would be easy to find information outside the Holy Bible to support his or her point of view.

Are New Testament Christians required to tithe?

In the early years of the Christian Church there were some men who insisted that a Christian had to follow all the laws of the Jewish faith. Their reasoning was simple: Jesus was a Jew and Jesus obeyed all the Jewish laws and therefore anyone who wanted to be like Jesus also had to follow all the Jewish laws.

Peter and Paul were constantly in opposition to this point of view because they knew that salvation was by faith in Jesus Christ and that nothing except faith was required to obtain the grace and mercy of God.

Unfortunately there were "legalists" who were constantly infiltrating Christian Churches and they taught that Christians had to obey the dietary rules of the Jewish religion, and they had to be circumcised, and they had to obey all the other laws as taught by Moses. This issue was finally settled by the Christian Church Council at Jerusalem and this group of men included Peter the disciple, James the brother of Jesus, and Paul the apostle.

Peter spoke to the Church Council and said:

Acts 15:10-11
"Now then, why do you try to test God by putting on the necks of the disciples a yoke that neither we nor our fathers have been able to bear? No! We believe it is through the grace of our Lord Jesus that we are saved, just as they are."

After much discussion and prayer the Jerusalem Church drafted and sent the following letter to the Christian Churches:

Acts 15:23-29
The apostles and elders, your brothers,
To the Gentile believers in Antioch, Syria and Cilicia:
Greetings.
We have heard that some went out from us without our authorization and disturbed you, troubling your minds by what they said. So we all agreed to choose some men and send them to you with our dear friends Barnabas and Paul -- men who have risked their lives for the name of our Lord Jesus Christ. Therefore we are sending Judas and Silas to confirm by word of mouth what we are writing. It seemed good to the Holy Spirit and to us not to burden you with anything beyond the following requirements: You are to abstain from food sacrificed to idols, from blood, from the meat of strangled animals and from sexual immorality. You will do well to avoid these things.
Farewell.

Based on the above scripture New Testament Christians are not required to obey the Old Testament Jewish regulations about tithing, or circumcision, or the distinction between clean and unclean animals. Christians can eat anything, except blood, or the meat of strangled animals, or food that has been sacrificed to idols. Christians are also to abstain from sexual immorality.

This interpretation is supported by the following scriptures.

Matthew 5:17
"Do not think that I have come to abolish the Law or the Prophets; I have not come to abolish them but to fulfill them."

Galatians 2:16,19-21
"... a man is not justified by observing the law, but by faith in Jesus Christ. So we, too, have put our faith in Christ Jesus that we may be justified by faith in Christ and not by observing the law, because by observing the law no one will be justified. ... For through the law I died to the law so that I might live for God. I have been crucified with Christ and I no longer live, but Christ lives in me. The life I live in the body, I live by faith in the Son of God, who loved me and gave himself for me. I do not set aside the grace of God, for if righteousness could be gained through the law, Christ died for nothing!"

Romans 7:4
So, my brothers, you also died to the law through the body of Christ, that you might belong to another, to him who was raised from the dead, in order that we might bear fruit to God.

Christians are the Children of God

Galatians 4:4-7
But when the time had fully come, God sent his Son, born of a woman, born under law, to redeem those under law, that we might receive the full rights of sons. Because you are sons, God sent the Spirit of his Son into our hearts, the Spirit who calls out, "*Abba*, Father." So you are no longer a slave, but a son; and since you are a son, God has made you also an heir.

Galatians 3:26
You are all sons of God through faith in Christ Jesus,

Ephesians 1:4
In love he predestined us to be adopted as his sons through Jesus Christ,

John 1:12-13
Yet to all who received him, to those who believed in his name, he gave the right to become children of God -- children born not of natural descent, nor of human decision or a husband's will, but born of God.

1 John 3:1-3
How great is the love the Father has lavished on us, that we should be called children of God! And that is what we are! The reason the world does not know us is that it did not know him. Dear friends, now we are children of God, and what we will be has not yet been made known. But we know that when he appears, we shall be like him, for we shall see him as he is. Everyone who has this hope in him purifies himself, just as he is pure.

1 John 5:19
We know that we are children of God,

Matthew 17:24-27
After Jesus and his disciples arrived in Capernaum, the collectors of the two-drachma tax came to Peter and asked, "Doesn't your teacher pay the temple tax?"
"Yes, he does," he replied.
When Peter came into the house, Jesus was the first to speak. "What do you think, Simon?" he asked. "From whom do the kings of the earth collect duty and taxes -- from their own sons or from others?"
"From others," Peter answered.
"Then the sons are exempt," Jesus said to him. "But so that we may not offend them, go to the lake and throw out your line. Take the first fish you catch; open its mouth and you will find a four-drachma coin. Take it and give it to them for my tax and yours."

All Christians are the adopted children of God and Jesus Christ is our brother. We have been set free from the law and we now live by grace and faith, and not by the laws of Moses. Since we are now the children of God we are exempt from the Old Testament laws, rules, and regulations. We are now accountable to God for how we behave as New Testament Christians under the new covenant established by the blood of Jesus Christ.

Therefore New Testament Christians are not bound by the law of circumcision, or dietary laws of clean and unclean animals, or the law of tithing.

What does the Bible say about Giving?

Although New Testament Christians are not subject to the law of tithing, we are commissioned to be generous givers. However, each Christian now has the awesome responsibility of deciding how much he or she should give.

2 Corinthians 8:7
But just as you excel in everything -- in faith, in speech, in knowledge, in complete earnestness and in your love for us -- see that you also excel in this grace of giving.

2 Corinthians 8:12
For if the willingness is there, the gift is acceptable according to what one has, not according to what he does not have.

2 Corinthians 9:6-7
Remember this: Whoever sows sparingly will also reap sparingly, and whoever sows generously will also reap generously. Each man should give what he has decided in his heart to give, not reluctantly or under compulsion, for God loves a cheerful giver.

The amount given by a Christian needs to be determined by that Christian. This is a very important responsibility that God has delegated to each Christian. The amount we give should be in accordance to what we have and not according to some arbitrary standard set by someone else. For example, an extremely wealthy person might be able to easily give 25% of his or her weekly income and it would not impact his or her family's standard of living in any way. But a person living in extreme poverty who has significant problems providing for his or her family's most basic fundamental needs might cause his or her family some additional painful hardships if he or she were to give just 1% of his or her weekly income to the Church. This is why the scripture says give *"according to what one has, and not according to what he does not have."*

A Widow, a Tax Collector, and a Pharisee

Mark 12:41-44
Jesus sat down opposite the place where the offerings were put and watched the crowd putting their money into the temple treasury. Many rich people threw in large amounts. But a poor widow came and put in two very small copper coins, worth only a fraction of a penny. Calling his disciples to him, Jesus said, "I tell you the truth, this poor widow has put more into the treasury than all the others. They all gave out of their wealth; but she, out of her poverty, put in everything -- all she had to live on."

Luke 18:9-14
Jesus told this parable: "Two men went up to the temple to pray, one a Pharisee and the other a tax collector. The Pharisee stood up and prayed about himself: 'God, I thank you that I am not like other men -- robbers, evildoers, adulterers -- or even like this tax collector. I fast twice a week and give a tenth of all I get.'
"But the tax collector stood at a distance. He would not even look up to heaven, but beat his breast and said, 'God, have mercy on me, a sinner.'
"I tell you that this man, rather than the other, went home justified before God. For everyone who exalts himself will be humbled, and he who humbles himself will be exalted."

The above scriptures vividly illustrate that it is not how much you give that is important. Instead the important issues are the condition of your heart and the reason you give. The widow gave everything she had, the Pharisee gave a tenth, but the tax collector didn't give anything. Jesus complimented both the widow and the tax collector but not the Pharisee.

Chapter 86: What Does the Bible Say About Giving?

What does the Bible say about supporting the Church?

1 Corinthians 9:13-14
Don't you know that those who work in the temple get their food from the temple, and those who serve at the altar share in what is offered on the altar? In the same way, the Lord has commanded that those who preach the gospel should receive their living from the gospel.

Galatians 6:6
Anyone who receives instruction in the word must share all good things with his instructor.

Christians should support the Church they attend. The Minister of the Church should be paid from the donations given to the Church.

How often should Christians give to their Church?

1 Corinthians 16:1-2
Now about the collection for God's people: Do what I told the Galatian churches to do. On the first day of every week, each one of you should set aside a sum of money in keeping with his income, saving it up, so that when I come no collections will have to be made.

Every week, on Sunday the first day of the week, Christians are to give a part of their income to the Church. However, each Christian must decide how much that will be. But each Sunday we are asked to give something.

Other Scriptures

It is interesting to note that neither tithing nor giving is mentioned as one of the original Ten Commandments.

Christian tithing is not mentioned anywhere in the New Testament. However, Jesus did mention the Jewish law of giving a tenth when He spoke to the scribes and Pharisees. However, Jesus was speaking to these men as Jewish hypocrites and not as examples of good Christian behavior.

Matthew 23:23
"Woe to you, teachers of the law and Pharisees, you hypocrites! You give a tenth of your spices -- mint, dill and cummin. But you have neglected the more important matters of the law -- justice, mercy and faithfulness. You should have practiced the latter, without neglecting the former."

Luke 11:43
"Woe to you Pharisees, because you give God a tenth of your mint, rue and all other kinds of garden herbs, but you neglect justice and the love of God. You should have practiced the latter without leaving the former undone."

The above words of Jesus were **not** spoken to His disciples. But occasionally a person will take the above comment of Jesus out of the context in which Jesus spoke it and try to make it apply to all New Testament Christians. In other words, that person is trying to add one of the laws of Moses to the doctrine of the Christian faith. This is similar to trying to add the doctrine of circumcision to the Christian faith. Neither tithing nor circumcision is relevant to being a good Christian.

Some Christian denominations have combined Christian giving and tithing. These denominations insist that Christians must obey the Old Testament law of tithing and, in addition, they must also be generous givers. This is usually referred to as a Christian's responsibility to give "Tithes and Offerings." In other words, they have selected one of the Old Testament laws and they have added it to the rules that Christians need to live by. However, this is not consistent with the teachings of the New Testament as previously explained.

Chapter 86: What Does the Bible Say About Giving?

Charity and Treasure in Heaven

Matthew 10:42-11:1
"And if anyone gives even a cup of cold water to one of these little ones because he is my disciple, I tell you the truth, he will certainly not lose his reward." After Jesus had finished instructing his twelve disciples, he went on from there to teach and preach in the towns of Galilee.

Matthew 19:21
Jesus answered, "If you want to be perfect, go, sell your possessions and give to the poor, and you will have treasure in heaven. Then come, follow me."

Luke 12:22,33-34
Then Jesus said to his disciples: . . . "Sell your possessions and give to the poor. Provide purses for yourselves that will not wear out, a treasure in heaven that will not be exhausted, where no thief comes near and no moth destroys. For where your treasure is, there your heart will be also."

The above scriptures clearly say that if you give to the poor you will have treasure in heaven. The above scriptures do **not** say that if you give to your Church you will have treasure in heaven. Therefore it is important for a Christian to not only give to his or her Church but a Christian should also seek out opportunities to be generous to the poor.

If a Christian wants to be perfect then he or she should sell his or her possessions and give the proceeds from that sale to the poor. One way to do this is to make a donation to your Church with the stipulation that the money be used in a specific way by the Church. This is supported by the following scripture:

Acts 4:34-35
There were no needy persons among them. For from time to time those who owned lands or houses sold them, brought the money from the sales and put it at the apostles' feet, and it was distributed to anyone as he had need.

Please do not misinterpret the above scriptures. A person cannot buy his or her way into heaven by simply selling all his or her possessions and then giving that money to the poor or to the church. The only way a person can get into heaven is by accepting Jesus Christ as his or her Savior.

In addition, a person cannot become "perfect" by simply selling all his or her possessions and then giving that money to the poor or to the church. This would be an admirable thing to do but it is not enough to make a person "perfect." If we truly desire to become more "perfect" then we need to begin by accepting Jesus Christ as our Savior, and then we need to practice good Christian behavior, and we also need to follow the teachings of Jesus Christ that are recorded in the Holy Bible. For example, if we truly desire for our gifts to the poor to be acceptable to God then we should give our money anonymously:

Matthew 6:3-4
"But when you give to the needy, do not let your left hand know what your right hand is doing, so that your giving may be in secret. Then your Father, who sees what is done in secret, will reward you."

Conclusion

Galatians 4:16
Have I now become your enemy by telling you the truth?

Are you striving to become a good New Testament Christian, or are you striving to become a Pharisee? Do you believe in the Grace of Giving, or in the Law of Tithing, or are you trying to mix the two together?

The Holy Bible clearly saws that all New Testament Christians are to be generous givers. God did not put any limits, either minimum or maximum, on how much Christians should give. This is supported by Jesus' comment about the Widow's remarkable gift and the Tax Collector's lack of any gift.

Chapter 86: What Does the Bible Say About Giving?

Unfortunately many Christian Churches get their Church and their members into serious financial difficulties by encouraging their members to give beyond what they can afford and then to trust God to supply their needs. This is a matter of faith and we are told that faith can move mountains, but I have yet to meet anyone with this measure of faith.

Instead I think it is more reasonable to be good stewards of our financial resources and to give each week to our Church in proportion to our income as we are able. In other words, strive to be a cheerful voluntary giver and not a giver under the Old Testament law of tithing. If you will try this then you may discover that as time passes you will be able to give more than a tenth of your income and you will not even miss it because God will have blessed you with such abundance that it is easy to meet all the true needs of your family.

If God does increase your income then you should be a good steward of your additional money and you should not simply look for new ways to spend all that extra money on yourself. Instead you should try to think of how you could help the poor and how you could invest some of your extra money to further the kingdom of God and to spread the Gospel of Jesus Christ your Savior. In other words, voluntarily lay up treasure for yourself in heaven that will last for eternity.

Chapter 86: What Does the Bible Say About Giving?

The Mark of the Beast

When God made man there was only **one** rule to which man had to comply.
God said, "Do not eat from the tree of knowledge or you will surely die."

Satan said, "You will not die. The fruit will simply open your eyes.
You will be like God, knowing good and evil, and you will be wise."

Adam and Eve believed Satan and they ate from the forbidden tree.
And death entered the world because God's Word they did not believe.

- - - - - -

God said, "If you receive the mark of the beast on your hand or head,
I will punish and kill you and cast you into hell when you are dead."

Satan said, "You will not die. If my mark you will only receive,
then you may buy and sell, and become prosperous and wealthy."

Ugly painful sores gradually appeared on all who wore Satan's mark,
and God made them suffer in agony in extreme heat and in the dark.

Later 100-pound hailstones fell on them in the country and in the city.
Eventually through many plagues God destroyed all their prosperity.

Finally God took the beast and everyone with the mark of the devil,
and God cast them into the lake of eternal fire for being so evil.

- - - - - - -

At the end of this age each person will need to make a simple choice:
Believe God's Word and live forever, or believe Satan and perish.

Scripture References: Genesis 1:26-27, Genesis 2:7, Genesis 2:15-17, Genesis 3:1-9, Genesis 3:15-19, Revelation 13:11-18, Revelation 14:1-8, Revelation 14:9-12, Revelation 16:1-21, Revelation 18:17, Revelation 19:19-21, Revelation 20:1-6.

Poem: The Mark of the Beast

Chapter Eighty-Seven

Recommended School Books for
The Education of the Ones You Dearly Love

Introduction

Since 1984 I have been a full-time university professor. One of my daughters was a fourth-grade school teacher for several years before she got married and then she became the mother of three children. After her children were born she decided that her place was in the home instead of the school room.

The Declining Academic Performance of Public School Students

For over 25 years I have gradually observed the changing trends in our public school educational system in the United States of America. As a university professor it was relatively easy for me to determine the true outcome of those changing trends because the students who graduated from high school were the same students who attended my university classes.

It should be noted that the students who go to college are usually the better high school students. Therefore I can only comment on the quality of the education that those better students have received.

In the year 2011 I still teach some of the classes I originally taught in the mid 1980s. And in many cases we still use the same textbook, written by the same authors, but we do use the most recently updated editions of those textbooks. As the years have passed most of us at the university level have noticed a gradual decline in the fundamental educational skills of the students who are attending our classes.

Let me explain what I have observed by dividing our university students into three groups as follows:

1. **Gifted Students:** We have some students who are exceptional. They can absorb and understand information regardless of the manner in which it is presented to them. And they can apply that knowledge to situations that are not specifically discussed in one of the university lectures. In 1984 this group consisted of about 10 percent of our student body and it still does.

2. **Intellectually Challenged Students:** We have some students who, for one reason or another, cannot comprehend the information that is presented to them. These students either change their majors, or they voluntarily drop out of school, or they receive failing grades and they are forced out of school. In 1984 this group consisted of about 10 percent of our student body and it still does. This 10% does not include those students who drop out of school for legitimate other reasons, such as marriage, or accepting a full-time job.

3. **Normal Average Students:** We also have what I will refer to as the normal average student. This group consists of approximately 80% of our student body. In the mid 1980s every student in this group knew their multiplication tables by heart, and they could write a one-page essay on a topic that made sense the first time you read it, and they were motivated by a desire to improve their intellectual abilities so they could have a more prosperous and successful life. In the year 2011 this group still composes about 80% of our student body but their intellectual skills have changed as follows:

    a. Some of these students do not know their multiplication tables and they cannot do simple math without the aid of a handheld calculator or a computer.
    b. Some of these students cannot tell time by looking at the face of an ordinary clock and they can only tell you the time if they can see the readout on a digital clock.

c. Some of these students cannot write one paragraph that makes sense and these students have to take remedial English to continue their university studies.
d. Some of these students believe that the only thing that matters is to get a diploma and it really doesn't matter how you get that degree as long as you get it. Whether or not you learn anything during this process is not important to them.

Please remember that our university students do have a high school diploma, and they are usually the better high school students who have hopes of acquiring a college degree, and they will be the leaders of our society in the years ahead.

It is my personal opinion that the primary reason our young people are not as well educated when compared to a few decades ago is because God was expelled from our public school systems. A few ungodly individuals were successful in having some laws passed that prohibited prayer and the mention of the name of Jesus or God in any public school in the United States of America. These laws also forced the public school systems to use textbooks that were atheistic and which provided no moral direction for our young people. Without God our young people have had to individually decide what was right and what was wrong. As a result a large number of students are now cheating on assignments and on tests as part of their normal daily routine.

Forcing God out of our public school systems has resulted in a serious decline in the quality of the education our children have been receiving for several decades. It is my personal opinion that expelling God from the classroom is the fundamental reason for the continuous steady decline in high school achievement test scores, and the lack of respect for anyone in authority, and the moral justification of lying, cheating, and stealing, and the use of drugs by an ever increasing number of students, and the steady increase in the number of teen suicides.

In the mid 1990s I decided that I wanted my grandchildren to have the opportunity for a better education than what was currently available in the public school system. Therefore I investigated the field of home schooling very carefully. Since I had a full time job as a university professor I knew it would not be possible for me to stay home and teach my grandchildren on a daily basis. However, I also realized that if I had a reasonable set of home reference materials then I could easily help my grandchildren with their homework assignments in such a way that they would learn how to teach themselves. This became my goal and it guided me in the choice of the books I purchased and put on the bookshelves in my home for my grandchildren to consult.

I am sharing the following list of books with you because I believe there are many parents and grandparents who are now in a situation similar to the one I faced. You have a full time job and you must keep that job in order to provide shelter and food for your family. But you also want to be able to help your children, or grandchildren, when they need assistance with their homework. But you do not want to do their homework for them. Instead you want to be able to provide them with some good resources so they can do their homework with just a little bit of assistance from you and in the process also learn how to teach themselves.

The following is a partial list of the most important books in our family's home school library. I know this list does not match any list of home school literature that is currently recommended on the internet. But the following books are the ones I believe are the most practical for our young people. You will notice that I have included some religious books for each age group because I firmly believe that without God a person will not be able to enjoy life, or become a "true" success in his or her chosen field of study as an adult, or become a good spouse in a healthy marriage relationship. A good spouse is someone who knows how to compromise and how to work toward realistic and important family goals to enhance the quality of life for everyone in their family unit.

Preschool

You will need to read to your children or grandchildren from the following books. The books have beautiful color illustrations and they will capture a child's interest and excite their imagination. If you will read to your children, or grandchildren, while they are very young then they will become very fond of books and they will not be intimidated by books as they grow older. After you begin reading these books to a child you will soon discover that the child will pull the book out of the bookcase and start looking through the pictures and he or she will pretend to read the words on each page. There is no better way to help a child learn how to read than to provide something for the child to read that the child is very interested in.

You should also consider reading a Bible story to your children each day from the Bible Story Book that is recommended for Elementary School Students in the next section.

1. **The Children's Treasury: Best Loved Stories and Poems From Around the World,** First Glance Books, 63 Different Stories and Poems, 1987, 388 Pages.
2. **Walt Disney's Story Land: 55 Favorite Stories,** Golden Book, 1974 or 1991 edition, 320 Pages.
3. **Walt Disney Classics Collection Storybooks,** Mouse Works, Hardcover, Full Color Big Picture Books with Big Print about some of the Walt Disney Animated Movies, about 95 pages per book.

Elementary School

1. **Adventures in Art, Art & Craft Experiences for 7 to 14 Year Olds,** Susan Milord, Williamson Publishing, 1990, 160 Pages.
2. **Now I Am Big I Can Tell the Time,** Brimax, Cardboard Pages with Round Cutouts and a Plastic Clock Face with Numbers and Moveable Hands, 1997, 18 Pages.
3. **Step into Reading Series,** Assorted Titles Available, Random House, Small Thin Paperback Books for each reading level from Preschool through Grade 4, between 30 to 48 pages per book.
4. **The Core-Knowledge Series, What Your ... Grader Needs to Know,** 1st through 6th Grades and Kindergartener, E.D. Hirsch, Jr., Doubleday Book, 1993, about 240 pages per book.
5. **Everything You Need to Know About ... Homework series,** including American History, English, Geography, Math, Science, and World History, Scholastic Home Reference Series, 1994, each book has between 131 to 136 pages.
6. **Great Illustrated Classics Series,** Assorted Titles, Playmore Inc. Publishers, Hardcover books, Black and white pen drawn illustrations are on every other page of a condensed classic, such as "Treasure Island," approximately 240 pages per book.
7. **The Children's Illustrated Atlas of the World,** Templar, 1996, 79 Pages.
8. **DK Merriam-Webster Children's Dictionary,** DK Publishers, 2008, 960 Pages.
9. **Golden Book Encyclopedia,** 20 Volume Set, Golden Books, about 96 pages per volume.
10. **The Reader's Digest Children's Songbook,** Reader's Digest, 1985, 252 Pages.
11. **Children's Favorite Bible Stories, From the Old and New Testament,** Landoll, Inc., Cartoon illustrated with big print, 1996, 360 Pages.

Middle School

1. **The DK Geography of the World,** DK Publishing, 1996, 304 Pages.
2. **The Kingfisher Illustrated History of the World,** Kingfisher Books, 1993, over 761 Pages.
3. **Visual Encyclopedia of Science,** Kingfisher Books, 1994, 320 Pages.

Chapter Eighty-Seven: Recommended School Books

4. **Math Doesn't Suck, How to Survive Middle School Math**, Danica McKellar, Penguin Group, 2008, 296 Pages.
5. **Favorite Poems Old and New**, Helen Ferris, Doubleday Book, 1957, 598 Pages.
6. **The Young Oxford Book of Astronomy,** Mitton, Oxford University Press, 1993, 160 Pages.
7. **The World of the Microscope,** Usborne Science & Experiments, Oxlade & Stockley, Usborne Publishing, 1989, 48 Pages.
8. **It Couldn't Just Happen, Fascinating Facts About God's World**, Lawrence O. Richards, Word Publishing, 1987, 191 Pages.
9. **The Golden Children's Bible, The Old Testament and The New Testament**, Golden Book Western Publishing Company, Inc., Color Illustrations, 1993, 510 Pages.

High School and College

1. **History of the World**, J.M. Roberts, 1993 Edition and **not** the 2003 Edition, 952 Pages.
2. **Usborne Illustrated Dictionary of Science** (includes Physics, Chemistry, & Biology), 2001, 382 Pages.
3. **Basic Math and Pre-Algebra, Cliffs Quick Review**, 2001, 176 Pages.
4. **Pre-calculus, Cliffs Quick Review**, 2001, 128 Pages.
5. **Teach Yourself Calculus**, Abbott and Neill, 2003, 336 Pages.
6. **Basic Calculus Textbook**, Alexander J. Hahn, 1998, (Note: Buy a good used copy.), 546 Pages.
7. **Chemistry: Concepts and Problems, Wiley Self-Teaching Guide**, 1996, 320 Pages.
8. **Chemistry Principles, The Quest for Insight**, Third Edition, Atkins & Jones, 2005, (Note: Buy a good used copy.), 1024 Pages.
9. **Basic Physics, Wiley Self-Teaching Guide**, Kuhn, 1996, 320 Pages.
10. **General Physics Textbook**, 2nd Edition, Sternheim & Kane, 1991. (Note: Buy a good used copy.), 912 Pages.
11. **The Elements of Style, the Original Edition,** William Strunk, Jr., (Note: This is **not** one of the Strunk and White editions.), Waking Lion Press, 2009 Printing, 56 Pages.
12. **Writing, Grammar, Usage, and Style, Cliffs Quick Review**, 2001, 224 Pages.
13. **Merriam Webster's Collegiate Encyclopedia,** 2000, 1792 Pages.
14. **DK Illustrated Oxford Dictionary,** 2003, 1008 Pages.
15. **The Firefly Five Language Visual Dictionary - English, Spanish, French, German, Italian,** 2009, 1004 Pages.
16. **Interlinear Bible - Hebrew, Greek, English,** 2005, 2936 Pages.
17. **Strong's Exhaustive Concordance of the Bible,** James Strong, 2001, 1685 Pages.
18. **Holman Illustrated Bible Dictionary,** 2003, 1704 Pages.
19. **Zondervan NIV New International Version Matthew Henry Commentary,** 1999 or before, 2062 Pages.
20. **Nelson's NKJV New King James Version Study Bible,** 2005, more than 2200 Pages.

Chapter Eighty-Eight

Recommended Books for Hard Times Survival

Basic Self-Sufficiency

1. **SAS Survival Handbook**, Collins Gem, John "Lofty" Wiseman, Highly Recommended.
2. **Survival Gunsmithing**, J.B. Wood, 1986.
3. **Effective Defense: the Woman, the Plan, the Gun**, 2nd Edition, Written for women by Gila Hayes, 2000.
4. **Deerskins into Buckskins**, 2nd Edition (not the 1st edition), Richards, 2004.
5. **Complete Modern Blacksmith**, Weygers, 1997.
6. **Bicycle Maintenance and Repair**, 5th Edition, Todd Downs, 2005.
7. **Reader's Digest Complete Guide to Sewing**, 1976 or 2002 Edition.
8. **Back to Basics**, Reader's Digest, 1997.

Food Preparation, Food Production, and Food Preservation

1. **Fannie Farmer Cookbook**, Paperback or Hardcover, 1995 or before. (When the 100th anniversary edition was published in 1996 the book was revised for "modern cooks" and some of the traditional cooking information was omitted.)
2. **Joy of Cooking**, Rombauer and Becker, 915 pages, 1975 Edition or before. (The 1975 edition was reprinted for many years until at least 1986. When the book was finally changed from 915 pages, the really good information was replaced with quick recipes and microwave cooking.)
3. **New Illustrated Guide to Gardening**, Reader's Digest, 2000.
4. **Seed Sowing and Saving**, Turner, 1998.
5. **Big Book of Preserving the Harvest**, Costenbader, 2002.
6. **Backyard Livestock**, Thomas and Looby, 2007 or before.

First Aid Books, Medical Reference Books, and Herbal Reference Books
(This is not medical advice and it is not a medical recommendation.)

1. **The Medical Advisor**, Time Life Books, Hardcover, 1996.
2. **Reader's Digest Guide to Medical Cures & Treatments,** Hardcover, 1996.
3. **Merck Manual of Medical Information**, 2nd Home Edition, 2004, Paperback, more than 1900 Pages, Highly Recommended.
4. **American Red Cross First Aid & Safety Handbook**, Kathleen A. Handal, M.D., 1992.
5. **DK First Aid Manual**, American College of Emergency Physicians, 2004.
6. **Kelley's Textbook of Internal Medicine**, 4th Edition, 2000.
7. **Surgery Book, Illustrated Guide to 73 Operations**, Youngson, M.D., 1997.
8. **Oxford Handbook of Clinical Dentistry**, 4th Edition, Mitchell et. al., 2005, a small reference book.

9. **Tooth Extraction, A Practical Guide,** Robinson, 2000.
10. **Improve Your Vision without Glasses or Contact Lenses**, Dr. Beresford, Dr. Muris, Dr. Allen, Dr. Young, 1996.
11. **Heart & Hands, A Midwife's Guide to Pregnancy & Birth**, Elizabeth Davis, 1997.
12. **Remington's Pharmaceutical Sciences**, 14th Edition or before, 1970 or before.
13. **DK Natural Health Encyclopedia of Herbal Medicine,** Andrew Chevallier, 2000.
14. **The Complete Medicinal Herbal,** Penelope Ody, 1993.

Books for the Preservation of Knowledge for Future Generations

1. **Fundamentals of Building Construction**, 4th Ed., Allen & Iano, 2004.
2. **Microhydro, Clean Power from Water,** Davis, 2004.
3. **Basic Electronics**, Bureau of Naval Personnel, 1973.
4. **Annapolis Book of Seamanship**, 3rd Edition, Rousmaniere, 1999.
5. **Boat Building**, Howard I. Chapelle, 1994.
6. **Introduction to Internal Combustion Engines,** 2nd Edition, Stone, 1999.
7. **Illustrated Guide to Aerodynamics**, 2nd Edition, Smith, 1991.

Spiritual Books

1. **The Golden Children's Bible, The Old Testament and The New Testament,** Golden Book Western Publishing Company, Inc., Color Illustrations, 1993.
2. **Nelson's NKJV New King James Version Study Bible,** 2005.
3. **Holman Illustrated Bible Dictionary,** 2003.
4. **Zondervan NIV New International Version Matthew Henry Commentary,** 1999 or before.
5. **Interlinear Bible - Hebrew, Greek, English,** 2005.
6. **Strong's Exhaustive Concordance of the Bible,** James Strong, 2001.

Highly Recommended Out-of-Print Books (if you can find them)

1. **Marks Standard Handbook for Mechanical Engineers**, 9th Edition or before.
2. **Civil Engineering Handbook,** any Edition 1990 or before.
3. **Fix-It-Yourself Manual**, Reader's Digest, (not the Do-It-Yourself Manual), 1977.

Other Suggestions

Books $20 or less can be purchased **new** but books over $20 are usually a better value in "Like New" or "Very Good Used Condition." There are exceptions, however, depending on the book and its importance to you. Books listed in "Good" or "Acceptable Condition" should usually be avoided, if possible. However, if the book is important to you and better copies are not available, then you will have to make the decision of whether or not to purchase the used book.

A book listed as a "Remainder" is a new book that a Publisher has liquidated in volume at a huge discount and each remainder copy has a small mark or stamp on it to identify it as a Reminder so it cannot be returned to the Publisher for a full refund. Except for the small mark or stamp these books are in new condition and they are an excellent value, in my opinion.

Chapter Eighty-Eight: Recommended Books for Hard Times Survival

Many engineering books published after 1990 have been updated with the latest technological advances and they have gradually deleted some of the older traditional concepts due to space limitations and the fact that those older methods and procedures are no longer being used because they have been replaced by computers and technology. If you wish to preserve the old knowledge I suggest the purchase of Engineering Handbooks published in the year 1990 or before. When doing book searches alternate using the search words "Engineering Handbook" and "Handbook for Engineers" along with the appropriate discipline such as Mechanical or Civil.

If you already own some good books in your area of expertise then you should add them to the books you intend to preserve for your future descendants.

You might also wish to purchase an Automobile Repair Manual written specifically for your primary vehicle.

Some books attempt to cover too many topics in one volume. Those books frequently have really good information on a few of the topics but they only provide an introductory overview on many of the other topics. They also do not have enough specific information to help you analyze and correct all the different types of problems you might encounter in a specific topic area.

A college level textbook can educate a teacher and the teacher can then scale down the knowledge to any grade level. However, a sixth grade textbook is **not** useful for high school students or college students or for educating a teacher.

Some of the recommended books may be of no interest to you and you know you would never read them. However, our children and our grandchildren do not always share our interests and the above selection of books would give your future descendants the opportunity to learn about a variety of different subjects so they could better select a profession they really enjoyed.

Any book you purchase primarily for the preservation of knowledge for future generations should be vacuum sealed inside a plastic bag using an ordinary food vacuum sealer. This is particularly useful for older books that have already started to show signs of aging, such as page discoloration.

Can You Imagine?

Can you imagine what it would have been like
if you could have stood beside the angels and watched
as God originally created the heavens and the earth and then later
watched as Satan was cast out of heaven and to the earth he fell?

Can you imagine what it will be like
when God appears on His Throne and the earth and
the sky vanish into the nothing from which they were made
and Satan and all his followers are cast into an eternal hell?

Can you imagine how all Christians will feel
when we stand beside the angels and watch
as God creates a new heaven and a new earth
and there in the presence of God we forevermore dwell?

This Poem is Dedicated to My Grandson **Jason Cleveland Gobert III.**

References: Genesis 1:1-31, Isaiah 14:12-15, Revelation 20:11-15, Revelation 21:1-5.

Chapter Eighty-Nine

Paperback Novels for Entertainment

During a serious long-term hard times tragedy event you will probably discover that each day will primarily consist of one of the following two activities:

1. During good weather you will begin work at sunrise and you will not stop working until it is too dark to see at the end of the day. You will stop to eat when you get hungry but there will be so much work that absolutely must be done that you will not be able to just sit down and do nothing for a hour or so during the day.

2. During bad weather you will not be able to work outdoors. On these days you will do any household chores that need to be done indoors. But you will also probably discover that you have a reasonable amount of free time and you will want to do something to relax and enjoy yourself.

If you don't have any electricity then watching television will not be an option.

If you have a battery operated radio, some rechargeable batteries, and a solar battery charger, then listening to your favorite music will be an option. You could also catch up on the international news from around the world if your radio is a shortwave radio.

If you have some board games, such as the Ancient Board Games and Solitaire Games From Around the World, then you will be able to engage in an intellectual challenge for entertainment.

If you have some paperback books then you will be able to read to pass the time and to relax and entertain yourself. The great thing about paperback novels is that they work just fine when there is no electricity.

Each person in your family can select a different type of paperback novel based on what they find to be enjoyable. If you have very young children then you can read one of the "classics" to them and you will be entertaining yourself and your children.

The average person will not truly appreciate the value of a paperback novel until they are in the middle of a serious long-term hard times tragedy event. At that time the entertainment value of paperback novels will become obvious to almost everyone. Therefore before the hard times get to be really serious it would probably be a good idea to invest in some gently used paperback novels.

A gently used paperback novel is one that has been read by someone else but it is still in like new condition, except you can tell it has been read. It will not have any writing or stains on its pages and the cover will be in excellent condition. It will not have a musty or bad smell, such as what typically happens to a paperback novel if it has been read by someone who smokes.

You can usually find gently used paperback novels selling for about 25-cents each at the Thrift Stores in your area, or at Yard Sales or Garage Sales in your area. In most cases you will not be able to find a good price on used paperback novels at a "Used Book Store" because that store depends on the profit from their book sales as their only source of income.

If you can afford it then you should consider buying at least 100 used paperback novels for about 25-cents each. This would be a total investment of about $25. On the other hand, if you can afford to spend more, then it would not hurt to have several hundred paperback novels in storage for your future entertainment pleasure during a long-term hard times tragedy event.

In order to provide some variety you should consider purchasing gently used paperback novels in a variety of different literature categories. It is okay to purchase the majority of your books in the category you prefer most. But as time passes you will probably discover that you will occasionally want to read something different to provide some entertainment variety. The only categories that I suggest you **not** invest in would be horror novels and romance novels. Both of these categories can influence the thinking of younger readers and lead them down a path they should not go.

I suggest you consider purchasing paperback novels in all the following areas:

1. **Adventure,** a broad category that includes spy novels and authors such as Jack London.
2. **Best Sellers,** such as previous New York Times Best Sellers.
3. **Children's Books,** such as comic books or children's fairy tales or children's stories.
4. **The Classics,** such as "Tom Sawyer" or "The Secret Garden" or "The Swiss Family Robinson."
5. **Historical Fiction,** such as medieval times or a story about the 1800s.
6. **Fiction,** a broad category that includes almost everything except true biographies.
7. **Mysteries,** such as Agatha Christie and Rex Stout and Sir Arthur Conan Doyle.
8. **Science Fiction,** any type of story that takes place in the distant future or is based on magic.
9. **Short Stories,** a collection of short stories by the same author of by different authors.
10. **Westerns,** such as Louis L'Amour, Zane Grey, Max Brand, and Luke Short.

Chapter Ninety

Music for Entertainment

One of the ways your family can maintain a positive and healthy attitude during a serious hard times event is by singing together. You don't have to have a great singing voice to sing-along with your own family. Everybody can join in and everyone will have their spirits lifted.

The following books are recommended for a home music library. The instrument music books are written in a self-teaching style so you can learn how to play the instrument yourself.

You don't have to be a skilled musician to learn how to play a very simple musical instrument such as a kazoo or a tambourine. To play a kazoo simply hum the song into the kazoo. Don't blow into the kazoo -- hum into it. A simple plastic kazoo can be purchased for less than $2 at many stores, including some of the Dollar stores and some Walmarts. Look for a kazoo and not a "recorder." A recorder looks like a long plastic flute and it has several finger holes on top.

Two Kazoos

If you don't already have some type of musical instrument in your home then may I suggest a basic harmonica such as the one recommended below. During a long-term hard times event you can gradually learn how to play the harmonica if you also purchase either one of the two recommended harmonica books below.

Songbook:
The Great Family Songbook, A Treasury of Favorite Folk Songs, Popular Tunes, Children's Melodies, International Songs, Hymns, Holiday Jingles and More for Piano and Guitar, 2007, 272 Pages.

A Harmonica and Harmonica Books:
Harmonica by Lee Oscar Major Diatonic in C, in Plastic Carrying Case.
Idiot's Guide to Playing the Harmonica, 2nd Edition, Melton, 2006, 272 Pages.
Harmonica for Dummies, Yerxa, 2008, 360 Pages.

Guitar Book:
Hal Leonard Guitar Method, Complete Edition (contains books 1, 2, and 3), with CD, Hal Leonard.

Piano Book:
How to Play Popular Piano in 10 Easy Lessons, Monath and David, 1984, 141 Pages.

Trumpet Book:
Play Trumpet Today, a Complete Guide to the Basics, with DVD, Hal Leonard, 48 Pages.

Drum Book:
Complete Idiot's Guide to Playing the Drums, 2nd Edition, Miller, 2004, 320 Pages.
Drums for Dummies, Strong, 2006, 384 Pages.

Christian Hymn Book:
Celebration Hymnal, Songs and Hymns for Worship, 1997, 865 Pages.

The Great Resurrection

In the town of Nain a young man was being carried in his coffin to his grave.
    Jesus felt sad in His heart because the man was the only son of a widow.
Jesus stopped the funeral and He said, "Young man, I say to you, get up!"
    Instantly the dead man sat up and spoke, and Jesus gave him to his mother.

The twelve-year old daughter of the ruler of the local synagogue had died.
    Jesus entered the room where the dead body of the little girl lay on her bed.
Jesus spoke softly to her and He said, "Little girl, I say to you, get up!"
    Immediately the little girl stood up, and walked around, and was fed.

For four days Lazarus was dead inside his tomb in the small town of Bethany.
    Then Jesus requested that the stone in front of his tomb be rolled away.
Jesus spoke in a loud voice and He said, "Lazarus, come out!"
    And Lazarus walked out of his tomb, and he ate with Jesus later that day.

Jesus always spoke directly to **one** person when He spoke to the dead.
    If Jesus had not specified **one** person each time He spoke His command,
All the dead would have heard, whether in the seas, or as ashes in the wind,
    and all the graves under the earth would have split open across the land.

Unless Jesus returns first, then one day I too will be resting in my grave.
    And slowly but surely my dead body will gradually begin to decay.
But one day Jesus will return and with a loud voice He will shout,
    "All my followers, arise!" -- and I will hear and I will obey.

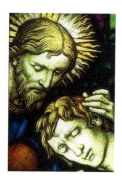 

Scripture References: Luke 7:11-15, Mark 5:35-43, Luke 8:51-56, John 11:43-44, First Timothy 4:16-18, Job 19:25-27, Isaiah 26:19, John 5:24-27, John 5:28-29, Daniel 12:2-3.

Chapter Ninety-One

A Deck of 52 Playing Cards and Some Card Game Books and Five Common Ordinary Dice

One entertainment option that does not depend on electricity is an ordinary deck of 52 **plastic coated** playing cards.

An ordinary deck of 52 playing cards can be used to play hundreds of card games and solitaire games, including Hearts, Spades, Rummy, Bridge, Go Fish, War, and Old Maid (after you temporarily remove three of the queens from the deck). A simple deck of playing cards will help your children recognize and understand the meaning of the numbers two through ten because each card has the same number of symbols as the printed number on the card. And a simple two-dollar investment in a quality deck of 52 playing cards will provide hundreds of hours of entertainment each year for one person, or for two people, or for your entire family.

The cheaper playing cards are usually not plastic coated. This means they have a tendency to stick together and they more easily acquire stains and rough edges and bent corners. Therefore I personally would prefer to have one quality deck of **plastic coated** playing cards than two cheap decks because the quality deck of cards will easily outlast two cheap decks of playing cards. If you have young children and you can afford it then you should probably invest in a few spare decks of **plastic coated** playing cards for future years because young children can easily wear out a deck of good cards in one year. However, two dollars is a cheap investment if it keeps your children quietly occupied for a few hundred hours each year.

I suggest you purchase a deck of cards with a generic back design as opposed to a design that includes gambling symbols, or gambling words, or the Bicycle brand because it shows a naked person riding a bicycle.

If you have a deck of 52 plastic coated playing cards, and some books on card games and solitaire games, then you and your family will be able to entertain yourselves for hours.

Some good card games books are the following:

1. **Official Rules of Card Games**, Morehead, 1996, 327 Pages.
2. **New Complete Hoyle Revised,** Hardbound, 1991, 720 Pages.
3. **The Complete Book of Solitare and Patience Games**, 225 Games, Morehead, 1983, 192 Pages.

If you enjoy card games then you should also purchase a deck of **Uno** playing cards.

Finally, a set of five common ordinary six-sided dice would allow you to play a variety of dice games, such as Yacht. Complete instructions for the dice game of Yacht may be downloaded from the following web site: http://boardgames.about.com/od/yacht/a/yacht_rules.htm

Say You're Sorry Before It's Too Late

After a person is caught doing something he or she shouldn't have done,
then he or she will usually say, "I'm sorry. I promise I won't do it again."
But it is the fear of punishment that causes these words to be spoken.

When there is a very small chance of being caught and found guilty,
most people will have no reason to apologize and say they are sorry.
Instead they will just wait until they die and appear before the Almighty.

Then they will loudly exclaim, "I'm so sorry. Please have mercy on me."
But then it will be too late and they will be cast into hell for all eternity,
and there they will know they waited too long to ask God for His mercy.

But today, right now, it's not too late if you truly want to be forgiven.
All you have to do is believe in Jesus Christ, God's one and only Son,
and then ask God in Jesus' name to forgive you for all you have done.

Scripture References: Matthew 5:25-26, Jude 1:14-15, Revelation 20:11-15, Luke 2:11-12, John 11:25-26, John 8:24, Ecclesiastes 7:20, Romans 3:23, James 2:10, Matthew 16:26, Romans 6:23, Romans 10:9-10, Mark 1:15, Second Corinthians 6:2.

Chapter Ninety-Two

What to Do Right Now if the Hard Times Have Begun and You are Not Prepared

There are two possible scenarios for the beginning of hard times:

1. **Scenario One:** You have some money and many of the local stores are still open for business.
2. **Scenario Two:** You don't have any money, or you do have some money but the stores are all closed.

The overwhelming vast majority of people who have thought about the possibility of hard times are expecting the hard times to unfold according to the first scenario above. Therefore they have not done anything to prepare for any type of hard times. The reason they don't prepare is because they believe they will have plenty of time at the beginning of the hard times to buy all the things they will need. Although this might work it is my personal opinion that this strategy has about one chance in a million of being successful.

The most likely scenario will probably be the second one above. In the second scenario:

A. A person will not have any money, or
B. A person will have some money but he or she won't be able to get to it because the banks will all be closed, or
C. A person will have some money and he or she will really, really want to spend it on the things he or she desperately needs but all the stores will be closed because the stores are now empty and they have nothing left to sell.

The second scenario is the one that occurs when an area is destroyed by a hurricane or a tornado or an earthquake. The people living in Japan on March 11, 2011 discovered how quickly an unexpected hard times event (an 8.9 earthquake and a 30-foot tsunami) could completely disrupt their normal life style and thrust them into a day-by-day survival mode where they had to deal with radioactive fallout, limited amounts of food and water, and intermittent utility services. Simple things, like batteries, or a flashlight, or a battery operated radio, were unavailable in Japan after March 11 and during April of 2011. Many, many people in Japan really wanted to buy these things but all the stores in Japan were sold out of these items. The only individuals who had these items were the people who had purchased them before the earthquake and the tsunami hit the island of Japan.

Hard times are inevitable. The only things we do not know about hard times in advance are:

1. the trigger event,
2. the severity of the hard times, and
3. the duration of the hard times.

The trigger event could be anything, such as an earthquake, or a tornado, or a hurricane, or a nuclear plant meltdown, or a world war, or hyperinflation, or a simple common ordinary worldwide famine. Severe famines depopulate entire regions and they cause massive population relocations that result in a huge number of refugees who die of starvation or starvation related health problems. And severe famines always convert a significant percentage of common ordinary people into ruthless savages who live by the "law of the jungle" or "survival of the fittest." This has been historically documented so many times in the past that to believe that a severe famine will unfold differently today is ludicrous. It really doesn't matter if you and 5% (or 30%) of the rest in the people in the world can afford to buy food, or if some percentage of families already have an emergency food supply. The people who can't afford food and who do not have an emergency food supply will not simply sit down and wait to die a peaceful quiet extremely unpleasant death due to starvation. They will do the same things today that starving people have always done in the past. It will begin with just a few people in each area reverting to savage behavior. Then you will hear about small organized groups of people who are engaging in savage behavior. Then each geographical region will be overrun by a huge uncontrollable mob of people who are starving and they will do anything to anybody in order to survive. This mob of starving people will first sweep through their immediate area, then they will descend on nearby suburban areas, and then they will overflow into the nearby rural areas and they will loot and destroy every farm and ranch they find. Many of the people in this mob will die or be killed during this looting process. But some of the people in this mob will survive for a little longer on the food they steal. However, after they have eaten all their stolen food the vast majority of them will still die of starvation because:

1. they don't know how to grow food, or
2. they do know how to grow food but they have absolutely no previous real world gardening experience, or
3. they simply have no desire to grow food.

And there will be no one they can turn to for assistance because they will have already murdered the farmers and ranchers who had extensive experience in growing food and managing livestock.

Is a worldwide famine in your future? I don't know. But I do pay attention to the news and I do know that the United States of America is having serious planting problems with millions and millions of acres of their agricultural land in the Spring of the year 2011. And many of the other major food exporting countries around the world are also experiencing severe planting and/or harvesting problems this year. And many, many news commentators are now predicting a significant increase in food prices later this year. If food prices significantly increase at the same time that tax revenues are down and the true unemployment rate is exceptionally high, then this combination of events could easily lead to massive worldwide unrest due to a simple ordinary worldwide famine. If this happens then living conditions will be leveled worldwide and everyone everywhere will be living in a nightmare third-world economy. The reason is because politicians and governments can't simply create food by passing new laws or making long speeches. All they can do is try to deceive people into believing that they have everything under control and that the horrible growling noise that everyone is hearing from their stomachs is just their imagination playing tricks on them. This is the one speech that nobody is going to believe and when that happens then the people of the world will revolt in a most unpleasant fashion.

The above is just one example of a worst case breakdown in society. The good news is that it may not happen during your lifetime. In fact, some people believe that a worst case breakdown in no longer possible or feasible in today's modern world. These individuals believe that our leaders will somehow be able to do all the following:

1. **Water:** Keep the water flowing in their faucets. However, as time passes the quality of that water gradually declines. At first it contains just a few tiny black things, and later it also contains some nasty chemicals, and finally it even contains radioactive particles. But the people gradually become accustomed to the constantly decreasing quality of their water and they accept their poor quality water as being normal.
2. **Sewer:** Keep the sewer systems working. Otherwise human waste will begin to accumulate inside and outside their dwellings. If this were to happen then sickness and disease would quickly exceed the capacity of their local medical facilities and people would just start dying. Therefore their leaders would never allow this to happen.
3. **Food:** Keep food on the store shelves. However, as the quality of that food gradually begins to decline, and as the price of that low quality food gradually begins to increase, people become accustomed to their weight loss and their frequent dietary related illnesses and they accept it as part of their new lower

standard of living. And they also gradually accept the fact that many older people, and many younger children, are now starving to death. And they accept the fact that some people can no longer afford the expensive low quality food and that those people are now stealing from other people in order to survive.

4. **Electricity:** Keep the electricity flowing to their homes. People gradually accept the fact that their electricity is only on for a few hours each day. Then they gradually accept the fact that the quality of that electricity is so unstable that it ruins the appliances in their homes.

5. **Heat**: Keep the propane or the gas flowing to their homes in the winter so they don't freeze to death. However, as the cost of that fuel increases many families will not be able to afford it and therefore many people will suffer during the winter and some will die as a result of the freezing weather.

6. **Employment and Housing:** Keep the economy healthy so that most people still have jobs and a place to live. However, as time passes more and more businesses go bankrupt, and more and more people lose their jobs and their homes. The lucky ones are able to move in with their relatives. The unlucky ones find a place to sleep below a bridge, or in a temporary tent city, or in a shanty built from scrap stolen from a junk yard. And with each passing month the true number of unemployed individuals increases and the number of tent cities and shanty towns also increases.

7. **Police Protection:** Maintain the illusion of law enforcement. People gradually accept the fact that the number of thieves, looters, rapists, and murderers is constantly increasing. And gradually they accept the fact that these criminals are not being punished when they are caught. Finally, they accept the fact that their government and their police are not helping them but they are causing some of their problems.

8. **Money and Inflation:** Keep some type of paper money flowing through the economy. People simply accept the fact that their smallest denomination bill is 1,000. And a short time later their smallest bill is 10,000 and all their other bills have a lot more zeros on it than that.

The above is an example of a slow collapse of an economy. Living conditions gradually continue to get worse and worse over a long period of time and people simply adjust to each new reduction in their standard of living. And with each new reduction in their living conditions the above people believe that they have now reached bottom and things couldn't possibly get any worse.

What the above individuals refuse to believe is that one day the poor quality water in their faucets may cease to flow, that their sewer systems may stop working, that there may be no food for sale anywhere, that there may be no electricity of any type, and that nobody in the entire world will accept their paper money. These individuals may be correct and this may not happen during their lifetimes. But to say that it is impossible and that it could never happen is not being very realistic when you consider everything that is currently happening around our world at this time.

That's enough "worst case doom-and-gloom." For the purposes of this chapter let's assume both of the original hard times scenarios are possible and let's examine the most practical strategy for each of those two scenarios.

The First Scenario:
You do have some money and
the local stores are still open for business.

If you already own an item in the following list then you don't need to buy another one. However, if you don't own one or more of the following recommended items then this may be your last chance to purchase one of these "necessities."

Obviously the most reasonable course of action would have been to have bought the following items before the onset of hard times. But if you have procrastinated and the hard times are now here, then you should not wait any longer.

If possible purchase at least one of all the following items. It would be better to have at least one of everything than to have lots of one thing and none of several other things. Use your money intelligently. This may be your last chance to acquire the things your family will need to survive.

If you are like most of us you probably only have a limited amount of money and you will need to

prioritize your spending. Therefore the following list has been separated into three sections:
1. Highest priority items.
2. Extremely important items.
3. Very important items.

Section One: Highest Priority Items

1. One, two, or three good quality heavy-duty tarps in sizes from 8 feet by 10 feet, up to a maximum size of approximately 20 feet by 30 feet. These can be used to capture rainwater or they may be used as an emergency shelter, or they may be used for both purposes at the same time. Do not waste your money on a tent.
2. At least 100 feet of nylon or polypropylene cord 1/4 inch or 3/8 inch thick.
3. At least 100 feet of 20 gauge black wire (hardware section) or 22 gauge green wire (floral section).
4. A box of 1,000 paper matches and at least two good quality butane lighters made by two different companies.
5. If you do not already own a good hunting knife then buy a Buck Model 119 hunting knife.
6. If you do not already own a good flashlight then buy a L.E.D. 2AA Mini Maglite flashlight. Buy an elastic head band in the sporting goods section.
7. A battery operated radio that uses AA batteries. Either buy an Emerson at Walmart or buy a Grundig G6 at Radio Shack. Read the chapters in this book about radios.
8. At least sixteen rechargeable AA NiMH batteries that are already pre-charged. These should be the same size batteries that operate all your battery operated equipment.
9. At least one 1,200 yard spool of thread in the sewing section at Walmart. Also buy one package of thin hand sewing needles and one package of thick heavy-duty craft sewing needles. A hand sewing needle has the point at one end of the needle and the thread hole, or eye, at the opposite end of the needle. Also buy one small package of assorted color thread that also contains needles and a needle threader.
10. A good pair of waterproof work/hiking boots, either brown or black, with ribbed soles and reinforced toes. Invest in boots that are about 1/2 size larger than what you have worn in the past to prevent foot blisters and to allow you to wear two pair of socks at the same time in the freezing cold winter months. Try the boots on and make absolutely sure they are comfortable to walk in.
11. A good quality portable first-aid kit. The kit should contain a variety of practical useful items and not just an assortment of bandages.
12. A fever thermometer that is the shake-down type and not one that is battery operated.
13. Four extra boxes of bandages in 3/4 inch or 1 inch widths.
14. One 2-inch wide or 3-inch wide elastic bandage.
15. At least one extra roll of sterile gauze and some white bandage tape.
16. A reasonable supply of the over-the-counter medications and ointments your family has used in the past, such as pain and fever reducers, anti-diarrhea medicine, anti-itch cream, etc.

17. At least 12 bars of pure "Ivory" brand soap for each member of your family, if your family is not allergic to Ivory soap.
18. At least one extra toothbrush for each member of your family and several tubes of toothpaste and several containers of dental floss.
19. A variety of vegetable seeds. If you can't find vegetable seeds for sale then buy one Roma tomato, two potatoes (either red or baking), some dry pinto beans, and two Golden Delicious Apples:
    a. Slice the tomato, carefully remove and save the seeds, and then eat the rest of the tomato. You can grow a tomato plant inside your house in a plastic pot in front of a window that gets good sun most of the day. Read the chapter on how to grow vegetables.
    b. Let the potatoes grow sprouts and then cut off and plant the sprouts. You may then eat the remainder of the two potatoes. Read the gardening chapter on how to plant potatoes.

    c. Do **not** eat the dry pinto beans. Save the dry beans so you can plant them as seed to grow more pinto beans. Pinto beans will grow to maturity in 65 to 90 days (depending on your climate and soil) whereas most other beans usually take between 90 to 110 days to grow to maturity. If your grocery store doesn't have dry pinto beans then buy dry kidney beans or any other type of dry beans your family will eat. Any type of dry bean may be planted as seed to grow more of that same type of bean. Beans contain protein, carbohydrates, vitamins, and lots of calories.

    d. Carefully remove and save the seeds from the apples and then eat the apples. Read the chapter on how to grow fruit trees from seed.

20. A garden shovel with a pointed blade and a total length of about 54-inches from the tip of the blade to the end of the handle. Also buy one garden hoe.
21. A water hose that is at least 100-feet long (or two 50-feet long hoses) and a water hose nozzle.
22. At least a one-year's supply of food for each member of your family. Read the Food Chapters in this book.
23. If you don't have a firearm then buy a firearm. A semi-automatic 22LR caliber rifle is the minimum investment. If you can afford it buy an original design AK-47 and a Glock Model 22 that shoots 40 caliber ammunition. Read the firearm chapters.
24. If you don't have ammunition then buy at least 500 to 1,000 rounds of 22LR ammo and several boxes of ammo for your other firearms. If possible pay cash to avoid leaving a paper trail.
25. One pair of safety eyeglasses for each member of your family.
26. If you don't already own one, buy a "Holy Bible."

If you can still buy things over the internet then buy the following items. Many of these items may be purchased from sellers on amazon.com or on ebay. Or you may do a simple web search and locate online sellers of the following products:

A. A good quality stainless steel gravity water filter system, such as the Berkefeld or the Aquarain, and at least four filter elements. If the stainless steel systems are on backorder then it is okay to buy four or more of the replacement filter elements with O-ring seals and wing nuts. You can use them to make your own homemade water filter following the instructions in the Water Filter Chapter in this book.
B. At least one good quality gill net to make it easier to catch fish for the frying pan. (http://www.texastastes.com/p129.htm) Read the chapter on gill nets.
C. At least three steel pan traps and three conibear traps for capturing wild animals for food. Read the chapter on traps and snares.
D. At least one solar battery charger that will recharge AAA, AA, C, and D rechargeable NiMH batteries. Read the chapter on batteries.
E. At least one portable mono-crystalline solar panel that will provide at least 15 watts of power per hour. Do not invest in a solar panel that provides more than 60 watts of power per hour. It is better to have several smaller capacity solar panels instead of one big solar panel. If one of the smaller panels malfunctions you will have only lost a small part of your total investment.

Section Two: Extremely Important Items

1. At least 24 double rolls of toilet tissue for each family member.
2. 500 to 1000 yards of 10 pound to 25 pound monofilament fishing line.
3. An assortment of fish hooks, swivels, and lead weights.
4. At least 500 feet of strong twine or string. Walmart sells 249-feet of #18 Catfish Nylon Twine (113 pounds tensile strength) for about $3. They sell 486-feet of #36 Catfish Nylon Twine (235 pounds tensile strength) for about $9. These are twisted nylon twines and they are not fishing line. This twine can be used whenever you need some string or twine to tie something and since it is nylon it may be used outdoors and it will not rot easily like cotton string.
5. In the sporting goods section buy a Magnesium Fire Starter. This unit has "fire steel" and it has magnesium so you could start a fire in almost any type of weather in an emergency.

6. In the sporting goods section buy a good quality compass with a dial needle that points north. The compass should be completely enclosed inside a plastic carrying case that you can open and close to protect the face of the compass. Do **not** purchase a battery operated electronic compass. Do not buy a cheap compass.
7. In the sporting goods section buy a camping solar shower bag that holds four or five gallons of water. Fill the bag with water in the morning, place the bag in the sun, and in the evening you will have hot or very warm water for a personal shower. Being able to take a simple shower after a hard day of work and cleaning the sweat off your body will allow you to get a really good night's sleep. A good night's rest is critical during hard times. If you can afford it you should buy a solar shower bag for each member of your family.

8. A Leatherman Wave multi-tool (usually sold in the sporting goods section near the knives).
9. At least twelve pair of extra socks for each member of your family.
10. At least one 12-volt marine (or golf cart) deep cycle battery. This battery can be charged with a portable solar panel. The battery could then be used to recharge many of your battery operated electrical appliances that have a cigarette lighter adapter, such as your cell phone or your laptop computer.
11. At least one 12-volt cigarette lighter adapter plug for charging battery operated items. This is the type of adapter that can be connected to the two terminals of a 12-volt deep cycle battery. These are sometimes sold in the electronics section or the automotive section of a store or at a Radio Shack store.
12. If you don't already have a reasonable assortment of ordinary hand tools then buy a good quality pre-assembled case of general purpose hand tools inside their own special plastic carrying case. The set should have a hammer and screwdrivers and pliers and wrenches and a tape measure. There is a big difference between a set of socket wrenches and a general purpose tool kit. A general purpose tool kit will usually contain a few socket wrenches but it will also include other items such as a hammer and pliers.
13. If you do not have a wood saw then purchase a Stanley Sharptooth 15-inch wood saw.

Section Three: Very Important Items

1. Several pair of gloves for each member of your family.
2. If possible buy a ski mask, or a cap with ear flaps, for each member of your family.
3. Some cast iron cook pots with lids, such as the "Combo Cooker" cast iron cook set that is sold at hardware stores and in the sporting goods section of some Walmarts.
4. If you do not already own one, buy a medium size backpack and buy a folding luggage carrier. A school backpack would be fine. Many of the camping backpacks will probably be too big. You will only be able to load a backpack with about 30 pounds for an adult male, and about 25 pounds for an adult female, and about 20 pounds for a teenager, and about 10 or 15 pounds for a child. The child's backpack should contain his or her spare clothes and some of his or her favorite small toys, such as a doll, or small hot wheels cars, or coloring book and crayons.
5. An outdoor mercury-filled thermometer and an indoor mercury-filled thermometer. Do not purchase battery operated thermometers.
6. One AA battery-operated quartz wall clock with hands that only shows the time of day.
7. One AA battery operated quartz clock that has an alarm and that keeps track of the date, and the day of the week, and maybe even the internal room temperature.
8. At least one 12-volt portable electric fan that has a 12-volt cigarette lighter adapter. These are sometimes sold in the hardware section or in the automotive section of stores or at Recreational Vehicle dealers. If you have relatively high summer temperatures in your area then you will truly appreciate the comfort of an electric fan.
9. A 1,200 watt inverter. These are sometimes sold in the automotive section or the electronics section of stores, or at Radio Shack. If possible do not buy an inverter that provides less than 1,000 watts or more than 2,000 watts of continuous power. Do not make your decision based on the momentary peak power

rating of the inverter which will be higher than the inverter's continuous power rating. You may need to purchase this item on the internet.

10. At least two portable fire extinguishers that will work on all types of fires.
11. If possible buy a mosquito head net for each member of your family. During hard times the insect population multiplies. All types of flying insects will fly around your head and they will annoy you and distract you and seriously reduce your productivity and your effectiveness in whatever you are trying to accomplish. The simple solution to the flying insect problem is to purchase a mosquito head net for each member of your family. The head net can be worn under a hat or over a hat or with no hat at all. These head nets sell for less than two-dollars in the camping section of many stores. The net will keep the tiny insects out of your ears, eyes, nose, and mouth and you will not experience the unpleasant gagging reflex caused by inhaling a gnat. (Note: A mosquito head net, and a thin lightweight long-sleeve shirt, and a pair of lightweight gloves will eliminate the need for insect repellent during "bug season.")
12. One large mosquito netting for each member of your family. During hard times flying insects increase exponentially and a mosquito net can be placed above and around each person's bed so that person can get some undisturbed sleep each night. During hard times you may become displaced from your normal residence and a mosquito net will make a big difference in your comfort each night wherever you may be forced to sleep.
13. At least one case of bottled water in the 16 ounce or 20 ounce plastic bottles. Save the empty bottles and the screw on caps. Refill the water bottles with water yourself when they are empty. These water bottles are a convenient size for personal consumption and they will allow you to keep track of how much water you are drinking each day. This will allow you to consume your water on a planned schedule. During hard times you should always boil your water for one-minute and then allow it to cool. Boiling will kill all the pathogens that might be in the water but boiling will not eliminate radioactive particles or dissolved chemicals. Read the Water Chapter in this book.
14. One good quality 100% stainless steel manually operated hand-crank can opener.
15. At least ten disposable razors.
16. 75 square feet of Reynolds Heavy-Duty Aluminum Foil (18 inches wide and 16.67 feet long), and one box of 5 Reynolds Oven Bags. You will also need to download the instructions on how to build a Solar Oven from this web site:
http://www.oksolar.com/samples/sunoven1.html
17. At least one deck of good quality plastic coated playing cards.
18. Some paper, some ink pens, some pencils, and a small pencil sharpener with an internal razor blade.

Depending on your current situation, such as where you live and the skills and special needs of your family members, you may need to change the priority of some of the above items from one category to another category. For example, if you have a job where your appearance is critical to keeping your job, then razors should be moved to the first category of items. You may also need to add some things that are unique to your family's specific situation.

Depending on your past life experiences you may or may not understand the critical importance of all the items in the above list. Just because you don't understand why an item is important does not mean that item is not important. If the hard times you are currently experiencing continue to get worse with the passage of time then the importance of each and every item in the above list will gradually become obvious to you. It would be sad if you decided to ignore the above advice and not buy an item just because you currently believe it is useless, and then discover later that your long-term survival actually depends on that item you decided you would not buy.

The Second Scenario:
Either you don't have any money or
you do have some money but the stores are all closed.

Recycling: Do **not** throw anything away unless it is worthless. As time passes you may discover a very practical use for some of the things you perceived as "trash" at the beginning of the hard times.

Water: Fill every container that will hold water with water. Save every plastic bottle and jar that has a screw on top. If you have a case of bottled water, or bottled Gatorade, or bottled soda, then rinse and save every empty plastic or glass bottle and its screw on cap. If you are not absolutely sure about the quality of your water then you should boil your water for one-minute during hard times to destroy all the harmful microorganisms that might be in your water. However, boiling will not remove dissolved chemicals or radioactive particles.

Fire: This includes matches and butane lighters. Do not waste these precious resources. Learn how to divide a paper match into four pieces before you waste one match. Learn how to start the maximum number of fires using a butane lighter. Learn how to start a fire without a match or a butane lighter by using the coals from a previous fire. Read the Fire Chapter in this book.

Food: Do not believe everything you hear or read. You may or may not receive some more food in the near future. Don't bet your life and the lives of your family members on a "promise" that food is on its way and you will have lots of food real soon. Until you actually have the food in your possession you should not bet your life on something you don't have. Therefore immediately ration your food and your salt. Do not add any salt to commercially processed food because that food already contains an adequate amount of salt. Save any salt you may have for the future when you may have some fresh meat or fresh vegetables. If you don't have very much food and you don't know when you will be able to get some more food, then go hungry for a day or two before you eat anything. Only eat one very small meal each day. Your objective is to stay alive. If you consume all your food during the first few days then you will starve to death. Consume your food as slowly as possible. This may mean that you have to skip a day or two between meals. One week's worth of food could keep you alive for seven weeks if you only eat one very small meal every two or three days. This is **not** easy to do but you need to focus on long-term survival and not on short-term appetite gratification. (Note: The one obvious exception would be pregnant women or nursing mothers -- they will need more food because they are feeding two people.)

Seeds: If you can find vegetable seeds then either buy them or trade for them. If you can't find seeds for sale then try to find the following **fresh** food (not cooked, canned, or frozen): tomato, potato, dry beans, corn on the cob, cucumber, any type of melon that has seeds, peppers, fruit, and raw peanuts in the shell (not roasted or salted). Learn how to save the seeds inside these items, or how to sprout and plant these items. Learn how to grow your own food. Read the Gardening Chapters in this book.

Shelter: Make a decision on whether you should remain where you are right now or whether you should relocate to a safer area. Do not let your emotions guide you. Instead let your mind guide you. Do not allow an emotional attachment to your current location interfere with this decision. Do not let your financial investment in your current location interfere with this decision. This is not a simple decision. Read the Shelter Chapters in this book. If you decide to relocate then each family member should take his or her favorite pillow with them if that is possible.

Clothing: Wear your most practical set of footwear. Read the chapter on shoes and boots. You will need warm clothing and warm blankets for the cold weather months.

Pets: Read the chapter on pets and livestock.

Toilet Tissue: Conserve any toilet tissue you still have as if it were gold. Do not waste your toilet tissue removing makeup, or wiping up spilled liquids, or anything except cleaning your bottom when it becomes necessary. Be diligent when cleaning your bottom but do not be wasteful with your toilet tissue when performing this necessary task. Read the Toilet Paper Chapter in this book.

Protection: Obey the firearm and knife laws in your area. If possible, always carry a pocket knife. If possible and it is legal in your area, also carry a hunting knife. If you have a concealed carry permit, carry a handgun. Do not waste one round of your ammunition on target practice. Conserve your ammunition as if it were gold. You may never have any more ammunition than what you have at the beginning of the hard times. Don't waste one round of your ammo. It is much too precious.

Psychological: Be intellectually prepared to see the dark side of people you may have known for many years. This may include some people you are related to by blood or by marriage. Read the Social Breakdown Chapters in this book.

Footnote: Firearm Selection

If you do not already own a rifle and a handgun then now would be a good time to seriously consider making this investment. If you visit a variety of different web sites you will quickly notice that almost every web site has multiple firearm recommendations. Each firearm is reviewed based on its strengths and weaknesses and the types of situations in which it would be appropriate. In a very short period of time the amount of information on firearms can quickly become overwhelming. This makes it extremely difficult for someone to make an informed choice that would be appropriate for his or her specific circumstances. Therefore please allow me to summarize this topic based on what I have recommended for many, many years.

Handgun: I strongly recommend a semi-automatic pistol instead of a revolver or a single-shot handgun. My first choice in a handgun would be a Glock Model 22 with a 15-round magazine that shoots the 40 caliber bullet. This is the same handgun that the overwhelming vast majority of law enforcement officers in the United States select as their primary sidearm. These men and women are intelligent individuals and they know that their lives may occasionally depend on their handgun selection. The Glock handgun is an exceptionally high quality firearm, it is very reliable, and the 40 caliber bullet has an impressive law enforcement history of being an effective man-stopper. The 40 caliber bullet (40 S&W) generates a reasonable and controllable amount of recoil so it is also an accurate firearm. My second choice in a handgun would be a Glock Model 21SF (SF = Slim Frame) with a 13-round magazine that shoots the 45 caliber bullet (45 ACP or 45 Auto but not the 45 GAP). The 45 caliber bullet also has an impressive law enforcement history that is almost identical to the 40 caliber bullet. However, the grip of the Model 21SF is 1/4 inch greater in circumference than the Model 22 and this makes it more challenging for a person with a smaller hand to comfortably grasp. The recoil of the 45 caliber bullet is also more than the 40 caliber bullet and this makes it more challenging for many individuals to shoot accurately. One very important consideration in the selection of a handgun is that it should feel comfortable in your hand when you hold it. Finally, if you are the only person in your family who can comfortably grip and shoot a 45 pistol, and you should become incapacitated for any reason, then nobody else in your family would be able to use your 45 for effective defense or protection. Regardless of which Glock model you purchase you should also install an internal laser sight made by LaserMax. You should also invest in a holster that contains a spare magazine compartment at the front of the holster. Finally, if you can afford it, you should invest in 1,000 rounds of ammunition for your handgun.

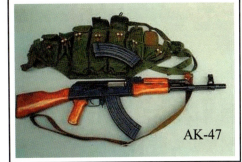

AK-47

Rifle for Hunting and Self-Defense: I strongly recommend a semi-automatic rifle instead of a bolt-action rifle or a lever-action rifle. My first choice in a rifle would depend on where I lived. If I lived in an area where the vast majority of my shooting would be done in areas where the normal visibility was 200 yards or less then I would invest in an original design AK-47 that shoots the 7.62x39 bullet. This bullet has a normal average trajectory of plus 1.5 inches at 110 yards and minus 1.5 inches at 175 yards (3 inch total

Chapter Ninety-Two: What To Do if the Hard Times Have Already Begun

circle) and it is lethal out to 240 yards. If I lived in an area where the vast majority of my shooting would be done in areas where the normal visibility was more than 200 yards then I would invest in an AR-10 that shoots the 7.62x51 bullet (308 caliber). This bullet has a normal average trajectory of plus 3 inches at 125 yards and minus 3 inches at 260 yards (6 inch total circle) and it is lethal out to 600 yards. I strongly recommend that you add a sling and a good scope to your rifle using see-through scope mounts. The scope mount has a significant impact on the stability and reliability of your scope so I recommend a mount that has four screws on each mount that holds the scope to the mount (total of eight mounting screws on both mounts). You can buy good scopes for less than $100. If you can afford it then you can spend more on a scope but my opinion is that most people will find that a scope that cost between $40 to $100 will perform very well for all their shooting. Finally, if you can afford it, you should invest in 1,000 rounds of ammunition for your rifle. (Note: If possible, purchase an AK-47 with a folding rear stock instead of a wood stock, and a black plastic front hand grip instead of a wood front hand grip. The folding rear stock should fold over against the side of the rifle.)

AK-47 GP WASR-10 (Semiautomatic 7.62x39)

22 Caliber Semi-Automatic Rifle: If you can afford it then my first choice in a 22 rifle would be the Ruger Model 10/22 with detachable 10-round magazine. If you can afford it then purchase a 10/22 with a stainless steel barrel rifle. My second choice in a 22 rifle would be the very affordable Savage Arms Model 64F semi-automatic rifle with a detachable 10-round magazine. Regardless of your rifle choice buy some extra magazines. Install a sling and a reasonable quality scope ($30 to $60) on your rifle using see-through scope mounts. If you can afford it, purchase 5,000 rounds of 22LR ammunition for your rifle.

Ruger Model 10/22 (Semiautomatic 22LR)

Savage Arms Model 64F (Semiautomatic 22LR)

Shotgun: I have not recommended a shotgun in the past and I do not recommend one to a new shooter. However, if you wish to purchase a shotgun then I strongly suggest a semi-automatic shotgun.

Concealed Carry: My first choice for a concealed carry handgun would be the Ruger LCP that fires the 380 ammunition. I strongly suggest that you install a Crimson Trace laser sight on this pistol. The laser sight is automatically activated when you grip the pistol in your hand. If you purchase the Crimson Trace laser it will include a nice carrying pouch that can be used to transport the Ruger LCP in your pocket. The reasons I suggest this specific pistol are: it is an exceptionally high quality very reliable semi-automatic 6-shot pistol, it is relatively flat (less than 3/4-inch) which means it can fit into your pants' pocket without creating the normal silhouette outline of a gun, it is very light weight even when fully loaded (12

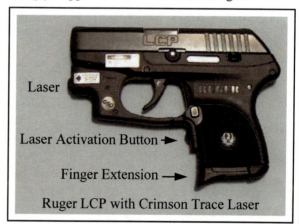

Ruger LCP with Crimson Trace Laser

ounces), and it fires a 380 caliber bullet which is very similar to the 9mm bullet. I also recommend that you install the finger extension on the bottom of the 6-round magazine to make the pistol more comfortable to grip and to shoot accurately. Also purchase at least 500 rounds of hollow-point ammunition for this pistol.

Chapter Ninety-Two: What To Do if the Hard Times Have Already Begun

Firearm Summary: I don't mind if you disagree with the above suggestions and you purchase something entirely different. You are an adult and you have the right to make whatever firearm choices you believe would be best for your family and your particular situation. However, please allow me to caution you against believing everything you read about firearms. It is relatively easy to make a very convincing argument for almost any type of firearm in any caliber if the person only focuses on the strong points of that firearm and that caliber and neglects to mention the shortcomings of that firearm or that caliber. Before you make a firearm choice you should learn as much as you can about that firearm including all of its potential shortcomings. Regardless of your choice in firearms you should learn all the firearm safety rules and you should consistently use your firearm safely and correctly.

Caliber of Ammunition: One of the very important issues in firearm selection that should not be compromised (unless you have some extremely good reasons) is that the firearm should use a caliber of ammunition that is very common and easy to obtain. During a long-term hard times event ammunition may become scarce and extremely difficult to acquire. However, common caliber ammunition has a much better chance of being available for a lot longer than any caliber that is a special caliber or that has very low historical sales. Examples of common caliber ammunition are the 22LR, 7.62x39, 7.62x51 (308), 40 S&W, and 45 ACP (or 45 auto but not the 45 GAP). The 380 caliber that the Ruger LCP requires is not a common caliber. Therefore a person would have to have some very good reasons to purchase any firearm that shoots the 380 caliber. Those reasons were listed above for the Ruger LCP as a concealed carry pistol.

Number of Firearms: Finally, you do **not** need to invest in a huge arsenal of weapons. If you have a limited amount of money to spend then you will need to select the most logical rifle and pistol for your particular situation. However, if you have lots of money and you really like firearms then you can buy all the weapons you wish. On the other hand, during serious hard times it is not unusual for a family to have to unexpectedly evacuate their current residence for an extremely valid reason, even though they originally believed they would never leave their home. For example, a fire may be headed your way and in about one-hour your home is going to become a pile of glowing cinders. Your only option for long-term survival will be to quickly load your escape vehicle with equipment and supplies and then abandon everything else to the fire. In this situation most people will select one rifle, one pistol, and at least 1,000 rounds of ammunition for each of those firearms. Then they will load their escape vehicle (or vehicles) with as much other practical equipment and supplies as they can depending on the amount of time they have available, and then they will drive away and never look back. In this type of situation the rifle you select should be suitable for hunting and self-defense, and your pistol should be primarily for self-defense. The weight of that rifle, and the bulk and the weight of the ammunition for that rifle, will also be important factors in this situation. My personal opinion is that most families will discover that an AK-47 is the rifle that will simultaneously satisfy all these requirements. However, if you live in an area where the AR-10 and the 308 caliber is the best option then you should select it instead.

Footnote: Candles or Battery Operated Flashlights

The next topic I would like to discuss is candles. Except for the emergency heating of canned foods, I have not recommended the purchase of candles. Instead I have consistently recommended the purchase of an L.E.D. flashlight and rechargeable batteries. However, on many survival internet web sites I frequently read discussions on the advantages and the disadvantages of the different types of candles, along with the recommendation that a specific type of candle be purchased in large quantities.

Let me begin by saying I don't mind if you invest in some candles. Everyone should have a few candles in the event of an emergency. I have about two dozen short round candles for an emergency. However, I do not have a huge inventory of candles because I do not intend to use the candles for light or for heating canned food. The candles are simply my "backup" plan in the event my primary plan doesn't work for some totally unexpected reason.

The reasons I personally do not intend to use candles are as follows:

1. A candle needs to be lit with a match or a butane lighter or some other source of a flame.
2. A candle provides a very weak source of light.
3. A candle should not be used for reading.
4. A candle consumes oxygen and this is a disadvantage in a small confined space.
5. A candle emits smelly fumes and this is a disadvantage in a small confined space.
6. A burning candle can be smelled from a reasonable distance away and this might lead someone to your place of refuge.
7. When a candle has been used up it is gone and it must be replaced with another candle. In other words, a candle is not a renewable resource.
8. A reasonable supply of candles would take up space and add weight to an emergency backpack or bug-out-bag.

On the other hand, a flashlight has the following advantages:

1. A flashlight does not consume oxygen or emit any type of odor.
2. A flashlight provides a strong source of light that can be focused into the distance or it can be used to light an entire room.
3. A flashlight may be used to provide light to read comfortably.
4. A L.E.D. flashlight bulb will last for approximately 100,000 hours so it will not need to be replaced during your lifetime. A L.E.D. flashlight bulb consumes less power than an ordinary flashlight bulb.
5. A flashlight will work using rechargeable batteries. You can recharge batteries using the sun. Therefore, a flashlight, plus some rechargeable batteries, plus a solar battery charger, is a renewable resource that will last for many, many years.
6. The above items would not take up much space in your emergency backpack or bug-out-bag.

The sun is a source of renewable energy. If you had a solar panel and a 12-volt deep-cycle marine battery or a golf cart battery, then you could capture and store the sun's energy inside your 12-volt battery. You could then tap that battery whenever you needed power. For example, you could recharge your portable computer, or your cell phone, or the AA batteries you use in your radio or flashlight. If you also had a 1,200 watt inverter then you could run 110-volt electrical appliances for short periods of time, such as an electric drill, or a printer, or a small microwave oven. This means you could heat some canned food to a reasonable temperature inside a small microwave oven using the sun's energy you previously stored inside a 12-volt deep-cycle battery. Solar power is such a practical option that every family should have their own solar generator.

A solar generator can be easily constructed by almost anyone using the following items for a total cost of about $275:

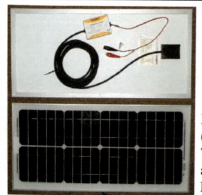

12-volt Adapter with three 12-volt outlets and wiring.

Left: Two 15 Watt Solar Panels ("Instapark" Monocrystalline)
Top = Back side with controller and red & black wires & end clips.
Bottom = Front of one solar panel.

1,200 Watt 110-volt Inverter. Two 110-volt outlets on front with on/off switch and meters.

1. One 15-watt monocrystalline solar panel. These panels are sometimes sold with an optional charge controller attached to the wiring to prevent overcharging of the 12-volt battery. ($75)
2. One 12-volt deep cycle marine battery or golf-cart battery. ($80) (Note: During a serious emergency you could use your automobile battery but your car battery is not a deep-cycle battery so it would not store as much energy as a marine battery or a golf cart battery.)
3. One 12-volt cigarette lighter adapter with three outlets for a cell phone, or laptop computer, or similar devices. ($17)
4. One 110-volt inverter that provides at least 1,200 watts of continuous power or 2,400 watts of peak power. An inverter normally has either one or two of the three-prong 110-volt outlet sockets built into the front panel of the inverter so you can easily plug your 110-volt appliances directly into the inverter without making any modifications to your appliance plugs. ($100)
5. About ten feet of 12-gauge electrical wire in two different colors such as red and black. ($3)

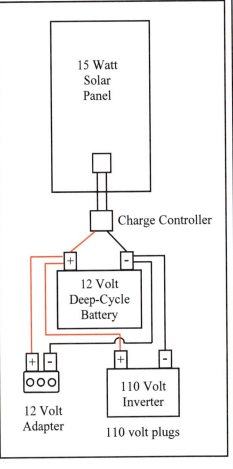

Connect the two color-coded alligator clips from the solar panel to the positive (red wire) and negative (black wire) terminals of the battery. Connect the two color-coded wires from the 12-volt adapter to the battery. Connect the 110-volt inverter to the battery using some of the 12-gauge electrical wire.

On sunny days you will need to place your solar panel so that it is facing directly at the sun. Depending on where you live you have two basic options for positioning your solar panel as follows:

1. Place your solar panel inside your home in front of a window or a glass door where the sun shines for many hours each day. This would protect the solar panel from high winds, and unexpected hail storms, and from theft. It should not attract any attention from someone who was casually passing by unless that person stopped and looked inside your window or door.
2. Hang the solar panel outside a window in a secure fashion so the panel is facing directly at the sun. Bring your solar panel inside in the evening to prevent it from being stolen.

Your solar panel needs to be in direct sunlight so that no part of the solar panel is covered by a shadow. This is easier to do with smaller solar panels because you can usually find sunny spaces on each side of a shadow that is big enough for a smaller solar panel.

The rest of your solar system should be inside your home below the window on the floor. When you need to recharge a device that has a 12-volt adapter just plug it into the 12-volt female plug of your solar generator. When you need to use a 110-volt appliance just plug it into the 110-volt inverter.

Practice the same safety precautions when you plug something into the 110-volt inverter that you use when you plug something into a 110-volt wall outlet. Even though the power is coming from a 12-volt battery it has been increased to 110-volts at the two outlets on your inverter.

The single 15-watt solar panel and single battery system will only store a small amount of power in your 12-volt battery. Therefore you should use that power wisely and not waste it on something frivolous such as a hair dryer or some other heat generating appliance. It would be enough power to keep all your AA batteries charged for your flashlights and your radio, and you could keep your cell phone charged for text messaging, or you could watch one DVD movie per day on your portable computer, or you could briefly heat one or two simple meals per day in a small microwave oven. If you add another solar panel and another deep-cycle battery then you could double the amount of electricity that you would have available each day.

Chapter Ninety-Two: What To Do if the Hard Times Have Already Begun

To recharge your rechargeable flashlight batteries you could plug a standard battery charger into the 110-volt inverter and you could then transfer the power from your 12-volt battery into your smaller 1.2-volt rechargeable batteries.

You could also add the Grundig G6 portable radio ($99) to this system and you would have an AM/FM/Aircraft/Shortwave world band radio to keep track of uncensored news as it was being reported by stations broadcasting in different parts of the world. The G6 radio also contains an internal charging system that will recharge two AA batteries when plugged into a 110-volt outlet. This means you could plug your Grundig G6 into your 110-volt inverter and it would recharge two AA batteries. You could then remove those two AA batteries from the radio and use them in a flashlight or any other device that uses AA batteries, such as an electric toothbrush. The Grundig G6 will not recharge AA batteries as quickly as a standard battery charger so it should not be used in place of a standard battery charger but it could be used as a supplement to a standard battery charger.

Although there is a numerical difference between 110-volts, and 115-volts, and 120-volts, these voltages are all the same when it comes to electrical appliances. Therefore anything you now plug into a standard wall outlet you could also plug into the outlet on a 110-volt inverter even if the appliance says it is 110-volts, or 115-volts, or 120-volts.

220 Volts: If you have the basic electrical knowledge about home wiring systems, then you could install a second 12-volt battery, and a second 110-volt inverter, and create 220 to 240-volt power for your 220, 230, or 240 volt appliances. However, you could not run these appliances for very long because you are using battery power. However, you could run one of these appliances for a few minutes each day. This might be very useful if you have a 220-volt well pump, or if you live in a country where the standard voltage is 220 to 240 volts. If you are a knowledgeable, experienced certified electrician then you could install a 110 to 220-volt transformer on a single 110-volt inverter to increase the voltage to 220-volts.

Wire Sizes: Generally the larger the wire size the more efficient your solar generator will be. If the electrical openings in your solar generator equipment will allow you to use 12-gauge wire then you should do so. However, some of the components may have smaller openings and they may require 14-gauge or 16-gauge wire. Therefore read the instructions that come with your solar equipment before you purchase your wire. The one exception is if you have more than one 12-volt battery. You

should connect your batteries together using standard automobile 2-gauge cable. Depending on where you intend to house your 12-volt batteries you may need to position them either side-by-side or end-to-end with at least 1/4-inch of air space between the batteries. After you have your batteries positioned then you could cut your battery cables to the optimum length so you have a slight bend in the wire between batteries. A battery cable may be cut with a metal saw or a hacksaw or a jig-saw. One way to do this inexpensively is to buy the longest 2-gauge battery wire you can find (or 0-gauge battery wire), and then cut it to the lengths you need, and then install a battery connector clamp on the bare end of the battery wire that you just cut. These are the same type of battery connectors that are used on your automobile battery and you can find them in the automotive section of most stores. The clamp connectors in the illustration have a red clamp for the positive terminal and a black clamp for the negative terminal. Or you can purchase the solid brass clamps.

Additional Information: Some additional detailed information about solar power and a solar power generator is in the Solar Power Chapter in this book.

Conclusion:
Will You Just Barely Survive or Will You Thrive?

There are three possible futures for your family during a serious long-term hard times event:

1. You and your family could perish.
2. You and your family could just barely survive on a day-to-day basis.
3. You and your family could thrive and prosper.

The title of this book is "**How to Survive and Thrive During Hard Times.**" Some of the people who will read this book will be content to just barely survive. But some of the people who read this book will want to do more than just survive -- they will want to thrive.

The secret to surviving and thriving during hard times is really very simple. First, you should do all that you can to provide for your family's needs. Second, you should pray and trust God to watch over your family and you should ask God to protect your family from harm and misfortune.

Regardless of how much money you have, and how much food you have stored, and how well equipped your retreat might be, there is no way you can protect your family from everything. Something simple like an airborne contagious pathogen, or a laboratory created virus, could kill everyone in your family in a very short period of time and there would be absolutely nothing you could do to stop it. Or something simple like a heart attack (my mother), or a disease of the intestines (my first wife), or a disease of the feet (my brother), or a tumor in the brain (my best friend), could kill or disable specific individuals within your family or your closest friends.

Therefore if you want to have the best chance of surviving and thriving during a serious long-term hard times event then you will need to include God in your plans. It is my personal belief that the only way you can effectively do this is to believe that Jesus Christ is the one and only true Son of God, that He was born as a baby in Bethlehem, that He grew up and taught the truth about God, that He performed many miracles while He was here on this earth, that He voluntarily allowed Himself to be humiliated, beaten, and crucified, that He died on the cross, that He was buried in a borrowed tomb, that God raised Him from the dead on the third day, and that He is alive today at the right hand of God interceding for everyone who will put their faith and their trust in Him.

In conclusion, surviving and thriving means that you do everything you can to provide for your family, and you also trust Jesus Christ to take care of all the things you can't do for your family.

Respectfully,
Grandpappy.

The Adventure: A True Story

Let me tell you about a true story I once read in a very, very old book of great antiquity.

The book begins with a snake talking to a woman in a faraway land of peace and great beauty.
The woman does what the snake tells her to do and she releases a great evil and sets it free.
Then the evil takes possession of her oldest son and he kills his younger brother ruthlessly.

The book then tells what happens to the woman's other descendents down throughout history.
For example, one day fire falls down from the sky and two evil homosexual cities cease to be.
A woman walking along a road disobeys an angel and she turns into a statue of salt instantly.

Later nine jealous brothers sell their despised half-brother as a slave for a very small fee.
Time passes and the half-brother is cast into prison for a crime for which he is not guilty.
Later the half-brother becomes a great ruler and all his brothers bow to him on bended knee.

A man speaks to the sun and the sun stands still in the sky for an entire day so the man can see.
A man breaks the ropes that bind him and kills 1,000 soldiers with the jawbone of a donkey.
A group of homosexual men abuse and kill a helpless young woman to satisfy their depravity.

A donkey is given the ability to speak and it warns its master of danger the master cannot see.
A witch calls up a dead man from under the earth so he can tell a king what the future will be.
Twice each day some ravens bring some meat and bread to an old man who is very lonely.

A man rides a chariot pulled by a team of blazing horses up into the sky and then into eternity.
An orphaned slave girl becomes the queen of a great nation and then she sets her people free.
Three men are thrown into a blazing furnace but they walk out unharmed for everyone to see.

In the middle of the night an ordinary fisherman walks on top of the water across a raging sea.
Two men from the ancient past appear to four men on top of a very high mountain in Galilee.
A man dead for four days walks out of his tomb and later he eats a meal with his entire family.

A man born with withered feet is healed and he stands up and walks and jumps triumphantly.
An innocent man chained to a prison wall is freed by an angel who leads him out into the city.
A man falls out of a third floor window and dies but he returns from the dead for all to see.

This amazing book does not end like any other adventure book you may have read casually.
This book contains a special final chapter about **you** and how **you** are a part of this true story.
And it also tells you how **you** can drink from the river of living waters and live for all eternity.

You can read all these exciting stories yourself in the Holy Bible, if you can just find a copy.
Start on page one and as time permits continue to read until you reach the end of the story,
and you will read many other adventures and you will learn the secret of eternal life in glory.

Scripture References:
Genesis 2:15-18, 3:1-6, 3:13, 3:17-19, 3:23, 4:1-2, 4:6-8, 19:24, 19:17, 19:26, 37:26-28, 39:20, 41:41, 43:26-29, Joshua 10:12-14, Judges 15:13-15, 19:22, 20:4-5, Numbers 22:25-33, 1 Samuel 28:8-15, 1 Kings 17:5-6, 2 Kings 2:11, Esther 2:5-7, 2:17, 8:3-4, 8:7-8, Daniel 3:21-27, Matthew 14:29-33, 17:1-3, John 11:17, 11:43-44, 12:1-2, Acts 3:1-10, 12:6-10, 20:9-12, Revelation 22:1-2, 22:17.

This Poem is Dedicated to My Granddaughter **Ashlyn Victoria Cagle.**

Index

A

Accuracy	259,275
Air Mattress	23,24,165
AK-47	271,284,412,479
Alcohol	441
Almond Trees	126
Amateur Radio	229
Ammunition	309
Antennas	226
Ant Hills	145
AquaRain Water Filter	47,157
Appetite Fatigue	53
Apple Trees	123
AR-10	480
AR-15	270,281,288,294
Arrows	381,383
Asparagus	107
Aspirin	195
Automatic Transmission Fluid	297

B

Bacteria	41
Backpack	339,476
Baking Powder	58
Baking Soda	58
Baptism	431
Barberry	200
Barter Items	14
Baseball Caps	177
Batteries, Cable	484
Batteries, Deep Cycle	231,483
Batteries, Flashlight	209
Beans	57,102,107,135
Beck's Silver Pulsar	201
Bee Stings	203
Beets, Regular	102,107,135
Beets, Sugar	102
Berkefeld Water Filter	46,157
Bible	417
Bicycles	343
Blackberry Bushes	127
Black Tuesday	1
Black Walnut Trees	125
Blanket, Emergency, Space, Solar	72
Blast Match	239
Bleach	42,146
Blueberry Bushes	127
Boiling Water	42
Bolt-Action Rifles	259

Books, Cards	469
Books, Music	467
Books, Paperback	465
Books, School	457
Books, Survival	461
Boots	183
Borax	20
Bouillon Cubes	58
Bow	381
Breathing	279
Broccoli	108
Brussels Sprouts	108
Budget	21
Bug-Out-Bag	339,476
Bullets, Homemade	318
Bullies	399
Bull's-Eye	275
Butane Lighters	238,373

C

Cabbage	108
Cabin Cave	24,167
Caliber	283
Calories	54,64
Campers	155
Campfires	79
Camp Stove	77
Candles	79,481
Can Opener	60
Canteens	49
Cards	469
Carrots	102,108
Cast Iron Cookware	79,359
Cast Iron Grates	356
Cast Iron Stoves	356,360
Cauliflower	109
Celery	109
Cell Phones	227
Chainsaws	355
Charcoal	257
Charcoal Grill	77,360
Charity	363,447,453
Cherry Trees	123
Chestnut Trees	126
Chiggers	203
Children	26,408
Chives	109
Chlorine	42
Christianity	419,427

Clothing	177
Clothing, Colors	181
Cloth Mittens	258
Coat	180
Cobbler, Shoes and Boots	184
Coffee, Coffee Pots, Grinders	91
Coghlan 6-Function Compass	339,373
Colloidal Silver	201
Colt-45 Pistol	411
Combo Cooker Cast Iron Set	82
Community Defense	414
Compasses	373,375,476
Compost	139
Concealed Carry	257
Conibear Traps	387
Condensation	39
Corn	102,109,136
Corn Starch	58
Cot, Folding	23,24,166
Craft Sewing Needles	182
Cream of Tartar	48
Creation	420
Crime	417
Criminals	27,408
Cross Wind	293
Cucumber	110

D

Dark Side	27,407
Darning Socks	179
Dental Floss	186
Dependability	270
Depression	3
Dehydrated Food	58,134
Dental Tools	193
Dew	37
Dice	488
Dirt, All-Purpose	120
Dirt Quality	120
Distilled Water	48
Dogs	408
Draw Knife	169
Dry Fire	278
Drying Food	134
Duck Tape	340
Dutch Oven	58,80,360

E

Echinacea	199
Eggplant	110
Elevation	296,300
Emerson Portable Radio	219
Evolution	420
Eye Protection	182

F

Famine	4,471
Fans, 12-volt	157
Feminine Pads	186
Fertilizer	121,131
Fig Trees	124
Fire	237
Fire, Emergency	241
Fire Steel	239,339
Fireplace	78
Firearm Accuracy	259,275
Firearm Cleaning Chemicals	297
Firearm Cleaning Kit	296
Firearm Dependability	270
Firearm Lemons & Cherries	297
Firearm Maintenance	260
Firearm Myths	273
Firearm Safety	258,298,412
Firewood	355
First Aid	191,474
Fish	391
Flashlights	217,482
Folding Oven	58
Food, Freezer, Frozen	60
Food, Heating Options	77
Food, One-Year Supply	69
Food Preservation Methods	133
Food Safety	61
Food Shelf Life Studies	61
Food Storage	53
Food Storage Areas	55,71
Food Supplies	17
Food, 30-Day Supply	63
Freeze-Dried Food	58
Fruit Trees	122

G

Gardening Skills	99
Gasoline	26
Germination	130
Gill Nets	391
Glock	274,304,411,479
Gloves	79,178
Grape Vines	126
Great Depression of the 1930s	1
Green House	29
Grinder, Coffee	92

Grinder, Meat	95
Grinder, Pepper	90
Grinder, Wheat	97
Group Think	8
Grundig Radios	221,223,484
Gunpowder	314
Gunsmith Screwdriver Set	260,297

H

Handguns	282
Handwriting on the Wall	9
Hard Times Categories	409
Hatchets	353
Hats	17
Head Lice	204
Heirloom Seeds	101,115,129
Herbal Home Remedies	198
Hide Tanning	182
Hole Size	119
Human Waste	139
Hybrid Seeds	101,115,129
Hygiene	184

I

Ice	34,37
Insect Stings	203
Inverters	232
Iodine	43
Ionic Silver	201
Iron Sights	292
Ivory Bar Soap	20,182,185

J

Jacket	179

K

Katadyn Pocket Water Filter	45,349
Kohlrabi	110
Knives	371,410

L

Large Bodies of Water	257
Lasers	282,301
Laundry	51,182
Law of the Jungle	5, 11,471
Lead Safety Hazards	318
Leatherman Wave Multi-Tool	354
Leeks	110
Lettuce	110
Lice	204

Liquid Alox	320,326,334
Livestock	368
Long Underwear	180
Luggage Carrier	342,344
Lye Water	253

M

Magnesium Fire Starter	239,339
Mainstay Food Bars	341
Maple Sugar, Maple Syrup	258
Maps	339
Matches	238
Meat Tenderizer	58
Melchizedek	443
Melons	111
Microwave Oven	77,482
Milk, Instant	60
Mittens	258
Moccasins	184,371
Moon	376
Moral values	2,19
Mosquito Head Net	178,477
Motor Oil	297
Mulch	143
Multivitamins	58
Music	467

N

Nail Polish	293
Natural Disasters	417
Needles	182,474
NiMH Batteries	209
North Star	243,376
Nut Trees	125

O

Oil Lamp	79
Okra	111
Onions	103,111,136
Ordinary People	407

P

Panniers	348
Pan Traps	387
Paperback Novels	465
Parsley	111
Pathogens	38,40,41
Peach Trees	124
Peanuts	103,111
Pear Trees	124

Peas 111
Pecan Trees 125
Pellet Air Rifles 335
Pepper, Green 112,136
Peppercorns, Black 57,89
Pets 367
Plague 404
Plum Trees 124
Polaris, North Star 243,376
Population Density 147,152
Potatoes 104,112,136
Presidential Executive Order 6102 1
Primers 311
Prisoners 28
Propane 77,157
Protozoa 40
Pumpkins 112

Q
Quality 14

R
Radios 219,221,223
Radishes 99,104.112
Rain 36,149,153
Rapture 437
Razors 186
Rechargeable Batteries 298
Recreational Vehicles 155
Refugees 28
Relatives 24
Reloading 305,309,328
Render Animal Fat 252
Rental Storage Space 25
Retreat Location 147,151
Revolvers 259,271
Rhubarb 113
Rice 56
Rimfire Rifles 310,480
Root Cellar 133
Rules of Survival 407
Ruger LCP 380 Caliber Pistol .. 305,480
Ruger 10/22 Rifle 338,480
Rutabaga 113

S
Safety 22
Safety, Firearm 258,298
Safety Glasses 22,182
Salt 57,87
Salvation 427

Satellite Phones 228
Savage Arms 64F 22LR 338,480
Saws, Wood 353
School Books 457
Scopes 285,289,292
Secrecy 26
Seeds 101,115,129
Self Defense 259
Self-Sufficiency 13,18
Semi-Automatic Firearms 259
Sewing 182,340,474
Shelters, Government 24
Shelters, Permanent 167
Shelters, Temporary 23,159
Shoes 183,349
Shooting Positions 277
Shortwave Radio 225
Shotguns 283,302,309
Shower 185,476
Silver, Colloidal 201
Silver, Generator 201
Silver, Money 115
Silver Protein 201
Silver Pulsar 201
Silver Solutions 201
Ski Mask 177
Skunk Deodorizer 208
Sleep 23,165,477
Snares 385
Snow 37
Soap 20,185,245
Socks 179
Solar Battery Cables 484
Solar Battery Chargers 210
Solar Generator 232,482
Solar Oven 79,477
Solar Panels 231,483
Solar Power 231,482
Solar Shower 185,476
Solar Still 39
Solder 323
Special Humanitarian Teams 401
Spinach 104,113,136
Spinning Wheels 29,182
Sport Wash 182
Squash 113
Stainless Steel Cookware 360
Stars 376
Starvation 404
Steel Traps 79,367,387
Sterno Cooking Fuel 78

Stock Market Crash of 1929 1
Storage Containers 134,175
Stratification 130
Strawberries 127,136
Suicide 423
Sun 119,376
Sundial 243
Survival of the Fittest 5,11,471
Survival Plan 17
Swish Chard 113

T
Target Practice 275,281,334
Tarps 173,340
Teflon Coated Cookware 360
Tents 23
Texas Fireframe 358
Thermal Underwear 180
Thread 29
Ticks 203
Tin 323
Tire Sandals 184
Toilet 51
Toilet Tissue 186,187
Toilet Tissue Alternative 190
Tomatoes 104,113,136
Tools 353
Toothbrushes 185
Toothpaste 185
Trade Items 14
Trajectory 286
Traps 387
Three-Ring Binders 184
Trivet 81,83
Turnips 105,114,137
Two-Way Communication 227

U
Unnecessary Complexity 20

V
Vacuum Food Sealer ... 59,137,342,463
Vegetable Recommendations 101
Vegetable Seeds 115
Vehicles 23
Viruses 41
Vitamins 59
Volt - Amp Meter 213
Volt Meter 234

W
Walnut Trees 125
Water 33,148
Water Cooler 32
Water Conservation 50
Water Filters 31,44
Water Heater 34
Water Purification Tablets 44
Water Well 35
Weaving Loom 182
Wheat Berries 60
Wheel Weights 322
White Rice 56
Wind 293,299
Wire 340
World War II 1
World War III 5
Worst Case Breakdown 399
Wristwatch 378

X

Y
Yacht 488
Yeast 57

Z
Zipper Freezer Bags ... 134,340,342,389

Index
491

About the Author

Robert Wayne Atkins, P.E. (Grandpappy)
Born in 1949.

Accepted Jesus as Savior in April of 1976.

George Washington High School, Danville, Virginia, June 1967.

B.S. Degree in Industrial Engineering & Operations Research,
  Virginia Polytechnic Institute and State University,
  Blacksburg, Virginia, June 1972.

Master of Business Administration, Major in Marketing,
  Graduated with High Honors (3.87 GPA),
  Georgia State University, Atlanta, Georgia, March 1985.

Licensed Professional Engineer (P.E.), Florida 1980, Georgia 1982.

Ordained Deacon in Christian Church, Ocala, Florida, 1980.

FCC Amateur Radio License, 1996, Extra Class License.

Author of Nine Computer Software Games, including "**The Lost Crown of Queen Anne,**" 1988-1991.

Contributing Author to "**Maynard's Industrial Engineering Handbook,**" Fifth Edition, 2001, p. 5-10.

Listed in "**Who's Who in America,**" 64th Edition, 2010.

Listed in "**Who's Who in the World,**" 29th Edition, 2012.

Robert is a descendant of the early European settlers in Virginia who married American Indian Cherokee wives.

In 1976 Robert began writing down his favorite recipes for his daughter, Renee, who had just been born. As the years passed he began writing down more of the things that he knew were of timeless value and that would one day be of interest to his children and his future descendants. However, he suspected he would probably be with our LORD before his children or his grandchildren would be old enough, or wise enough, to appreciate the simple practical knowledge he possessed.

In the year 2003 he began writing down what he had learned from the Holy Bible after more than 25 years of reading it on a daily basis. But he suspected his children would probably never read what he wrote if he put it into a sermon format. Therefore he began writing short Christian poems because he hoped that his children, grandchildren, and his other future descendants might take the time to read a short poem even if it was Christian oriented.

Later it occurred to him that some of his knowledge might be of interest to other people. Therefore he began publishing some of his writings on his web site. Based on the favorable email feedback he received he continued to freely share his knowledge on his web site. After several years and at the request of many of his readers he eventually consolidated some of his writings into the books listed below.

Other Books by this Same Author:
1. Grandpappy's Recipes for Hard Times.
2. How to Survive and Thrive for Several Years in a Hostile Wilderness Environment.
3. Ancient Board Games and Solitaire Games from Around the World: Volumes One and Two.
4. Grandpappy's Christian Poems.
5. The Four Pillars of Prosperity: Governments, Businesses, Religions, and Banks